What Others Are Saying About
Tracking the Soul

This book is a marvelously imagined integration between western astrology and Indian metaphysic. Joe Landwehr displays a wide-ranging mastery of the material and communicates it crisply and clearly to his audience. Readers interested in deepening their understanding of chakra theory in its application to astrology would do well to open this treasure house of ancient knowledge written from a modern psychological perspective. - **Brad Kochunas**, author of *The Astrological Imagination: Where Psyche and Cosmos Meet*.

This excellent book describes the relationship of astrological symbols to the psychology of the chakra system. Joe Landwehr shows how the natal chart and transits become a basis for inner work and transformative yoga, helping us work through the emotional issues and energetic blocks associated with each chakra, to become progressively liberated on every level. Joe writes with heart and humor, focus and fire, drawing the reader into a deeper personal experience of astrology as a living spiritual philosophy and a tool for consciousness growth, This book is inspiring reading for astrologers of all levels. Highly recommended. - **Greg Bogart**, author of *Astrology and Meditation: The Fearless Contemplation of Change*

Joe Landwehr's 'Tracking the Soul' is a fascinating and eloquent look the spiritual dimensions of astrology. His take on the relationship between astrology and the chakras is original, and bound to stimulate further discussion on this important topic. Highly recommended. - **Ray Grasse**, author of *The Waking Dream* and *Signs of the Times*

Once the definitive history of the last one hundred years is written, I suspect the dominant intellectual theme will be the collision/fusion of psychology and religion. The funky realities of our inner lives and the soaring glories of our souls' potentials will emerge as interdependent and synergistic. The more deeply we embrace our humanity, the higher our souls climb - and the more we fear engaging with our juicy, crazy humanity, the more we become schizoid and shattered. Joe Landwehr's book, "Tracking the Soul, is smack on the cutting edge of this paradigm shift. He's done his homework, both metaphysically and psychologically. And we, his readers, are the lucky winners." - **Steven Forrest**, author of *The Inner Sky, The Night Speaks*, and *Skymates*.

Tracking the Soul

With An Astrology Of Consciousness

Joe Landwehr

Ancient Tower Press
Mountain View, Missouri

www.ancient-tower-press.com

FIRST EDITION
First Printing, 2007

Cover design by Anne Marie Forrester
Interior Design by Joe Landwehr
Copy-editing by Annie Woods Tornick

Publisher's Cataloging-in-Publication
(Provided by Quality Books, Inc.)

Landwehr, Joe.
    Tracking the soul : with an astrology of consiousness
  / Joe Landwehr.
        p. cm. ~ (The astropoetic series ; v. 1)
    Includes bibliographical references and index.
    LCCN 2006909996
    ISBN-13: 978-0-9747626-1-6
    ISBN-10: 0-9747626-1-X

    1. Soul. 2. Chakras (Theosophy) 3. Astrology
  I. Title. II. Series.

  BD421.L363 2007   128'.1
                              QBI06-600551

Ancient Tower Press
230 West First Street #119
Mountain View, Missouri 65548

www.ancient-tower-press.com

About the Author

J oe Landwehr is an astrologer of 36 years experience, seeking an eclectic integration of astrology, spiritual psychology and ancient wisdom teachings. After an initiatory reading in 1971 by an astrologer in Ashland, Oregon known only as Sunny Blue Boy, Joe began his own study of astrology in earnest. About this time, Joe also began a serious study of kundalini yoga with Yogi Bhajan, moving to southern California where he became senior editor at the Kundalini Yoga Institute. While there, Joe also functioned as the resident astrologer, taught kundalini yoga and meditation in the surrounding colleges, and obtained a masters degree in Marriage, Family and Child Counseling. It was here that he began the integration of ideas drawn from psychology, yogic philosophy and astrology that led to the writing of this book.

Upon leaving the ashram in 1977, Joe moved to Florida, where he continued to study, write and teach. In 1978, he was introduced to the teachings of Swami Muktananda, and began to supplement his knowledge of yogic philosophy with the theory and practice of Siddha yoga. Over the next 15 years, Joe developed an international mail order astrology practice with clients from Canada, England, Germany, Japan, and Thailand, as well as the US. Combining a Rudhyarian approach to astrology with a strong foundation in spiritual psychology, Joe focused his readings primarily upon the underlying spiritual opportunities at the heart of his client's issues and concerns.

In 1993, Joe had an epiphany in which he realized that he could better serve his clients by teaching them astrology, rather than simply decoding the symbolism for them. He started an intimately personal correspondence course called The Eye of the Centaur, and for the next 8 years, worked intensively with a small number of dedicated students, willing to let the crucible of their own lives be their classroom. Throughout the 90s, Joe wrote numerous articles for The Mountain Astrologer, The International Astrologer and other publications, sharing insights he had evolved in the teaching of his course.

In 2001, Joe took a sabbatical from his course to research and write *The Seven Gates of Soul: Reclaiming the Poetry of Everyday Life* – a 6000 year history of ideas about the soul, drawn from religion, philosophy, science, psychology and an intuitive form of astrology called astropoetics. This book – *Tracking the Soul With An Astrology of Consciousness* – is the sequel to that book. In 2005, Joe resumed teaching his correspondence course, now transformed into The Astropoetic School of Soul Discovery.

Additional information about astropoetics, The Astropoetic School, and the author's current workshop schedule can be found at www.astropoetics.com. The author can be contacted at jlandwehr@astropoetics.com or jlandwehr@ancient-tower-press.com.

Acknowledgements

Though it only took about three years to write, this book has been gestating since my ashram days more than thirty years ago. My astrological studies and my serious practice of kundalini yoga began simultaneously in 1971, the former initiated by Sunny Blue Boy, the latter by Gurujohn Lamenzo, my first yoga teacher. Gurujohn sent me to California in 1973, where my teachers became Gurucharan Singh, Shama Kirn Singh and Rama Kirn Singh. After leaving the ashram, Ram Butler introduced me to the teachings of Swami Muktananda, while Charity James graciously hosted the weekly satsang group where I began to absorb them. Sunny Blue Boy pointed me toward the writings of Dane Rudhyar, who subsequently became an abiding inspiration throughout my astrological studies. I met him once and had a brief conversation in an elevator at a conference in Virginia Beach in 1980. All of these people are important links in the chain of fortuitous events that lead me to write this book, and I want to thank them here, even though we have long since gone our separate ways.

In 1977, I published a series of articles encompassing the ideas explored in this book in Skylight Magazine, published by Penny Biemiller in Saint Petersburg, Florida.

Thirty years later, these ideas have found their way into this book with the gracious assistance of a number of additional people, who read my manuscript in its formative stages: Jann Burner, whose philosophy of soul often served as the grain of sand in the oyster that made my pearl what it is; Leslie Ullman, who felt the poetry and the flow beneath my ideas and encouraged it; and Fran Laakman, who has drawn forth the teacher in me, and helped bring him into clearer focus. I am also grateful to Brad Kochunas, Ray Grasse, Greg Bogart and Steven Forrest who took time out of their busy schedules to read the rough draft and help me make sure my astro-logic was sound.

Last, but not least, I want to thank Anne Marie Forrester for her gorgeous cover design, and my copy-editor, Annie Woods Tornick, for helping me tighten my message and take more forceful ownership of it.

This book is dedicated to my teachers: Yogi Bhajan, Swami Muktananda, Dane Rudhyar and my grandfather.

Table of Figures and Charts

Table of Contents

CONTENTS

CONTENTS

CONTENTS

◇◇

Preface To The Astropoetic Series

In my previous book, *The Seven Gates of Soul: Reclaiming the Poetry of Everyday Life*, I suggest that before we can talk in a meaningful way about the soul, we must speak a language that allows the soul to feel its journey pulse beneath its feet at every step. Such a language ideally recognizes in a non-judgmental way the value of everyday existence – this life in the here and now – as the focal point of the soul's experience. It understands this life as a precious opportunity for trial-and-error learning, tending over the course of a lifetime toward a more conscious, creative and intimately personal embodiment of Spirit. It appreciates the suffering inherent in the human condition to be a primary catalyst for the learning process. It approaches an understanding of the soul's experience, not with the rational, objective mind, bent on articulating an external reality we can agree upon, but through a more subjective fusion of sensory input, feelings, and imagery unique to the individual. It facilitates an intimate qualitative understanding of the individual's purpose and place within the larger Whole – one that honors the color of the soul's shifting moods, the taste of its obsessions, the sound of its pain and its joy.

I further suggest in *The Seven Gates of Soul*, that a modified form of astrology – called *astropoetics* – can potentially serve as the basis for such a language of soul. My word for this language is a composite of two references that I believe will prove to be a useful synthesis. The second half of the word, *-poetics*, is meant to suggest that the ineffable mystery of soul is best approached through a poetic language. A poetic language is one that conducts its quest for the truth obliquely – through simile and metaphor, image and symbol, suggestion and allusion, rather than direct, dogmatic statement of fact. The first half of the word, *astro-*, is meant to suggest that the soul can be observed in its movement through various cycles, which wax and wane in predictable rhythm, and are mirrored in the movement of the larger cosmic patterns that routinely coalesce and disperse in the sky. Since tracking these cosmic patterns and their relevance to the soul is the province of natal astrology, it seems natural to suggest that a poetic approach to astrology can provide a useful template for a viable language of soul. Such a language – born from the marriage of poetic sensibility and awareness of cycles – will empower the soul to dream and to awaken within the dream, to wrestle with and surrender to the archetypal forces at the heart of its most pressing dilemmas, and to create a life that shimmers with the potency of self-knowledge consciously embodied.

In discussing this possibility, I speak of astrology's role in qualified terms, because before astrology can be truly useful as a language of soul, it must be liberated from certain bad habits absorbed through centuries of osmosis from religion, philosophy, science, and psychology, as well as through its own history of development. The astrology of the individual, as it is practiced today, co-evolved with these other disciplines, and although it is nearly universally disavowed by them all today, it nonetheless shares many of their underlying assumptions about the nature of reality, and about how reality might be known. These assumptions – as I demonstrated in some detail in *The Seven Gates of Soul* – present barriers to a true understanding of soul, whether sought by a spiritual seeker, a philosopher, a scientist, a psychologist or an astrologer.

The Astropoetic Impulse

Meanwhile, despite the vociferous rejection of astrology by these other disciplines, the central idea at the heart of the astrological quest – the notion that there could be a meaningful symbolic correlation between the movements of the greater cosmos and what is going on inside an individual human life – remains as compelling today as it was in the 17th century, when astrology was still taken seriously. As human beings, we long to know who we are – not just in human terms, but in relation to the larger patterns that connect us to the grand seemingly intelligent design that permeates this vast, unfathomable universe. I call this desire to know who we are in relation to the grand design, the *astropoetic impulse*, because despite astrology's shortcomings and the low esteem in which astrology is nearly universally held, no other discipline speaks quite as eloquently or with as much sophistication to this desire. When astrology is approached poetically – as a whole-brain contemplation of imagery and symbolism, reflected in uncannily descriptive ways by everyday life – it potentially holds the key to an understanding of soul that eludes these other disciplines.

For all the faith that we place in these other disciplines, especially science, they all seek an understanding of the human predicament that systemically excludes essential ingredients of the whole picture by which the grand design must be understood. Religion seeks to understand our relationship to God or Spirit, but generally looks upon our relationship to the material realm and the body with disdain. Science studies our relationship to the physical universe in great detail, but fails to acknowledge its spiritual dimension or the existence of soul. Psychology discusses the soul, either strictly within the parameters imposed by science – which is to say, not at all – or with reference to only the human dimensions of its experience. Only astrology – with its inherently poetic language animated by gods and goddesses, connecting earth and sky through their perpetually changing dance – seems broad enough to entertain the thought that earth, human, and cosmos could conceivably be part of a larger all-inclusive pattern. To the extent that astrology can be weaned from its bad habits – discussed at some length in *The Seven Gates of Soul* – it lends itself quite succinctly to an articulation of the astropoetic impulse.

Astrology seeks specific understanding of the correlations between human experience and the patterns formed by planets, stars, and other astronomical phenomena. In this sense, it is potentially the ideal language for focused expression of the astropoetic impulse. But the astropoetic impulse itself – the quest to understand the larger patterns in which our lives acquire meaning – is not limited to astrological expression; it is intrinsic to human nature. This impulse is not completely unfamiliar, even to those who know nothing or could care less about astrology.

Artists of all persuasions routinely exercise an astropoetic sensibility in the creation of their art, although they likely do not call it that, whenever they depict the individual seeking to intuit his or her place in a mysterious universe beyond human comprehension. Psychotherapists not wedded to a medical model of psychology will exercise astropoetic sensibilities, as they approach a deeper, symbolic understanding of their client's experience through dreams, projective tests, art and music therapy, or somatic modalities aimed at a holistic understanding of human behavior. Spiritual teachers, particularly those from indigenous or pagan traditions, often unconsciously use astropoetic imagery in their attempt to articulate the unknown, and draw it within experiential range of their students and followers – largely through ritual ceremonies that embrace the Sun, the Moon, the planets and the elements as co-participants in a dance of transmutation and release. Even many visionary scientists – from Aristotle to Einstein – who draw their inspiration from sources that transcend the mere facts they study, give expression in their own way, to the astropoetic impulse.

We do not necessarily recognize the astropoetic nature of these pursuits, because there is no explicit use of astrological language, no recognition of the relationship between signs, houses, or planetary dynamics and human experience that compose the vocabulary of the astrological worldview. The use of such language – except within the astrological community itself, and in certain New Age circles – is something of a cultural *faux paus*[1]. Since the 17th century, serious discussion of astrology has largely become intellectually taboo, and few people today other than astrologers would dare use astrological language to seriously articulate their perspective. Our modern conception of astrology has been distorted by centuries of denigration by religious authorities and scientists, most of whom know little about it, and by the popular media, which tends to trivialize whatever it touches. However, this does not mean that the astropoetic impulse is not at work in our non-astrological attempts to make sense of our lives.

Making sense of our experience in terms of larger patterns is part of what it means to be human. We all strive to do this as a matter of course, every day – even if all we ever talk about is the weather and last night's tv shows. Stripped of its jargon and the cultural baggage that has been heaped upon it, astrology is merely a useful language for articulating our relationship to these larger patterns. To the extent that we reach for this

◇◇

kind of understanding, by whatever means, our efforts are an expression of the astropoetic impulse. To the extent that giving expression to the astropoetic impulse is important to us, then a poetic understanding of astrology can be a useful place to begin.

Viewed dispassionately, astrology provides a rather sophisticated methodology to bring our astropoetic awareness of larger patterns into clearer focus. Like science, astrology strives to articulate interrelationships within the larger pattern. Unlike science, astrology is more interested in the symbolic implications of these interrelationships than their literal, material, or causal dimensions. Science attempts to understand larger patterns as they can be described objectively as part of consensual reality, while natal astrology attempts to understand and describe these same patterns subjectively, as part of the intimately personal reality of each individual. Astrology and science pose two very different perspectives, which under the best of circumstances, ought to complement and balance each other. Unfortunately, since the importance of the astropoetic impulse is not generally acknowledged, and science likes to present itself as the only legitimate worldview, the astrological perspective, potentially useful as it can be in giving expression to the astropoetic impulse, is in danger of being negated altogether.

While few non-astrologers would likely mourn the loss of astrology per se, the denigration of the astropoetic impulse is also being felt in less obvious ways, because of the dominance of science. Whenever a school cancels its art and music programs for lack of funding; whenever an insurance policy dictates that interactive forms of psychotherapy, not based on pharmaceutical intervention, are ineligible for reimbursement; or wherever religious dogmatism breeds an environment of intolerance and closed-mindedness, it will be because the astropoetic impulse – by whatever other name we might call it – is not recognized or valued. Wherever we stop sensing, feeling, imagining and intuiting our way into a recognition of larger patterns of meaning and purpose, beyond the reach of the strictly rational mind, we function at less than our full capacity as human beings. This is a great loss, regardless of how we feel about astrology.

In *The Seven Gates of Soul*, I outlined the historical process by which both astrology and the dominant worldview became corrupted by the gradual loss of astropoetic sensibilities. I also began to explore what an astropoetic language of soul might look like once it had been recognized and liberated from its conditioning. In this book, and in the series of books that will follow, I wish to discuss the syntax of this language in some detail, and develop a cohesive methodology by which it might contribute to a deeper understanding of the human experience. In order to do this, I will borrow heavily from astrology, and at the same time, restore a broader foundation of symbolic logic to astrology that is intrinsic to the astropoetic impulse at the heart of its nature.

✧✧✧

Astro-logic

This specifically astropoetic form of logic, or astro-logic, as I like to call it, is not the same as the linear, analytical, left-brain logic developed by the early Greeks, which later came to serve as the foundation of both astrology and science. It is essentially a poetic logic of simile and metaphor, suggestive of possibilities, rather than descriptive of literal facts. It is an invitation to contemplate experience with the whole of one's being – with the senses, emotions, and imagination, as well as the rational mind. It is a trigger for the intuition, stretching into realms of subjective awareness inaccessible to mere rational analysis. It is rooted in the power of the symbol to evoke visceral recognition, rather than a purely intellectual interpretation of data. It speaks not just to the mind, but to the soul, and attempts to place the soul within a larger, more cosmic context. It strives to reveal something universal in recognition of the whole of which we are part, even as it expresses itself through an intimate exploration of our uniqueness. It seeks to recognize and articulate symbolic correlations between the larger patterns unfolding around us (referred to by astrologers as the macrocosm) with the smaller patterns that weave through individual lives (the microcosm).

To reclaim the astro-logic that underlies the astropoetic impulse, we do not necessarily need to believe in astrology, nor encumber ourselves with knowledge of arcane, intellectual techniques. In fact, astrology itself has in many ways become less astro-logical – in the way that I am defining it here – as it is impacted by the same loss of astropoetic perspective that is affecting us all. Under pressure from critics both within and outside the astrological community, astrology has largely become too rational, left-brained, and analytical to adequately serve as a useful language of projective imagination. This book, and those that will follow, are intended to remedy this situation, and to promote a more basic relationship between the astrological language and the rules of astro-logic by which a more whole-brained, intuitive, and poetic expression of the language might evolve. Meanwhile, my broader purpose is to rediscover and elaborate the astropoetic impulse at the heart – not just of astrology, as it was practiced in some golden, pre-scientific age – but of our shared human nature, as it can be experienced in the here and now.

The Roots of Astro-logic in Symbolic Astronomy

Given that astrology is the language *par excellence* for exploring the astropoetic impulse, we might suspect that astrology had a more exalted position within the historical development of western thought than is generally acknowledged. Instead, those who know little about astrology or philosophical history often assume that it sprouted like a weed, a foreign opportunistic species that rooted in the cracks of

◇◇◇

our civilization, despite the fact that it was alien to our culture. Nothing could be further from the truth. Astrology grew up as the twin brother of astronomy, the right-brain echo of its scientific sibling's left-brain focus on literal fact. Both astronomy and astrology studied cosmos – one with an eye toward measurement of its material parameters, the other toward an illumination of the mystery at the heart of our relationship to the infinite, incomprehensible vastness of space. A mere four to five centuries ago, both were practiced together as part of the same pursuit by astropoetically inclined astronomers like Nicholas Copernicus, Johannes Kepler, and Tycho Brahe. These astronomer/astrologers attempted to describe, not just the mechanical workings of a material universe, but also the cosmic order, or grand pattern of the Whole, as it manifested in the movements of celestial objects. Until the 7th century, the same word – *astrologia*, meaning "logic of the stars" – was used to describe both.

While science has long since disavowed its relationship to astrology, the astro-logic at the heart of both astrology and astronomy was originally an expression of the astropoetic impulse. Science became increasingly uncomfortable with the metaphysical implications of astro-logic, and gradually divorced itself from all speculative concerns with meaning or purpose that might incidentally be found in the larger patterns it was attempting to study. Astrology became marginalized as the pre-scientific view, though it kept the flame alive. As discussed in *The Seven Gates of Soul*, however, it did so in a way that was inevitably distorted by science, the dominant paradigm – its bigger, stronger, bully of a brother – to which it was compelled to pay allegiance by cultural mandate.

As we turn our attention back to astro-logic, we will explore the intimate connection between astrology and astronomy that engaged the earliest astropoetic astronomers. The literal facts of astronomy – not just those available to the ancients, but also those that modern astronomers have since discovered – will serve as one important source for the rules of astro-logic. Rather than take these facts literally, however, we will use them as a springboard for an intuitive assessment of relevant similes and metaphors. If the Moon appears to move through phases from the total darkness of New Moon to the haunting luminescence of Full Moon, we shall take this to say something – not just about the astronomical movements of Sun, Earth and Moon, but also about the metaphorical waxing and waning of our relationship to all things lunar – feelings, dreams, memories, and the mysteries of life, death and rebirth. If the Sun appears to rise, culminate, set, and anti-culminate, as the Earth rotates about its axis, we shall take this as symbolic evidence of the shifting focus of consciousness, as it is reflected in the rising and setting of the life force within us. And so on. In the realm of astro-logic, every astronomical fact will have its symbolic correlates, suggestive of various astro-logical truths.

◇◇◇

The Roots of Astro-logic in Qualitative Mathematics

More fundamental to astro-logic than astronomy is the mother tongue of mathematics, which makes possible both astronomical and astrological calculations. Implied in the pursuit of science is the ability to measure, and implied in the ability to measure is the power of numbers to illuminate something about the object of measurement. Science assumes that what gets illuminated by numbers is a quantifiable fact. Astro-logic, however, is inherently more interested in the *quality* of experience – the similarities that make something part of a symbolic family, or the underlying sense of resonance that makes a given image an apt metaphor for a process to which it is otherwise unrelated. Science denies the qualitative nature of both numbers and the material objects that numbers are capable of measuring. But this is exactly the cornerstone cast aside that proves useful as a foundation for the rules of astro-logic we will explore. It is indeed the very essence of the astrological art.

The quality at the heart of numbers was of great interest to Pythagoras, and later to Plato and the Neoplatonists. Pythagoras is credited with discovering the mathematical underpinnings of music, and of harmony and discord, which reverberated throughout the measurable universe in countless qualitative ways. He and his followers believed that numbers were the key to understanding the Divine Order, the intention of the Creator, as reflected in the various ways in which He constructed the manifest universe. In this perspective, everything, which in some way, partakes of the nature of a given number, resonates on the same harmonic wavelength, or put another way, becomes part of the same family of symbolic gestures. Numbers become not just units of measurement, but far more importantly, organizing principles of the astro-logic implied in the manifest world. Since the embodied soul is also very much of the manifest world, numbers also become an organizing principle in the more internal logic of each individual soul – though not just in the literal, objective way that scientists would like to believe they do.

Though much of the Pythagorean system has been lost, the notion that numbers have symbolic implications, which in turn describe something of the nature of the soul's experience is a central tenet of the astro-logic that we will seek to cultivate in this series. Everything astrological can be understood as a manifestation of the qualitative dimension of number – the twelve signs of the zodiac, the twelve houses, the four elements, the three modalities, the various angular relationships between planets, the harmonics that underlie those angular relationships, the larger planetary patterns that underscore certain harmonics, and the numbers associated with the duration, shape and permutations of each astrological cycle under scrutiny. Understood in the spirit of Pythagoras' qualitative approach to numbers, these numerical relationships can be considered part of the astro-logic by which any birthchart becomes illuminated as a symbolic statement about the soul. Beyond the usual astrological uses of numbers, a qualitative assessment of numbers will also be useful in establishing a broader, metaphysical context in which to understand astro-logical information.

The Roots of Astro-Logic in Mythology

A third primary source of astro-logic lies in the inextricable relationship between astrology and mythology. As pointed out in some detail in *The Seven Gates of Soul*, no small part of the discomfort experienced by proto-scientists, when contemplating the astro-logic they shared with astrology, was the fact that this astro-logic was rooted in the mythopoetic culture science sought to supplant. Entangled in these roots was the mystical notion that the material bodies revolving around the Sun were the actual bodies of the gods and goddesses for which they were named. Venus was not just a neighboring planet, closer to the Sun than Earth, but also the literal embodiment of the Greek goddess, Aphrodite, and a symbolic harbinger of everything associated with the mythology of Aphrodite – an archetypal conduit through which experiences of erotic love, sensual pleasure, artistic passion, and the perpetual quest for a deepening relationship to beauty could find their place within human experience. The subsequent movements of Venus in relation to the Earth and the other planets was not just a matter of measurable orbits and gravitational forces, but also one of mythological intercourse with repercussions and corresponding melodramas within the realm of human affairs.

While early astrologers, particularly those who were magically inclined or versed in the Hermetic arts, often took these correspondences literally, it is the symbolic and experiential implications of the mythological dimension of astrology that will provide an opening to an articulation of the astro-logic that we seek. All things that resonate on some level in the mythology of Venus, will form the basis for a nexus of symbolic correlates to the appearance of the planet in the birthchart. By the same line of symbolic reasoning, the four elements, the directions associated with the angles of the chart, and the interplay of any combination of planets in mutual aspect to one another, among other possibilities, will all have their mythological correlates.

While western astrology is traditionally rooted in Greek and Roman mythology, the mythology of cultures throughout the world, as well as that from post-mythological cultures, folklore, literature, art, music, theatre and film, might all potentially provide source material for the astro-logic implied within a given astrological symbol. Indeed, once we identify the rules of astro-logic by which these threads weave their patterns, the patterns themselves will be recognized to pre-exist in places where even veteran astrologers might not previously have thought to look.

◇◇

The Flowering of Astro-logic in Subjective Experience

The most obvious and critical place to look for the proliferation of astro-logical patterns is within the life stories of the individuals in whose birthcharts these patterns are described. The rules of astro-logic extracted from a symbolic consideration of mathematical, astronomical and mythological truths will provide a lens through which we can more skillfully glimpse the patterns that compose a life, but the patterns themselves will take on nuances and, in some cases, entirely unfamiliar personas that are intimately unique to the individual. Each life has its own inherent astro-logic, and often this more subjective patterning of symbolic elements is discovered only when the rules of astro-logic are applied with an open mind that is prepared to be surprised in discovering something new that the rules could not have prepared one to anticipate.

Essential to understanding how the astro-logic of any life reveals itself, is a process of self-observation. Everything astrological evolves through some cycle – whether the daily rotation of the Earth about its axis, the annual revolution of the Earth or any other planet around the Sun, the movement of two planets in relation to each other, or some more esoteric cycle less tangibly measured. Each of these cycles represents an opportunity to observe and collect information about the astro-logic of the various factors converging to create the cycle. A Mars-Venus cycle, for example, is an opportunity to learn something about Mars and Venus and the way they interact. The passage of a planet through a sign or a house is an opportunity to learn something about how that planet functions within that sign or house. A Saros cycle, or series of related eclipses, is an opportunity to learn something about the astro-logic that ties the series together as a symbolic whole.

Astrologers routinely build their collective pool of astrological knowledge through their shared observation about events and processes that occur simultaneously, or synchronistically, with the unfolding of various cycles. The same principle can be applied within the context of an individual life. Indeed, the evolution of a cogent language of soul will demand it, for it is only this more subjective form of self-observation that yields a true understanding of the soul that is living the patterns reflected in the birthchart. Many beginning and intermediate astrologers assume that the principles of astro-logic alone are sufficient to describe the soul in question. They are not. It is not until the principles of astro-logic – culled from mathematical, astronomical and mythological correlates, and from the cumulative observations of the astrological tradition – are observed within the unique context of an individual life, that the astropoetry of that life will reveal itself.

Thus, a deeper, ultimately more intensely personal and potent source of what we might call esoteric astro-logic will evolve through the application of the familiar exoteric astro-logic of tradition within the context of a real life story, observed and understood cyclically. This esoteric astro-logic – infused with the subjective wisdom of the individual soul – will only emerge slowly, over the course of many years of self-observation.

Since most of us begin the process of self-observation somewhere in mid-stream, penetrating to the heart of this more esoteric form of astro-logic also involves a process of self-remembering. The freshest information will always be that which can be gleaned in the moment. But also of great importance are memories related to key moments in the cycle under observation. Ideally, the effort to remember can best be undertaken while a given cycle is currently being activated, and consequently ripe for observation. Remembering is also greatly facilitated by keeping a personal journal, to record significant thoughts, feelings, events and processes, and to map them to various cycles.

Memory is a tricky affair – selective at best, often blocked, frequently distorted by pain, creative reconstruction, wishful thinking, or denial. Likewise, observation can be skewed by biases, blind spots, and false beliefs. The subjective quest for truth is necessarily flawed, because we are flawed as observers and rememberers. But if we are to get at the truth of our soul's existence, discover our purpose in this life, and find our place within the larger scheme of things, we can only do so from within the context of our own experience, however imperfectly perceived or remembered. If we are sincere in this attempt, and our intentions are clear, the rules of exoteric astro-logic will provide us with a set of tools to help us more clearly perceive the esoteric astro-logic at the heart of our experience. If we just start where we are, the process will gradually deepen, and take us where no mere exoteric astro-logic can possibly go.

Astro-logic and the Evolution of Consciousness

Implied in this recognition of esoteric astro-logic is the understanding that the meaning of any birthchart depends in part on the consciousness that is channeled through it. In *The Seven Gates of Soul*, I argue that consciousness is the preeminent expression of Spirit functioning within a body, and the mechanism for a trial-and-error learning process through which the soul gradually learns to more fully embody Spirit. At different times, each of us will bring varying degrees of consciousness to the task at hand, and it is this variable – more than anything overtly astrological – that will determine the most relevant meaning of the correspondent symbolism in any birthchart.

Seen astropoetically, an astrological birthchart is a thing of great beauty. It is an aerial photograph of the interior landscape of the human psyche, a landscape I like to refer to as soul space. For those with eyes to see, it also describes the shape, texture, scent and tone of an individual life, echoing in countless ways through the real life experience of the native inhabitant of the soul space that it describes. Translated in temporal terms, it outlines an evolutionary timetable for the various shaping influences that will forge the soul in the crucible of its experience. As cycles interweave with cycles, and the wheel of time turns around the birthchart as its axis, the soul comes into more conscious being as an astropoetic articulation of its symbolism. No two charts are alike, and even for souls born in adjacent hospital beds at exactly the same moment, the colors and the nuances of expression that breathe life into the chart, will mark each as a unique signature of singular majesty, divine genius, and rare beauty.

As beautiful and compelling as the birthchart is, it must be considered an abstract portrait of potentialities until the being whose actual life is mirrored by the birthchart enters into our consideration of it. Everything astrological can be understood to function on multiple levels of possibility, and interpretation of a birthchart – according to the most common approach to astrology – is nothing more than educated speculation about possibilities. The best astrologers speculate with ample input from the client about whom they are speculating, realizing that without the client, the birthchart would be nothing more than an elaborate algebraic equation.

A generation ago, seminal astrologer Dane Rudhyar suggested that "astrology is fundamentally the algebra of life. But its applications are as numerous as the types of life it coordinates, integrates, and to which it gives the significance of order" (18). Although Rudhyar was speaking of a broad range of applications – including not just natal astrology, or the astrology of the individual – it is nonetheless a corollary of his statement that its application to a given soul depends upon the "type of life" that individual is living. The type of life an individual lives, in turn, will be a function of the consciousness that individual brings to life, evidenced perhaps most clearly at each juncture, by the choices that she makes. If this is so, then an understanding of these choices is necessarily a prerequisite to understanding any birthchart.

The choices that we make at the important junctures of any cycle will determine which of the many possible meanings for the astrological correlates to that cycle are most valid – not in an exoteric sense as a statement of generic fact, but in an esoteric sense as an expression of subjective truth. One person with Saturn square the Sun will experience the Saturn-Sun cycle as a series of frustrating ordeals, perhaps like Sisyphus, endlessly pushing that rock up the hill, only to have it roll back down again. Another person with the same natal aspect will more effectively rise to the occasion, and through the Saturn-Sun cycle gradually evolve a solid sense of increasing competence, commitment, integrity, and personal authority.

One might argue – and some astrologers have – that astrological context (sign and house placements, other mitigating natal aspects, concurrent transits to each juncture of the cycle, etc.) is sufficient to account for the difference. I tend to believe that it is more fundamentally a matter of consciousness, and that consciousness is something that we bring to the birthchart, not something inherent within the chart itself. Unless we know how a given soul has responded to the symbolism through the choices made in relation to it, we simply cannot know what the symbolism means.

With this understanding, the exoteric astro-logic presented in this series of books will be built upon a model that recognizes various levels of consciousness upon which any symbol – from the smallest detail to the birthchart as a whole – might manifest. This model will encompass the astrology practiced by most astrologers – based on an understanding of the symbolic implications of number, astronomy and mythology, and rooted in our cumulative tradition. It will not depart significantly from the common understanding of basic principles, nor will it attempt to rewrite the language in some foreign tongue. It will instead strive toward the application of astrology within a spiritual context – as a template of possibilities amenable to the exercise of consciousness – that allows its more intentional development as a language of soul.

Endnotes

[1]   Thankfully, this has been slowly changing due to the pioneering work of Project Hindsight and ARHAT in translating classical astrological texts from Greek and Latin into English; the degree programs in astrology being offered by Kepler College in the Seattle area and Bath Spa University in England; and the inroads into academia and professional circles made by pre-eminent astrologers like Liz Greene, Nick Campion, Demetra George, Patrick Curry, Glenn Perry, Richard Tarnas and others. But this recent development is still in the nascent stages and will no doubt take at least a generation to begin to bear fruit that is noticeable and acknowledged by the mainstream.

Tracking the Soul

With an Astrology of Consciousness

Introduction
The Astro-logic of Consciousness

Although few astrologers would argue that any birthchart is written in stone, beyond the exercise of free will, choice or consciousness, little is written about the subjective interplay between astrological symbolism and the consciousness exercised in relation to it. The astrological community has little to say about consciousness – neither in terms of how it impacts the subjective perception of a birthchart, nor the way the meaning of a birthchart changes as the symbolism is embodied more or less consciously. As the first in a series elaborating an astropoetic approach to astrology, this book will be a partial attempt to remedy this glaring omission. For as we discuss the various tenets of exoteric astro-logic – hoping to feel our way into a more esoteric place of subjective wisdom – we can only do so within a framework recognizing the primacy of consciousness as the overarching context within which everything astrological must be understood.

Exoteric astro-logic can be helpful as a language of inquiry into the nature, meaning and purpose of life experience – as I will demonstrate in some detail in this book – but it is the inquiry that is primary. Ultimately, the birthchart and the exoteric astro-logic that infuses it with abstract meaning are only really useful as the point of departure for an exploration of the life that colors it with subjective nuance and the intimate particulars of actual experience. To put it bluntly: without an assessment of the choices made by the soul living the chart, the chart cannot be interpreted, except as an exercise in speculation. Our ability to say anything at all about a chart depends upon knowing something about who or what the chart refers to.

Interpretation as an Exercise in Consciousness

We must begin by recognizing that the astrological inquiry itself is an exercise in consciousness. What we "see" in a birthchart will depend upon the consciousness that we bring to it at various stages of our inquiry. However astutely it is approached in the moment, the birthchart is not something that reveals itself all at once, nor will it necessarily reveal itself in the same way tomorrow as it did yesterday. What we see when we look within it changes as we change. The same chart will be ours throughout a lifetime of experience, but it will not mean the same thing at age 47 that it does at age 7. The exoteric astro-logic we apply to the chart may be consistent, but the fruit of our application – the esoteric understanding that we gather – will ripen with age and spiritual maturity. Both life and our understanding of life as it is reflected in our birthchart are thus primarily a reflection of the evolution of our consciousness.

INTRODUCTION

If we are attempting to understand our own birthchart, the quest is necessarily one that will evolve over the course of a lifetime. If this is true of each of us end-users of astrology (hopefully each practicing astrologer is also an end-user), it must be an even more profoundly humbling realization when we turn our attention to the birthchart of another. For what we see in any birthchart, and how we interpret what we see will depend upon who we are as souls, where we have been in our own spiritual journeys and what we are capable of seeing.

At best, when we interpret the birthchart of another, we stand outside of that life, attempting to peer through its walls with the x-ray vision afforded by our exoteric knowledge of astrology, and hoping to grab a snapshot of a moving human work-in-progress that the subject of the snapshot will recognize as theirs. Although many astrologers do accomplish this minor miracle on a routine basis, the ability to do so is at heart a profound demonstration – not of astrological prowess per se – but of the capacity of the astrologer to enter into the experience of the client and see it within the framework that astrology provides. It is not just our competence as astrologers that allows us to do this, but also – and perhaps primarily – our maturity as souls endowed with empathy, an awareness of the human tendency to project, and a high level of responsibility for our own subjective state of being.

This self-evident truth is rarely acknowledged among astrologers, who are weaned along with the rest of our culture on the expectations inherent in a dominant scientific paradigm. As discussed in some detail in *The Seven Gates of Soul*, science has vigorously sought to neutralize, if not eliminate altogether the impact of the observer on the observation. Through double blind experiments, endless replication by other experimenters, and other rigorous procedural checks and balances, the subjective is effectively squeezed out of any statement of scientific fact. Despite the fact that some of the more scientifically-minded in our community call for scientific rigor in the articulation of exoteric astro-logic, few practicing astrologers I know would feel comfortable knowing they are not an integral part of the equation by which the truth in a birthchart reveals itself in the course of a reading. In the best readings, a synergistic magic takes place that is as much a product of the interaction between the astrologer and the client – as two human beings in dialogue – as it is of mere astrological knowledge. Any practicing astrologer who has experienced this must acknowledge that the consciousness that the individual astrologer brings to the actual practice of astrology matters profoundly.

Most astrologers celebrate the fact that different astrologers bring different perspectives to the same birthchart, but we tend to consider our differences mostly in terms of preferred techniques, or of astrological orientation, rather than the more intangible factors that each of us brings to our work – personal history and background; cultural, socio-economic, political and religious biases; individual strengths and weaknesses; life experiences; unresolved psychological issues; personal beliefs about the meaning and purpose of life; temporary moods and mindsets at the time of a given reading, etc. Our focus is almost exclusively on astrology and our relationship to the language – even though each of us will speak a different language and see a chart differently – not just because of what we know about astrology, but also because of who we are.

It is important to acknowledge that the picture in the mirror gets passed through an additional set of filters when a professional astrologer "reads" the birthchart for a client. In order to function as a clear intermediary between a birthchart and its rightful owner, the professional astrologer must possess, in addition to his exoteric training, a deep esoteric understanding of his own chart and who he is in relation to it. Ideally, he will be consciously and intentionally on his own spiritual journey, preferably one facilitated by the application of astrology to his own life process. In addition to standard counseling skills, he must cultivate the ability to astro-empathize – to listen with astrologically trained ears for the subjective truth behind the symbolism of the chart. To do this effectively, he must set the intention to "get out of the way," be upfront and honest about any personal biases that may skew a reading this way or that, and suspend his exoteric knowledge of astrology so that new information – supplied by the client – can register. In this way, his presence in the reading can become as transparent a filter as possible, and a genuine guide to self-knowledge for those who come to him for perspective.

Astrology as a Language for Self-Inquiry

Although I know from personal experience that this can be done, I have gradually shifted my own focus away from reading charts for other people to helping them to read their own. In 1993, after 25 years of professional practice, I began to promote self-reliance in the quest for guidance by teaching a correspondence course called Eye of the Centaur to those wanting to learn astrology to facilitate their own process of self-discovery. This book is written to serve this same student base and audience, as well as conscientious professional astrologers who wish to use an esoteric knowledge of their own chart as a platform for their practice.

Each individual, armed with a knowledge of exoteric astro-logic, and taught a few techniques of self-observation and memory work, is in a much better position to intuitively penetrate to the heart of the deeper esoteric understanding of the symbolism than any stranger, however well-versed in astrology they might be. We all need help from time to time, and well-trained professional astrologers can be a godsend in this capacity. But in the end, each of us must make sense of our own lives, and bring as much consciousness to it as possible. Astrology is even more valuable as an aid to this more personal, solitary process.

Some would argue that it is not possible to be objective about oneself. However, since it is actually subjective wisdom that we seek, and not mere astrological information, it is only as we attempt to see the image reflected in the mirror for ourselves that we can find what we're looking for. It may take time, but it is not something that can just be handed to us, even by the most skilled astrologer. What we seek in this mirror is not just a static interpretation of symbolism, but rather an evolving sense of self, reflected through the dynamic track record of choices mapped to various astrological cycles. This mapping of choices to cycles, in turn, renders the birthchart comprehensible to us as a useful reflection of the evolving consciousness we have brought to it.

The Birthchart as a Template
For the Tracking of Consciousness

Having established the primacy of this track record of personal choices, and encouraged the reader to explore her own, we are now in a position to understand how the birthchart itself might reveal, purely on the level of exoteric astro-logic, the tracks upon which consciousness will tend to travel. In *The Seven Gates of Soul*, I suggested that in the age-old argument between fate and free will, the birthchart represents a template of fate, while free will is what each of us brings to the template. Here I would add that fate can be understood, in part, as a set of habits of consciousness, which we are free to indulge unconsciously or to break with new awareness. Exercising this freedom is the essence of the choice we make at each juncture of our journey. Thus, the choices we track as we explore the birthchart are essentially between a set of defaults and a departure from habit, which broadens and deepens our way of being. Claiming the broadest and deepest possible way of being is then tantamount to fully incarnating as Spirit within a body – of becoming a fully embodied soul.

Astrology can be helpful in this process by revealing the default position from which we attempt to expand and deepen. Or put another way, the natal birthchart can be understood as a template of habit patterns, in the exercise of consciousness, against which we can measure our subsequent growth. In Part Two, we will look in some detail at how this template is constructed. We will map various states of consciousness to the appropriate astrological correlates, and develop a system through which any birthchart can be understood explicitly as a template for the awakening and development of consciousness. In Part Three, I offer additional suggestions for moving beyond the system into a more open-ended awareness of the evolutionary process at the heart of the life behind the birthchart. First, however, it will be helpful to differentiate between various states of consciousness, discuss the psychology that governs each state, and explore the habits of default that are implicated at each level.

Consciousness is a fluid media, and any attempt to discuss it in terms of discrete states is somewhat contrived. On the other hand, having a conceptual framework in which to explore the spiritual psychology of consciousness can be a useful point of departure for evolving a system of exoteric astro-logic conducive to a more nuanced quest for subjective esoteric wisdom, so we will persist a while longer in this folly.

The Yogic Model of Consciousness

An elegant and relatively simple system for understanding consciousness was conceptualized at least four thousand years ago (Judith 5) by yogic practitioners of a Hindu mystical tradition[1], postulating a series of seven *chakras*[2], through which primal energy and consciousness rise in the course of spiritual evolution. These practitioners were intent on charting their spiritual progress and articulating the inner work yet to be done, and used the *chakra* system as a point of reference. The system was passed down to successive generations of disciplines as an oral teaching, and eventually codified in writing a couple centuries before the birth of Christ. Though other frameworks are possible, in my experience none speaks quite so simply or eloquently to the possibility of human evolution. This perspective gains immensely in power and clarity when synthesized with astrology, as I will demonstrate comprehensively in this book.

Our modern understanding of the *chakra* system comes primarily through a Hindu teacher known as Patanjali, who lived three centuries before the birth of Christ. His teachings were first written down as a set of aphorisms in the *Yoga-Sûtra*, c. 100-200 CE, elaborated in the 16th century by Tantrik Purnanda-Swami in a text called *Sat-Chakra-Nirupana*, and transmitted to the West largely through the promotional activities of the Theosophical Society, an esoteric metaphysical group founded in New York 1875 by Madame Helena Blavatsky and Colonel H. S. Olcott. The Society counted among its members early western *chakra* authorities such as Alice Bailey, Annie Besant, and Charles Leadbeater. In the late 19th century and on into the early 20th, the Society published a number of translations, and sponsored various East Indian teachers in the US and western Europe, who brought with them variations of this ancient yogic wisdom teaching. In the 1960s and 70s, the *chakra* system was further popularized by spiritual teachers such as Parmahansa Yogananda, Swami Satchidananda, Gopi Krishna, Swami Kriyananda, Yogi Amrit Desai, Haridas Chaurhuri, Sri Chimnoy, Yogi Bhajan, Swami Muktananda, and others who traveled from India and established ashrams in both the US and Europe. More recently, knowledge of the *chakras* has been refreshed by a new wave of teachers, such as spiritually oriented psychologist Anodea Judith, medical intuitive Caroline Myss, and energy medicine pioneer, Rosalyn Bruyere.

My understanding of the *chakra* system comes from both Yogi Bhajan and Swami Muktananda, with whom I studied intensively from 1971 – 1979. This understanding necessarily differs from more traditional teachings through a consideration of this system within an astrological context, as well as through allowing my understanding of the system to percolate through a quarter century of life experience. While I have no interest in reinventing the wheel, I do intend to turn that wheel in kaleidoscopic fashion to reveal a layered multi-dimensional perspective that to my knowledge is not available elsewhere.

The Five Levels of Manifestation

Our discussion of *chakras* will be further developed through reference to a second, lesser-known system, as described by the Hindu concept of the five *koshas*, or levels of penetration of Spirit into matter. In *The Seven Gates of Soul*, I speak of the soul's experience of embodiment as an inhabitation of the body by Spirit. Here, I will elaborate that understanding through reference to the *koshas*, which describe in more detail the extent to which Spirit has penetrated the material realm. Reference to this second complementary system lets us assess not only the quality of consciousness brought to focus through each astrological pattern that we study, but also the depth of awareness the embodied soul is being called to by its experience.

Within the Hindu framework, the *koshas* exist as intermediate states of receptivity to Spirit along a continuum of being that lies between pure matter, or *prakriti*, at one end of the scale, and pure consciousness, or *purusha*, at the other. *Kosha* is roughly translated as "sheath," implying that within the yogic system, Spirit is essentially clothing itself with matter at various levels of transparency. At one end, Spirit wears the thick winter clothing of matter, and the soul is essentially oblivious to the presence of Spirit within the body. At the other end, Spirit is essentially naked, and the soul is fully conscious and essentially identified with Spirit.

Between the endpoints of pure matter and pure consciousness are distinct but interrelated levels of *kosha*, or sheathing, that find their expression within the human body. According to the yogic system, these are *annamaya kosha*, or the physical body itself; *pranamaya kosha*, or the vital energy body; *manomaya kosha*, or the realm of sense perception, emotion, memory, and ego-consciousness; *vijnanamaya kosha*, or the intuitive, meditative mind; and *anandamaya kosha*, or the ongoing state of bliss in which a full embodiment of Spirit is being realized in each moment.

While the five *koshas* can be understood as a hierarchy along which a soul becomes increasingly more conscious in the embodied state, it is also useful to understand that Spirit is continuously manifesting concurrently on all five levels. It is our awareness that draws one or more of the *koshas* into focus at any given time. Those *koshas* seemingly activated by our awareness will in turn determine the apparent circumstances of our lives. At any given time, however, it is possible to shift our awareness from one *kosha* to another, in order to understand more deeply how Spirit is available to us on a deeper or more all-encompassing level of penetration. Such a shift can suggest strategies for more effectively coping with whatever life issues appear to be related to the more obviously activated *kosha*.

For example, if you have just been diagnosed with cancer, then obviously your attention is being directed to *annamaya kosha*, or the physical body – that is to say, the densest layer of clothing assumed by Spirit. If you choose traditional allopathic treatment for this cancer, the available healing modalities of radiation, chemotherapy, and surgery will all be directed exclusively to this level. Cancer – or any seemingly physical manifestation of Spirit in the body – is, however, never *just* a physical manifestation. It also reverberates throughout all five *koshas*, whether we are aware of these reverberations or not.

If you move to *pranamaya kosha*, or the vital energy body, and ask what is going on there, for example, you might well notice how you feel shut down on an energetic level, as though you don't quite have the vital force you need to cope on the physical level. Going more deeply still, to *manomaya kosha*, or the realm of sense perception, emotion, memory, and ego-consciousness, you might then trace these feelings back to an incident of betrayal five years earlier by someone you loved deeply, from which you have never fully recovered. Moving to *vijnanamaya kosha*, or the intuitive, meditative mind, you might then realize the necessity for forgiveness and letting go, and understand – in a way that a merely medical model of intervention could never fathom – that your healing and recovery in some sense is actually more dependent on your ability to do this, than any drug you might take or operation you might choose to undergo. Were you able to accomplish this inner task, you might then become aware of how Spirit was manifesting on the level of *anandamaya kosha*, and suddenly know beyond a shadow of a doubt, that regardless of what appeared to be happening on the physical level – whether you cured your cancer or not – you would be absolutely fine.

This is a hypothetical example. But as we will explore later in this book, what happens at each *kosha*, and the interplay between *koshas* can be tracked with exquisite detail as we view life through an astrological template. Each astrological indication, including the birthchart as a whole, can be interpreted at the level of each *kosha*, so that it gives one level of meaning relevant to the functioning of our physical bodies, another relevant to the flow of energy through our vital body, another relevant to the ongoing operation of our sensory-emotional experience, and so on. Each level of interpretation will parallel, confirm, and enhance our understanding at every other level, creating a developed synthesis of observations at all five *koshas* that can provide a much more complete astrological picture than a mere consideration of astro-logic alone. For this reason, as we discuss the astrology of consciousness, I will employ the *koshas* as a useful component of the system.

The Chakra System Revisited

The primary component of this system – the seven *chakras* – is more familiar to western seekers, since it has been part of our common vocabulary since the integration of eastern and western religious cultures in the late 1960s and 1970s. The word, *chakra* means "circle," "wheel of light," or "vortex" and refers to a state of consciousness through which life energy, or *prana*, is processed and released into expression. The *chakras* are not explicitly physical in nature, though each is associated with an endocrine gland and with a group of nerves called a plexus. Each *chakra* also has its psychological correlates, which in turn determine the needs, desires, source of motivation, intention, and characteristic patterns of fear and resistance that can be associated with the *prana* or life energy that is channeled through it.

Chakras are sometimes also referred to in the Vedantic literature as *granthi*, meaning knots, or *sankhocha*, meaning contractions, implying that as we work through the blockages of fear and resistance associated with each center, we rise to a higher level of consciousness[3]. Thus, within the system of seven *chakras*, we have everything we need to understand the consciousness that is brought to bear upon our perception of the birthchart. We also have a broader context in which to place our study of astro-logic that recognizes the central role consciousness plays in the soul's evolution through the patterns represented by the birthchart.

Before we explore this system in more detail, I wish to present a perspective about the system as a whole that is somewhat different than that which originally governed the yogic practitioners that developed it. These practitioners envisioned the system as a hierarchical progression of evolutionary states that paralleled and in some ways depended upon the raising of *kundalini* energy up the spine from one *chakra* to the next. *Kundalini*, sometimes referred to as *shakti*, was a reserve of psychic energy thought to rest at the base of the spine like a coiled serpent. Various yogic practices were designed to arouse the *kundalini*, and draw it up the spine where it would open and activate higher centers of awareness. Through the ongoing practice of *kundalini yoga*, coupled with an ascetic life based vows of chastity, minimal concern for material needs, and non-violence, the higher *chakras* could be opened on a more permanent basis, and serve as the energetic basis for a life of refined motivation and expression.

While *kundalini yoga* is still practiced in both India and the West today, one need not subscribe to the practice in order to benefit from an understanding of the *chakra* system. Indeed, our purpose here is not to facilitate the practice of *yoga*, but to provide a context in which ordinary, everyday life might be understood with reference to consciousness, and a system of astro-logic might be used more consciously to map ordinary life as a vehicle for soul growth. From this perspective, it is somewhat misleading to think of the system in hierarchical terms, because everyday life is not a simple matter of progression from one state to the next.

Even within practice of *kundalini yoga* itself, spiritual progress is rarely a strictly linear proposition. One may experience the temporary opening of a so-called higher *chakra*, for example, before a so-called lower one is completely purified. One may also find it necessary to return to more intensive work on a lower *chakra* in order to sustain one's experience at a higher level. In fact, while the aim of *kundalini yoga* is to raise consciousness up the scale, in practice, the real work of spiritual growth often requires going down the scale to deal with unresolved issues connected to the lower centers.

Since the ultimate goal – in the practice of *kundalini yoga* and in life – is to experience all *chakras* open and vibrating at an optimal level, even the notion that we are moving up or down the scale can impede our understanding of the process. In practice, our spiritual work, however we choose to pursue it, will involve moving between various centers and learning to negotiate more skillfully and gracefully the energy dynamic between them. For this reason, I prefer to think of the seven *chakras* as being arranged in a circle, rather than as a straight line, as this allows us to work with them conceptually in a more flexible way.

The Chakras Considered as a Circle of Circles

Some precedence exists for this view among Taoist yogis, who speak in modern terms of the microcosmic orbit (Chia 6), through which *ch'i*, or the Taoist equivalent of *kundalini*, circulates through the *chakras* in a continuous circuit. While energy flows up through the *chakra* system along the spine at the back of the body, it flows down through the same system in front of the body. Anodea Judith also speaks of the necessity for balancing the upward flow of energy through the *chakras*, which she calls the "current of liberation," with a downward flow, the "current of manifestation" (14-15).

Conceptualizing the *chakras* as a circular continuum also creates a practical advantage in visualizing how they work together as a system. Among practitioners of both Taoist and Hindu *yoga*, there are known connections between various *chakras* that are not successive in nature – such as that between the second, or sexual center and the fifth or throat *chakra*, or that between the root *chakra* at the base of the spine and the crown at the top of the head. A circular model more easily allows for consideration of these kinds of connections, particularly within the context of spiritual psychology that is not dependent upon strict physiological correlates. The advantage of this will become clear as we proceed.

A third reason for moving away from a hierarchical model is that hierarchies invariably encourage judgment, which is nearly always detrimental to a clear understanding of the soul's process. The natural assumption in contemplating any hierarchy is that higher is better than lower, but in the case of the *chakra* system, especially as it is considered from the perspective of spiritual psychology, this is not always the case. Energy medicine pioneer, Rosalyn Bruyere points out that it was the Victorian mindset, prevalent throughout the age of British Colonialism that endowed the lower *chakras* with their negative associations. She calls for a less judgmental approach that distinguishes between the frequency of energy moving through a *chakra* (consciousness) and the *chakra* itself (58)[4].

Outside of the context of yogic discipline, it is a mistake to make judgments on the basis of which *chakras* seem more open than others, or where the major concentration of energy lies. This is necessarily so, because different processes experienced at different points in the evolutionary process, or within different life contexts, may require a different mix of energies, and so-called lower *chakras* may well play as important, if not a more important role, than so-called higher *chakras*.

A young couple, desirous of children, for example, may be appropriately focused on clarifying issues within their second or sexual centers and their fourth or heart centers, while an older, solitary writer may be almost exclusively focused in her fifth or creative/ expressive center. This does not mean, as a hierarchical interpretation of *chakras* might suggest, that the process of writing is a higher, more evolved activity than starting a family. Within the context of a quest for subjective wisdom, such judgments are, in fact, quite meaningless.

In *The Seven Gates of Soul*, I suggest that a major conceptual barrier to understanding soul process is the judgment projected onto that process, largely by religion. As the by-product of a religious orientation, the *chakra* system must also be purged of its judgmental overtones, before it can be truly useful. From a symbolic perspective, this can readily be accomplished by arranging the *chakras* conceptually within a circle, rather than along a straight line.

This approach also nicely mirrors our understanding that the circle is the basic foundation for all subsequent development of a cogent system of astro-logic. By synthesizing the astro-logic of the circle with a circular interpretation of the *chakra* system, we have the basis for understanding the movement of circles (*chakras*) within circles (the birthchart as a whole, and the various planetary cycles that circulate within it). Such a conceptual basis is itself astrological, since it employs the same symbol to explore the connection between the conscious evolution of an individual soul and the circulation of consciousness throughout the larger Whole or Cosmos of which the individual is a part.

A Word About the Psychic Correlates to the Chakra System

Before we can make the leap to a broader system of astro-logic, it will be necessary to briefly explore each of the seven *chakras*, and discuss their related psychologies. In the Hindu system, each *chakra* was part of an elaborate system of symbolic correspondences, involving animals, colors, a particular number of petals, and sounds. Since these are often suggestive on a subliminal level, and may intuitively engender a more personal set of associations, I will include them here for the reader to ponder, mostly without additional comment. Other aspects of the Hindu symbology can be rather esoteric, and are perhaps less meaningful or useful to the Western mind.

Although there is not universal agreement on these correspondences, the descriptions I have chosen come from a scholarly classic, *The Serpent Power: The Secrets of Tantric and Shaktic Yoga* by Arthur Avalon (Sir John Woodroffe), who translated them from original *Tantric* texts, written in Sanskrit, including Tantrik Purnananda-Swami's *Sat-Chakra-Nirupana*. Woodroffe spent half his life locating these documents, which were well-guarded secrets of esoteric literature, and we can be reasonably sure they are as close to the source of the original teachings about the *chakras* as it is possible for modern western scholars to get, though certainly not the final word on the subject.

Even though we can talk about *chakras* as an objective system, *chakras* are by nature a subjective phenomena that will be experienced differently by different people. As Theosophist authority Charles Leadbetter notes, referring to the wide divergence of opinion regarding the colors to be associated with each *chakra*, "It is not surprising that such differences as these should be on record, for there are unquestionably variants in the *chakras* of different people and races, as well as in the faculties of observers" (97).

Woodroffe's correspondences, drawn from original texts, are best understood as corroborated observations made by yogic practitioners whose intention was to purify and cleanse their *chakras*, not necessarily replicable by contemporary observers viewing the auras of ordinary people. On the other hand, the modern tendency to simply map the *chakras* to the colors of the rainbow (Bruyere 79, Judith 2) – while conceptually appealing – is probably not any closer to the actual truth for most people. For the sake of comparison, I include observations by Leadbetter, Judith, Bruyere, and Myss, where they differ from Woodroffe's translations of *Tantric* texts.

The Chakras as a Model of Psychological Process

Given that our interest here is not the psychic correlates to the *chakras*, but rather their relevance to a psychology of soul, I offer this brief taste of the ancient teachings only as an appetizer to the main course. The primary discussion will revolve around an exploration of each *chakra* in more contemporary psychological terms, as it manifests on the level of each *kosha*. The psychology of each *chakra* will be most visible on the level of *manomaya kosha*, or the realm of sense perception, emotion, memory, and ego-consciousness – and it is largely here that we will look for the perceptual framework that makes the mirror of the birthchart what it appears to be at each level of consciousness. *Manomaya kosha* is where most of us focus most of the time, since this is where the melodrama of the soul's everyday journey appears to be playing itself out. Yet, the melodrama is often merely the most noticeable manifestation of a process that is unfolding concurrently at all five *koshas*.

Each *chakra* will function not just in terms of psychology, but also on the level of the physical body, on an energetic level, as an intimately personal play of suggestive imagery that speaks directly to the intuitive mind, and as a statement of spiritual purpose, where even the most mundane of life circumstances becomes grist for the mill of our awakening. Most modern interpretations of the *chakra* system assume that the so-called lower *chakras* are closer to the physical end of the spectrum, while the so-called higher *chakras* are more spiritual (Myss 68-70, Bruyere 44-47, Anodea 7). This conception largely comes from the linear arrangements of the *chakras* up the spine, in which the lower *chakras* are literally closer to the earth. Using the circular model, by contrast, allows us to think of each *chakra* as a neutral domain in which Spirit can manifest on various levels of penetration as indicated by the *koshas*.

At shallower depths of penetration by Spirit, the first three *chakras* will appear to encompass a psychology that revolves primarily around earthly concerns, and to some extent, there will be a developmental progression to less worldly concerns as one moves into the fifth, sixth and especially the seventh *chakra*. But there will also be situations in which a deeper level of penetration of Spirit into matter in one of the so-called lower *chakras* can spark a powerful spiritual awakening, or conversely where shallow levels of penetration by Spirit in the upper *chakras* can manifest physically. In any case, spiritual development will not be a strictly linear progression from physical manifestation at the lower *chakras* to awakening of Spirit in the higher centers, and a dual system allows greater latitude in considering the actual course of the evolutionary process.

The Astro-Chakra System

In many ways, the *chakra* system – as understood by the ancient practitioners and modern adherents alike – constitutes a stand-alone approach to spiritual psychology. The depth and sophisticated simplicity of the system, refined through thousands of years of observation and practice, rivals anything modern psychology – still in its infancy – has to offer. This is especially true to the extent that modern psychology is built upon a scientific model, since, as discussed in *The Seven Gates of Soul*, such a foundation precludes serious consideration of the spiritual implications of psychological experience.

As many have pointed out, astrology is also a stand-alone system of spiritual psychology, refined through thousands of years of observation and practice. Any attempt to combine the two systems might seem an exercise in redundancy, were it not for the fact that each contributes something unique to the synthesis. As discussed earlier, astrology lacks an explicit understanding of the way in which consciousness alters the meaning of its symbolism, nor does it inherently include a discussion of consciousness as a framework for spiritual evolution that the *chakra* system offers. Individual astrologers may bring a sense of this to their work, but it is not intrinsically a part of the astrological language.

What astrology does contribute is the unparalleled ability to personalize the spiritual process, and to time it. Each chart is a unique signature of possibilities for spiritual growth belonging to a particular soul, and encoded within each chart is a timetable for the outworking of those possibilities. For all its sophistication, the *chakra* system lacks these two essential ingredients. For this reason, bringing the two systems together – in a creative synthesis I will call the astro-chakra system – can only serve to enhance them both.

As we correlate astrological patterns with various *chakras* and *koshas* in Part Two, we will gradually evolve a larger conceptual framework in which the birthchart can be understood as a multi-dimensional template for the tracking of consciousness through the life of an embodied soul. The astro-chakra system will provide a point of access to the esoteric wisdom beyond the exoteric logic of astrology's symbolism. It will render an astrology more fully capable of articulating the astropoetic impulse at the heart of the human experience and of facilitating answers to the deepest, most intimate questions the soul is capable of posing. It will also provide a solid foundation on which subsequent volumes in The Astropoetic Series – exploring the astro-logic of number, astronomy and mythology – can proceed toward the development of a true language of soul, which must necessarily have a systemic appreciation for the interplay of consciousness and symbolism at its base.

Endnotes

[1] As Bruyere points out, the *chakras* were known to other cultures as well – including the Egyptians, the Chinese, the Greeks and Native Americas – "although they may have called them by different names" (27).

[2] Unfamiliar terms, from various spiritual traditions, specific to the astro-chakra system, or unique to the practice of astropoetics can be found in the glossary, beginning on

page 425.

3   According to Ken Wilbur, "Liberation . . . is not the actual untying of these knots, but rather the silent admission that they are already untied. Herein lies the key to the paradox of the *chakras*: They are ultimately dissolved in the realization that they need not be dissolved" (121).

4   This fearful attitude toward the lower centers was also adopted by the Theosophists, who often focused it toward the second or sexual center, which they replaced by the spleen. In a footnote to his classic, *The Chakras*, Leadbeater acknowledges this when he says, "The spleen *chakra* is not indicated in the Indian books; its place is taken by a centre called the *Svadhisthana*, situated in the neighbourhood of the generative organs. . . From our point of view the arousing of such a centre would be regarded as a misfortune, as there are serious dangers connected with it" (7).

Part One
The Chakras

Chapter One
The First Chakra

In the Hindu system, the first or root *chakra*, associated with the nerve plexus at the base of the spine, was known as *muladhara*. It is described as crimson, four-petaled, related to the earth *tattwa* or element, and symbolized by the elephant (Avalon 116-117). Drawing upon Hermetic tradition, Bruyere instead correlates this *chakra* with the element of fire (53) and points out that in various cultures, the first *chakra* has been portrayed by worms, spiders and lizards (indigenous peoples of North and South America), dragons (pagan cultures of Europe), serpents (Egypt, Babylon, India and China), horses (ancient Greece) and bumblebees (Crete and Egypt) (111-118). Myss connects this *chakra* with the *sefirah* of Shekhinah (in the Kabalistic Tree of Life), which she says is "symbolic of the the spiritual community of all humanity and to the feminine spirit of the earth known as Gaia" (104).

The root *chakra* is the most fundamental level at which the fusion of Spirit and matter takes place, and the most basic resting place of consciousness within the human body. At this most fundamental level, Spirit infuses the body with the gift of life, and we depart on a quest to secure, explore, and extract a sense of meaning and purpose from this gift. It is where the embodied life takes root, and where we begin to grow as embodied souls, reaching through our embodiment toward the Light.

The motivational pattern seeking expression at this level of consciousness is related to survival needs, although the satisfaction of those needs means something quite different at each *kosha*, and it is not until all these needs are met on the level of all five koshas that the first *chakra* can be said to be functioning at its optimum level. When this level of optimum functioning is reached, the *chakra* opens, and survival needs cease to be a part of a person's conscious motivational repertoire. For the most part, these needs will recede into the background, and seemingly be taken care of as a matter of course, without a great deal of conscious attention necessary. Since the embodied soul, however, is destined to one day face its own mortality, we are never entirely done with the first *chakra*. How we understand what survival means, and how well-equipped we are to face our mortality will be a function of how much awareness we can bring to all five koshas on which this *chakra* functions. As our survival needs are met at successively deeper levels of *kosha*, the concept of survival itself takes on broader connotations that ultimately transcend our physical mortality.

◇◇◇

Annamaya Kosha

Before we can make this conceptual leap, however, it will be necessary to understand how the first *chakra* functions at each of the five koshas. On the level of *annamaya kosha* (the physical body), at the first *chakra*, we are primarily concerned with the process of elimination. In the body, the first *chakra* is associated with organs such as the liver, kidneys and gall bladder that process toxins, and organs such as the colon, the urethra, and the skin that eliminate them. The first order of business in the first *chakra* is to eliminate everything that poses a threat to a sustainable life, and on the level of *annamaya kosha*, it is largely through urination, defecation, and sweat that we accomplish this purpose.

The concept of elimination, however, also has broader metaphorical implications that extend the function of the first *chakra* on *annamaya kosha* to other activities that are not strictly physiological. Anytime we become aware that something is harmful to us, and seek to eliminate it, avoid it, or refrain from indulging in it, we are acting on a first *chakra* impulse that has manifest on the level of *annamaya kosha*. In the most primal way, normally frowned upon in civilized society, this impulse might manifest as the need to kill potential predators – that is to say, those who would kill us. Society as a whole acts on this impulse, for example, when it sentences a murderer to death row, gives life in prison to someone considered dangerous to the lives of others, or goes to war. On a less dramatic level, we also act out this impulse whenever we eliminate from our diets certain foods that seem to disagree with us, avoid physically abusive people, refrain from touching a hot stove, or stop for a fast moving train before attempting to cross the railroad tracks.

We may also act out this impulse in relation to situations that are not objectively threatening us in any way. The key principle here – as in all matters of consciousness – is perception. For on this level, we may also seek to avoid people who remind us of an abusive parent, whether or not the comparison is justified; skirt around a confrontation, if the memory of a fist fight on a childhood playground has made us timid; or refuse to go skiing ever again, if we once broke a leg in an earlier downhill run. Anything can become a threat to our survival, if we perceive it to be so. To the extent that we subsequently seek to eliminate, avoid or refrain from experiencing it – whatever it is – then we are acting out a first *chakra* impulse on the level of *annamaya kosha*.

Pranamaya Kosha

On the level of *pranamaya kosha*, or on the energetic level, the process of elimination can be understood more consciously in terms of the movement of energy at the heart of the strategies we employ to achieve our goal, and as greater awareness of the true nature of the goal itself. When we eliminate something, for example, we are expelling it from our body, and/or from the larger space that comprises our embodied world. When we avoid something, we are excluding it or shutting it out; when we refrain from participating or experiencing something, we are erecting a psychological, if not a physical barrier between ourselves and whatever we perceive to be somehow threatening to our existence. What happens at the level of one *kosha* is not different from what happens at any other level. We are merely shifting our perspective to encompass a broader and more deeply spiritual understanding of our process.

Thus, if we are eliminating something at the level of *annamaya kosha*, for example, we are still eliminating at the level of *pranamaya kosha*. Seen from this vantage point, however, the process of elimination can be understood more consciously as a deeper penetration of Spirit into matter, or conversely as a greater receptivity to the functional purpose of Spirit as it manifests at that level. On an energetic level, we are not just eliminating; we are also establishing boundaries. We are seeking protection behind those boundaries from forces and influences that we perceive to be in some way threatening to our survival. Our elimination, avoidance, and refraining, in other words, has a purpose, and that purpose can be understood as protection.

Knowing this, we begin approaching our first *chakra* issues in a slightly different way. Instead of simply asking, "how can I eliminate this unwanted influence from my life?" we ask, "how can I protect myself from it?" The difference is subtle, but important, for it changes the way we approach the necessary task of survival. Instead of avoiding dark alleyways, we may choose to buy a gun, study martial arts, or hire a bodyguard. Instead of refusing to ski, we may take lessons, learn how to fall safely, and stick to the beginner's slopes until we build our confidence. Instead of eliminating hot Indian curries from our diet, we may learn to temper their fiery danger to our gastrointestinal tract with milder spices or a cooling side dish of yogurt and cucumbers. We respond to our first *chakra* task of survival differently because protection is not necessarily dependent on elimination, avoidance or refraining from something altogether. We have a wider range of options, because we understand the purpose for which we are attempting to eliminate, avoid or refrain. Spirit has penetrated more deeply into matter, and we have risen to greet it at a slightly more empowered level, so we are now more conscious in relation to our first *chakra* issues than we were before.

Manomaya Kosha

The process continues to evolve as we move to the level of *manomaya kosha*, or the level on which we experience ourselves as sensory, emotional beings with a memory and a sense of identity. Again, on this level, we are still eliminating and protecting, but we are

◇◇

also beginning to evolve a broader perspective that allows a greater range of options in our response to the first *chakra* task of survival. For it is at this level of manifestation that we begin to become aware of who it is that we are protecting, and why protection is a desirable goal. To this point, elimination and the desire for protection have largely been instinctual, but as Spirit penetrates to the level of *manomaya kosha*, we begin intentionally seeking a life-sustaining relationship to the embodied world, and our soul's journey increasingly becomes a matter of conscious choice.

Beyond simply shutting out everything from which we feel a need for protection, at the level of *manomaya kosha*, we begin to realize that what we are really seeking behind the walls of our protection is a healthy relationship with our bodies and with the embodied world that is life-sustaining. We also become identified, for the first time, with the being at the heart of the life we are hoping to sustain. Put another way, it is at this *kosha* that the embodied soul becomes aware of its own existence, and begins to approach its journey as a matter of conscious intent.

It is also here that a psychology of intention and resistance, fear and suffering comes into play, and begins to condition how we perceive and interact with the embodied world. Our intentions at the first *chakra* will naturally revolve around fostering conditions that are conducive to the maintenance of health and physical vitality, and may well involve establishing regular patterns of diet, elimination, sleep, and personal hygiene. They will, however, also invariably extend to personal finances, job and career, and to other issues that are perceived to be central, on some level, to our survival. Finding a place on earth where we can feel at home, connected, grounded, and rooted in the soil, sweat, and blood of both the earth and the local community sustained by the earth, is likewise a focus for fundamental first *chakra* intentions. In astrological language, these more obvious first *chakra* concerns will be related to the element of earth, which in general governs the practical, everyday process of working to keep body and soul functioning well together, and establishing a viable, functional connection to the embodied world.

Ultimately, however, the concept of survival, as it is encompassed by the first *chakra*, will also extend to other less earthy dimensions of our being. Emotionally, for example, we all need to feel that we are loved, that we belong, that we are appreciated for the contribution we are making, that others care about us, and our existence matters to those who are impacted by it. From the perspective of the embodied soul, these emotional experiences are every bit as essential to our survival as food, water, and air.

Scientific experiments have shown that monkeys separated from their mothers at birth experience a lower survival rate (Harlow & Zimmerman). To the extent that the absence of love, caring, and a sense of belonging contribute to a sense of lowered vitality, a depressed will to live, and a compromised instinct toward survival, dealing with issues that arise around these deficiencies can be considered a first *chakra* process, and the intentions that we set around dealing with these issues will be first *chakra* intentions. Judith speaks of first *chakra* traumas that revolve around separation anxiety at birth, abandonment, neglect and abuse (70-75), all of which stem from a sense of emotional deprivation in the first *chakra* at the level of *manomaya kosha*. Myss also speaks of fear of abandonment by the group, or tribal culture, as a first *chakra* wound (105-112). I will discuss this specific wound in more detail when we get to the sixth *chakra*, but to the extent that belonging to a group is felt as a necessity for survival, anything that undermines that basic sense of belonging will have important first *chakra* repercussions.

If our sense of belonging depends upon growing up in a familiar environment, then moving from place to place can also be a source of first *chakra* trauma. Perhaps in childhood, moving meant having to start over again with a new set of friends in a strange place at a school where it was necessary to find one's place all over again. If so, then moving in adulthood might bring up these same fears that the very foundation under one's feet were in jeopardy. With such a trauma at the root of a first *chakra* issue, one might fail to take advantage of job opportunities later in life that require one to move, experience a breakdown in marriage to a spouse who felt drawn to return to college in a different town, or even suffer undue anxiety when a favorite store went bankrupt. Anything that we experience as threatening to our survival, whether or not it actually is, will be experienced by the soul as a source of resistance to change, rooted in our first *chakra*.

A similar source of disturbance within the first *chakra* will be felt when any bottom-line need is not being met. Regardless of the particulars of our life, each of us needs to be able to communicate, to cooperate with others, and to exchange our talents, skills, and services for monetary compensation. We need to find work that sustains our interest and invokes our creative passion, and in general cultivate a sense of meaning and purpose sufficient to make us want to get out of bed in the morning and live. Spiritually, we need to feel a larger sense of connection to Spirit, or God, or Something that extends beyond our immediate sense of self. In the long run, and within the context of soul process, all of these basic needs may in one way or another ultimately prove necessary to our survival. To the extent that they are, our ability to satisfy them will be part of the spiritual psychology associated with the first *chakra*. Though a more traditional understanding of the *chakra* system would perhaps not recognize these as first *chakra* issues, anything that fuels our motivation for living, or conversely adversely impacts our will to survive, can serve as a focal point around which first *chakra* issues and the intentions we create to address them revolve.

✧✧

On this level, too, may arise more enlightened concerns with many environmental issues, especially those revolving around contamination of air, water, food, and threats to public health and the health of the biosphere. Once we are able to make the connection between personal survival and the larger ecological systems on which all of life on earth depends, we will begin to migrate to the deeper levels of penetration posed by *vijnanamaya* and *anandamaya koshas* (representing the intuitive mind and union with Spirit respectively). When we personally feel threatened by these larger threats to the environment, our involvement with these issues will also be a *manomaya kosha* (ego-based, psychological) process. The protection of our personal space can and will take any number of forms, depending on how that personal space is defined, and what we perceive to be threatening to its safety.

The will to survive can also manifest on less obvious, more subjective, and often more dysfunctional levels, and be experienced in realms that are not normally associated with survival. If, for example, we grew up with parents who insisted that we suppress our anger and punished us severely when we did not, we may reach adulthood believing, at some core level of our being, that the suppression of our anger is necessary to survival. Within the *chakra* system we are discussing here, this can be understood as a first *chakra* issue. Likewise, if one of our parents dies in our early childhood, we may feel a profound sense of abandonment. Subsequent adult relationships in which we take extraordinary measures to ensure we are not abandoned by our partner may well be rooted in first *chakra* issues – since we unconsciously associate abandonment with death. While on the emotional and psychological levels first *chakra* issues can take any number of forms, at the root of each will be some fear that our survival is being threatened.

At the level of *manomaya kosha*, these fears will begin to become more conscious, and we will feel motivated to do something about them. If our health is deteriorating, we may see a doctor, start dieting, or vow to begin exercising on a regular basis. If we have lost our job and feel the weight of the unpaid bills on our desk as a threat to survival, we will become motivated to seek employment. If we don't feel a sense of connection to the earth and the community where we are living, we will long for the greener grass on the other side of the fence, and perhaps be drawn to explore it. Intentions arise at the level of *manomaya kosha* whenever we perceive that our survival is being compromised or threatened.

Since everything in this embodied existence is balanced by a polar force tending in the opposite direction, no sooner will we set an intention than resistance will arise to meet it. As soon as we begin dieting, obsessive cravings for rich German pastries begin to consume us. As soon as we have psyched ourselves up for the necessary job search, cumulative memories of rejection, humiliation, and endless waiting in line flood through our tender psyche and wash us up on the shores of creative procrastination. As soon as we vow to move, the weight of all that stuff in the garage, and the kids' attachment to school, and countless other little strings that tie us down where we are, begin to complicate the burning intention to change that initially seemed so clear. This is the nature of intention. It invariably arises and seeks actualization within an inherent context of inertia.

In the case of first *chakra* intentions, there is also an additional source of resistance endemic to the very issue of survival. For as discussed at length in *The Seven Gates of Soul*, the inescapable counterforce staring us in the face whenever we assert our will to survive is our own mortality. Ultimately, despite our best and most heroic efforts to ensure our survival, this being that we identify as "I" will one day no longer be. This horrible truth is especially troublesome on the level of *manomaya kosha*, for it is here that our sense of "I" is asserting its most tenacious foothold upon our consciousness. We are not prepared at this level, to consciously entertain the notion of our own mortality. But the forces of entropy work against us nonetheless, and form the nucleus around which all resistance to our first *chakra* intentions will constellate.

Even assuming we are successful at our diet, our job search, or our move to a more life-sustaining location, eventually the forces of entropy will catch up with us. One day, no amount of dieting will matter – our bodies will wither, the life force will ebb within us, and dust will return to dust. No matter how successful we are at our careers, one day, it will be over – we will retire, happily or not, and gradually lose the interest, the will, and/or the ability to work at all. Though we may find the perfect spot for us on earth, one day, we will have to leave it behind in order to enter a less tangible, more etheric realm. Perhaps at a deeper level of penetration, none of this will matter so much, even in the first *chakra*, where survival is the issue at hand. But on the level of *manomaya kosha*, the relentless force of entropy is what we are working against in a match that is doomed from the start. Every sand castle we could possibly build, on any beachhead we might establish, will one day wash out to sea.

Meanwhile, every smaller tug of inertia we feel in the face of our first *chakra* intentions will be a recognition, largely unconscious, of this larger force of entropy at work, against which we are ultimately powerless, regardless of the strength of our intentions. Inescapable though it may be, this entropy is not the problem. As suggested earlier, behind every resistance is a fear, and it is this fear we must ultimately confront, if we are to resolve the underlying issues our intentions are conceived to address. Behind the resistance posed by the inevitability of death will be the fear of death, and it is this fear that will keep us scrambling to build sand castles on the beach at high tide.

Overcoming this fear is not a matter of clinging to our intentions with futile desperation, but gradually learning that we can survive in all kinds of situations that previously seemed threatening. The first time we fall off a bike, first *chakra* fears are likely

◇◇◇

to be raised. But if we keep at it, soon we learn to ride, and those fears begin to subside. If we lose a job, and discover that we can move on to whatever comes next with relatively minimal disruption of our lives, then the next time we get laid off, we might almost welcome it as an opportunity to create something better for ourselves. If we discover that no one dies when we get angry, then something inside of us shifts to allow a lessening of the fear behind our resistance. We may well continue building sand castles on the beach, because that is what we humans do, and we will be just as doomed by the relentless encroachment of the ocean as we were before, but somehow, as we live through our fears of death, the washing away of sand castles will not be nearly as problematic as it once was.

Eventually, as we are penetrated more deeply by, and become more receptive to Spirit, our understanding of what it means to survive, and who or what it is that actually dies will undergo a profound shift in a direction that will greatly lessen our fear of death. At the level of *manomaya kosha*, however, where we are tenaciously attached to a limited, ego-bound definition of self, this fear of death will prove to be a major source of suffering, for it will limit our participation in life to what seems safe. Since change is the little brother of death, and any change will necessarily involve risking the unknown, to the extent that we are controlled by our fear of death, we may enter a vicious cycle in relation to our first *chakra* issues. We will feel some threat to survival, seek to eliminate, avoid or refrain from engaging it, build walls against it, and then hunker down waiting for the ocean to come pounding against those walls. If you've ever attempted to shore up a sand castle at high tide, you know what a labor-intensive struggle it is. The same is true for all of our efforts to resolve first *chakra* issues, as long as the fear of death is fueling our intentions and creating our resistance to them. Not only do we defeat our own purpose, but the very effort expended in doing so wears us down, saps our vitality, and jeopardizes the survival we are struggling to protect.

This struggle can be played out on a thousand different stages, depending upon the specific astrological context in which it is implicated. When we explore the planetary dynamics related to first *chakra* issues later in this book, we will take a more detailed look at the spiritual psychology behind this struggle. For now, it is enough to know that the root *chakra* governs the basic health of the connection between Spirit and the body, and between the individual soul and the embodied world that it inhabits. Where these fundamental relationships are comprised by some threat to survival, issues will arise that generate pain and suffering within the domain of the first *chakra* – mostly on the level of *manomaya kosha*, which is where the spiritual psychology related to each of the chakras unfolds in living color.

Vijnanamaya Kosha

At the level of *vijnanamaya kosha*, or the intuitive, meditative mind, images begin to arise that point beyond the dilemma posed at *manomaya kosha*. The good news underlying the struggle at *manomaya kosha* is that sincere intentions are an attractive force that do not go entirely unrewarded. Not only do they attract resistance, but they also attract guidance from a deeper place within ourselves. The yogic traditions from which we are borrowing these concepts would attribute this guidance to higher mind, which in their estimation is closer to Spirit than the lower mind with which we struggle at *manomaya kosha*. But my experience is that getting pushed to the wall of the resistance is the prerequisite to evoking the guidance. In some mysterious way, the guidance arises out of the resistance, and this typically occurs not on the mental level at all, but on a sensory and an emotional level that defies rational analysis.

Resistance is a potent force within any struggle, largely because the fear that fuels it remains unconscious. It arises not as an idea, but viscerally as a dry lump in our throats, a gnawing in our bellies, an uncontrollable twitch or an itch that no amount of scratching will alleviate. It also arises as an irrational emotional response to that which overwhelms us and often cannot be put into words. We do not think, "I am afraid of death." We sob in our pillows at night; we rage at those closest to us; we tremble in fear when no one is looking. We don't have names for our resistance, but we feel it our bones and in our hearts when it overtakes us.

And we inevitably surrender to it. Surrender comes when we realize that this thing we are struggling against is much bigger than we are. It is not the weight problem, the job, or the sense of isolation that has pushed us to the wall, but the belief that we ought to be able to stave off death through the sheer force of our intentions. This belief is a hoarse whisper pitted against the endless roar of the ocean, as it echoes in every cell of our bodies, and it is a belief destined for major review. When we finally feel the untenable nature of this belief, we stop pushing against the ocean, and the ocean floods in to greet us.

In this moment, something miraculous begins to happen. As the ocean surrounds us, and permeates us, we begin to get a sense that we are no different than the ocean. We contain the ocean, and the ocean contains us. All the power of the ocean is available to us, and everything we have been pushing against becomes our source of strength once the pushing stops. When the pushing stops, and our sense of struggle subsides, we also discover that the natural buoyancy of the ocean will allow us to float, if we let it.

It is at the level of *vijnanamaya kosha* that we stop struggling and begin to learn how to float. This is not something that happens all at once, but to the extent that we are able to surrender to what appears to be larger than we are, we gradually allow Spirit to penetrate to the point where it enlarges us. It should be noted here that the surrender of which I speak is not the same as resignation, which is merely giving up in the face of issues we can't resolve. Surrender is actually closer to what American Buddhist nun Pema Chodron speaks of when she tells us to drop the story line - the struggle with our specific issues, in this case, our survival issues - and move into the soft spot of vulnerability (called *bodhichitta* in the language of Tibetan Buddhism) (88). When we connect with this soft spot of vulnerability, we realize that we are in the same boat as every other soul bobbing in the same ocean. We realize that this boat is Life itself, and how foolish it is of us to struggle against the very thing that carries and sustains us.

In the life of the soul, such a realization is priceless, for it opens the door to a much larger vision of survival than can possibly be entertained by the small ego, struggling to maintain its sand castles on the beach. This vision does not gel until Spirit penetrates to the final level of *anandamaya kosha* (where identification with Spirit is complete). But at the level of *vijnamaya kosha*, we are blessed with an endless procession of clues - in our dreams, in the symbolic implications of our daily lives, in synchronistic encounters with people, objects, and omens of endless shapes and forms - all pointing toward a synthesis of everything we are already feeling in our bellies, bones and hearts, but don't yet have a name for.

In *The Seven Gates of Soul*, I speak at length about the image-making process, and how the imagery that arises speaks directly to the soul on a sensory and emotional level. I also hint that the astropoetic practice of astrology is nothing less than the cultivation of an ability to articulate these images, while suggesting earlier in this book that this practice also marks the transition from an exoteric from of astro-logic into a more esoteric realm of subjective wisdom. Here, I will add that one can only really begin to enter this realm when Spirit has penetrated to the level of *vijnanamaya kosha*, where the spontaneously arising imagery of the unconscious points the way toward surrender into a larger sense of self.

In *The Seven Gates of Soul*, I share a pivotal dream I had, which illustrates this process. In this dream, I am walking home in semi-darkness, being followed by, and sometimes following, a gray wolf with red eyes. I manage to elude him and get inside my house, when I notice that a door on the second floor is open. In trying to secure the door, I inadvertently knock down the entire wall, and can only surrender myself to the inevitable encounter with the wolf that I know is imminent. In the wake of this dream, I went out into the desert and cried uncontrollably for myself, but also for all the suffering throughout the world. It took several years to assimilate the meaning of the dream on a conscious level, but in my surrender to my tears, I had already started bobbing in the ocean where all story lines dissolve into *bodhichitta*, and where surrender sows the seeds for a larger understanding of life, death, survival, and the soul that is struggling to survive.

Anandamaya Kosha

At the last stage of penetration by Spirit, *anandamaya kosha*, the meaning beneath the imagery is assimilated, the individual soul merges completely with Spirit, and even the boat becomes an unnecessary protection against the ocean. This is the state that is described in all the mystical literature throughout the world's religions as the ultimate goal of all spiritual practice. More specifically, in terms of our discussion of the first *chakra*, at the level of penetration of Spirit posed by *anandamaya kosha*, survival is tantamount to the attainment of spiritual immortality. Immortality cannot be understood in the usual way in which we understand this word, however, since at this stage, the very notion of survival loses its meaning altogether. There is no longer anyone in danger of dying, and no death that could occur that wouldn't feel like an expansion into an embrace of more abundant and all-inclusive life. I won't pretend to have attained this level of realization myself. I can, however, tell a story, which will at least hint at the possibilities inherent in this state.

One day in the late 1970s, while spending time in an ashram in the Catskills, I was waiting along with hundreds of other devotees for Swami Muktananda's *darshan*, or blessing. We would typically wait for hours on end for a few seconds of his undivided attention. He would generally smile and nod, perhaps say a few words through his interpreter, or ask you a question, then bop you on the head with his peacock feather, and that was that. This went on every day, day after day, for several hours at a time. Or at least, this is how a casual observer might interpret the scene. To those of us who were studying with him, however, it was an amazing experience. The room literally buzzed with electricity, and you could have a *kundalini* experience just sitting there. When he did look into your eyes, for those few seconds that you were before him, receiving his blessing, it was as though he could see right down to the very core of your soul, and everything else just melted away. The most amazing inner transformations happened in that room with the mere flick of a feather and a mischievous glance.

But as laid back as he often seemed to be, and as routine as the *darshan* line might have been for a lesser being, Muktananda was as fresh and as present with the last person in line as he was with the first, and extremely focused with each. He gave each person exactly what she needed, and he was an irrepressible trickster. If someone came to him and asked, "Oh Babaji, what should I do with my life?" he would suddenly turn into a basket case, throw up his hands in mock bewilderment, eyes wide and loosed from their moorings. If someone came to him in an open-hearted space, he would melt in their presence, and shower them with grace. If someone else came to him closed and skeptical,

◇◇

he would cross his arms in front of his chest, and his eyes would go shifty. And so on. He was an amazingly accurate mirror for everything anyone ever brought to him, and in the mirroring that he did, barriers to soul were removed – most a little bit at a time, but some, just like that, in the blink of an eye. So even though the waiting was endless, most of us didn't want to miss a thing.

One day, a strange looking character came to the front of the *darshan* line and pulled a gun on him. Muktananda feigned mock horror, then proceeded to roll in the aisles with laughter. The tears were streaming down his cheeks. The man with the gun was completely unnerved. He started shaking, and the gun fell from his hands, as Muktananda's bodyguards hauled him away. Everyone in the hall was beside themselves with a mixture of all sorts of emotions - fear, amazement, anger, grief, disbelief - it all came up at once, from that one incident. Meanwhile, Muktananda stopped laughing, and turned his undivided attention to the next person in line as though nothing at all had happened.

It took many years for me to digest this experience, but what I finally got out of it was the realization that here was a man who literally had nothing to lose. He was so connected to Spirit, that whether he was alive or dead, he would still be in the same place. He thought it hilarious that this man who presumed to pull a gun on him thought that by killing him, anything would change. The rest us had a major knot in the pit of our stomachs that day, but Muktananda was as unruffled as a daisy in the sunshine – apparently completely free from all fear of death. In retrospect, I can only assume that his first *chakra* was thoroughly penetrated to the level I am describing here as *anandamaya kosha*. He had surrendered completely, and as a consequence, he was invincible.

Chapter Two
The Second Chakra

In the Hindu system, the second or sexual *chakra* was called *svadisthana*. Represented as a vermillion lotus with six petals, this center is located at the root of the genitals, and is symbolized by water, lightning and the crescent moon (Avalon 118-119). In keeping with the metaphor of the rainbow, Judith (8) and Bruyere (42) consider this *chakra* to be orange in color, while Leadbeater quotes one yogic source that calls it "sunlike" (97). As mentioned earlier, Leadbetter and the Theosophical school in general, shifted the location of this *chakra* from the genitals to the spleen (7). Myss associates this *chakra* with the *sefirah* of Yesod, which in the paternalistic Kabbalah is correlated with the phallus, and "the male energy of procreation" (130).

Psychologically this *chakra* is connected not just with procreation, but also with sexuality for its own sake, with the watery realm of feelings, and with instinctual behavior, desire, passion, and the pursuit of pleasure on every possible level. It is the center of both procreativity and creativity, attraction and manifestation. It is where consciousness begins to assert itself with imagination, adaptability and resourcefulness. A balanced *svadisthana* will result in an overall sense of well-being, as well as free-flowing sensuality, emotions that are expressed easily in a balanced way, playfulness, creativity ingenuity, and spontaneity.

As discussed at some length in *The Seven Gates of Soul*, a balanced *svadisthana* was eyed with great suspicion by both eastern and western religious traditions, which feared the sexual freedom it encompassed as a recipe for licentious promiscuity, social chaos, and political anarchy. As we shall explore in more detail when we discuss the psychology associated with the second *chakra* at the level of *manomaya kosha*, many of these same societal and cultural fears get played out neurotically within the psyche of the individual soul. The psychology of the second *chakra* has been discussed *ad nauseum* by Freud and countless others, and I will not attempt to recreate that discussion here. In contrast to traditional religious teachings, I do want to suggest, however, that a flowing, uninhibited, playful, joyful expression of sexuality is a vital step on the spiritual path, and a necessary prerequisite to so-called higher states of being – including the capacity to create, the power to visualize and to manifest one's vision, and the ultimate attainment of psychological integration, spiritual balance, and wholeness. The process by which we attain this level of freedom – sexually, emotionally, psychologically, and spiritually – is encompassed by the second *chakra*.

It is telling to note that within the hierarchy of *chakras* as it was originally conceived, the tasks encompassed by the second *chakra* are secondary only to the necessity for

◇◇◇

securing our survival. To be sure, the Hindu yogis who developed this system were mostly obsessed with keeping second *chakra* energies tightly under control, largely out of fear for their rampant expression. Yet, if we are able to step back from the religious stigma they placed on sexual license, it is possible to see that what is at stake in opening and freeing the second *chakra* is no less than the capacity to enjoy life.

Once we can be reasonably assured that we have safely landed in this garden paradise, and reasonably well protected against anything that might abruptly terminate our presence here, it seems the next order of business is to open our senses and learn how to take pleasure in all the beauty that surrounds us. The pursuit of pleasure is not something sinful, as western religion has taught, nor is it a dangerous stage of self-indulgence on the way to more important spiritual attainment, as it was mostly considered in the east. It is a major cornerstone of our foundation as embodied souls seeking a deeper and more complete embrace of our wholeness. It is in the spirit of this recognition, then, that I would like to explore the spiritual psychology of the second *chakra* as it manifests on the level of all five *koshas*.

Annamaya Kosha

On the level of *annamaya kosha*, or the physical body, the energy of the second *chakra* manifests as the reproductive system and the sexual organs associated with it. Obviously, on one level, our capacity to reproduce can be understood as an extension of the primary first *chakra* task of survival, since our entire species would soon become extinct without it. Whereas our collective goal within the domain of the first *chakra* might be understood to be carving out and securing an ecological niche for ourselves, the second *chakra* speaks more directly – both on a collective level and on an individual level – to what we shall actually do within that niche. For to reproduce is to participate in creation as a co-creator, as a giver and a nurturer of life.

On the level of *annamaya kosha*, we might envision couples in loving embrace, mothers breast-feeding their children, and the fertility rites of spring on the beach at Fort Lauderdale or on the streets of pre-Katrina New Orleans at Mardis Gras as a celebration of our capacity to participate in the creation and sustenance of life. As we saw, once we reach *manomaya kosha* in relation to the first *chakra*, elimination and protection against unwanted influences gradually give way to the more intentional cultivation of a life-sustaining relationship to the embodied world. This impulse is apparently built into the psychology of the second *chakra*, from the most basic level of awareness, where it registers not merely as a useful strategy for survival, but as a pleasurable activity that is its own reward. Assuming for the moment that the healthy exercise of our physical sexuality can be experienced free from psychological baggage, the fact that it is inherently pleasurable makes it conducive, not just to survival, but to a celebration of the embodied life, and of our capacity to participate in it.

Because this is so, I also associate the second *chakra* – at the level of *annamaya kosha* – with sensory awareness in general. As discussed at some length in *The Seven Gates of Soul*, the senses are the first and most fundamental vehicle through which we become aware of the presence of Spirit, as consciousness, within the embodied state. Here I would add that it is largely within the second *chakra* that this initial, primal awakening takes place. As we see the proliferation of colors and shapes that fill the embodied world with interest and intrigue, and as the symphony of sounds surrounding us fills our ear with wonder and delight, it begins to dawn on us that the entire embodied world is inhabited by a living Presence, and that we are somehow in relationship to that Presence. As we touch our world and it touches us, as we inhale the ancient smells and remember an evolutionary journey our minds are too small to grasp; as we taste of all of the fruits in this earthly garden of delights, we move beyond a mere will to survive and realize that we are of the earth and it is of us. We belong here, in a way that invites further exploration.

To be sure, not all sensory experiences will be pleasurable. As pointed out in *The Seven Gates of Soul*, it is in learning what is pleasurable and what is not, that we slowly gravitate to our place within the whole, and begin to understand who we are in the larger scheme of things. Most of this is probably unconscious at the level of *annamaya kosha*, but even at this most basic level of penetration by Spirit, every exercise of our sensory capacities holds the potential to teach us something about our relationship to the embodied world, and to the animating presence of Spirit within that world and within us. This happens naturally as part of our ontological development as infants wiggling our fingers and our toes, and spiritually as souls touching each other and feeling our way into the texture of life's exquisite sensory nuances.

Pranamaya Kosha

On an energetic level, the second *chakra* is governed by the principle of attraction. In *The Seven Gates of Soul*, I suggested that each soul exists in a resonant field of soul space, where like attracts like, and where we naturally gravitate to experiences that hold some potential for teaching us who we are, where we belong within the whole, and what our personal path is back to a complete and unencumbered embrace of our Wholeness. Here, I would add that this process begins in the second *chakra*, as an expression of what happens on the level of *pranamaya kosha*. Whatever we are attracted to – on the most basic sensory level – becomes part of our resonant field. We are drawn to enter a relationship because of our resonance with it, however fleeting that relationship may be, and through that resonance, we have the opportunity to learn something new about ourselves, and the embodied world that we inhabit.

From this perspective, life is a field of flowers and we are the bees that pollinate that field. Each flower has a unique shape, is adorned by its own characteristic combination of colors, and emits a signature fragrance that draws forth from within us a desire to participate in its beauty and dance with it – for a moment or a lifetime. In that dance, we learn how we are like that flower and how we are different, and when the dance is over, we move on to the next flower, carrying the nectar of greater self-recognition. If, for the moment, you can imagine that every experience you encounter in the course of your lifetime, every relationship, every involvement, every moment of connection is a dance of learning and self-discovery with a flower to whom you are attracted, then you have an apt image of what happens in the second *chakra* on the level of *pranamaya kosha*.

Of course, flowers often come with thorns or with toxic secretions cleverly designed to discourage would-be hungry insects that see only lunch within the beauty. Likewise, within the context of our metaphor, that to which we are attracted will not always prove pleasurable or benign. One of the first lessons learned in the second *chakra* is that attraction and the pursuit of pleasure are not always synonymous. Often, in fact, that to which we are attracted proves downright painful, or in some cases, even detrimental to our well-being. Any heroin addict will tell you about the unparalleled pleasure of that first fix, and the nightmare that ensues. Though most of our learning experiences will be less extreme, we all gravitate to the promise of pleasure, not for pleasure itself, but for the potential for learning what lies unseen, pulsing at the heart of pleasure.

Since we are the primary source of attraction at the center of our own resonant soul space, what we attract depends upon who we are. To the extent that we are aware of and connected to Spirit dwelling within us, we will naturally attract beauty and pleasure into our lives. To the extent that we are wounded, and believe ourselves unworthy to participate in the glorious majesty of this divine creation, then we will attract those experiences designed to reflect back to us just what we are doing to ourselves with these beliefs. We do this, not as punishment for our sins, nor even as an expression of our neuroses. We attract these learning experiences in the second *chakra*, on the level of *pranamaya kosha*, so that we can make the necessary course correction. On this level, pain and pleasure are both navigational tools, and what we learn when we pay attention to them is where the path to a more complete, and more enjoyable embrace of our wholeness actually lies.

Manomaya Kosha

Since *manomaya kosha* is inherently associated with sensory experience, there is a natural affinity between this *kosha* and the second *chakra*. Spirit cannot penetrate to this level of awareness, at any *chakra*, without stirring a second *chakra* response. Or put another way, as the psychology of any *chakra* is triggered, there will be a sensory and emotional response that registers in the second *chakra* as pleasure or pain or some exquisite combination of the two. Conversely, one cannot begin awakening the second *chakra* – through sexual activity or through intentional sensory stimulation or both – without inviting Spirit to penetrate to the level of *manomaya kosha* in every *chakra*. This is one reason why sexual relationships often serve as a potent trigger for all of our core issues, while each of those issues will have identifiable sensory and emotional correlates.

Having said that, it is important to note that the second *chakra* has its own inherent psychology, which is evoked as Spirit engages the soul on the level of *manomaya kosha* within it. Though pleasure and pain will both be part of our second *chakra* experience, the psychology of the second *chakra* will be primarily driven by the instinctual gravitation toward pleasure. Freud often discussed the pursuit of pleasure in the same breath with an acknowledgment of our natural tendency to also want to avoid pain, but from the perspective of spiritual psychology, the two are actually very different functions that must be assigned to entirely different *chakras*. Since pain is normally perceived on some level to be threatening to our survival, eliminating that which is painful and/or somehow buffering ourselves from it is a natural function of the first *chakra*, and whenever sensory or emotional pain arises in the second *chakra*, we will naturally gravitate back to the first *chakra* in order to address it. But to the extent that we remain engaged in the second *chakra* itself, we will instinctually gravitate toward that which is pleasurable.

This will be true, even when pain arises. Pleasure naturally stimulates the second *chakra*, for in contrast to the first *chakra* – which often requires us to build walls and shut out the flow of life – the second *chakra* is first and last about opening. It is entirely possible within the overall scheme of things in which *chakras* are considered simultaneously, that one might strive to open more completely to life in the second *chakra* while also attempting to shut out some unwanted influence in the first. Indeed, such contradictory, self-defeating dynamics are the stuff of which all sexual and many psychological neuroses are fashioned. Left to its own uncompromised devices, however, the second *chakra* will always yearn toward a deepening of enjoyment, connectedness and the will to participate with full consent in the embodied life, and it is around this irrepressible desire that the psychology of the second *chakra* revolves. At the level of *annamaya kosha* (the physical level) and *pranamaya kosha* (the energetic level), this psychology will largely be instinctual and unconscious. On the level of *manomaya kosha*, the soul will begin to make deliberate choices and set intentions that promote increased pleasure, enjoyment, and celebration of life in support of the natural function of the second *chakra*.

On this level, we will evolve a set of personal preferences that we perceive will make us happy. Of course, not everything that we perceive will make us happy actually will,

◇◇

but as with all movement at the level of *manomaya kosha*, perception is key. At the second *chakra*, perception takes the form of desires, and it is by pursuing the object of our desires that we gradually learn what makes us happy and what doesn't.

We also learn how much of a good thing is good, and how much turns counterproductive in the quest for pleasure. As Judith points out, second *chakra* issues can just as easily revolve around excessive desire in need of containment as it can a deficiency or sense of deprivation (146-152). After a first encounter with chocolate sets our endorphins buzzing, we may feel a sudden obsessive desire to stock our cupboards with a lifetime supply of Dove Bars, Snickers, or Godivas. Twenty pounds and a face full of fresh zits later, we may rethink this strategy. In the pursuit of desire, we learn something, our perception about what makes us happy is refined, and we gradually grow toward a more realistic understanding of who we are in relation to chocolate. As with chocolate, so too with every object of desire it is possible to encounter in the second *chakra*.

Intentions in the second *chakra* naturally revolve around the fulfillment of desires. Resistance to the satisfaction of desire will usually take the form of guilt or shame. We are all conditioned – by religion, by our parents, and by the culture at large – to believe that an unbridled pursuit of pleasure is bad. Where the line sits will differ, according to the level and the form that our particular brand of conditioning has taken, but it will almost never coincide with our natural inclinations to seek pleasure, nor will our definition of pleasure often coincide with what is deemed "normal" by religious and/or psychological authorities, or conversely by the media. It is in the gap between what is true for us, and what our conditioning tells us ought to be true, that guilt and shame – and the resistance inherent within the psychology of the second *chakra* – arise in counterbalance to our conscious intention to maximize pleasure. Guilt, in this case, can be understood to be a complex of conflicting emotions about some specific action, which our conditioning tells us is bad. Shame is the more global sense that we are bad, because we do not fit the conditioned ideal of "good" or "normal."

Beneath this resistance is the fear that we will be punished for our sins and transgressions – that we will be booted from the garden, sent unceremoniously straight to hell, and forced to break rocks for eternity with the hot sun on our backs and heavy iron shackles on our legs. This is the primal fear exploited by religion – a development, as I pointed out in some detail in *The Seven Gates of Soul*, that is detrimental to the soul. Here, I would add that the psychological damage inherent in this view registers primarily in the second *chakra* on the level of *manomaya kosha*, and the fear that breeds resistance to the natural function of the second *chakra* is also evoked in many other ways, on many other levels, wherever individual desires butt up against societal mores.

In a conservative society that promotes a monolithic definition of sexual propriety that excludes gays, those who are single and sexually active, and the polyamorous community, fear of social sanction, discrimination and even violent recrimination can cloud the free, unencumbered expression of sexuality, desire, and natural preferences. Media images that evoke ideals of weight, breast or penis size, and sexual attractiveness can evoke fears of social ostracism within those who do not fit these ideals – which is to say, most of us – and fuel such unnatural second *chakra* distortions as anorexia, bulimia, silicon implants, penis enlargement, liposuction, and botox injections. On the other side of the equation, environmental zealots promoting childlessness as an antidote to the disproportionate consumption of resources in Western culture can evoke guilt and fears of punishment through ecological devastation in those who are sensitive to the truth in these messages, but whose natural desires tend toward having more than the politically correct number of children.

From the soul's perspective, as long as one is respectful of the rights of others to sexual self-determination, there is no right or wrong way to pursue the desires that arise within the second *chakra*. To the extent that one's natural propensities take one in directions that run contrary to religious, psychological, or societal ideals, then fear of punishment, ostracism, or retaliation by the collective will tend to compromise the natural expression of second *chakra* desires on the level of *manomaya kosha*. Myss suggests that "the energy of the second *chakra* helps us evolve beyond the collective energy of the tribe" through the conscious exercise of choice (132), but to the extent that our capacity to choose freely is hampered by cultural, social or religious conditioning, the fears of punishment lodged in the second *chakra* can be very deeply rooted in the mores of the tribe. Fear of punishment on this level is not limited to the expression of overt sexual desires, but extends to the expression of any desire or natural preference.

A young boy with poetic sensibilities, for example, growing up in a macho culture where males are expected to be interested in football, hunting, fast cars, and fast women may fear repercussions for daring to be who he is when in the judgmental presence of his family or his peers. A young woman who prefers homemaking to a professional career might fear punishment – through exclusion, social stigmatization, or ridicule – by the more upwardly mobile, feminist, or corporate-minded women in her community. Astrologers attempting to practice in fundamentalist Christian communities, Islamic fundamentalists seeking spiritual community in post-9/11 society, and environmentalists promoting sustainable timber management practices in traditional logging communities may all operate within a climate where fear of punishment is a compromising factor in the exercise of their natural preferences.

As with the first *chakra*, there may also be instances where the fear of punishment is less obviously justified, but no less of a distorting factor within the second *chakra* psychology of the individual soul. A child whose parents forbade the reading of comic books, for example, may grow up to be a collector, wracked by guilty pleasure, married to a spouse who holds her partner's passion in punishing contempt. A young man, having suffered through a messy and costly divorce after several years of her serial infidelity, may awkwardly avoid women to whom he is attracted in the future for fear of a repeat performance. A political activist, receiving death threats in response to her efforts to create what she perceives to be a better world, may well back away from political activity, even though she must deny a strong dimension of her being in order to do so.

Obviously, fear of punishment experienced in the second *chakra* can trigger first *chakra* concerns about survival and a consequent shifting of energy to that *chakra*. To the extent that fear of punishment also interferes with the natural expression of some desire, natural proclivity, or definitive activity that is inherent in our being, then it also compromises, if not shuts down completely, our second *chakra*. Shutting down desire, denying natural proclivities, and curtailing activities toward which we are naturally drawn results in less enjoyment of life, diminished pleasure, and a sense of being excluded from the garden of earthly delights that surrounds us. When this happens, we experience the suffering that is associated with the second *chakra*, and the crystallization of second *chakra* issues on the level of *manomaya kosha*.

Vijnanamaya Kosha

We also experience a psychic response, designed to restore equilibrium to the soul. As Jung and many others have pointed out, whatever is consciously denied reasserts itself into our consciousness with a vigor that is commensurate to the force with which we repress it. In the case of the second *chakra*, what is repressed is at core, no less than the Life Force itself, which is ultimately irrepressible. From the highest possible perspective, this Life Force can be understood as Spirit infusing the embodied world and everything in it with the animating power that fuels its existence. To recognize that is to realize that we can no more keep this Force from moving through us than we can keep the flowers from blooming in spring, or protons and electrons from intermingling on the atomic level, or new galaxies from being born. When the psychology of the second *chakra* results in a shutting down on the level of *manomaya kosha*, we may well experience both a depletion of energy on the level of *pranamaya kosha*, and physical symptoms that are somehow symbolic of our repression on the level of *annamaya kosha*. We will, however, also invariably experience the emergence of imagery on the level of *vijnanamaya kosha*, which, if we are open to it, can point the way toward a restoration of balance.

We see this process at work on a societal level, for example, in the proliferation of sexual images in the media and our ambivalent obsession with them that lies in stark contrast to our avowed conservative ideals of discretion, modesty and sexual privacy. Movies, prime time television shows, readily available Internet porn, Broadway plays, magazines, and billboards all proclaim a sexual freedom, range of expression, and preoccupation with sex that few people are likely to experience in real life. Standing in any checkout line in any grocery store in America, one can learn of 101 ways to take one's lover to unparalleled heights of sexual ecstasy. Any night of the week, one can find one or more cable channels supplying images to fuel any sexual fantasy ever conceived. Check your email and you are bound to encounter spam offering cheap Viagra, penis or breast enlargement opportunities. Walk down any main street in any major city in the world, and you will be accosted by images catering blatantly to your every unexpressed or latent desire. To the extent that you have suppressed your desires, sexual or otherwise, on the level of *manomaya kosha*, you will also likely attempt to shut out, filter, ignore, decry, or denigrate these images. But on the level of *vijnanamaya kosha*, these images are nonetheless extending an invitation to you to reclaim what has been lost through your denial and repression. You would not experience the reaction to them that you have, or give them the psychic weight that you do, if this were not so.

Consider, in this regard, the public outcry to Janet Jackson's brief exposure of a breast during the halftime show of Superbowl XXXIX. Though the incident itself lasted no more than half a second, it became the subject of endless debate for months afterward, and was followed by legislation stiffening fines for "indecency" on the public airwaves. This is obviously a strong expression of repression at the level on which the second *chakra* is experienced collectively, but it is also a call to heightened awareness on the level of *vijnanamaya kosha* – on which imagery holds the power to evoke a collective response. Given the disproportionate attention that this incident has received, we must ask not just how we can prevent this from happening again, but why should the mere image of a breast during prime time television evoke such a strong reaction?

Those who condemned the incident cited its potential corrupting influence on children. But children for whom the second *chakra* is functioning in a healthy manner would naturally associate the breast with the comfort, warmth, and nurturing pleasure of a mother's embrace, and not be disturbed by such an image. Teenagers who have not already seen a breast by the time they are old enough to be interested in sex are living a sheltered life, indeed. Similarly, indigenous cultures living close to nature, for whom breast exposure is a fact of everyday life, would not experience such an adverse reaction.

If the most innocent and natural among us would see nothing to be alarmed about in the image by which we are so disturbed, then perhaps the problem lies not in the image itself. Perhaps it is only to the extent that we as a culture have attempted to shut the second *chakra* down through induced guilt, shame, and conditioned fear of punishment,

◇◇◇

that the brief image of a breast exposed becomes capable of serving as the focal point for such public outrage. To the extent that we can entertain this possibility, then we must also consider this image of a breast exposed as a call to the restoration of balance in our unnatural attitude toward a natural and innately human expression – regardless of the tastelessness or lack of judgment with which it was presented.

As it is on the societal level, so too will it be on the personal level. To the extent that we have repressed any natural desire, sexual or otherwise, then images will arise – in our dreams, in the books we are drawn to read, in the movies we are drawn to watch, and in the synchronistic events of everyday life – that will attempt to restore those desires to their natural place within our psychic repertoire. Spiritual autobiographies are filled with stories of saints and sages troubled by incessant, relentless sexual imagery in their dreams, visions, and unwanted intrusions into the meditative state. Conversely, those who are engaged in excessive or addictive behaviors with regard to their desires will encounter images that encourage restraint and moderation. The compensatory function of dreams has been well-documented by several generations of psychoanalysts. By a similar unconscious mechanism, we routinely find ourselves in relationship to others who live out our images for us, push all our buttons, and evoke in us our harshest judgments. To negotiate such relationships, we are often required to meet the offending person somewhere in the middle – where our own natural balance invariably lies.

These images demand our attention to the extent that we have pushed their message of balance, desire, and natural expression away. We are ultimately no match for them, and it is by taking them seriously that the road to healing and wholeness resides. All images evoked at the second *chakra* on the level of *vijnanamaya kosha* invite us to embrace a wider, broader, deeper range of options than our conscious mind considers appropriate, necessary or possible. Whatever we think we are, whatever we think is ok or not ok about us, the truth is we are much bigger than that. We are – in Essence – the Life Force funneled through a particular form, and we identify mostly with the funneling. At the level of *vijnanamaya kosha*, we are always called to identify with the Life Force itself, and its infinite repertoire of disguises. Wherever we think it is not, that is where second *chakra* images of *vijnanamaya kosha* will lead us.

On the wall behind my desk at the cabin retreat where I am writing these words hangs a favorite quote by Nietzsche, framed to remind me of something I am often prone to forget. The quote reads, "You must carry a chaos inside you to give birth to a dancing star." The truth is I am terrified of that chaos, though I very deeply desire to give birth to a dancing star. Here then is a classic second *chakra* dilemma. Without getting too psychoanalytical about it, I'm sure on some level I learned my fear of chaos from my mother, who stressed the importance of being neat, organized, and disciplined. To win and keep her love, I undoubtedly molded myself around these preferences and evolved a sense of fear around breaking the code, for fear of losing her approval, affection, and affirmation of my worth.

While I don't remember ever being beaten or outwardly traumatized by failing to live up to her code, I do recall one incident that epitomizes the second *chakra* issue she triggered in me. I remember not being allowed to leave the dinner table and play with my friends until I cleaned my plate. I remember sitting at the table in despair, unable to eat my corned beef hash, or chopped liver, or whatever it was that disgusted me, yet believing on some unconscious visceral level, that the path to my mother's unconditional acceptance depended upon doing just that. The ultimate slap in the face came when my mother would scrape the uneaten food on the table, and stomp off in disgust to wash my plate. There it was – the cold, unwanted lump of amorphous chaos sitting uncontained in front of me, signaling to the world my badness, my failure to live up to expectations, my unworthiness to partake of the dancing star that was life in paradise, infused by a mother's love.

To avoid a repeat of this incriminating scenario, I grew up being neat, organized, and disciplined. Invariably over the years, I have also drawn to me other people for whom clutter, disorganization, and undisciplined spontaneity was a way of life. Typical of this pattern is a relationship recently ended. For a time, my partner and I lived together in a house that was filled with stacks of unopened boxes, too much furniture and a menagerie of pets constantly pooping, shedding, and chewing on the woodwork. We had few shared routines, and getting coordinated to accomplish any mutual goal was a major undertaking. I often felt a sense of despair in relationship to her that somehow resembled that uneaten lump of cold, chopped liver on the table before me.

Yet, I was attracted to this woman precisely because she also happened to embody the dancing star that I aspire to be. Her joy, her capacity for spontaneity and playful celebration of life were my living image of what the second *chakra* restored to balance would look and feel like, were I to allow it to open more completely within myself. To embrace her, I had to also embrace the chaos that she carried with her, and that I resisted inside myself. On the level of *vijnanamaya kosha*, she gradually taught me where the place of balance might be found. Over time, as my fear of chaos subsided in love for her, I opened more completely to the Life Force within myself, and learned to relax into a space of greater enjoyment, celebration, and a more complete fulfillment of desire – where messiness and clutter were no longer quite the triggering issues they used to be.

Anandamaya Kosha

As discussed at length in *The Seven Gates of Soul*, the embodied life is inherently conditioned by polarities – life and death, male and female, light and dark, hot and cold, order and chaos. Within the second *chakra*, we naturally position ourselves somewhere along each of these continuums, and define ourselves accordingly. I prefer order to chaos, warmth to cold, acknowledge my female side but know myself to be predominantly male, and so forth. My desires are predicated around these definitions of self, and on the level of the second *chakra*, I conduct my life accordingly.

Yet to become fully conscious of the presence of Spirit within the embodied world is to realize that all of these polarities are but a figment of my embodied imagination. To identify with Spirit, not just intellectually through some belief system, but in actual fact, I must realize that Spirit is neither male nor female, but both and neither at the same time. Though religion invariably identifies God with the Light and labels that good, while assigning darkness to the Devil and labeling that bad, Spirit is inevitably large enough to encompass both light and dark. The philosophical dialogue that led to the scientific revolution emphasized and idolized the rational mind, but as anyone who has ever found insight in a dream will attest, Spirit speaks to us not just through reason, but through the senses, the emotions, the fantasies and everything we label irrational as well. Whatever dichotomy we can conceive, and whatever dance we do on the level on which opposites intermingle, Spirit is beyond all that. To the extent that we are able to allow Spirit to penetrate to the final level of *anandamaya kosha*, we must also move beyond awareness of polarity to an innate, experiential embrace of the wholeness and unity of Life.

Jung called this realization of unity the *hieros gamos* and conceived of it as a marriage between male and female that took place within the individual rather than in some outside relationship. When I reach this state, for example, no longer will I need to look to my partners to play out the chaos that balances my preference for order. I will be equally capable and comfortable with both. This state of balance and self-containment is symbolized by the figure of the hermaphrodite, who was both male and female. While such a figure invariably invokes a measure of discomfort within us, such discomfort is at its core a measure of the extent to which we have yet to fully open our second *chakra*. For at the level of *anandamaya kosha*, we become large enough to embrace all that is.

Just as there is no nook nor cranny of this manifest creation that Spirit is not, so too, do we fill the resonant space available to us and become all-inclusive, embracing all, rejecting nothing, when we allow Spirit to fully penetrate our second *chakra*. Everything we encounter that appears to be Other on the way there, is merely an invitation to foreplay on the way to orgasmic bliss. The Sanskrit word, *ananda* means bliss, and it is this state to which we aspire - whether we are aware of it or not - on the level of *anandamaya kosha*, or deepest possible opening of the second *chakra*.

Chapter Three
The Third Chakra

The third *chakra*, or *manipura*, is said by Hindu tradition to be as lustrous as a gem, red in color, composed of ten petals, related to the element of fire, and symbolized by the ram (Avalon 119). Judith (8) and Bruyere (42) consider it to be yellow in color (the next color up the rainbow), while Leadbetter quotes widely divergent "authorities" who perceive it to be blue, golden, or "various reds and greens" (97). Most modern authorities agree with ancient sources in associating the third *chakra* with the element of fire, but Bruyere feels it is more akin to air (43). Myss proposes an affinity between the third charka and the *sefirah* of Nezah, representing "the Divine quality of endurance" and the *sefirah* of Hod, symbolizing "the majesty (or integrity) of the Divine" (168).

The third *chakra* is generally located between the navel and the solar plexus and represents a motivational pattern having to do with self-esteem, sense of competence, and personal power. Psychologically, this *chakra* governs the establishment of the ego, the pursuit of personal excellence and effectiveness within the world. A balanced third *chakra* will yield worldly success, a sense of satisfaction in the work that one does, the ability to adapt to changing circumstances gracefully, a respectful relationship with one's peers, and prosperity.

Invariably, the third *chakra* is where our involvement with the embodied world takes its most activated, extroverted form, and where the embodied life we are living takes its most characteristic shape. It is here that we are most likely to forget completely that we are souls on a journey that encompasses, but also transcends this life, and identify completely with the particulars of our earthly life. Consequently, it is also here that we have the greatest opportunity for awakening to the presence of Spirit within us – an awareness that transforms ordinary life into a learning experience with deeply spiritual implications. All the attainments that were possible in the classical yogic model of spirituality, and which take place at the so-called higher *chakras*, depend upon this awakening at the third *chakra*. Ironically, this transformation generally does not come without a breakdown in the very quest for worldly attainment that occupies us at this level of awareness.

A classic spiritual story illustrates this process. One day, an earnest disciple asked his teacher, "Master, what must I do to attain enlightenment?"

"Enlightenment can be easily attained," the master replied with sly irony, "by completing one simple task. Fetch me a cup of water from the well, and you shall be enlightened."

"Piece of cake," thought the excited disciple to himself, as he accepted the master's favorite cup, and trotted down the street toward the well, which was a mile down the road between two villages. As coincidence would have it, a young maiden from the other village was approaching the same well at the very moment that the young man arrived, and the young man was distracted by her beauty. Putting his task on hold for just a moment, he struck up a conversation with the maiden, and hormones racing, was soon madly, head-over-heels, obsessively in love. The maiden, also attracted to the young man, returned his affections, and invited him to accompany her back to her village. The young man accepted, and the rest, as they say, is history. They were soon married, had children, and settled into a full and active life together.

Many years later, as they sat around the dinner table one evening for their supper, a knock came on the door. When the young man, now grown old, opened the door, he was shocked to see his ageless master standing before him. "Are you still planning to fetch my cup of water," he asked, "or must I do it myself?"

On the level of the third *chakra*, we are all in the position of this young man. We have all incarnated to embody Spirit as consciously as possible, each in our own way. We anchor ourselves in the first *chakra*, so that we might be sustained in this all-consuming task. In the second *chakra*, we orient ourselves, evolving a sense of direction through pursuing what gives us pleasure in accordance with our nature. In the third *chakra*, we acquire the skill and the competence necessary to embody Spirit in a way that suits us, along a path we have chosen. But in the third *chakra*, we become enamored of the path itself, abandon ourselves to embodiment and forget that it is Spirit we are attempting to embody.

This is where the embodied world becomes the realm of *maya* or illusion, spoken of in Hindu religious teaching, or where from the Western perspective, life becomes an endless soap opera, its meaning or purpose hidden from our view. When something goes wrong – where death in all of its many metaphorical guises comes calling – the master knocks on our door, and we remember why it is we have come, and what it was we intended to do. While it doesn't always work this way, the opportunity exists for remembering the soul's journey at the third *chakra* in a way that it does nowhere else, and it is the exposure to the opportunity around which the psychology of the third *chakra* revolves.

Annamaya Kosha

At the level of *annamaya kosha*, third *chakra* energy manifests as the solar plexus, and the digestive system, encompassing more broadly the mouth, salivary glands, esophagus, stomach, and intestines. This is where we take in the food, or raw substance of life, and begin to break it down to basic nutrients that can be used by the body. If in the second *chakra*, we are attracted by the smell, taste, and texture of certain foods, in the third *chakra*, we partake of the feast to which our senses have drawn us. On every level on which this could possibly have meaning, the third *chakra* is where we become part of the spiritual food chain – where we eat the food that sits before us on the table provided by Life, and where we are eaten by Life in return.

Being eaten by Life is the price to be paid for admission to it. Or put another way, it is impossible to participate in life without being altered by it. At the level of the second *chakra*, Life calls us to it, and we begin moving toward it, but we are still separate from it. On the level of the third *chakra*, this separation is no longer possible. We become what we engage, and the engagement consumes our identification with Spirit in exchange for identity. This was the fall from grace depicted in the story of the Garden of Eden that led to our ouster from paradise. It was an act of eating – of the fruit of the knowledge of Good and Evil – you will recall, that led to the fall. Within this model of consciousness we are presenting, this act of eating can be understood as the quintessential third *chakra* act.

On the level of *annamaya kosha*, eating can be understood literally as an act that sustains and forms the body. On a metaphorical level, this same function can be understood as the accumulation of life experience that constitutes the embodied life. Embodiment is the entry of Spirit into a particular body and particular set of circumstances. The act of embodiment forms a focal point of consciousness, which in turn both attracts and projects the life of a unique individual into being. It is this unique sense of individuality that is discovered and cultivated at the third *chakra*.

From the yogic perspective, this sense of individuality emanates from the solar plexus. At birth, this is the place where the umbilicus connects a child to her mother, and it is when this cord is cut that the newborn infant becomes an individual in her own right, with a body that must learn to function on its own, and a separate identity that will begin evolving through the learning process.

In martial arts training, the solar plexus is the center through which the individual accesses and channels his personal *ch'i* or life force in service to a focused intention, moves that *ch'i* outward and establishes a sense of territory. In life, the solar plexus is likewise the center through which an individual accesses the Life Force within, makes the decisions that shape life in a particular way, and establishes the range and scope of the resonant soul space in which life plays itself out.

Pranamaya Kosha

On the level of *pranamaya kosha*, the third *chakra* manifests as digestive metabolism, or the process of assimilation. As with other *chakras*, what happens at the level of *pranamaya kosha* reveals the nature and purpose of the purely physical act that takes place at the level of *annamaya kosha*. We eat, not merely for the sake of eating, but to nourish the body, to replenish its store of energy, to rebuild cells that have aged, decayed or broken down, and to grow new cells capable of continuing and sustaining life. Before the food we have eaten can be utilized in this way, it must be metabolized. It is this metabolic process that forms the essence of the third *chakra* at the level of *pranamaya kosha*.

On a metaphoric level, it is not just experience that we are seeking, but an assimilation of the lessons to be learned within our experiences. From the soul's perspective, this learning process is the very essence of the embodied life, and it is in the third *chakra* at the level of *pranamaya kosha* that we begin to consciously engage ourselves in it. Assimilation of our life lessons depends upon the clear and open functioning of the third *chakra* at this level of manifestation.

As discussed at length in *The Seven Gates of Soul*, this learning process proceeds as we orient ourselves with all the various polarities that give the embodied life its color: light and dark, male and female, hot and cold, wet and dry, and so on. We experience our natural preferences in relation to these polarities in the second *chakra*, and then we learn from our preferences in the third, where preferences often lead to excess. By moving too far toward one end of any spectrum, we experience an internal feedback mechanism commonly known as pain or suffering that pulls us back to a place of balance. As we find this place of balance, and gravitate toward it, we become the unique individual that we are, aligned with Spirit and with the embodied world in a way that reflects who we are as a soul.

The quest for balance then, is the second function of the third *chakra* at the level of *pranamaya kosha*. As we assimilate life lessons, taught to us by the experience of being out of balance in relation to one or more of the polarities that condition our existence, we gradually align ourselves with the truth of our being and increasingly live from this place of alignment. This, of course, is the ideal; in reality, there are countless distractions and seductions capable of drawing us off balance, but within the context of the third *chakra*, this simply becomes part of the learning process through which we assimilate new information and fine tune our alignment.

Manomaya Kosha

This alignment with our true nature will coincide with a gradually increasing sense of self-confidence, competence in our chosen field of endeavor, and sense of self-worth. The psychology of the third *chakra* outwardly revolves around the cultivation of a healthy ego, which will generally manifest externally as an increasing ability to function with ease and comfort within the embodied world. With a healthy ego, we are able to define a sense of territory, or sphere of influence, and to rise to a certain level of respect and recognition among our peers. The most visible arena in which this evolutionary process plays itself out will be career. But since our sense of alignment with ourselves in general governs how comfortable we are in our own skin, it manifests across the board through feedback about how well we are doing in the art of living the embodied life, and in meeting its many challenges.

At the third *chakra* will also be manifest all those places in our lives where a chronic sense of misalignment causes ongoing difficulties in meeting the challenges of embodiment. It is here that the psychology of the third *chakra*, at the level of *manomaya kosha*, will be triggered. On this level, our core issues begin to reveal themselves to us in living color.

Manomaya kosha in general is associated with the psychology of core issues, but it is only at the third *chakra* that this psychology begins to make itself accessible to the conscious mind. At the first *chakra*, all we know is that something appears to be threatening our survival or our well-being; it never occurs to us that the threat may be a reflection of something within us capable of attracting the threat to us. At the second *chakra*, all we know is that we feel bad, and our preference is to move in some other direction that is more pleasurable. We do not yet understand that it is impossible to move away from our pain, because it is ultimately rooted in issues that we have incarnated to try to resolve. At the third *chakra*, we gradually become aware that we will meet our destiny on the very road that we take to avoid it, and that the only way beyond our pain is to move more deeply into it and then through it.

At the level of *manomaya kosha*, this realization gradually crystallizes as an intention to confront our issues and work through them. The necessity for confrontation arises because not everything consumed at the level of *annamaya kosha* is digestible. Not everything assimilated at the level of *pranamaya kosha* is conducive to a healthy embrace of the soul's totality. Some of what we take in from a learning environment designed to ferret out and trigger our internal imbalances will fester within us, cause chronic conditions of psychological, emotional and physical pain, and generate problems that are not easily solved by choosing pleasure over pain. Core issues are core issues precisely because their resolution eludes us. It is at the level of *manomaya kosha* in the third *chakra* that we encounter these issues, and are forced to acknowledge their hold upon our psyche.

As children, we are vulnerable to every impression projected upon us by our parents, our teachers, our religious authorities, and society. Occasionally, someone will recognize something within us that is truly a part of our essential nature and encourage its development. Invariably, most of these projections will be a more accurate statement about the unrecognized talents, character traits, or propensities of those who are doing the projecting. We are the repository for these projections, often simply because as impressionable children, we are open to them. This openness is centered at our third *chakra*, and it is here – as part of the process of eating and assimilating – that we take these impressions, both true and false, into our psyche and learn from them.

It is here that a father, battered about by a world indifferent to his talents, and unable to advance very far in his career, will impart the message to his son that "no matter how hard you try in life, you just can't win". Until the son has his own body of experience that contradicts this message, he will proceed through life as though his father's worldview were reality, and this small piece of bad wisdom will cause him pain and suffering.

It is here that a woman, taught by her mother and the Church to believe that her sexual desires were dirty, or wrong, and somehow needed to be kept in check, will teach the same lessons to her daughter, and punish her when her natural sexual curiosity is aroused. The daughter may later rebel against these early messages by becoming sexually promiscuous, or pregnant at too young an age, or engaging in extreme behavior designed to shock her mother's puritanical sensibilities. Underneath the rebellion, the messages will still reverberate as a catalyst to imbalanced behavior that causes pain. To the extent that these messages contribute to our belief system or our image of the world, they are more likely understood as the province of the fifth and sixth *chakras*. To the extent that form the basis of an identity that does not quite fit, they will generate third *chakra* issues.

While many of these messages will be negative in tone, some of them will appear to be positive, while still doing injustice to the true nature of the soul. The successful businessman who automatically assumes his son will follow in his footsteps, even though his son has no inclination to move in that direction, will generate an indigestible projection that his son must eventually regurgitate. The son will suffer under the weight of trying to measure up to his father's expectations until he realizes his father's path is not for him. A mother who always wanted to be a classical pianist, but never had the talent, may project that unrealized talent onto her daughter, who grows up resenting the many hours she was forced to practice without ever attaining the heights toward which her mother was pushing her.

I experienced a false positive projection of this kind as part of my own third *chakra* process. My grandfather was an imminently successful immigrant who worked himself up the ladder of success by sheer will, but who never went to college. Before I was old enough to understand what was going on, my grandfather started saving for my college education, and referred to me not by name, but as "the professor." Since he appeared to care deeply about my well-being and future, I naturally sought to please him. It wasn't until graduate school, nearly ten years after his death, that I suddenly realized I was struggling to live out his unrealized dreams, following a path that he had imagined for me, and not my own. This realization was a third *chakra* awakening that propelled me on a more conscious journey to find my own path and claim it, creating an embodied life for myself at the level of *manomaya kosha* that fit my true identity as a soul.

It is here that any caring person might want to suggest that all the pain and suffering precipitated by these false projections ought to be unnecessary. But from the perspective of the soul, it is exactly this pain and suffering – the psychological equivalent of death – that forces each of us to claim our most precious, though hard-won, wisdom. Because he had to struggle against his defeatist father's faulty assessment of the world, the young man in our first example might well be motivated to work harder and rise to greater heights in his career than he would have if he could have taken his success for granted. The daughter in our second example will inevitably learn to find a level of peace and comfort in relation to her sexuality that was never available to her mother or her grandmother, simply because their conditioning never rose to the level of awareness – centered in the third *chakra* at *manomaya kosha* – where it could precipitate a learning process. Through my own experience, I have learned the value of struggling against these false projections to find the truth, and have created a life of much greater interest and vitality than I believe I would have, had I simply lived out my grandfather's dream in quiet desperation. It is at the level of *manomaya kosha* in the third *chakra* that our suffering crystallizes into specific life issues, and then transmutes into growth as we give these issues the quality attention they require. As we engage our issues, we grow into the fullness of our being and become who we were meant to be.

Not every manifestation of a core issue will automatically result in growth, but at the level of *manomaya kosha*, the challenge and the opportunity will be extended. Myss suggests that cultivating a healthy, empowered sense of self – the primary task in the third *chakra* – is a four stage process involving: 1) revolution: breaking away from the projections of the tribe; 2) involution: a process of gradually discovering who we are; 3) narcissism: indulging ourselves in our newly formed identity, at times becoming caricatures of ourselves; and 4) evolution: learning to operate from a quiet, steady place of personal integrity (187-192).

While not all core issues will revolve specifically around the cultivation of self-esteem, finding the courage to face and heal any core issue will result in a more genuine identity, as we gradually learn to be true to ourselves. As we will see in Chapter Five, this challenge becomes the central focus of the fifth *chakra*. In the third *chakra*, the nascent emergence of a more genuine identity will be a natural by-product of dealing directly and intentionally with whatever core issues cause us pain and suffering.

❖❖

The cultivation of genuine identity (or what the Existentialists have called authentic being) is not always easy, since it involves risking rejection by the tribe; and enduring additional projections by those who are locked into rigid ways of being and in some way threatened by our growing freedom. But the reward, experienced at the level of *manomaya kosha* in the third *chakra* will be personal power, healthy self-esteem, increased autonomy, competence and the capacity to make a difference in the world.

Some will deal with their third *chakra* challenges by retreating to the second *chakra*, where the intention to face their issues head on reverts to a more instinctual quest for pleasure. This is the strategy promoted, for example, by the pharmaceutical companies who promise biochemical relief from the pain of psychological issues. The issues do not go away, but medication allows the sufferer to slide into the relative comfort of a second *chakra* immersion in pleasurable numbness. This will be true at least until the inevitable side effects of the drug kick in and precipitate a fresh round of pain, which in turn may act as a catalyst back to the third *chakra*. When the individual soul finally realizes that there is no easy fix for her suffering, she will begin to center herself in the third *chakra* with a clearer intention to address the core issues that arise there on the level of *manomaya kosha*.

Jung recognized the false messages at the heart of our core issues to be the nucleus around which the psychological shadow was formed. This shadow was the guardian of the threshold to the process of individuation, through which a soul could attain true individuality that was no longer distorted by false conditioning. It is in the third *chakra*, at the level of *manomaya kosha*, that the shadow is first encountered, and it is largely coming to terms with the shadow that serves as the pivot point around which the psychology of the third *chakra* revolves.

Within the context of this psychology, the process of projection will work both ways, for invariably, the false conditioning that we must work out within ourselves will be mirrored back to us by other people, onto whom we will project our issues so that we might see them more clearly. The woman struggling to free herself from her mother's false conditioning around sexuality will inevitably draw to herself partners with that same false conditioning, who treat her accordingly as a sex object with whom they can satisfy their guilty desires. The son of the businessman, ushered onto the wrong path by a well-meaning father, will invariably meet other mentors who make the same projections and push the son more deeply into his pain. In finding my own path, I had to first encounter a series of grandfather surrogates who sought to harness my creativity and intelligence to help them realize their own elusive dreams. It is through these projections that the patterns of false identification assimilated in childhood repeat themselves until we clearly and more consciously see them for what they are.

It is also within the context of these relationships that the resistance to our best intentions toward growth begins to arise. This is so because there is something attractive about these relationships that draws us to them, even though they harbor within them the same false projections against which we are struggling. It took me many years to realize that just because my grandfather loved me and had my best interests at heart, it did not mean that he saw my best interests clearly. But because of that love, and because I also loved him, I forgot that I wanted to free myself from the expectations that he unconsciously imposed upon me. Later in life, when I encountered others with agendas of their own to which they desired to harness me in a supportive role, I bit the poison apple because its sweetness was an irresistible attraction. Those I encountered were friends I respected, and their agendas were worthy ones in which I saw I could make a difference. It was easy to forget that I had something of my own to do, which could not be accomplished until I became immune to the seductive projections of others about what those accomplishments ought to be.

And so it is with each of us, in our own way. The shadow issues we must confront at the third *chakra* on the level of *manomaya kosha* are complicated by the fact that we were once dependent upon the love, approval, caring, acceptance, and respect of those who projected them. Often we got love, approval, caring, acceptance and respect to the extent that we took them in and made them our own. The bitter pill which we must later spit out was sugarcoated, and it is that sugar – or the promise of that sugar, realized or not – that poses the strongest counterforce to our intentions toward growth at the third *chakra*. Even in the worst case scenario – situations, for example, where children are physically abused, and grow up to be abusers – it is the promise of love, or redemption for our sins, or something better, less painful, more affirming that drives us back into the dysfunctional patterns that characterize our core issues, again and again and again.

The fear underlying our resistance to working through core issues then, is the fear of losing the love, approval, caring, acceptance, and respect of those who originally wounded us and of their surrogates later in life. This loss is not just a third *chakra* issue, since the love is – or was at one time – essential to our survival (first *chakra*) and at least potentially a source of pleasure (second *chakra*). At the level of the third *chakra*, however, this fear also becomes a loss of identity, since our identification with the chronic misalignment that is causing us pain is anchored by the survival value and potential for pleasure – rightly or wrongly – that we have attached to it. In order to work through this fear, we must be willing to endure a period of confusion, disorientation, and unknowing, while we let go of false attachments to the projections of others and open to a more genuine connection with our true nature. This is not a process that happens overnight, and there will often be much backsliding toward the old identity which really no longer fits.

Once I realized that I was only going to college because I had assimilated the unrealized dreams my grandfather projected on me, I dropped out of graduate school. Because there was nothing to take its place, however, I eventually returned, finished my degree, and spent several years trying to make it work as a source of my identity in the world. Only when the pain of failure was met with creativity born of desperation did I gradually and painfully find my way into a relationship to the embodied world on my own terms. To break our identification with the false projections assimilated at the third *chakra*, we must access great courage in the face of the unknown, and find a reservoir of self-love within ourselves deep enough to replace that which we fear we stand to lose. This is a process that takes time, and to the extent that we are not there yet, we will suffer the ambivalence of having one foot in both worlds – the world of false projections from which we are attempting to escape, and the world of genuine being to which we are attempting to gain entry.

Vijnanamaya Kosha

In *The Seven Gates of Soul*, I speak about the process of taking a cyclical history, or viewing the life story in segments, each related to a critical juncture in the movement of some planetary cycle. Since memory is a function of the psyche that first manifests at the level of *manomaya kosha*, this is a process that can be useful once the resolve to tackle core issues has been aroused at the third *chakra*. Within the story related to the outworking of a given issue are key events and peripheral images, objects, people, and circumstances that form the psychic backdrop to the drama of life as it revolves around these issues. When these events, images, objects, people and circumstances are considered metaphorically, they can reveal a deeper, more intuitive level of truth that somehow transcends the sense of being stuck that often pervades the third *chakra* at the level of *manomaya kosha*, when one is caught in the throes of an activated issue.

In *The Seven Gates of Soul*, for example, I outlined a pattern related to my tendency to be broadsided by forces seemingly beyond my control, then traced the pattern through its many guises by studying the relevant cyclical history for clues. Among those clues were a dream about a wolf (reiterated in Chapter Two), and a seemingly peripheral encounter with a book about ravens that in retrospect seemed to converge to offer central clues about how I might more effectively deal with the issues related to the pattern. The important point here is that these images are extracted from my real life experience, as it is manifesting at the third *chakra* on the level of *manomaya kosha*, while my intention to understand and work through the pattern triggers an intuitive awareness on the level of *vijnanamaya kosha* that sheds new light on my predicament.

While *vijnanamaya kosha* can be accessed in any *chakra*, the conscious need to address core issues - first experienced in the third *chakra* at the level of *manomaya kosha* -

allows the images at the level of *vijnanamaya kosha* to be evoked, accessed and consciously harnessed to the healing agenda, as an act of intention. Images arising on this level at the first and second *chakras* generally arise spontaneously and often remain inaccessible to the conscious mind. We are constantly being given clues by a universe designed to act as a mirror to our subjective attitude toward ourselves and the world. But until the third *chakra* has been sufficiently opened, and we have determined on the level of *manomaya kosha* to address the core issues that cause us chronic pain, our relationship to these images remains largely unconscious, or literal, A bird is just a bird; a wife is just a wife; a job is just a job.

When the third *chakra* is open, however, and the intention to address core issues has been set, these same mundane entities become infused with metaphorical significance on the level of *vijnanamaya kosha* and begin pointing toward a higher level of possibility. A bird may become a harbinger of change; a wife may suddenly reveal herself to be an ingenious fusion of mother and goddess; a job may be recognized as a reflection of old patterns of competitive behavior first manifest in relation to siblings. And so on. The whole world opens up to become an arena in which everything becomes symbolic of a deeper process of integration at work.

The third *chakra* in general governs the use of will, which among other functions, is the faculty that allows us to set intentions. When the intention that is set relates to the healing of core issues, the will can be harnessed at the level of *vijnanamaya kosha* as a kind of ritual magic. Magic, of course, can be harnessed to any intention, even those tainted by anger, a desire for revenge, or an obsessive need to control or dominate. Such magic can have disastrous consequences, and will invariably rebound to the detriment of its perpetrator like a rubber band stretched to its limit and released at the wrong end. The universe is reflexive in nature, and will always seek to restore balance in the opposite direction to which it was bent by some act of will. If, however, the will is harnessed to a desire for alignment with one's true nature, then the reflexive universe will work to restore the already distorted rubber band to a less dangerous and more balanced place of harmony. The images that arise at the third *chakra* on the level of *vijnanamaya kosha* can also be harnessed to this same agenda by an act of will.

My Third Chakra Vijnanamaya Story

Several years after I had the realization that my grandfather's loving projections onto me had set me off on a false path to self-realization, I had the opportunity to do a vision quest. The vision quest is a Native American rite of passage, generally a time spent alone in wilderness, during which an intentional openness to the images of *vijnanamaya kosha* can greatly facilitate healing and alignment with one's true nature. The vision itself is a potent convergence of images around the healing intention. It is also a form of ritual magic, as discussed above.

As part of the preparation for my vision quest, I took what is called a medicine walk. During a medicine walk, one spends an entire day in nature, walking in an attitude of openness, with the intent to become clear about what is possible during the quest itself. One is specifically looking for some image or talisman with a strong sense of resonance that will reveal the nature of the work to be done. It is natural to assume that one's reasons for wanting to undertake a vision quest would be readily accessible to the conscious mind, but this is not always the case. Often it is a more subliminal sense that something is not right – or out of alignment – coupled with a desire to return to alignment, that precipitates the desire to quest. The underlying issues reveal themselves only gradually as one consents to the process of the quest and opens oneself to the level of *vijnanamaya kosha* on which the quest becomes symbolic as well as literal. The medicine walk is, in this sense, both a signal of intent to the reflexive universe and an opportunity to practice opening to the realm of imagery and symbolism available at *vijnanamaya kosha*.

While there were several images that came to me during my medicine walk, the most powerful by far was a freshly shed snake skin, about two feet long, and completely intact. I immediately recognized that a major theme for this quest would be the shedding of old skins, and old outmoded identities. In retrospect, I can see this as a manifestation of my desire to work through the false projections I had taken in, at the third *chakra*, so that I could get on with my own life in a more conscious way, from a place of more genuine alignment with my nature. Since I had decided to take this vision quest at the tail end of the period I spent struggling with great ambivalence to find a job related to my graduate degree, it is inevitable that I would gradually be lead by a trail of images and symbols back to my grandfather.

Later, at the beginning of the quest itself, I chose a *rune* to shed further light on the true nature of my journey from the soul's perspective. I picked the *rune* Othila, which according to a book of translations (Blum 68) suggested

> . . . a time of separating paths. Old skins must be shed, outmoded
> relationships discarded . . . a peeling away . . . radical severance . . . real
> property is associated with this rune . . . however, the benefits you receive,
> the 'inheritance,' may derived from something you must give up. This can
> be particularly difficult when that which you are called upon to give up or
> abandon is part of your background, your cultural inheritance. For then
> you must look closely at what, until now, you have proudly claimed as your
> birthright.

This *rune* seemed to echo the intuitive association I had made earlier to the snake skin, but it also pointed more specifically to the nature of the old identity to be shed. The words "inheritance" and "birthright" made me think of my grandfather, and how it was time to release him, or rather to release those aspects of his imprint upon me that were holding me back.

I made a list describing attributes of my grandfather's projection onto me that I wanted to release, and gradually began to envision an appropriate ceremony that would ritually symbolize this release. At the time, I was wearing a ring that my grandfather had given me, and within the context of the imagery of *vijnanamaya kosha* that was revealing itself to me on this quest, the ring became a symbol of both my connection to him and the loving bondage into which he had unwittingly placed me through his projections.

I gradually made my way to a rock face with a series of catacombs that somehow seemed like a good place to do the ceremony. I placed some sage and a piece of the snakeskin from my medicine walk in one of the catacombs, and made a small fire in my grandfather's honor. I then placed the ring he gave me on the burning sage, and released those aspects of my connection to him that I put on my list, thinking about each one in turn, and then consciously letting it go. After the sage had finished burning, I placed some flowers I had picked earlier on top of the ring, left it in the catacombs, and then turned to go back down the hill without it.

As I finished my ceremony, the morning sun was just creeping over the edge of the rock face, and a chipmunk was playing down below. I took the chipmunk to be a symbolic reflection of the animal spirit of my inner child, now released to playfully find its own way without the burden of projection, and the rising sun in the east to be the symbol of new birth. In the days that followed, the process of finding my own way, free from my grandfather's projections, was more of a gradual emergence than a single dramatic, identifiable event, but on that day of my vision quest, I was able to take a quantum leap forward through an intentional opening to *vijnanamaya kosha* at the level of the third *chakra*, where desire for change had crystallized.

Anandamaya Kosha

As we gradually assimilate the core lessons we have incarnated to learn by following the trail of clues before us on the level of *vijnanamaya kosha*, we rise to a certain level of mastery in relation to those issues. We become living experts in facing the very dilemmas that used to cause us so much pain and suffering. This expertise may translate externally as success in life, but much more importantly from the soul's perspective, it also translates into a certain depth of being capable of meeting difficulty with grace, dignity, humor, and creative ingenuity. As we aspire to this depth of being – which is a possibility, but by no means a given – we rise toward the level of *anandamaya kosha* at the third *chakra*.

In this blessed state, we become aligned with our own true nature in such a potent way that nothing within the embodied world can dislodge us from this alignment. To use a common phrase bandied about among spiritual seekers, we are now "in the world, but not of it." This is not a state of being that can simply be assumed by avoidance, escape, or detachment from the world, as some spiritual seekers attempt to do. Rather, it is the hard-won fruit of a long intentional engagement with the world, in which the healing resolution of core issues has served as the conscious pivot point around which we have prioritized our involvements and activity.

Few of us actually choose to live this way because it is generally painful – at least until we realize the pain to be a product of false conditioning that can be shed. Unless we are willing to go more deeply into our pain in order to understand its origin, we will either slide back down to the relative comfort of the second *chakra*, or remain stuck at the level of *manomaya kosha* in relation to the third *chakra*. Attaining the blessed state of *anandamaya kosha* in relation to the third *chakra* is reserved for those willing to do the hard work that our core issues require of us.

Chapter Four
The Fourth Chakra

In the Hindu system, the fourth *chakra*, located near the heart, is called *anahata*. Like the third *chakra*, this *chakra* is also red, but has a lotus of twelve petals, and is home to a deity seated on a black antelope. It is said to harbor the "sound which comes without the striking of any two things together" and is depicted as "the steady flame of a lamp in a windless place" (Avalon 120-121). Following the rainbow, Judith (8) and Bruyere (42) consider it to be green in color, while Leadbeater quotes yogic authorities who see it as deep red, golden or vermillion (97). Most authorities associate this *chakra* with the element of air, but in Bruyere's system, it is an earth *chakra* (43). Myss correlates the fourth *chakra* with the *sefirah* of Tif'eret, "symbolic of the beauty and compassion within God" (198).

Psychologically, the *anahata* governs the formation of relationships, learning to love self and others, the awakening of empathy and compassion, and the urge toward community. In the fourth *chakra*, the concept of *dharma* also comes into play, as we begin to heal the wounds that have previously blocked us, walk a path uniquely our own, fulfill the purpose for which we have incarnated, and make a contribution to the larger whole of which we are part. A balanced *anahata* will be experienced as satisfying relationships and a sense of interconnection, a strong sense of purpose and a steady experience of quiet joy.

In *The Seven Gates of Soul*, I speak of the psychic space the soul inhabits as a resonant field, in which it naturally gravitates toward people, places, ideas, activities and experiences to which it is attracted. As we pursue our attractions, we instinctually form relationships that contain our resonance with others and allow it to be explored. When these relationships are considered in their entirety, the embodied world in which the soul functions and gradually discovers itself becomes a field of opportunities for learning and growth. Here I would add that it is largely in the fourth *chakra*, that one's awareness of this resonant field – first awakened in the second *chakra* – comes into its most potent focus as the arena in which the soul works through its issues and takes its place as an integral part of a larger whole. Our relationships and relationship issues often appear to dominate the fourth *chakra*, but beneath whatever outer melodramas ensue, will invariably be the soul's attempt to integrate not just that with which it resonates, but also that which seems utterly foreign to its nature.

The resonance that leads to relationship is first awakened in the second *chakra*, where we gravitate to those life experiences that promise pleasure. At this level, we instinctually seek to surround ourselves with that which feels familiar and comfortable

◇◇◇

and in harmony with our essential nature. If one is "hot' by temperament, one will naturally gravitate to the experience of heat in all the ways that this might be available: intense, passionate, emotionally volatile interactions with other people; ideals worth fighting for that often need fighting for; dangerous, competitive sports; a desert climate and so on. The particulars will vary greatly from individual to individual, but the shared essence of heat will provide a common link that ties the resonant field together as a whole. To the extent that we then build a life around this type of resonance – which we might call resonance by affinity – we enter the realm of the fourth *chakra*, where the relationships that embody our affinities become the focus of our learning process.

As discussed in Chapter Three, the choices that we make on the basis of our affinities often have consequences, which precipitate opportunities for learning in the third *chakra*. As these opportunities begin evolving into relationships, we experience a second type of resonance in the fourth *chakra* that we might call resonance by wounding. Resonance by wounding occurs when we are attracted to various people, places, things, ideas, and experiences that hold the potential for triggering our core issues – often causing us pain, but also presenting us with an opportunity to work on our issues and gradually heal them. This type of resonance is likely to be a much more unconscious source of attraction than resonance by affinity, because few of us consciously choose to move toward that which promises to cause us pain. Yet because each of us is here in part to address our core issues, and heal our wounds, resonance by wounding will be an important factor in determining the nature of the relationships we form at the level of the fourth *chakra*.

Resonance by wounding will almost always take the form of too much or too little. The hot soul in our example above will invariably be drawn into situations that are too hot. The intense, passionate, emotionally volatile interactions with other people into which the hot soul is drawn may turn violent or destructive; the ideals worth fighting for that often need fighting for will invariably lead to conflicts that get out of hand; the dangerous, competitive sports may produce injuries or take one a bit too close to death for comfort; on a milder scale, a desert climate may produce dry skin, dehydration, or heat rashes. Every resonance by affinity holds the potential to lead to excess of the very quality to which we are attracted, and this propensity for excess will invariably lie at the heart of many of our core issues.

A necessary corollary to the natural tendency toward excess will be some intrinsic deficiency. Our hot soul, for example, will necessarily be lacking in cold. In the midst of a hot relationship, she will likely lack the ability to dispassionately step back from the heat of involvement to make a cooler, more detached assessment of her situation. In fighting for her ideals, she may lack the skills to discuss her position without alienating others or provoking their anger. In pursuing dangerous, competitive sports, she may not be able to deal with losing gracefully, nor know how to pace herself for the long haul. In each of these situations, she could benefit from cultivating a relationship to everything metaphorically cold that could potentially balance her hot nature. Through resonance by wounding, her soul space will become too hot, so that she might be moved to seek this balance.

A third type of resonance – that I call resonance by contrast – arises once the movement toward balance has begun. Since the antidote for too much heat is cold, our hot soul will eventually begin gravitating toward cold, despite the fact that cold is seemingly not in harmony with her nature. The truth, from a spiritual perspective, is that each soul must embrace its wholeness – its coldness as well as its hotness, its maleness as well as its femaleness, its darkness as well as its light – before it can attain the balance that ensures the resolution and healing of its core issues. Core issues are the catalyst in each life that propel the soul toward wholeness, and resonance by contrast is the mechanism for moving forward on this journey. Together all three forms of resonance encompass our experience of relationship within the embodied world, as we experience it in the fourth *chakra*.

Annnamaya Kosha

On the level of *annamaya kosha*, the fourth *chakra* manifests as the physical heart and the circulatory system – the network of arteries and veins that pump blood from the heart to all the vital organs and back again. Many early cultures and some Greek philosophers believed that the physical heart was the seat of the soul. This is literally true on the level of *annamaya kosha*, since it is the beating heart that marks the difference between a living being and one that is dead. As discussed in *The Seven Gates of Soul*, this point of view was eclipsed in the 17th century when Descartes and others began to replace the concept of soul by a more limited focus on the mind, which science then physically located in the brain. The soul – which encompasses not just the intellectual capacity of the mind, but also the emotions and imagination – nonetheless continues to depend upon the metaphorical, if not physical, heart for its sense of direction.

Conditioned as we are by contemporary culture to make our decisions rationally, most people would not consider the heart to be their primary compass. Yet, it is only when the heart is fully engaged that the quality of life we experience sustains our interest in living. Where the heart is not engaged, we are merely going through the motions, and although our lives may look healthy and "normal" to an outside observer, from the soul's perspective they are likely to feel impoverished. Within the context of our discussion of the fourth *chakra*, we feel impoverished because the life we are living is not one with which we resonate. We are attempting to adapt to some external model to which we feel we

◇◇

ought to conform, rather than following our heart, or our bliss, to use Joseph Campbell's well-known suggestion.

The exact quote in which Campbell gave us this advice provides an excellent summary of the soul's task at the level of the fourth *chakra*: ". . . if you follow your bliss you put yourself on a track that has been there all the while, waiting for you, and the life you ought to be living is the one you are living" (Power of Myth 150). To follow your bliss, you must be willing to stop trying so hard to figure out what it is you are supposed to be doing, and instead open your heart, so that you might feel your way into a more emotional and imaginative answer than your mind alone is capable of generating. While we are talking primarily about the feeling heart here, and not the physical heart, on the level of *annamaya kosha*, the condition of the physical heart becomes a barometer of how well we are doing in the attempt to follow our bliss.

It is no coincidence that as the Industrial Revolution accelerated during and immediately following World War II, heart disease rose to become the number one cause of death in the United States (CDC), and was declared the world's most serious epidemic by the World Health Organization. Medical science has declared the cause of this epidemic to be a more sedentary lifestyle, facilitated by labor saving technology, and a diet high in cholesterol. Certainly, on the merely physical level, these factors play their part. Yet, on a deeper, more spiritual level, the increasing incidence of heart disease may well be a byproduct of the fact that fewer people in a society geared toward production are free to follow their hearts. Instead, for the most part, they trade their freedom for a paycheck, work a soul-deadening job, then watch television and stuff their faces with sweet, greasy food in an unconscious attempt to fill the aching void.

In the 21st century, production has largely shifted to the Third World, while we now deal mostly in information and service. The mentality that fuels the predominant business model throughout most of the commercial world, however, remains the same – with little emphasis on putting heart into one's work. The goal is still to crank out as much work – or "product" – as possible in as little time as possible, and quality is normally considered at all only to the extent that it affects the bottom line. Such work is just as deadening to the soul as the industrial production of a previous era, and it continues to take its toll in the fourth *chakra*. When the heart's internal sense of direction is chronically ignored or negated in order to fit the mold of business as usual, the physical heart can begin shutting down. This is not a scientific statement, but I propose it here as an assessment of spiritual probability.

The second function of the fourth *chakra* on the level of *annamaya kosha* –namely circulation – is also compromised when the heart and its inner promptings are ignored. On a purely physical level, the leading factor in life-threatening heart disease is arteriosclerosis, or clogging and hardening of the arteries. When arteries become restricted, the circulation of blood throughout the body is impeded, and the body becomes starved for oxygen and the necessary nutrients to sustain life. Likewise, when decisions are made without the participation of the heart, the soul's mobility is impaired, and life can become a prison sentence. People easily become trapped by lives that they seemingly did not choose, when they fail to follow their heart's internal sense of direction. Conversely, the extent to which life is characterized by freedom of mobility, flexibility, and choice becomes the measure of clarity within the fourth *chakra* on the level of *annamaya kosha*.

Pranamaya Kosha

On the level of *pranamaya kosha*, the heart's compass becomes a source of attraction. A healthy fourth *chakra* draws to it whatever it needs from its environment in order to function at its optimal level of efficiency and effectiveness, as well as those experiences that hold the greatest potential for growth. All three forms of resonance – by affinity, wounding and contrast – are a function of the fourth *chakra* at the level of *pranamaya kosha*. The more we pay attention to the callings of our heart, the more active and reliable this attractive power becomes. As we fine tune this ability, it becomes necessary to expend less energy in seeking to manipulate or maneuver through the realm of possibility. Life increasingly becomes a matter of envisioning outcomes, setting intentions, and opening to receive.

Taoists call this effortless, heart-centered approach to life *wu-wei*, roughly translated as the art of non-doing. *Wu* means "not" or "non-" and *wei* means "making", "doing", "striving", "straining", or "busyness". The idea behind *wu-wei* is that by stepping back from the hustle and bustle of external life, and taking the time to listen internally to the heart, we can more clearly assess where we are in relation to what is happening around us. This assessment then allows us to orient ourselves to the outside world from a place of inner alignment, which makes striving, straining, and struggling unnecessary. In the third *chakra*, growth may often be a matter of expending effort, of rising to the occasion and actively harnessing talents and resources in order to meet the challenge at hand. In the fourth *chakra*, it is this alignment and not our effort that makes possible a life of meaning and fulfillment. If we are not aligned with our own souls, no amount of effort will produce satisfactory results. If we are, then very little effort is required.

This Taoist understanding was immortalized in the George Harrison song, *The Inner Sky*, adapted from the 47th stanza of the *Tao Te Ching*:

> *Without going out of my door, I can know all things on earth.*
> *Without looking out of my window, I can know the ways of heaven.*

The farther one travels, the less one knows,
The less one really knows.

Arrive without traveling.
See all without looking.
Do all without doing.

Wu-wei is not a matter of sitting in your room, avoiding life, and contemplating your navel, but rather of approaching life from a place of fluid adaptability, which in turn produces a natural resonance with everything around you. English Philosopher Alan Watts tells us that "*wu-wei* is a kind of "intelligence" that comes from "going with the grain, rolling with the punch, swimming with the current, trimming sails to the wind, taking the tide at its flood, and stooping to conquer" (76). In practing *wu-wei*, in other words, we do not resist the flow of life; we merge with it, and in merging, we experience a meaningful exchange with everything in our environment that has something to teach us.

When we seek to understand this flow, and to move in harmony with it, we automatically circulate through the embodied world as an integral part of it – as a natural expression of balanced resonance by affinity. No effort is required, since doing on this level is really a matter of being. This does not mean we won't make effort, but when the fourth *chakra* is clear on this level of penetration, there will be a buoyancy to our effort that carries us forward – like riding a wave into the shore. It takes an initial thrust of energy to merge with the wave, but once the merging has occurred, the wave does all the rest. In those places where we are most wounded, this kind of merging will not be possible, and effort will meet resistance and produce strain. The harder we push, the harder the universe will push back, and the more likely that resonance by wounding will lead to the learning that comes through resonance by contrast. As we then seek contrast to balance our propensity for excess and complete our deficiencies, we will naturally gravitate back toward the effortless place of *wu-wei*.

Manomaya Kosha

On the level of *manomaya kosha*, fourth *chakra* experiences manifest as feelings and emotion. Feelings come and go like breath, waves upon a shore, or weather patterns. Emotions are chronic feelings that have solidified through our ongoing identification with them. Emotions are much more durable than feelings; they become the psychic atmosphere in which we live our lives - the air we breathe, the ocean in which waves rise and fall, the climate zone through which weather patterns move. Regardless of the shape they take, and regardless of whether or not we judge them to be bad or good, pleasant or unpleasant, helpful or unhelpful, emotions are a fourth *chakra* signal that core issues being triggered. We naturally prefer pleasant emotions to those that appear to cause us pain, but it is our clinging to them, regardless of their nature, that is problematic. In the fourth *chakra*, our emotional attachments cause pain, because – like the clogging of an artery – they impede the circulation of feelings through the heart.

The antidote to this pain is love. Though love can be an emotion, when unencumbered by attachment, it is more than that. Love is the natural state of the heart when it is open and clear. Love is what generates the inner strength to allow feelings to come and go without attachment. Love is the alchemical elixir in which all core issues dissolve, the Universal Solvent in which all emotion is released. A friend once said, "There is no problem that more love cannot fix." Though at the time I thought his words a bit overly optimistic, if not delusional, I have since come to see the wisdom of this simple approach to life. At the very least, there is no problem that more love cannot benefit. Regardless of the outer face of our core issues, at the fourth *chakra*, the remedy will on some level always be opening the heart to an increased capacity for love.

Conversely, there is no deeper pain and no more insidious core issue than one that revolves around the many variations of love's absence or dysfunction. Most of the issues that take root in the fourth *chakra* will be those that get in the way of our ability to love self and others: from a deeply ingrained sense of unworthiness to be loved, to jealousy in the face of rivalry for love, to love through appeasement and self-compromise. There are a thousand and one faces to this primal dilemma, and since human love is inherently imperfect, no one is immune from its wounded underbelly. So much has been written about love and relationships that spending much time on them here would be somewhat redundant – except to say that on the level of the fourth *chakra*, every issue we could possibly encounter in relationship to another will mirror back to the self what is as yet unknown, unclaimed, unresolved, or in need of quality attention within our own stable of core issues.

The fourth *chakra* presents an interesting paradox, born of the fact that it lies midway between the first three (so-called lower) *chakras* and the last three (so-called higher) *chakras*. In the first three *chakras*, the focus is invariably upon self; in the fifth, sixth and seventh, the focus is increasingly upon taking one's place as part of a larger integrated whole. When fourth *chakra* issues arise, they often reflect the awkwardness of having one foot in both worlds – not yet fully centered as a self, yet not content to remain focused solely on the self. In such a transitional state, reaching out invariably triggers a wound with the memory of insufficient or imperfect love at its core – so that we can heal and move toward a place of wholeness that will allow us to participate fully in the life of the whole.

Today, for example, I am feeling discouraged about the return for effort I've expended to promote my first book. However much I might want to blame my discouragement upon a cold, indifferent world, the deeper truth is that my core issues have been triggered. The strong emotions I am feeling in the throes of these issues are a signal that I am out of alignment with myself. I am not loving myself enough, and this lack of love is causing an echo of my wounding in the world around me.

Stepping back ever so slightly from my identification with discouragement, I must readily acknowledge that the feeling of discouragement comes and goes. The other day I was feeling elated because I had just received word that my first review was to be published in a well-respected astrological journal. In prior communication with the editor of this journal, I had gathered that the review would be positive in tone. I felt hopeful that it would boost my visibility and translate into increased sales to a wider audience. In contrast to my present mood, this sense of hopeful elation would appear to be preferable, though apparently difficult to sustain. Yet if I take both moods together, it becomes impossible to ascertain which is a true measure of my experience. Both seem valid in the moment in which I experience them, but neither is durable enough to cling to for any length of time. Could it be that neither tells the truth about who I am as a writer, nor why I write, nor what purpose my writing serves in the overall scheme of my soul's evolutionary agenda?

The truth is that I write because it seems to be in my nature to do so. Or to use an eastern phrase, it is my *dharma*. The *dharma* of a candle is to burn; the *dharma* of an eagle is to fly; the *dharma* of each human soul is to express themselves through the gifts that they have been given, and through the exercise of talents that give them joy. The fulfillment of my *dharma* requires that I give consent to the words that seem to want to flow through me. Giving this consent helps align me with my core identity as a soul.

There are many obstacles to the fulfillment of *dharma*, however, since within the resonance of soul space, the world often conspires to trigger issues and attendant feelings capable of derailing us from our alignment with it. It takes a steady inner flame of self-love to keep allegiance to *dharma* alive within the face of other feelings that call it into question. How I feel about what I am doing as a writer will necessarily fluctuate, at times from day to day, or even moment to moment. These feelings will come and go, and to the extent that I am aligned with my *dharma*, solidly rooted in self-love, I will not be moved by them to depart from the steady flow of life force through me. I will simply immerse myself in this flow, and experience my creativity as an expression of *wu-wei*. Through simply being who I am doing what I do, I will effortlessly merge with the flow of life and experience fulfillment through my participation in it.

On the other hand, when I get caught up in the momentary feelings that swirl around the fulfillment of my *dharma*, and cling to them as though they were a measure of my worth – or a statement about who I am – I will begin resisting the flow of life and/or pushing against it. When I feel disillusioned, and allow myself to be moved by disillusionment, I sink into lethargy and hold myself back from a full participation in my *dharma* and in my life. "What's the use?" I tell myself, and the flow of *wu-wei* is impeded by this heaviness. When I feel elated or hopeful, and allow myself to be moved by these feelings, I begin straining in the opposite direction and try to push the river faster than it wants to go, thinking that if I act while the momentum of life seems to be on my side, I will somehow accelerate the process. But the flow is what it is, and I can only move with it or against it. Whether I hold myself back, or push myself forward, I am out of harmony with this flow. Through my identification with my temporary feelings, they have now gelled into emotions, capable of moving me out of alignment with the flow of *wu-wei* in relation to a changeless steady expression of *dharma*.

The antidote to this fall from grace is to keep writing, and to center myself in the process, while letting my feelings about the process simply rise and fall like waves upon the shore. In fact, having done that for the past three hours, I'm already feeling better, and the disillusionment I felt earlier this morning has begun to fade. It is the resonance with the art of writing and the loving affirmation of self that arises through giving consent to my *dharma* that is the important thing here, not the outer results of those actions.

A major fear behind my obsession with outer success, of course, is that maybe I am not a writer after all, and this is yet another false path in the pursuit of a *dharma* that remains ill-defined and elusive. But affinities come as naturally to us and are as essential to our well-being as breathing, and when we allow ourselves to be dissuaded from their pursuit at the fourth *chakra*, we suffer a loss of soul. This loss of soul is not an ordinary garden-variety of emotion, but a self-denial and a little death with reverberations throughout the *chakra* system. When we do not whole-heartedly pursue our affinities, we languish in a state of mediocrity in relation to our talents and abilities at the third *chakra*, we enjoy life less at the second *chakra*, and our will to live diminishes at the first *chakra*. In the fourth *chakra*, we suffer a disconnection from our *dharma* and experience the world as a loveless place.

Following the path with heart (to use Carlos Castenada's phrase (122) is the task of the fourth *chakra*. Following the path with heart without becoming attached to the feelings that rise and fall in the course of the journey is the specific task at the level of *manomaya kosha*. When the fourth *chakra* is open and clear, there will be a steady candle flame of quiet joy, self-sustaining in its simple, effortless expression of being. Feelings may come and go, but there is no clinging and no need to cling. There will a natural merging with the flow of life and a sense of interconnectedness, of being an integral part of the whole.

This sense of flow and interconnectedness is not a state of being that we can force. It will evolve as we keep our heart open in the face of everything that seemingly conspires to shut it down – in my case today, the apparent indifference of the world to my best efforts. Protecting the heart - which is our natural tendency whenever we feel wounded - diminishes the power of attraction and lessens the likelihood that we will draw to ourselves that which our heart most deeply desires. It can be a vicious cycle, the antidote to which often feels counterintuitive. For to keep the heart open, we must continually move in the direction of our fears and vulnerabilities and in so doing, discover a power within us that transcends them. When I can live in this place - when I can love myself enough - the issues with which I struggle today will no longer exist.

Whatever melodramas are produced in the fourth *chakra* on the level of *manomaya kosha* are meant to be potent emotional teaching devices designed to lead us toward a deeper alignment to *dharma* - to a core sense of self, not utterly devoid of ego, but now aligned with a deeper sense of purpose that transcends ego. The more aligned we are with this core sense of self immersed in *dharma*, the more we have to give, the more naturally we are compassionate and caring, the easier it is for us to reach out and help make this world a better place for all of us, and the more naturally and effortlessly we take our place within it.

Vijnanamaya Kosha

At the level of *vijnanamaya kosha*, the feelings that crystallize as emotions color our entire relationship to the embodied world in which we live. The world itself does not change, but our perception of it does, according to our mood. When I am feeling elated, the world becomes a brighter place; I feel more connected to it, more interested in it, and more willing to participate. When I am feeling disillusioned, the same world becomes a darker, sadder, colder place; I feel disconnected from it, less interested in it, and less willing to participate. When I am caught up in my core issues, resonance by wounding will predominate, and I will feel less resonance by affinity with anything. Paradoxically, the way back to affinity will be through resonance by contrast, but I won't become aware of the healing nature of contrast until I can attain a certain level of detachment from my issues. Before I reach that blessed state, contrast will only serve as affirmation that the world is an inhospitable place. Everywhere I look will be something with which I cannot resonate, and what I see - from this place of identification with wounding - only serves to increase my alienation and anxiety.

The human condition entails a tremendous amount of vulnerability. So many things in life seemingly lie beyond our control - from the parents that raise us, to the world we encounter once we leave the family nest, to the inescapable fact of our impending death, not to mention global warming, nuclear proliferation, impending terrorist attacks, and genetic mutation of deadly viruses. At every turn, there is something to remind us just how fragile and precarious is this fleeting human existence.

Most of us find ways to erect walls of protection against these potential reminders of vulnerability, and life goes on somehow despite it all. But whenever our core issues get triggered, our barriers of protection dissolve and we are back in that scary place where the illusion of control breaks down. The good news is that this is also our personal invitation to an opening of the heart.

The hardest thing we will ever have to do in this life is to open our hearts in a place of vulnerability. The instinctual response is to shut down, because at every *chakra* below the fourth, shutting down makes perfect sense. From the perspective of the first *chakra*, we shut down to protect ourselves as a matter of survival; at the second, we naturally shield ourselves as much as possible from our pain and suffering; at the third, shutting down affords us a modest measure of self-control, and keeps the ego intact. At the fourth *chakra*, however, shutting down is paradoxically a recipe for diminished living. We choke off our relationship to the embodied world, and to the flow of spiritual vitality that moves from our center into the world. On the emotional level, shutting down leads to more suffering, not less, because shutting down cuts off the flow of love that lubricates the difficult places in our lives, and diminishes our capacity to cope.

The supreme spiritual test that we face at the fourth *chakra* is opening the heart to embrace our inherent vulnerability. This involves great risk, because it will evoke fear in each of the preceding *chakras*. We stand to lose a great deal, if the gamble we take is misguided or wrong. Opening the heart in the wrong place at the wrong time can be the act of a fool, and the fear that reminds us of this, at each of the first three *chakras*, can crystallize into a powerful force of resistance.

This fear is not entirely ungrounded. To the extent that fear is present at all, our reality will mirror that fear back to us, and what we fear is what we get. If the antidote to fear is an open heart, however, then opening the heart means mustering enough self-love to counterbalance and neutralize whatever fear keeps it shut. To the extent that we can muster this love in the face of our vulnerability, then our fear subsides. When fear subsides, we become receptive to grace – which can be understood as the primary experience of the soul at the fourth *chakra* on the level of *vijnanamaya kosha*.

Grace is awakening to the understanding that this life is a gift. Death may be inevitable, but life is not. The fact that life exists at all – that Earth is just the right distance from the sun and has the necessary ingredients to support life; the fact that life has taken this unique, complex shape it is possible to identify as "I"; the very notion that dead, inert matter can become conscious enough to sense, feel, think and imagine – is something of a miracle, is it not? If vulnerability is the realization that there is nothing that we can do to guarantee our survival, avoid our fair share of pain and suffering, or exercise absolute control over our existence, then grace is the capacity to view these same uncomfortable truths from the other end of the telescope. For there is also nothing obvious we have done to earn the right to our existence; it is a gift that is given to us. Though we may high-five our buddies when pleasure comes around, as though we were smart enough to navigate our lives into it, the fact that pleasure exists and is possible to experience is also a gift built into the fabric of this universe. Though we pride ourselves on everything that we create or accomplish in this life, our talents and abilities arise within us unbidden as a dispensation of grace. To open to this realization is to penetrate to the level of *vijnanamaya kosha* in our experience of the fourth *chakra*. We will know when we are there, because of the gratitude we feel for everything and everyone around us.

This attitude of gratitude, in turn, makes possible the appearance of images and symbols that can help heal of our core issues and our wounds. For if life, pleasure, and affinity are all gifts of grace, then perhaps death, pain, and wounding are as well. This is a realization that does not really come into focus until we reach the fifth *chakra*. In the fourth, it is enough to know that the opening of the heart in the face of vulnerability that leads to an experience of grace is also an opening to the healing power of the symbols and images that present themselves to us in everyday life.

As discussed in Chapter Three, we also encounter these images at the third *chakra*, when we feel the necessity and set the intention to address our core issues. To the extent that we are engaging these issues at the third *chakra*, however, it will appear that the images we encounter arise as a response to our intention, and that they are amenable to the magical manipulation of our will. This is not necessarily an illusion, but it is an incomplete understanding of the nature of the symbolic realm. For these images are part of the elfin realm of the anima – described by Jung so eloquently in his masterwork, *The Archetypes and the Collective Unconscious* (28-32) – in which the ego must relinquish its control in order to open to a deeper dimension of symbolic meaning.

This surrender is necessary before grace becomes available. When the heart opens to grace through the surrender of ego, we begin to realize at the level of *vijnanamaya kosha*, that these symbols and images with which we interact are woven into the very fabric of the embodied universe as clues, waiting for our discovery. They too, are part of the grace that pervades this manifest universe – a part that is apparently personal to us. As in the old Grimm Brothers fairy tale about Hansel and Gretel, these symbols and images are the trail of breadcrumbs Spirit leaves for us so that we may find our way back through the dark forest of this life. The world is filled with breadcrumbs, and each of us will follow a unique trail of them back to the same place from which we all emerged.

Though there are many ways to approach this trail of breadcrumbs, astrology is one of the most sophisticated paths to increasing awareness of just how intricately placed these breadcrumbs are. Until the fourth *chakra* is open, however, the astrological practitioner will not be conscious enough to use astrology as a revelation of grace. We will begin exploring this level of astrological possibility in Part Two. For now, suffice it to say that on the level of *vijnanamaya kosha* – where everything has symbolic implications – an opening of the heart yields an ever-deepening appreciation for the grace that is always available everywhere within the embodied world.

Anandamaya Kosha

When Spirit finally penetrates to the level of *anandamaya kosha* at the fourth *chakra*, the world becomes filled with grace, and the soul becomes the embodiment of love and compassion. Having tasted the vulnerability that necessarily precedes the opening of the heart, the soul blessed to reach this level will have great empathy for the suffering of others, and great tolerance for their struggle to alleviate this suffering, however unconsciously it might be undertaken. At this level, one becomes not merely a recipient of grace, but also its willing agent, for despite the inherent vulnerability within the human condition, there is – at this level – no longer anything that would impede the flow of love, and thus no resistance to block the dispensation of grace from Spirit. All is *wu-wei*, and in the spirit of *wu-wei*, miracles proceed unimpeded.

In the Siddha tradition, out of which my former teacher, Swami Muktananda emerged, there was a saint known as Zippruana. As was true of most of the Siddha saints, Zippruana had a most unorthodox way of dispensing grace. He would sit at the outskirts of town on a heap of dung at the local dump. Those souls brave or foolhardy enough to seek his blessing had to venture to the dump and meet him there. When a would-be disciple approached him, Zippruana would jump up and down and yell obscenities. He would then reach down, scoop up a handful of dung and throw it at the bewildered soul who had dared disturb his meditation. This was hardly the kind of behavior one would expect from a saint, and any lesser being doing the same thing would undoubtedly be committed to a mental institution, or be carted off to prison.

But because Zippruana's heart was open, and active at the level of *anandamaya kosha*, his actions were merely the vehicle for cutting through the vulnerability and fear of those who approached him to reveal the miracle of grace at work beneath it all. When the dung hit its intended target, it burst into the most sublime fragrance, and left the astonished soul with an experience of unexpected bliss. Upon leaving, Zippruana's visitors were utterly transformed by a glimpse of the grace available within even the shittiest of experiences. Such is the power of the open fourth *chakra* that has been penetrated to the level of *anandamaya kosha*.

Chapter Five
The Fifth Chakra

In the Hindu tradition, the fifth *chakra*, located at the throat, is called *visuddha*. Here we find a smoky purple lotus of sixteen petals, a white elephant, a circle, and an androgynous god depicted as half white and half gold. Here can also be found three forms of time, the seven subtle tones, and "the gateway of the Great Liberation" (Avalon 122). For Judith (8) and Bruyere (42), this *chakra* is blue, while Leadbeater reports a range of observations – from "blue, silvery, gleaming" to smoky purple to brilliant gold to "moonlike" (97). Bruyere (43) and Leadbeater (106) associate this *chakra* with ether, while Judith correlates it with sound or vibration (7). Myss relates the fifth *chakra* to the *sefirah* of Hesod – "the love or mercy of God," and Gevurah – "the judgment of God" (220).

Psychologically, the throat center relates to expression, communication, the capacity for living and teaching one's truth, and the dawning of spiritual awareness – that is to say, awareness of one's place within the outworking of a larger cosmic design. Those with a balanced *visuddha* will be articulate, willing and able to communicate the subjective truth of their being in each moment, receptive to divine grace, at peace with the seeming imperfection in the world, often amused by the cosmic humor that pervades it, and in a position spiritually to teach others.

If at the fourth *chakra*, one begins to move through the resonant field of soul space and form relationships by affinity, wounding, and contrast, the process culminates in the fifth *chakra* as one discovers and increasingly inhabits a sense of place. A sense of place arises out of a deepening self-acceptance in relation to the natural affinities that make the individual soul who and what it is – an acceptance that comes through the hard work of healing core issues, and cultivating resonances by contrast that balance the soul's tendency toward excess or deficiency. This does not mean that the soul will not occasionally express itself in ways that embody these imbalances – which after all, may be a part of the unique expression of a particular soul. But as the fifth *chakra* opens, this will increasingly become a matter of choice in conscious response to a specific situation. Finding its place, the soul will become at home in any situation, at peace with the world, and able to influence the world through its mere presence rooted in a sense of place within it. A sense of place also encompasses the concept of dharma, developed in the fourth *chakra*, but at this level, dharma is unimpeded by doubt and comes as naturally to the soul as breathing.

A corollary development to this growing sense of place, at the fifth *chakra*, is a similar sense of timing. The soul begins to move in a more synchronistic way with the cycles of its life, and as it does, it becomes more cognizant of the uncanny alignment of inner process and outer events, understood from a metaphorical perspective. These cycles can be observed and mapped astrologically – as I demonstrated in *The Seven Gates of Soul* and will again demonstrate later in this book – but to the extent that the fifth *chakra* is open, they can also be simply intuited. The soul is naturally aware of the juxtaposition of time and space, and allows this awareness to guide it to the right place at the right time, in the spirit of *wu-wei*, with a minimal amount of deliberate design.

At the fifth *chakra*, this growing sense of place within space and time will be accompanied by the ability to speak, write, and teach what the soul is learning. The yogis and yoginis that originally devised the *chakra* system to measure spiritual progress often referred to a special power that arises at this *chakra*, called *Vach siddhi* – the power to speak the truth. The soul with *vach siddhi* not only had the power to discern and articulate what was going on beneath the surface of appearances, but could also make something true simply by speaking it out loud.

This power is, at core, the power of intention we first observed being cultivated in the third *chakra*, amplified by a sense of alignment with an integrated center developed in the fourth *chakra*. In the fifth *chakra*, the power of intention is taken to its culmination as inner alignment allows the soul to take its place within the cosmic order. *Vach siddhi* can also be understood as the art of *wu-wei* taken to a higher level. If one has mastered the art of being in the right place at the right time, then one witnesses the flow of life as one participates, and gradually develops the capacity to anticipate it. This is not divinatory magic, or prophecy, or the power to predict the future as some would claim, but – from the perspective of the developed fifth *chakra* – merely an instinctual awareness of the cyclical movement of time along knowable trajectories.

Obviously, this power to speak something into being would seem to hold great potential for abuse, but the ingenious safety catch built into the system is that in order to abuse *vach siddhi* one would have to step out of the profound sense of inner and outer alignment that produces it in the first place, at which point, the power would dissipate.

What *vach siddhi* does allow the soul to do is to begin to teach and guide others. This is not something that the soul can decide to do. It is something that happens, as the soul's alignment with space and time attracts those who are seeking direction. There will be a powerful sense of resonance by affinity between the soul with the developed fifth *chakra* and those who could benefit from the wisdom of his experience, and when the teacher is ready, the students will come.

Both my spiritual teachers in the 1970s – Yogi Bhajan and Swami Muktananda – were powerfully magnetic beings, attracting thousands of students, disciples and followers from around the world. They could fill a room just by promising to enter it, and their words held great power. Yogi Bhajan spoke imperfect English, while Swami Muktananda had to speak through interpreters, and often the words themselves were difficult to interpret or understand, but the energy and spiritual vitality coming through the words were unmistakable, and the student often got the message before his mind could comprehend what was being said.

At the fifth *chakra*, one begins to discern the cosmic order – which is at once exquisitely beautiful, ingeniously constructed and infused with a delightful sense of humor. As a consequence, with the capacity to speak the truth and teach, generally comes a childlike capacity for wonder and delight. There is a sense of compassionate peace even in the face of the most gruesome suffering, and a sense of humor that can at times be infuriating to those who don't understand its source. In *Miracle of Love* – American spiritual teacher Ram Dass' wonderful book of stories about his guru Neem Karoli Baba – Ram Dass shares the following anecdote (140):

> In 1962, during the India-China war, I told Maharaji, "Chinese forces have entered Assam. Our forces have acted like spectators. If they continue not to fight, the Chinese will come to the plains."

> Maharaji said, "Nothing will happen. Chinese will retreat. India is a place of rishis (sages) and self-sacrifice. Communism can't come."

> "But, Maharaji," I continued, "why have the Chinese forces come?"

> "Just to awaken you," he replied.

As the fifth *chakra* opens, one begins to see that everything – even the most horrendous turn of events – exists for the sole purpose of awakening us all, individually and collectively. This then becomes the wisdom that one imparts to those who are drawn by the power of the soul's alignment with the cosmic order. The extent to which we don't get it, is the measure not of the teacher's delusion, but of our own lack of alignment. The extent to which we protest is the extent to which our resistance to alignment is more powerful than our desire to align. We sweat and strain, adamant about holding onto our limited understanding, while the teacher winks and nods, laughs and rolls his eyes, seemingly indifferent to our predicament, and yet all the while holding us in a place of unconditional love and utter compassion. The true teacher – the one whose fifth *chakra* allows her to see and speak the truth – is fully capable of seeing us as we truly are, in perfect alignment with ourselves, the embodied world, and the cosmic order, even when we can't see ourselves that way because of our wounding. Meanwhile, any effort we can expend to see ourselves from the teacher's point of view moves us that much closer to the alignment that otherwise eludes us.

Annamaya kosha

At the level of *annamaya kosha*, the fifth *chakra* manifests as the organs of speech – mouth, throat, palate, tonsils, tongue, larynx – and thyroid gland, all contained within the neck region of the body. As might be suspected through our discussion of sound and communication above, the throat is also intimately connected to the ears through the Eustachian tube. In this region is also the nose, which medical professionals will tell you works in close harmony with ears and throat to form a system. This system is affected, for example, when you have a cold, a sinus infection, or more serious bronchial infection extending down into the lungs.

The first thing we can notice about this system is that it includes most of the organs through which something external to us can enter our body. We use our mouth, throat and esophagus for eating, our nose for breathing, and our ears for taking in sound. The female sexual organs, associated with the second *chakra*, and at times the anus, associated with the first *chakra* can also be associated with intake, as can the skin (a permeable membrane that I would associate with the boundary and territorial issues that arise in the third *chakra*), and the eyes, which we will discuss in the next chapter in relation to the sixth *chakra*. These exceptions aside, we hear and breathe all the time, and usually eat several times a day, and by far the predominant intake activity of the body can be associated with the fifth *chakra*.

What this means metaphorically is that the fifth *chakra* is where we attempt to receive from the embodied world. It is where we take in what is not available to us within the boundaries of our own being, and where we allow the embodied world to supplement and complement what is missing. We eat to replenish the nutrients our bodies need to function. We breathe to obtain the oxygen we need to vitalize the body with a fresh supply of life energy. We listen both within and without to know who we are and where we stand in relation to the world around us. All three of these activities allow us to form a connection to the world that is potentially nourishing, vitalizing, and educational.

In Chapter Three, we discussed eating in relation to the third *chakra* and the formation of identity. Here, the same function takes on added significance as the source of growing awareness of our connection to the embodied world. In the third *chakra*, we eat to grow a body and an embodied sense of self. In the fifth *chakra*, there is an exchange that takes place, and as we absorb nourishment, energy, information and qualitative essence from those things, people, ideas, places, and activities with which we resonate, we take our place among them and give back through our presence within the resonant field that we share.

Sometimes what we absorb from our environment produces an adverse reaction, and proves – in the short term at least – not to be good for us. This is reflected by the fact that the physiological organs associated with the fifth *chakra* – ear, nose and throat – are where most of the primary infections we experience first take root. We get sick, usually, because of some virus, bacteria, or other infectious organism that we take in through our mouth or nose. The fifth *chakra* then has a great deal to do with our essential vulnerability as embodied souls, and with whatever sense of immunity or lack of immunity we experience in relation to this sense of vulnerability.

To some extent, vulnerability will be experienced at each of the *chakras* – the vulnerability of some threat to our survival at the first *chakra*; of pain at the second *chakra*; of failure at the third *chakra*; and of conflict at the fourth *chakra*, to name a few possibilities. We also spoke of this vulnerability more specifically in relation to the fourth *chakra* as it is experienced on the level of *vijnanamaya kosha*, where it is a prelude to an opening to grace. In the fifth *chakra*, this sense of vulnerability is met more actively – even at the shallowest levels of penetration by Spirit – with a response that stems directly from the vitality of our being. On this level, there is a natural immunity to the "slings and arrows of outrageous fortune" of the embodied life that arises to the extent that we are aligned with our own center, and rooted within our place in the larger cosmic scheme of things. This sense of immunity, on whatever level it exists, is a function of the fifth *chakra*.

On the level of *annamaya kosha*, we are speaking primarily of the strength of the body's immune system in fighting off disease. It should be obvious by now that issues related to physical health can be rooted in any *chakra*, at the level of *annamaya kosha*, and will likely manifest in the correspondent physiological system associated with the *chakra*. Colon cancer, for example, will likely be related to first *chakra* issues, genital herpes with the second *chakra*; ulcers with the third *chakra*; heart disease as already discussed with the fourth. The first *chakra* will necessarily be involved in any life-threatening illness, since the will to live, a psychological function of the first *chakra* will by nature be evoked. The third *chakra* – which governs the defense of soul space – will be involved with the body's attempt to fight a disease that has entered the body, and therefore with an autoimmune response.

Within this somewhat more complex model, the fifth *chakra* on the level of *annamaya kosha* will specifically be related to the body's inherent vulnerability to disease, as a consequence of its openness to outside influences that are detrimental to it. In a global sense, it will govern how vulnerable we are to detrimental influences, as a consequence of misalignment with our center and imperfect inhabitation of place. These two factors, in turn, will govern how immune we are to taking in what is not good for us, while how conscious we are in the fifth *chakra* will determine how discriminating we can be. The power to "just say no" to that which is not in alignment with our nature comes through a clear and open fifth *chakra*, and the process begins at *annamaya kosha*, as we become more conscious of that to which we expose ourselves.

More specifically, diseases related to an imbalance in the fifth *chakra* might include any compromise to the respiratory system – lung cancer, asthma, bronchitis, pneumonia and the like; allergies; laryngitis; sinus infections; hearing difficulties; canker sores; colds and flu; acute poisoning; and environmental sensitivities.

Pranamaya kosha

At *pranamaya kosha*, the process of intake serves to shift the soul in a new direction on one or more qualitative scales. For example, an individual that has a resonant affinity to all things wet, might be drawn to live near a lake where he could go boating, drink beer on weekends, and date moody, sensual women with a poor sense of boundaries. During an emotional crisis with his girlfriend, such an individual might be inclined by nature to drink a bit too much, and be a bit more reckless when he takes his boat on the water. In relation to the fifth *chakra*, the intake of excess alcohol, in particular, will tend to move him into the red zone on the wet scale, creating a condition of excess that could potentially be dangerous.

If our hypothetical friend continues along this path, he may well have an accident, or do something he will later regret that serves as a wakeup call, triggers his core issues, and attracts troublesome circumstances through resonance by wounding. He might have a boating accident, or a blow-out argument with his girlfriend that ends the relationship, or experience a series of black-outs related to his alcohol consumption. As a consequence of this wake-up call – assuming an ideal scenario – he may then be inspired to join Alcoholics Anonymous, face his underlying emotional issues, and in general seek to balance his tendency toward excess wet with a discovery of the drier side of life.

All the while, he will be exposing himself to various influences at the fifth *chakra*, gradually learning to be more discriminating in what he chooses to allow into his resonant soul space, and on the level of *pranamaya kosha*, fine tuning his sense of place on the wet-dry scale. This process of fine tuning will gradually reduce unnecessary vulnerability along this scale, and increase his innate immunity to conditions of excess wet. Through his experiences, he will have learned something about what happens when he crosses a certain line, and he will tend to become more discriminating about those influences that tend to push him over the line. Will he continue to make the same mistakes? Probably. But gradually, at the fifth *chakra*, on the level of *pranamaya kosha*, he will find his place of balance.

As discussed previously, this is a learning process that begins in the third *chakra*, and continues to evolve in the fourth. With each successive stage in the process, the lessons remain the same, but our awareness shifts to encompass a perspective unique to the *chakra* at which the issues are resonating in any given moment. In the third *chakra*, we become conscious in some way that we are over-exposed, usually because of resonance by affinity that leads to excess. In the fourth, we find ourselves more frequently drawn to situations and relationships that trigger our wounding, and learn to experiment with contrasts that complement our deficiencies. In the fifth, this experimentation continues, but with a greater sense of conscious control. On this level, we know where the point of balance is; we know how to get there; and we can choose to dwell in this place of balance or not.

In the fourth *chakra*, resonance by wounding and resonance by contrast are still fairly instinctual responses to the consequences of our imbalanced affinities. In the fifth *chakra*, we become increasingly aware of the element of choice, and the power to choose differently. We move beyond the instinctual clinging to our affinities in the second *chakra*, and gradually beyond the necessity for additional wounding in the fourth, to a more consciously cultivated skill at self-regulation. Psychically speaking, we learn to mix our hot and cold to just the right temperature, without getting scalded or freezing ourselves when we step into the shower. One day, we may prefer a hotter shower, another day a cooler one, and we can adjust the mix of hot and cold accordingly. We widen our range of options and claim the wisdom of our experience. Ultimately, we gain the freedom of the character in a story that by now will be familiar to many readers:

> A man walks down a street and falls into a hole he fails to see.
> The man walks down the same street, sees the hole, but falls in anyway.
> The man walks down the same street, sees the hole and walks around it.
> The man walks down a different street.

Since the fifth *chakra* is associated with sound and the faculty of hearing, it should be noted here that one huge area of learning related to the fifth *chakra* is in processing information. It is here that we take in much of the information that later becomes entrenched as our belief system and our worldview. Beliefs and worldview are more accurately understood as the province of the sixth *chakra*, and we will discuss them in more detail in the next chapter. But learning to discriminate between truth and fiction in what we hear is specifically the province of the fifth *chakra*, as is learning what information is germane to our soul process and what is merely background static.

This is especially critical in the current information age, when we are constantly bombarded by more information than we can effectively process, much of it of no redeeming social or spiritual value whatsoever. Some information also comes through the eyes, and I will address this more specifically when I talk about the sixth *chakra*. Meanwhile, at the fifth *chakra*, we are more exclusively concerned with the information that we hear. At the fifth *chakra*, we must learn to filter the verbal spam that enters our resonant space through our ears, and then actively seek out information that facilitates our soul's evolution.

The learning process begins in childhood, as we are exposed to the family worldview through the verbal messages that we receive from our parents: "you'll never amount to anything," "a woman's place is in the home," "big boys don't cry," or whatever it might be for us. The fifth *chakra* hosts all those verbal messages that lie at the core of our wounding. As children we lack the discrimination to know that these messages are often false projections, but through a trial and error learning process – centered in the fifth *chakra* – we will gradually learn to weed out messages that are not in alignment with our own highest good. At the level of *pranamaya kosha*, this will take the form of exploring qualities associated with the forbidden side of life. Our big boy that was told it was not ok to cry, for example, will inevitably learn the perils of being too dry, and gradually be moved by his wounding to discover the wonderful world of wet, in all its many guises.

That which was not spoken in childhood can also present a special challenge at the level of the fifth *chakra*. As discussed by Judith, family secrets that children are admonished to keep (e.g., daddy's drinking or mommy's mental breakdown), or subjects that are forbidden in family discourse (e.g., sexual feelings or unhappiness) can create a tremendous psychic burden that must eventually seek release (320-321). These secrets can create blockage in the fifth *chakra* on the level of *pranamaya kosha*, as can a family atmosphere marked by lying, verbal intimidation, or even the lack of meaningful conversation. On the level of *pranamaya kosha*, the fifth *chakra* demands that the truth be acknowledged, freely told, and openly lived to keep the life force flowing freely.

Manomaya kosha

The issues that arise in the fifth *chakra* on the level of *manomaya kosha* are those that in some way prevent us from speaking and living our truth and finding our place within the natural order. Some of these issues will revolve around false or toxic messages, although to the extent that these messages have gelled into a belief system or a self-reinforcing image of the world, they will more effectively be dealt with in the sixth *chakra*. On a more basic level, many fifth *chakra* issues will involve the necessity for correcting imbalances that are reinforced by family messages. Sometimes our excesses are caused by our natural affinities. At other times, however, they can be caused by dysfunctional messages taken to heart as faulty guidance. Faulty guidance serves to complicate our issues on the level of the fifth *chakra*, though at times, it may amplify and exacerbate tendencies toward excess that already exist within our nature. Whatever the message, the task at the fifth *chakra* is to discover what is actually true for us and then learn to live that truth.

It is here, for example, that a woman who was taught by her family to take a secondary, supportive role to her husband becomes too soft. As a consequence, she winds up with no support when her husband leaves her, and chooses to get harder in

✕✕

order to correct that imbalance. She may find a job where she can be competitive, work out at the local gym, and learn to practice tough love in relation to her children. It is here that the man who has discovered the pitfalls of being too tight, after suffering a stroke, learns to relax, delegate responsibility, and cultivate a broader range of interests outside of work. It is here that the shy become more vocal, the loud learn to listen, and the cold learn the necessity for and joys of warmth - usually because some life crisis has forced an acute awareness of an imbalance that only tells a partial truth about who they believed themselves to be.

In short, the fifth *chakra*, at the level of the *manomaya kosha*, is where we cultivate the essential life wisdom that is ours because of the dues we have paid, and the lessons we have had to learn the hard way. Once these lessons are learned, we are much less easily thrown out of balance by the external influences that impinge upon our lives. On this level, we've been there, done that, and have no need to do that again. We begin to shape ourselves as souls, in ways that are relatively unique to us, as a consequence of the lives that we have lived, and through the shaping process, we find some essential clue to immunity that serves as the pivot point for a life in which we gladly take our place and learn to occupy it with greater skill.

At the fifth *chakra*, we come full circle from our first discovery of our affinities in the second *chakra*. We still have the same affinities at this level, but now we know the consequences of overindulgence, and have learned the lessons of wounding through overindulgence. We can now choose to overindulge or not. We also know how to balance our tendencies toward excess or deficiency with contrast, and can adjust the mix to suit our mood and/or the requirements of a given situation. Awakening this *chakra* is in essence a matter of taking the Delphi Oracle to heart by knowing ourselves, and seeking all things in moderation. It takes work at all the *chakras* to master these two commandments, but it is in the fifth that our hard work in all the other *chakras* begins to distill into something we might call subjective wisdom.

Despite the fact that subjective wisdom is uniquely ours, it also often carries within it a desire to be shared. Our reformed alcoholic in the example above may be moved to serve as a mentor to other alcoholics in recovery. A mother who has learned hard lessons about teenage pregnancy will likely want to pass those lessons onto her own teenage daughter, who may or may not be receptive to them. A friend of mine who has survived breast cancer now counsels other women who are going through the same ordeal. It is at this level that we become a resource to those who are moving through the resonance-by-wounding stage of their own process to discover the healing power of resonance by contrast.

The fifth *chakra* can become blocked when one of the messages received in childhood is that one does not have the right to impose his truth on another. This kind of blockage can arise, for example, in individuals growing up in families where they were shouted down by bolder siblings or intimidated by parental authority (Judith 322-323). While discrimination in the speaking of one's truth can be a valid mark of sensitivity to the rights of others, there is a fine line between its exercise and self-denial. For we do have the right – indeed the obligation – to honor what we have learned about life through our own experience, to live from a place of alignment with our own deepest truth, and to speak our truth with conviction wherever it is necessary to secure these rights.

Inevitably there will be those with whom we disagree, but the job is not to convince others that they are wrong. It is to be true to ourselves. We cannot take our place within the larger scheme of things without the willingness to do this; and it is at the fifth *chakra*, at the level of *manomaya kosha*, that all issues of self-doubt in the expression of subjective truth must ultimately be resolved. To the extent that the resolution of these issues is a work in progress – as it will be for most of us – the suffering we experience will be in direct proportion to the compromises we feel compelled to make to our sense of integrity.

Vijnanamaya kosha

Normally when we think of imagery and symbolism, we think in visual terms, and almost always the imagery and symbolism that arise on the level of *vijnanamaya kosha* will have a visual component. At the fifth *chakra*, however, we also experience aural imagery through the meaning that we ascribe to various words and sounds. If, for example, we remember the sound of a door slamming as a prelude to parental fights in childhood, we may still have a visceral response to doors slamming in adulthood that includes anticipation of confrontation, even though from an objective standpoint, that may or may not be an impending possibility.

Words will likewise have subjective connotations that depend upon our personal experiences of the "objective" reality that the words point to. Consider the word "love." Anyone hearing the word in a sentence will have no problem recognizing and understanding it as an identifiable word. There may even be definitions for the word "love" that most of us could agree on. But for one person, "love" brings a romantic vision of hearts and flowers, jacuzzis and warm fuzzy emotions, while for someone else, "love" may have more to do with honesty, trust, and intimate verbal sharing. For a third, "love" may be a signal that another is trying to control and manipulate them; while for a fourth, "love" may be a prelude to rejection and abandonment. It's the same word in each instance, but each of us will load the word with connotations that skew the meaning of the word in distinctly personal directions.

This is, in fact, what we do routinely at the fifth *chakra*, on the level of *vijnanamaya kosha*. Few words in any language can be spoken without being heard through subjective

✧✧

filters, and when the filtering process is taken into account, it is a wonder that we can ever communicate at all. Political election campaigns, divorce proceedings, and late night talk shows are all exaggerated examples of the "he said, she said" dynamic that flows through this *chakra* at this level when it is still relatively unconscious. As the fifth *chakra* opens and clears, one gains the ability to hear what is really being said beneath and beyond the words that are being spoken. One becomes a good listener, and adept at responding in a way that fosters understanding and rapport. The soul is endowed with the capacity to bring clarity to difficult issues and facilitate a deeper recognition of subjective truth in those to whom one is listening.

Like sound, smells also carry with them deeply personal connotations. Scientists have begun to document the relationship between smell and memory, particularly memories that have strong emotional content (Web India 123). Since the memories triggered by smell are necessarily subjective, the olfactory signature of any situation carries symbolic associations that register differently for each of us at level of *vijnanamaya kosha*. These highly individual associations with the sense of smell are a function of the fifth *chakra* at this level of manifestation.

In the original *yogic* system from which this system of *chakras* and *koshas* we are exploring is extracted, smell was traditionally associated with the first *chakra* and the *tattwa* (element) of earth. Smell was considered to be the most primitive of the senses, and thus ontologically the first to awaken. Logically, many of the earliest smells we encounter will be related to our earliest efforts to anchor Spirit within an unfamiliar body and with survival. Yet, as we acquire a body of experience, various smells can also become associated with other *chakras* – the smell of peaches, for example, with the pleasure of the second *chakra*; the smell of morning coffee, perhaps, with the activation of the third *chakra*; the smell of freshly baked bread with a favorite grandmother, whose memory is now a part of our resonant soul space centered in the fourth *chakra*; and so on. Memories related to smell can, in fact, be rooted in several *chakras* at the same time. The internal process by which smells become attached to certain experiences and the emotional components of those experiences are a function of the fifth *chakra* at the level of vijnanmaya *kosha*.

Anandamaya kosha

At the fifth *chakra* on the level of *anandamaya kosha*, the teacher emerges. When we take our place of balance within the cosmos, when the art of listening is mastered, and the hard work of neutralizing the spoken or unspoken messages behind our core issues has been done, the soul opens to a clarified channel of information from a deeper source of wisdom within. One listens, both within and without, hears and then speaks. The flow of words that comes through the being who has reached this level at the fifth *chakra* is infused with *vach siddhi*, because it is no longer being filtered through personal biases born of wounding. It is instead a direct expression of Spirit, operating within and through an embodied soul, using speech as its faculty of expression.

Those familiar with New Age philosophy might recognize this as a form of channeling, but what is being channeled here is not some other entity. It is the soul, still embodied, but relatively free of the wounding that embodiment necessarily entails. I speak of the soul at this level as being "relatively" free, because the process is always along a continuum that stretches out to infinity in both directions. The more deeply the fifth *chakra* extends into the material realm, the more difficult speech is at all; the farther into the realm of Spirit it extends, the more transparent a vehicle for Spirit and the more deeply truthful speech becomes.

Words themselves necessarily imply a filtering process, since even the best, most carefully chosen words only point at what they are attempting to convey – at least one step removed from the experience itself. The words of a master, operating from a place of *vach siddhi* at the fifth *chakra*, on the level of *anandamaya kosha*, however, carry a certain energy which is capable of triggering the experience to which it refers. This power is illustrated by the following story told by Paul Reps in his classic work, Zen Flesh, Zen Bones (51):

> Just before Ninakawa passed away the Zen master Ikkyu visited him. "Shall I lead you on?" Ikkyu asked.
>
> Ninakawa replied: "I came here alone and I go alone. What help could you be to me?"
>
> Ikkyu answered: "If you think you really come and go, that is your delusion. Let me show you the path on which there is no coming and no going."
>
> With his words, Ikkyu had revealed the path so clearly that Ninakawa smiled and passed away.

An unevolved mortal uttering Ikkyu's words, "Let me show you the path..." might simply be another snake oil salesman. But one who had opened the fifth *chakra* and attained the level of penetration by Spirit experienced at *anandamaya kosha* would not only speak the words, but reveal the truth of the words in the speaking. Such a being lifts a veil between words and their meaning, and opens a door to understanding.

In truth, the veil is frequently lifting, but one must have eyes to see what is truly there to be seen – a subject to which we will return in the next chapter. One must also have ears to hear, for beyond all the verbiage and outright noise that pervades the embodied world wherever humans congregate, there is beneath it all a single, simple vibration out of which everything else springs.

CHAPTER FIVE

In the Bible, it states at the very beginning that God said, "Let there be light," and then there was. Using His infinite powers of *vach siddhi*, He created the manifest universe. But what language was God speaking? It most certainly wasn't English; chances are it wasn't Hebrew either. My guess is that God simply gave voice to the subtle sound, or *shabda*, as it is called in *yogic* practice, that vibrates at the heart of everything.

Throughout my studies with both Yogi Bhajan and Swami Muktananda, the practice of *shabda yoga* or chanting was emphasized. The chants we practiced were Sanskrit phrases, usually praising some attribute of divinity. *Yogic* doctrine has it that the Sanskrit language itself was derived by *yogic* practitioners who spent many hours listening to the sacred *shabda* at the heart of every sound, then translating these sounds first into spoken, then written language. Of primary importance were the sounds associated with each *chakra*, for a faithful reproduction of these sounds had the power to open and cleanse the *chakra* with which they were associated. When I lived or spent time at one of Yogi Bhajan's or Swami Muktananda's *ashrams* (monastic centers), we would chant for hours on end, usually before sunrise, in order to saturate our minds with these sounds, which would then reverberate on their own throughout the day.

Earlier chapters on the second and fourth *chakras* discussed at length the soul's alignment with the its natural affinities. In the fifth *chakra*, this process continues and deepens to become an alignment with the cosmic order - being in the right place at the right time, in balance, offering exactly what is needed in the moment. On a mundane level, this deeper alignment manifests as a sense of place and timing. But ultimately - at the level of *anandamaya kosha* - it is an alignment with the creative power of Spirit that has evoked this manifest world into being. Sound was and continues to be the vehicle for this evocation, and to the extent that one allows Spirit to penetrate to the level of *anandamaya kosha* at the fifth *chakra*, the soul begins to hear the holy *shabda* that makes all creation possible, and to echo that sacred sound in every thought, word and deed.

Chapter Six
The Sixth Chakra

The sixth *chakra*, or *ajna*, is a simple lotus of two white petals between the eyebrows, home of *manas* or mind (Avalon 126). Judith (8) considers this *chakra* to be indigo, while for Bruyere (42) it is purple, though both are following the rainbow in assigning colors to the *chakras*. Leadbetter quotes authorities who see it variously as yellow and purple, white or red (97). Judith (7) associates it with light or luminescence, Bruyere (43) with the element of radium. Myss correlates the sixth *chakra* with the *sefirah* of Binah representing "divine understanding" and Hokhmah, or "divine wisdom" (238).

Psychologically, this *chakra* is associated with mental functions, thoughts, beliefs, internal imagery, dreams, intuitive understanding, and the faculty of vision. In *The Seven Gates of Soul*, I speak of the image as a constellation of our projections into the embodied world, which in turn determines how the world is perceived and experienced by the soul. Here I would add that it is in the sixth *chakra* that the image is formed. In the fourth *chakra* we are attracted to certain experiences through various forms of resonance. In the fifth, our resonant experiences tend to reinforce themselves through repetition, leading us in turn to a certain sense of place within the cosmic order. In the sixth, this sense of place crystallizes to become our image of the world.

This is not to say that the image we hold of the world is etched in stone. It does evolve and change as we evolve and change. Within the image, however, is a certain inertia, especially to the extent that we approach the world from a place of wounded fear. When our core issues are activated, those experiences to which we are attracted through resonance by wounding can be preferable to less painful experiences, simply because they are familiar. The image is, by nature, self-reinforcing, because it is ingrained within us by positive feedback at each *chakra*.

At the first *chakra*, the image arises through the will to live, and the world becomes what it needs to be in our eyes, in order to ensure our survival within it. Imagine, for example, a man whose father was unpredictable – professing to love him in one moment, and beating him in some fit of irrational anger in the next. Such a man might well grow up believing the world is a dangerous place where he must constantly be on his guard, and maintain as much control over the circumstances of his life as he can. This is not necessarily what the world is, but since this particular soul has experienced it this way, it becomes his image of the world. To the extent that he acts as though the world fits this image, his survival will appear to be ensured, and his image of the world will be reinforced. At some point, this man may realize that the world is not quite as dangerous as he initially believed it to be, but until then, he will take his image of the world for granted and proceed accordingly.

As with the first *chakra*, so it will be with each successive *chakra*. At the second *chakra*, our image of the world will be one that attempts to maximize pleasure and minimize pain. The vigilant soul in our example above might avoid bald men with mustaches, who remind him of his father that beat him, and seek out meek women who strive to please their partners, who remind him of his mother, the one source of solace in his childhood years. Eventually, he will learn that all bald men with mustaches are not inducers of pain, and not all meek women who strive to please are a source of solace. But until he has experiences that counteract his image of the world, it will continue to dictate his behavior. Such behavior may appear irrational to an outside observer, but it will make perfect sense within the context of subjective logic that informs his image of the world.

In the third *chakra*, the image is reinforced by the worldly success that we experience. In the fourth *chakra*, the image is further strengthened by the love, approval, respect, and affirmation we receive for being a certain way. In the fifth *chakra*, the image becomes a reflection of the internal messages that we verbalize to ourselves and others. In the sixth *chakra*, the image becomes a reflection of our beliefs, reinforced by the seemingly self-evident truths that inform those beliefs.

As the sixth *chakra* begins to open and clear, we begin to realize that all beliefs and consequently all images of the world are relative to our perspective. That perspective becomes more flexible, and we gradually attain the capacity to see the world from many different perspectives, each of them equally valid in their own right. Consequently, we become less attached to our pet image of the world, and increasingly free from its limitations. Our vigilant soul, who was beaten by an unpredictable father, for example, would learn to take risks, relax his need to maintain control, and even seek out danger as an antidote to his own prior timidity. At times, he would appear to become something other than what others believe him to be. In an ironic mirroring of his early childhood relationship to his father, he would become unpredictable himself. To the extent that his sixth *chakra* was open, and functioning at optimum efficiency, his unpredictability would in fact be a dynamic exercise of choice among a wide range of options.

I witnessed the exercise of this ability firsthand with Swami Muktananda. As mentioned earlier, one of the most fascinating features of his daily *darshans* (dispensations of blessing) was his amazing capacity to be fully present with each person, and a perfect mirror to the image that was presented to him. With one person, he would be shy and retiring; with the next, strong and controlling; with a third, light and chatty. Sometimes his facial features would change and he would appear to be an entirely different person.

In *The Seven Gates of Soul*, I speak of the personality as a form of adaptation to the world that is in turn a reflection of our image of the world. I finally came to the conclusion, watching Muktananda, that he had no personality, because his image of the world was entirely adaptable to the situation at hand.

In shamanic language, Muktananda was what I would consider to be a shapeshifter. Shapeshifters are generally described as beings who frequently take the form of their animal allies in order to accomplish something that they could not accomplish in human form. They might, for example, become an eagle in order to gain an aerial perspective; or a bear to endure long periods without food; or a gazelle in order to cover long distances quickly. Although Muktananda didn't turn into an animal, he apparently did possess the ability to change his demeanor at will, and appear in different ways to different disciples. In retrospect, I understand this to be a capacity that is cultivated when the sixth *chakra* becomes open and clear. In the fourth *chakra*, we align with our center; at the sixth *chakra*, we gain the ability to align with multiple centers, and function with equal facility at each one.

The Yaqui sorcerer Don Juan called the center to which we align, our assemblage point. In Carlos Castenada's book, *The Fire From Within*, he discusses the tenets of the image-making process in shamanic terms (108):

> There is no objective world, but only a universe of energy fields which seers call the Eagle's emanations.
>
> Human beings are made of the Eagle's emanations and are in essence bubbles of luminescent energy; each of us is wrapped in a cocoon that encloses a small portion of these emanations.
>
> Awareness is achieved by the constant pressure that the emanations outside our cocoons, which are called emanations at large, exert on those inside our cocoons.
>
> Awareness gives rise to perception, which happens when the emanations inside our cocoons align themselves with the corresponding emanations at large.
>
> Perception takes place . . . because there is in each of us an agent called the assemblage point that selects internal and external emanations for alignment. The particular alignment that we perceive is the product of the specific spot where our assemblage point is located on our cocoon.

Elsewhere in the book, and throughout his teachings, Don Juan suggests that the ability to see beyond the veil of appearances that we might associate with a given image

◇◇

of the world is a matter of moving the assemblage point, and consequently seeing from a different vantage point: ". . . one of the most important breakthroughs for the new seers was to find that the spot where that point is located on the cocoon of all living creatures is not a permanent feature, but is established on that specific spot by habit" (118). In *The Seven Gates of Soul*, I speak of the habits of mind by which our image of the world is constructed. As Don Juan discusses in more psychic terms, these habits are bendable through an act of intention. I would say it is actually a matter of intention being met by grace, but we both agree that bendable habits of mind result in a capacity to see the world differently, and form a different image of it. Here I would simply add that this shifting perspective is a function that is centered in the sixth *chakra*.

Beyond merely seeing the world differently, however, shifting the assemblage point and our image of the world actually changes the nature of the world and who we are in relation to it. In the past I have referred to this capacity as spider medicine ("Cutting Away" 122), evidenced by a spider's capacity to completely dismantle its web, and spin a new one. I have witnessed this capacity in myself and many of my friends, as well as in many of the most successful of artists, musicians, writers and actors, when we all periodically "re-invent" ourselves and our lives. The corporate executive who renounces materialism and joins a Buddhist monastery, the cab driver who buys a sailboat and sails around the world, the transvestite who undergoes a sex-change operation are all calling on spider medicine to re-invent their lives. To the extent that these changes arise from some profound shift in perspective that has altered the very nature of their being and their relationship to the embodied world, it can also be a reflection of a sixth *chakra* awakening.

As we gain the ability to shapeshift and reinvent ourselves, through opening and clearing the sixth *chakra*, we gain freedom from the limitations inherent in a world bound by physical form, time and space. The center we cultivate in the fourth *chakra* becomes mobile, and the sense of place we cultivate in the fifth becomes the capacity to align with our center in any situation, and be at home wherever we happen to be. Ultimately, as a consequence of opening and working through the sixth *chakra*, the soul's very attachment to form increasingly becomes a matter of choice, and how, when, and where, one attaches, a matter of intention.

Annamaya Kosha

On the level of *annamaya kosha*, the sixth *chakra* is associated with the physical eyes, the faculty of sight, and the psychological process of perception. In Chapter Six, I spoke of the ears, nose and throat associated with the fifth *chakra* as the primary intake system of the human body - together serving as the conduit through which various messages about reality become crystallized as one's worldview. This crystallization process, in turn, determines what one sees at the level of the sixth *chakra*. The so-called objective world, measured by scientists and reinforced through a common language, is perceived differently by each of us, according to the subjective belief systems that we bring to it. This subjective perception of the world – referred to here and in *The Seven Gates of Soul* as the image – is translated at the level of *annamaya kosha*, as the ability to see, and the tendency to see selectively that which tends to reinforce our worldview.

It has been said that when a pickpocket encounters a saint, all he sees are pockets. So it is for each of us, according to what we have been conditioned to believe is available to be seen. Through the exclusion of various dimensions of reality that do not enter into our perception of the world, each of us is blind to entire worlds of possibility. In his landmark book, *The Doors of Perception*, British philosopher Aldous Huxley speaks of the brain as a filtering mechanism by which the infinite amount of information available to us in any given moment is reduced to a manageable level. As this information is filtered, we entertain a certain level of blindness at the sixth *chakra* on the level of *annaymaya kosha*. This makes reality seem more amenable to our control, but at the same time, limits our range of creative mobility within the world. This limitation, in turn, can be the source of pain and suffering, which drives us to claim a higher level of illumination and insight. On the level of *annamaya kosha*, this process can often translate into literal problems with our eyesight.

When I was three years old, I suffered an early formative incident that had a profound influence on my initial image of the world. I was playing king of the mountain on a huge pile of ashes in my grandfather's back yard, with several other neighborhood children, all older than I. Somehow I had managed to make it to the top of the mountain, only to be attacked and dragged back down to the bottom. Of course, this is the very nature of the game, and even at three, it should not have been unreasonable for me to expect this sudden reversal of fortune. In the process of being dragged to the bottom of the mountain, however, I had ashes stuffed into my nose and mouth, stopped breathing and started turning blue. If the commotion had not brought my grandfather out of the house to see what was going on, I might have choked to death. As it was, my grandfather cleared my mouth, nose and throat, chased the other kids away, and called an ambulance. After a short bout with pneumonia, I was released from the hospital relatively intact.

My image of the world, however, had been dramatically altered. The world was no longer a safe place, and my place within in was now limited by what I believed would ensure my safety. More specifically, the childhood game of king of the mountain became a metaphor for my relationship to the world, with the wounded understanding that getting to the top of the mountain, or winning the game, was dangerous. As a consequence, I became acutely aware of the mountain, and at the same time, blind to my own capacity to reach the top, for to recognize and cultivate that capacity would – according to my image of the world – put me in danger. I learned to hide my true talents and abilities, and became adept at being second best at everything I attempted.

Shortly after this incident, I also developed problems with my eyesight. By the time I entered the first grade, I wore thick glasses to compensate for farsightedness and visual dyslexia, or crossed-eyes. I could easily see the distant goal – the top of the mountain – but could not negotiate the path to get there. What was directly in front of me – and thus attainable – got pushed to one side by my dyslexia. My eyesight, in other words, adapted itself to reflect my image of the world as it played itself out at the sixth *chakra*, on the level of *annamaya kosha*. Subsequent attempts to work through the limitations associated with this image of the world and my relationship to it, and various inevitable setbacks in those attempts, have likewise tended to be reflected through fluctuations in my literal ability to see.

Pranamaya Kosha

If seeing is believing – as suggested by the well known adage – then the logic of the sixth *chakra* dictates that what is seen at the level of *annamaya kosha* forms the basis for our belief system at the level of *pranamaya kosha*. Beyond the formation of belief is Huxley's filtering mechanism, which in turn makes the world a manageable place. On the level of *pranamaya kosha*, this filtering by belief is the function of the sixth *chakra*. At this level, our experience of the world gives rise to our image of the world – a subliminal constellation of impressions – that governs what we see and don't see on the level of *annamaya kosha*. What we see and don't see then crystallizes into and reinforces our beliefs about the world and who we are in relation to it, thus effectively filtering out whatever evidence – visual or otherwise – contradicts those beliefs.

Closely associated with the filtering process and the formation of beliefs is the loss of innocence that each of us experiences in our own way, when the world proves itself to be something other than what it initially appeared to be. Innocence is the state in which all things are possible, and we are at the center of the universe of unlimited possibility. There are no beliefs in this place, because we have not yet experienced the need for filtering or protection. This need arises when innocence is shattered by the realization we are not the center of the universe, and that even though all things are possible, all things are not necessarily equally desirable. Inevitably each of us is wounded in some way early in this life, and this act of wounding – by betrayal, abandonment, rejection, or abuse – causes a schism in our thinking. This schism is conceptualized by many cultures as a fall from grace, and becomes built into the very fabric of our relationship to the world as a set of judgments about good and evil that automatically filters our existence through a set of taboos – both personal and culturally conditioned. Restoring our sight, at the level of *pranamaya kosha* at the sixth *chakra* – and subsequently, restoring our innocence – then becomes a process of breaking taboos, and rethinking the filtering beliefs that have led us to impose them upon ourselves.

For many years after the ashpile incident, I had imposed upon myself a taboo against winning. Throughout high school, I got mostly As and a few Bs, and managed to do quite well, although I was always behind one or two other students. In Boy Scouts, I rose to the rank of Life Scout, but never attained the top rank of Eagle. In band, I always played second tenor saxophone, never first. In sports especially, I managed to lose, often badly. It wasn't until my freshman year in college, when I won an essay contest, and realized that no one was going to knock me off this particular mountain, that I found I could breathe easily again, and dare to win at the game of life. Not coincidentally, it was shortly after winning this contest that I "accidentally" broke my glasses, and decided not to replace them. I managed to see quite well without them for the next 25 years, until age and the strain of long days in front of a computer screen began to reclaim my eyes from innocence restored.

Manomaya Kosha

On the level of *manomaya kosha*, it is possible to see how our belief system tends to constellate around and reinforce our core issues. Since the fall from grace inevitably involves a primal wounding, and through this wounding we first become aware of the need for filtering our perceptions, what we eventually come to believe has a profound relationship to the wounds that we experience. Thus the psychology of the sixth *chakra* – typically experienced at the level of *manomaya kosha* – generally revolves around working through the limitations associated with our beliefs. It is in this domain that cognitive psychologists – those who trace our psychological problems to the beliefs that condition them – have the most to contribute to an understanding of soul process.

On the level of *manomaya kosha*, the intentions associated with opening the sixth *chakra* arise when we become aware of the ways in which our beliefs limit us, and feel a desire to work beyond those limits. The woman who grows up believing that all men are abusive pigs, in the wake of an incestuous rape by her father, may wake up one day horribly lonely, even though she is surrounded by men who genuinely care for her. The man who grows up believing that expression of anger is not ok because he was beaten for it as a boy, may be inspired to question that belief when he develops ulcers working for a bully of a boss. The devout Christian opposed to abortion, who subsequently gets pregnant with a child determined to be congenitally deformed while still in the womb, will have her beliefs severely challenged. When this happens, perhaps the original belief will prevail, in which case, an intolerable situation will become the defining characteristic of a life of chosen imbalance.

Or perhaps the soul caught in the intolerable situation will have an epiphany that dissolves the limitation imposed by the belief, and frees the soul for a broader, more balanced experience. The lonely woman in our example above may let down her guard and begin reaching out to men she instinctively trusts. The man afraid to be angry may be pushed far enough back to the wall that one day he stands up to his boss and discovers a power he never suspected he had. Our devout, pregnant Christian may develop a deeper sense of compassion for other women she previously judged for their choices.

In any case, an awakening of the sixth *chakra* on the level of *manomaya kosha* exposes the soul to what psychologists call a double bind – a moment of reckoning in which one must make a choice, and all of the available choices threaten to make life worse. Psychologist R.D. Laing has recognized the irresolvable double bind to be a core factor in clinical schizophrenia. In what has come to be known as the school of uncommon therapy, other psychologists have learned to use the double bind as a deliberate tool in precipitating therapeutic change.

One famous story of this practice is told by seminal hypnotherapist Milton Erickson, describing his encounter with a patient who claimed to be Jesus Christ. "Just the man I wanted to see," exclaimed Erickson. "I've been wanting to remodel my house, and can use your superb carpentry skills." Realizing that he knew nothing at all about carpentry, the deluded patient was forced to acknowledge he couldn't possibly be Jesus Christ. Not every double bind is this easily resolved, nor did this one led to a permanent "cure." Most double binds are intensely stressful situations with no easy exit, and few of the beliefs that put us in these impossible situations are that easily relinquished. Double binds do expose the untenable nature of our beliefs, however, and are potent catalysts toward the cultivation of a sixth *chakra* intention.

Resistance to our intention to question and reevaluate our beliefs is rooted in the even more insidious belief that doing so will, on some level, invoke the wrath of God. The beliefs most closely associated with our core woundings first arose because we believed that adopting them would protect us from further wounding. To suspend, change or abandon them is therefore associated with a fear of exposing ourselves to further wounding. If we entertain the idea that all men are not pigs, then we could get raped again. If we consider the possibility that maybe in certain situations, it is ok, even desirable to express our anger, then maybe we'll be beaten again, as we were in childhood. To relax our adherence to the religious injunction against abortion will inevitably expose us to hellfire and damnation, as warned by the priestly guardians of those beliefs. In each case, we cannot deviate from the code without risking death – in the metaphorical, if not the literal sense of the word, as discussed in Chapter One of *The Seven Gates of Soul*. Yet to the extent that we are caught in a double bind, clinging to these old beliefs will also appear to be killing us, and our suffering will appear to be equal to our resistance.

Ironically, it is in confronting the beliefs designed to protect us against death in all its many guises that we experience our most profound opening to soul. For when these beliefs are suspended, we are able to see the world anew, and to understand our place within it without the intermediary of protective filters. Each belief that stands between us and the core woundings that shut us down is conversely the gateway to a larger, expanded, more empowered sense of being. Each belief relinquished through some immense act of courage in the face of possible death is a quantum leap along the path toward reclaiming our wholeness. To realize that beliefs are relative to our experience and ultimately expendable is to take the first step toward becoming a shapeshifter – one whose center is mobile, and whose place within the universe is wherever one happens to be at any given moment.

Vijnanamaya Kosha

The images that arise on the level of *vijnanamaya kosha*, once the desirability of change is realized, invariably stand in stark contrast to the beliefs that hold us hostage. Freudian psychologists, for example, have long spoken about the compensatory nature of dreams - that is to say, their ability to compensate for the attitude adopted by the conscious ego. An individual who is too timid in waking life, out of a wounded belief that boldness invokes ridicule or rejection, may dream of heroic deeds and bold, ostentatious gestures. A monk sworn to vows of celibacy will have pornographic dreams wild enough to make a prostitute blush. An angry young woman may dream of sailing on clear mountain lakes. In each case, the compensatory nature of the imagery in the dreams will point the way toward a restoration of balance, and invite the conscious mind to entertain thoughts outside the limiting box of its belief systems. This compensatory function of dreams will be awakened to the extent that Spirit has penetrated to the level of *vijnanamaya kosha* at the sixth *chakra*.

At a further stage in the same process, waking life will become colored by a constellation of images that appear to challenge our belief systems. The timid individual will encounter bullies, damsels in distress, and double binds of seemingly epic proportions that require a leap of faith to a bolder way of being. The celibate monk may suddenly be charged with the task of providing religious instruction to pre-pubescent girls to whom he is sexually attracted. The angry young woman may join the Sierra Club and discover a more peaceful side of her being in settings of unparalleled natural beauty. In each case, waking life will provide images that provide balance to belief systems that have unnecessarily limited the soul to a restricted range of motion.

We have discussed this compensatory mechanism earlier as a kind of resonance by contrast. In fact, resonance by contrast can operate at multiple levels of consciousness simultaneously. At the second *chakra*, it will tend to balance our preferences with a broader palate of flavors and tastes. At the fourth, it will expose us to the healing power of relationship with others unlike ourselves. At the sixth *chakra*, resonance by contrast will invite us to change our minds about who we are, and how we take our place within the larger scheme of things. To the extent that the sixth *chakra* has been penetrated by Spirit to the level of *vijnanamaya kosha*, the world will appear to be something other than we originally believed it to be.

Our experience of this shift can be very much like awakening from a dream. It can also be quite disorienting, as it exposes us to what Carl Jung has called the elfin logic of the anima/animus. According to this logic – which is quite illogical within the context of our beliefs – all the usual rules are suspended, including the unspoken internal rules that govern our outward behavior. Indigenous cultures speak of *heyokahs*, or sacred clowns, whose function it was to do everything backwards from the way it was normally done, or in stark contrast to what might be expected, in order to challenge rigid thinking wherever it occurred. Such beings were the living incarnation of the sixth *chakra*, at the level of *vijnanmaya kosha*, for they lived according to elfin logic and broke all cultural taboos as part of their daily routine. When we are in the throes of a sixth *chakra* process at the level of *vijnanamaya kosha*, we ourselves become *heyokahs*, shattering the images others hold of us, as we give expression to the uncharacteristic urges that seize us.

I'll never forget the moment in third grade when I balanced precariously on the back legs of my chair (which at the time, was somehow widely considered a form of rebellion), and the entire class cheered. After the ashpile incident, I had become seriously focused on the distant goal, while being perpetually frustrated at my seeming inability to achieve it. Or as my father might have put it, I had become way too serious for my age. On that day, when I dared to relax enough to break the rules, I broke my own image of myself, and the change was immediately recognized. This was Spirit penetrating to the level of *vijnanamaya kosha* at the sixth *chakra*, to remind me that the world was not just the mountain I had made it out to be in my perpetually unrealizable dream of wanting to be king, but also a playground where king of the mountain was only one of many games to be played, and perhaps not the most interesting or rewarding game at that. Not that I wouldn't forget again, almost immediately, but in that moment, the subsequent opening to grace was an invitation to set my beliefs aside and just play at being, instead of trying to be a limited, living image of my beliefs.

Anandamaya Kosha

Beliefs often lie at the very core of our identity, and the images we hold of the world are invariably mirror images of our beliefs about who we are. As the sixth *chakra* opens, we begin to experience these beliefs about ourselves as flexible, if not suspendable altogether. Experiences precipitated at this level are cosmically designed to show us just how much larger we are than the identity we have adopted as a consequence of our beliefs. By the time Spirit has penetrated to the level of *anandamaya kosha*, the very concept of identity becomes too limiting to contain the essence and the volume of Spirit flowing through us. At this level, we essentially become channels for a transpersonal energy that does not depend upon identity, personality, or belief for its expression.

This transpersonal energy is free to take multiple identities as it functions within us. As each moment is understood as an opportunity for awakening to a deeper alignment with Spirit, we adapt ourselves to the need and the opportunity it presents to us. We become shapeshifters, liberated by the secret knowledge that identity is merely a disguise behind which Spirit enters each life in order to precipitate certain experiences capable of teaching us what we need to learn. As Spirit penetrates to the level of *anandamaya kosha*, within this *chakra*, we catch a more sustainable glimpse of this hidden agenda, and mold ourselves to it at will. Beings functioning at this level can often baffle their less enlightened peers, but written within the choreography of their movements is the intent behind their dance, and to watch them is itself an education in observing the movement of Spirit within the seemingly mundane flow of everyday life.

It is also an education in the true meaning of rebirth and immortality. From the limited perspective of one functioning primarily through the first *chakra*, a belief in the possibility of rebirth is held within the context of a belief in the inevitability of death. When the sixth *chakra* is open, however, one begins to see that both beliefs are ultimately misleading. The question arises, "Who is it that dies and is reborn?" To the extent that one is invested in identity, the answers to these questions will appear to be a question about what happens to identity in the face of death. But as we begin to relinquish our attachment to identity, the question becomes one about what lies beyond identity, and we are freed, while still in the body, to reach toward it. What lies beyond identity, of course, is Spirit, and on an intellectual level, we might begin to take comfort in this fact. But beyond the intellect is experience, and to the extent that we have experienced a lessening of our attachment to identity, Spirit automatically rushes in to fill the void. Within this flow, the very concept of death is washed away, and with it our vulnerability in the face of death.

As I finish this chapter, I happen to be attending a gathering of relatives in the wake of a friend's father's death. I would not presume to try to assess the level of consciousness

◇◇◇

on which Lowell lived his life, but in his death, I do see evidence that the whole notion of identity is far too limited to encompass all that we are. Tomorrow, we will each tell our stories in remembrance of him, but today it is not hard to look around the room at his children, grandchildren and great-grandchildren and see the many faces of Lowell proliferating far beyond the limited range that his own personality could possibly encompass. Today, we are celebrating the sixth birthday of his great-granddaughter, Alejandro, and in her smile and twinkling eyes, it is clear that Lowell lives on. Such a realization will likely fade again as I pick up my own life, revolving around my own sense of identity, in the days following this gathering. But in this moment out of time, it is possible to glimpse what it must be like beyond the belief in death, when all of life is understood to be one continuum with many faces, alternately looming large, then fading from the screen upon which our collective image of the world is projected.

Chapter Seven
The Seventh Chakra

The seventh *chakra*, or *sahasrara*, is depicted as a thousand-petalled lotus of indescribable hue, located at the top of the head or crown, and containing all possible combination of sound (Avalon 143). For Judith, this *chakra* is colored violet (7), while Bruyere (42) breaks with the metaphor of the rainbow and considers it white. Leadbeater does not assign a color to this *chakra*. Judith associates the seventh *chakra* with thought or consciousness (7), while Bruyere assigns it the element *magnetum*, which she says is unknown to science, but mentioned in the *Hermetica* (56). Myss correlates the seventh *chakra* with the *sefirah* Keter, which represents "nothingness, the energy from which physical manifestation begins" (266).

Psychologically, the seventh *chakra* is the place of transcendence, the gateway between this physical realm and realms beyond the reach of human imagination. When the *sahasrara* is open and in balance, one becomes a pure channel for Spirit, and one's every thought, word, and deed becomes a vehicle for spiritual awakening. One's purest spiritual essence is expressed without impedance through the personality and one becomes a god or goddess in physical form. At this point in the journey, the soul is faced with a choice: either remain in physical form to grace other sentient beings with her Presence – a commitment known in Buddhism as the *vows of the bodhisattva* – or leave this plane to merge with Spirit on some other plane, incomprehensible to mere mortals on this one. There are no words in our language to describe this experience of reunion with Spirit, although mystical poets throughout the ages have tried. If the soul at this level takes the *vows of the bodhisattva*, the rules governing ordinary spiritual evolution no longer apply, and the entire system we have been discussing in Part One of this book begins to dissolve.

Needless to say, few human beings ever reach this level of attainment, at least in the sense in which the *yogis* and *yoginis* aspired toward it. Within the context of our current discussion, however, we have agreed to consider each *chakra* not as a hierarchical ladder toward some idealized state, but as a circle of possibilities, each resonating with equal capacity to impact the total expression of any human being. Various situations will engage various *chakras*, and not all *chakras* will be equally engaged by every situation that arises. But all will be available in each moment as a point of reference to which one can attune one's perspective, given sufficient depth of intention and spiritual will. Considered in this way, the seventh *chakra* becomes a perceptual resource that can transform ordinary human life beyond the concerns, struggles and moments of triumph that appear to define it.

◇◇◇

The seventh *chakra* is where we have the opportunity to relinquish what Buddhist nun Pema Chodron has referred to as the "story line" of our lives – the unique set of circumstances and our response to them that has made us what we believe ourselves to be. This story line – which is the root source of our identity as human beings and as souls upon a journey – forms the nucleus around which the spiritual processes discussed in Part One of this book revolve. At each *chakra*, the process is necessarily understood differently, although it is the same story line that is being perceived. At the seventh *chakra*, our identification with the story line dissolves, and the processes that previously appeared to revolve around it reveal themselves to have been but passing dreams.

In Part Two, we will explore the ways in which these shifting perceptions of passing dreams are mapped to the story line at each level of consciousness, within a larger astrological framework connecting the microcosm of the individual soul to the macrocosm of the divine order unfolding. At the level of the seventh *chakra*, the microcosm is absorbed into the macrocosm, and all that is left is Spirit reflecting itself back to itself. The being that we have heretofore identified as "I" ceases to function as a separate entity and all the information we have gathered through our participation in life at the other *chakras* reveals itself to be dust on the diamond we only dimly sensed was there, before this seventh *chakra* was awakened.

Just as a dream appears to linger, once we awaken, so that for a short time dream reality and waking state reality exist simultaneously, so too does the seventh *chakra* experience of the diamond reverberate throughout our normal human preoccupation with the dust at every other *chakra*. Every moment in which we prevail against some first *chakra* threat to our survival, we touch the possibility of immortality that characterizes the seventh *chakra*. Behind every second *chakra* experience of pleasure is the seventh *chakra* experience of perpetual bliss. Within each third *chakra* attainment of worldly power is a taste of otherworldly seventh *chakra* omnipotence. Within each fourth *chakra* pattern of resonance is an eternal seventh *chakra* echo of the interconnectedness that weaves our personal life into a larger Whole that contains and transcends it. Even as we find our fifth *chakra* place in space and time, space and time dissolve in the seventh *chakra* to reveal a timeless place where there are no boundaries of separation and eternity pulses in each moment. Through each sixth *chakra* shift in shape is the seventh *chakra* Shapeshifter, changeless, yet boundless in its creative capacity to reflect the ever-changing moment. The undying truth that pervades everything and anything that could possibly happen on each of the previous six *chakras* is that we are this eternal yet ever-changing Spirit, dancing simultaneously within and beyond the reach of the dance. In each moment where we see the diamond through the dust, we stir the seventh *chakra*, and awaken – however slightly – its potential to utterly transform everything we think we know about our story line into a hymn of praise to the Unknowable Mystery.

The seventh *chakra* is also awakened each time we penetrate on any *chakra* to the level of *anandamaya kosha*, for this is where there is no difference between embodied soul and Spirit. The Immortal One, the Blissful One, the Master, the Embodiment of Love, the Teacher or Sage, and the Creative Shapeshifter are all facets of the Diamond Body reverberating with Light and fully awakened Consciousness at the Seventh Chakra. It is impossible to experience ourselves at this level of penetration without also awakening a deeper identification with the Awakener at the heart of our every experience. Yogi Bhajan was fond of saying that awakening can come in the twinkling of an eye, and it is the ever-silently reverberating seventh *chakra* where this possibility perpetually exists.

Annamaya Kosha

On the level of *annamaya kosha*, the energy of the seventh *chakra* manifests as the pineal gland and the anterior fontanel, or soft spot on a baby's head. The pineal gland is considered the master gland in the body, regulating the hormonal secretions of every other gland, and by esoteric implication, the activity of every other *chakra*. The primary function of the seventh *chakra* can thus be understood as regulation – not in the sense of control, but in a more expansive sense as divine orchestration. Just as a conductor leads an orchestra, transforming a potential cacophony of independent players into a seamless synthesis of voices, so too does Who We Are at the seventh *chakra* orchestrate our lives. Though we don't often identify with this Orchestrator in the heat of our experience, the level of invincibility, bliss, *wu-wei*, resonance, grace and place that we do experience is a measure of our capacity to cooperate with this divine orchestration. Conversely, the level of vulnerability, pain, suffering, fear and resistance we experience is a measure of our inability to open to this more empowered set of possibilities. As we shift back and forth between these two poles of our existence, the diamond beneath the dust begins to twinkle.

I experienced this twinkling made manifest in human form through an exposure to Sufi teachings in the 1980s. The Sufi Master Pir Vilayat Khan was known in the 1960s, 70s, and 80s for his orchestration of elaborate dances, mostly on the West Coast, in which thousands of participants moved to different rhythms, chanting different chants, yet all somehow contributing to an amazing blending of energies that was far more than the sum of its parts. While I never had the privilege of participating in one of his legendary cosmic dances, I did experience them on a smaller scale, as they were taught by professional dancer, and beloved Sufi teacher, Zuleika.

In a large room of a hundred people, Zuleika would start by asking five or six people to chant a simple one-syllable chant and sway together as a core, arms across shoulders and waists. When this core group began functioning seamlessly as an integrated whole,

97

◇◇

Zuleika would set another group in motion. She would perhaps choose a somewhat larger group of fifteen to twenty people to form a ring around the first group, moving slowly in a clockwise direction, chanting a different chant that complemented that being sung by the first group. Piece by piece, she would add groups moving in different directions or in different ways, chanting different chants, until all one hundred people were contributing to a larger orchestrated body of movement in praise to Spirit. When everyone was resonating to this larger possibility, she would break various groups into subgroups, combine smaller groups into larger groups, change either the motion or the chant, or both, of one or more groups, and constantly alter the interweavings of the group as a whole. Gradually, she would lead us all to the same movement and the same chant, then let the chant go, and gradually bring the silent movement to a place of stillness.

During the chant and the movement I often lost track of myself, and experienced myself to be part of a larger whole, in the same way that each cell of my body is part of a larger whole. As the group gradually descended into a place of silence and stillness, so did I experience a timeless space of unity and peace. Inevitably, there would also be a warm glow at the top of my head in the area of my seventh *chakra* that I learned earlier to associate with an awakening of that center in my body. Whatever problems or concerns I had brought to the dance would by this time, be gone, and through this orchestration of outer movement, I would feel an inner alignment, orchestrated from the highest possible place within my being. Inevitably, the sense of orchestrated alignment would dissipate when I left the dance, but I will be eternally grateful for the seventh *chakra* touchstone that this experience provided me, for now I know what it is like to be in that place where I am simply privileged to participate in the ongoing orchestration of divine design that pervades this manifest universe at every level.

A second function of the seventh *chakra* at the level of *annamaya kosha* is suggested by its association with the anterior fontanel (the soft spot on the top of the skull). Psychically, this physiological separation of bone and cartilage is associated with the entry of the Spirit into the body. The fact that it is relatively open and soft after birth, but closes and hardens shortly after birth suggests that Spirit descends to enter the body, and is trapped for the duration of life. This was the view taken by Plato and passed on to the Western religious tradition, as discussed at some length in *The Seven Gates of Soul*. Conversely, upon death, it is understood by many spiritual traditions that Spirit exits the body through this same aperture. From this perspective, it can be intuited that the anterior fontanel and the seventh *chakra* symbolize the tentative vertical relationship between Spirit and matter that characterizes the embodied experience.

If, however, we combine this awareness with our knowledge of the orchestrating function of the seventh *chakra*, then we might postulate that the seventh *chakra* encompasses a horizontal function as well. If the seventh *chakra* is both the point of entry for Spirit into the body and the central hub out of which all emanations at the other *chakras* are orchestrated, then it is not so great a stretch to imagine that the seventh *chakra* is also the point at which the presence of Spirit within the body is disseminated – as consciousness – throughout the entire chakra system. That is to say, the seventh *chakra* becomes the point at which mundane life becomes an adventure of soul – a possibility waiting for us to embrace it, as we recognize Spirit in the many guises it assumes within us.

As consciousness is disseminated from the seventh *chakra* through the first, we feel our fundamental internal reservoir of strength – or as German poet Rilke put it, "that within us that will live longer than the suns." In the second *chakra*, consciousness manifests as pleasure, enjoyment, bliss, and ultimately as an abiding sense of contentment that transcends the inevitable rise and fall of our momentary satisfactions. In the third *chakra*, we experience consciousness as a growing sense of competence, mastery and flow, tasting of the omnipotence of the Creator and participating in the ongoing Creation through the exercise of our Spirit-given talents and abilities. In the fourth *chakra*, consciousness manifests as love, compassion, and caring. In the fifth, it enables us to take our place and empowers us to speak our truth. In the sixth, consciousness manifests as the detachment that brings perspective, enabling us to move into a neutral place of witness to the ongoing miracle that is the divine plan unfolding all around us. Whenever we experience any of these states of being, it is because the seventh *chakra* is resonating in association with one of the other *chakras* through which it is disseminating the presence of Spirit – as consciousness – within us. On the level of *annamaya kosha* it is this disseminating function of the seventh *chakra* that makes all things – collectively known as life – possible.

Pranamaya Kosha

On the level of *pranamaya kosha*, the seventh *chakra* serves the energetic function of integration. At this level, all the seemingly separate and contradictory parts of our being become a seamless, cohesive whole. Just as I lost track of myself in the trance state of the cosmic Sufi dance led by Zuleika, so too do all individual pieces of the whole puzzle lose their separate identity when the seventh *chakra* is activated at the level of *pranamaya kosha*. Like the scene in The Matrix – where Neo sees Agent Smith and the entire world in which Agent Smith appears to be real as source code – when the seventh *chakra* is activated at the level of *pranamaya kosha*, everything becomes a transparent container for the Source from which it emanates.

A friend who studied *kundalini yoga* under a different teacher and within a different system than I, once suggested that all strong emotion was just food for the spirit, if you could see it that way and take it in without judging or interpreting it. At the time, his remark seemed a fanciful notion, perhaps a more ostensibly spiritual cousin of the historical fear of emotion that governed the evolution of religion, science, and psychology, as documented in *The Seven Gates of Soul*. Now, in retrospect, I can see it as an expression of the way reality works on the level of *pranamaya kosha* at the seventh *chakra*. On this level, everything is just energy moving in and out of form, and all the names we place on our experiences in order to help us better understand them comprise a veil that can be lifted once the need to label everything subsides. If we can do this with our emotions – which is where we are most engaged in the illusion of whatever story line we are entertaining – then we can do this in every corner of our lives.

This is not a spiritual attainment that can be faked – for as discussed earlier, any emotion that does arise is an indication that some core issue has been activated, and core issues are not dismissed by simply deciding to conceptualize them in energetic terms. On the other hand, since the seventh *chakra* governs the pineal gland, which in turn orchestrates the entire endocrine system through which emotions are given their hormonal impetus, then perhaps it also makes sense to understand strong emotions as an opportunity to practice seeing the source code beneath the outer appearances of whatever experiences trigger them.

I experienced such an opportunity the other day, when a car failed to stop for me as I attempted to cross an intersection. Instinctively, I lashed out as the car was passing and hit its side with a bag I was carrying. The car stopped, and the driver got out, infuriated. For a few seconds, we traded vulgar epithets, and huffed and puffed at each other. Then suddenly, I just stopped and walked away. The driver silently got in his car and left.

If I were going to analyze this interaction in terms of the *chakra* system we have been discussing, I would have to admit that what happened did not take place upon the integrated, orchestrated, transcendent level we have been associating with the seventh *chakra*. We were both fiercely defending our sense of personal territory, and functioning from a place of anger – both strong indications that what was going on between us was a third *chakra* encounter. My decision to walk away was perhaps as much a secondary reverberation in the first *chakra*, born of my assessment that he would probably prevail in any fight that might ensue – that is to say, a choice designed to ensure my survival.

On the other hand, given that a dissemination of energy through the seventh *chakra* is implicated in any experience we could possibly have on any other level, it is also possible to see this encounter as a simple transmutation of energy. Most interesting to me was that as I walked away, I felt my anger immediately dissipate. I continued the aborted dialogue that might have ensued between us within my own head, and from time to time the anger would resurface. But mostly, as I see it now in retrospect, the dialogue was my attempt to gain some perspective. Who was this being that felt violated? What was the core issue being triggered within me? And how could I have handled the interaction more gracefully, channeling more consciousness through an experience cleverly designed to push my buttons? There are no easy answers to these questions, but in my asking them, I have already shifted the energy from the third *chakra* to the fifth – where the quest is for understanding.

Implied in this shift is the larger behind-the-scenes orchestration of Spirit through my seventh *chakra*. This orchestration was possible because of a long history – or story line – in which such encounters did previously result in protracted fights, some of them physical. Having grasped on a cellular level that this approach to conflict resolution simply does not work, I was in that moment, ready to try something new. In this readiness, born of lessons learned the hard way, the seventh *chakra* opened, ever so slightly, and in that opening was the possibility for learning a different kind of dance. Every time we entertain the possibility of letting the story line go, because of what we have learned through our past experiences, a small jolt of energy ripples through our seventh *chakra* on the level of *pranamaya kosha*.

Manomaya Kosha

Manomaya kosha is typically associated with the outworking of core issues – the emotions that they trigger, the string of memories associated with the triggered issues and emotions, and our trial-and-error attempts to address, resolve, and heal the wounds underlying these issues. But when we enter the seventh *chakra*, and begin to see the source code through the outer trappings of our experience, core issues begin to lose their power to derail, frustrate, infuriate and otherwise bend us out of shape. Like Neo, punching listlessly at his arch enemy Agent Smith, who no longer has the power to hurt him, we begin to perceive our issues as transparent conveyances for an increased intake of spiritual energy, and as catalysts to spiritual awakening. In light of the awareness flowing through the seventh *chakra* at the level of *manomaya kosha*, our issues show themselves to be the hollow projections of an imbalanced imagination that they ultimately are. This does not mean that we won't continue to wrestle with them within the other *chakras* on which they have meaning. But to the extent that we can engage them at the seventh *chakra*, we gain a certain level of detachment from them. In that detachment, we find the freedom to let the story line go, basking in the amplified presence of Spirit in the here and now. In this place, even the thorniest issues dissolve without effort.

Ultimately, this dissolution is a testament to the power of focused attention. The simple but potent truth waiting patiently for discovery at the seventh *chakra* is the fact that bringing anything into the full light of attention changes it. Most of our core issues remain unresolved, even through a lifetime spent wrestling with them, because we never quite focus on them clearly in the here and now with the full power of our undivided attention. Whatever else they might be, core issues are always a measure of our most intense investment in the story line of our lives, and it is often this story line that captures our attention before we can focus ourselves within the current chapter of the story. We sense our core issues through our peripheral vision, long before they emerge to take center stage, and by the time they do, we have already been distracted by the memory of what has come before. We flinch, expecting to be hit again, and in that flinching, we miss what is actually happening.

When the seventh *chakra* opens, our attachment to the story line begins dissipating, and we are empowered to bring more of our attention into the present moment. When we do, we see that the shadow looming large on the wall is, in fact, just a shadow. To protect ourselves against the pain and suffering inherent in any core issue, we register a great many sensory and emotional clues about each episode in which our core issues get triggered. If your mother wore a red dress when she abandoned you at age three, the color red worn by any woman is a signal to the limbic brain to be cautious. If your father always started pacing the floor before he stomped out the door to go on a drinking binge, then this behavior in others will tend to make you nervous. If you were feeling boredom the instant before you were attacked by the dog on your way to school, then any hint of boredom in the here and now will set you scrambling for something to fill the empty space. When the story line begins to fade at the seventh *chakra*, however, we are free to see these peripheral clues for what they are – raw data with no intrinsic meaning, other than what we have given them. Or as Freud is reputed to have said, "Sometimes a cigar is just a cigar." It is at the seventh *chakra* that this truth has its most liberating ring.

At every other *chakra*, the symbolic dimensions of ordinary reality contains a rich motherlode of information useful to us in our quest for meaning. At the very heart of astropoetics is the intent to plumb this motherlode for everything we might possibly extract from it. At the seventh *chakra*, however, there is nothing left to extract, for it is here that we experience the ultimate truth of our existence without the necessity for interpretation of intermediary symbols. To the extent that this *chakra* is open and clear, the entire psychology associated with intention, resistance, fear, and suffering at *manomaya kosha* begins to break down, along with the dissolution of the core issues this system is designed to help us understand.

The only intention necessary at the seventh *chakra* is the will to be. At this level, we are aligned and identified so completely with Spirit, the consent to be is all that is necessary to allow the divine plan to unfold within and through us. There is no longer any resistance to this plan, and no core issues to arouse our resistance. We become superconductors to the will of the divine, and are no longer in the way. Our every breath becomes an expression of *wu-wei*, and consequently, there is no longer any suffering to be experienced.

On a deeper level still, we need not even consent to be, for there is no longer anyone to give or withhold consent, and nothing that would not happen anyway, with or without our participation. We are, in fact, free to go. Religious traditions considered this freedom from embodiment the ultimate goal of the spiritual quest, but the great irony in the seventh *chakra* is that by the time we reach this blessed level, there is nowhere to go, nothing to be liberated from, and no one to be liberated. We are Spirit, and Spirit simply is. This is both the end and the beginning of the story, the answer to the riddle that this embodied existence poses. What comes next, when we transcend the need for embodiment, we can't possibly begin to imagine.

Vijnanamaya Kosha

Given that the very need for symbolism at the seventh *chakra* ceases to exist, one might rightfully wonder what could possibly take place at the seventh *chakra* on the level of *vijnanamaya kosha*, which is where the symbolism related to any *chakra* is evoked. Assuming the soul whose seventh *chakra* is fully opened makes the decision to be - that is to say, takes the *vow of the bodhisattva* - her every action becomes the expression of a living symbol, with many levels of information to be mined by others. At this level, the living soul itself becomes the motherlode, and the story line with which the living soul no longer identifies becomes a parable with transformative power for those who feel a resonance with it.

It is on this level, for example, that Christ's crucifixion and resurrection become symbols with the power to bring countless millions to their knees; that the Buddha's meditation under the Bodhi Tree becomes the template for millions more following in his wake; that every mythical gesture in the mysterious life of Lao Tzu becomes a teaching to Taoists around the world, thousands of years after his death, if indeed he ever lived at all. In a sense, because these beings - all of whom had presumably opened their seventh *chakra* and been penetrated at least to the level of *vijnanamaya kosha* - were so identified with the blinding Light of Spirit, we cannot look at them directly. We can only begin to understand them through the clues they left to the true nature of their Being in the gestures that compose their lives. These gestures, available to us on the level of *vijnanamaya kosha* at the seventh *chakra*, are their ultimate gift of grace to us.

I once experienced such a moment of grace with Yogi Bhajan. At one of the many spiritual gatherings over which he presided, I was charged with the task of making sure that others did not sit in an area roped off for a few dignitaries he had invited as his special guests. Feeling honored to be asked to assume this important task, I naturally became enamored of my own importance and the power of my position. I got to tell others, "No, I'm sorry, but you can't sit here. Babaji has reserved this space for some important guests." My third *chakra* was buzzing with delight, especially since one of my core issues in this life – centered within the third *chakra* – is a sense of invisibility. In the midst of this moment of respite and perhaps redemption – or so I thought – from this issue, Yogi Bhajan arrived with his entourage, backed into the area where I was keeping guard, and would have sat down right on top of me, had I not moved. I had to scramble to get out of his way, and fell awkwardly and unceremoniously out of the roped area, into the crowd that I had previously been holding at bay.

Immediately, whatever sense of self-importance I had managed to squeeze out of this task I was assigned was deflated, and I was placed in a double bind – of the kind discussed earlier in relation to the sixth *chakra*. Either one of two things was true: Yogi Bhajan hadn't seen me or known I was behind him when he sat down, in which case, the "I" that was so self-important a moment ago, was in fact, still every bit as invisible as my core issues constantly reminded me that I was; or, he had known that I was behind him when he sat down, in which case, he appeared to be making a deliberate statement about how little I mattered, visible or not, in the larger scheme of things. In the midst of this double-bind into which his actions had suddenly placed me, the whole issue revolving around whether or not I was visible to him, and the implications of that visibility or invisibility, became a bit of a moot point. To the extent that I could rise to his level, at the seventh *chakra*, the entire issue that precipitated my dilemma would dissolve. In the moment, I could not quite stretch that far, but in retrospect, I can see that this was the gift of grace he was offering.

The objective truth of the matter is that in that moment, as in every other moment, he was just being himself – allowing Spirit to flow through him unimpeded by the usual considerations we place upon our actions within the world. Whether he saw me or not, he was just sitting down. On the level of the *vijnanamaya kosha* at the seventh *chakra*, this action meant nothing other than that. At this same level, however, his meaningless action was nonetheless a gift of grace to me, with the power to offer a momentary dissolution of everything that kept me separate from Spirit in my own psyche, provided I could open to the ultimate truth of the moment. To the extent that I couldn't, it was a trigger to my issues. Such is the power of enlightened beings to transform all those who come into their presence, just by being, engaging in the ordinary acts of everyday life – sitting down, standing up, winking, nodding, picking their nose. It doesn't matter. On the level of *vijnanamaya kosha*, such actions contain the symbolic power to set us free, provided we can take them in and experience them at the same level on which they are freely given.

Anandamaya Kosha

At the level of *anandamaya kosha*, the gateway symbolized by the anterior fontanel dissolves, as there is no longer any separation between Spirit and matter, or between soul and Spirit. There is no identity other than Spirit, no journey, no destination. All is here now, and in the here and now all opposites fuse and the world of duality that characterizes the embodied world collapses, along with the embodied world itself. The embodied world continues to exist on all the other levels, but in the seventh *chakra* at the level of *anandamaya kosha*, all that exists is the pure tone of *shabda* or cosmic sound, present at the dawning of creation, still present after the creation has been absorbed back into its Source.

There is not much that can really be said about this level of being, at least within the language of mere words that we have available to us. The question remains, however: is it possible for an individual soul to actually reach this level while still in a body, and what happens when it does? These are, of course, primal questions about the Great Mystery itself, and I do not think there are definitive answers. My sense about it, however, is that the very concept of individuality ceases to have meaning at this level, and what happens at this level is not something that can be experienced, in the sense in which we understand the concept of experience on this side of that blessed state.

On the other hand, there must be some reason why the One chose to splinter into all the myriad forms through which Spirit permeates the embodied world. Could it be that when the individual soul moves through this final gateway, it gets to experience life simultaneously from every cell in every body that still draws breath, just as Spirit does all the time? I find myself tickled by the thought that I am not just me, but also this tree, this sky, this mountain, this bird, this flower, this storm, and everything else I see and don't see outside this limited window through which I observe my Self.

To think such a thought is to think like a poet, and to think this thought within a framework of cycles that encompass our coming and our going in and out of form is to think like an astropoet. It is to such thinking that we will turn our more detailed attention in Part Two of this book, and in the other books in this series.

Chapter Eight
Interchakra Relationships

Thus far we have been discussing the *chakras* as though they were separate, discrete states of consciousness and/or being. This is an artificial device that allows us to gain some perspective on a complex dynamic that is in constant flux and would otherwise be fairly unwieldy. While *chakras* can be understood to have unique physiological correlates, govern distinct arenas of psychological function, and encompass discrete worldviews - each with their own characteristic flavor, tint, and feel - real life is rarely quite so neatly packaged. From a practical as well as from an energetic standpoint, there is much commerce between *chakras*, and most core issues around which the life of the soul revolves will likely involve two or more *chakras* resonating in tandem. While it is possible for *chakras* to be mutually engaged in this way in any possible combination, there are a few classic relationships that bear special mention. In this chapter, I will briefly discuss each, so that we may approach our application of these principles to astrology and to life with a broader, more multi-dimensional palette.

Chakras Arranged By Directional Flow Between Spirit and Matter

In *The Seven Gates of Soul*, I describe soul as an embodiment of Spirit, whose purpose it is to bring Spirit into the material realm through the vehicle of consciousness. Spirit's inhabitation of matter is what makes possible the actualization of this purpose. The process itself evokes within the soul an increasing recognition of its ultimate Unity with Spirit that can be understood as a gradual return to It. Given that the *chakras in toto* describe the manifestation of consciousness within the embodied state, they can also be understood to play their part within the actualization of the soul's purpose.

Within this context, the seven *chakras* can be divided into groups of two, with the seventh being a special case. The first two *chakras* describe the phase of the process in which Spirit enters matter and securely anchors itself within it. In the first *chakra*, where the motivation is survival, we work to eliminate threats to the union of body and Spirit, and create a safe space in which it is possible to live a life of meaning and purpose. In the second *chakra*, we discover and indulge what we enjoy, and through an awakening of pleasure, make a decision to embrace the gift of life and participate in its possibilities. These two functions - securing our survival and discovering the pleasure available within embodiment - constitute what I will call the incarnation phase of the self-actualization process. As we work through the challenges and issues associated with the first two *chakras*, we are essentially seeking to more fully and consciously inhabit these bodies we have been born into.

In phase two, encompassed by the activity in the third and fourth *chakras*, the task is to use this incarnation as a vehicle for bringing Spirit more deeply into the embodied world through our participation in it. In the third *chakra*, we work toward the mastery of talents and skills necessary to effectively make a contribution. In the fourth *chakra*, we awaken to a deeper sense of purpose and a nexus of resonant relationships that makes possible a higher, more integrated level of co-creativity. Within this phase individual effort fuses with individual effort to produce culture and civilization, which – from the perspective of the soul – constitute an awakening of Spirit within the embodied world on a larger, more collective scale. As we work through the challenges and issues associated with the third and fourth *chakras*, we are essentially doing the work of Spirit – which is to say, infusing the embodied world with consciousness. I will call this phase of the self-actualization process, encompassed by the third and fourth *chakras*, the awakening phase.

As the awakening proceeds, we gradually begin to identify more completely with Spirit, so that there is less and less separation between our individual identity and the larger Identity of Spirit with which we are merging. In the fifth *chakra*, we are opening to the power of Spirit to create through us, and to the grace that flows when we inhabit our natural place within the larger scheme of things. In the sixth *chakra*, we learn of the mobility of our personal center as we align increasingly with S/He whose "center is everywhere and circumference is nowhere to be found." In both the fifth and sixth *chakras*, we are learning to identify more completely with Spirit, and through that identification, opening to a range of creative power and motion that transcends what can be encompassed within the normal limitations of the embodied state. For this reason, I will call this grouping of fifth and sixth *chakras*, the transcendence phase of the self-actualization process.

As I speak of the self-actualization process, I am referring to the ideal. In actuality, real life is likely to be more problematic, and issues will invariably arise at each phase of the process. Within the context of this tri-fold grouping, however, these issues can be more consciously addressed through reference to the relevant phase of the self-actualization process. A rape victim, for example, unable to enjoy sex with her partner, will likely be dealing with an incarnation issue that is rooted in both the first (fear for survival in the wake of trauma) and second (inability to open to pleasure) *chakras*. A mid-level executive who becomes paranoid about his co-workers when his job is on the line in the wake of a corporate merger, is – from the soul's perspective – dealing with a blockage to awakening that is rooted in both his third (self-doubt and insecurity) and fourth (mistrust of others) *chakras*. A concert pianist, suddenly bored with Chopin and Beethoven, but unable to stop the momentum of a successful career, may well be dealing

◇◇

with an issue of transcendence, in which the fifth (disillusionment) and sixth (fear of change) *chakra* are both implicated. Working through these issues – which appear to be mundane crises within the embodied life – moves one farther along the path of self-actualization. This work – which is the soul's journey – allows us to more fully incarnate, awakens us to a larger sense of identity and purpose, and empowers us to surrender to a more flexible, more all-encompassing sense of Self.

In the seventh *chakra*, these distinctions begin to break down, for here we are simultaneously incarnating, awakening, and transcending the embodied state in which the entire process occurs. In this state, the veils lift – however briefly – and we realize there was never anyone to incarnate, awaken, or transcend – other than an image projected onto the screen of the embodied world with which Spirit has momentarily identified. It is Spirit that incarnates, and awakens, and the transcendence is merely a recognition of this truth that resonates on every level of our being. A chant, taught to me by an old long lost friend, Jim Spittler, describes this recognition more succinctly than anything else I have encountered:

> I am not leaving home,
> I am not leaving home,
> I am returning.
> Mountains, rivers and streams living in me.
> I am returning.
> I am not leaving home,
> I am not leaving home,
> I am returning.

We might be tempted to call the seventh *chakra* the return phase of the self-actualization process, except that even the concept of return is ultimately illusory. Spirit is here now, in this moment, in us, as us, as in every blade of grass, every rock, every passing cloud. There is no place to return, nor need for returning. This is not to say that we do not get caught up in this illusion from time to time, or even live our entire lives there. At the seventh *chakra*, the impulse toward suicide as a path of liberation – such as that entertained by the disciples of Marshall Applegate or Jim Jones – can be a self-destructive illusion rooted at the seventh *chakra*. To a lesser extent, the longing for escape, including many addictions to various paths of ecstasy, can all be understood as aberrations within the seventh *chakra* that must be worked out essentially as issues of return.

The Alpha and Omega

Working out these issues of return ultimately requires the soul to integrate the seventh *chakra* and the first, which together form a second important combination of *chakras* that are often mutually engaged. When the *chakras* are considered, not as a hierarchy the way they were in the *yogic* system, but rather as a circle, as we have been doing here, then the seventh and the first can be understood to be the alpha and the omega, or the point at which the circle both begins and ends. From this perspective, whether we discuss the process by which Spirit anchors itself in the body (as we would when focused solely on the first *chakra*) or the process by which the embodied soul gradually rises in consciousness to realize her identity with Spirit (as we would when focused on the seventh *chakra*), we are discussing the same process. We cannot effectively return to Spirit without realizing in every fiber of our embodied being that Spirit is returning to us in each moment, and to the embodied world through us.

To the extent that we have not yet understood this, we begin another round of existence at this point where the omega of the seventh *chakra* and the alpha of the first come together. The reader will undoubtedly recognize this as a description of reincarnation, or the belief that the same soul enters into a succession of bodies in order to continue to evolve toward a reunion with Spirit. But given that the alpha and omega merge in this moment of reunion, the belief in reincarnation can be understood as a reflection of the same illusion that gives rise to the apparent necessity for it. Taken as a metaphor, however, the idea of reincarnation can be a useful way of understanding how the same patterns of confusion tend to repeat themselves - both within the context of an individual life, and on the world stage as perennial human dilemmas.

The recurrent nature of our core issues is also encoded in the astrological worldview, which understands everything terrestrial as a reflection of celestial cycles. As we will begin to see in Part Two, these celestial cycles and the patterns they mirror can be mapped to specific astrological symbols and to the interplay between them, as well as to specific *chakras*. At this point, we might simply reflect upon the possibility that the cycle itself is - from the standpoint of consciousness - the result of this bridge between the alpha and omega points, the first and seventh *chakras*, understood as a continuum. The cycle is both an embodiment of Wholeness, attained when the individual soul realizes its identity with Spirit, and a vehicle for working through the various issues that block this realization. The promise of realization within the process is encoded in the coming together of the first and seventh *chakras*.

The Chakras Divided by Polarity

Short of the point where alpha and omega come together in a realization of Oneness with Spirit, everything within the embodied world, including the soul itself is marked by duality. This idea of duality need not be understood in negative terms, as it is by many of the world's religions, but can be understood as a deeply spiritual polarity that affords each soul the opportunity for balance and creative synthesis of the opposites on every level of being. In *The Seven Gates of Soul*, I speak of this opportunity within the context of a sexual metaphor, both to suggest that the process of self-discovery it entails is meant to be pleasurable, and to underscore the compelling power of magnetic attraction, intercourse, and co-mingling of energies by which the movement toward realization of identity with Spirit proceeds.

Just as in a relationship with a lover, our relationship to the embodied life guarantees that we will be attracted to a set of life circumstances through some combination of affinity, wounding and contrast. We will then seek by trial and error a place of balance within those circumstances, and learn more about ourselves and our capabilities through the process of seeking balance. As we gradually learn to find our place of balance within all circumstances, we naturally experience an expansion of identity that is ultimately rooted in Spirit. This process is made possible by the inherent polarity that is built into the embodied world at every level – from the dance of protons and electrons in the nucleus of the atom, to the dance of gender in relationship, to the birthing of new galaxies and the imploding of old stars that fuels the drama on the largest, most cosmic of stages.

The interplay of polarities is also encoded within the *chakra* system. The odd numbered centers of consciousness – one, three and five – constitute what I will call the *yang chakras*, while the even numbered – two, four and six – compose the *yin chakras*. The seventh, as in our previous grouping, is a special case that we will discuss in a moment. I use the Taoist words *yin* and *yang* to describe the others, instead of the more familiar western terms, masculine and feminine to avoid any false association of these terms with men and women. Men must learn to open, activate, and balance their *yin chakras*, as well as their *yang*; women must form an intimate relationship with their *yang chakras*, as well as their *yin*.

The *yang chakras* are those in which we must reach out to form a more active, participatory connection to the embodied world, and/or stretch more consciously in order to access Spirit. The *yin chakras* are those in which the embodied world appears to invite us to fuller participation, and Spirit appears to stretch toward us in order to make a more recognizable contact. Opening, activating and balancing *yang chakras* is a matter of conscious intention, deliberate action, and learning through consequence. Opening, activating and balancing *yin chakras* is a matter of opening, allowing, and learning through surrendering to grace.

In the first *chakra*, the task is to grab hold of the life we have been given and find a foothold in this embodied life through our will to be. Without this will to be, nothing else is possible. Before Spirit can reveal itself to us at the heart of this embodied life, we must first consent to be embodied. This is essentially a *yang* act, which begins before birth, while we are still in the womb. From a spiritual perspective, it is our intention to be born that propels us into this life, and from the perspective of the first *chakra*, this intention is the *yang* gesture that calls Spirit into the body and produces life. Without the intention to be born, Spirit cannot respond with the gift of life, for there is no foothold where life can take root.

Through parallel *yang* gestures, we reach toward a more conscious and deliberate expression within the embodied world in the third *chakra* as we learn to navigate its tricky shoals with increasing skill and competence, and we intentionally begin to address those issues that keep us separate from Spirit. In the fifth *chakra*, we give back something of all that we have learned through our participation by teaching, by speaking and living our truths, by offering the hard-won fruits of our personal wisdom to others who are in a position to benefit. This offering, known in many Native American traditions as the *giveaway*, is the gesture that completes the circle and allows a larger, more all-encompassing identity with Spirit to gradually emerge.

It should be noted here that the fifth *chakra* also has a strong *yin* component, for as discussed earlier, it is the place where we take energy in through our environment - food, breath, and sound, which encompasses those verbal messages that inform our relationship to the embodied world. In the transcendent *chakras* - the fifth and sixth - the polarity between *yin* and *yang* is already beginning to break down. I nonetheless place the fifth *chakra* within the *yang* grouping because it is our willingness to take what we have been given and give back - through what the Buddhists call *right action* - in alignment with our own truth, that opens, activates and balances this *chakra*, and this willingness to give back and make a contribution to the larger world in which we live is essentially an expression of the *yang* side of our nature.

On the *yin* side of the equation, the feeling and the spiritual task required of us is much different. In the second *chakra*, we first open to the beauty and the wonder within the embodied life through a sensory awakening. We discover what is pleasurable, not by intending to, but by opening to it as it reveals itself to us. Likewise in the fourth *chakra*, we discover ourselves to be a part of a network of resonant relationships, each of which carries an unexpected opportunity - unbidden through any act of intentional summoning - to learn something about ourselves through association. In the sixth *chakra*, we open to other perspectives, which in turn begins to grace our lives with a certain psychic flexibility and range of motion that we could not begin to muster through our own initiative. It is our willingness to surrender our own point of view and entertain other possibilities that makes this kind of grace possible, and this surrender is essentially a *yin* process.

As with the other transcendent *chakra*, however, the sixth also has a strong *yang* component, for this *chakra* also encompasses the internal image, or worldview, which we then project into the embodied world. This *chakra* is included in the *yin* grouping, because the projection of the image is the root source of problems, issues, and challenges associated with this *chakra*, while clearing the *chakra* involves the *yin* gesture of letting the image go, allowing the vacuum to be filled with an open-minded and open-hearted embrace of that which previously seemed foreign to our nature, and a surrender of attachment to everything we have previously defended as ours.

In the seventh *chakra*, as we might by now expect, the whole dichotomy between *yin* and *yang* breaks down completely. Here is where we experience the synthesis of *yin* and *yang* that Jung referred to as the *hieros gamos*, or sacred marriage, and where all opposites come together in unity and graceful balance. As Spirit infuses the embodied world so thoroughly with its presence as to be indistinguishable from it, every act of intention becomes its own realization; every action meets an immediate response; every gesture of giving becomes its own gift.

Cross-Polar Relationships

In the hierarchical system of *yogic* philosophy, the distinction is often made between the lower *chakras* – first, second, and third – which are considered to be aligned with our animal nature, and the higher *chakras* – fifth, sixth and seventh – which are considered to be aligned with our divinity. As we have observed in various ways so far throughout this discussion, however, any *chakra* that is not entirely clear or balanced can be the home of unresolved issues that bring out the beast in us, while even the so-called lower *chakras* can be sublime in their expression to the extent that we have done the work each requires of us. Because this is so, we will not emphasize this distinction between higher and lower in our grouping of *chakras*, except to note that the heart serves as a pivot point around which our identification within the embodied world will shift. *Chakras* "below" the heart center our awareness firmly within the boundaries of a self that appears to be separate and apart from a world which is more or less foreign to it, while *chakras* "above" the heart center our awareness within an embodied world in which we seem to have a place and play a part.

It is not that this awareness of place is higher than an awareness of self, since both are necessary to a full realization of our identity with Spirit. But we will approach life differently with this sense of place than we will without it. We might call the perspective that arises in the first three *chakras* self-centered, and the perspective that arises in last three *chakras* place-centered. It should be noted that the term "self-centered" is not meant to imply selfishness, but rather a state of awareness that refers all experience to an identifiable self, which is felt to exist as a mediating pivot point at the center of that experience. In place-centered *chakras*, by contrast, experience is understood as a reflection of one's relationship to the rest of the embodied world, in which one plays a more peripheral, though no less vital, role.

Creativity

Of notable importance within our present discussion of *chakra* combinations are two cross-polar relationships that span this divide between separate self and interconnected place. The first of these is between the second *chakra* (yin/self-centered) and the fifth (yang/place-centered). I call these two *chakras* together, *creative*, because working in tandem they produce the sensibility, if not necessarily the capability of the artist. I use the word "artist" here in the broadest possible sense of the word as one who, aligned with an intentional sense of self that is endowed with purpose and a receptive awareness of connection that seems to want to invite further exploration, is compelled to give expression to something that transcends the self and enriches the embodied world.

The artistic intention comes through the fifth *chakra*, where one is compelled to speak and live one's truth. At the same time, the truth that one is compelled to speak and live comes through an opening to beauty and pleasure at the heart of this world that takes place through the second *chakra*. As these two *chakras* synthesize, this *yin* opening to beauty and pleasure becomes the self-centered surrender that allows one to more actively take one's place within the larger scheme of things as a *yang* gesture of self-affirmation. At the same time, the *yang* intention to speak and live one's truth within the world fuels the place-centered action necessary to open more deeply to Spirit – a *yin* process of surrender. What emerges from this blending can take any number of forms, but it will invariably be infused both with a clear sense of self, freely given, and with an appreciation for one's relationship to the rest of the embodied world, often engaged with great delight.

Obviously, this is the ideal, and in any interchange between the second and fifth *chakras* there can and most likely will be issues that make the quest for the ideal more challenging and perhaps more interesting. If the complicating issue is lodged in the second *chakra*, one may have the sensibility of the artist, but be driven by pain to produce works that are disturbing in their dark intensity. If the complicating issue is lodged in the fifth *chakra*, one may lack the ability to articulate the wonder one senses and feels, but consequently be provoked as an artist to mix media and evolve new techniques.

Even if second and fifth *chakras* are clear, other issues lodged in other *chakras* may pose complications and lend their own range of nuances to the palette of possibilities. In the life of a photographer doing candid portraits of real people living in a war zone or dealing with the aftermath of a hurricane, the first *chakra* will also likely be engaged. In the life of a stockbroker seeking to balance the needs of her clients with pressure from the companies she represents, the third will perhaps play a part. In any attempt to give expression to one's creativity – whether building a better mousetrap, revealing the hidden life of bees, or raising children – the interplay between the second and fifth *chakras* is likely to be a primary axis, with other *chakras* contributing color and subjective nuance.

Power

The second cross-polar relationship of note is between the third and sixth *chakras*. The third *chakra* represents a *yang*, self-centered perspective, while the sixth is *yin* and place-centered. Together these two *chakras* govern the alignment of individual will with what has been called divine will. Divine will need not necessarily be understood as the will of an actual divine being, but can be more secularly understood as the natural order which pervades the manifest creation of the embodied world with intelligent design. This distinction is important to make, because the concept of divine will has been used to justify all manner of atrocity – from genocide, to torture, to the development of weapons of mass destruction. Attunement with natural law, by contrast, is a state of being marked by flowing adaptability to the moment, harmony (or *right relationship*, as the Buddhists would say) with everyone and everything in one's environment, synchronicity, and an effortless, intuitive understanding of the symbolic implications of everyday life. Natural law cannot be codified into dogma, although religions around the world have tried. Rather, it must be felt as an inner sense of alignment with one's own nature, and an ability to function gracefully as oneself within the world.

In the sixth *chakra*, we internalize our experience of the world (a *yin* process) as an image, around which our belief system takes shape. In the third, we act out that belief system (a *yang* process), and intentionally mold ourselves accordingly. Because the third *chakra* is a self-centered state of being, our tendency functioning from this *chakra* alone is to take our sixth *chakra* belief system as gospel truth, and to defend it against attack as though we were defending ourselves. As the sixth opens and clears, we realize that all beliefs are place-centered, or relative to the experience of the individual, and we learn to co-exist, co-operate, and even co-create with those who harbor very different beliefs. With third and sixth working in tandem, we evolve a way of being in the world that respects and tolerates the beliefs of others, even when we disagree. This does not mean we no longer hold strong convictions, but it does mean we no longer insist upon everyone else believing as we do. Tolerance evolves into compassion and compassion opens a door to miraculous change and a profound ability to influence others – not by coercing or manipulating them, but by simply being who we are.

When the third *chakra* functions without the balancing perspective of the sixth, we often have individuals driven by what neopagan activist Starhawk refers to as *power-over* – the attempt to dominate, control, manipulate and otherwise harass others with the Truth. Third and sixth functioning together, by contrast, produce what she calls *power-from-within* – arising from our deep, primal connections to the earth and to each other (3-4). This is not a personal power, but rather a power in which we participate through consent, the clarity of our intention, and our sense of belonging to a larger, cosmic order. "When we plant," says Starhawk, "when weave, when we write, when we give birth, when we organize, when we heal, when we run through the park while the redwoods sweat mist, when we do what we're afraid to do, we are not separate. We are of the world and each other, and the power within us is great, if not an invincible power" (14).

Beings with both third and sixth *chakras* open and functioning in harmonious tandem with each other, gain the power to change the world. As with the *creative chakras* (second and fifth), the power *chakras* can be and often are distorted in their expression as they move together through a trial and error process of harmonization. To the extent that the third is unclear, that is to say, until issues associated with the third have been resolved, one will invariably seek power over others. To the extent that the sixth *chakra* remains clouded by unfinished business, one will be subject to manipulation and coercion by others. In either scenario, difficult life lessons will ensue which provide motivation toward balance. In any situation where the individual soul seeks a higher level of self-empowerment, while learning how not to trample or disrespect the rights of others to the same privilege, you can be sure that the power *chakras* are being engaged.

Heart Chakra Combinations

The last category of *interchakra* relationship I wish to discuss is the relationship of each *chakra* with the fourth. From the hierarchical perspective, the fourth *chakra* was often considered the point of mediation between the lower self and the higher self, while the opening of the heart was considered to be the primary gateway to a spiritual path. There is some truth to this perspective, since until the heart is open, one experiences oneself as functioning in isolation, apart from the embodied world, even though one is apparently forced to function within it. As the heart opens, one enters a field of resonant relationships within which one is given the opportunity to learn the lessons necessary to evolution of the soul. For this reason, the opening of the heart, the capacity to love, and the ability to reach out across the abyss between self and sense of place is the act that invites Spirit to enter a life and transform it. Love is the ultimate antidote to any wound it is possible to experience in this life, and the transformation that comes through opening the heart to this love extends specifically to each *chakra* in which the issue arises that triggers the longing to be healed.

Between the first and fourth *chakra* is the recognition that we would not be given the gift of life if we did not also have the capacity somewhere within us to survive. Being cast utterly defenseless into a hostile world is not usually the lot of any soul – although there are exceptions – and as one gradually relaxes into the experience of being loved, usually through relationship to one's mother, a bond is formed between the first and fourth *chakras* that can and will serve as a touchstone in times of difficulty. This bond will be tested many times throughout the course of a lifetime, but each time we reach down inside ourselves for a deeper memory of that Love of which every human expression is merely an echo, we strengthen the bond, and anchor our survival at a deeper level of our being.

When the second *chakra* is awakened in tandem with the fourth, we re-enter a garden of Eden in which we are not only the recipients of pleasure, suckling the breasts of Divine Mother, but also givers of pleasure, co-creators of a pleasurable world. This combination of energies and perspectives is evoked most powerfully when we fall in love, and the world becomes a lover's playground. Of course, there are all sorts of issues in any relationship to render this idyllic state a fleeting tease at best, but to the extent that we are committed to working through these issues and barriers with the ones we love, we strengthen the second-fourth *chakra* bond, and with it, our capacity to create a life of joy, satisfaction and contentment. The experience of this bond is not limited to erotic love, but can instead radiate throughout every aspect of one's life, and through every relationship as a pervasive capacity for loving enjoyment, when these two *chakras* are open, clear and functioning in harmony with each other.

We discussed the relationship between the third and fourth *chakras* earlier, in speaking about the awakening phase of the self-actualization process. Here I would simply add that until the fourth *chakra* is open, one will experience the third *chakra* primarily within the context of competition, conflict and growth through struggle within the world. With this opening comes the capacity to engage others not in combat, but as dancing partners in a process of mutual growth and awakening. No longer "me against the world," the third and fourth in tandem produce an awareness of "me within the world" that evolves in the fifth and sixth *chakras* as increasing alignment with Spirit and flexible sense of place.

The mutual awakening of the fourth and fifth *chakras* produces the power to heal and to alleviate the suffering of others. In the fifth, we actualize power of intention, or *vach siddhi*, as it was called by the *yogis* and *yoginis* who sought to awaken this *chakra*. When the attainment of this power is accompanied by an opening of the heart, one's intentions naturally become aligned toward the highest good of all concerned, for one cannot both care about another being and intentionally do them harm. Of course, unintentional harm occurs – mostly because love is often misconstrued when it is experienced by wounded beings, but when the fourth and fifth *chakras* are open and working together in harmony, every action ultimately becomes a catalyst to healing, even if in the short term it must sometime reopen old wounds before they can be healed.

When the fourth and sixth *chakras* are functioning together in balance and harmony, one gains the perspective of the sage. One sees the relativity of one's point of view, and can mold it compassionately to the deepest needs of the one seeking truth. The wounded temptation in the sixth *chakra* is always to cling to one's truth as though it were The Truth, and then to impose it upon others. This is no longer possible when the heart is open, for in this *yin* state of being, imposition gives way to allowing. When one sees the truth and yet allows others to make their mistakes and learn from then, without judgment or interference. one gains the capacity to serve as a clear mirror to the truth for anyone it is one's destiny to engage. I believe this was the place Swami Muktananda functioned from in the *darshan* line, as discussed earlier in Chapter Six on the sixth *chakra*. Had his heart *chakra* not been open, he might have used his power to impose his worldview on others. Instead, he mirrored, and in the compassionate neutrality of this act, he changed many lives.

Lastly, when both fourth and seventh *chakras* are open and clear, one becomes a *bodhisattva*, an avatar, or an enlightened being like Christ or Buddha. There is no longer anyone to get in the way of Spirit, and one becomes a clear channel for the functioning of Spirit within form. Every act becomes a benevolent dispensation of grace; every gesture, a teaching; every word, a creative force set in motion. The opening of the seventh alone produces clarity of meditation and communion with Spirit within the privacy of one's heart. But until the heart opens wide enough to contain the entire embodied world within it, the work of Spirit remains incomplete. It is when both seventh and fourth are fused into one expression that Spirit becomes fully incarnate in human form – a rare occurrence perhaps, but the ultimate goal of any legitimate spiritual path.

Other Combinations, Other Chakras

In a system of seven *chakras*, 28 combinations of two *chakras* are possible, and obviously we have not discussed them all in this chapter. There are also a number of minor *chakras* – in the hands, and feet, at the nape of the neck, outside the body, and scattered throughout various locations by various systems (Bruyere counts 122 (41) – that I will decline to discuss in this book. Rather than providing the definitive word about every possible combination, this book is meant to demonstrate a process by which even a working knowledge of the basic system can serve as the basis for a new way of thinking about and processing one's own experience. It is not an exhaustive encyclopedia we are aiming for here, but the outline of guiding principles and the demonstration of a process that can then be applied creatively to any situation that might arise.

As the reader will discover, this will also be my approach to everything astrological discussed in this and other books. If you understand the "logic" of a given system, you can exercise that logic under your own authority, without the exact formula being written down for you. It is my goal, as your guide in this book, to gradually lead you to the place where you feel comfortable doing that. To the extent that you have grasped the principles

◇◇

presented in Part One, you will be empowered to approach any situation with a sense of which *chakras* might be involved. Conversely, you will be able to consider any *chakra* combination not covered explicitly through a contemplation of principles.

In considering the relationship between the first *chakra* and the sixth, for example, you already know something about each *chakra* individually. You know that the first is the alpha point, the point of entry of Spirit into the body. You know that it is reflective of the incarnation phase of the self-actualization process, while the sixth is reflective of the transcendence phase. You know that the first is *yang* and self-centered, while the sixth is *yin/yang* and place-centered. Using your imagination to put these *chakra-logical* facts together in a synergistic way, you can begin to feel your way into the possibilities for manifestation that might arise, both when *intrerchakra* issues are evoked and when both *chakras* are functioning in tandem from a state of relative clarity and balance.

Likewise, when you are faced with a given set of life circumstances, you should be able to intuit which *chakras* might be involved, using your knowledge of the *chakras* and of the various combinations as a springboard to your own inner knowing. I would invite you to the same process of discovery in Part Two, when I make astrological suggestions for approaching the birthchart from the perspective of each *chakra*. This entire system is not presented dogmatically, but rather as a mutual enrichment of both *yogic* psychology and astrology capable of adding dimension and perspective to any contemplation of life circumstances. If you can find the courage to begin doing this through the application of the ideas and suggestions presented in Part Two, this book will have served its purpose as a catalyst to your own process of creative synthesis.

Part Two
The Astro-Chakra System

Chapter Nine
The Astro-logic of the Five Koshas

Having outlined the nature of each *chakra* in Part One, it will be our task in Part Two to map each *chakra* to the astro-logic that reveals its presence and relative prominence within the birthchart. Likewise, we will discuss the five *koshas* in terms of their astro-logical ramifications. Each birthchart will reflect a composite of all seven *chakras* operating at the level of all five *koshas*, but each will also emphasize certain *chakras* and de-emphasize others. Even emphasized *chakras* will not always function visibly at the level of all five *koshas*. All *chakras* come into prominence at some point in each life through activation by various transits and progressions which echo or temporarily trigger the astrological features with which they are associated, and at various times this activation takes place at the level of one or more *koshas*. By assessing any natal birthchart in terms of these astrological factors, we can establish a meaningful context through which it might be understood as a map of the soul's evolutionary journey.

We begin our discussion of the astrological factors associated with each *chakra* by observing that the birthchart itself is depicted as a circle. The circle is the preeminent symbol for wholeness, but we will experience this wholeness – which is who we are at core – differently as our consciousness shifts from one *chakra* to another. As we approach the birthchart from the perspective of each *chakra*, the very nature of the circle encompassing the birthchart shifts in meaning, and creates an entirely different context in which everything within it must be understood. Signs, houses, planetary dynamics, and every other component of the astrological language must be approached differently, depending on which *chakra* (or *chakras*) are being evoked in a given moment, or in reference to a given question. In Part Two, we will summarize the major astrological ramifications of each *chakra*, and outline the astro-logic that distinguishes one *chakra* from another.

As we discuss the astrology of each *chakra*, I will provide a case study that suggests how the system can be useful in real life application. Each case study will include a relevant cyclical history, a technique introduced in *The Seven Gates of Soul* as a way to map memories, life experiences, and shifts in consciousness to the astrological cycles that represent them. Through the cyclical history, we will observe how the esoteric astro-logic of each case study birthchart can be a useful framework for tracking the process related to the *chakra* under study.

Chakra Charts and Sub-Charts

Because we must shift our point of view in approaching the same chart from the perspective of each *chakra*, we might postulate that each soul has not one chart, but seven – let us call them *chakra* charts. Each *chakra* chart emphasizes certain planetary placements, aspects and aspect patterns and de-emphasize others. Each also represents an entirely different perspective on life in general and on the issues that are encompassed by a specific *chakra*. The same life circumstances, events and processes, in other words, can be understood very differently as we shift our perspective from one *chakra* chart to the next.

For purposes of nomenclature, we will distinguish between them by placing the number of the *chakra* chart under scrutiny in the center of the circle. Each *chakra* chart can also be understood from the perspective of all five *koshas*, yielding a total of 35 secondary charts. We will indicate the level of penetration at the *chakra* under scrutiny by a series of letters representing the *koshas* – a for *annamaya kosha*, p for *pranamaya*, m for *manomaya*, v for *vijnanamaya kosha*, and n for *anandamaya kosha*. In this way, a chart labeled 3p indicates that the dynamic of the chart is best be approached as a third *chakra* matter, experienced on the level of *pranamaya kosha*, while a chart labeled 5v describes a fifth *chakra* chart, at the level of *vijnanamaya kosha*.

Certain *chakra* charts are more potent for each of us than others. We are all prone to view the natal chart from the perspective of our emphasized *chakra* charts, but have difficulty seeing it – or our lives – from the perspective posed by less dominant *chakra* charts. This same tendency lies at the root of our core issues, and may be a factor in the seeming tenacity of those issues. Periodically, certain transits and progressions will provide opportunities to shift our perspective, and approach these issues with fresh insight. Growth in consciousness also requires making an intentional effort to shift our perspective, with or without the help of temporary astrological alignments.

For example, if a compulsive gambler is struggling with an addiction rooted in her third *chakra*, manifest as low self-esteem seemingly related to a dead-end job where she is not appreciated, she may well have an emphasized 3m chart – the m referring to the activation of her problem on a psychological level – where feelings of despair, hopelessness, and despondency are foremost in her awareness of her predicament. The solution to her problem will involve cultivating a clearer sense of her core strengths, and moving toward a more satisfying job that draws upon those strengths. At core, this is a matter of working to clear, balance and strengthen her third *chakra*, and to work out her difficulties on the level of *manomaya kosha*, where she suffers low self-esteem and is most actively engaged in the day to day drama of her life.

But given that she is clearly stuck at this level, progress may also be a matter of learning to see herself and her natal chart more clearly as a second *chakra* chart on the level of *pranamaya kosha* (2p), where what is being emphasized is the more basic question of what really turns her on and gets her vital, creative juices flowing. It may be that the energy to break free from her dead-end job is just not there, because something more fundamental has yet to be addressed. Learning to view her chart as a 2p, instead of a 3m, can help her to approach the task posed by her third *chakra* chart more effectively.

All core issues revolve around certain habits of mind that are an expression of the level of consciousness at which they are formed and maintained. Working through core issues often requires shifting our perspective to entertain a different point of view – one that is represented by a different *chakra* chart, through which different habits of mind can be cultivated, and new possibilities considered. Having 35 possible charts at our disposal, instead of the one or two with which we naturally resonate, and in which we are probably stuck, greatly expands our repertoire and makes possible the desired shift in consciousness in relation to our core issues.

The Astro-logic of Elemental Dynamics

In the next chapter and throughout the remainder of Part Two, we will explore the astro-logic of each *chakra* chart. As a prelude to that discussion, I will briefly outline the astro-logic of the five *koshas*, which remains the same regardless of which *chakra* chart we consider. In the astro-logic of any *chakra* chart, certain signs, houses, angles, planets, aspects, midpoints, transits and/or progressions are emphasized. Each of these astrological features also correlates with one or more *koshas*, primarily through their associations with the four elements – earth, fire, water, and air – and with various disparate combinations of elements that produce tension.

Disparate elements are those combinations of elements that do not function in natural harmony with each other. Since fire and air share a certain level of compatibility, their juxtaposition in a birthchart produces a generally harmonious interaction that reinforces both elements. A similar relationship exists between earth and water. By contrast, the other four possible combinations – air and water, air and earth, fire and water, fire and earth – create challenges that must be addressed before a working synthesis of inherently incompatible elements can take place. I associate these various disparate combinations of elements with an internal pressure – often mirrored externally – that I call alchemical tension, because this working synthesis is not possible without a deeper opening to Spirit, and a consequent transformation of being. Achieving this synthesis requires growth in consciousness – that is to say, the opening, activation, and cleansing of one or more *chakras*, and the penetration within a given *chakra* to deeper levels of manifestation by *kosha*.

The correlation of earth, fire, and water with the first three *koshas* will be intuitive and self-evident to anyone following the discussion so far. Both earth and *annamaya kosha* refer to the physical dimension of our experience. Similarly, fire and *pranamaya kosha* refer to the energetic, and water and *manomaya kosha* to the emotional and psychological realms. The correlation of *vijnanamaya kosha* and *anandamaya kosha* to various combinations of disparate elements requires a more elaborate explanation. Air is significant within this system only to the extent that it combines with other elements – either enhancing the function of fire on the level of *pranamaya kosha*, or forming a disparate combination with earth or water. We will see why when we discuss the astro-logic of *vijnanamaya kosha* – the obvious correlation to air, were we to continue the sequence in a strictly linear fashion.

Association to the elements is made through traditional patterns of rulership as follows: Aries, Leo and Sagittarius are fire signs; the 1st, 5th and 9th houses are fire houses. Taurus, Virgo and Capricorn are earth signs; the 2nd, 6th and 10th houses are earth houses. Gemini, Libra and Aquarius are air signs; the 3rd, 7th and 11th houses are air houses. Cancer, Scorpio and Pisces are water signs; the 4th, 8th and 12th houses are water houses.

Planetary rulership is a bit more complicated. Traditionally, before the 18th century, five of the seven primary planets – Mercury, Venus, Mars, Jupiter and Saturn – were assigned dual rulerships as follows: Mercury ruled both the airy sign of Gemini and the earthy sign of Virgo; Venus ruled the earthy sign of Taurus and the airy sign of Libra; Mars ruled the fiery sign of Aries and the watery sign of Scorpio; Jupiter ruled the fiery sign of Sagittarius and the watery sign of Pisces; and Saturn ruled the earthy sign of Capricorn and the airy sign of Aquarius.

This dual rulership essentially means that each of these planets can be associated with one of two elements, depending on their sign placement in a given birthchart. Mercury, for example, functions as an air planet when it is placed in an air sign or house, but as an earth planet when it is placed in an earth sign or house. Since air is traditionally considered to be compatible with fire, and earth with water, we might also speculate that Mercury functions as an air planet when it is placed in a fire sign or house, but as an earth planet when it is placed in a water sign or house. We can make a similar designation for each of the other planets with dual rulership: Venus functions as an earth planet in an earth or water sign or house, but as an air planet in an air or fire sign or house; Mars functions as a fire planet in a fire sign or house, but as a water planet in a water or earth sign or house; and so on. As we shall see when we discuss the individual *koshas*, some of these placements also have functions specific to the deeper *koshas* (*vijnanamaya* and *anandamaya*).

Some astrologers may balk at the notion that Mars could function as a water planet, since Mars is nearly universally considered to be a quintessential fire planet – associated with energy, action, initiation and other classical masculine or *yang* functions. Mars also has a more reactive side, however, which can be understood as a *yin* expression, more appropriately associated with water. When an angry Mars, for example, is rooted in subconscious patterns that make it defensive, vindictive, or passive-aggressive, it functions as a water planet, governed not by a driving, animating spirit, but by festering emotional residues which have no clear outlet for expression. In a more positive sense, Mars can also be watery when it is moved by subliminal instincts, visionary impulses with no rational basis, or altruistic service-oriented sentiments that place the needs of the collective before one's own agenda. This *yin* side of Mars is more clearly emphasized when Mars is in a feminine sign – earth or water.

Similarly, it may be difficult for some astrologers to conceptualize Mercury – classically known as a quintessential air planet – as an earth planet. Mercury, however, has its earthier side: its organizational aptitude, its inventive genius, its affinity for crafts and hands-on activities, and its association with trade and commerce. These earthy functions are likely to be more clearly emphasized when Mercury is in a feminine sign.

In similar fashion, Venus is earthy in the sensual, erotic dimension of its expression, but airy in its quest for aesthetic appeal, social grace and balance. Saturn is earthy in its rulership of commitment, discipline and perseverance toward tangible goals, but airy in its capacity to strategize, organize and administrate. Jupiter is fiery in its passion, vision and cause-oriented leadership, but watery in its swollen appetites, indulgences, and compassionate altruism. When these planets of dual rulership fall in signs of a given gender, matched by a house of a compatible element (e.g. Jupiter in Scorpio in the 6th house or Venus in Leo in the 7th), they will tend to fall clearly on one side of the line or the other in their expression (e.g. Jupiter will function as a water planet, and Venus as an air planet).

A more ambivalent situation arises when any of these planets of dual rulership is placed in a sign of one type, but a house of the other type. Mercury in an air sign and an earth house, for example, will function simultaneously as both an air and earth planet; Mars in a fire sign and an earth house will function simultaneously as a fire and a water planet; Saturn in a water sign and an air house will function simultaneously as an earth and an air planet; and so on. When this occurs, the sign will take slight precedence over the house, so that Venus in an air sign and an earth house will be slightly more airy than earthy, while Jupiter in an earth sign and a fire house will be slightly more watery than fiery. Where the discrepancy between sign and house involves a combination of disparate elements, there will be alchemical tension, albeit relatively mild, inherent in the placement.

The Sun, ruler of fire sign, Leo, and no other sign, will always be a fire planet. The Moon, ruler of water sign, Cancer, and no other sign, will always be a water planet. Uranus, co-ruler of the air sign, Aquarius, functions as an air planet. Neptune, co-ruler of the water sign, Pisces, functions as a water planet. The placement of any of these planets in signs or houses of the opposite polarity creates a disparate elemental combination.

As co-ruler of the water sign, Scorpio, and fire sign, Aries, Pluto functions like any other planet of dual rulership –as a water planet when placed in an earth or water sign or house, and as a fire planet when placed in a fire or air sign or house.

It should be noted that within the yogic model of consciousness we are considering, the transpersonal planets – Uranus, Neptune and Pluto – serve a more complex function in relation to both the *koshas* and the *chakras* that transcends their elemental placements. Regardless of placement, the transpersonal planets are alchemical agents that work to open, activate, and cleanse each *chakra*. This alchemical function is especially noticeable when the transpersonal planets form natal patterns by aspect with other planets that carry the alchemical tension of disparate elements, or when they activate such patterns by transit. Within each *chakra* being activated, they also work toward a deeper level of penetration, triggering awareness at *vijnanamaya kosha* and *anandamaya kosha* through the activation of various forms of elemental tension – a process we will soon discuss in more detail. First, let us briefly examine other factors that can indicate elemental associations or emphasize a particular element, then take a closer look at each *kosha* in turn, to see how its activation may be indicated in a given chart.

Various Factors Indicating Elemental Emphasis

A planet that is conjunct an angle of the birthchart is traditionally considered to be emphasized. To the extent that this is so, the element(s) associated with the planet may also be emphasized, depending on which angle and which side of which angle it is found. The Moon in Pisces, for example, provides the strongest possible signature for water when it is close to the Nadir in the 4th (water) house, or to the Ascendant in the 12th (water) house. It is also greatly strengthened when it is found close to the Midheaven on the 10th house side or the Descendant on the 6th house side (in earth houses).

On the other side of these same angles, the Moon in Pisces is also strengthened, with additional alchemical significance. On the 3rd house side of the Nadir, or the 7th house side of the Descendant, the Moon in Pisces becomes a disparate placement, precipitating an alchemical tension between water and air. On the 9th house side of Midheaven or the 1st house side of the Ascendant, the Moon in Pisces precipitates an alchemical tension between water and fire.

Two planets emphasizing a given element in aspect to each other strengthens that element exponentially. The Moon in Pisces in the 4th house trine Neptune in Scorpio in the 12h house is much more watery than the Moon without this aspect. The Moon in Pisces in the 4th house sextile Mercury in Taurus in the 6th house is likewise a strong boost to both water and earth. These examples are artificially skewed in the direction of elemental reinforcement to make a clear, unambiguous case. In real life, the elemental balance will be more mixed, at times possibly giving rise to alchemical combinations. These will be spelled out in more detail as we consider each *kosha* and their elemental associations.

Aspects themselves can affect the elemental balance in a chart. Conjunctions, sextiles, trines and oppositions naturally reinforce the elements in which they occur, since they generally occur within elements that are compatible with each other. For purposes of this discussion, we will call such aspects soft, noting that traditional astrology considers the opposition hard, as well as certain conjunctions between planets of disparate natures. Semi-sextiles, semi-squares, squares, sesquiquadrates and quincunxes – referred to here (and in traditional astrology) as hard aspects – are generally indicative of alchemical tension. These rules of thumb are altered if and when an aspect is out-of-sign. A trine between one planet at the beginning of a water sign and another at the end of an air sign is a disparate combination, while a square between one planet at the beginning of a fire sign and another at the end of an air sign is not.

Often planets in soft aspect to one another will give somewhat contradictory information that must be reconciled before an aspect can be assumed astro-logically to contribute to a particular elemental disposition. In this case, the slowest moving planet will take precedence, in accordance with astrological tradition. Within the context of a trine between Mars and Mercury in water signs, for example, Mars would function as a water planet, while Mercury would function as an earth planet. Since Mars moves more slowly than Mercury, it will tend to dominate, and the aspect as a whole would be considered watery. With hard aspects, the contradiction tends to produce disparity and alchemical tension, which will not be reducible to one element or the other. A square between Mars in a water sign and Mercury in an air sign will be neither watery nor airy, but will create alchemical tension between water and air.

In general, planetary patterns formed by planets in soft aspect to each other – stelliums, wedges, bowls, kites, half-kites and grand trines – will tend to reinforce the element that is emphasized and provide an important opening to the *kosha* (*annamaya*, *pranamaya* or *manomaya*) associated with that element. Planetary patterns formed by planets in predominantly hard aspect to each other – t-squares, grand crosses, and yods – will create elemental disparity and provide openings to the deeper *koshas* (*vijnanamaya* and *anandamaya*).

Any planet conjunct the lunar North Node receives reinforcement if it is airy or fiery, and becomes a disparate combination if it is earthy or watery, because the North Node is the *yang* pole of the nodal axis, while the South Node is the *yin* pole. Conversely, any planet conjunct the South Node receives reinforcement if it is earthy or watery, and becomes a disparate combination if it is fiery or airy.

Midpoints between planets either reinforce a given element or produce a disparate combination, depending on the planets involved and where the midpoint happens to fall. The midpoint between Venus in Gemini and Saturn in Libra is especially airy when it falls in Leo, but more disparate in Cancer (air-water) or Virgo (air-earth). The midpoint between Venus in Gemini and Mars in Scorpio is disparate by nature (air-water), wherever it lands. Midpoints do not generally add significantly to the natal koshic signature, unless they actually form a planetary picture involving three or more planets, but they can represent points of activation of various *chakra* charts by transit or progression.

Transits and progressions, in general, can produce temporary emphasis on various elements or elemental combinations. In addition, any natal factor emphasized by strong aspect (particularly conjunction, semi-square, square, sesquiquadrate or opposition) to a New or Full Moon (particularly an eclipse) or direct or retrograde station will greatly emphasize the elemental association of the planet being so contacted. Since any syzygy (conjunction or opposition of Sun and Moon) will automatically entail a disparate combination – fire and water – it provides an opening to the deeper *koshas*. Full Moons are more watery (Moon-dominated); New Moons are more fiery (Sun-dominated) in nature. Eclipses will reverse this designation: solar eclipses are more watery, while lunar eclipses are more fiery[1].

The Astro-logic of Annamaya Kosha

The elements represent not only the material substances with which they are symbolized, but also the resonant fields in which issues and concerns metaphorically associated with each element can be found. Earth, for example, represents those aspects of our embodied existence in which we cultivate all that is tangible, stable, constant, and practical – or the areas of concern where these attributes are the desired goal, as well as issues where these attributes prove to be elusive or excessive. Within the realm of earth, we are concerned with the health and well-being of the physical body, our relationship to the earth and the physical environment in which we live, our material concerns – job, career, money, possessions, wealth and abundance or lack thereof – and everything else that grounds us in the physical dimension of our lives.

Knowing something about the astro-logical correlates to the element earth, it should not be hard to see that what happens within this realm essentially happens on the level of *annamaya kosha*, which likewise within the yogic system, represents the physical realm. Astro-logically, earth (and *annamaya kosha*) will be implicated whenever a planet involved in the signature for a given *chakra* chart is found in an earth house (2, 6 or 10) or an earth sign (Taurus, Virgo or Capricorn). The natural rulers of these signs – Venus, Mercury and Saturn – point an especially strong finger at *annamaya kosha* when they are in a feminine sign or even-numbered house, and stronger still when conjunct, sextile or trine each other. Any of these planets conjunct the Descendent (on the 6th house side of the angle) or the Midheaven (on the 10th house side) are particularly potent indicators of *annamaya kosha* emphasis. Any of these planets conjunct the South Node, featured as a singleton planet in a feminine sign and/or even-numbered house, or at the apex of some planetary pattern in a feminine sign and/or even-numbered house, also provides a point of entry to *annamaya kosha*.

If the earth element is not emphasized in the natal chart, it can be triggered by progression or transit, producing periods in an individual life when the gateway to *annamaya kosha* is wider than usual. Progressed Mercury or Venus or transiting Mercury, Venus or Saturn moving through a feminine sign or even-numbered house can temporarily open the gate to this *kosha*, as can a conjunction of any of these temporal factors to the South Node, or any aspect of transiting Neptune or Pluto (in a feminine sign or even-numbered house) to a natal *yin* Mercury, Venus and/or Saturn or the midpoints between them. A Full Moon or solar eclipse that takes place in a feminine sign or even-numbered house, especially when it aspects Mercury, Venus or Saturn, can also be a point of entry into *annamaya kosha*, as can any station of transiting Mercury, Venus or Saturn – retrograde or direct – in a feminine sign or even-numbered house.

The Astro-logic of Pranamaya Kosha

Pranamaya kosha is associated with the element of fire. Like *pranamaya kosha*, fire governs what happens on the energetic level – including the basic overall vitality of the body; the enthusiasm, passion, inspiration and excitement we bring to our interests, activities and involvements in the embodied world; our sense of vision and purpose, and the quest for meaning. Since fire is volatile, transformative, voracious and expansive, it also governs our experiences of growth, change, and the transmutation of our sense of identity that occurs over the course of a lifetime of experience. As a point of entry into the realm of *pranamaya kosha*, everything within the resonant field of fire serves to move the process associated with any *chakra* forward with the sheer momentum of the energy moving through it.

Astrologically, *pranamaya kosha* is indicated wherever fire is implicated in a given *chakra* chart. Fire is implicated whenever a planet involved in a *chakra* chart signature is in a fire house (1, 5 or 9), or a fire sign (Aries, Leo, or Sagittarius). The natural rulers of these signs – Mars, the Sun, or Jupiter – can point a strong finger at *pranamaya kosha* when they are in a masculine sign or odd-numbered house, and becomes even stronger when these planets are conjunct, sextile or trine each other. Any of these planets conjunct the Ascendent (on the 1st house side of the angle) or the Midheaven (on the 9th house side) are particularly potent indicators of *pranamaya kosha* emphasis. Any of these planets conjunct the North Node, featured as a singleton planet in a masculine sign and/or odd-numbered house, or at the apex of some planetary pattern in a masculine sign and/or odd-numbered house, also provides a point of entry to *pranamaya kosha*.

If the fire element is not emphasized in the natal chart, it can be triggered by progression or transit, producing periods in an individual life when the gateway to *pranamaya kosha* is wider than usual. Progressed Sun or Mars or transiting Sun, Mars or Jupiter, moving through a masculine sign or odd-numbered house can temporarily open the gate to this *kosha*, as can a conjunction of any of these temporal factors to the North Node, or any aspect of transiting Uranus or Pluto (in a masculine sign or odd-numbered house) to a natal *yang* Mars, Sun and/or Jupiter or the midpoints between them. A New Moon or lunar eclipse that takes place in a masculine sign or odd-numbered house, especially when it aspects Mars, the Sun or Jupiter, can also be a point of entry into *pranamaya kosha*, as can any station of transiting Mars or Jupiter – retrograde or direct – in a masculine sign or odd-numbered house.

The Astro-logic of Manomaya Kosha

Manomaya kosha shares the nature of the water element, as within their respective systems, both are where the psychology of core issues tends to get worked out. Water governs what happens on the emotional level of our lives – it is where the endocrine system of the body is triggered by some response on the emotional level; where our unresolved issues govern our behavior on an unconscious level; where imagination and fantasy color our image of the world; where we enter the murky alchemical waters of sexual and emotional intimacy with others, as well as mystical intimacy with Spirit; where we engage our creative and procreative fertility; and where we must surrender to mysterious forces beyond our conscious control. Because water is fluid, adaptable, solvent and reflective, it governs our experiences of intimate relationship, the level of emotional investment we have in our lives, and our connection to the unfathomable mysteries that lie beyond the reach of our rational minds. As a point of entry into the realm of *manomaya kosha*, water allows us to engage life on the level at which our core issues simultaneously block and serve as catalysts for the awakening of the soul.

Astrologically, we can tell that we are dealing on the level of *manomaya kosha* wherever water is strong in a given *chakra* chart. Whenever a planet involved in a *chakra* chart signature is in a water house (4, 8, or 12), or a water sign (Cancer, Scorpio or Pisces), *manomaya kosha* is being emphasized. The natural rulers of these signs – the Moon, Mars and Jupiter – and their co-rulers – Pluto and Neptune – can strongly indicate *manomaya kosha* when they are in a feminine sign or even-numbered house, and stronger yet when these planets are conjunct, sextile or trine each other. Any of these planets conjunct the Ascendant (on the 12th house side of the angle) or the Nadir (on the 4th house side) are particularly potent indicators of *manomaya kosha* emphasis. Any of these planets conjunct the South Node, featured as a singleton planet in a feminine sign and/or even-numbered house, or at the apex of some planetary pattern in a feminine sign and/or even-numbered house also provides a point of entry to *manomaya kosha*.

If the water element is not emphasized in the natal chart, it can be triggered by progression or transit, producing periods in an individual life when the gateway to *manomaya kosha* is wider than usual. Progressed Moon or Mars, or transiting Moon, Mars, Jupiter, Neptune or Pluto moving through a feminine sign or even-numbered house can temporarily open the gate to this *kosha*, as can a conjunction of any of these temporal factors to the South Node, or any aspect of transiting Neptune or Pluto (in a feminine sign or even-numbered house) to the natal Moon, Neptune, *yin* Mars, *yin* Jupiter, and *yin* Pluto or the midpoints between them. A Full Moon or solar eclipse that takes place in a feminine sign or even-numbered house, especially when it conjuncts Moon, *yin* Mars, *yin* Jupiter, Neptune or *yin* Pluto, can also be a point of entry into *manomaya kosha*, as can any station of transiting Mars, Jupiter, Neptune or Pluto – retrograde or direct – in a feminine sign or even-numbered house.

The Astro-logic of Vijnanamaya Kosha

Vijnanamaya kosha is like the air element in that both are involved in the generation of the image that we project into the embodied world. Astrologically, air is associated with all matters related to thought, ideas, belief, communication, education, social exchange and human commerce. The qualities of air – extreme mutability, interconnectiveness, transparency, and insubstantiality – are well suited to the process by which fleeting impressions and the constant influx of information contribute to the formation of our worldview as it is revealed to and through us on the level of *vijnanamaya kosha*.

Since *vijnanamaya kosha* is a matter of attunement to the symbolic realm, however, it is also somewhat watery in nature, since nothing becomes symbolic without reaching down into the irrational depths of the unconscious, governed by water. For this reason, a true activation of any *chakra* on this level requires the juxtaposition of air and water – that is to say, the alchemical tension formed by this disparate combination. If air is missing, we are most likely dealing with a situation manifest at the level of *manomaya kosha*. If water is missing, it must be supplied by transit or progression before a true opening to *vijnanamaya kosha* can occur. Natal Mercury in Gemini in the 3rd house, for example, would provide only a potential opening to *vijnanamaya kosha*, while any Neptune transit to this Mercury would activate the potential.

Astrologically, air is emphasized whenever a planet involved in a *chakra* chart signature is in an air house (3, 7 or 11), or an air sign (Gemini, Libra or Aquarius). *Vijnanamaya kosha* is emphasized whenever a planet involved in a *chakra* signature chart is in an air house and a water sign, or vice versa – the latter being a somewhat stronger indication. The planet Uranus (always an air planet) will create an opening to *vijnanamaya kosha* when placed in any water sign or house, while the Moon or Neptune (always water planets) will do the same in any air sign or house.

Since the natural rulers of the air signs – Mercury, Venus and Saturn – become earth planets in water signs or houses, they do not provide openings to *vijnanamaya kosha* when so-placed. Conversely, Mars, Jupiter and Pluto become fire planets in air signs or houses, and as such, provide openings to *pranamaya kosha* in these positions. An opening to *vijnanamaya kosha* does occur when any air planet – Uranus and *yang* Mercury, Venus or Saturn – aspects a water planet – Moon, Neptune and *yin* Mars, Jupiter or Pluto.

Any air planet conjunct the Ascendant (on the 12th house side of the angle) or the Nadir (on the 4th house side), or any water planet conjunct the Descendant (on the 7th house side) or the Nadir (on the 3rd house side) create strong *vijnanamaya kosha* emphasis, particularly when an aspect is involved – e.g, Mercury in Libra in the 12th house square Jupiter in Capricorn in the 3rd house. An air planet featured as a singleton planet in a water sign and/or house, or water planet singleton in an air sign and/or house; an air planet at the apex of some planetary pattern emphasizing water, or a water planet at the apex of some planetary pattern emphasizing air also provide points of entry to *vijnanamaya kosha*.

If the air-water combination is not emphasized in the natal chart, it can be triggered by progression or transit, producing periods in an individual life when the gateway to *vijnanamaya kosha* is wider than usual. Progressed Mercury or Venus or transiting Mercury, Venus, or Saturn in a masculine sign moving through a water house can temporarily open the gate to this *kosha*, as can progressed Mars or transiting Mars, Jupiter or Pluto moving through a feminine sign in an air house. Progressed Moon or transiting Moon or Neptune moving through an air sign or house, or transiting Uranus moving through a water sign or house can also create an opening to this *kosha*.

A solar eclipse that takes place in an air sign or house can be a point of entry into *vijnanamaya kosha*, especially when it conjuncts an air planet, as can any direct or retrograde station of Uranus in a water sign or house, or Neptune in an air sign or house.

The Astro-logic of Anandamaya Kosha

Within the fusion of disparate elements air and water is born the symbolic dimension of experience, where a literal interpretation of reality gives way to a multidimensional range of symbolic implications for creative participation in the embodied life. At the level of *anandamaya kosha*, the alchemical fusion of the other three disparate combinations – earth and fire, earth and air, or fire and water – reflects an opportunity for the final penetration of Spirit through whatever illusory barriers of separation keep us from fully inhabiting this entire multidimensional range. If the demands of the disparate elements can be reconciled, the soul will move toward a closer identification with the Source out of which the soul arises. If the soul is ready, the possibility exists that the illusory barrier between soul and Spirit will collapse completely, triggering an experience of true spiritual awakening. The juxtaposition of disparate elements associated with *anandamaya kosha* is no guarantee that this degree of penetration will be achieved by the soul, but it does often present a compelling invitation to explore the potential for it.

The juxtaposition of earth and air most closely mirrors the predicament of the soul, which as we explored in some depth in *The Seven Gates of Soul* is an alchemical union of Spirit (as consciousness) and matter (within the physical body). When earth and air are juxtaposed in the bithchart, it will extend an invitation to the soul to become more aware of the spiritual implications of everyday life, or conversely to anchor some spiritual vision, awareness, or recognition of truth on solid ground. As one attempts to do this, one inhabits the life of the soul with greater awareness and clarity of intention.

The juxtaposition of earth and fire mirrors the primary task of alchemy itself – to turn base matter (that which is unconscious, symbolized by lead) into a purified substance (that which is fully conscious, symbolized by gold). As Jung points out, most alchemists were operating under the Platonic belief that Spirit was imprisoned in matter, and needed to be set free before the necessary purification could take place (Psychology and Alchemy 299-300). My view, as outlined in detail in *The Seven Gates of Soul* is somewhat different – namely that it is our task is not to free Spirit *from* matter, but to awaken Spirit *within* matter. Be that substantial difference as it may, either view requires a purification process symbolized by the juxtaposition of earth and fire. Fire is potentially an agent of purification; earth is any situation where the soul remains unaware of the presence of Spirit within it. Purification in this sense, means burning away whatever veils of illusion and healing whatever wounds keep one separate from Spirit.

The third alchemical challenge – posed by the juxtaposition of water and fire – speaks to the apparent duality at the very heart of the embodied world, between light and dark, male and female, hot and cold, life and death, and the quest for balance in relation to each of these polarities. As suggested throughout this book and *The Seven Gates of Soul*, spiritual growth is largely a matter of identifying with the Tao that is neither one side nor the other, but both together in synergistic harmony. Where this place of optimal balance lies will vary from situation to situation and from moment to moment, but the art of finding that balance and living is the path to enlightenment – itself a fusion of opposites:

the embodied soul and bodiless Spirit. In any chart where a juxtaposition of fire and water exists, there will be alchemical pressure toward this place of optimal balance in relation to some polarity within which the soul identifies too strongly with one side or the other. Put another way, wherever fire and water work together in a birthchart, there will be a gradual transition from the resonance by affinity that leads to excess and deficiency to the resonance by contrast through which balance is restored.

The simplest possible opening to *anandamaya kosha* exists in a birthchart when a planet associated with one element is placed in a sign or house associated with the second element of each alchemical pair. When Venus, Mercury or Saturn, for example, are placed in either a feminine sign (normally making them earth planets) and an odd-numbered house (normally making them air planets), there is an internal alchemical tension between earth and air that produces an opening to *anandamaya kosha*.

When these same planets are placed in a fire sign (normally making them air planets) but also in an earth house (normally making them earth planets), we have a similar alchemical tension. Venus, Mercury, and Saturn placed in air signs will produce an opening to *anandamaya kosha* when placed in earth houses, but will tend to produce an opening to *vijnanamaya kosha* instead when placed in water houses. When Uranus (an air planet) is placed in an earth sign or house, there is a similar alchemical tension (born of the juxtaposition of air and earth), which provides an opening to *anandamaya kosha*. Uranus in a water sign or house will produce an opening to *vijnanamaya kosha*.

By a similar line of astro-logical reasoning, when Mars, Jupiter or Pluto sit in a masculine sign (normally making them fire planets), but also in an even-numbered house (normally making them water planets), we have a different alchemical opening to *anandamaya kosha* – through fire and earth, or fire and water. Alternately, Mars, Jupiter or Pluto in a feminine sign (normally making them water planets), but also in a fire house (normally making them fire planets), would produce the same effect. Mars, Jupiter, or Pluto in a feminine sign (as water planets) in an air house would produce an opening to *vijnanamaya kosha*.

The Sun – always a fire planet – does not become a water planet when placed in a feminine sign or even-numbered house. Nonetheless, these placements do produce alchemical tension and an opening to *anandamaya kosha*, since the Sun is compelled to function in a context that is quite foreign to its nature. The Sun in a masculine sign or odd-numbered house experiences an enhancement of its fiery nature, and produces a stronger opening to *pranamaya kosha*.

The Moon and Neptune – water planets regardless of placement – will produce an opening to *anandamaya kosha* when placed in fire signs or houses. The Moon and Neptune in air signs or houses will tend to produce an opening to *vijnanamaya kosha*.

When these planets are placed in feminine signs or even-numbered houses, they will experience an intensification of their watery natures and produce a stronger opening to *manomaya kosha*.

Uranus – an air planet regardless of placement – will produce the requisite alchemical tension when placed in earth signs or houses. Uranus in a fire sign or house will produce an opening to *pranamaya kosha*, while Uranus in a water sign or house will produce an opening to *vijnanamaya kosha*. Uranus in an air sign or house will simply contribute air, often in excess, to any other aspect or planetary pattern in which it is involved. It will also serve as a latent trigger to *vijnanamaya kosha*, awaiting the proper progression or transit (from a water planet) to actualize its potential.

Proximity to the angles of the chart will add alchemical potency to the opening of *anandamaya kosha*, especially on the disparate side of the angle – e.g. Mercury in a feminine sign on the 1st house side of the Ascendant; Mars in a masculine sign on the 4th house side of the Nadir; Saturn in a feminine sign on the 7th house side of the Descendant.

Simple planetary placements are usually insufficient in and of themselves to precipitate a very potent opening to *anandamaya kosha*, but become much more significant when they aspect other planets providing the same opening. Squares between planets showing some potential for the requisite alchemical tension are especially powerful indicators of compounded emphasis on *anandamaya kosha*. Modern psychological astrology recognizes the square to be a primary catalyst for spiritual growth, as well as to the core issues that must be addressed for growth to occur. Within the astrological model of consciousness presented here, we can see that this is so, because squares exist by definition between placements that span the disparate elemental combinations associated with an opening to the deeper *koshas*.

Normally (unless out of sign) a planet in an air sign or house will be square to a planet in either a water sign or house (producing an opening to *vijnanamaya kosha*) or a planet in an earth sign or house (producing an opening to *anandamaya kosha*). A planet in a fire sign or house will normally be square to a planet in either an earth or water sign or house (producing an opening to *anandamaya kosha*). Likewise, a planet in an earth sign or house will usually square a planet in a fire or air sign or house, while a planet in a water sign or house will usually square a planet in an air or fire sign or house. Any square (unless it is out of sign) will thus provide an opening to either *vijnanamaya* or *anandamaya kosha*, and pose a potential opportunity for deepest possible penetration of Spirit into the embodied life.

Squares are especially potent openings to these deeper *koshas* when both planets harbor an inherent alchemical tension related to the *kosha* in question. The Moon in

Gemini (a disparate juxtaposition of water and air) in the 3rd house (an air placement), for example, square Uranus in Pisces (a disparate juxtaposition of air and water) in the 12th house (also a disparate juxtaposition of air and water) would produce an especially potent opening to *vijnanamaya kosha*. Mars in Cancer (making a water planet) in the 11th house (making Mars a fire planet) square Jupiter in Aries (making Jupiter a fire planet) in the 8th house (making Jupiter a water planet) would produce a formidable opening to *anandamaya kosha*.

Semi-sextiles and quincunxes also generally take place between disparate elements. T-squares and grand crosses can greatly expand and deepen these openings, as can finger of God configurations, which by definition involve two quincunxes, or disparate patterns where one planet sits at the midpoint of two other planets sextile (in harmony) to each other.

Any fire planet conjunct the South Node opposed any *yin* planet conjunct the North Node will provide a higher potency alchemical opening to *anandamaya kosha*. So will a planet of one elemental disposition featured as a singleton planet in a sign and/or house of some disparate disposition; or a planet of one elemental disposition at the apex of some planetary pattern emphasizing some disparate disposition – e.g., Mercury in Gemini (air) at the apex of a t-square with Venus in Virgo (earth) opposed Saturn in Pisces (earth).

If the requisite disparate combination is not emphasized in the natal chart, it can be triggered by progression or transit, producing periods in an individual life when the gateway to *anandamaya kosha* is wider than usual. Progressed Mercury or Venus or transiting Mercury, Venus, or Saturn in a masculine sign moving through an earth house or in an earth sign moving through an air house can temporarily open the gate to this *kosha*, as can progressed Moon or transiting Moon or Neptune moving through a fire sign or house. Progressed Sun or Mars, and transiting Sun, Mars, Jupiter or Pluto can also produce an opening to *anandamaya kosha* moving through a fire sign in an even-numbered house, as can progressed Mars or transiting Mars, Jupiter or Pluto moving through a feminine sign in a fire house.

A conjunction of any of these temporal factors to the lunar node of disparate polarity (fire planet to South Node or feminine planet to North Node), or of any transiting transpersonal planet to a planet of appropriate disparity – e.g. transiting Neptune (water) to a *yang* Sun (fire); or to the natal midpoints between two such planets – e.g., transiting Uranus (air) to the midpoint of Venus in Virgo (earth) and Saturn in Gemini (air); or transiting Pluto in the 5th house (fire) to the midpoint of Mars in the 2nd house (water) and the Sun in the 9th (fire) – can temporarily provide the necessary elemental tension. Any lunation or eclipse taking place in the fire or water sign or house of opposite polarity can be a point of entry into *anandamaya kosha* (especially a lunar eclipse (fire) in a feminine sign or even-numbered house or a solar eclipse (water) in a fire sign or house. Direct or retrograde stations; progressed or transiting air planets in earth houses, earth planets in odd-numbered houses, water planets in fire houses, or fire planets in even-numbered houses can also produce the requisite alchemical tension.

Obviously these rules can get quite complex, although at their core is a simple understanding of the way elements combine. With a careful analysis of the juxtaposition of elements within a given birthchart, the various openings within the birthchart to each of the five *koshas* should easily become clear. For those who would like the application of the most important of these rules spelled out for them, please see the Appendices. In the next chapter, I will demonstrate how these rules might be applied to a number of sample charts.

Endnotes

[1] Although a New Moon is fiery by nature (Sun dominating Moon), a solar eclipse (occurring at the New Moon) is watery, because the Moon appears to block the Sun, and is thus temporarily dominant. Likewise, although a Full Moon is watery by nature (Moon dominating Sun), a lunar eclipse (occurring at Full Moon) is fiery, because the Earth's penumbra casts the Moon in shadow, leaving the Sun temporarily dominant.

Chapter Ten
Case Studies Illustrating
the Astro-logic of the Koshas

The preceding principles of astro-logic are not meant to be hard and fast rules, but rather a perceptual framework through which it might be possible to see the evolution of consciousness within the context of everyday life. Such information is generally missing from astrological analysis, when the astrologer merely assumes it, and then projects her own consciousness onto the symbolism being interpreted, The astro-logic of consciousness, as it is being presented in this book, is meant to recognize the multidimensional nature of the symbolism, and then map those dimensions as a prelude to approaching the symbolism itself.

Because consciousness is ultimately what each of us brings to our chart – and not something inherent to the symbolism itself – it can only be fully assessed through reference to our actual life experience. Applying the exoteric astro-logic of consciousness to a birthchart, we can see the tracks on which the train will run, but it is the train itself that is of interest. In this chapter, we will use the principles outlined in the preceding chapter to practice identifying tracks, with minimal reference to the train itself. In subsequent case studies for each *chakra*, later in this part of the book, we will look much more closely at how the train negotiates the tracks it has been given.

The sample charts presented in this chapter will reference only the astro-logic of the five *koshas*. It is important for the student to assimilate this material, before moving on to the more complex analysis of core issues as they are played out within the framework of consciousness posed by the *chakra* system.

It is also important to note before presenting these sample charts that rarely, if at all, is there a birthchart that does not represent a multifaceted mix of elements, and therefore of the *koshas* on which they depend. Life is always lived at every level, consciously or unconsciously, and often it is the mix of *koshas* that makes a given experience, or a life taken as a whole, the intriguing exercise in penetration of Spirit into the embodied life that it is. The sample charts in this chapter are chosen for their clear presentation of a given *kosha*, realizing that such clarity will typically be the exception, rather than the rule. Where relevant, I will also show how various *koshas* interpenetrate when implicated in the same planetary pattern.

Annamaya Kosha

Our first sample chart, representative of a strong signature for activation of *annamaya kosha*, is that of James Dean, a popular actor in the 50s and early 60s, known for his bad-boy persona as displayed in his three films: "Rebel Without a Cause," "Giant," and "East of Eden." His brilliant, but short-lived career was an inspiration to many other artists, actors and musicians, who considered him a seminal influence. Among actors, he was known for his ability to enter a part so completely, he became the character he was portraying. Said Dennis Hopper of his talent, "Jimmy was not only an internal actor, but an expressionist, which came partly from his studying dance. He would physicalize actions, such as the way he lifted himself up on the windmill in Giant, or goose-stepped measuring off the land, or his sleight-of-hand gesture as Jeff Rink." Dean died in a car crash and became a cult hero to an entire generation of rebellious youth.

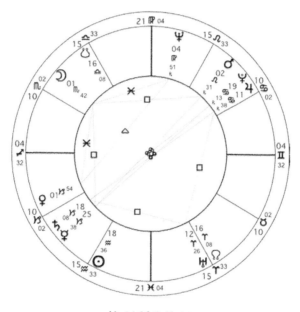

JAMES DEAN

What makes Dean's chart a strong trigger for *annamaya kosha* is the placement of all three earth planets – Venus, Mercury and Saturn – in the same earth sign. Two of these – Saturn and Mercury – are loosely conjunct in the earthy 2nd house. Saturn opposes a watery Jupiter/Pluto in the 8th house, while Mercury opposes only Pluto. The Saturn-Jupiter opposition adds strength to the signature for *annamaya kosha* (Saturn – earth placement; Jupiter - water placement; Saturn (slower moving planet) is dominant; water supports earth = *annamaya kosha*).

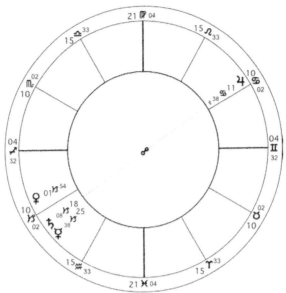

JAMES DEAN'S ANNAMAYA KOSHA CHART

Saturn/Mercury-Pluto acts as an opening to *manomaya kosha* (Saturn/Mercury – earth placement; Pluto - water placement; Pluto (slower moving planet) is dominant; earth supports water = *manomaya kosha*). Both ends of this opposition square Uranus in the 4th house (an air-water placement), triggering *vijnanamaya kosha*, and accounting for Dean's status as a cultural icon, a living symbol onto whom we have collectively projected our archetypal image of The Rebel. This opening to *vijnanamaya kosha* and Dean's role as cultural icon are both underscored by Uranus' conjunction to his fiery North Node (in Aries in the 5th house).

The second *annamaya kosha* chart belongs to Louis Pasteur, 19th century founder of microbiology, developer of the purification process that bears his name. and a man of many tangible achievements, despite being paralyzed by a stroke at age 46.

Again we see all three earth planets in earth signs, in this case forming a trine to each other, spanning the 3rd and 7th air houses. The fact that Mercury and Venus not only conjunct each other, but also participate in a six-planet earth stellium greatly enhances the potency of this opening to *annamaya kosha* (see chart on page 142), while the juxtaposition of earth and air creates a concurrent opening to *anandamaya kosha* that perhaps reflects the way Pasteur greatly advanced our collective understanding of matters related to life and death - mysteries at the very heart of Spirit's presence within the embodied world.

JAMES DEAN'S VIJNANAMAYA KOSHA SIGNATURE

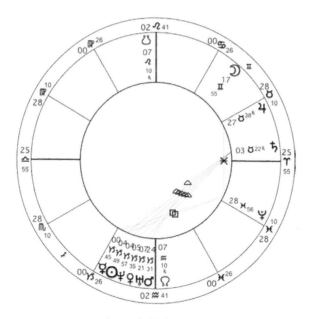

LOUIS PASTEUR

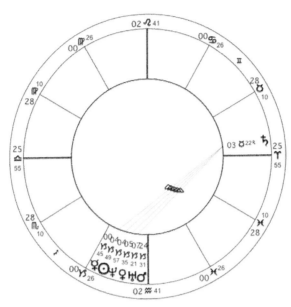

LOUIS PASTEUR'S ANNAMAYA KOSHA CHART

The last *annamaya* chart I wish to share is that of my ex-partner, described in Chapter Two as a creature of chaos, living "in a house that is filled with stacks of unopened boxes, too much furniture and a menagerie of pets constantly pooping, shedding, and chewing on the woodwork."

As with James Dean, all three earth planets are in the same earth sign. Venus and Saturn are in the watery 4th house, a supportive placement for emphasis on earth. In addition, their association with *annamaya kosha* is strengthened by Venus' proximity to the Nadir and Mercury's conjunction to the South Node.

Mercury's placement in the airy 3rd house provides an opening to *anandamaya kosha* (through the juxtaposition of earth and air), suggesting that underlying the relatively external *annamaya* task of bringing order to the chaos within the home is a deeper issue, the resolution of which promises to a major stepping stone on her spiritual path. Meanwhile the sextile between Mercury and Uranus in the 12th conjunct the Ascendant (a strong air-water combination) provides an opening to *vijnanamaya kosha* (see chart on page 144), which is where I am drawn to project my image of her as a dancing star (the epitome of Nietschze's quote – see page 40).

MY EX-PARTNER'S CHART

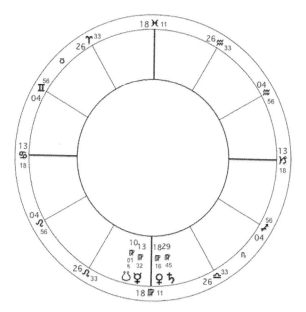

MY EX-PARTNER'S ANNAMAYA KOSHA CHART

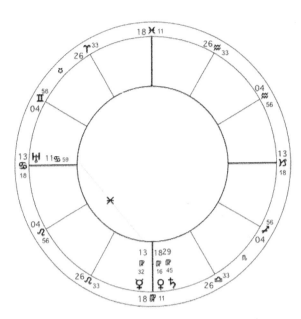

MY EX-PARTNER'S VIJNANAMAYA KOSHA SIGNATURE

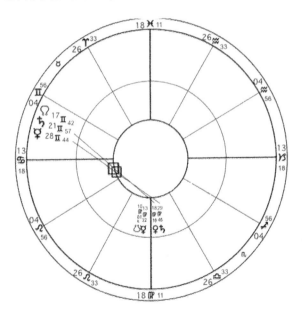

FLOOD TRANSITS TO MY EX-PARTNER'S ANNAMAYA KOSHA CHART

A traditional astrologer would look at this stripped down configuration and yawn, since it does not represent anything particularly noteworthy. As a lens through which to view my ex-partner's embodied life, on the level of *annamaya kosha*, however, it is capable of revealing a great deal. In July, 2002, for example, there was noteworthy flooding in the town where we lived at the time, that destroyed a large storage unit of her possessions, which we sorted through for salvage and then carted – much to my chagrin – to our backyard. Using the guidelines offered by traditional astrology, one would suspect a Neptune transit to the 2nd house, or at the very least to this constellation of earth planets clustered around the Nadir. Instead, there was a relatively innocuous triggering of these earth planets by the same planets – Saturn and Mercury – but now in Gemini in the 12th house, where conjunct the North Node they represented a juxtaposition of air and water, or an opening to *vijnanamaya kosha*. The flood was nothing if not a symbolic outworking of the fears and the attachments that made this inconspicuous nest of *annamaya kosha* planets a potential viper's den. While the spread of planets might seem a bit wide, the midpoints of the natal configuration (including South Node) and the transiting triggers (including North Node) were less than 2 degrees apart.

Pranamaya Kosha

Our first *pranamaya kosha* chart is that of popular creative homemaker, marketing mogul, and recent temporary inmate Martha Stewart (see natal chart on page 146), who is known for her tireless energy channeled into an ever-evolving panoply of projects, large and small.

The *pranamaya kosha* signature in this chart (on page 146) is formed by fire planets Sun and Pluto conjunct in Leo in the fiery 9th house, near the Midheaven, trine to fiery can-do Mars in Aries, with fire planet Jupiter (in Gemini) at the apex of a wedge pattern with both ends. There's nothing complicated here, but there is obviously a great deal of energy which will naturally tend to manifest – from the soul's perspective – as Spirit penetrating to the level of the energy *kosha*. Jupiter's placement in a water house and Mars placement in an earth house offer modest openings to *anandamaya kosha*.

The next *pranamaya* chart belongs to well-known mythologist, Joseph Campbell (on page 147), whose oft-repeated admonition to "follow your bliss" has become the battle cry for spiritual seekers everywhere. Within the context of our discussion here, it should not be hard to hear this as a recipe for activation of consciousness at the level of *pranamaya kosha*. Campbell was perhaps best known for his landmark book, *The Hero With a Thousand Faces*, with the archetype of the hero being central to the elemental dynamic of fire and of *pranayama kosha*.

MARTHA STEWART

MARTHA STEWART'S PRANAMAYA KOSHA CHART

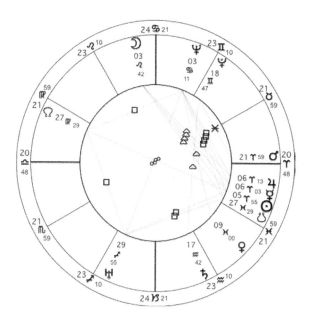

JOSEPH CAMPBELL

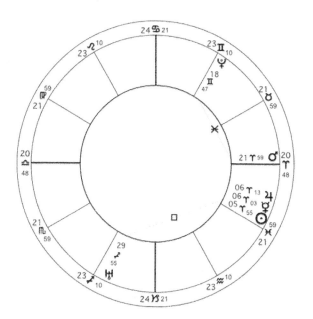

JOSEPH CAMPBELL'S PRANAMAYA KOSHA CHART

◇◇◇

Here the signature for *pranamaya kosha* is presented by Campbell's Aries stellium near the Descendant, including all three fire planets – Mars, Sun and Jupiter. Sun and Jupiter are conjunct within a degree, and Mars is especially powerful in its position conjunct the Desendant, in the airy 7th house, sextile fire planet, Pluto in the watery 8th. Mercury (an air planet) in the midst of this stellium, adds supportive fuel to the fire of the *pranamaya kosha* signature, as does the out-of-sign square from air planet Uranus in a fire sign and an air house.

The juxtaposition of fire and water in the 8th (Pluto in a masculine sign and even-numbered house), and fire and earth in the 6th (Jupiter and the Sun in a masculine sign and an even-numbered house) provides an opening within this signature to *anandamaya kosha* – which according to *yogic* tradition, is where Campbell's bliss is to be found, and where Campbell himself is empowered to live a life of deepest possible connection to Spirit. Certainly, if his prodigious writings are any indication, he is privy to secret knowledge about the inner workings of Spirit within the human psyche and the embodied life of the soul. We will take a closer look at Campbell's chart in relation to his life when we explore the fifth *chakra*.

As a last illustration of *pranamaya kosha*, we have Richard Speck, a 24-year-old sailor, who murdered eight student nurses in 1966.

RICHARD SPECK

In this chart, the signature for *pranamaya kosha* is a tight half-kite pattern formed by all three fire planets – Mars in Aries in the supportive air environment of the 7th house sextile to Jupiter (as a fire planet in Gemini) in the fiery 9th house opposed the Sun in Sagittarius in the supportive airy 3rd house trine Mars. Furthermore, this entire pattern is underscored in bold red letters because its backbone (the fiery Jupiter-Sun opposition forms a grand cross with the nodal axis. Pluto also functions as a fire planet here (in Leo in the airy 11th house, and is trine the Sun, although too far out of orb to a trine to Mars to complete what is almost a grand trine in fire – a pre-eminent *pranamaya kosha* signature, especially when formed by fire planets in odd-numbered houses.

RICHARD SPECK'S PRANAMAYA KOSHA CHART

Obviously what Speck chose to do with his opening to *pranamaya kosha* was very different than the path taken by Campbell and Stewart. I would note here only that these other examples had openings to the deeper *koshas* tied to their *pranamaya kosha* signatures – Campbell through the placement of fiery Pluto in the watery 8th and fiery Sun/Jupiter in the earthy 6th, and Stewart through the placement of Jupiter in the watery 8th. There are no such mitigating factors in Speck's chart, and thus ultimately no clear pathway to a deeper penetration of Spirit with regard to the use of this energy. This is not to say that Speck could not have chosen differently, but that the tracks upon which these deeper *koshas* could have been accessed were not there. Fire is the most difficult of all elements to channel consciously, and when it is not, it can and does become destructive.

Manomaya Kosha

Manomaya kosha, emphasizing the element of water – with its association to creativity, sexuality, and psychological complexity – is naturally a dimension of being that shows strength among many artists, musicians and writers drawn to explore the interface between psyche and art, in the broadest sense of that term. Not every artist will exhibit an affinity for this *kosha*, but of those that do, there will tend to be a certain psychological intensity that is both compelling and potentially overwhelming in its intensity. Among such artists are Nirvana's lead signer/songwriter Kurt Cobain. Cobain was one of the pioneers of the Seattle-based grunge rock revolution of the 1990s, and spokesperson for a generation of angst-ridden teenagers. Tragically, he committed suicide at the very beginning of what was promising to be a stellar career.

KURT COBAIN

Cobain's chart displays a remarkable water kite, involving all 10 planets, with water planet Pluto conjunct the Ascendant. I include Mars and the Sun in this pattern, even though they are too far out of orb to be direct participants, because the Sun is part of a Pisces stellium that contributes to the pattern, and Mars in Scorpio in the 2nd house is a strong water placement. Mars and Neptune straddle the South Node, further reinforcing water. Moon and Jupiter are in Cancer; the Moon is in an earth house, which likewise reinforces water. Water planets Jupiter and Neptune form the wedge portion of Cobain's water kite with Pluto.

Water planet Pluto's conjunction to air planet Uranus in a house that supports air produces an opening to *vijnanamaya kosha*, as does Neptune's placement in the airy 3rd house, sextile Uranus. The presence of three earth planets in the airy 7th house at the heavy end of Cobain's water kite provides an opening to *anandamaya kosha* through the juxtaposition of earth and air, while the square between his Pisces 6th house Sun and Neptune provides an additional opening to *anandamaya kosha* through the juxtaposition of fire and water. The Sun itself offers a complex opening to *anandamaya kosha* through its placement in Pisces (juxtaposition of fire and water) and the 6th house (fire and earth), as well as its tight trine to Mars (fire and water). Nothing is wasted in this chart. Everything contributes either to the predominant *manomaya* signature or to an opening to one of the deeper *koshas* through which the creative psychological energy generated at *manomaya kosha* could potentially be released. In Cobain's case, however, the intensity of this complex, richly interpenetrated pattern unfortunately proved too much for him to bear.

A much simpler *manomaya kosha* signature can be found in the chart of beat poet Allen Ginsberg, noted for his raging anti-establishment polemics. Ginsberg also had a mystical side, more typical of the watery realm of *manomaya kosha*, and was institutionalized for 8 months after a psychotic episode in 1948.

ALLEN GINSBERG

The signature for *manomaya kosha* is formed in Ginsberg's chart by the placement of water planets Moon and Mars in Pisces in the watery 12th house. Mars is conjunct the Ascendant, while the Moon is trine water planet Pluto in the watery 4th house.

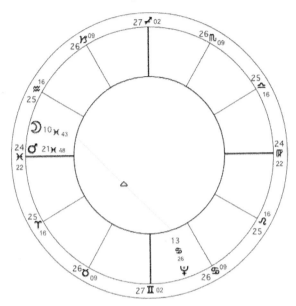

ALLEN GINSBERG'S MANOMAYA KOSHA CHART

Pluto's conjunction to the North Node provides additional emphasis, as well as an opening to *anandamaya* and *vijnanamaya koshas* through the juxtaposition of fire/air and water. Fiery Jupiter in the watery 12th house opposed water planet Neptune creates an additional opening to *anandamaya kosha*, while Uranus, loosely conjunct Mars/Ascendant in Pisces, provides an additional opening to *vijnanamaya kosha* through its placement in Pisces (air planet in a water sign).

Our last *manomaya kosha* chart belongs to Nancy Reagan, wife of former president Ronald Reagan, best known in her own right for her "Just Say No" campaign against drugs. As we will see, Nancy Reagan's chart also provides a potent opening to *vijnanamaya kosha*. Historically, drugs have been a watery link between the emotional/psychological domain of *manomaya kosha* and the symbolic realm of *vijnanamaya kosha*. The fact that Nancy Reagan spoke so vehemently against drugs, while functioning within the context of a chart in which a poet like Allen Ginsberg or a musician like Kurt Cobain might have found a beckoning haven, perhaps speaks to the fact that the chart alone cannot reveal how it will be used, or the choices that will be made in the face of the internal pressures it represents.

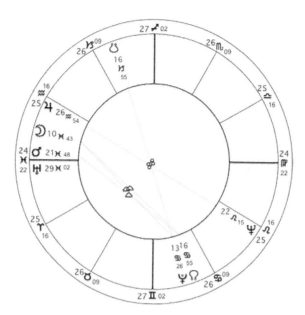

ALLEN GINSBERG'S VIJNANAMAYA & ANANDAMAYA KOSHA SIGNATURES

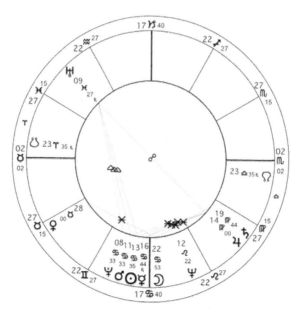

NANCY REAGAN

153

◇◇◇

The intention that forms at the heart of the psychology of *manomaya kosha* can just as easily form around resistance to the opening, as it can to the opening itself. While it would be presumptuous of me to suggest which was true in Nancy Reagan's case, it is clear that her relationship to the strong *manomaya kosha* signature in her chart stands in strong contrast to that within the charts of Cobain, Ginsburg, and many of her other *manomaya kosha* chart compadres – including Miles Davis, Eric Clapton and Jimi Hendrix – for whom drugs were a two-edged catalyst to the deeper exploration of the potentials within their patterns.

The *manomaya kosha* pattern in Nancy Reagan's chart begins with a Cancer stellium straddling the watery Nadir that includes water planets Pluto, Mars and Moon with her Moon in the watery 4th house. A watery Mars sextile a watery Jupiter then completes the pattern.

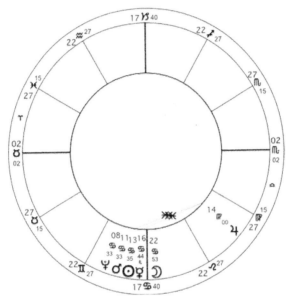

NANCY REAGAN'S MANOMAYA KOSHA CHART

Jupiter in turn opposes airy Uranus in Pisces, which then trines most of the planets in the Cancer stellium. The opening to *vijnanamaya kosha* mentioned earlier comes through Uranus in the 11th house (air) in Pisces (water) trine the Cancer stellium (water), most of which sits in the airy 3rd house. This *vijnanamaya* signature provides a astrological reflection of the power of her anti-drug slogan to lodge itself in the collective consciousness as a symbol of the shifting cultural tides of the 1980s.

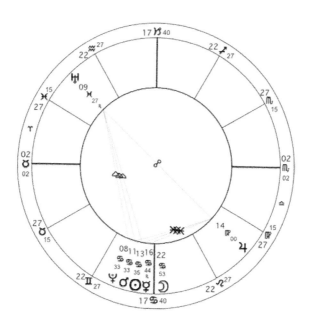

NANCY REAGAN'S VIJNANAMAYA KOSHA SIGNATURE

Vijnanamaya Kosha

Nancy Reagan's status as a representative of *manomaya kosha*, as well as *vijnanamaya kosha* underscores the importance of approaching an interpretation of any astrological signature with an open mind and as few preconceived notions as possible. It is tempting to say, for example, that since *manomaya kosha* governs the psychological realm where core issues arise and are addressed, psychologists as a class are likely to exhibit a strong signature for *manomaya kosha* in their charts; or that since artists as a rule deal with symbolism in their work, they ought to display an astrological affinity for *vijnanamaya kosha*. In practice, such statements get in the way of discovering how and why these various openings exist, and more importantly, how they are approached in actual experience by those whose charts suggest them. For answers to these deeper questions, we must look more explicitly to the actual life process of the person behind the chart, and it would be a mistake to make assumptions about the life in question with nothing more to guide us than blind reference to the chart alone.

Our purpose in using these charts of relatively famous people to illustrate the various possibilities for identification of one or more *koshas* is not to draw definitive conclusions about whose chart is likely to harbor what signature, but rather to explore the various ways in which each *kosha* might be represented. As we look at each *chakra* in more detail in the chapters to come, we will go more deeply into the lives behind the patterns to explore the dynamics involved. Here we merely want to gain some practice in pattern recognition.

Another illustration of *vijnanamaya kosha* is the chart of Isadora Duncan, a 19th century pioneer in the evolution of expressive dance, a woman whose every gesture on and off the stage was a broad stroke of flamboyant excess seeking expressive release. In addition to her remarkable career, Duncan had three children by three different lovers. Two were drowned, the other was stillborn. Her poet husband hanged himself, and she died in a freak accident in which her scarf got caught in the spokes of the wheel of her sports car. From the standpoint of *vijnanamaya kosha*, her life – in many ways larger than life – was a standing invitation to ask the deeper questions about meaning and purpose that define the life of the soul – for her, and for all of those who bore witness to her soul's journey.

ISADORA DUNCAN

Duncan's *vijnanamaya kosha* signature is formed by a dramatic grand cross, involving seven of ten planets. One of the two primary oppositions that define this pattern is formed between Moon in Scorpio in the 8th house and Pluto in Taurus in the 2nd, presenting an extremely strong expression of water which in turn is square to Uranus in Leo in the 5th house, a contrasting air placement. Uranus is opposed to Mars in Aquarius in the 11th house. This is technically a fire placement, but with Uranus the dominant planet within this opposition, and with Mars in an air sign and an air house, the aspect as a whole is decidedly airy. The air-water mix within this signature is amplified by the presence of air planets Mercury and Venus in Gemini adjacent to water planet Pluto in the second house. Air planet Mercury is within range of an opposition to water planet Moon, though out of sign. The Sun, while technically a fire planet, adds to the air through its participation in the Gemini stellium.

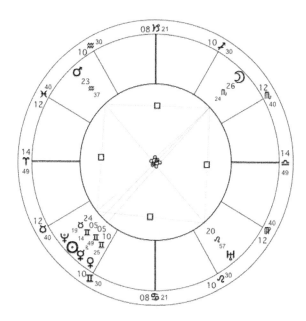

ISADORA DUNCAN'S VIJNANAMAYA KOSHA CHART

Our next example of a strong *vijnanamaya kosha* chart is Prince (on page 158), otherwise known as the Artist formerly known as Prince. Known for his erotic lyrics and stage presence, as well as his cutting edge mix of musical styles, Prince has gradually built a solid career as a post-rock era incarnation of Elvis Presley – not to imply that his music is at all reminiscent of Presley's, but rather that his persona and his art carried the same capacity to shock and push the envelope in the 1980s and 90s as Presley's did in the 50s and early 60s. Prince is also known for changing his name to a symbol in order to break a $100 million contract with Warner Brothers and regain his artistic freedom. With an unpronounceable symbol for a name, the Artist formerly known as Prince entered the realm of *vijnanamaya kosha* in a very graphic way.

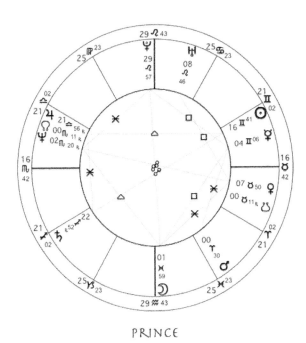

PRINCE

Prince's *vijnanamaya kosha* signature begins with an intensely watery Moon in Pisces conjunct the Nadir in the 4th house square to an intensely airy Mercury in Gemini in the 7th house. Mercury is loosely sextile Uranus, amplifying and intensifying air, while Uranus is loosely square a very watery Neptune in Scorpio in the 12th house conjunct the North Node (creating a water-air and water-fire juxtaposition). To complete this unusual circuit, watery Neptune is trine watery Moon.

Our last example of *vijnanamaya kosha* is the chart of acid-guru, and former Harvard psychology professor Timothy Leary. In contrast to Nancy Reagan's admonition to "Just Say No," Leary became the inspiration for an earlier generation's collective desire to "Tune In, Turn On, and Drop Out." Whereas the reaction to drugs on the level of *manomaya kosha* was oriented around their capacity to alleviate and at times to exacerbate the psychological intensity of the emotional realm, on the level of *vijnanamaya kosha* on which Leary and other pioneers of the drug culture explored them, they were an opening to altered states of consciousness and a deeper awareness of the symbolic and spiritual implications of everyday reality. Leary pursued this interest in various ways throughout his life – from his early immersion in cutting edge psychology, through the blatant experimentation with and promotion of LSD for which he is known, to his lesser known latter-day incarnation as an advocate of the use of electronic stimulation as a vehicle for consciousness expansion. Throughout all of this activity, he sought to open a wider channel of access to *vijnanamaya kosha* – both for himself and for the culture at large.

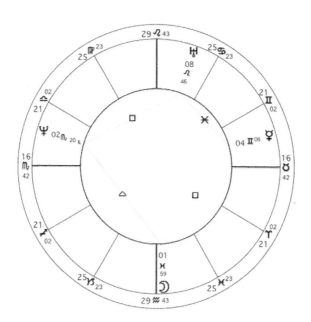

PRINCE'S VIJNANAMAYA KOSHA CHART

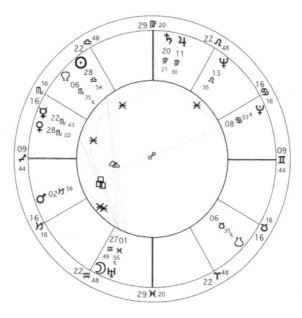

TIMOTHY LEARY

In contrast to Nancy Reagan, Isadora Duncan and Prince, Leary's *vijnanamaya kosha* signature is quite simple: Moon (water planet) in Aquarius in the 3rd house (air placement) conjunct Uranus (air planet) in Pisces (water placement) trine Sun in Libra in the 11th house (though technically still a fire planet, one that displays a strong air placement). Pluto in Cancer (a water planet) in the 7th house (air placement) loosely trines Uranus (air). Leary's chart is testimony to the fact that one need not have a dramatic chart to make optimal use of a given *kosha* signature.

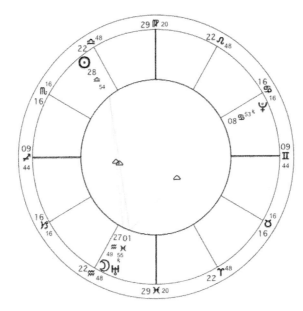

TIMOTHY LEARY'S VIJNANAMAYA KOSHA CHART

Anandamaya Kosha

While there was an opening in Leary's chart to go beyond *vijnanamaya kosha* into *anandamaya kosha* (mainly through his 9th house Jupiter/Saturn conjunction in Virgo (a watery Jupiter and an earthy Saturn in a fire house), Leary's sidekick, Richard Alpert (better known as Ram Dass) was a walking manifestation of *anandamaya kosha*. While Leary was still enamored of the possibilities of psychotropic drugs, Ram Dass' hunger for what he called the "crisp trip" - a total identification of the soul with Spirit - took him to India, through a deeper meditation practice, and into a life that has become a shared public teaching on every level he has experienced it.

Ram Dass' complex *annamaya kosha* pattern begins with a conjunction between a watery Jupiter in Cancer in the 12th house and a watery Pluto in Cancer in the fiery 1st house tightly conjunct the Ascendant. Pluto is opposed to an earthy Saturn in Capricorn in the airy 7th house. Both ends of this opposition in turn form a t-square with a tight Sun/Uranus conjunction in Aries conjunct the North Node (strong fire/air with air dominant) in an earth house. A second component of this signature occurs when earth planet Venus in Pisces in the fiery 9th house squares water planet Moon in fiery Sagittarius in the 5th house. Venus opposes a watery Neptune that also squares Ram Dass' fiery Moon. Venus-Neptune in turn forms a half-kite pattern with an earthy Mercury in Taurus in the airy 11th house.

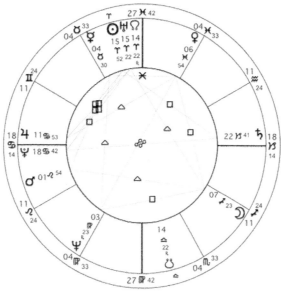

RAM DASS

The only planet that is not unequivocally part of Ram Dass' overwhelming *anandamaya kosha* signature is Mars (quite at home as a fire planet in both Leo and the 1st house), creating an unambivalent opening to *pranamaya kosha*. Mars does trine the Moon (in a fire sign and a fire house), but as the slower moving planet in relationship to a faster moving water planet besieged by fire, fire trumps water in this case, and creates only small opening to *anandamaya kosha*.

As with Kurt Cobain's signature for *manomaya kosha*, very little is wasted in this chart, and Ram Dass perhaps presents as pure a picture for *anandamaya kosha* as it is possible to achieve. This is not necessarily to say that Ram Dass will become an enlightened being or actually experience a complete penetration of the embodied soul by Spirit, but it would appear to me, knowing something about his life, that he is nonetheless taking every possible advantage of the opportunity that has been granted him.

◇◇

Lest we get carried away with the enticing assumption that openings to *anandamaya kosha* are reserved for spiritually-oriented beings, let us note a second strong signature for *anandamaya kosha* in the chart of Nazi General Hermann Goering, among those responsible for the return of millions of Jews to the realm of Spirit in a way that has been universally condemned as one of the worst atrocities of all time.

HERMANN GOERING

In Goering's chart we have a fiery Mars in Aries in the watery 4th house (fire-water juxtaposition) loosely conjunct a fiery Jupiter in Aries in the 5th house square the Sun (a fire planet in an earth sign and house). Mars sextiles Neptune (creating an additional juxtaposition of fire and water) and Pluto (a fire planet). Goering's fire is given additional fuel by airy Saturn, which completes a half-kite with Neptune/Pluto and a very loose cardinal t-square with Sun and Mars/Jupiter. The juxtaposition of air and water (Saturn square Neptune) provides a secondary opening here to *vijnanamaya kosha*, through which Goering's acts (in service to the Nazi regime) had the power to lodge irrevocably as a symbol of evil in the collective consciousness.

Our last example of *anandamaya kosha* is found in the chart for Bob Dylan (on page 164), prolific troubadour extraordinaire, criticized by many lesser beings for all sorts of reasons: a voice like a strangled frog; lyrics that sound deep, but are often merely clever; and a chameleon-like capacity to reinvent himself in the image of what the cynics perceive as a more commercially-viable persona. The fact remains, however, that Dylan has continued to produce memorable music for nearly half-a-century. If anyone within the Pluto in Leo Baby-Boomer generation has earned a shot at immortality (total identification while living with a identity that transcends that of the embodied soul), for all his human faults, Dylan would have to be one of the first in line.

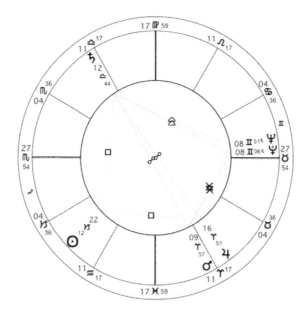

HERMANN GOERING'S ANANDAMAYA KOSHA CHART

Dylan's opening to *anandamaya kosha* starts with a spreading seven planet stellium in Taurus and Gemini, stretching in the fiery 5th house from an earthy Saturn in Taurus (earth-fire), to the Moon (water-fire), to Uranus in Taurus (air-earth), to water planet Jupiter (in Taurus) that forms an out-of-sign conjunction to a fiery Sun (water-fire) in the 6th house (fire-earth), to an airy Venus in Gemini in the 6th (air-earth), to the pure expression of air (Mercury in Gemini in the 7th house) conjunct the Descendant. Mercury in turn is square Neptune conjunct the North Node in the 9th house (water-fire). A fiery Pluto in Leo in the watery 8th house sextiles watery Jupiter (fire-water), and lastly, Mars in Pisces in the 2nd house (a pure water placement) squares the Sun (a fire planet). Again we see nothing wasted in this signature, granting Dylan an unparalleled opportunity in this life to reach maximum penetration by Spirit – if he so chooses.

These few examples are by no means exhaustive of the opportunities for opening to various *koshas* that are prevalent among charts of well-known people. Hopefully, they

◇◇

will illustrate the many ways it is possible to observe these openings in actual practice. As we continue through Part Two, we will explore in more depth the process through which Spirit penetrates to various levels of involvement in the embodied life, using core issues at each of the seven *charkas* as a vehicle for penetration.

BOB DYLAN

Chapter Eleven
The First Chakra Chart

The *koshas*, as discussed in the preceding two chapters, are a measure of how deeply Spirit is invited by the individual soul to penetrate into the embodied life. Since each soul is an expression of Spirit released into manifestation for a specific purpose, there is no judgment that deeper is necessarily better, nor is there any guarantee that given the possibility for experiencing penetration at a given level, the individual soul will rise to the occasion and be able to take advantage of the opportunity. Where the signature for a given *kosha* is strong, there will be pressure – both from within and without – to evolve a life that is a reflection of an opening to the level of penetration offered. But the life can just as easily crystallize around resistance to that opening as it can around the opening itself.

As we turn our attention from the *koshas* to the *chakras*, we will begin to see how and why these patterns of resistance arise, for this level of analysis reveals all the core issues that provide a focal point for the evolution of consciousness within the embodied life. How well a given soul is able to take optimal advantage of the *kosha* opening offered will depend upon how successful she is in addressing and healing the core issues posed by the *chakra* charts to which the *kosha* signatures are related.

In the remaining chapters of Part Two, we will discuss each *chakra*, and provide an example in which the signature for that *chakra* is strong. We will take the time to explore the issues revealed by the *chakra* in some detail, drawing from the actual life experience of the soul living it. By tracking consciousness through a relevant cyclical history, we will demonstrate how the pattern related to the *chakra* signature provides a template and a timeframe for growth in relation to the issues encompassed by the *chakra* under study. In discussing the sixth *chakra*, we will also demonstrate how this information could be used in real time - as in an actual session with a client - through a transcribed interview with a former client who has a strong sixth *chakra* pattern in her chart.

The Astro-logic of the First Chakra Chart

A depiction of the first *chakra* in any chart can be understood as a first *chakra* chart – that is to say, a partial chart in which only those features that contribute to potential first *chakra* issues are displayed. Wherever these features form a major pattern or seem to predominate in some way, we would note a strong first *chakra* chart and speculate that first *chakra* issues might be a factor in the spiritual psychology of the individual whose chart we are viewing. Such speculation must be confirmed by actual life experience, but with a strong first *chakra* chart, there would be a basis for pursuing a line of inquiry that would either confirm or refute our speculations.

Since the first *chakra* is where we secure our survival on the physical plane, and on every other level on which survival has meaning for us and/or appears to be threatened, the first *chakra* chart describes how we go about accomplishing this most fundamental task. Everything within the first *chakra* chart is interpreted in terms of how it either contributes toward or seems to undermine our basic sense of security. The chart itself is a measure of our survival instinct, shows where and how that instinct is most likely to be aroused, and maps an optimal path toward ensuring that the body (and the embodied life) serve as a fitting container for the journey of the soul through this life.

We might begin by envisioning the circle that forms the first *chakra* chart as a perimeter or circumference. Everything within the circumference of the circle is enclosed within a protective aura of safety; everything outside the circle is potentially a threat to our existence. Although the symbolism within the chart is by definition inside the circle, entering into a dynamic relationship with the chart essentially means learning to feel safe with each component of the chart taken as a whole, and as a synthesis of separate pieces. We must psychically bring what the symbolism suggests is ours to experience into the circle of safety. This goal requires a learning process in which we gradually work through our fears until potential threats to our survival are perceived to be less traumatic. In support of this learning process, the circle as circumference becomes a source of containment, protection, safety, and limitation.

Establishing the Parameters of a Chakra Chart

Within the circle itself, we can make further distinctions. The first of these, in relation to each *chakra*, involves the arrangement of patterns in astrological space – with reference to the hemispheres, quadrants, and houses of the birthchart. At the level of consciousness associated with each *chakra*, the soul tends to identify with certain sections of astrological space where there is a natural affinity with the circumstances, activities, and/or areas of focus the space encompasses and the spiritual challenges posed at the *chakra* in question. An antipathy or tendency to want to avoid certain other sections of astrological space will also play its part in the psychology of each *chakra* chart. Often, the resolution of core issues and growth in relation to these issues involves risking movement beyond the soul's comfort zone into those areas of the birthchart that are less familiar, comfortable or safe.

While *chakra* charts can and do arrange themselves throughout astrological space, the most potent patterns – those likely associated with core issues – tend to be aligned with sections of astrological space where there is a natural sense of affinity. *Chakra* charts indicating core issues often cluster in areas of familiarity and preference and form bridges by aspect to those areas of astrological space where growth is required. However a *chakra* chart is arranged, its potency and potential evolutionary impact can be assessed with reference to these areas of affinity and antipathy.

A second consideration in exploring *chakra* patterns involves planetary dynamics. Most astrological models of the *chakra* system assume that each *chakra* is governed by a single planet (Grasse 204)[1], or a dual rulership (Oken 155)[2]. By contrast, the underlying assumption of this system is that any planet can function within any *chakra*, and that each *chakra* is potentially the arena in which a given planetary dynamic might play itself out. However, I do believe that each *chakra* tends to involve several key players, and when three or more of them form planetary patterns by mutual aspect – especially from those sections of astrological space associated with the *chakra* in question – we can feel more confident in declaring that a given *chakra* chart will reflect an important core issue related to that *chakra*[3]. *Chakra* charts that don't involve key players or span key sections of astrological space still serve as triggers to processes related to the *chakra* in question, but are less likely to reflect a dynamic that is central to the soul's evolutionary process.

In practice, many of the most identifiable planetary patterns in any chart will involve more than one *chakra*, as well as planets that aren't key players at that level of consciousness. They may also span areas of the chart associated with multiple *chakra* charts. In establishing a template for each *chakra* chart, we must first consider a few basic guidelines, and establish a baseline against which any deviance from the template might be measured and taken into account. In Part Three, I will discuss in more detail how this system is designed to be used as a platform for exploration that by its very nature, defies and transcends the system. But first, we will look in some detail at the astro-logic of the system itself.

The Astro-logic of Soul Space

To establish a template for a given *chakra* chart, we must first imagine the soul functioning at this level of consciousness, from within each of the hemispheres and quadrants of the birthchart. We then get an intuitive sense both of where the soul prefers to gravitate when it is functioning in a given *chakra*; what sorts of issues might be harbored by the other sections of astrological space that are less comfortable, familiar or safe at this level of consciousness; and how the soul must stretch and grow in order to claim the wholeness that is its birthright within the *chakra* chart under scrutiny. Out of this analysis, we will suggest a reasonable set of guidelines for locating a *chakra* pattern within astrological space.

The astro-logic of hemispheres, quadrants and houses derives from the daily rotation of the Earth about its axis. As the Earth rotates, each planet, including Sun and Moon, appear to move around the birthchart in a clockwise direction – rising at the Ascendant, culminating at the Midheaven, setting at the Descendant, and anti-culminating at the Nadir. Everything below the horizon of the birthchart will – by metaphorical implication – tend to be invisible, internal, and relatively unconscious, while everything above the horizon is at least potentially visible (some planets only with the aid of a telescope, and all planets only at night), external and accessible to consciousness. Everything to the east of the meridian is rising, while everything to the west is setting. Traditionally, the east is also associated with self-determination and a more willful, assertive approach to life, while the west is associated with relationships and a more passive, projective, and/ or responsive approach to life. Putting these basic observations together, we arrive at a further distinction for each quadrant as follows:

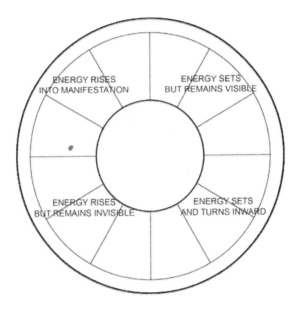

ENERGY RISES INTO MANIFESTATION

ENERGY SETS BUT REMAINS VISIBLE

ENERGY RISES BUT REMAINS INVISIBLE

ENERGY SETS AND TURNS INWARD

MOVEMENT OF ENERGY THROUGH THE QUADRANTS

Through liberal association by analogy, we might now extrapolate from actual planetary motion to the symbolic implication of a planet in a quadrant, as it reflects the soul's movement through its evolutionary journey. If a planet in the NE quadrant is rising but invisible, then we might speculate that here the soul is inwardly formulating the intention, the motivation, and the strength necessary to propel itself into visible, tangible manifestation. NE quadrant planets are those that are related to desires, other motivating factors, and subterranean impulses that inspire the soul toward self-revelation. Similarly, if a planet is found in the SE quadrant, then it is in some way involved in the soul's more visible effort to reveal itself through some outward form of expression. A planet in the SW quadrant is more likely one around which the consequences of this expression arise, and life lessons constellate – often within the context of relationships. A planet in the NW quadrant is one that can serve as a catalyst to self-reflection and the extraction of meaning from experiences above the horizon.

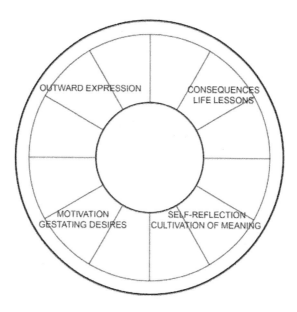

ASTRO-LOGIC OF THE QUADRANTS

Lastly, we can make a final distinction within each quadrant through considering the angular, succedent and cadent houses. Given the placement of succedent houses within the middle of each quadrant, we might assume that these houses are most characteristic of the quadrants that they occupy, and that here the soul is most intensely involved with the process associated with the quadrant. Given that we are considering the movement of planets through astrological space as a reflection of their apparent clockwise motion through it (see Landwehr "Clockwise Motion" for a more detailed explanation of the rationale for this approach), we must approach angular and cadent houses in a slightly different way than they are normally understood.

From this perspective, angular houses are not the beginning of the quadrant, but rather the end. The astro-logical suggestion here is that planets residing in the angular houses have experienced all there is to experience in that quadrant and are ready to move on. Angular houses immediately precede the next quadrant, where any planet is about to make a major shift – e.g. rising into visibilty (in the 1st house); beginning to set after a period of rising (in the 10th house); setting into invisibility (in the 7th house); and beginning to rise after a period of setting (in the 4th house). This moment of poise on the edge of major change after the completion of a certain course of experience is – from this perspective – what gives the angular houses the potency with which they are associated.

By contrast, cadent houses represent the beginning of each quadrant from the clockwise perspective. As such, they represent an adjustment phase, in which planets entering a new quadrant must gradually adapt to a new way of functioning. They are by nature sections of astrological space where the soul becomes more tentative and in some ways more experimental, as it adapts to new unfamiliar conditions, and gradually orients itself to the evolutionary demands of the quadrant it has just entered.

A full explanation of the astro-logic of soul space is worthy of a book unto itself (and will be covered later in *The Astropoetic Series*), but hopefully this brief synopsis will serve as an adequate foundation for establishing a pattern of correlations between various *chakras* and their preferred hemispheres, quadrants, and houses. As we consider each *chakra*, we will elaborate the astro-logic of soul space with reference to the specific psychology of the *chakra* we are discussing.

The Placement of First Chakra Planets in Astrological Space

We begin by considering the horizon and how the soul functions on either side of this axis, at the level of the first *chakra*. Since the primary motivation of the soul at this level is the quest for an assurance of survival, we will approach this task by imagining how the soul is helped or hindered in seeking such assurance, above and below the horizon, given what we know about these sections of astrological space. From an objective vantage point, where first *chakra* concerns are not an issue, no one section of astrological space will be any more advantageous than any other. But from within the mindset associated with the first (or any) *chakra*, perceptions will be skewed by the astro-logic associated with each section, and it is this pattern of perception – and not objective reality – that we are interested in exploring.

As we do this, we are immediately presented with an interesting dilemma. On the one hand, what is below the horizon represents that which is internal, familiar, close to home, and probably within the safe embrace of the soul's comfort zone. On the other hand, what is below the horizon is also often largely unconscious, invisible, and beyond the reach of one's conscious control, especially at a level of consciousness where there is typically very little sense of self. Conversely, the area above the horizon, representing the external world, is where most threats to survival are experienced, yet it is also here that life is most visible, amenable to conscious control, and most easily kept at bay when necessary.

At the most basic, instinctual level, if you can see something, you can somehow deal with it; if you can't, it may prove dangerous.

In reality, threats to survival can come from anywhere. Southern hemisphere threats to survival are perhaps more obvious and more identifiable, but northern threats – from family members, from latent health issues, from dormant unconscious patterns capable of erupting unexpectedly with the right provocation – are more insidious and, in the end, far less easily defused. On the other hand, given that the northern hemisphere is internal, it is also womb-like and initially holds forth greater promise of security than that which lies outside, which is relatively unknown and has yet to prove itself safe. At this level of consciousness, the soul is unaware – not just of specific threats that might lie dormant within, but of the possibility that there could be internal threats at all. Within the perceptual framework encompassed by the first *chakra*, inside feels safe, while outside is perceived as far less certain.

For this reason, the soul caught in the throes of a first *chakra* pattern is likely to look for safety and security below the horizon, while the most serious threats to survival will appear to be above the horizon – thus establishing the pattern of preference and avoidance at this *chakra*. Invariably, the soul's process, both in being wounded and in working toward the healing of its first *chakra* wounds, will involve learning that not everything below the horizon is safe, and not everything above it is a potential threat. But initially, at this level, it will instinctually gravitate to the north and approach the south only to the extent that its base of security has been firmly established.

For similar reasons, planets in the eastern hemisphere – associated with self, will likely to be perceived as safer than those to the west – associated with other people, who are by nature, relatively unknown factors inherently beyond the soul's control, and who have yet to prove themselves safe, trustworthy allies in the quest for survival. At the level of the first *chakra*, the sense of self is relatively undeveloped, for it is not until we reach the third *chakra* that survival instincts begin to revolve around an actual sense of self that is the subject of self-preservation. Nonetheless, there is an instinctual identification with planets in the east, and a wariness of planets in the west that will tend to be reflected by the positioning of first *chakra* patterns in astrological space.

Putting these two principles together, we might speculate that the quadrant of preference for the soul centered in the first *chakra* will be the NE or 1st quadrant, where energy is internal, but gradually rising (from the perspective of planets moving toward the eastern horizon in the pre-dawn hours encompassed by this quadrant). This is the most womb-like of all the quadrants, and thus the safest from the first *chakra's* perspective, yet the momentum is out into the embodied world, where the soul must anchor itself at this first stage of the incarnation process.

Conversely, the most dangerous quadrant within a first *chakra* chart will be the 3rd or SW, for this is where the soul is most exposed to unfamiliar forces – usually taking the form of other people – over which it has little or no control, and whose potential impact on survival is unknown. Again, the fact that this is a projected assumption, and not necessarily an objective or accurate description of reality, makes it no less real within the context of the first *chakra* chart perspective. Working through these first *chakra* issues (or any core issue for that matter) is often a matter of learning that appearances can be deceiving – that perceived threats are not always real, and that true safety is not always where the soul instinctually thinks it ought to be.

Astrologically, this growth in awareness will be by symbolized by movement from the preferred NE quadrant west, into the bosom of family relationships symbolized in the NW quadrant, and south, into a gradually expanding comfort zone of exploration within the outside world represented by the SE quadrant. The leap into the SW quadrant is generally not possible from the first *chakra*, but will rather depend upon commensurate and simultaneous development in the second and third *chakras*.

What this means in terms of our first *chakra* chart template is that astrological patterns representing first *chakra* core issues generally take one of three forms:

1) the planets forming the pattern will cluster in the NE quadrant (the quadrant of safety), perhaps with tendrils extending into the SE and/or NW quadrants;

2) the NE quadrant will be relatively empty, with a planetary pattern bracketing it from the SE and NW; or

3) there will be a strong cross-quadrant dynamic between the NE quadrant and the SW quadrant.

Of these patterns, the third is the most difficult to negotiate, since it poses the greatest apparent threat to survival. The second possibility requires developing an internal sense of safety and security where the world appears to afford none – also a difficult task. The first pattern will generally detail a more manageable course of development – from a stronger more internally developed sense of security and/or strong will to live, toward an expanded range of motion within the SE and NW quadrants.

Not all first *chakra* charts will exhibit one of these three patterns. As previously mentioned, *chakra* charts can and will take any number of forms. Where they do revolve around the affinity of the first *chakra* for the NE quadrant and/or antipathy for the SW quadrant, we would have our first reason to suspect that a first *chakra* core issue is at work. Where they do not, we would simply note that the first *chakra* chart – however it is arranged in astrological space – is likely the template for first *chakra* concerns operating as background factors in the life of the soul, rather than as pressing core issues.

The First Chakra and Angular Planets

Since survival – especially within the southern hemisphere – often appears to depend upon vigilance, planets near the angles of the chart, and/or in angular houses, where they become emphasized, tend to represent important resources in working out first *chakra* issues. Planets near the Nadir (the most internal and thus safest angle of the chart) tend to describe characteristic coping mechanisms – faculties through which the individual works to set safe boundaries and erect barriers of protection. Venus near the Nadir, for example, might describe someone who believes that by staying close to home and surrounding himself with familiar objects that hold special appeal, he will ward off opposition; while Mercury at the Nadir (within the context of the first *chakra* chart) might represent the kind of person who will try to remain silent and thus invisible, hoping to avoid confrontation.

By the rules of astro-logic, the houses associated with the Nadir (the 3rd and 4th) can be understood as extensions of the safe space in which the first *chakra* individual feels most in control, and thus most capable of protection. Since the 3rd house is actually within the NE quadrant of choice, it will often play a role in first *chakra* dynamics – particularly as the house representative of the early childhood environment in which coping mechanisms are first learned. Less obviously, the 4th house, being angular, will in some ways offer the first *chakra* soul a greater sense of control over his own safety, and planets here will tend to represent a more solid foundation from which the soul might begin to more actively and intentionally address survival needs.

A similar twist of astro-logic will govern planets near the Ascendant. The 1st house, which is below the horizon, and thus within the realm of safety, is technically the most likely home for first *chakra* planets in that section of astrological space. Traditionally, the 1st house is associated with basic personality, and those inherent strengths with which one most closely identifies. At the level of the first *chakra*, however, the soul tends to not know itself very consciously, nor is it typically aware of strengths, except as an instinctual response to danger. Meanwhile, 12th house planets and the strategies they represent provide a sense of buffer against the unknown in the outside world and may often feel safer than 1st house planets, even if they are more dysfunctional.

The 12th house is where unconscious, often preverbal, clues about what is expected of one are projected onto an infant by the family, and the growing child learns to adapt himself to those expectations seemingly as matter of survival. Often certain behaviors are expected of the child which seem to be the keys to love, approval, acceptance, or in the most severe cases, avoidance of physical abuse. The child then molds himself to these behaviors as a survival mechanism, which invariably proves problematic later in life.

Astrologers traditionally associate the Ascendant with the persona, or a mask each of us adopts in order to cope with the outside world. It is my sense, however, that it is primarily on the 12th house side of the Ascendant – which is within the external realm of the southern hemisphere – where the persona is formed and employed. With Jupiter in the 12th house, a false hyper-cheery, optimistic persona might overcompensate for rampant fear, while Saturn in the 12th house might reflect a cautious, serious persona that instinctively keeps others at arms length.

Since the persona is a first line of defense for the soul in dealing with an unfamiliar and potentially unsafe world, many first *chakra* issues can be traced to these 12th house planets and the planetary patterns in which they participate. Planets in the 1st house represent a more natural expression of the soul in its most essential sense of internal identity. Within the context of the first *chakra* chart, these will remain relatively unconscious, while planets in the 12th house will be more critical to an understanding of the primary survival mechanism. This will be especially true, when 12th house planets form hard aspects to planets – mostly likely by square to planets in the 3rd or 4th houses, and/or by opposition to planets in the 6th house.

In general, 6th house planets are more likely to be associated with first *chakra* issues than 7th house planets, because of their placement in the internal (safe) portion of the chart, below the horizon. Unlike the Ascendant – where planets are rising from the womb-like NE quadrant into the far less protected SE quadrant – in the west, planets at the Descendant are setting – that is to say, returning from the more vulnerable southern hemisphere to the relative safety of the internal northern hemisphere. Thus, within the context of a first *chakra* pattern, planets in the 6th typically represent strategies of retreat. The Moon here, for example, may reflect a tendency to use relationships with women – beginning with Mom – as a safe haven and a buffer to the world. Mars in the 6th may manifest as a workaholic tendency that allows the soul an excuse to avoid a broader, more meaningful participation in life beyond work.

Planets near the Midheaven are less likely to be involved in first *chakra* patterns, simply because the incarnation phase of the evolutionary process (first and second *chakras*) is by nature a more internal affair. When they do participate in a first *chakra* pattern, they typically represent overt threats to survival, or external conditions upon which perceived threats to survival are projected. The Sun at the Midheaven, for example, might depict a person who though outwardly successful is fragile and vulnerable to the exposure that fame produces. With Uranus at the Midheaven, an individual known for her rebellious spirit and willingness to push the envelope may inwardly be trying to stay one step ahead of forces beyond her control. It should be emphasized, however, that these scenarios will generally only refer to first *chakra* patterns when they also involve other planets – and especially classical first *chakra* planets – at other more common first *chakra* stations:

near the Nadir, conjunct the Ascendant on the 12th house side, and/or conjunct the Descendant on the 6th house side.

Saturn's Role in First Chakra Dynamics

While any planet placed at these positions can be associated with first *chakra* issues, certain planets are more readily associated with the first *chakra* than others. Since the primary source of motivation in the first *chakra* revolves around a desire for safety and protection, such motivation is likely to be amplified when Saturn - the planet most associated with safety and protection - is prominent. With Saturn near the angles of the chart - especially in the 12th, 6th, 3rd or 4th houses, or placed in hard aspect to another planet in one of these key positions, it is not unlikely that some first *chakra* issue lies at the core of the soul's process. Such assumptions must always be confirmed or refuted through reference to the appropriate cyclical history, and to the specific first *chakra* issue determined through the life story that emerges through this history. But on an exoteric level, the astro-logic of the first *chakra* often involves the planet Saturn.

Saturn's involvement in the first *chakra* as an agent of safety and protection is usually something of a mixed blessing. It provides a solid circumference to the circle and enfolds a space in which the soul can take root within the embodied world, but it can also become a prison - a source of limitation and confinement from which one must break free in order to resolve the issues that have evoked the need for protection.

In Greek mythology, Cronus (Saturn) is known as an ogre who swallows his own children before they are born, and it is this stillborn journey from womb to tomb that Saturn helps the fearful soul negotiate, usually at tremendous price. The *ouroborous*, or serpent who swallows his own tail, is a symbol of Saturn's function within the first *chakra*, since it represents both a state of self-containment and a kind of living death out of which the soul must awaken, if it is to offer an hospitable habitat in which Spirit can take root and flourish.

The Moon's Role in First Chakra Dynamics

As Erich Neuman points out so eloquently in his seminal book, *The Great Mother*, the *ouroborous* state is often associated with one's relationship to the mother, who in childhood represents the ideal haven of safety and protection - at least in theory[4]. In real life, however, all mothers are imperfect, and inevitably there comes a time when the child realizes that his mother is not the infallible refuge he wanted her to be. Even where a mutual desire exists on the part of both mother and child to seal the pact by which this desire is guaranteed, inevitably the protection fails, and the child is unwittingly wounded. This moment of rude awakening is the primal act that sets the true first *chakra* journey in

◇◇

motion, for it is when the protection of the mother fails that the child is forced to begin his own journey toward self-reliance in the assurance of his own protection.

Most of us get past this moment relatively unscathed, learn to pick ourselves up after a fall, and gradually grow into adults fully capable of taking care of ourselves and dealing with whatever threats to our survival manifest along the way. If, however, our mother (or father or any adult to whom we look for protection and safety) is abusive, or neglectful, or abandons us in some critical moment of vulnerability, a first *chakra* issue can become the nucleus around which evolves a lifetime quest for the safe haven one never had when it was most critical.

Astrologically, this place of eminent vulnerability (particularly in relation to the mother) is symbolized by the Moon. Thus, when there are hard aspects between Saturn and the Moon, especially spanning the positions we have associated with the first *chakra*, we are likely to have a full-blown first *chakra* core issue to contend with. In traditional astrology, these planets are associated with parents in general, reflecting the fact that often the chronic sense of unprotected vulnerability that crystallizes first *chakra* issues arises through a problematic relationship to both parents, or to parents suffering from chronic tension in their relationship to each other. Whatever the dynamic (which must ultimately be understood within the story associated with the pattern), it is the juxtaposition of Saturn and Moon, appropriately placed, that signifies a first *chakra* issue.

Pluto's Role in First Chakra Dynamics

These issues are greatly exacerbated when this basic Saturn-Moon signature also involves one or more transpersonal planets. While any transpersonal planet can up the ante in the game through which an individual soul must work out her first *chakra* issues, the greatest threat by far is signified by Pluto's participation. In traditional astrology, Pluto is associated with death – both literal and metaphorical – and it is exactly this experience of death, on every level on which it is experienced, against which first *chakra* protection is invoked. In *The Seven Gates of Soul*, I speak of death as the great catalyst to an awakening of soul. Here I would add that within the context of first *chakra* issues, Pluto is often the agent of an experience that evokes a literal fear of death and a potent opening to a deeper awareness of soul – especially when it triggers a first *chakra* Saturn-Moon signature, either natally or by transit.

Within the context of the *yogic* model we are exploring, Pluto can also be understood as the manifestation of *kundalini*. *Kundalini* is often envisioned as a serpent (a more dynamic cousin of the *ouroborous*) coiled three and one half times at the base of the human spine. In its dormant state, the *kundalini* quietly and unobtrusively generates enough energy for us to carry on the daily affairs of life. In its awakened state, however, the *kundalini* unleashes a vast reservoir of latent creativity, infusing life with a numinosity and a mythological dimension not previously experienced. It is this numinosity of *kundalini* that is invoked in all magical rituals and in all incubative ceremonies of healing and empowerment. Within the context of our first *chakra* dilemma, *kundalini* is what empowers us to become self-reliant in the quest for safety and protection. *Kundalini* is the power within which allows us to rise above our fears and create a sacred space in which the life of the embodied soul might unfold without undue fear of imminent annihilation.

To the extent that we fail to grab hold of this serpent and claim its power, we will appear to be at the mercy of Plutonic forces bent on our destruction, and we will look outside ourselves for protection. As we begin to assimilate the raw power of *kundalini* through a series of first *chakra* crises – precipitated by Pluto's passage in relation to our first *chakra* signatures, the circumference of protection becomes a living, breathing membrane within which we cultivate, and through which we express, our power within the embodied world. Though it may take countless forms, this is essentially the path encompassed by the soul within the domain of the first *chakra*. Although first *chakra* issues can involve other planets, the journey down this path will be most in evidence in those birthcharts where Pluto forms a hard aspect pattern with Saturn and the Moon across the sections of astrological space associated with the first *chakra*, especially during Saturn or Pluto transits or points of contact from the progressed Moon to this same natal configuration[5].

As the lower octave of Pluto, Mars can also be associated with first *chakra* issues, but usually only as a secondary agent[6]. That is to say, if Pluto is not part of a first *chakra* signature, the mere presence of Mars within such a signature will not add much to it. If both Pluto and Mars are present, the combination will be especially potent. Mars is often the antidote to the vulnerability experienced by the Moon in the face of first *chakra* issues, and it is the heroic agent through which the protective but stifling walls imposed by Saturn are pushed back far enough for Pluto to carve out enough psychic space for *kundalini* to begin rising. When Mars and Saturn learn to work together, it is often reflected by our increasing capacity to protect ourselves rather than look to some outside source of protection. This will invariably be a huge step forward in the healing and resolution of first *chakra* issues.

The First Chakra Chart

The strongest *chakra* charts are those that revolve around core issues associated with the *chakra* in question. Strong first *chakra* charts will involve a planetary pattern (usually but not always a hard pattern like a t-square) between the Moon, Saturn and Pluto stationed near the Nadir, on the 12th house side of the Ascendant and the 6th house side of the Descendant. Alternately, there will be a concentration of planets (usually but not always a stellium) in the NE quadrant, involving these same three planets at a minimum. A third form of first *chakra* issue will be indicated by a core opposition between one or more of these three primary first *chakra* planets near the Midheaven (especially on the 9th house side) and the rest in the NE quadrant.

A somewhat less potent first *chakra* issue can be indicated when a planetary pattern forms between these three planets, but off the angles and/or away from the NE quadrant. The Moon in hard aspect to either Saturn or Pluto, but not both, may indicate a hybrid core issue with first *chakra* flavor, but one that involves other *chakras* as well.

If none of these planets occupy the classic first *chakra* stations, or form aspects to each other, we probably don't have a first *chakra* core issue. In this case, we can still construct a first *chakra* chart by noting any other planets in these positions and their aspects to each other. If there are no other planets near the Nadir, on the 12th house side of the Ascendant or the 6th house side of the Descendant, we would look to the rulers of these three angles and any aspects between them. Additional planets may be drawn into the *chakra* chart if they closely conjunct any of the other primary planets forming the pattern. Jupiter would be part of a first *chakra* pattern signified by a Moon/Jupiter-Saturn square, for example, even though Jupiter is not a classic first *chakra* planet, and does not rule the Ascendant, Nadir or Descendant of the chart we've been looking at. Ideally, we would like to see at least one aspect representing each *chakra*, but occasionally a weak *chakra* chart will be composed of three unaspected planets.

A more detailed demonstration of the construction of all seven *chakra* charts in relation to the same natal chart is presented in Part Three of this book.

Endnotes

[1]   In an email (10/24/06), Grasse acknowledges that "the particular astrology/*chakra* set of correlations I use in my writings aren't actually mine (though the interpretative techniques I use are) ~ I got them from Goswami Kriyananda, and his teacher Shelly Trimmer, who got them from Yogananda. . . Beyond the Kriya Yoga tradition, one also finds the same approach used by Marc Edmond Jones (in his unpublished Sabian Assembly notes) – he may well have learned it from Yogananda, but I don't know for sure – and Jeffrey Green (in his book *Uranus*) –where he got it I have no idea – and in passing by David Frawley".

[2]   Oken's approach derives from the teachings of Alice Bailey and the Theosophist school.

[3]   Hodgson offers a similar multi-planet system of chakra association in her book *The Stars and the Chakras: The Astrology of Spiritual Unfoldment*. Hers is mostly a sign-based

system, derived from an integration of the astrology of Alan Leo and A. G. S. Norris and the channeled teachings of a being called White Eagle. Each chakra is associated with an element, the signs of that element, and the planets she associates with (not necessarily ruling) those elements.

4   This role can also be played by the father, if he is the one with whom the child most readily identifies security and protection – or perhaps this role will be shared by both parents. Regardless of the gender of the protective parent, however, the process of subsequent wounding is one in which a lunar bond of trust, familiarity, and safety is broken or betrayed.

5   Hodgson is in agreement with me about the participation of Saturn and the Moon at this level of consciousness (81). Grasse assigns Saturn to this *chakra* (through a conceptual scheme that moves mostly from the outer planets inward as a reflection of rising consciousness) (204), while Oken notes the rulership of the first *chakra* by the Moon in conjunction with Mercury (155).

6   Hodgson considers Mars to be a primary player in the first *chakra* because of its exaltation in Capricorn, an earth sign. She also associates Mars with *kundalini*, which could partially account for this minor discrepancy in our respective views.

Chapter Twelve
A First Chakra Case Study

The most poignant example of a first *chakra* chart within my collection is that of a former student in my correspondence course – let us call her Mary.

Mary's first *chakra* chart is formed by an out-of-sign square between Pluto/ Moon in the 12th house and Saturn at the Nadir. Saturn is also loosely conjunct Mars, also at the Nadir in the 4th house. Mars is loosely conjunct the North Node, both in Sagittarius. Since Jupiter is also tightly conjunct both Pluto and the Moon, and the dispositor of both Saturn and Mars, I include it in this pattern, even though it is not one of the classic first *chakra* planets.

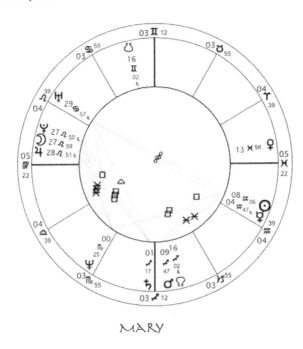

MARY

In passing, we would note here that this first *chakra* chart encompasses a dramatic juxtaposition of fire and water within the 12th house stellium and through the placement of a fiery Mars/North Node in the watery 4th house. There is also a juxtaposition of air and water through the square between her 12th house Moon and air planet Saturn in the 3rd conjunct the watery Nadir. These disparate elemental combinations provide openings to both *vijnanamaya* and *anandamaya kosha*, suggesting that whatever first *chakra* issue may be associated with this pattern will present a potent opportunity for penetration by Spirit – that is to say, spiritual awakening.

MARY'S FIRST CHAKRA CHART

We would also note that this pattern largely surrounds an empty NE quadrant, suggesting that Mary's task with regard to this pattern will be to evolve an internal sense of safety and security where the world appears to afford none – a task we will soon see reflected and confirmed by her story.

Mary's Unwounded Soul Essence

As noted earlier, the Moon represents the point of maximum vulnerability within this pattern, and it is here that I would like to begin my discussion of Mary's chart within the context of her life. If we temporarily remove the intense alchemical pressure of Saturn-Pluto, the Moon represents who Mary would be (and is, at the very core of her soul essence) were she not encumbered by the first *chakra* wounding imposed by the pattern as a whole. It is who she was before the initial wounding occurred, and who she will become at a more conscious, more deeply penetrated level of her being, as she gropes toward healing these wounds.

This unencumbered being is often most clearly in evidence before the age of 3 or 4, which is when transiting Saturn forms its first semi-square to its natal position (and by hard aspect to the rest of the pattern) and presents the first major challenge to the natural, unencumbered expression of lunar innocence. Often the primal wounding takes place at this time, although the wounding can also be triggered by exposure to a chronic state of affairs, and may or may not manifest as a tangible, identifiable event. Usually by the age of 7, when transiting Saturn forms its first square to its natal position (and simultaneously or successively aspects the remainder of the first *chakra* pattern), the wounding is in full display.

In the two years that I worked with Mary, I experienced her to be an extremely intelligent, creative woman with the capacity for mastering any body of knowledge or set of skills to which she turned her attention. This creative intelligence is perhaps most accurately understood as a reflection of her Uranus-opposition to Sun/Mercury in Aquarius in the 6th house, with Mercury as the ruler of her 10th. But at a deeper, more emotional level, fueling this intelligent creativity was a fiery passion for life, a desire to engage life creatively, and to receive acknowledgement for her creative contribution – all of which can be understood as a manifestation of her Moon in Leo, rising or rather attempting to rise within the context of this challenging first *chakra* pattern.

As Mary described herself growing up, she was "a talented and sensitive child who had been placed in a stifling and unresponsive family[1]." Her fondest memory before the age of 7 was "of joyously running around the house naked. . . and [her] mother affectionately laughing at the sight." This moment would obviously be before her mother's inherent flaws proved fatal to Mary's sense of safety. One of Mary's early teachers, who contributed to her wounding (at Saturn's first transiting square to the natal pattern) felt a need to "take her down a notch" because she was exhibiting "'too much self-confidence' and . . . [her] opinion of [herself] was too high." This confident, talented, self-assured child, running naked through life with joyful merriment was who Mary was (and is) at the heart of her unencumbered soul essence, as revealed astrologically by Moon in Leo, augmented no doubt by Jupiter's jovial and expansive presence tightly conjunct the Moon.

Mary's Primal Wounding

Given the fact that Mary's Leo Moon sits at the heart of a powerful first *chakra* chart signature, however, it was inevitable that this naked, carefree, precocious child would experience a clipping of her wings. True to form, the initial wounding associated with this first *chakra* pattern took place at the age of 4 (around the time of transiting Saturn's first semi-square to the pattern), when her father left his marriage to her mother, and moved out of the household. Before that, Mary was compelled to function in an atmosphere she described as "embattled" by constant fighting between her mother and father. The tension finally erupted during the semi-square, when her father walked out. While it is likely that her father's decision had absolutely nothing to do with her, Mary suffered a wounding of abandonment in this moment, and a serious breach of the circumference of the family circle, that previously at least held forth the possibility of protection.

After this traumatic event, Mary became "the one who 'started things'. It seemed to be [her] role in the family to bring things out into the open at any cost (Mars driving her from within). And yet at the same time, [she was] terribly sensitive to the others and would become tortured and depressed over their slightest disapproval or misunderstanding.... [She was] a bundle of sensitivity and violent emotions with no idea how to handle them. (Moon/Pluto square Saturn/Mars)." By the age of 8, shortly after the incident with her teacher, Mary became "rather withdrawn,. . . while *angry* at the same time." This is a succinct but accurate description of Mars at her Nadir, faced with the perpetual dilemma of needing and wanting to get the anger (and the energy) out, while not being emotionally or psychologically equipped to deal with the consequences of outer expression.

Much of Mary's anger was directed toward her mother, whom she "hated . . . for many years." Even as an adult, she "became defensive and closed down" in her presence. Her mother "had the effect of making [her feel] drained and exhausted," and Mary deliberately "limit[ed] the amount of time [she] spent with her." No doubt, within the context of her first *chakra* wounding, Mary blamed her mother for driving her father away and felt her mother's part in this breach of the protective circumference as a betrayal. Beneath the blame was likely the unconscious identification with mother (astrologically symbolized by Moon) and the terrible realization – no less a force of wounding for its lack of basis in reality – that Mary, too, must on some level, be responsible for driving her father away. In the twisted logic of the wound, this essentially means that genuine Mary is not ok, and must somehow be suppressed in order to ensure that vulnerable Mary does not get wounded again. The betrayal by mother, abandonment by father, and internalized sense of irrational responsibility for her parents' separation, together became the trigger for Mary's first *chakra* wound.

Mary's wound was further exacerbated in childhood by her sisters, who constantly invaded her privacy and sought to humiliate her in front of family and friends. Mary's 3rd house of siblings is ruled by Pluto, which squares Saturn in the 3rd, forming the backbone not only of a classic first *chakra* pattern, but one in which siblings could also potentially be a catalyst. While humiliation and invasion of privacy are not nearly as threatening to survival as abandonment and betrayal by those Mary most needed to count on for protection, within the context of this first *chakra* pattern, her troublesome relationship to her older siblings was nonetheless experienced as a matter of life and death.

In Mary's words, her sisters were attempting to "squash any of [her] tendencies to stick out in both negative and positive ways." Since "sticking out" is what the Moon in Leo most deeply desires to do, having these tendencies squashed was tantamount to annihilation of the Moon. Like Cinderella, Mary was "hardly ever allowed to be part of [her sisters'] plans or activities.. . . [Yet they] were... the chief violators of [her] highly valued privacy." Within the context of her first *chakra* wound, this violation of privacy can also be understood as a denial of her right to exist or to occupy her own space.

Though naturally curious, highly intelligent and an innovative thinker, Mary spent her time at school "hid[ing] out," and seeking refuge from "the sometimes daily abuses at home." She tried looking toward her teachers "for someone to serve as mentor or surrogate parent who would not be shocked by the confidences [she] longed to share, [but she] never found anyone who felt safe enough to confide in.... [She] felt like [she] could not let on about the truth of (her) pain and kept *a* stern outer countenance even though [she] might have tears running down [her] face." After the age of eight, she withdrew and squelched her previously expressed natural enthusiasms and talents. This is the portrait of an intensely lonely child, for whom the world was not a safe space for her to be who she was, nor within which the inhabitants could be trusted. Mary summarized this first *chakra* dilemma by saying "I constantly wondered why I had been born, and secretly and fearfully thought that it might have been to experience intensity in the form of emotional pain." In the face of this pain (Saturn-Pluto), she (Moon/Jupiter) shut down.

Of course, no one is born to feel intense emotional pain, yet within the throes of our wounding, inevitably, we all do. The fact that in Mary's case, this wounding seemed to be directly tied to her reason for being, makes it an identifiable first *chakra* wound. Under pressure from Saturn-Pluto – in this case, taken the form of this intensely painful and lonely world within which Mary needed to be vigilant against further abandonment, betrayal or abuse – Moon/Jupiter simply imploded. While Mary had previously been outgoing, carefree and precocious, after the primal wounding, she became sullen, cautious and withdrawn, occasionally erupting in anger, despite her caution, as an attempt to create more breathing room for herself. The only safe space was inside Mary's own troubled psyche, and so this is where she retreated – as an act of self-preservation.

Astrologers will recognize this introverted withdrawal as a Saturnian coping mechanism. In mythology, Saturn ate his own children to prevent them from usurping his power and authority. Here – in Mary's life – Saturn can be seen swallowing everything that is most intensely Mary in order to prevent her from invoking further punishment, or put another way, from usurping the power and authority of her wound. This is not some external force, however, but one that Mary herself wields. Why anyone would want to do this defies the logic of the rational mind, But within the unconscious logic of her first *chakra* wound, it makes perfect sense. Since it was her father (also symbolized by Saturn) that initially triggered the wound by abandoning her, her continued protection in his absence (and her survival) required that she take his place. She did this by becoming more

Saturnian – that is to say, by swallowing everything about her that would otherwise make her proud (Moon in Leo).

In describing her childhood, Mary said, "I do not think anything terribly malicious took place in the family." But the 12th house planets involved in Mary's wounding often represent preverbal messages which get reinforced throughout childhood in countless ways, which often fail to register as anything tangible on which the soul can readily put its finger. It's as if 12th house patterns are inhaled like an invisible gas, and precisely because there is nothing solid for the soul to resist, that which it takes in by osmosis becomes all the more fixed for its invisibility.

Meanwhile, the hidden treasure at the heart of Mary's wound is the promise that this child (Moon/Jupiter) shall one day be set free from the invisible chains that bind (Saturn-Pluto) – perhaps with a vengeance, stronger and more powerful for its ordeal than it otherwise would have been. Freeing this child – the naked, carefree Moon in Leo buttressed and fortified by Jupiter – and allowing her to take her rightful place as the pivot point of Mary's existence – is also the task imposed by Mary's wound. Succeeding at this task will require Mary to discover, inevitably through a lifetime of fits and starts, that she is stronger and more powerful than the forces that seemingly conspired to inflict intense emotional pain upon her in childhood.

The Seeds of Healing Within the Wound

It should come as no surprise that both as a child and an adult, Mary's anger – and her Mars in general – was often the agency through which this self-discovery process took place. As mentioned earlier, this is often typical of the dynamic in first *chakra* charts where both Pluto and Mars are involved. At first Mary's anger was projected outward toward those who had abandoned, betrayed and abused her. But gradually, and unconsciously at first, she found ways to reclaim her western Mars and use it on her own behalf.

Throughout childhood, Mary would "cut [her] arms with a razor. . . (an extreme Martian behavior) to ground [her]self in physical pain as opposed to emotional, [and] this had a strangely calming effect on [her]." I suspect that within the distorted logic of a first *chakra* wound, it also gave her a sense of increased control over her pain along with tangible evidence for her own existence amidst forces that seemed to deny it. Mars in Sagittarius in the 4th house often precipitated "a struggle with [Mary's] demons, which loom[ed] large, creating tempests in teapots, [and] a fight with [her] own ego," but it also gave her the strength of the heroine necessary to do battle with those demons and emerge victoriously claiming their power as her own.

In many ways, the struggle for Mary's existence – her first *chakra* dilemma – was a battle between Saturn (tightly bound to her wounded pattern) and Mars (on the other side of the Nadir, bound to Saturn and the North Node by conjunction). Ultimately these two planets would have to learn to work together, but within the context of Mary's first *chakra* wound, Saturn was the adopted protection against further wounding, while Mars was the redeemer of the wounded child. To redeem the child, Mars would often have to fight the protector for custody.

At one point in our work together, Mary suggested that all her problems could be solved if she could just "surrender [her] ego to God." This popular notion has a certain appeal, since we are often the architects of our own self-imposed disasters, and if we could just get that bumbling idiot out of the control booth, we would all be better off. In Mary's case, however, I argued that quite the contrary – it was the resurrection of a healthy ego that ought to lie at the heart of Mary's quest. At the core of every first *chakra* wound is the belief that "I don't have a right to exist," and although annihilation of the ego is attractive as a spiritualization of this belief, it is also a clever way to remain in the wounded state – a guaranteed victory for Saturn, the child-eater, now justified as an expression of pseudo-evolution.

"For even though the storm is much bigger than you," I told her, "you are the protagonist in the middle of it, experiencing everything through your tender, and receptive Moon, and you can no more remove yourself from the storm than you can control it.... Without a strong and healthy ego, the storm will simply sweep you away. You need a strong ego in order to weather the storm, and to feel worthy enough to find that place at the eye of the storm where you can sink the roots of your soul and begin to grow, despite the onslaught that rages around you.... If the challenge of living were merely a matter of surrendering the ego, you would long ago have simply been squashed like a bug under the heel of a shoe.... It takes a strong sense of will and purpose to follow a spiritual path to its conclusion, and if that sense of strength does not come from ego (which after all, is really only a focal point of consciousness that calls itself "I"), where is it going to come from?"

The task at the heart of any first *chakra* wound – including Mary's – is to cultivate a sense of self that is strong enough to align itself firmly with the soul's agenda and begin to grow, even at the heart of whatever forces seem to perpetually threaten its very existence. Mars was for her a fitting agent for this task.

The Astrological Timing of the Wounding/Healing Process

Having identified the natal pattern related to Mary's first *chakra* wound, it should come as no surprise that the timing of events related to both the wounding and the healing process would correlate with transits to this pattern. Since Saturn and Pluto are the two outer planets associated with first *chakra* wounds, it is natural to assume that Saturn and Pluto transits (particularly by hard aspect) would be critical triggers to both the wounding, and the process by which the soul – in this case, Mary – gropes toward healing.

We have already identified Saturn's role in the initial wounding. Transiting Saturn was semi-square its natal position (and sesquiquadrate to the natal pattern including Mars) within a one-degree orb from January, 1960 – November, 1961. This was when her father left the marriage to her mother, and the initial wounding by abandonment took place.

To this point in Mary's life, transiting Pluto was also making its way through the entire pattern, setting a more chronic background tone of ongoing catharsis within the family dynamic. When Mary's father abandoned her, transiting Pluto was exactly square her Mars, essentially bringing the whole simmering stew to a boil. This transit was in effect within a 2° orb, from November, 1960 - June, 1964, encompassing the period that began at age 4 with her angry acting out and "bringing things out in the open at any cost," and ended at age 8, with her shutting down and withdrawing. From November, 1960 – November, 1961 – the critical year of abandonment and betrayal – both Saturn and Pluto (the two agents of wounding in first *chakra* patterns) were simultaneously triggering the pattern by hard aspect.

While it is beyond the scope of this case study to trace the entire cyclical history of Saturn and Pluto transits to Mary's natal first *chakra* pattern, a few poignant examples should suffice to illustrate how the pattern gets triggered and played out in the subsequent events of Mary's life. During one hard Saturn transit to the natal pattern, for example, Mary found herself in the middle of a "desperately unhappy time. . .; [she was] miserable in [her first] marriage in which [she] felt trapped" by the Hasidic Jewish community to which her first husband belonged. These feelings of entrapment came to head during this period, when she experienced "serious complications" during a pregnancy. "[Her] husband didn't adequately care for [her] during [her] recovery.. . . [She] felt terribly isolated and unable to tell anyone about what had happened." She was, in short, essentially betrayed and abandoned by her first husband, in an uncanny repeat of the primal wounding she experienced at age 4.

The Re-enactment of Mary's First Chakra Wounding in Present Time

It was perhaps no coincidence that I began working with Mary during another critical phase in the outworking of these primal wounds, shortly before transiting Pluto began conjuncting her natal Mars in late December, 1998. At that time, she was just about to move to a foreign country to join her fiancé, a man 23 years her senior – obviously a father figure, and a suitable stand-in for Saturn in this fresh chapter of the ongoing saga through which Mary sought healing for her first *chakra* wounds. Mary finalized her wedding plans to this man – whom we will call John – while both transiting Pluto and transiting Mars were conjunct her natal Mars.

At first blush, John appeared to be the perfect partner in this dance of healing that Mary had embarked upon. He was a spiritual teacher, seemingly capable of providing a gentle, but unflappable container for the volatile emotions that lie just beneath the surface of Mary's wounds. As Mary described him, "he seemed to have a peaceful core that was not ruffled or bent out of shape no matter what [she] said or did. He was not one to be controlled or be in control, and he had a way of handing [her] issues squarely back to [her] when there was any conflict.. . . [She] remain[ed] in awe of his ability to simply let the small stuff wash over and drift away of its own accord." .

If the unconscious message that Mary carried into this relationship from her residual father wounding was "I must be bad to drive my father away," then having an older father surrogate for a partner who was not that easily driven away would seem to be ideal. Given that Mary had gravitated to this relationship during a critical phase of the cycle that encompassed her wounding, however, it was inevitable that she would be testing this emotional hypothesis throughout her relationship with John. If she threw everything she had at him, and he didn't leave her, then this would prove to the wounded child inside of her that she must be ok after all – or so the unconscious logic of her first *chakra* wounds went. If, on the other hand, John finally threw up his hands, and said, "I'm out of here," then the hypothesis she was testing must be true, and she would prove to be as bad as her wounding told her she was.

Of course, the objective truth is that she was not bad, nor was she responsible for her father leaving, but to the extent that the wounded child inside of her didn't really know this yet, she would necessarily be engaged in a process of testing her partner's resiliency in the face of her wounds. This is what she did through October, 2000, when transiting Pluto moved beyond a two-degree orb to Mars for the last time. Fueled by Pluto's alchemical intensity, Mary would act out a rebellious, out-of-control Mars, while projecting her Saturn (symbol of the abandoning father as well as of the need for control) onto John, along with her wounded expectation of eventual abandonment. Though "not one to be controlled or be in control," John would nonetheless unconsciously evolve to embody her projection.

Despite John's uncontrolling nature, Mary soon began to experience herself "without rights, means, or emotional support," and acutely aware of "all the constrictions and incompatibilities" she was "forced" to live with within the context of her relationship. Again, as in childhood and as in her marriage to her first husband, she began to feel trapped – that is to say, from an astrological perspective, she began to feel Saturn's protection as imprisonment.

At the same time the relationship became claustrophobic, John began to express "the wish that he could be free of [Mary]," quite in conformance to Mary's wounded expectation. At the beginning of her marriage to John, Mary hoped "that [she] would come to this fresh situation, unencumbered by the things and people from [her] past, willing to learn a new way of being in the present,. . . [and that] John would guide [her] to a higher way of living," but what she found when she got there was that her past followed her to her new location into her marriage, and that John was incapable of being anything other than what her unresolved first *chakra* issues dictated that he must be.

This repeat of the primal episode came to a head during the Christmas holidays, as John "pulled away emotionally and [told her] he didn't know if the relationship was salvageable." Mary was utterly disappointed in him, because of "his shutting off emotionally and becoming critical and judgmental in moments of stress.. . . [Her] every flaw got reported to [her] . . . [and she found it]. . . very hard to maintain [her] equanimity in what had become an atmosphere of dislike and disapproval. [Her] pattern was to react out of fear, which. . . just produced more recrimination and complaints."

As in childhood, Mary felt – among other complaints – that her need for privacy was dishonored. In accordance with his spiritual training, John considered her desire for privacy to be an "ego game," uncannily echoing her early relationship to sisters who routinely invaded her space, shamed her, and then took delight in tormenting her when she got upset. Having grown up with such a juxtaposition of experiences as part of her first *chakra* wounding, Mary now unconsciously associated privacy with shame and vulnerability. Thus when John told her that her desire for privacy was just an ego trip, she believed on some level he must be right, because she carried these negative experiences of the quest for privacy inside of her. Outwardly she rebelled against his suggestion, but inwardly she took it to heart. The challenge for her here was to allow herself this fundamental need without judgment – a challenge she made great strides in meeting throughout transiting Pluto's fresh triggering of these wounds.

Transforming the Wounded Moment Into an Opportunity for Healing

During this critical Pluto transit, Mary nearly broke up with John twice. But she hung in there and at one point found herself marveling that "someone with fixed Saturn at Nadir squaring that fixed stellium in the 12th house" could move into a childlike space of fun and play. As I tried to remind her, however, there was nothing inherent in the symbolism of her chart that precluded this possibility. Quite the contrary. As noted at the very beginning of this case study, Moon in Leo, which is the tender heart of her pattern, is a playful essence. Moon conjunct Jupiter in Leo is capable of playing voraciously, and

◇◇◇

taking great delight in life's abundant adventure. For all of Pluto's painful intensity, it is not astrologically inconceivable that Pluto was pushing her toward a reclaiming of this Moon/Jupiter essence – which is also a major source of her power.

Even Saturn, the ogre who ate his own children, squaring (and seemingly putting a damper on this possibility from its hidden station in the 4th house) is, in another manifestation, farther up the scale of consciousness, associated with Santa Claus. Saturn rules Capricorn, the astrological season in which Christmas occurs and that brings Santa Claus down our chimneys with a bag full of toys. In pagan days, Christmas was celebrated as Saturnalia, a bacchanalian orgy of feasting, dancing and celebration of the abundance of life. Could it be then that the promise beneath the wounded signature in Mary's chart was that she would gradually learn of Saturn and Pluto's secret conspiracy to prod the wounded child toward its own private Christmas morning?

This is not to say, of course, that Mary's first *chakra* wounds could be easily dismissed by a glib affirmation of this positive interpretation of the difficult first *chakra* pattern in her chart. Even traditional astrologers would be stretching the limits of credibility in suggesting that Mary's path through life would be a free-wheeling skip down the yellow brick road. For whatever reason, Mary chose a more arduous route, and both the identification of the first *chakra* pattern in Mary's chart and the tracking of the story line associated with this pattern bear this out.

From an astropoetic perspective, we would go so far as to say that the painful journey through Mary's first *chakra* hell and back again was necessary before Mary could realize the abundance carried within her by the carefree, naked child. In the end, she would likely receive a more potent gift because of the trials and tribulations she endured on the path to its discovery. Nor would this be a one-time realization. With this pattern in her chart, Mary was seemingly fated to awaken to the highest possible potential encoded in the pattern only through many false starts. As she realized during the Christmas of 2000, however, being fated by this pattern did not mean she was not free, whenever she was ready, to drop the story line, and claim the gold at the end of the rainbow. Since this is a first *chakra* wound, the gold at the heart of the story line is the right to be here in all of her naked, carefree glory – a right that Mary would inevitably claim, or not, as her natal pattern was triggered in various ways throughout the various cycles in which it participated.

Endnotes

[1] All quotes in this chapter are from my correspondence with Mary over the course of our work together.

Chapter Thirteen
The Second Chakra Chart

The second *chakra* chart is formed by extracting and noting the factors in any birthchart associated with the second *chakra*. Where these factors are strong, we might reasonably expect – provided the story behind the pattern corroborates our suspicion – that a second *chakra* issue is critical to the spiritual life of the person living the chart. Even where the second *chakra* chart is not particularly strong, it will function in the background of any life, and can come to the fore when it is triggered by the appropriate transit or progression.

As discussed earlier, the second *chakra* is where we begin to turn our attention from securing our survival to the proactive creation of a pleasurable and joyful existence. It is where we discover our natural predispositions, innate desires, and natural rhythms, and learn to relax into them through a process of deepening self-acceptance and increasing self-permission to be who are without apology or compromise. The second *chakra* is often associated with sexuality, and indeed it is through the second *chakra* that sexuality is discovered and explored. Along with this discovery inevitably come whatever dysfunctional patterns of guilt, shame, or self-distortion we have learned in relation to our sexuality through our conditioning, both familial and cultural. The true meaning of the second *chakra*, however, extends far beyond the expression of overt sexuality to encompass a more profound awakening to the erotic dimension of our experience.

At the heart of this erotic dimension is the realization that we are in relationship to the rest of this manifest creation and everything in it, and that the true nature of that relationship is enjoyable, filled with the promise of pleasure, abiding joy, even ecstasy. This is not to say that this promise will be realized in every instance, nor that there are not cases in which seeking its realization would be unwise. Within the domain of the second *chakra*, however, an enjoyable and intensely meaningful exchange of essential life energies becomes the holy grail of every quest worthy of the name.

The second *chakra* chart is a description of this erotic quest. It describes how and where we seek pleasurable connection within the embodied world, and – in the case of a wounded second *chakra* – where and how we experience blockage, inhibition, or some other form of resistance to our deepest capacity for abiding joy. Everything within the second *chakra* chart is interpreted in terms of how it contributes toward or seems to undermine the free expression of our erotic desires. Encompassed within the story behind the second *chakra* chart is the journey of every soul to recreate the garden paradise that is inextricably ensconced in its most primeval memories – from the most

◇◇◇

innocent gravitation of the child to non-sexual pleasures, to the awkward grappling of the adolescent with the explosion of hormones, to the seasoned adult in mid-life and beyond who is less and less willing to settle for anything that does not deeply satisfy. In its entirety, the second *chakra* chart is a measure of our subjective instincts toward the good life, shows where and how these instincts are most likely to be aroused, and maps an optimal path toward the liberation necessary to their fulfillment.

The circle that forms the second *chakra* chart takes special note of the fact that every point of the circle is balanced by another point across from it, and is nestled against points on either side of it. Within the circumference of the first *chakra* chart is an infinite variety of potentially pleasurable discoveries to be made, and it is through movement around the circle that the journey toward them is set into motion. Everything within the second *chakra* chart – even its most difficult features – can be understood as an expression of preference, of desire, of natural predisposition. Sextiles and trines, for example, normally associated with ease of expression and comfortable flow, might naturally be an astro-logical reflection of what is pleasurable, and what is naturally a part of one's preferred state of being. But even where the quest for desire seems thwarted, or the natural tendencies seem compromised by harder aspects such as the square or opposition, its function within the second *chakra* dynamic is no less erotic. The difficulties associated with the harder aspects, in fact, ultimately only add intensity to the experience of pleasure, increase the obsessive pull of our desires, and drive us more insistently toward the satisfaction of our innate preferences.

In *The Seven Gates of Soul*, I discuss the necessity for suspending judgment as a prerequisite for a true experience of the soul. Here I would add that it is in the second *chakra* that we learn how to do this. Behind whatever judgments traditional astrologers might place upon the features of a given birthchart is the astropoetic notion – brought to its most cogent expression in the second *chakra* chart – that everything in the chart and in life is exactly how the soul is predisposed to choose it. Even the more difficult patterns in the birthchart represent choices made by the soul, not out of some perverse desire to torture itself, but as an optimal pathway to alignment with its own essential nature. However arduous the journey might appear to be, the promise encoded in the second *chakra* chart is that this alignment will ultimately result in optimal pleasure, sustainable joy, and creative satisfaction in a life of well-being and abundance.

The Placement of Second Chakra Planets in Astrological Space

In Chapter Eleven, we postulated that planets in the first *chakra* chart above the horizon and to the west of the meridian would tend to be experienced as areas of potential danger, while the relative womb-like atmosphere of the NE quadrant – where energy is rising toward participation in the world, but also still protected by its invisibility – was considered ideal. Within the context of the second *chakra* dynamic – still part of the incarnation phase – protection, containment and safety are still important, but now within the context of providing an untroubled arena for exploration of the erotic dimension of our existence. This movement toward safe exploration of everything new and different is symbolized astrologically by a gravitation westward, but still below the horizon. While the west is suspect at the level of the first *chakra*, in the second *chakra*, where everything unknown is potentially a source of increased pleasure or joy, the west is likely to hold a special attraction.

From an erotic perspective, it is often the dark (northern) and mysterious (western) hemispheres that are most compelling, and so it is natural to assume that planets in the north and/or west will contribute most to the second *chakra* signature. The northern hemisphere also affords a sense of containment that separates the garden paradise from the wild chaos of the tangled jungle, so that the soul seeking to ground itself in a pleasurable relationship to the world will have a less compromised, complicated or ambivalent experience. Obviously, real life will often be compromised, complicated and ambivalent, and this will be reflected in any astrological signature we might ascribe to the second *chakra*. Second *chakra* experience will also invariably extend into the chaos of the jungle – especially where outer planets are involved. But here we are simply talking preferences, and to the extent that pleasure is a vehicle for deepening our embodiment (as it is in the incarnation phase), then the soul will prefer the NW quadrant as a base of operations.

This is not to say that planets above the horizon or to the east will not also play their part in second *chakra* patterns, nor that there is any particular problem with such placements from the perspective of the second *chakra*. Indeed, these placements may well be points of natural disposition from which the second *chakra* quest proceeds. But movement within a strong second *chakra* chart will tend to be down and to the west, where the promise of safe and pleasurable experience within the realm of the unknown holds special erotic appeal.

Where the most dangerous quadrant from the perspective of the first *chakra* chart was the SW, from the perspective of the second *chakra*, this will be a natural area for expansion and growth. For most of us, erotic exploration of the world is played out within the context of our relationships, and it is within the SW quadrant that relationships come into their own as a vehicle for life experience. Second *chakra* patterns may also be tied to the NE quadrant, particularly where issues of self-worth compromise the second *chakra* experience, or conversely where erotic experience is a primary vehicle through which a more cogent, secure and durable sense of self is evolved. The SE quadrant will not necessarily be considered dangerous from the perspective of the second *chakra*, but will generally be of less interest, and thus less often represented in second *chakra* charts.

Strong second *chakra* charts indicating core issues at this level of consciousness will generally take one of two forms:

1) the planets forming the pattern will cluster in the NW quadrant (the quadrant of choice), perhaps with tendrils extending into the SE and/or NW quadrants

2) the NW quadrant will be relatively empty, with a planetary pattern bracketing it from the NE and SW

In the first instance, the erotic tendency will be strong – perhaps at times, too strong, and the impetus toward growth through second *chakra* exploration will tend to be a major theme. In the second instance, there will tend to be avoidance of, strong taboo against, and/or disinterest in second *chakra* matters, until they erupt into consciousness – often dramatically – when triggered by progression or transit of second *chakra* planets through the NW quadrant and/or in aspect to the second *chakra* pattern.

The Second Chakra and the Succedent Houses

Whereas first *chakra* planets are most likely to be harbored near the angles of a chart, second *chakra* planets are more likely to be found in succedent houses. Since succedent houses are in the middle of the quadrant in which they reside, they represent life at its deepest level of engagement. This is where we are most actively participating in our lives on a day to day, moment to moment level, and thus – from the perspective of the second *chakra* – where the greatest potential for pleasure and erotic intensity of connection are to be found. While angular planets describe who we are in our most poignant statements of being and most potent moments of transition (as noted from a clockwise perspective), succedent houses describe what happens to us when we merge with the flow of life and, in a sense, disappear into life – that is to say, where we become so thoroughly engaged in the living of life that we forget ourselves in the moment. From the erotic perspective, it is this surrender to the moment – experienced most intensely during orgasm – that represents the highest possible, most deeply treasured attainment.

From an astro-logical perspective, it is in the succedent houses that this attainment is to be found. In the earthy 2nd house, we discover our bodies, the embodied world, the pleasure to be found within it, and what we value about it. The 5th house, associated by astrologers with sex, romance, and erotic play is perhaps the most archetypal second *chakra* house – appropriately nestled at the very heart of the preferred NW quadrant. In the fiery 5th house, often associated with the spirit and vitality of the child, we discover what gives us pleasure and brings us joy, experiment with our capacities for creativity and play, and gravitate toward a natural expression of being that is inherently a reflection of our most innocent, organic, uncompromised sense of self. This house describes our most basic passion for life, and the bliss (in Joseph Campbell's sense of the word) that we naturally feel drawn to follow. In the watery 8th house, associated by modern astrologers with, among other things, interpersonal chemistry, we take our desires and pleasures into the realm of intimate relationships, where the erotic potential of merging with the flow of life and with each other is realized and/or frustrated in some way, and where everything tends to become more intense. In the airy 11th houses, perhaps the least erotic of the succedent grouping, we nonetheless take Epicurean pleasure in the company of kindred spirits, and explore the potential for co-creativity in the building of a society that reflects our values and our preferences. Planets in any of these houses, but particularly the 5th, 2nd and 8th – can likely be considered the denizens of the second *chakra* chart.

Measurement of the exact range of succedent houses is one of the abiding areas of controversy within traditional astrological circles. Depending on which of a dozen or so possible house systems one uses, the boundaries of these houses will shift, at times up to half a sign or more. While each astrologer has their preferences and biases, my own tend toward the Porphyry house system, which recognizes the sacrosanct angles of the chart, and then simply divides the resulting quadrants in equal thirds – beginning, middle and end. Sometimes, shifting from one house system to another may reveal a second *chakra* pattern where it was previously not apparent. Whatever system one chooses, it seems astro-logical to assume that the closer any planet is to the midpoint of a quadrant (a point not normally considered in traditional astrology, but easily calculated), the more potent it will be as a potential second *chakra* planet.

It should also be noted that despite a preference for succedent houses, there will be times when a second *chakra* pattern shifts into the angular houses. Such may be the case, for example, with film stars or others, whose erotic explorations and second *chakra* issues are on public display. Among them, Marilyn Monroe had a strong second *chakra* pattern on public display formed by an upward half-kite in angular houses.

Second *chakra* patterns in cadent houses will be much less common.

Venus' Role in Second Chakra Dynamics

Given that the second *chakra* chart revolves around the erotic quest, it should come as no surprise that the planet Venus – associated with the erotic pursuit of pleasure, intimate relationships, and creativity – is often an important player in any second *chakra* chart[1]. This will be especially true when Venus sits in a succedent house, near the midpoint of a northern and/or western quadrant. Again, as with the first *chakra* chart, such potential must be confirmed by reference to the actual story that plays itself out in relation to the second *chakra* signature, but where Venus is strongly situated by astro-logical reference to the second *chakra*, it seems reasonable to look to the story to confirm a second *chakra* focus.

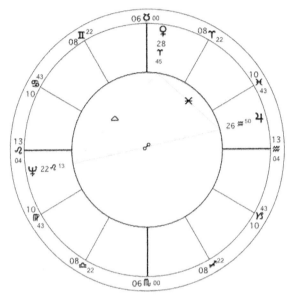

MARILYN MONROE'S SECOND CHAKRA SIGNATURE

Since the second *chakra* chart is ultimately an expression of that which is pleasurable, a source of joy, conducive to a life of well-being and bliss, any discussion of second *chakra* issues – particularly of core issues, worthy of a lifetime of struggle, pain, and hard learning – might seem to be an oxymoron. Of course, anyone who has ever been in a sexual relationship, watched 30 seconds of any soap opera, or walked through any red light district anywhere in the world knows that a vast universe of thorny issues weave precariously through the second *chakra* rose garden. We would not, in fact, be the first to observe that the human world as we know it, largely revolves around these issues. Given that this is so, it would be hopelessly naïve of us to suggest that the second *chakra* chart could be anything but a rich and fertile field for harvesting of life's most bittersweet fruit.

The seductive, but often deceptive nature of the second *chakra* world is a reflection of Aphrodite, who in one of her many guises as the goddess of erotic love and pleasure, presides over that world. Just as Saturn's protection proved to be a mixed blessing in the first *chakra*, so too does Venus' promise of unbridled ecstasy come at a price. In myth, Venus not only brought intense pleasure to those she blessed with her sensual touch, but also brought to the surface every pocket of unworthiness, guilt and shame, jealousy, vanity and petty rivalry for affection it was possible to dislodge from the trembling psyches of those who were caught in her erotic web. Yes, the second *chakra* describes what the Garden of Eden looks and feels like for us, but it also describes who and what we are behind whatever fig leaves we feel we must hide behind to withstand the intensely naked openness to experience required by the Garden.

In the first *chakra*, we strive to keep everything beyond the Garden walls at bay. In the second *chakra*, safe within the Garden, the question becomes not how much we can keep out, but how much of the Garden we can actually let in. With a weak second *chakra* chart, we can easily manage to stumble through life, accepting whatever moments of pleasure life affords us, but with a strong second *chakra* chart, we will be compelled to push back the limits of our capacity for pleasure, joy, and satisfaction. Everything that pushes back at us, also inherently reflected by the second *chakra* chart, then becomes the pivot point around which our second *chakra* issues will form.

Saturn's Role in Second Chakra Dynamics

In the language of astrology, any talk of limits or pushing back invokes the intuitive sense that Saturn might be involved. Indeed, in the psychology of any *chakra*, our resistance is likely in one way, shape or form, to involve Saturn. Thus in any chart, where Venus is counterbalanced by Saturn – particularly by hard aspect (semi-square, square, opposition, sesquiquadrate or conjunction) – the full experience of the second *chakra* will be compromised by our resistance to it.

Where this happens, resistance will generally take the form of retreat to the first *chakra*. In other words, as the intensity of the second *chakra* becomes too much for the soul to bear, Saturn's connection to Venus provides a convenient retreat behind the wall of safety afforded by the first *chakra*. Pleasure is diminished by moderation, joy is tempered by sobriety, and the unbridled pursuit of the good life is curbed by responsibilities and pragmatic considerations. But the fear of falling into, being swallowed by, and disappearing in the bottomless well of pleasure – or of being consumed by guilt or shame – is kept at bay.

When Saturn's presence becomes overbearing, the second *chakra* can become blocked, and compromised by issues which inhibit, censor or otherwise thwart the natural flow of the erotic impulse. Such issues can manifest as overt sexual dysfunctions, but also less obviously as chronic poverty, a debilitated sense of self-worth or worthiness to enjoy whatever abundance life has to offer, the absence of joy, and/or self-righteous judgments directed toward the more self-accepting quest for pleasure undertaken by others not similarly compromised. The mere presence of Saturn in juxtaposition with Venus is not sufficient, in and of itself, to indicate a blocked second *chakra*, but where such an aspect is part of a larger pattern (especially a hard aspect pattern) spanning succedent houses, it would not be out of line to look for confirming evidence of a second *chakra* issue within the life story of the person behind the chart.

Neptune's Role in Second Chakra Dynamics

Second *chakra* issues of a very different kind tend to arise when Saturn is not a tempering influence by hard aspect to Venus, but Neptune (and/or to a lesser extent, Jupiter) is. Neptune tends to push simple desire over the line into addiction, often never really knowing where that line is, or even that it exists. Under Neptune's unconscious pressure, the pursuit of pleasure becomes tinged with escapist urgency; the natural preference of the soul for experiences that are positive, joyful, satisfying and conducive to well-being tends toward denial in the face of experiences that are not; and relationships with erotic potential become neurotic adventures in which boundaries erode, jealous paranoia runs rampant, and fear of loss fuels possessive, clingy behavior. Venus and Neptune together can also produce genuine ecstasy, sublime works of art, and soul-stirring intimacy. But when lodged in a hard aspect across succedent houses, the combination tends to function like an enticing tropical pool with quicksand on the bottom.

To some extent, Jupiter (which is Neptune's astrological sibling) will function in the same way. Certainly, it will amplify and exaggerate Venus' natural functions, often to the point where the quest for pleasure becomes excessive and imbalanced. But like the function of Mars in first *chakra* patterns, the mere presence of Jupiter in juxtaposition (hard aspect or not) with Venus is insufficient to indicate the presence of a second *chakra* issue[2]. Jupiter and Neptune both in combination with Venus – as in Marilyn Monroe's chart – will be far more potent than Venus and Neptune alone.

Pluto's Role in Second Chakra Dynamics

Pluto, active as an agent in first *chakra* issues, is again often a significant player in second *chakra* issues. As the natural ruler of the 8th house, and the sign Scorpio, Pluto is often associated with sexuality, and especially with those aspects of sexuality that are obsessive-compulsive and out of control of the conscious ego. Anyone who has ever fallen in love will understand the irrational power of this obsessive-compulsive component of the sexual impulse to make us think, do, and attempt to be something outside of the box of our normal personality. It is though we are swept away by hormonal forces that don't care what becomes of us in the rush to merge with, consume, be consumed by, and saturate ourselves in the object of our erotic desire. Left to its own devices, the second *chakra* naturally functions as a compass designed to lead us toward our rightful place within the erotic web of possibilities. Under Pluto's alchemical pressure, it is as though the compass sits on top of the mother lode, spinning in directionless frenzy.

At this center, Pluto is also associated with breaking taboos. Wherever Pluto is locked into some astrological embrace with Venus, there will tend to be a desire to explore everything that was off-limits within the context of childhood conditioning. If Mom said oral sex was disgusting, oral sex will tend to hold a stronger than usual attraction. If the Church condemned homosexuality or society frowned upon interracial unions, then these forms of sexuality may become fertile fields begging for investigation. If an outraged teacher caught you masturbating in the girl's room during recess, then you might find the prospect of getting caught in the act to be the core of an enduring erotic fantasy.

The erotic compulsions existing within Pluto's repertoire will not be limited to overtly sexual behaviors, but may also include artistic expressions that push the boundaries of what society finds acceptable, non-sexual association with "undesirable elements," a refusal to conform to society's ideal of productivity and a strong work ethic, or the passionate embrace of anything shunned by those setting standards in any arena. The condemnation of these behaviors, sexual or otherwise, by authority figures will not likely be the sole source of attraction, but it will add a dimension of erotic compulsion to whatever natural tendencies or desires already exist. Nor will the goal of such Pluto-driven second *chakra* complexes be to shock others – unless Uranus is also implicated in the pattern – but rather to broaden the scope of one's erotic investigations, often without serious forethought, regard for consequences, or concern about the opinions of others.

These tendencies are exacerbated when Pluto and Neptune impinge upon Venus together in a planetary pattern involving them all. It is in such combinations that love really does go blind – losing all sense of boundary or limit under Neptune's dissolving fog, and being pushed over the edge by Pluto's volcanic insistence. Of special note in this regard is the t-square, or grand cross spanning succedent houses, but because the second *chakra* can be considered a *yin* center of consciousness – opened through surrender, permissive receptivity, and allowing – softer patterns involving these three patterns can also be indicative of second *chakra* issues. Among these are kites and half-kites, and grand trines.

Mars' Role in Second Chakra Dynamics

Again, as with first *chakra* patterns, it is not inconceivable that Mars will also play some part in second *chakra* patterns – in part as a more garden variety echo of Pluto's sexual proclivities, but without the obsessive-compulsive dimension, or preoccupation with breaking taboos. Unlike the first *chakra*, however, where Mars is insufficient to indicate a core issue without the presence of Pluto, Mars does play its own role in second *chakra* dynamics, and can precipitate a second *chakra* pattern (in tandem with other second *chakra* planets) without the necessity of Pluto's participation[3].

Mars is the planetary agency through which we actively seek to satisfy our desires, pursue the objects of our erotic attraction, and seek to generate the satisfaction and well-being our heart's desire. Mythologically and astrologically, Mars is the counterpart to Venus, providing a yang balance to Venus' erotic receptivity. If Venus extends the invitation, it is Mars that responds and actively seeks consummation of whatever promise has been held forth. Together Mars and Venus are the archetypal lovers. Though the second *chakra* is a *yin* center of consciousness, in which our task is to open more deeply to desire, pleasure, joy and abundance, the erotic quest is incomplete if desires cannot be fulfilled, pleasure cannot be actively sought, one must wait passively for joy, or do nothing to open the floodgates of abundance. Since Mars is the planetary agency through which we are driven to meet Venus in the Garden, and taste of the apple Venus offers, it can hardly be understood as a minor player within the realm of second *chakra* issues.

There is an entire class of issues, in fact, that is precipitated when either Mars or Venus is missing from the second *chakra* chart. When Venus is present, but not Mars, desires can be consuming without ever being met; pleasure can remain perpetually beyond one's reach; and one may crave champagne on a beer drinker's budget. Conversely, one may suffer from knowing how to take, but not give, thus precipitating imbalance, resentment and drawing forth a dysfunctional response from Mars (anger, retaliation, violence) in whatever erotic exchange one might otherwise enjoy. When Mars is present, but not Venus, one may try too hard to achieve one's desires, without ever really being able to enjoy the fruits of one's efforts. Giving can become a distorted attempt to control or manipulate or force the affection of another, without ever allowing the other person sufficient space to respond, or give, or contribute to the exchange. The troubled soul with a Mars-driven second *chakra* complex may have the sexual charisma or power to have anything or anyone she wants, but not the capacity to truly meld with another in erotic dissolution of boundaries.

The Second Chakra Chart

When three or more of the five second *chakra* planets – Venus, Neptune, Jupiter, Pluto and Mars – or any two plus Saturn (not really a second *chakra* planet, but capable of impacting second *chakra* issues) are involved in a planetary pattern, especially across succedent houses, you will have the astro-logical basis for a strong second *chakra* chart[4]. The more second *chakra* planets involved in the pattern, the stronger the pattern is likely to be. When all five second *chakra* planets are involved, or any four plus Saturn, the second *chakra* chart is likely to become dominant within the overall psychology of the individual soul.

A strong second *chakra* chart can also be indicated with a concentration of planets (usually, but not always a stellium) in the NW quadrant, particularly the 5th house. Alternately, there may be a larger pattern formed by three or more planets (including at least one second *chakra* planet) in the NW quadrant, extending tentacles by aspect to other second *chakra* planets in the SW and/or NE quadrants.

A somewhat less potent second *chakra* issue can be indicated when two second *chakra* planets form an aspect to each other that involves some third planet other than the one of the primary five. Here, we may have a hybrid pattern including the second *chakra* with some other. A t-square between Moon/Mars, Venus and Saturn, for example may be a hybrid first-second *chakra* pattern, if the life story bears this out.

As mentioned earlier, a planetary pattern involving three or more second *chakra* planets in angular houses can be a second *chakra* core issue put on public display. Such a pattern spanning the cadent houses may be a weak second *chakra* issue, or – as we shall see later – a sixth *chakra* issue. Planetary patterns formed by other "non-second *chakra*" planets – Sun, Moon, Mercury, Saturn, or Uranus[5] – in succedent houses may also indicate a weak second *chakra* planet.

If there are no planetary patterns formed by three or more planets in succedent houses, then we would look to the rulers of the succedent houses (particularly the 5th, 2nd, and 8th) for additional clues. If any of these planets form aspects with each other or with classic second *chakra* planets, these aspects would constitute our second *chakra* chart – although it is not likely in such a case that we are dealing with a second *chakra* issue. This kind of weak second *chakra* chart would most appropriately be understood as providing a low-level background indication of second *chakra* activity, perhaps with periods of foreground activation by transit or progression.

Endnotes

[1]   It seems odd to note that neither Grasse, Oken, nor Hodgson associate the second *chakra* with Venus. I can only speculate that this must be, in part, a reflection of the unconscious influence that Theosophical thought has had upon our collective understanding of the *chakras*. As mentioned earlier, the Theosophists felt the overt sexual energy (and by implication, the erotic impulse) to be so threatening, and so antithetical to spiritual development, that they relocated the second *chakra* from its original location near the sexual organs to the more innocuous spleen. Although I doubt that any of these other astrological authors are quite so repressed with regard to their sexuality, on a conceptual level, I think the Theosophical influence still holds court. Hopefully, this book will help to break that pattern and restore Aphrodite to her rightful place on the throne of second chakra pleasures.

2   Grasse and Hodgson disagree with me here, both postulating Jupiter as a primary player in second chakra dynamics. As with Judith's and Bruyere's association of the rainbow with the color scheme of the *chakras*, there is great conceptual appeal in making a simple correlation of the Chaldean order with the rulership of *chakras* by planets. In actuality, however, I suspect a more complex dynamic is at work. It is not that Jupiter is wrongly associated with this chakra, but I tend to think that Neptune represents a more intensely alchemical version of Jupiterian pressures around which issues in this *chakra* tend to constellate.

3   Hodgson identifies Mars as a primary player in this *chakra*, mainly through its traditional rulership of water sign Scorpio (93).

4   Hodgson specifically mentions the Moon (as ruler of water sign Cancer) in relation to this *chakra* (93).

5   Oken assigns Uranus rulership of the second *chakra* (155).

Chapter Fourteen
A Second Chakra Case Study

A strong second *chakra* chart is displayed by another student in my correspondence course, whom we shall call Irene.

Irene's second *chakra* chart is formed by the potent square between second *chakra* planets Mars in the succedent 2nd house and Neptune/Jupiter in the succedent 5th house. Since the Sun is part of this 5th house Libra stellium, conjunct Neptune/Jupiter, I would include it in this pattern. Mercury, forming an out-of-sign conjunction to the Sun, is also present, but less critical. Lastly, Mars is conjunct the North Node – always giving a boost in importance to whatever *chakra* pattern it emphasizes by contact.

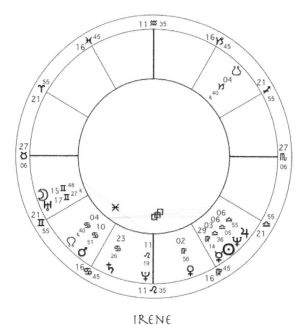

IRENE

While Venus is not a direct participant in this pattern, it is the ruler of Irene's chart and the dispositor of her 5th house Libra stellium, which is part of her second *chakra* signature. With the pre-eminent second *chakra* planet playing such a dominant role in Irene's chart, it could hardly fail to contribute to a strong second *chakra*. Yet, as we shall see later on in this case study, the fact that Venus does not participate directly in Irene's second *chakra* chart has its own set of implications for the nature of her particular second *chakra* issues.

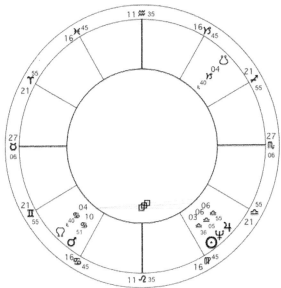

IRENE'S SECOND CHAKRA CHART

In a similar fashion, since Pluto sits tightly conjunct Irene's Nadir (the angle spanned by her second *chakra* pattern), it is also a silent participant in Irene's second *chakra* process. All five second *chakra* planets are thus active in shaping Irene's evolutionary intent, and hers is likely to be a life dominated by a second *chakra* quest. This is not to say that Irene is a one-dimensional being. Knowing her personally, I can attest to the fact that nothing could be farther from the truth. Nonetheless, within the context of this case study, we will explore the ways in which this pattern has at times been the dominating, all-consuming preoccupation we might expect it to be.

Lastly, we would note that although Saturn is not directly aspecting Venus (or any of the other second *chakra* planets in Irene's chart, Pluto does sit within 2° of the exact midpoint of Saturn and Venus. This midpoint pattern fits neatly inside the more obvious Mars-stellium square, thus suggesting an internal struggle (coalescing around the Nadir) between an attraction toward taboo and a restraint in the pursuit of it, which will become apparent as we explore the story related to Irene's second *chakra* issues. This can also be understood as a hybrid first-second *chakra* issue, in which the breaking of taboos can be experienced on some subliminal level as a threat to survival.

This somewhat obscure connection also illustrates an important point related to the identification of *chakra* signatures – namely that they come in many shapes and sizes that are not always obvious at first glance. In Irene's case, the presence of the complex square between a succedent Mars and a succedent stellium, involving three of five second *chakra* planets alerts us to the probability that some second *chakra* process lay at the heart of her life story. But to fill in the details that will illuminate the whole story, we must get creative and look beyond simple aspect patterns to other connective factors, such as dispositorship and midpoint trees. While our focus will be on observing the cyclical patterns related to the more obvious planetary pattern in the discussion that follows, we will also observe how these other, less obvious factors play into the dynamic.

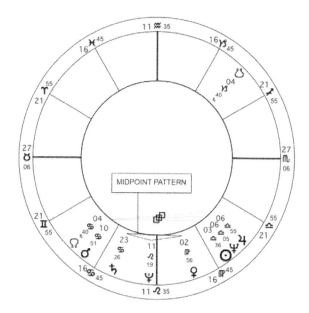

IRENE'S SECOND CHAKRA MIDPOINT PATTERN

In passing, we would note that Irene's second *chakra* chart encompasses a strong juxtaposition of fire and water – a watery Mars square water planet Neptune in a fire house, bracketed by fire planets, Jupiter and the Sun. This juxtaposition of fire and water, within the context of Irene's second *chakra* pattern suggest that the issues related to the pattern will provide an opening to *anandamaya kosha*, and an important opportunity for spiritual growth.

Irene's Unwounded Soul Essence, Part One: Mars

Just as we looked to the personal planets in our analysis of first *chakra* patterns (the Moon) for the unwounded essence of the soul, so too will we look to the personal

◇◇

planets in this second *chakra* pattern for evidence of Irene's unwounded soul essence. In this case, however, we must look for two very different images – one for Mars, the more obvious protagonist in Irene's second *chakra* story, and one for Venus, the less immediately involved, but equally important undertone for all second *chakra* issues and for Irene's chart as a whole. Again, as with the first *chakra*, these images of unwounded second *chakra* essence will come relatively early in life, usually before the age of 3 or 4.

First, let us look for Mars. As Irene described herself growing up, she was a "tomboy," whose earliest memories were of "fun, care-free romps on the farm, surrounded by bigger-than-life farmer uncles and aunts. . .[1]" She also notes "feeling that [she] was a disappointment to [her] father, because his oldest child was a girl. And all [her] natural tom-boyishness was constantly being reigned in because it wasn't lady-like. . . Whatever time her Dad had for [his] kids, it was usually spent with [her] brothers doing 'boy things' that [she] was excluded from." Here, of course, we are really discussing an aspect of Irene's wounding – involving a perceived rejection by her father for being of the "wrong" gender. But it is possible to see, in this description, nonetheless, a clear desire to be doing "boy things" and a strong identification with Mars, the planetary agency through which "boy things" are done. We would also note in passing that within the context of Irene's upbringing, the "boy things" toward which she naturally gravitated were somewhat taboo – off limits to a girl growing up in her family – and thus charged with the Plutonian edge common to many second *chakra* issues. In Irene's case, we see this astrologically through the semi-sextile (an aspect of friction) between her Mars and her Pluto.

If Irene did not get support for the aspect of her soul essence encompassed by Mars from the adults in her family, she did get some from her brothers, who accepted her as one of their own. She was, in fact, quite close to all her siblings (three sisters and three brothers), but it was the two brothers closest to her in age that encouraged the development of her Mars. In her words, they "looked up to [her] as a protector, defender, and leader (particularly on the ball field)." This statement, can of course, easily be translated astrologically as "they looked up to her as an embodiment of Mars," thus reinforcing her own identification with this planet. "They didn't reject [her] for being 'just a girl,' but saw [her] as a person with talents and abilities, and they still do. They taught [her] that [her] athleticism and leadership could be appreciated and respected, and they helped [her] earn a position of trust and acceptance in a 'boy's world'."

Irene's Unwounded Soul Essence, Part Two: Venus

When asked her fondest memory before the age of seven, Irene recalled "sitting on [her] paternal grandmother's lap on the back porch of the farm, wrapped up in her softness, [her] hand tucked into the top of her housedress, resting on her massive bosom.

It was a time of complete peace and serenity, warmth and comfort, and as [she had] come to realize, unconditional love." There is obviously a lunar quality to this image, suggesting that unlike Mary, for whom there was little sense of bonding with the Feminine source of life, Irene was literally and figuratively enfolded in the "bosom" of first *chakra* security.

This is reflected in her chart by the Moon's sextile to first *chakra* planet Pluto, the fact that first *chakra* planet Saturn is disposited by (in a sense, governed by or subservient to the needs of) the Moon, and the wide trine between Moon and Jupiter that forms the boundary of her entire chart, and broadens the lunar influence in her life. Only the conjunction with Uranus stands to possibly complicate her lunar bounty, but this is probably not a complication she will experience in the first *chakra*. As both the primal image of Grandma and these astrological indications suggest, we may safely assume that Irene's is not primarily a first *chakra* issue – although as we will see later, Pluto tightly conjunct the Nadir (the Moon's angle) does connect her second *chakra* issues to the first, as does its midpoint pattern with Venus and Saturn.

Meanwhile, we can also view this image of grand maternal love as an expression of Venus, satiated within the bosom of life's erotic embrace. There is a definite sensual quality to the image – given an innocent Venusian undertone through the soft warmth of her grandmother's lap, and the tiny hand on the breast. Obviously, at the tender age at which this image was first implanted in Irene's psyche, there could have been no erotic intent behind her attraction to grandma's comforting gift of unconditional love. Yet, as pointed out by generations of Freudians, it is a mistake to believe that the moments of bonding we experience in childhood do not have erotic implications that reverberate throughout our adult lives. As we shall see, when we get farther into Irene's story, the quest for the return to Grandma's lap, where love was uncompromised and happiness complete, lay at the heart of a lifetime of erotic adventure and misadventure. Thus, in terms of Irene's second *chakra* pattern, I think it safe to assume that this image of first *chakra* security is also an image of second *chakra* bliss, and that who Irene is within the context of this image, represents the embodiment of her unwounded Venusian soul essence.

There is another image from Irene's childhood that also speaks to Venus. On July 9, 1950, Irene "distinctly remember[ed] [her] father leaving to go to Korea on the day of an aunt and uncle's wedding. . . [She] was the flower girl, and it was both an exciting, happy day and a fearful, sad one at the same time." If we can temporarily extricate this moment from the fear and sadness, we have an unmitigated image of Venus, as this flower girl, pollinating a wedding ceremony with petals of beauty and love. To the extent that the quest for healing of our deepest issues is at heart a desire to return to the place of sacred innocence we once knew before we were wounded, then within the happiness and excitement beating in the small breast of this flower girl lies a key to Irene's redemption.

CHAPTER FOURTEEN

Irene's Primal Wounding

It would, of course, be impossible not to notice that this image of Irene's Venusian soul essence was clouded by the departure of her father for the Korean War. In the tenderly beating breast of a young girl, such moments are inevitably experienced as abandonment, since at that age, there is no capacity for understanding the complex worldly forces behind her father's departure. In Irene's case, however, this event merely serves to underscore a more internal and I believe more deeply damaging sense of abandonment – where she felt rejected by her father for not being a boy, and was excluded from doing "boy-things" with her father and her brothers. This deeper wounding precipitated a deeper identification with Mars, and when her father left, Irene also left the Venusian flower girl behind to embark upon her own quest for healing and reclamation of all that was rejected by her father.

Before we get to this story, however, there is one important point I wish to make. When we explored Mary's first *chakra* wound, we saw that hers was also precipitated by father abandonment. Looking at the outer events of both lives, a casual observer might conclude that the wounding experienced by both women must essentially be the same. Indeed, this would the path taken by most contemporary schools of psychological thought, and by more traditionally-minded astrologers unconsciously conditioned by these schools. But I am proposing here that the inner experiences of these two women are different enough, despite the similarities in the outer events of their lives, that it is worth distinguishing between two different kinds of father wounds. Before moving on, then, it will helpful to look at what exactly these differences are – both psychologically and astrologically.

From a psychological standpoint, Mary's father abandonment was experienced as a betrayal by mother, and as banishment to a world where it was impossible for her to gain a solid foothold. There was, within this world, no real security, no privacy, no support for her existence as a person. Irene, by contrast, was left in the care of an extended family that loved her and supported her, among them brothers who encouraged her in the development of the masculine side of her soul essence, a paternal grandmother whose nurturing lap was the epitome of security, and a mother who diligently provided for her material, if not her emotional needs. Here the abandonment was not banishment to an unsafe world, but to a world where "boy things" (Irene's natural gender identification) were taboo, and where her father – the primary teacher of "boy things" – though never really available to her, was now physically gone. Thus while Mary's quest was for safety and for a secure foothold within the circumference of the circle, Irene's was for an unconditional, loving embrace of her gender essence. Mary's father wounding can therefore be understood to belong to the first *chakra*, while Irene's is more accurately approached as a second *chakra* wound.

Astrologically, there is also a clear difference. Mary's father wound is reflected by a signature involving Saturn and Pluto, Saturn being traditionally associated with the father. Irene's wound, by contrast, does not involve Saturn, but the Sun, which is closely conjunct Jupiter/Neptune. The Sun is also classically associated with father, but in this case, the proximity to Jupiter/Neptune tells a very different story than Pluto. As Irene describes her father, he was "a social alcoholic and would often come home from official (military) functions completely intoxicated." Seasoned astrologers will recognize a living description of Irene's Mars-Jupiter/Neptune square in this quote, while I would also point out that this seemingly irresponsible, addictive behavior (the antithesis of Saturn-Pluto's rigid intensity) is a classic expression of the kind of second *chakra* wound that arises in the absence of Saturn's mitigating influence. Irene was spared this fate by her mother, who embodied the Saturn her father was apparently lacking, for when her father came home drunk, her mother, "an abstainer, would go on a rampage. It was usual at this time that (Irene's parents) had horrible and sometimes violent arguments."

Again, we can see an outer similarity to Mary's situation, in which life before her father's abandonment of the family was described as "embattled." While Irene did not go into detail about the nature or style of her parents' arguments, one "particularly violent episode (that) left a major emotional scar on [Irene's] psyche" shows how hers was clearly a second *chakra* wound. This incident took place shortly after her paternal grandmother (earliest image of unwounded Venus) died, around the age of 8, close to transiting Saturn's first square to its natal position. As Irene describes the parental fight, again after her father came home drunk:

> I remember huddling in the hallway with my brothers . . . since we were unable to sleep through the commotion, and evidently needing each other's comfort. The basic argument was that Dad felt held back in his career because of his responsibilities to a wife and four children. . . I felt I might be responsible for these arguments, and perhaps my brothers felt the same, but there was no comfort possible for that feeling. At some point, my mother pulled us in from the hallway, put my baby brother in my arms, got one of my dad's shotguns, handed it to him, stood behind us and said, 'If we're such a millstone around your neck, go ahead and get rid of us all right now!' In the moments that it took my weaving, drunken father to register what was happening, the terror I felt was almost unbearable. My brothers were crying, and I felt absolutely helpless to do anything to protect them, particularly (the) brother in my arms, who seemed the most vulnerable and innocent.

Obviously, this would have been a classic first *chakra* dilemma, except for one small detail: instead of brandishing his weapon in a life-threatening way, Irene's father broke out laughing, at which point her "five-foot-four-inch mother hit (her) six-foot-two-inch

◇◇◇

father so hard that she knocked him back over the coffee table and he hit his head on the edge of the couch, where he crumpled like a sack of potatoes, completely unconscious." Meanwhile, "[Irene's] emotions went from the fear of [her and her siblings] deaths to the fear that [her] father was dead." This is obviously an unbearable psychic load for an eight-year old girl to handle, and it undoubtedly triggered a potent first *chakra* response.

Beyond the fear of death, however, I believe that Irene was also placed in what we might construe as a powerful second *chakra* double bind, for the real question for her here was one of identity and function. As Irene framed the question, looking at the incident from the perspective of 50 years' distance, "Am I my father, guilty of feeling a 'millstone around his neck' with the pressure (of) family responsibilities, or am I my mother, guilty of setting up the situation that threatens the life of the relationship, or am I the helpless child, unable to defend herself and those she loves?"

When we explored this fundamental question in more depth, Irene concluded; "The scary part is that I sense I am all three, which only keeps me frozen in one spot.... Whenever someone becomes very angry with me, I will do anything to keep the shotgun from coming out." This became evident in a subsequent series of intense, melodramatic relationships where the shotgun was invariably on the table between Irene and her partners. She took disproportionate responsibility for the well-being of each lover, bending over backwards to accommodate their every need in order to avoid being seen in their eyes as a millstone. This heroic effort (Mars) often extended to the megalomaniac presumption (square Sun/Neptune/Jupiter) that she ought to be able to rescue her partners from the consequences of their own wounding. In the end, she invariably felt helpless to do this, and developed a cumulative sense of failure. Meanwhile, the flower girl languished in a perpetual limbo where whatever promise of true happiness might have been there at the beginning, soon wilted in the heat of entanglement between her partners' unresolved issues and her own. This pattern then became the template for the outworking of her second *chakra* wound.

The Astrological Timing of the Wounding/Healing Process

While a great deal of valuable information can be found tracking any outer planet transit to Irene's second *chakra* signature, the most immediately relevant will be a cyclical history of hard Neptune transits to her natal square. Since Neptune moves slowly, we might include the semi-square and sesquiquadrate along with the square, opposition and conjunction, in order to provide more data. In the following case study, I won't necessarily include every piece of data gathered, but will mention a few salient points that do emerge from Irene's Neptune story.

The first hard aspect from transiting Neptune to Irene's natal square was a semi-square to Sun/Neptune/Jupiter and sesquiquadrate to Mars lasting in total from December, 1963

– November, 1969. Growing up Catholic, Irene "tried to be a good Catholic girl, thinking that would secure [her] relationship with God and get [her] to heaven. [She] followed the rules as much as possible, felt guilty and fearful when [she] didn't, and bought the 'one true Church' dogma." In true Neptunian fashion, this unnatural effort to be the "good Catholic girl" extended to a brief flirtation with the idea of becoming a nun.

At the beginning of this first Neptune transit to Irene's second *chakra* pattern, at age 18, however, this strategy "fell apart when [she] came to realize that this 'child of God' was a flawed model in the eyes of the Church." No small part of this perception arose in the dawning realization that Irene was lesbian by disposition, and therefore not acceptable within the context of the religious life she was contemplating. She left the convent in early 1964, and embarked upon a more overtly erotic adventure, where she could more freely explore her sexuality and seek healing of her second *chakra* wounds.

Needless to say, claiming her true gender identity was a journey complicated not only by her father's rejection but also by the highly judgmental atmosphere of her religious conditioning. Struggling to free herself of this conditioning, she contracted venereal disease at age 20, "after having sex with two boys in college in an attempt to be straight."

By the end of this period, Irene had migrated to her first lesbian lover. She wrote "two volumes of ardent and philosophical poetry" in the heat of their initial romance, only to end the relationship as transiting Neptune was forming a direct station 2+ degrees beyond its last exact sesquiquadrate to natal Mars. As Irene described the break-up, "I had turned angry and verbally abusive toward her .... I wallowed in my worthlessness, got drunk on cheap beer and tragic love, and chased dark thoughts down the spiral of rejection and obsession. The deeper I went, the more afraid I became, started questioning my own sanity and contemplated suicide." Might we safely assume that Irene's second *chakra* wound, born of the rejection of her father, the Church and her own self-rejection, was now being triggered by what she perceived to be a new rejection by her first lover?

Thankfully, Irene did not commit suicide, but a year later, as transiting Jupiter and Neptune both transited Venus' angle in her chart (the Descendant) – a classic second *chakra* moment – she found herself being voluntarily committed to a state mental institution (like the convent, another Neptunian refuge). Before entering, "totally delusional and trapped by irrational fears and obsessive thoughts, [she] wept or moaned uncontrollably for hours and couldn't be left alone." In the hospital, she played Hearts with a deck of 50 cards, "trying to sort out what 'crazy' and 'normal' behavior was all about and where [she] fit in the continuum." She left a few days later in the good company of a new lover, "a bartender at a college watering hole,... who was (also) on the rebound."

At the beginning of the next hard Neptune transit to Irene's second *chakra* pattern (square to Sun/Neptune/Jupiter and opposite Mars – from January, 1985 – November,

1990), Irene moved overseas. Prior to the move, she had just experienced a relatively blissful phase of an on-again, off-again relationship with a lover she first encountered as a girl in summer camp, where Irene was a camp counselor, during Neptune's previous semi-square/sesquiquadrate period, discussed above. Irene's relationship with this lover began with tremendous guilt that she might have wounded this woman by introducing her to lesbian sexuality, at a time when Irene was still struggling with "religious guilt and self-loathing in dealing with [her] own lesbianism." Nonetheless, after several additional stormy, but passionate interludes, in 1985, they parted on amiable terms, and Irene thought that was that, as she began her new life abroad. But in the evolutionary plan for the healing of Irene's second *chakra* wounds, this smooth and easy ending ultimately proved to be merely another in a series of "opening farewells."

Irene's relationship with this lover was typical of her pattern, mirroring back to her and amplifying her own self-rejection in the distorted funhouse image of dysfunctional romantic love. Of this relationship, Irene wrote, "she often accused me of being 'stupid' when I did not agree with her, found it difficult to follow her line of reasoning, or was unaware or insensitive to her feelings and/or needs. My own lack of boundaries (a typically Neptunian dilemma) and insecurities usually led me to agree with her, acquiesce, or apologize, even when I didn't think I was being stupid or had done anything wrong." Is this not an echo of Irene's earlier statement that she would do anything to avoid the shotgun? This lover would alternately seduce, then blame and reject her, while Irene did a spastic dance of hungry atonement for sins real and imagined, futilely trying to protect herself from the abuse that deep down she believed she deserved. This went on for the better part of 25 years,

Nearly two years into this period, this lover formed a serious relationship with another woman. Irene was left to pine for what might have been, and to endlessly torture herself with fantasies about what she might have done differently. On the verge of moving on, however, this lover appeared again on her doorstep in 1989, and "just as [Irene] feared, [she] could not resist her (lover's) seductions and [they] ended up in bed together after a few weeks had passed," even though her lover was still in this other relationship. Irene felt a "twisted sense of triumph" in being "the desired mistress rather than the cuckolded mate" but "still... had the feeling that [she] was in a no-win situation." In retrospect, after an invitation to join a ménage a trios with both women, and a new somewhat more complex dance of flirtation, seduction and rejection, Irene concluded that "to say that I felt like a gullible idiot again is a bit of an understatement."

Bringing the Second Chakra Dance into Present Time

Fast forward to March, 2005, and Irene once again enters a hard Neptune transit to her second *chakra* pattern (sesquiquadrate to Sun/Neptune/Jupiter and semi-square to

Mars). A few years before this period began, at age 56, Irene wrote, "I harbor no illusion about actually having another relationship, much less an appropriate and fulfilling one.... I am in fact ready to die a failure at relationships.... I used to think that being happy and being in love (and getting laid) was synonymous (clearly a second *chakra* attitude), but I don't really believe that any more. Oh, there are plenty of times that I forget that, but for the most part, I want the sexual monkey off my back."

Nonetheless, a few short months later, she found herself in yet another relationship – this time with a colleague, who was vivacious, cultured, well-educated, well-traveled, and heavily medicated. As Neptune entered this new round of activation of Irene's second *chakra* pattern, serious problems began to surface. This new lover was clearly an erotic adventuress, in the best sense of that word, yet it soon became apparent that she expected Irene to foot the bill for these adventures. Beneath the hyper-extroverted drive of her new mate, which was largely drug-induced, lay a veritable rats nest of demons lurking for the opportunity to surface and remind her why she needed medication in the first place. Through a series of illnesses, accidents and crises at work, Irene became a caretaker (on multiple levels) to her new friend, lost all sense of personal space, and watched her savings dwindle. About this situation, Irene wrote, "I sometimes feel as if I'm responsible for filling a bottomless well of needs that is beyond my capabilities, megalomania notwithstanding! She may say she does not expect me to take care of her, but her actions and attitudes say otherwise, and that is what I tend to respond to and not without some resentment." Once again, Irene had apparently been duped into proving her worthiness in relationship to another woman with an uncanny ability to trigger her issues.

Groping Through the Second Chakra Fog Toward Healing

At the bottom of Irene's ongoing dilemma lay a profound sense of self-rejection and unworthiness. Despite the fact that this is a second *chakra* wound, ostensibly centered in the erotic quest for pleasure, joy, and blissful union, there is very little joy to be found in Irene's story. Sex – the quintessential second *chakra* experience – is not the issue. As Irene wrote, "I love sex with the woman I love – the pure physical sensuousness and the transcending spirituality of it. It is the one place I feel all of me work in sync." But within the context of her issues, sex has only been the gateway into a psychological morass in which the original rejection that wounded her in childhood gets played out in an infinite variety of permutations. The antidote to Irene's pain is clearly not sex, even great sex with a loving partner, but rather a much deeper self-love that only she can give herself.

It is telling from an astrological perspective that Venus – the primary second *chakra* pattern – is not involved in Irene's second *chakra* signature. It is bound instead by a much less obvious midpoint structure, Pluto = Saturn/Venus. Saturn/Venus combinations are often a signature for diminished pleasure, compromised joy, and inhibition of the capacity to open to the erotic dimension of life and receive its blessing, Pluto inevitably pushes any complex to its unbearable limit, at which point, there is either transformation or death, or some unfathomable and devastating combination of the two. Often, the subject (some would say victim) of Pluto's alchemical attentions must be broken, before she can feel the light that penetrates the cracks in her shattered identity. As battered as Irene has been in relationship, my guess is that she is not quite there yet.

Meanwhile, it is clear that this combination of first *chakra* planets in juxtaposition with her Venus forces a deeper reckoning. For behind the wall separating Irene from her joy is the image of the shotgun (Pluto), ever ready to put an end to her misery as the imagined millstone (Saturn) around the neck of every lover it has been her mixed blessing to encounter. To prove she is not that millstone, Irene has sacrificed her joy (Venus) on the altar of hyper-responsibility (Saturn again). To reclaim her joy, Irene must love herself enough to lift the yoke from around her own neck and release herself from bondage. With six more years to go in this current Neptune transit of Irene's potent second *chakra* pattern, the golden opportunity will be there for her, for some time to come.

Endnotes

[1]   All quotes in this chapter are from my correspondence with Irene over the course of our work together.

Chapter Fifteen
The Third Chakra Chart

The third *chakra* chart is a symbolic description of the process by which we stake out our territory within the embodied world. It is here that we evolve an ego, which then serves as the pivot point around which we grow as individuals capable of making a difference in the world in which we live. The ego has gotten a bid of bad rap in certain New Age circles, since it implies a certain level of politically incorrect selfishness, antithetical to so-called higher spiritual ideals of altruistic generosity, group-mindedness, and selfless service. Yet, as Yogi Bhajan was fond of saying, "Without ego, you do not have the strength to follow a spiritual path." Ego is merely the rudder on the ship we are each sailing across the cosmic ocean back into the heart of the Sun. At some point, the ego simply melts into the Ocean under the intensity of the Sun's penetrating gaze. But the ship will never get close enough for that to happen, unless the ego is there to chart the course and steer.

At a certain point in my study with Yogi Bhajan, he developed the vision to create a research facility that would scientifically document the physiological and psychological effects of various yogic practices. When it came time to staff the facility, which he named the Kundalini Research Institute, he slyly chose not one director, but four. When asked years later why he did this, he remarked that it was the best way he knew to accelerate the growth of the four directors he had chosen. "They were the ones with the biggest egos," he confided, "and it was by butting egos that they would gradually attain the spiritual strength necessary to manifest my vision."

The process was undeniably ugly, as it brought up every core issue these four directors had lurking beneath their shiny spiritual persona, but in the end, they accomplished far more than any one of them would have been able to accomplish alone. They did this by gradually staking out territories of authority and expertise within the organization they were entrusted to guide. One of them became Director of Research, another Director of Publications, a third Director of Applied Research and Counseling, and the last Director of Community Relations. It was an ingenious division of talents that allowed each of them to excel, and all of them together to work synergistically as a team, without sacrificing their individuality or autonomy.

In retrospect, it is possible to understand this entire process as a metaphor for what happens within the embodied world, on the level of the third *chakra*. Each of us is earnestly seeking to claim our place within a crowded arena of others also jockeying for position. In the end, no one else can claim our place but us, and we are all meant to function synergistically as integral parts of a whole. But until our third *chakra* issues are resolved, it often appears as though we are in perpetual competition for resources that are scarce, seeking to establish boundaries that overlap and violate each other, and struggling to overcome obstacles placed in our path by others. Collectively, we engage our egos in an adult version of bumper cars, fight holy and unholy turf wars, and cut tenuous deals to try to gain advantage. The current wave of popular television shows, including *Survivor*, *The Apprentice*, and *American Idol* are cartoonish displays of third *chakra* histrionics at their worst.

Can it be done another way? Perhaps. But as Yogi Bhajan used to say, "the spiritual journey is one that can be measured by a hand with outstretched fingers," which happens to be the distance between the physiological location of the third *chakra* and the fourth. At the fourth, we gain our first sense of being part of a larger integrated whole, at the center of our own field of resonance. At the third, however, it appears to be every soul for herself, and in the race toward center, it is unfortunately not always the best among us who win. What the fiery process teaches us, however, is that we occupy the center of our own world to the extent that we become centered in alignment with ourselves. When that happens we discover a reservoir of strength within that sustains us regardless of what does or does not happen on the third *chakra* battlefield.

Given the nature of this process, we might imagine that the third *chakra* is symbolized by the circle with a dot at its center. In the second *chakra*, we recognized an affinity of relationships to be explored in the juxtaposition of points next to and across from each other in the circle. At the third *chakra*, what emerges that was missing at the earlier phase is a sense of the one who is exploring, the "I," the primary protagonist in the quest for relationship. All points in the circumference of the circle are now referenced to a central point of awareness, through which everything in soul space finds its place.

Everything within the third *chakra* chart can be understood, in relation to this symbolism, in terms of how it either contributes to or thwarts the cultivation of an empowered central sense of self. While pleasure was inherently a good to be sought for its own sake in the second *chakra*, pleasure can be either conducive or antithetical to the strengthening of identity and purpose sought at the third. Likewise, though survival is the unquestioned goal of the first *chakra*, the price to be paid for safety and protection may at times be antithetical to third *chakra* goals. Once the center of the circle is established, there is impetus to explore the territory past the circumference, and one is willing to take a risk that is just not part of the first *chakra* dynamic – even when pushing past the circumference becomes uncomfortable or even painful at the level of the second *chakra*.

In *The Seven Gates of Soul*, I speak of how the embodied world is an arena for learning through finding one's center along the continuum marked by a number of primal polarities – light and dark, male and female, self and other, hot and cold, near and far - to name just a few. At the second *chakra*, we seek our natural place of preference along each of these continuums. At the third *chakra*, we push past the place of balance into imbalance, in order to explore what exists on the other side. We push, and the universe pushes back - often, as my earlier anecdote about the Kundalini Research Institute suggests, in the form of other people vying for the same territory. It is at the third *chakra* that we experience excess and the tendency toward conflict that arises as a consequence of excess. Or, if we are lacking in some essential skill or quality, we may experience the universe pushing us more insistently to develop it.

The third *chakra* chart will show where in our lives we are likely to experience and/or gravitate toward excess, or suffer deficiency, and how we will tend to get in trouble because of it. In this chart are the seeds of interpersonal friction, and at a deeper level, of ambivalence within ourselves regarding our place along one or more polarities from which we have chosen to learn. The third *chakra* chart shows how interpersonal friction and conflict can contribute toward a stronger, more integrated sense of self, and ultimately points beyond the need for conflict or friction. Once we realize, as did the old cartoon character Pogo, that "we have met the enemy and he is us," we no longer need to project our battles outside ourselves, but can turn instead to the battle raging within as an increasingly skillful mediator. While third *chakra* dynamics can turn ugly in the struggle toward this realization, from a spiritual perspective the work in the third *chakra* is always about dealing with anger effectively, moving beyond blame, and cultivating a vehicle that is strong enough to contain and channel the intensity of our personal power. The third *chakra* chart shows us where the triggers are for this kind of learning, and how we might approach the tasks involved with consciousness and creativity.

The Placement of Third Chakra Planets in Astrological Space

In the third *chakra*, we experience our first inclination to actively explore the southern hemisphere. Now that a sense of safety has been established, and we have identified our own desires, preferences, and natural inclinations, we have effectively anchored our existence in the embodied world, and that world begins to beckon us. The third *chakra* agenda revolves around the opportunity to test, prove, and establish ourselves within a larger arena of our choosing, and it becomes clear to us at this level, that this opportunity exists primarily across the other side of the horizon. While the incarnation phase of the evolutionary process demands the dark, protected, underground containment of the northern hemisphere, the awakening phase proceeds full throttle in the south.

As with the first *chakra*, the natural preference in the third *chakra* is the east - identified with the cultivation of a sense of self, and the capacity to take initiative in the pursuit of a personal agenda. The east is particularly important to the soul wrestling with third *chakra* issues, for it is here that the soul must go to cultivate ego strength. The deepest internal sense of self will be found in the NE quadrant, and it will be natural for the third *chakra* soul to retreat here from time to time for guidance and renewal. The real work in the third *chakra*, however, will involve testing and refining the ego in the real world laboratory provided most poignantly in the SE quadrant. The NE quadrant, will often be a source of strength within third *chakra* dynamics, but the SE quadrant will represent the cutting edge of its growth.

The western hemisphere is a bit more problematical at this level, in that it often represents that area of soul space with the highest potential for conflict. Those with strong third *chakra* charts may gravitate here, but will generally find themselves butting against other egos also seeking to establish a sense of personal territory. Mentors and teachers are often found at the cadent end of the SW quadrant (9th house), but rivals and outright enemies will tend to be attracted at this level at the angular end (7th house).

In the 3rd quadrant, the primary challenge will involve dealing with projections – both positive and negative – through which we misperceive our mentors and our enemies. The task in relation to these projections is invariably owning qualities, attributes, or features with which we don't identify – essentially everything encompassed by Jung's shadow. However, this is rather advanced work for a soul struggling with typical third *chakra* issues – developing an ego, cultivating talents, skills and abilities, and discovering what one is capable of accomplishing within the world. Within the context of third *chakra* dynamics, the soul is more likely to do battle with its projections than own them.

The battle takes place largely in the SW quadrant, while the possibility for owning projections will tend to be a NW quadrant process, mostly beyond the range of the third *chakra*. Still, the farther we push out into the world, the more deeply the world tends to extract from within us what we would prefer to keep hidden, and in some cases, there may be a cross-quadrant undertow, pulling the soul into the NW quadrant, despite its preference for the open field of the southern hemisphere.

In summary, astrological patterns related to third *chakra* issues will generally take one of three forms:

1) the planets forming the pattern will cluster in the SE quadrant, with tendrils extending into the NE and/or SW quadrants;

2) the SE quadrant will be relatively empty, with a planetary pattern bracketing it from the NE and SW;

3) there will be a strong cross-quadrant dynamic between the SE quadrant and the NW quadrant.

In the first instance, the soul will tend to experience a relatively normal course of third *chakra* development, primarily through the pursuit of career – with periodic bouts of soul-searching and/or work-related conflicts with bosses, co-workers and possibly employees. In the second instance, third *chakra* development will tend to be more problematic as personality, self-confidence, and competence (all either in excess or deficiency) become potential obstacles to success within the world, and/or interpersonal conflicts block one's forward progress. In the third instance, when a third *chakra* pattern spans the SE and NW quadrant, there will be higher stakes and potentially higher rewards. Here is where chronic patterns of family wounding can interfere with the cultivation of individuality and the pursuit of an individual path. Seemingly irreconcilable conflicts between career and family responsibilities can add significantly to the stress of third *chakra* development; or ongoing health issues can create an unlevel playing field – to suggest a few of the more common possibilities. On the other hand, working through these deeper, more unyielding third *chakra* issues can generate a great deal of personal power and vision, allowing one to carve out a unique niche for oneself on the more public side of the horizon.

The Third Chakra and Angular Planets

As with the first *chakra* chart, planets in the third *chakra* chart will most likely be found on the angles of the chart, although with a different meaning. Whereas at the level of the first *chakra*, planets on the 12th house side of the Ascendant were often cultivated as an assurance of safety, protection, and survival within the childhood environment, these same planets can and will be the triggers for conflict as third *chakra* patterns are triggered. At this level, they are the internal psychological obstacles – the personal guardians of the threshold – that must be overcome if progress is to be made in establishing one's area of expertise within the world. Someone with Mars here, for example, may need to learn to assert himself more effectively, stand up to bullies, and fight for what he believes. Someone with Venus here may need to learn to cooperate, cultivate people skills, and see the beauty in the world before she can conquer it.

Planets in the 1st house, especially those near the Ascendant, represent energies, faculties, and/or resources held in abundance, which provide the engine for the push across the line into the world. Unlike with first *chakra* dynamics, these planets are not difficult to own or assimilate at the third *chakra*. Quite the contrary, the soul with a strong third *chakra* chart is likely to identify with these planets to a fault, or at a disproportionate level to their importance within the whole chart. To the extent that the third *chakra* dynamic takes center stage, one with Mars here might well be the assertive bully the 12th house third *chakra* Mars needs to stand up against. One with Venus here might be a people person, perhaps self-sacrificing at times in self-sabotaging counterbalance to her own third *chakra* agenda.

Planets in the 10th house are often pressed into third *chakra* duty, as these are the planetary vehicles through which we most actively and effectively pursue our careers (a primary arena for the outworking of third *chakra* dynamics). Planets in the 9th house can also contribute to third *chakra* issues, especially when they are in hard aspect to planets near the angles of the chart. In this context, they often represent projections directed toward authority figures, bosses, teachers, mentors or others in a position to guide us in the cultivation of third *chakra* skills, the gradual development of competence and confidence, and assumption of our place in the world. In some cases, the projections onto 9th house planets can be in the opposite direction – toward us, directed by those in whose footsteps we are following. When this is the case, the third *chakra* task becomes disentangling ourselves from those projections so we can get on with our own lives.

Planets in the 7th house are also convenient targets for our third *chakra* projections, although here the relationships in which they are projected tend to be more horizontal than hierarchical, relationship with equals – typically rivals – rather than with those we look up to by choice or necessity. When Mercury is here, we tend to argue vociferously with those who disagree with us. With Saturn here, we may struggle with a dominant spouse who imposes burdensome demands upon us. Planets on the 6th house side of the horizon, especially those near the Descendant, are more likely to represent internal qualities with which we struggle, because they appear to get in the way of our third *chakra* agendas. With Mercury here, our arguments tend to be more internal, and may manifest, for example, as the inability to make a decision, or take a committed stand on a divisive issue, or clearly articulate to ourselves our goals and priorities. With Saturn here, we may tend to be especially vulnerable to the judgments of others, especially when they are questioning our competence or pointing out our limitations, because the outer words echo our own opinions of ourselves. The struggle here, in relation to our critics, is not with them, but with the self-judgments that they echo, although almost invariably third *chakra* issues will be projected across the horizon into the angular 7th house, where they can be openly dealt with, projected or not.

Lastly, planets near the Nadir can contribute to third *chakra* dynamics by exposing the hidden roots of whatever external conflicts play themselves out in our lives. However, these more subterranean planets will rarely be part of a third *chakra* process, since the tendency at this level is not to dig quite so deeply – except where Type 3 patterns are in play. When this is the case, angular planets at the Nadir can either represent forces that hold us back or that push us out into the world in disproportionate measure to our own desires or inclinations. The parent who insists their child follow in their footsteps though she is ill-suited for such a journey can be found here in the third *chakra* chart of the child (usually on the 4th house side of the line), as is the parent whose self-doubts have infected their child's own third *chakra* drives. On the 3rd house side of the line is found sibling rivalries, out of which spring adult imitations of the childhood dynamic, or conflicts with neighbors or co-workers that appear to hold one back until one comes to terms with the projections they embody.

As with the other *chakras*, third *chakra* issues are underscored where there are aspects between planets at more than one of these stations – principally on the 1st house side of the Ascendant, the 7th house side of the Descendant, and on either side of the Midheaven. Especially difficult are squares or oppositions, and planetary patterns formed by hard aspect between planets in these houses.

Mars' Role in Third Chakra Dynamics

While Mars plays a secondary role in first *chakra* dynamics (behind Pluto), and a more active role in second *chakra* dynamics in counterbalance to primary second *chakra* planet, Venus, Mars comes into its own in the third *chakra*[1]. This cannot be surprising to any astrologer following this discussion so far, since Mars is the planet most readily associated with all activities and expressions of the third *chakra* – self-determination; procurement and territorial defense of personal space; the cultivation of competence, confidence, and expertise; and the downside associated with interpersonal friction, cutthroat competition, and conflict.

Given the closeness of this match, we might postulate that anywhere Mars sits on the angle of a chart (especially the Ascendant, Descendant and Midheaven), some third *chakra* dynamic is likely to be involved – particularly if it sits in hard aspect to another third *chakra* planet. Mars need not be angular, however, to be a third *chakra* indicator, if it is otherwise emphasized by placement. For example, if it sits at the apex of a t-square, or is a singleton planet, or rules the sign on the Ascendant (Aries or Scorpio), it can serve as the focal point around which a third *chakra* pattern might revolve.

Just as Saturn and Venus presented a mixed blessing to the soul, seeking fulfillment through the first and second *chakras* respectively, so too does Mars demand a price for facilitating the third *chakra* agenda. In moderation, and channeled with clarity of intention, there is no better planet than Mars for fueling the journey toward self-actualization and skillful navigation of one's personal sphere of influence. By nature, however, Mars is a planet given to excess, and unless it is counterbalanced – by Saturn, placement in an earth sign, or retrogradation, to name a few common possibilities – it will tend to precipitate the difficulties that naturally come with excess: competence can easily lead to recklessness; confidence inevitably crosses the line to become arrogance; self-assertion ramps up as aggression; territorial defense becomes a stepping stone to conquest; and so on. Mars demands movement, and when it reaches the natural edge of its rightful kingdom, it may not know how to stop.

◇◇

Wherever Mars has a burr in its saddle, through hard aspect to other planets, especially other third *chakra* planets, the potential for a third *chakra* core issue is vastly increased. Most core issues in this *chakra* will revolve around Mars' tendency toward excess, although it is also possible to struggle with a deficient Mars that is debilitated through difficult placement, usually in hard aspect to Saturn or Neptune.

The Sun's Role in Third Chakra Dynamics

If Mars is the agency through which we attain the skills, competence and confidence to take our place within the world, then the Sun represents who we become as we attain third *chakra* mastery and struggle with whatever obstacles lie on our road toward that end[2]. The Sun is traditionally considered to be the central protagonist of any soul's journey – it is the "I" who undertakes the journey, the ego who negotiates the journey according to its own sense of identity, intention and purpose, and the central self out of which identity, intention and purpose spring. The Sun (and everything it represents) only begins to enter the stage of our awareness at the level of the third *chakra*. Before that, it exists as mere potential, a guiding force that acts subliminally at the first *chakra* to ensure its own survival, and instinctively at the second *chakra* as it gravitates toward experiences that feed it and spark it into life. Only at the third *chakra* does the Sun becomes a conscious force tending toward actualization of the potential that was only dimly sensed at previous *chakras*.

It is no coincidence that the glyph for the Sun – a circle with a dot at its center – is identical to our earlier description of the circle as it exists symbolically at the third *chakra*. The entire process of self-actualization being discussed in relation to the third *chakra* is very much a solar journey. It is why we are here, and its destination is our soul's destiny. The Sun itself, however, is not a planet capable of self-actualization. It is an expression of being, and ultimately of Being out of which all souls arise. Caught in the melodramatic throes of the third *chakra* dynamic, we are more likely to be aware of Mars as the active agent through which the third *chakra* agenda of self-actualization is realized. But at the heart of that agenda reverberates the Sun, the spark of the divine at the center of each soul, that propels it into and through this embodied existence. While Mars drives the soul toward self-actualization, it is the Sun that is actualized as Spirit within the living form of each individual soul[3]. The Sun has multiple levels of reality waiting to unfold and be discovered, many of which transcend the third *chakra* altogether, and the highest of which transcend this embodied existence. But it is at the third *chakra* that our awareness of the being encompassed by the Sun, first emerges.

In this function, the Sun can be understood to be a seed, sometimes called a *bindu* in yogic terminology, around which the soul forms, gradually comes into more conscious being, and evolves through much trial and error toward a full identification with its source in Spirit. Swami Muktananda often spoke of the awareness of *bindu* as a much-desired goal of meditation, the attainment of which was said to put the entire journey of the soul into spiritual perspective. Just as the physical Sun is the source of light within the embodied world, so too is this spiritual Sun, the source of radiance that illuminates the spiritual path.

> In the center of this radiance there is a blue dot, the blue bindu, which is marvelous to behold. When you see that light, you know that you are really divine. This blue bindu should be honored very highly. It is by means of this blue bindu that a man is born and reborn, and by means of the blue bindu one can see all of the different worlds in meditation. The blue bindu is the foundation of the body; and if it were to leave, the body would be as lifeless as a corpse. All of the bodily functions: the respiratory rhythm, the circulation of the blood, and the action of the nervous system are regulated by the blue bindu. It is like a small sesame seed, and the writers of the sacred books call it the seed of the heart. The whole animate and inanimate universe lives inside this heart seed.... We call it the radiant blue bindu. We can also call it the inner Self, and we can also call it our God.

In this passage (<u>Understanding Siddha Yoga</u> 118-119), Muktananda speaks of the Sun as it exists and is experienced in the *sahasrara* or seventh *chakra*. Most spiritual teachers, including both Yogi Bhajan and Swami Muktananda, considered the experience of this *bindu*, or all-potent seed, to exist in stark contrast to the everyday garden-variety ego that normally guides our soul through its embodied journey, and the goal of much spiritual practice seems to be to transcend the ego so that *bindu* might be experienced in its place. Since my study with these teachers, however, I have come to believe that the ego and the *bindu* are not opposites, but rather phases of the same being, emerging only gradually as one discovers and experiences it from various perspectives. Put crudely, the ego is the *bindu* in third *chakra* drag.

Ego is both the vehicle for learning, and the being that learns. Though we like to think that the *bindu* is who we are, when all of this worldly preoccupation with ego falls away, without the learning process centered in the third *chakra* around the experiences of the ego, this is never going to happen. We don't transcend the ego so much as we shed various layers of its skin, until the radiance of the *bindu* shines through our transparency. Ego is simply *bindu* in a relatively unconscious state. As we grow in consciousness, the ego gradually evolves into *bindu*, which sits at its core all the while radiating with pure intention. This process is encoded astrologically by the symbol of the Sun, which exists at the third *chakra* as ego, and at the seventh as *bindu*, and continues to reverberate, silently invoking the particulars of our journey, at every stage in between.

When the Sun is involved in a third *chakra* pattern, through placement in aspect to Mars, it functions mostly as ego, but not without reference to its spiritual reality in *bindu*. *Bindu* can be understood as the central dot within the third *chakra* circle, the ultimate vantage point from which to perceive the circle of life encompassing the embodied world. At the level of the third *chakra*, this circle of life is an arena in which the soul must assert its presence, and take a place that fits its nature. But the nature of the soul itself *is bindu*, and as the soul grows in relation to its third *chakra* agenda, its place within the circle of life will increasingly honor its awareness of this central truth – harbored astrologically by the Sun.

To the extent that Mars serves the third *chakra* agenda with skill and awareness, Mars will facilitate a learning process that allows ego to exist and function in harmony with *bindu*. To the extent that Mars tends toward excess, and mistakes the means (its own fiery capacity for doing) with the end (the full illumination of being), Mars and the Sun will be at odds with each other, and a third *chakra* core issue will crystallize. To the extent that Mars is rendered incapable of manifesting the sense of place required by the Sun on the level of the third *chakra*, a different sort of core issue will arise. The determining factor that skews Mars toward either excess or deficiency will often be other planets to which Mars and/or the Sun are bound, usually but not always by hard aspect.

Planets Contributing to Third Chakra Excess

Planets contributing to conditions of excess Mars are Jupiter, Uranus, and Pluto. When any of these planets are in aspect to Mars, especially an angular (or otherwise emphasized) Mars in hard aspect to the Sun, we have the signature for a potential third *chakra* core issue marked by excess. It should be noted that soft aspects are just as potent, sometimes more potent, as indicators of third *chakra* excess as hard aspects. Any hard aspect, even by a sympathetic planet, will produce some friction, which ultimately slows Mars down. Though Jupiter and Mars both share a capacity for fiery excess (especially when both are in masculine signs), Jupiter square Mars will pit Jupiter's capacity for perspective against Mars' short-sighted impulsiveness; Jupiter's concern with social sanction with Mars' rabid individualism; and Jupiter's sense of altruistic generosity with Mars' tendency toward selfishness. Similar dichotomies will exist when Mars is in hard aspect to Uranus and Pluto. Whatever shape they may take, these dichotomies tend to mitigate and counterbalance Mars' tendency toward excess. When Mars is in soft aspect to these planets, however, their similarities tend to reinforce each other, and Mars is given a more unbridled path toward excess and often encouraged to travel it.

When Mars and Jupiter are in soft aspect, Mars becomes Mars on steroids. Jupiter often exaggerates, inflates, and increases whatever it touches, and when it touches Mars,

Mars becomes over-confident, careless, oblivious to what it happens to run over in its enthusiasm, spread too thin, and/or more likely to crash headlong into other souls making their way through the third *chakra* arena. When Mars also sits in hard aspect to the Sun, or conjunct to it, these behaviors marked by excess will in some way, interfere with the solar agenda of evolution toward *bindu*.

The Sun itself will distort to reflect this imbalance, and begin exhibiting all the attributes that have given ego its bad-boy reputation. As Mars/Jupiter breeds over-confidence, the Sun becomes proud, and as the saying warns us, "pride goeth before a fall." When Mars/Jupiter is careless, *bindu* goes out of focus, and the Sun becomes a dim and sloppy imitation of its most radiant self. When Mars/Jupiter begins banging into other souls, because of its oblivious, cavalier, reckless nature, the Sun is forced to defend itself as a separate entity, forgetting its interconnectedness at the Source of All-That-Is and becomes but a pitiful ego, puffed up with its own self-importance. This will also be the case where the aspect of excess is between Sun and Jupiter.

When Mars and Uranus join forces through soft aspect, Mars becomes reckless, accident-prone, unreliable, unpredictable, and anarchistic. In reflection of these excesses, the Sun is forced to shift its attention from self-actualization to damage control, and ego loses the focus of *bindu* as it is forced to ground itself and re-establish its equilibrium amidst rapidly shifting circumstances. Though individuals with Sun-Mars-Uranus complexes will be perceived as spontaneous free-wheeling surfers of the cosmic wave, beneath the flash and glitter, they will tend to perpetually be one-step behind themselves, never quite sure if the next step will land on solid ground. It is hard to grow toward a deeper embodiment of the radiance of *bindu* when you are constantly blinded by the light, especially one that is strobing in syncopated rhythm on a dance floor constantly shifting beneath your feet.

In hard aspect, Uranus can provide some counterbalance to Mars. While both Mars and Uranus are individualistic by nature, Uranus thrives on the stimulation of other free spirits, whereas Mars prefers to work alone. Mars functions best when it can establish a rhythm and a momentum; Uranus will constantly disrupt both, as the inspiration of the moment strikes it. While Mars is not afraid of conflict, indeed often thriving in the midst of it, Uranus is more of a laissez-faire kind of energy, for whom conflict holds no inherent attraction. Each of these differences can present obstacles to the unbridled expression of Mars, although any of them can also contribute to a third *chakra* core issue, where Mars must fight its allies, while the Sun gets caught in the middle as ego in a perpetual bind.

Mars is often called the "lesser octave" of Pluto, suggesting a natural affinity between these two planets similar to that between Venus and Neptune in the second *chakra*. When we discussed the first *chakra*, we saw how on that level, Mars contributed emphasis and intensity, as well as a mechanism for working through first *chakra* core issues, in situations where Pluto was a primary player. In the third *chakra*, Pluto can easily support Mars and easily lead it toward excess, when both are involved in a third *chakra* pattern. This will tend to be true whether Mars and Pluto are in soft or hard aspect, but more pronounced in soft aspects and the conjunction. Pluto is, in many respects, an intensified, over-the-top, no-holds-barred caricature of Mars at its most hyperactive self: mythic warrior Rambo to Mars' ordinary soldier; speed demon Mario Andretti to Mars' everyday driver; ferocious linebacker Ray Lewis to Mars' garden-variety defender of territory.

Imagine everything Mars is good at, and then amplify it to the point where it becomes too intense for most situations that will arise in the course of the soul's embodied journey through life. Where Mars is courageous, Mars/Pluto can be as fiercely fearless as a berserker; where Mars is competitive, Mars/Pluto won't rest easy until it has squashed the competition; where Mars seeks to stake out its territory, Mars/Pluto must conquer and subjugate what it claims for its own. Such attitudes inevitably breed conflict and retaliation, and where the Sun seeks only to shine, it is often pressed into active duty as a target and a shield whenever Mars and Pluto join in third *chakra* shenanigans. Sun-Pluto combinations can produce an obsessive, relentless, ruthless agenda that pushes Mars to the limit of its capacity. Regardless of how these planets are arranged in relation to each other, the combination is a recipe for hyper-aggression, behavior that tends to antagonize, and eventually for burn-out.

When Mars and Pluto function together in hard aspect, Mars is still driven to excess, but here there are likely to be consequences, which can slow Mars down. Soliders driven by berserker energy do get wounded; race car drivers crash; even ferocious linebackers meet their match and occasionally go down. All of this provides tremendous opening for soul – as outlined in some detail in *The Seven Gates of Soul* – particularly through the activation of a third *chakra* core issue involving Mars, Pluto and the Sun.

Planets Contributing to Third Chakra Deficiency

While Jupiter, Uranus and Pluto contribute to third *chakra* patterns marked by Mars' excess and the consequences of that excess, Saturn and Neptune can contribute to third *chakra* patterns where the problem is Mars' inability to muster the necessary internal resource to serve the evolutionary agenda of the Sun. As with patterns of excess, these contributing planets work either in soft or hard aspect. Soft aspects can provide smooth sailing through third *chakra* waters, provided the Sun is not also in hard aspect to a deficiency planet, for in moderation, these influences can curb just enough of Mars' tendency toward excess that it functions optimally within third *chakra* territory. Where the Sun is also impacted by these planets of deficiency, however, what curbs Mars may also curb the Sun, and both may be resigned to a low-energy manifestation of third *chakra* possibility.

If, for example, Saturn sextiles Mars and simultaneously squares the Sun, which in turn semi-sextiles Mars, there tends to be a friction between Mars' interest in worldly success and the Sun's reach toward a higher, more spiritual agenda that manifests as a depressed and depressing ambivalence in the face of opportunity. Good old-fashioned hard-aspect patterns like the t-square or grand cross can also breed third *chakra* core issues marked by deficiency, but some of these less obvious combinations of hard and soft aspects can be just as problematic. However they combine, where Mars (especially an angular Mars) and Sun (especially in hard aspect to Mars) join Saturn or Neptune, you have the makings of a third *chakra* core issue marked by deficiency.

Each of these planets will impact Mars in different ways. Saturn is very much the gnarly old task-master, who initially seems to present nothing but impossible tasks to his unruly, cocky pupil. Blocked at every turn, the pupil either implodes with frustrated rage, or gradually rises to a level of mastery in relation to the third *chakra* challenges it would be impossible to reach without the tutelage of the master. Both experiences are likely along the path that these two very different planets will walk in tandem. To the extent that Mars is forced to labor under the yoke of impossibility in the face of its own limitations, its service to the evolutionary agenda of the Sun will be hampered by a sense of deficiency. Even where Mars is able to rise to a certain level of competency and mastery against impossible odds, the struggle can be wearing and take a cumulative toll. Nothing will come easy to Mars with Saturn on its back, and even the most impressive accomplishments will tend to be marred by an internal anticlimactic sense of "too little, too late."

If Saturn presents a wall of resistance to Mars' push forward, Neptune does just the opposite – offers no resistance at all[4]. Here the warrior hero enters a forest glen shrouded in thick fog. There is no resistance here, no visible enemy to fight, no clear pathway forward. In such fog, it is difficult for Mars to rise to any level of competence at all, since neither the rules of engagement, the measures of success, nor the stepping stones by which skill might be attained are clear. Confidence is elusive, since Mars can never be quite sure what game it is playing, what strategy might be effective in moving toward a mirage on the horizon, or even what winning would look and feel like. Ambition is rife with ambivalence, as it is difficult to identify values, set priorities, or establish goals. Movement is hampered by the shifting, yielding quicksand under Mars' feet, and progress often proves to be illusory in retrospect. The enemy seems to be more internal than external, and when outer battle become necessary, it takes place in a landscape painted by Salvadore Dali, in which nothing is ever as it appears to be at first glance.

It is possible for Mars to become aligned with a higher transpersonal sense of purpose under Neptune's tutelage, but in order to reach such a lofty goal, it must essentially surrender everything that would have previously identified Mars as Mars. Mars/Neptune can become the spiritual warrior but not without first wrestling with the profound paradox that such a concept poses. Like the student of Zen faced with a koan his mind can't possibly solve, Mars/Neptune walks toward its enlightenment with all its usual faculties tied in knots. The awkward nature of this walk presents a conundrum that can be understood as a third *chakra* dilemma, especially where the Sun is involved in some larger aspect pattern that contains all three planets.

The Third Chakra Chart

A third *chakra* issue is likely indicated whenever Sun and Mars form a mutual aspect to one or more planets of excess (Jupiter, Uranus or Pluto) or deficiency (Saturn or Neptune). The strongest complexes involve multiple aspects to Sun and Mars, while the most complex third *chakra* issues are indicated when Sun and Mars are mutually aspected by planets of both excess and deficiency. The potency of any third *chakra* issue is increased when these planets cluster in the SE quadrant or sit on the appropriate angles (Ascendant, especially the 1st house side, Midheaven, and Descendant, especially the 7th house side).

Weaker third *chakra* issues may be indicated when the Sun or Mars – but not both – forms a planetary pattern with other planets of deficiency and/or excess at these third *chakra* stations, or weaker still, elsewhere in the chart.

If no clearcut signature exists for a third *chakra* issue, as described above, then we would look to the rulers of the Ascendant, Midheaven and Descendant for additional clues. If any of these planets form aspects with each other or with Mars or the Sun, these aspects would constitute a more ordinary third *chakra* chart. This chart would most appropriately be understood as providing a low-level background indication of third *chakra* activity, perhaps with periods of foreground activation by transit or progression.

Endnotes

[1] Mars is noted as a third *chakra* planet by Oken (155), Grasse (204) and Hodgson (107), the latter two whom note its association with fire (through rulership of Aries), and the importance of fire to the dynamic of the third *chakra*.

[2] The Sun is noted as a third *chakra* planet by Hodgson, primarily because of its rulership of fire sign Leo.

[3] With a similar understanding of the Sun's role in the third chakra, Hodgson says (111):

◇◇

The true power of the Christ Sun deep in the heart can only begin to shine forth when the desires and ambitions of the personal self have been to some extent outgrown, or until a denial of some dear desire has brought the soul to a point of crucifixion. In myths and stories within every religion, the Sun-Hero sacrifices his life for the sake of a person or a case. This sacrifice, or rededication of the solar energy, leads the soul to seek the true light, which is to be found in the heart center.

4   Following the esoteric teachings of Alice Bailey, Oken assigns co-rulership of the third *chakra* to Neptune.

Chapter Sixteen
A Third Chakra Case Study

In Chapter Three, I spoke about my relationship with my grandfather as a third *chakra* dilemma. Here, I would like to elaborate using my own chart and the story that goes with it, as a way to illustrate how such a dilemma can be mapped astrologically. My chart is reproduced below as a point of departure for this discussion.

MY CHART

My third *chakra* pattern is formed by Mars conjunct Saturn in the 9th house square an angular Sun in the 12th house. Saturn/Mars square Sun is part of a larger mutable t-square, involving Mercury and the Moon, but of more relevance here is the sextile between Sun and Neptune, given emphasis by Neptune's conjunction to the South Node. Although Mercury is not particularly known as a third *chakra* planet, I would include it in this pattern as a supplemental player, since it is angular, loosely conjunct the Sun, sextile Neptune and tightly square Saturn/Mars. It mimics the Sun in its aspects to the other players in this group, but also brings the pattern into a tighter focus. According to the criteria outlined above, we might approach this pattern and the story behind it as a classic third *chakra* condition of deficiency, involving Sun, Mars and both deficiency indicators.

MY THIRD CHAKRA CHART

To complete our analysis of this pattern within the system I am outlining in this book, I would note a juxtaposition of fire (Sun in Sagittarius) and water (Sun in 12th house square water planet Mars in Virgo and sextile water planet Neptune). There is also a secondary juxtaposition fire (fire planet Sun in Sagittarius) and earth (square earth planet Saturn in Virgo). Both of these juxtapositions provide an opening to *anandamaya kosha*, and underscore the deeply spiritual nature of the opportunity that is being presented to me here.

A Word About the Kosha Implications of Third Chakra Dynamics

In passing, I would note that all third *chakra* patterns involve fire by definition since the Sun (a necessary player in third *chakra* dynamics) is always a fire planet. Mars, the other necessary player in third *chakra* dynamics can either be a fire planet (when it is in a masculine sign) or a water planet (when it is in a feminine sign). When Mars functions as a fire planet, the third *chakra* pattern as a whole will tend to manifest on *pranamaya kosha*, and work itself out in terms of the basic overall vitality of the body; the level of enthusiasm, passion, inspiration and excitement we are able to bring to our interests, activities and involvements in the embodied world; and the energy dynamics between

231

those we must interact with as we fulfill our third *chakra* agendas – that is to say, how we affect others and how they affect us on the energetic level. The opening to *pranamaya kosha* is amplified when the pattern also involves planets of excess Uranus (always an air planet), Jupiter and/or Pluto in masculine signs, and planet of deficiency Saturn in a masculine sign.

When Mars functions as a water planet, the pattern as a whole becomes an opening to *anandamaya kosha* through the juxtaposition of fire and water. This opening is enhanced and deepened when the pattern also involves planets of excess Jupiter and/or Pluto in feminine signs, or planet of deficiency Neptune in any sign. When a third *chakra* pattern presents an opening to *anandamaya kosha*, it can be considered to be a focal point of the life in question, considered from a spiritual perspective, and representative of a core issue worthy of deeply focused investigation. This is true, in general, of all patterns that provide openings to the *koshas* of deep penetration (*vijnanamaya* and *anandamaya*). But since the third *chakra* is where we break through the psychological barriers in our lives to touch the spiritual implications of our most intractable struggles, it is also where the greatest potential for spiritual growth is often found.

My Unwounded Soul Essence

As discussed in Chapter Three, my third *chakra* wounding was precipitated by an ostensibly positive image that my grandfather had of me, as "the professor," a projection in part of all his own unrealized dreams. I was the first grandchild, and for those of my grandfather's generation (with both Pluto and Neptune in Gemini), education was the rite of passage to a better life. This generational hope was amplified in my grandfather's case by the fact that in his chart, Pluto/Neptune was opposed Venus/Jupiter in Sagittarius not far from my Sun. Ironically, my grandfather had a very good life (at least as seen from my perspective) though he never went to college. Meanwhile, given the close alignment of this potent signature in his chart with my Sun (and by extension, my entire third *chakra* pattern), I was the ideal candidate for the projection of this potent brew of energies in his chart.

I would also note here that my grandfather's Sun was sextile Mars, with both planets straddling his Venus/Jupiter conjunction, and forming a finger of God pattern with Pluto. This is a rather powerful third *chakra* signature, tending toward excess, and was manifest in my grandfather's life as the classic story of the immigrant who came to this country with nothing, and worked himself into a position of prominence, prosperity, and great respect. My grandfather became a master of the third *chakra* domain, often described by those who knew him as a "self-made man." I admired him to no end, even as his Pluto opposed my Sun (with his Sun semi-square my Mercury, and his Mars sesquiquadrate my Mars/Saturn) and through this alignment of our charts, he sent a projection of his unrealized dreams directly into the heart of my own third *chakra* pattern.

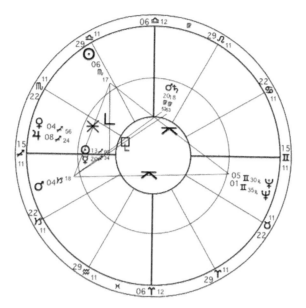

MY GRANDFATHER'S THIRD CHAKRA PROJECTION

Before we talk about how this seemingly positive projection wounded me, it is intriguing to note that in calling me "the professor," and envisioning for me a life empowered by college education, my grandfather was not simply shooting in the dark. He was, in fact, clearly perceiving my soul essence, but couching what he saw in terms that fit his socio-cultural worldview. With Mars/Saturn in Virgo the 9th house of higher education square Mercury in Sagittarius in the 1st of personal identity, I am indeed, a teacher, as well as a life-long seeker of philosophical, metaphysical, and astrological truth. Once I was able to orient myself to the educational system from a place of self-awareness, college did in fact become an intellectual springboard for many of the interests, ideas, and conceptual passions that carry me forward in my thinking to this day.

I loved my grandfather deeply, because of all the adults in my world, it was he who understood me best. He taught me how to play chess, encouraged me to read, ask questions and pursue what interested me, and modeled what it was like to create a life fueled by passionate self-discovery and actualization of possibilities. He encouraged me to be who I was, and I grew up wanting to follow in his footsteps – not necessarily doing what he did, but approaching life with the same attitude and spirit. Far from projecting onto me an image foreign to my nature, he was very much a guide and a mentor to the cultivation of my soul essence.

My Primal Wounding

My primal wounding came right on schedule around the age of 3 1/2, though to be honest, I have been unable to pinpoint the exact date, and don't really know what the aspects were at the time of my wounding. I do know that from March – September of that year, one or more outer planets was transiting my natal Mercury-Saturn/Mars complex within a degree of exact aspect, thus creating multiple triggers to this third *chakra* pattern we have identified in my chart. I also remember clearly that life was radically different from this point forward. I mentioned the incident previously in Chapter Six, as an example of the way childhood wounds can precipitate self-limiting beliefs in the sixth *chakra*. Here, I will discuss the same seminal experience from the perspective of the third *chakra* – illustrating the fact that most life experiences can be understood from multiple perspectives. Indeed, the astro-chakra system we are exploring here is designed to facilitate just that.

On the day the incident took place, I was playing with my friends (all of whom were older and bigger than I) in my grandfather's backyard. We were playing "King of the Mountain" on a pile of ashes my grandfather kept there for some purpose I no longer remember. At one point in the game, I had managed to make it to the top of the ashpile, and enjoyed a brief moment as "king." Then, much to my horror and surprise, my friends started attacking me. They knocked me down, and began stuffing ashes in my mouth.

Hearing my screams, my grandfather rushed out and chased the other kids away. By this time, I was choking, turning blue, and unable to breathe. My grandfather cleared my throat, then called the ambulance and I was rushed to the hospital. In the days that immediately followed, I contracted pneumonia, and throughout my childhood, suffered from a weakened constitution, and a heightened susceptibility to colds, flu and infectious diseases. Given that the core issue being triggered in my chart was a dance between fire and earth, it is not surprising that the symptoms of my wounding should appear on *annamaya* and *pranamaya koshas*, associated with earth and fire respectively. Astute readers will remember from Chapter Five that these symptoms can be associated with the fifth *chakra*, and it is not unlikely to assume that in addition to my sixth and third *chakras*, this incident also had ramifications for that center as well.

Since our focus here is the third *chakra*, what we want to explore are the implications of this wounding for the third *chakra* agenda of finding and taking a suitable place within the world. As a consequence of what I have come to refer to as "the ashpile incident." I began to believe that winning was dangerous to my health and well-being, that I was powerless against unpredictable forces much stronger than I, that other people could not be trusted, and that the world, in general, was not a safe place to be. Something shut down inside of me, and I became much more guarded, less willing to risk fully revealing myself, and less available to fully be myself in the presence of others. To the extent that these early decisions have influenced my choices and my behavior throughout my life, I have struggled to find a satisfactory place for myself within the world, attained only limited success in my creative endeavors, found it difficult to be close to other people, to be myself in group situations, or to feel as though I belonged anywhere, and could claim only limited freedom in situations where freedom was clearly mine for the taking. Since childhood I have made great progress in healing these patterns, and gradually evolving healthier responses to situations that retrigger the early wounding, but have come to appreciate the possibility that working through these core issues is a lifetime proposition.

In terms of our model of third *chakra* dynamics, this pattern can be understood largely in terms of Saturn's impact on Mars. By natural inclination, Saturn and Mars have often worked against each other and generated stress. Saturn has held back when Mars was ready to move forward; Saturn has sought security while Mars was hell-bent on adventure; Saturn has sought the sanction of tradition and social approbation, while Mars would have gone its own way without regard for consequences. In Virgo in the 9th house, this conjunction has at times manifested as an intense conflict with a critical father; frustration at dealing with a world seemingly callous and indifferent; difficulties in expressing my anger for fear of being inappropriate, out of control, or misunderstood; self-criticism, self-doubt, feelings of inadequacy and incompetence (classic symptoms of third *chakra* deficiency); awkwardness, restlessness, impatience, nervous tension, and poor digestion. There have, of course, been positive manifestations as well – self-discipline, organizational skills, responsibility, determination and perseverance among them – but these have come only as the initial wounding by Saturn began to heal.

The Astrological Timing of the Wounding/Healing Process

Hopefully the reader can easily see the astro-logic behind the difficulties I've experienced in my life as described above, the relationship between these difficulties and the third *chakra*, and the relationship between this third *chakra* wounding and the ashpile incident that triggered it. What may not be so readily apparent is how the ashpile incident distorted my soul essence, described by my grandfather in his depiction of me as "the professor." This missing link emerges in living color as I entered school. School can be understood as the training ground for everything this professor in me might one day embody, but it is also the first coherent microcosm of the world I had grown to mistrust, and thus the first battleground on which I encountered all of my third *chakra* demons.

CHAPTER SIXTEEN

Since day one of kindergarten, I rebelled fiercely against the very thought of having to spend my days cooped up in school. My fire did not like the oppressive rigidity of the system, which was quite tangible to me, any more than it liked the ashes being stuffed down my throat. It didn't take more than a few seconds for the same sense of claustrophobia and inability to breathe to register. Before my mother had even left the room on the first day, I walked up to some other kids playing with blocks, knocked their tower down, and got into a fight. Throughout kindergarten and the first grade, I fought nearly every day on the playground, and refused to settle down or cooperate with an educational system that I instinctively knew existed only to take away my freedom.

By the time Saturn's waxing square to Saturn/Mars was in play, the school authorities were responding to my rebellion. A conference was called between the principal, my guidance counselor, the school psychologist, my teacher, and my parents, and I was ordered to change my behavior or suffer unspecified dire consequences. Since by this time I had very few allies, either in the adult world, or even among the kids in my class, and because I did very much want to be accepted, at age 7 I began to seriously re-evaluate my strategy. I decided to change my tactics, did a 180 turn-around, and became a model student, shocking teachers and students alike. For me, however, it was a psychological survival mechanism that allowed me to get a foothold in a world I believed I had no choice but to enter. It was also my first moment of surrender to the calling of my soul essence, since assuming an identity worthy of my grandfather's moniker for me would require me to take my education seriously.

By the time my Saturn opposition rolled around, I had actually done quite well in school, and was contemplating college. My passion at this time, however, was my music, and while maintaining decent grades, I reveled in playing saxophone with a number of local rock and roll bands. Yet as I turned to face my future, I again felt the Saturnian pressure of parents, grandparents, and guidance counselors, who admonished me to "be practical." "Music is alright as a hobby," they told me, "but you'll never be able to earn your livelihood doing it." Under Saturn's pressure, I believed them, and turned my gaze toward what I thought would be a more practical career in chemistry.

Between my Saturn opposition and the waning square, I came to realize that the practical decisions that I made under Saturn's tutelage during the waxing square and opposition were a mistake. They did not allow enough space for my emerging individuality, which was far more Mercurial and Neptunian than Saturn had wanted me to believe. By my junior year in college, I had switched my major from chemistry to English. I began reading literature, philosophy and psychology, started writing poetry, became editor of the campus literary magazine, and felt in general like a huge weight had been taken off my shoulders. After college, I took off on a trip cross country with a friend, and wound up living in a commune called Funny Farm, where I experimented with soft drugs, and did lots of writing. Shortly after that, I discovered meditation, *kundalini yoga*, and astrology, and began to explore my spirituality. I was gradually throwing off the conditioning of my childhood and discovering the personal touchstones of my own path.

During the waning square of the Saturn cycle, I was living in a *yoga ashram*, under the direction of a Saturnian teacher, who ran a tight ship, and was quite paternalistic toward his students. One day, as he came upon me organizing some notes from a teacher's training I had just attended, he suddenly decided that my talents could be better utilized at another *ashram* across country. So I moved, and became part of the Kundalini Research Institute, where I embraced a wonderful opportunity to develop my skills as a writer, a teacher, and an astrologer. I also began graduate school at this time, and eventually earned a masters degree in counseling psychology. It was during this period that I began to build the creative foundation for the work that I am doing now. It was also during this period that I met and began studying more intently with Yogi Bhajan.

In the intervening years between the waning square and my Saturn return, I had learned all I could living at the *ashram*, and decided it was time to leave. I began feeling increasingly isolated from the rest of the world, and increasingly conspicuous belonging to a spiritual organization that deliberately set itself apart from the everyday lives of the people in the community that surrounded it. I wanted to share my knowledge and my service from a more egalitarian place.

Returning to the "real world," however, was definitely a shock to my system. Suddenly confronted with the necessity for earning a livelihood, and paying off my student loans, my perspective began to shift once again. I continued writing, teaching, and practicing astrology, but outside the context of *ashram* life, I found it impossible to pay my bills without supplementing my income. After unsuccessfully seeking work in the counseling profession, I found work as a painter, but became increasingly dissatisfied having to work for someone else at a job that did not engage my creativity.

During my Saturn return, I left a stifling painting job, where I was overworked and underpaid, and made the decision to actively pursue a long-standing dream. I decided that I no longer wanted to work for someone else, and that I wanted a simpler lifestyle that did not require me to spend all my time working to make money just to pay my bills. I left the town where my parents lived, and moved a thousand miles away, where I eventually bought some land and began to homestead. I did not really have a plan when I left, but my dream was strong and bright, and led me small step by small step to this Ozark cabin retreat where I sit to write this book today. I may still be relatively poor by society's standards, but in allegiance to my dream, I am living a life where my time is essentially my

◇◇

own. The decisions made during my Saturn return, were the basis of my rite of passage into ownership of this dream.

Since then, I have learned to function in the world. I've discovered that I share my grandfather's entrepreneurial spirit, and after having created and run several successful businesses. I am no longer afraid to climb the mountain – provided it is a mountain of my own choosing, where my passions are engaged, and my own agenda is being served. Not that I don't still occasionally get caught in the outworking of yet another subtle layer of wounding, but after nearly two full Saturn cycles ripe with opportunity for healing and growth, I have a perspective about the process that I couldn't possibly have had at 3 1/2 when the ashpile incident first derailed me.

I have also since come into my own as a teacher, having taught for many years at a ceremonial gathering in New Mexico, and in my own correspondence course, as mentor to intelligent and challenging students around the world. This was perhaps not the societal role envisioned for my by my grandfather, and it has not been the smooth passage up the academic ladder that a more traditional life, in his image, might have been, but in my own way, I have assumed the identity of the soul essence that he saw in me over 50 years ago.

A Word About Neptune's Role in My Third Chakra Dilemma

In analyzing my third *chakra* chart earlier in this chapter, I mentioned Neptune's role as a secondary player, contributing to the overall pattern of deficiency marked predominantly by Saturn's impact on Mars. Neptune does not form a direct relationship to Mars, but it does impact the Sun (and Mercury) by sextile, and its function in that capacity is worth mentioning here.

As previously discussed, the Sun symbolizes the gradual emergence of identity along an evolutionary track grounded in ego at one end of the journey, and cultimating in *bindu*, or union with the Source of All Being at the destination. With Neptune sextile to the Sun, the path along which this solar journey proceeds will tend to be somewhat elusive, though generally not to a debilitating extent, and more meandering. The ego is softened by Neptune, meaning in a positive sense that there is somewhat less attachment to the temporary roles being played as stepping stones to a higher, more all-inclusive sense of identity. On the other hand, there is also less ambition with which to take the journey at all, and a much greater tendency to languish in tangential backwaters along the way.

In my case, this influence of Neptune upon the Sun is amplified by the fact that my Sun is placed in the 12th house, which by modern astrological convention, is Neptune's domain. With Neptune in the 10th house, a strong arena for the outworking of third *chakra* issues, the implication is that finding my place within the world, or put another way, establishing a public identity, would not necessarily be an easy, or straightforward task.

Between the lines of my Saturn-Saturn/Mars story, Neptune's influence can be felt as a slowly-emerging, somewhat nebulous and illogical career path. From an early interest in music to an ii-fated attempt to study research chemistry in college to a Masters degree in Marriage, Family and Child counseling to a 7-year stint as a house-painter to the directorship of a non-profit to my current gig as teacher of astrology and writer of philosophy books, it would be difficult at best for any sane person to get a handle on where I am going with all of this. From an astro-logical perspective, each of these temporary traveling disguises is a symbolically consistent expression of Neptune. But within the eyes of the world where third *chakra* issues are worked out in real time, it appears that I am merely flitting across the stage of life with no clear, consistent sense of direction or purpose. The slowly solidifying alignment with a more internal sense of soul essence that constitutes the real evolutionary story behind this eccentric trail of disjointed stations is fairly invisible to anyone but me.

I like to think, however, that my path through life would be one that my grandfather would readily understand, for he followed a similar trail in his own third *chakra* process – immigrating to this country when he was 18 to take a job with the railroad, eventually buying his own milk delivery route, selling that and buying a restaurant, selling that and going into the construction business, then running for city council, working to develop and patent several inventions, and retiring to putter in his garden and build bird houses – all this in an era, where the norm was 50 years with the same firm for a gold watch and a pension.

Going back to the astrology of my relationship to my grandfather, we can remember that Neptune was part of the potent arrow of projection directed at my Sun (Pluto/Neptune opposed Venus/Jupiter). Within his chart, we might also note here that this arrow was more of a second *chakra* than a third *chakra* signature (although because I don't know my grandfather's time of birth, I can't say whether this pattern fits the succedent house profile that would seal this assessment). In any case, the implication here is that in calling me "the professor," what my grandfather really wanted for me was not worldly success, but the good life. College education and everything that this implied to him was not so much a measure of accomplishment along a career path, but rather an opening to increased pleasure.

Despite the pull of practical necessity (to be expected within a third *chakra* process dominated by Saturn), Neptune has asserted its steady influence upon my process by guiding me from one step to the next toward a path of gradually increasing pleasure and satisfaction. I've tried to follow my bliss, in other words, even as I struggled to gain a

◇◇

secure foothold in the world where third *chakra* egos jockey for position. To the extent I've been successful at this, despite having Saturn on my back, I've fulfilled my own third *chakra* agenda while also assimilating the tasty second *chakra* feast hidden at the heart of my grandfather's unwitting projection. I like to think that despite the meandering nature of my journey, it would be one that might have made my grandfather proud.

Chapter Seventeen
The Fourth Chakra Chart

As discussed in Chapter Four, the fourth *chakra* is where we enter a field of resonant relationships and learn to negotiate a balance of energies within the learning opportunities these relationships provide. Some relationships will be marked by affinity, where like attracts like, but also leads to the excess that creates imbalance. Some relationships will be an attempt to redress these imbalances by seeking qualities, experiences, and other people who are opposite to our nature (resonance by contrast). A third category of attraction within the realm of the fourth *chakra* will be to those people, places, and things with the capacity to trigger our core issues, so that we might encounter the opportunities for healing that are necessary to our growth (resonance by wounding). Through all three types of relationships, we gradually embrace the wholeness of our being, in all of its paradoxical complexity.

In the third *chakra*, we have been engaged in a *yang* quest for our place in the world, jostling other egos for position, gradually migrating to a niche that matches our soul essence with uncanny singularity. Until we attain this state, others are often viewed as competition for scarce resources, interlopers of limited space, and obstacles on the path to a strictly personal victory. The closer we come to a realization of interconnectedness - our spiritual goal in the fourth *chakra* - the more we become open to the possibility that this personal victory is merely a necessary stepping stone to a more integrated participation in a collective reality, where no one wins unless we all do. It is this possibility that we are impelled to explore in the fourth *chakra*.

As has been our pattern so far, the fourth *chakra* brings us back toward the *yin* side of the circle of life, just as the second *chakra* brought us back from the *yang* struggle for survival in the first *chakra* to a place of deeper receptivity to the pleasures of embodiment. In the fourth *chakra*, the task is no longer proving ourselves through assertion and initiative, but rather becoming receptive to the Other, in all the many guises that the Other is capable of assuming. Each manifestation of the Other has a gift for us, a resource that supplements what we are consciously able to muster for ourselves, a seemingly missing piece that completes the mysterious puzzle of our existence. With a third *chakra* sensibility, our inclination might be to grab this gift and run, but the gifts of the fourth *chakra* cannot be had by grabbing. We must instead, learn to open the heart and allow them in. As anyone who has ever been in a relationship knows, this is often easier said than done, since it is our vulnerability that is awakened in the fourth *chakra*, and unlike in the third, there are ultimately no defenses against this vulnerability that will move us forward on our path.

American Buddhist nun Pema Chodron speaks of this vulnerability as the soft spot – known in her tradition as *bodhichitta*. It's the place in us that reminds us of our essential humanity, our inherent fragility in the face of life's unpredictable harshness, and the notion that we transcend this fragility only by embracing it together and caring enough to be willing to ease each other's burden. This is a distinctly feminine way of being, in stark contrast to the "everyman-for-himself" mentality of the third *chakra*, It is not necessarily wrong to view the world in this way, as the world often *is* this way, and our participation in it often requires us to put our armor on and gear up for battle. But as Chodron and many other spiritual teachers remind us, behind the armor of the enemy is the same tender beating heart that pumps inside our own breast, and in the end, no amount of armor can shield us from this heart.

> *Spiritual awakening is frequently described as a journey to the top of a mountain. We leave our attachments and our worldliness behind and slowly make our way to the top. At the peak, we have transcended all pain. The only problem is that we leave all the others behind – our drunken brother, our schizophrenic sister, our tormented animals and friends. Their suffering continues, unrelieved by our personal escape.*

> *In the process of discovering bodhichitta, the journey goes down, not up. It's as if the mountain pointed toward the center of the earth instead of reaching toward the sky. Instead of transcending the suffering of all creatures, we move toward the turbulence and doubt. We jump into it. We slide into it. We tiptoe into it. We move toward it however we can. We explore the reality and unpredictability of insecurity and pain, and we try not to push it away. If it takes years, if it takes lifetimes, we let it be as it is. At our own pace, without speed or aggression, we move down and down and down. With us move millions of others, our companions in awakening from fear. At the bottom we discover water, the healing water of bodhichitta. Right down there in the thick of things, we discover the love that will not die (91-92).*

It is this "love that will not die" that we are seeking in the fourth *chakra*. The process is relationship – the ultimate container for all of the issues that come up when we attempt to open ourselves up to or wall ourselves off from the experience of *bodhichitta*. The process begins and ultimately ends with our relationship to the self, but the journey is inevitably populated by a cast of characters that mirror various unintegrated aspects of our being.

The fourth *chakra* circle is a solid red circle, formed as the dot at the center of the third *chakra* circle – which we might also visualize as red – expands to fill the entire circle.

The dot is still there, but now it is no longer separate from all the other dots that also fill the space. As the sphere of our relationships begins to encompass all that is, and ego evolves into a more all-inclusive sense of Self, we become the circle whose center is everywhere and whose circumference is nowhere to be seen.

The Placement of Fourth Chakra Planets in Astrological Space

In keeping with this metaphor, planets indicative of fourth *chakra* dynamics can be located in any hemisphere or quadrant. There is no need to stay close to home or avoid the unfamiliar; every quadrant holds something of interest to the soul centered in the fourth *chakra*, while no quadrant is beyond its reach. As a consequence, patterns indicating fourth *chakra* issues are generally not limited to certain sections of astrological space. In general, this is true of the so-called higher *chakras*, although here we are considering them as alternate states of awareness on a co-equal horizontal plane.

Having said this, however, it is important to note that the fourth quadrant sits midway between the first three *chakras* where issues are likely to remain relatively unconscious and be projected out into the world, and the *chakras* of transcendence, where the soul becomes increasingly conscious of and responsible for its own spiritual journey. The fourth *chakra* is often where spiritual awakening first occurs, but such awakening generally only arises within a place of vulnerability induced by the triggering of issues located in the first three *chakras*. Indeed, it is often these issues that create the blockages of fear, unworthiness and mistrust that must be worked through in the fourth *chakra*, before love and clear connection to one's *dharma* (or sense of purpose) can be experienced.

The fourth *chakra* also has its own issues, which generally center around difficulties in relationship to others that are reflected astrologically by planets in the SW quadrant of relationships. Unlike third *chakra* issues centered in the SE quadrant, fourth *chakra* issues are not perceived as a test of ego strength, nor do they tend to yield very well to conflict or confrontation. Instead, as befitting the yin nature of the western hemisphere, they require the soul to enter a more vulnerable place of *bodhichitta*, out of which will generally arise a deeper understanding and capacity for love, empathy and compassion.

Astro-logically, this may require the soul struggling with fourth *chakra* issues to enter the NW quadrant, into which planets set, as the Earth completes its daily rotation about its axis, and where the soul goes to contemplate and digest the consequences of its experiences (primarily of relationship) in the southern hemisphere. While the soul struggling with third *chakra* issues was only compelled to enter the NW quadrant when something broke down on the more extroverted side of life, the soul dealing with fourth *chakra* issues will find the NW quadrant a natural destination. This scenario will be underscored when a fourth *chakra* pattern spans the SW and NW quadrants.

When a fourth *chakra* pattern takes a more eastern flavor, involving the NE and SE quadrants, the issue will generally require the soul to form a deeper connection to itself (generally in the NE quadrant), as a prelude to actualizing a more integrated fulfillment of *dharma* (generally in the SE quadrant). This process will parallel the third *chakra* process of cultivating ego in order to function more effectively within the world, but generally arise from a deeper sense of connectedness (cultivated on the western side of the chart) and aim toward serving a more transpersonal agenda.

The exact meaning and focus of a fourth *chakra* pattern will depend on which quadrants are involved. As mentioned earlier, the fourth *chakra* is less restricted to certain sections of astrological space than the first three *chakras*, and this is generally a trend that continues as we move into the transcendence phase of the evolutionary cycle. At the same time, it is important to note that the fourth *chakra* completes the pattern of hemisphere and quadrant preference established by the first three *chakras*. Astute readers may have already discerned this pattern, but to spell it out more clearly, it is this:

CHAKRA	HEMISPHERE PREFERENCE
1	north/east
2	north/west
3	south/east
4	south/west

Souls dealing with issues lodged in first and second *chakra* charts (the incarnation phase) will show a preference for the northern hemisphere, while souls dealing third and fourth *chakra* issues (the awakening phase) will prefer the south. The *yang chakras* (first and third) find their natural home in the east, while the *yin chakras* are more at home in the west. The pattern is continued with the following distribution of preferences among the quadrants:

CHAKRA	QUADRANT PREFERENCE
1	4th (NE)
2	2nd (NW)
3	3rd (SE)
4	1st (SW)

Astrological patterns reflecting these dynamics will tend to revolve around the quadrant of choice, either through a convergence of planets in that quadrant or a conspicuous absence of planets there. This "rule" will be less applicable to the fourth *chakra*, which exhibits greater flexibility than the first three *chakras* in its occupation of astrological space.

The Fourth Chakra and Succedent Planets

A third pattern established by the first three *chakras* and continued in the fourth is this:

CHAKRA	QUADRANT PLACEMENT
1	angular
2	succedent
3	angular
4	succedent

Again, we see a division according to gender: planets in a *yang chakra* chart will prefer the angles of a chart; planets in a *yin chakra* chart will prefer the center of their chosen quadrant. As with hemispheres and quadrants, we also see an evolution from the incarnation phase (first and second *chakras*) to the awakening phase (third and fourth). In terms of the *yang chakras*, the shift seems to be from the cadent to the angular side of the angle. First *chakra* issues are often lodged near the angles, but on the cadent side of the line, where they are appear to be less consciously assimilated by the self – which is, at this point, relatively undeveloped. Third *chakra* issues are also likely lodged near the angles, but on the angular side, where we are more capable of owning them. Even when these issues are projected onto others or into the world at large, they are still referenced back to the emerging ego in the angular houses, where patterns of excess or deficiency require rebalancing.

A more subtle shift of emphasis takes place between second and fourth *chakra* patterns, which both tend to occur in succedent houses. Here the difference lies more in the meaning ascribed to each of the succedent houses, which is transmuted in the fourth *chakra* by the experience of *bodhichitta* and by the quest for connection to others within our resonant field. At the second *chakra*, the 2nd house is where we first discover our bodies and the pleasures inherent in the experience of embodiment. We are, at this level, aware of pain and suffering – that is to say, the outer manifestation of *bodhichitta*, but there is no awareness within our suffering of the door that *bodhichitta* provides to a deeper connection to soul.

Once the fourth *chakra* has been awakened, the 2nd house becomes the point of entry to a very deep experience of *bodhichitta*. This is necessarily so, because increased identification with the experience of mbodiment in the 2nd house entails increased awareness of our inherent mortality. Death is most often associated with the 8th house in traditional astrology, but it is in the 2nd house, below the horizon where our vulnerability in the face of death (on all the levels, actual and metaphorical, on which death has meaning) is felt most acutely. Thus, what was primarily experienced as an invitation to pleasure from the perspective of the second *chakra*, becomes enriched by an experience of psychological peril in the fourth *chakra*.

In addition to our vulnerability in the face of death, this peril often revolves around our sense of worthiness to be loved, which is called into question at the level of the fourth *chakra* through our relationships with others who mirror our self-doubts or lack of self-esteem. This is less an issue at the second *chakra*, because the self that would otherwise be capable of doubt and a sense of unworthiness exists only in nascent form as a nexus of impressions, inclinations and instinctual urges. This is not to say that the second and fourth *chakras* cannot be resonating simultaneously, within the context of the same core issues. But when they do, our experience will be multi-dimensional, with global sensations and instincts registering in the second *chakra*, and feelings referenced to a central self in the fourth.

The 5th house, associated with the vitality of the child, an expanded palette of pleasures, and the erotic impulse at its most intense in the second *chakra* also takes on an altered meaning in the fourth *chakra*. Here the soul must learn to reach out to others, and to balance its natural tendency toward self-gratification with a capacity to share. At the level of the fourth *chakra*, the unselfconscious lust of the child for life can become excessive, and create a blockage to further development. When fourth *chakra* core issues are centered in the 5th house, the natural self-centeredness of the second *chakra* is experienced as deterioration into selfishness; the quest for pleasure becomes caricaturized as hedonism and debauchery; and the erotic impulse can become an addiction that drives dysfunctional patterns of narcissism, self-indulgence, emotional manipulation, and disregard for the consequences of one's actions in the lives of others – ultimately all barriers to an opening of the heart and discovery of the capacity for love, compassion, and caring.

When this happens, the 5th house becomes another portal to *bodhichitta* through the experience of rejection by others, and the demand for emotional reciprocity and/or accountability that will invariably arise to greet the soul in the realm of relationships. These experiences are first imposed in childhood by parents as part of a normal upbringing, perhaps reaching critical mass during the terrible twos and again in adolescence. But to the extent that the 5th house is also implicated in natal fourth *chakra* patterns, they may also reverberate into adult relationships and cause interpersonal problems there. Conversely, at this level, the soul can also attempt to take too much responsibility for others to the detriment of the capacity for second *chakra* pleasures. The goal in addressing fourth *chakra* issues is not to deny or negate the child, but rather to teach him how to share the sandbox (and his capacity for enjoyment of the garden) with others.

In the 8th house, the erotic potential for merging with the flow of life and with others is realized at both the second and fourth *chakras*. At the latter, however, this union potentially takes place as the love that exists between two people on a broader level of give-and-take. To the extent that such love is unconditional, experiences here mutually reinforce each other in both the second and fourth *chakras* to produce the full bloom of sustainable romantic love at its juiciest. To the extent that love is conditional – which is true for most people, most of the time – the 8th house becomes the place where we work through whatever barriers of projected judgment or fear stand in the way of genuine intimacy. Obviously, these 8th house issues generate their own level of *bodhichitta* – the inherent vulnerability at the tender, exposed heart of love.

8th house core issues centered in the fourth *chakra* can also revolve around co-dependency, where excessive attachment ironically stands in the way of true union. This fourth *chakra* task has never been summed up more beautifully than by Kahil Gibran in his classic, *The Prophet*:

> You shall be together when white wings of death scatter your days.
> Aye, you shall be together even in the silent memory of God.
> But let there be spaces in your togetherness,
> And let the winds of the heavens dance between you.
> Love one another but make not a bond of love:
> Let it rather be a moving sea between the shores of your souls.
> Fill each other's cup but drink not from one cup.
> Give one another of your bread but eat not from the same loaf.
> Sing and dance together and be joyous, but let each one of you be alone,
> Even as the strings of a lute are alone though they quiver with the same music.

Lastly, the 11th house, least important among the succedent houses in terms of the second *chakra* agenda, becomes much more important in the fourth *chakra*. While taking pleasure in the company of kindred spirits, and exploring the potential for co-creativity in building a society that reflects our values and our preferences is generally of peripheral concern where the goal is opening to the pleasure of embodied life, it moves to very center of the game, when the goal is resonant relationship. For this is where we decide as a culture how we want to live – and especially whether or not we are responsible for, accountable to, and willing to take care of each other. Here, the fourth *chakra* process can have implications that extend far beyond the individual life into a broader spectrum of political, cultural, and social concerns – where *bodhichitta* becomes a collective experience reverberating throughout the larger embodied world that we share.

The Sun's Role in Fourth Chakra Dynamics

In the third *chakra*, the Sun played a secondary role behind Mars' heroic drive to stake out territory, assert, accomplish and conquer. Mars' is less useful in addressing the *yin* agenda of surrender required at the heart *chakra*, although as we shall see in Chapter Twenty Five, any planet can function in any *chakra*, not just those with which they are associated by natural affinity. Nonetheless, in the psychic landscape of the fourth *chakra*, Mars normally recedes into the background. The Sun, on the other hand, moves into a more prominent position as a major player[1].

In the third *chakra*, as discussed in the previous chapter, the Sun governs an evolutionary process tending from ego at the relatively unconscious end of the spectrum, to *bindu*, the spiritual seed around which soul takes shape and grows, much as a pearl grows around a grain of sand at the heart of an oyster. As *bindu* becomes activated through progress made in both the third and fourth *chakras*, it begins to radiate through the fourth, sending forth a vibrational beacon of sorts, which in turn resonates with other souls – either by affinity, wounding or contrast, or some combination of all three. This radiation of *bindu* at the fourth *chakra* can be understood – metaphorically, if not literally – as the mechanism by which the embodied world becomes a resonant field of learning opportunity.

In less esoteric terms, we might simply say that a soul whose fourth *chakra* has been activated on a solar level, through this radiation of *bindu*, becomes attractive to others. As soul singer, Ray Charles once put it, "Soul is a force that can light up a room." Here, we might refine his statement a bit by suggesting that it is an activated *bindu* at the fourth *chakra* that produces this light, commonly known as charisma. It should be noted here, however, that this soul force is not always comfortable or pleasant to be around. It is also capable of triggering wounds, and providing contrast to the excesses and imbalances generated in the resonant soul fields of others.

Swami Muktananda's soul force was, at times, so overwhelming that it literally felt as though I were burning up in his presence. From my training in yogic tradition, I understood this burning to be the activation of *kundalini*, more specifically directed as a purifying force called *tapas*. When *tapas* meets with resistance, usually centered physiologically at one or more knots, called *granthi*, heat is generated in the spine. In the process of working through these knots – as the soul force of a powerful being, radiating awakened *bindu*, meets our resistance to awakening – many strange reactions, called *kriyas*, can occur (Desai 72-73).

> *When the empowered prana (shakti) moves through the body, it creates various external and internal movements. On a physiological level one can experience the following: heat, cold, automatic breathing of various kinds, mudras (hand gestures), locks, postures (which are done with perfection even if the aspirant knows no hatha yoga), laughter, tears of joy, utterance of deformed sounds, feelings of fear, the curling back of the tongue, revolving of the eyeballs, temporary stopping of breath without effort, an itching or crawling sensation under the skin, and singing with ecstasy and joy. . . .*

> *On a subtle level, one may experience divine harmonies, the sounds of various instruments or mantras, the taste of divine flavors and the smell of sweet fragrances, or divine lights and colors. One may recall past lives, be poetically inspired, feel drunk with the ecstasy of divine bliss, have frightening dreams, or remain completely silent. . . . On an intellectual level, the hidden meaning behind the scriptures and spiritual texts are revealed. Intuition and psychic powers put one in touch with the divine, bringing security, peace, and a feeling of unseen guidance and protection.*

Among those gathered around Swami Muktananda, we also commonly used the term *kriya* to refer to the various melodramas that were played out in everyday life, once *kundalini* was activated. Successful doctors and lawyers suddenly decided to abandon their careers and take up pottery. Seemingly stable marriages began cracking at the seams, some ending in sudden, unexpected divorce. Chronic pain, cultivated over a lifetime of bodily neglect and abuse, just as suddenly disappeared. From a fear-based perspective, some might call this black magic or voodoo or psychic manipulation. But those of us who experienced Muktananda's grace, knew that he wasn't consciously doing anything. He was merely radiating pure, unconditional love, and we were resonating in whatever way we needed to respond.

This same power of love (or its absence) operates less dramatically among ordinary people going about the everyday business of their mundane lives. To the extent that the heart is open, or not, we impact those around us, and they likewise impact us. Learning to love ourselves and others as unconditionally as possible is a fourth *chakra* task common to us all, but when the Sun is involved in a strong fourth *chakra* pattern, there are likely to be core issues revolving around this task, which will produce melodramatic *kriyas* in our relationships with others.

◇◇

The Moon and Bodhichitta

We last spoke of the Moon in our discussion of the first *chakra* in Chapter Twelve as an experience of vulnerability, usually first triggered within us through some act of wounding by the mother. This lunar vulnerability is not essentially different than that which is discussed by Pema Chodron when she speaks about the soft spot of *bodhichitta*. The wounding we experience in the first *chakra* is, in fact, invariably some perceived withdrawal of unconditional love. Usually this is not a conscious or deliberate act on the part of the mother, but a simple consequence of the fact that we are all imperfect human beings, capable of loving imperfectly at best. I have never met a mother whose heart was not opened by the experience of giving birth, and to the extent that she is able to maintain this open space in her fourth *chakra*, the child will experience stability, safety and protection in the first *chakra*. To the extent that her own unresolved issues inevitably intrude upon this space of purity, she will experience a *kriya*, which in turn will burn a hole in the fabric of protection shielding her child's first *chakra*, and the child will experience a first *chakra* wound.

This wounding – which seems to be endemic to the human experience – is an experience of *bodhichitta*, but how it ultimately registers within the child, depends where the child is most vulnerable. To the extent that the mother's withdrawal of love is experienced as a threat to survival, the child will experience it as a first *chakra* wound. This usually occurs, for example, when the withdrawal of love takes the form of abandonment, rejection, betrayal, or abuse. To the extent that the same withdrawal is accompanied by projection, especially projection tinged with ongoing judgment or blame, it can also become a fourth *chakra* wound, translating in everyday experience as a sense of unworthiness to be loved.

If, for example, a young unwed mother unconsciously blames her daughter for robbing her of her own youth, while all her friends are out partying and enjoying lives relatively free of responsibility, her child may grow up feeling that she is somehow responsible for her mother's unhappiness. The daughter may then grow up bending over backwards to please first her mother, then her partners in life, and suffer from a chronic fourth *chakra* wound. Or it may be that a child put up for adoption develops a fantasy about his mother's perceived rejection that stirs a great deal of anger, which he then projects onto his partners in sporadic tirades of verbal and physical abuse. This may also be understood as a fourth *chakra* wound. Often fourth *chakra* wounds will have first *chakra* reverberations, since withdrawal of love can often be both a threat to survival and a perceived reflection of the child's unlovability. Fourth *chakra* wounds, however, will generally be played out on the stage of relationship, through *kriyas* that revolve around the inability to give or receive love, while first *chakra* wounds will be more accurately understood as an attempt to secure safety and protection.

The differences can be discerned astrologically, provided the life story matches the theory – a caveat that I personally would write in stone. First *chakra* wounds are often – if not always – indicated when the Moon is angular in hard aspect to Saturn and/or Pluto; while fourth *chakra* wounds are indicated when the Moon is succedent, in aspect to the Sun and one or more of the other fourth *chakra* planets – particularly Venus. One or more outer planets may also be involved, as discussed below. Obviously there will be overlapping scenarios here, especially when Saturn and Pluto participate, but through careful listening to the story in relation to the astrological context in which the story unfolds, it is possible to sort out the nuances within the parameters of this system.

The Moon and the Memory of Wounded Love

In the fourth *chakra*, the Moon plays an additional role, through its association with feeling and memory. At the heart of any soul wound is feeling, since it is through feeling that the soul is evoked, and the soul is evoked in no stronger terms than when it is wounded. As discussed at length in *The Seven Gates of Soul*, the soul is born through a fusion of body and Spirit, which is inherently a temporary arrangement. Because the body will one day fall away, the soul is innately vulnerable to the experience of death, both literal and metaphorical, on whatever level that takes place: the loss of a loved one, a divorce, getting fired from a job, getting sick, and so on. Out of the inherent vulnerability of the soul – that is to say, the experience of *bodhichitta* – in the midst of these predicaments, which are often beyond its control, a wide range of feelings can be evoked: sorrow, anger, depression, grief, despair, fear, anxiety, outrage, hysteria, manic denial, or crazy laughter, to name just a few possibilities. Giving expression to these feelings often provides relief, since feeling moves energy, like a river through the heart, keeping it eternal fresh and new.

When feelings do not have an outlet, or are evoked in the face of chronic conditions that do not change, wounds are formed. To the extent that feelings are able to be released, wounds can be healed, if indeed, they ever form in the first place. It is when feelings accumulate and become stagnant, that wounds fester and become toxic to the system. These stagnant feelings in turn become the nuclei around which wounded memories crystallize. We remember moments of intense feelings, because our attention is drawn fully into the present moment, and whatever is happening in that moment leaves a psychic impression. This is not to say that what we experience in the moment is perceived clearly; obviously we bring a certain subjective filter to every experience, and what we remember is often colored by the feelings taking shape in that moment.

◇◇

Each memory is also tinged by peripheral clues that in turn color our subsequent perceptions, especially to the extent that we have not been able to address or process the feelings related to the memory. A woman beaten in childhood by a father with a handlebar mustache may associate men with handlebar mustaches with the potential for being beaten, whether or not such a threat actually exists. A man locked in a closet as a boy, may become claustrophic as a man, have trouble committing in relationship, and arranging his life in such a way that he doesn't stay in one place long enough for feelings of claustrophia to develop. Having had ashes stuffed into my mouth in my childhood game of King of the Mountain, I have harbored certain expectations about winning or being the best at anything for many years that kept me perpetually in second place. We react to situations that remind us of our early experience of wounding as though we were going to be wounded again.

This instinctual response, which is largely unconscious, belongs to the Moon. Our attempt to cope with the experience of *bodhichitta* is evoked whenever our wounds are triggered. It is in the fourth *chakra*, commonly associated with the heart, that the feelings behind these instinctual responses to our essential vulnerability are lodged. Wherever the Moon is involved in a fourth *chakra* pattern, the antidote to all these troubled feelings is more love – a wider opening, not a shutting down – for the wounds of the heart are those which block our ability to give and receive love. Our instinctual response to situations in which these wounds are triggered will be to withhold love, or withdraw, or in some way to cringe in anticipation of whatever it is that has caused our wounding in the first place. The antidote is to allow the feelings behind the wounds to flow, and then to let them go – often easier said than done, but a process invariably guided by cultivating a more conscious relationship to the Moon.

The Moon as Shakti

There is one final function of the Moon related to the fourth *chakra* that should be mentioned here. Most translations of the word, *kundalini*, refer to a serpent coiled at the base of the spine, which is why in deference to tradition, I discussed *kundalini* within the context of the first *chakra*. But with a sly smile, Yogi Bhajan often spoke of *kundalini* as *kundalini shakti*, translating it as "the curl in the hair of the beloved," hinting – in my mind anyway – at a fourth *chakra* interpretation of this primal force. Just as the curl in the hair of the beloved has the power to evoke an awakening of the heart of her lover, so too does *kundalini* only really begin to rise and infuse the soul with the numinosity of a radiant *bindu*, when the heart is open.

This interpretation of *kundalini* requires an important shift in perception, for no longer is it a force initiated through *yang* activity, but rather one that responds to the *yin* receptivity of the soul who would evoke her. Yogi Bhajan taught *kundalini yoga*, which is a very active form of *yoga*, an intentional *yang* activity designed to deliberately initiate an awakening of *kundalini*. Yet, wise teacher that he was, he also understood that no amount of effort would result in such an awakening if the practitioner of *kundalini yoga* were not open to receive its powerfully transformative grace. "Getting it up is easy," he would caution us, "but keeping it up depends upon your purity of heart."

This feminine conception of *kundalini* is more overtly referenced when it is referred to as *kundalini shakti* or simply *shakti*. *Shakti* is a distinctly feminine force, the power behind all creation and all visible manifestation, ultimately a dispensation of grace from the goddess, Shakti, who in Hindu mythology is the Mother of All Things, consort to Shiva. Shiva, the destroyer God is the Hindu equivalent of Pluto, who in this context, is the serpent coiled at the base of the spine. It is only as Shiva is completed by Shakti, opening in love to "the curl in the hair of the beloved," that *kundalini* is invited to rise. As a physical approximation of this truth, we experience a rising of *kundalini* in the sex act, when male energy rises phallically to meet the receptive feminine. But the union of Shiva and Shakti is a fourth *chakra* experience, referred to by Jung as the *hieros gamos*, and as such requires more than the mere awakening of sexual energy.

Yogi Bhajan taught *tantric yoga* as well as *kundalini*, serving as a radiant *bindu* filter for hundreds of couples simultaneously sitting in meditation, seeking union at this more sublime level. *Tantric* is commonly understood in the west as sexual *yoga*, and often taught as a leisurely, non goal-oriented form of lovemaking with plenty of foreplay. In eastern yogic tradition, however, it is a potent spiritual practice designed to transmute sexual energy from a second *chakra* force into an alchemical cleansing agent of the heart, burning through whatever blockages to the free flow of unconditional love might be lodged there. This important distinction is clearly articulated by Swami Sivananda Radha. In explaining *kundalini* to westerners conditioned to equate *tantra* with sex (52), she says:

> In the kundalini symbololgy, the union of Shiva and Shakti is presented in one body, not two bodies united. Lord Shiva ultimately becomes half man and half woman. The meaning of this symbolism is lost today. True oneness is only achieved in a particular state of mind for which the sex act itself is not essential. The pleasure from the sexual act, which is often misinterpreted as spiritual union, is in fact only the registration of stimulation in the pleasure center of the brain. The experience of union has many levels, beginning with that of the male and female united in oneself. This has nothing to do with sex. The final level is union of the individual consciousness with cosmic consciousness. This experience is beyond the ability of language to describe.

When the Moon sits in aspect to the Sun, particularly in hard aspect (offering the opportunity for penetration to the depth of *anandamaya kosha*), this can be a potent invitation to the internal union of Shiva and Shakti in the fourth *chakra*. Whatever obstacles might exist on the path to this union will be indicated by the other planets involved in this pattern, and the journey will invariably be one of learning to open the heart – to the essential vulnerability of *bodhichitta*, to the healing capacity for love, and to the feminine grace that showers anyone whose purity of heart opens a clear channel for the radiance of *bindu* to serve as an attractive force. Relationships will most often be the vehicle through which these lessons are taught, but a devotion to art, selfless service and/ or dedication to a spiritual path can all be alternate or supplemental opportunities.

Venus' Role in Fourth Chakra Dynamics

Given the *yin* nature of the fourth *chakra*, and our definition of the fourth *chakra* as a field of resonant relationships in which the lessons of love are learned, it can hardly be surprising that Venus, goddess of love and relationship, should be a major player in fourth *chakra* dynamics[2]. We previously met Venus in our discussion of the second *chakra*, where she was the gateway to the erotic dimension of our experience: sensory delight, sexual pleasure, aesthetic appreciation for the beauty in nature, infused throughout the embodied world, and within each other. Just as *tantra* channels the energy of sexuality toward an opening of the heart, so too can this erotic dimension governed by Venus be an opening to the fourth *chakra* experience of *hieros gamos*.

Within the context of any relationship, sex provides the lubricant to the process of working through whatever blockages exist in the heart to prevent the free-flow of love. Sex cannot long be a substitute for the hard work of facing fourth *chakra* issues and opening the heart, but where the work is being done, sex can bind any couple into a more sustainable union, capable of lasting through the hard times on the way to the union of Shiva and Shakti. Yogi Bhajan used to say that marriage was the hardest and highest form of *yoga*. *Yoga* means "union," and in any fourth *chakra* dynamic, it is Venus who presides over this deep spiritual practice, as well as the pleasurable packaging of the practice in sexual embrace.

This statement bears a bit of explanation, for in Greek mythology, it is Hera and not Aphrodite who is generally considered to be the goddess of marriage. The irony here is that Hera's own marriage to Zeus, the head deity and lord of Olympus, was apparently one of those bonds of status and form, designed by matchmakers as a shrewd logistical move, but crawling with worms on the inside. Zeus was famous for his philandering, and Hera equally famous as a vengeful spouse, perpetually seeking to punish both her husband and his consorts for their promiscuity. Zeus, in fact, was bisexual, and would today possibly be considered a pedophile, as the story of his affair with the beautiful youth Ganymede suggests. In light of the reality of Hera's marriage to Zeus, one can only speculate - with tongue-in-cheek cynicism - that Hera is really goddess not of marriage, but of the longing for union that drives unlikely, incompatible couples together in desperation.

This is not to say that there was not love between Zeus and Hera, especially during the honeymoon phase of their relationship. As Hesoid describes their initial union (quoted in Morford 79):

> The son of Cronus clasped his wife in his arms and under them the divine earth sprouted forth new grass, dewy clover, crocuses, and hyacinths, thick and soft, to protect them from the ground beneath. On this they lay together and drew around themselves a beautiful golden cloud from which the glistening drops fell away.

If this classic piece of erotica does not hint that there might be more to this sham of a marriage between Zeus and Hera than meets the eye, then the entire edifice of Greek mythology must rest upon a shaky foundation indeed. This passage and others like it suggest that for all its melodramatic *kriyas*, their union was an evocation of Shakti at the most primal level of cosmic procreativity. What is notable here, however, is that it is an experience of erotic love, taken to its most intense *tantric* level that elevates this marriage to an alchemical *hieros gamos* - an experience governed by Aphrodite. Indeed, whenever Hera was intent on re-seducing her husband and thus renewing their marriage, she would borrow Aphrodite's girdle, a talisman for the erotic power that no god nor mortal could resist.

Out of this union, made possible by Aphrodite, came four children: Eileithyia, a goddess of childbirth; Hebe, cup-bearer to the gods, eventually replaced by Zeus' homosexual lover, Ganymede; Hephaestus, club-footed artisan extradordinaire, married to Aphrodite, who treats him as her father-in-law treats Hera; and Ares, hero god of war and one of Aphrodite's primary lovers. Thus even as Aphrodite triggers every possible fourth *chakra kriya* it is possible to experience on the arduous path to a true opening of the heart, within the context of marriage, she also makes possible four primary possibilities. In Eileithya, we have the most obvious metaphor - of the very literal possibility of children. In Hepheastus, we have the manifestation of a magical form of creativity, transcending the ordinary limitations of time and space. In Hebe, we have the capacity for divine nourishment at the level on which ambrosia is quaffed by the gods. Lastly, in Ares, we have an embodiment of passion and spiritual vitality that fuels and sustains itself.

While the full explication of these four gifts of Venus to the fourth *chakra* vessel of union is beyond the scope of our current discussion, suffice it to say that all four of these children of Zeus and Hera are manifestations of the rising of *kundalini* within the heart *chakra* as *shakti*. Wherever Venus is involved in an astrological pattern with Sun and Moon, we have a signature for a fourth *chakra* dynamic where this high level of alchemy is possible – usually, however, not without a saga worthy of the dysfunctional side of Aphrodite's legacy. Since Venus is never more than 48 degrees or so from the Sun, possible aspects of note would include the conjunction, semi-sextile and semi-square.

Other Planetary Players on the Fourth Chakra Stage

As an extension of Aphrodite's creativity on the dysfunctional side of her nature, the four primary asteroids – called "handmaidens of Venus" by Australian astrologer Pemo Theodore (58)[3] – can play a significant role in fleshing out the details of fourth *chakra* dynamics, especially when they are linked to Sun, Moon and/or Venus in a larger planetary pattern. As noted authority on asteroids Demetra George summarizes on the cover of her classic, *Asteroid Goddess*:

> *Ceres, the Great Mother, provides a model to understand the causes of co-dependency, eating disorders, child sexual abuse, and the challenges of single parenting. Pallas Athena, Goddess of Wisdom, refers to the dilemma of professional women who sacrifice relationship or children for career and the wounds from the father-daughter interaction. Vesta, the temple priestess, illuminates the need to reintegrate spiritual and sexual energies, and to find meaningful work. Juno (the Roman equivalent of Hera), Goddess of Marriage, speaks to the redefinition of significant relationships, changing sexual roles, and the plight of battered women and powerless wives.*

I highly recommend this book as a treatise on fourth *chakra* dynamics, along with the equally informative, *The Goddesses in Everywoman* and its companion, *The Gods in Everyman* by Jean Shinoda Bolen.

Any of the collective or transpersonal planets can also play their part in fourth *chakra* dynamics. Jupiter often joins Sun, Moon and Venus where infidelity is an issue. From Jupiter can also come the deep magnanimity of heart that allows one person to respond to another with compassion, caring, and altruistic intent.

Saturn can create blockages in the ability to give and/or receive love, often raising issues of worthiness, guilt and shame that can block one's capacity for satisfying relationships. In a more positive role, Saturn can also lend stability to a marriage where these blockages can potentially be worked through[4]. Saturn's contribution to the stability of marriage is very different than Venus', probably more clearly aligned with Hera's preoccupation with morality and social convention, as well as a mutual sense of responsibility (e.g to the children), but it can be an important positive factor keeping two people together long enough to experience a true and lasting opening of the heart, nonetheless.

In Greek mythology (or at least one version of the story), it is the castration of Uranus that gives birth to Aphrodite, suggesting that Uranus is – potentially at least – instrumental in helping transmute the second *chakra* energy of *tantra* into a true fourth *chakra* union. I believe this is possible mostly when Uranus is also active in the seventh *chakra*, where it facilitates the *hieros gamos* on a higher level of horizontal alchemy – as the fusion of all polarities. We will discuss this in more detail in Chapter Twenty Three. Meanwhile, at the level of the fourth *chakra*, Uranus can, especially in tandem with Jupiter, produce relationship patterns in which commitment is elusive and multiple partners complicate the potential for *hieros gamos*.

Neptune is often active in fourth *chakra* patterns as the planetary agency that facilitates genuine intimacy. Known for its capacity to dissolve barriers of separation, Neptune is instrumental on in any relationship where true union is genuinely sought. The paradox inherent in Neptune's symbolism is that it cannot really serve this function until each individual partner experiences *hieros gamos* within themselves – as discussed by Swami Sivananda Radha earlier in this chapter. To the extent that each partner looks to the other to complete them, Neptune will more likely precipitate experiences of co-dependency, and inappropriate blurring of personal boundaries. Neptune can be involved in early childhood wounding by incest, particularly where it works in tandem with Pluto.

Pluto can precipitate its own pattern of blockage to the free flow of unconditional love, primarily through the potential for physical and/or psychological abuse, power struggles in relationship, and/or the intense mistrust and fear of intimacy born of past abuse. But Pluto can also become manifest in the fourth *chakra* as the capacity of Shiva to open to the healing, redemptive power of Shakti and the deep longing for *hieros gamos* that draws it within range of possibility. One of the most potent catalysts to the experience of vulnerability in the fourth *chakra*, Pluto also is fully capable of cracking open hearts hardened by life, so that they once again become receptive despite the soul's determination to resist. Whether part of a natal fourth *chakra* pattern, or a transiting trigger to a natal fourth *chakra* pattern, Pluto brings us to our knees, so that the grace of *bodhichitta* might rekindle the spark of soul within us.

The Fourth Chakra Chart

Strong fourth *chakra* charts (indicating that this center of consciousness will be a major focus of learning and healing of core issues) are formed when the Sun, the Moon and Venus form a planetary pattern – especially either in the SW quadrant or spanning succedent houses. Such a pattern is made even stronger through additional planetary players and occasionally one of the "handmaiden of Venus" asteroids mentioned above.

Weaker fourth *chakra* patterns will involve either Sun or Moon in aspect to Venus, but not both. Where such aspects are lacking altogether, a fourth *chakra* chart (operating as a background factor) can be formed by aspects between Sun, Moon, Venus and/or the rulers of the succedent houses.

Endnotes

1 Oken assigns rulership of the fourth *chakra* to the Sun and Jupiter (155).

2 Following the Chaldean order, Grasse (204) and Hodgson (122-123) both assign rulership of the fourth *chakra* to Venus.

3 Theodore also includes the asteroids Psyche, Sappho, Eros, Cupido and Amor as additional fourth *chakra* players (60-64).

4 Hodgson considers Saturn an important fourth *chakra* planet, through its exaltation in Libra.

Chapter Eighteen
A Fourth Chakra Case Study

A strong fourth *chakra* signature can be found in the chart of Bill Clinton, who aside from his legacy as America's 42nd President, will be remembered for his infamous tabloid affair with Monica Lewinsky, and the impeachment trial that followed. However the media might have construed or misconstrued the events of Bill Clinton's life, and however he might be remembered by posterity, it is important to acknowledge that he – like every other soul alive in a body – was and is on a personal spiritual journey, learning or not learning from his mistakes, groping toward wholeness and integration of the many complex and contradictory facets of his being.

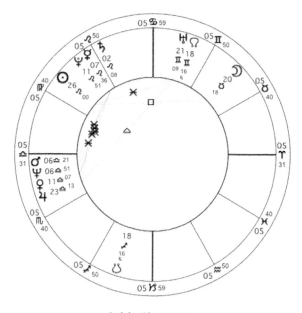

BILL CLINTON

In this case study, it is this more interior journey that we will attempt to coax out of his chart, placed in close juxtaposition to his life story. Perhaps we shall never know the real story, the whole story, the deepest spiritual significance of his saga - or of the saga of any public figure, for that matter. Nonetheless, since the known events of his life fit the profile under study well, I will comb the pages of his autobiography, *My Life*, for clues about the fourth *chakra* dynamic at the heart of his story. Wherever possible, I will attempt to explore his fourth *chakra* pattern using his words to illustrate my points. I will confess at the outset of this study that I admire and respect the man, although I did not always agree with his policies, so if that bias seeps through my words, the reader can take it into account.

What makes Clinton's fourth *chakra* chart so potent is the fact that 6 of 10 major planets in his chart are participating. The succedent 11th house Sun in its own sign Leo squares the Moon in Taurus (where it is exalted) in the succedent 8th house. The Sun also semi-squares Venus, ruler of his chart, placed in its own sign. It should be noted here that all three major players in this fourth *chakra* dynamic are strongly placed by sign, and two of them – Sun and Moon – are natally succedent. As we shall see in a moment, though natal Venus is not succedent, it does complete the perfect score by progressed house placement during the critical years that Clinton's fourth *chakra* wounds were being put on public display.

Venus sits at the heart of a stellium with Mars, Neptune, and Jupiter. Mars is not part of the classic fourth *chakra* signature, but it does participate in this one, through its tight conjunction with Neptune. Mars/Neptune then completes a sesquiquadrate to the Moon, thus closing the circuit binding Sun, Moon and Venus together.

Of special note in Clinton's chart is the presence of Juno (Hera) conjunct Jupiter (Zeus), at the edge of Venus' 1st house Libra stellium. Before we even begin to approach Clinton's story, as much as possible from the inside out, it is clear that this mythological duo and their marriage seemingly immune to infidelity plays a major role in Clinton's life, mirrored in his relationship to Hillary. Zeus/Hera is sextile Clinton's Sun, which is also sextile Uranus/North Node. Within the context of this pattern, Uranus stimulates Jupiter's tendency toward infidelity, while Hera stands by her man, Zeus, the philandering king. Finally, Uranus/North Node completes a wedge pattern with Sun and Jupiter/Juno by forming a trine to the latter.

The Koshic Implications of Clinton's Fourth Chakra Chart

On the level of koshic analysis, Clinton's fourth *chakra* pattern presents a relatively complex picture. Sun in Leo in the 11th house is about as fiery as one can get, while the Moon in Taurus in the 8th house is nearly as strong an expression of water. The square between the two then becomes a potent opening to *anandamaya kosha* through the juxtaposition of fire and water.

Clinton's 1st house Libra stellium is predominantly a fire/air signature. Mars and Jupiter in Libra are fire planets; Venus in Libra is an air planet. Uranus in the 9th house is also distinctly airy and fuels the fire/air mix through its trine to Jupiter. The combination of all four of these planets in Clinton's 1st house provides a potent opening to *pranamaya kosha*. Certainly by any standards, Clinton must be considered an energetic, passionately driven man with the capacity to mobilize others to action – such as the notorious FOBs (Friends of Bill) who, as legend has it, carried him to the White House on their shoulders – often despite tremendous opposition from his enemies.

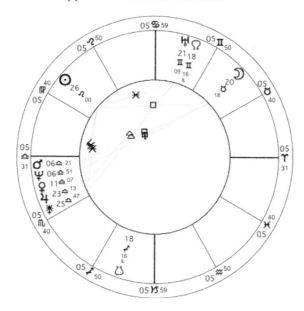

BILL CLINTON'S FOURTH CHAKRA CHART

Neptune is the only anomaly in this stellium, being the quintessential water planet surrounded by fire and air. Neptune strengthens the watery nature of the Moon through its tight sesquiquadrate to that body, as well as the fire-water dynamic discussed earlier, providing additional opening to *anandamaya kosha*. Through its watery presence in an air sign, conjunct the airy Venus, it also provides an opening to *vijnanamaya kosha*. In the midst of his public ordeal, Clinton was the perfect screen for the projections of all the angry Heras of the world, who were ready to lend a shoulder for the wounded Hillary to cry on, and crucify the king who had wounded her. With Mars so tightly conjunct Neptune and the Ascendant (a classic third *chakra* signature of deficiency), Clinton also became an easy target for the projections of his political enemies.

Clinton's Unwounded Soul Essence

Before we get to these fateful events, however, let's take a moment to see if we can't discern Clinton's soul essence, shining through the early years of his childhood, as it is

261

◇◇

portrayed in his autobiography. At the outset we might speculate that since the highest expression of the fourth *chakra* is the capacity to love and be loved, how well loved one is in childhood will necessarily be a measure of the strength of one's unwounded fourth *chakra* soul essence. By this measure, Clinton appears to have had a rather auspicious beginning. Raised by his grandparents, after his father died, and his mother went to back to nursing school, Clinton claims that his caretakers "were incredibly conscientious about me. . . . For all their own demons, my grandparents and my mother always made me feel I was the most important person in the world to them. Most children will make it if they have just one person who makes them feel that way. I had three" (9-10).

Clinton "adored" his grandfather, "an incredibly kind and generous man" and "felt pride that (he – Clinton) was born on his birthday" (10). His grandather had two jobs – one running a grocery store, whose customers were predominantly black. "It was rare to find an uneducated rural southerner without a racial bone in his body. That's exactly what my grandfather was. I could see that black people were different, but because he treated them like he did everybody else, asking after their children and about their work, I thought they were just like me" (11-12). Clinton was later remembered by a customer of his grandfather's store as " the only white boy in that neighborhood who played with black kids" (12).

After his grandfather's death, his mother happened to find some of his old account books. In them were many unpaid bills, mostly from his grandfather's black customers. "She recalled that he told her that good people who were doing the best they could deserved to be able to feed their families, and no matter how strapped he was, he never denied them groceries on credit" (12). Here we see an early demonstration of compassion that crosses cultural barriers that Clinton absorbed by osmosis because of his resonance with his kind and generous grandfather, his earliest solar role model. All that he absorbed in this way, we might then safely assume resonated strongly with Clinton's unwounded soul essence, demonstrated in later years as his untiring efforts in fighting Republican efforts to gut social programs, raise taxes on the working poor, and skew policies in favor of the wealthy.

Throughout Clinton's story, as told in the early chapter of his autobiography, it is quite clear that he cared about, appreciated, and respected most of the people around him for their humanity, just as his grandfather had taught him to do. "I saw a house burn down across the street," he says in describing an early lesson, "and learned that I was not the only person bad things happened to. . . I learned that what seems funny to the strong can be cruel and humiliating to the weak" (12). He learned not to judge others by appearances alone – that "the guy pumping your gas might have had an IQ as high as the guy taking your tonsils out" (15).

I learned a lot from the stories my uncles, aunts, and grandparents told me: that no one is perfect, but most people are good; that people can't be judged only by their worst or weakest moments; that harsh judgments can make hypocrites of us all; that a lot of life is just showing up and hanging on; that laughter is often the best, and sometimes the only response to pain. Perhaps most important, I learned that everyone has a story – of dreams, and nightmares, hope and heartache, love and loss, courage and fear, sacrifice and selfishness. All my life I've been interested in other people's stories. I've wanted to know them, understand them, feel them. When I grew up and got into politics, I always felt the main point of my work was to give people a chance to have better stories (15).

These childhood lessons are clearly the hallmark of an 11th house Sun, a man with a big heart, a tremendous capacity for caring and compassion, and a burning desire to use his talents, his powers of persuasion, and his political influence to make the world a better place for the people that lived within it. However history might judge his actions in retrospect, it is not hard to see that from the very beginning, Clinton's fourth *chakra* soul essence was vibrant and alive, a force intent on radiating as far and wide as the world would allow it to. Though he doesn't put it in these terms, Clinton grew up intimately acquainted with the vulnerability of *bodhichitta*, reflected in the eyes of the poor, but mostly decent southerners – black and white – around him. He also grew up appreciating the strength of character, the power of humor, tolerance and forgiveness, and the sheer humanity that made it possible to cope with pain and suffering. This awareness, resonating with something at the very core of him, is the unwounded soul essence that propelled him into his fourth *chakra* process.

Clinton's Primal Wounding

The story of Clinton's childhood, as he tells it anyway, is so buoyant, and so big-hearted an embrace of everyone and everything, that it is difficult to discern the wounding that was most certainly there – for awareness of *bodhichitta*, the essential vulnerability at the fragile heart of human nature, does not come without a first-hand acquaintance with pain and suffering. As Clinton describes his family life, he does mention considerable tension between his grandmother and grandfather, as well as his mother and step-father (reflected astrologically by his Sun-Moon square. This tension apparently came to a head one day, probably when Clinton was 4 or 5, when his stepfather lost control of his anger in a drunken stupor. As Clinton describes his stepfather:

Roger Clinton really loved me and he loved Mother (Clinton's unwounded fourth chakra soul essence speaking), but he couldn't ever seem to break free of

◇◇

> *the shadows of self-doubt, the phony security of binge drinking and adolescent partying, and the isolation from and verbal abuse of Mother that kept him from becoming the man he might have been (19).*

On that fateful day in 1950 or perhaps 1951, his mother and father were arguing Roger Clinton (20):

> *. . . pulled a gun from behind his back and fired in Mother's direction. The bullet went into the wall between where she and I were standing. I was stunned and so scared. I had never heard a shot fired before, much less ever seen one. . . . I'm sure Daddy didn't mean to hurt her and he would have died if the bullet had hit either of us. But something more poisonous than alcohol drove him to that level of debasement. It would be a long time before I could understand such forces in others or in myself.*

That is all Clinton says about the incident, but one has to wonder about the stark contrast between his grandfather's gentle kindness and the dark, angry energy apparently festering inside his stepfather, and how that might have ripped a hole in the otherwise seamless fabric of Clinton's unabashed love affair with life. Later, in junior high school, Clinton hints a bit further at the vulnerability within himself that his stepfather's demeanor and actions exposed. After a fight with an older boy who was picking on him, Clinton says (42):

> *I had learned that I could defend myself, but I hadn't enjoyed hurting him and I was a little disturbed at my anger, the currents of which would prove deeper and stronger in the years ahead. I now know that my anger on that day was a normal and healthy response to the way I'd been treated. But because of the way Daddy behaved when he was angry and drunk, I associated anger with being out of control and I was determined not to lose control. Doing so could unleash the deeper constant anger I kept locked away because I didn't know where it came from.*

Both this deeper constant anger with no apparent source and the drunken anger of his stepfather are represented in Clinton's fourth *chakra* chart by Mars/Neptune sesquiquadrate the Moon. The Moon, as discussed above, is the embodiment of *bodhichitta* within the context of the fourth *chakra* chart. In Clinton's case, it is a sense of vulnerability triggered by that within his nature that is seemingly out of his control.

Mars/Neptune brings a strong unconscious component to one's actons, at times propelling them beyond control, while Venus/Jupiter can incline one toward self-indulgence. The combination, in Clinton's case, produces not just a somewhat volatile temper, but also a weakness for sweet and fatty foods, and a prodigious sexual appetite capable of crossing the bounds of propriety. The inability to keep these potentially troublesome behaviors in check produces a sense of vulnerability, reflected astrologically by the Mars/Neptune sesquiqudrate to the Moon. To the extent that these out-of-control behaviors impact his relationships, and hurt the people he loves, then they become the source of lessons on the path of fourth *chakra* awakening.

As a child, the potential for out-of-control behavior capable of hurting loved ones was modeled for him by an abusive, alcoholic stepfather. His stepfather didn't abuse him, but took his frustrations out on Clinton's mother, triggering a confused sense of outrage in Clinton, as well as a troublesome sense of recognition that "there but for the grace of God go I."

These family problems got worse when Clinton was about 14, culminating in his parents' divorce, while transiting Uranus was conjunct his Sun and square his Moon. After a particularly violent episode, in which Clinton picked up a golf club and threatened to beat his stepfather unless he stopped hitting his mother, Clinton said, "I just couldn't accept the fact that a basically good person would try to make his own pain go away by hurting someone else. I wish I'd had someone to talk with about all this, but I didn't, so I had to figure it out for myself. I came to accept the secrets of our house as a normal part of my life. I never talked to anyone about them" (46). The fact that Clinton had no one to talk to about the tumultuous impact his stepfather's out-of-control behavior had on him no doubt contributed to his wounding. In his words, "secrets can be an awful burden to bear, especially if some sense of shame is attached to them, even if the source of the shame is not the secret holder (46)."

Of course, it is often the case that where we are most woundable is also where we are most capable of wounding others, and as Clinton recognized in an essay he wrote as a junior in high school (58):

> I am a person motivated and influenced by so many diverse factors I sometimes question the sanity of my existence. I am a living paradox – deeply religious, yet not as convinced of my exact beliefs as I ought to be; wanting responsibility yet shirking it; loving the truth but often times giving way to falsity . . . I detest selfishness, but see it in the mirror every day. . . I view those, some of who are very dear to me, who have never learned how to live. I desire and struggle to be different from them, but often am almost an exact likeness,

As history has recorded, Clinton would inevitably come to know his own capacity to hurt those he loved, keeping shameful secrets about his own out-of-control behaviors.

About the connection between his fourth *chakra kriya* with Monica and Hillary, Clinton says in retrospect (46-47):

> *. . . it became a struggle for me to find the right balance between secrets of internal richness and those of hidden fears and shame, and that I was always reluctant to discuss with anyone the most difficult parts of my personal life. . . I know now this struggle is at least partly the result of growing up in an alcoholic home and the mechanisms I developed to cope with it. It took me a long time to figure that out. It was even harder to learn which secrets to keep, which to let go of, which to avoid in the first place. I am still not sure I understand that completely. It looks as if it's going to be a lifetime project".*

Indeed, most core issues are. Neptune is the planet within Clinton's 1st house stellium most clearly associated with secrets, and probably also with shame – that is to say, secrets behind which there is a sense that he was not living up to the high standards of personal conduct his own vibrant fourth *chakra* dictated he ought to. Some of those secrets are undoubtedly connected to "the deeper constant anger (he) kept locked away because [he] didn't know where it came from," indicated astrologically by Clinton's tight Mars/Neptune conjunction. Others, however, would also be associated with Venus/Jupiter – Venus being the goddess of romantic entanglements and Jupiter being the philandering king. This, of course, is not to say that everywhere Venus and Jupiter appear in tandem, the dynamic between them will play out in this way. But given that Clinton's chart harbors them within the context of a fourth *chakra* pattern, brimming with secrets, it seems clear that working through "which secrets to keep, which to let go of, which to avoid in the first place" in relation to his love life, would be one of the lessons he must learn on his way toward healing his fourth *chakra* issues.

Uranus' Role in Clinton's Fourth Chakra Drama

With any core issue, there are numerous opportunities for self-observation that will yield useful information. In particular, it is often helpful to track the transits of the outer planets (from Jupiter through Pluto) that are involved in the pattern itself to the whole pattern. In Clinton's fourth *chakra* chart, there are three outer planets – Jupiter, Uranus and Neptune – and if we wanted to be really thorough, or if Clinton were a student of astrology wishing to learn more about his own patterns, it would be a useful exercise to track all three. Given the space limitations of our purpose here, I will just demonstrate a few of the possibilities, by tracking Uranus transits to his fourth *chakra* pattern.

Aside from his father's death, which actually took place while Clinton was still in his mother's womb, the first real breach in his buoyant fourth *chakra* worldview came while transiting Uranus was conjunct his Sun (and square his Moon), from October, 1960 – June, 1962. This encompassed the period of the first shotgun incident when he was 14 through his parents' divorce, discussed earlier in this chapter.

When transiting Uranus was conjunct Clinton's Mars/Neptune, from October, 1969 – September, 1970, Clinton wrestled with decisions surrounding his induction into the military at the height of the Vietnam War. While the chapter in his book devoted to this period makes an interesting story, it is less relevant to Clinton's fourth *chakra* story than what comes after. For the sake of brevity, it will suffice to say that during this period, Clinton was faced with another moral dilemma pitting his convictions against the war with his fourth *chakra* sensibilities that we are all in the same boat together and ought to take responsibility for each other. About his decision-making process during this period, Clinton says, "I had mixed feelings. I knew I had a chance to avoid Vietnam, but somebody will be getting on that bus in ten days and it may be that I should be getting on it too." Instead Clinton went to law school, and the rest – as they say – is history.

No small piece of that history occurred while transiting Uranus was conjunct Venus, from October, 1970 – September, 1971. In the spring of 1971, Clinton met Hillary in the Yale Law Library, and by mid May, they were starting to fall in love. Summer was coming, however, and Hillary had accepted an offer to work at a law firm in California, while Clinton had been asked to take a job as coordinator of the southern states for George McGovern, a tremendous opportunity no one in their right mind with Clinton's political aspirations would pass up. The trouble was, Clinton wasn't in his right mind. He was in his heart, and his fourth *chakra* pattern was being activated as he fell in love. About this dilemma, he wrote (184):

> Though I found the prospect of the campaign exciting, I feared . . . that it would simply be a way of formalizing my aloneness, letting me deal with people in a good cause but at arm's length. With Hillary, there was no arms length. She was in my face from the start, and before I knew it, in my heart.

Keeping people at arm's length is not a fourth *chakra* path. Nor was it Clinton's style, after 21 years of immediacy and caring in relation to everyone from the bus driver to the important political figures for whom he interned. Having someone in your face and in your heart is a fourth *chakra* recipe for maximum learning on the pathway to unconditional love. With his potent fourth *chakra* chart, Clinton took to it like a piece of freshly baked peach pie. He rejected the job offer from McGovern, and asked Hillary if he could accompany her to California. Incredulous at first, she agreed, and by the end of this period, and the beginning of the next school year, they were living together in New Haven.

By the following spring, Clinton had rejoined the McGovern campaign and got to have his pie and eat it too. After graduation, however, Bill and Hillary's paths led them in opposite directions – while Uranus was transiting his Jupiter (from December, 1972 – August, 1974) – Clinton took a job as law professor at the University of Arkansas in Fayetteville, while Hillary went to work with Marian Edelman's Children Defense Fund in Cambridge, Massachusetts. By the end of this period, he had made the decision to run for his first political office – a congressional seat in Arkansas. He lost, but fitting the imagery of Uranus' activation of Jupiter, the planet of law and politics, and the tail end of his fourth *chakra* stellium, his career as a progressive politician who wanted "to give people a chance to have better stories" was underway. By the time, transiting Uranus was opposed his Moon, ruler of his Midheaven and 10th house of career (from December, 1978 – November, 1979), Bill Clinton – at age 32 – had become governor of Arkansas.

From the very beginning of his first campaign, Hillary was by his side, cheering him on in his triumphs, consoling him in his defeats, despite her separate career. A few days after Nixon resigned, and she was offered a teaching position at the University of Arkansas in Fayetteville, she agreed to come to Arkansas. At the time, Uranus was finishing its transit of Clinton's Juno (Hera).

On October 11, 1975, Bill and Hillary were married. The Sun was conjunct the midpoint of natal Venus/Jupiter; Venus was semi-square this same midpoint. Jupiter was opposed its natal position and sextile Uranus. Saturn was making its return, while natal Saturn was being squared by transiting Uranus. Transiting Pluto was inching its way toward a conjunction with natal Venus, suggesting perhaps that the woman who was in his face and in his heart was the one who would also hand him his biggest lesson about the price of admission to the fourth *chakra* promise of unconditional love.

Clinton's Fourth Chakra Drama Through an Astrological Lens

In writing about his marriage, Clinton, who by his own admission, prefers to keep his private life private, said this (234-235):

> *Probably more has been written or said about our marriage than about any other in America. I've always been amazed at the people who felt free to analyze, criticize, and pontificate about it. After being married for nearly thirty years and observing my friends' experiences with separations, reconciliations, and divorces, I've learned that marriage, with all of its magic and misery, its contentments and disappointments, remains a mystery, not easy for those in it to understand and largely inaccessible to outsiders.*

Not wishing to be one of those who criticize and pontificate, I will restrict my astrological analysis of the events surrounding Clinton's marital saga to his fourth *chakra* dynamic as I have fleshed it out so far. On the journey of the soul through the difficult territory encompassed by any strong *chakra* pattern, mistakes are made, sometimes horrendous mistakes. But from a spiritual perspective this is how we learn, and as pointed out in *The Seven Gates of Soul*, losing our capacity to point fingers of blame is an important step on the path to learning. It is in that spirit that I approach the events of Bill Clinton's life, with which we are all too familiar.

Public suspicion of Clinton's extramarital affairs first began surfacing in mid-September, 1990, while Clinton was running for Arkansas governor for the last time. A "disgruntled former employee of the Development Finance Authority (359)" Larry Nichols accused Clinton of using agency funds to carry on affairs with five women. Clinton told the press to call the women, all of whom denied it, the story essentially died, and Clinton was re-elected by a comfortable margin.

Astrologically, this first breach in the secret wall shielding Clinton's personal life and marriage from scrutiny occurred while transiting Uranus was square his natal Mars/Neptune – one quarter cycle from the period in which he chose to go to law school instead of the military, by a circuitous route, wracked by guilt, ambivalence and second guessing. As with the earlier conjunction, Clinton was able to slide past his obstacles with relative ease, if not in the wake of actions that were entirely above suspicion – a capacity summed up by his critics' nickname for him: Slick Willie. His actions in relation to the Vietnam War era draft came up for later scrutiny during his first presidential campaign, but since they are not really part of the fourth *chakra* story we are tracking here, we will slide by them, too.

When transiting Uranus was square his natal Venus, through all of 1991, while Clinton was campaigning for the presidency, his fourth *chakra* challenges became more serious. One quarter cycle from his courtship and marriage to Hillary, and on the day before Uranus' first exact square to Venus, a story broke in the Little Rock media about one of the women on Larry Nichols list, Gennifer Flowers, who reversed her earlier story and said she had had a twelve-year affair with Clinton (which if true, would have started during transiting Uranus' previous opposition to Clinton's natal Moon). As the story gained momentum, Bill and Hillary appeared together on 60 *Minutes* and defended the viability of their marriage. When asked directly if he had an affair, Clinton toyed with the idea of using Rosalyn Carter's defense against a similar question in 1976, when she said, "If I had, I wouldn't tell you." Instead, Clinton took a more artful dodge. In his book, he describes his strategy this way (385):

> Since I wasn't as blameless as Mrs. Carter, I decided not to be cute. Instead, I said that I had already acknowledged causing pain in my marriage, that I had already said more about the subject than any other politician ever had and would say no more, and that the American people understood what I meant.

⟡⟡⟡

Six years later, during his deposition in the Paula Jones case, Clinton admitted having had an affair with Gennifer Flowers, though it did not apparently last for twelve years. But on that *60 Minutes* interview in early 1992, Hillary defended him, and later Larry Nichols withdrew his lawsuit, saying, "the media has made a circus out of this thing and now it's gone way too far. When that *Starr* article first came out, several women called asking if I was willing to pay them to say that they had had an affair with Bill Clinton. This is crazy" (386). This was but the first volley in a Republican vendetta that would dog Clinton for the better part of his presidency. It was also the first public view through a private window, behind which Clinton was struggling with his fourth *chakra* issues – out-of-control, self-indulgent behavior that hurt the people he loved most.

While the Republican feeding frenzy over Clinton's personal failings never let up, it did intensify right on schedule as Uranus squared Clinton's Jupiter, through most of 1994. This year, Clinton says (567):

> . . .*was one of the hardest of my life, one in which important successes in foreign and domestic policy were overshadowed by the demise of health-care reform and an obsession with bogus scandal. It began with personal heartbreak and ended in political disaster.*

The personal heartbreak came in early January, when Clinton's mother died. Along with Clinton's grandparents, his mother was one of the three people that had shown him the unconditional love that would nurture and encourage the opening of his own heart *chakra*, and the loss was tough. The political disaster, fueled by "obsession with bogus scandal" proved to be tougher. While Clinton was in Moscow, working to improve relations with the Soviets, Republicans and some Democrats back home were clamoring for an independent counsel to investigate an allegedly questionable real estate deal that came to be known simply as Whitewater. The deal in question would have been made in 1978-79, or around the time of transiting Uranus' opposition to the Moon (ruler of fourth house governing real estate), and Clinton's affair with Gennifer Flowers. The investigation began with relatively even-handed special counsel Robert Fiske, but by August 5, as transiting Uranus retrograde was less than half a degree from exact square to Jupiter, Fiske was replaced by the more conservative and partisan Kenneth Starr. We saw earlier how transiting Uranus conjunct Jupiter launched Clinton's political career. Now one quarter cycle later, that career is being seriously challenged, in part by secrets connected to out of control behavior.

Just as Whitewater was heating up, Clinton's wall of secrecy was dealt another blow, when Paula Jones filed a sexual harassment suit against him. Paula Jones was quoted earlier in an *American Spectator* article that she had wanted to be Clinton's "regular girlfriend." But when given a chance to clear her name at the Conservative Political Action Committee convention in February, 1994, she instead accused Clinton of making unwanted sexual advances, and claimed that she was denied annual pay raises in her employment with the state, when she rebuffed him.

Clinton and his lawyers managed to stay one step ahead of Kenneth Starr and his small army of prosecutors until late spring, 1997, when the Supreme court unanimously ruled that the Paula Jones case could go forward. Throughout this wrangling, transiting Saturn was opposing Clinton's Neptune/Mars, coming to its last partile aspect to Mars just as the Supreme Court made its decision. From the time Paula Jones first made her assertion of sexual harassment in 1994 through the dismissal of the case in April, 1998, progressed Venus was also moving through the succedent 2nd house and squaring Clinton's natal Sun, thus intensifying the activation of his fourth *chakra* pattern.

While the Jones case was dismissed without a trial because the judge had found no credible evidence to support her claim, Starr had gotten what he wanted – Clinton's famous false statement about his affair with Monica Lewinsky – and pressed on toward impeachment. Clinton vehemently denied the affair, to his wife, to the press, and in court. Hillary appeared on NBC's *Today* show to say she didn't believe the charges, and that a "vast right-wing conspiracy" had been out to destroy her and her husband since 1992. Despite the truth of this statement, Clinton had lied, and in mid-August, 1998, around the time of his 52nd birthday, Clinton was compelled to come clean.

On August 15, two days before his grand jury testimony, as transiting Uranus was trine Venus, Clinton told Hillary the truth about his affair. About this painful confession, he says (800):

> *She looked at me as if I had punched her in the gut, almost as angry for lying to her . . . as for what I had done. All I could do was tell her that I was sorry, and that I felt I couldn't tell anyone, even her, what had happened. I told her that I loved her and I didn't want to hurt her or Chelsea, that I was ashamed of what I had done, and that I had kept everything to myself in an effort to avoid hurting my family and undermining the presidency. . . I still didn't fully understand why I had done something so wrong and stupid; that understanding would come slowly, in the months of working on our relationship that lay ahead.*

I had to talk to Chelsea, too. In some ways, that was even harder. Sooner or later, every child learns that her parents aren't perfect, but this went far beyond the normal. . . I was afraid that I would lose not only my marriage, but my daughter's love and respect as well.

◇◇

These were tough fourth *chakra* lessons, played out on a public stage, perhaps as a modern-day morality play worthy of the great Greek tragedians of antiquity. Two days later (as transiting Pluto formed a direct station sextile to natal Mars/Neptune), Clinton admitted that "on certain occasions in 1996 and once in 1997 I engaged in wrongful conduct that included inappropriate intimate contact with Monica Lewinsky (801)." Throughout 1996, transiting Jupiter made a triple pass square to natal Venus, triggering an intensified round of the pattern of self-indulgence we have previously identified with these planets. In September, Starr sent his report to Congress, outlining eleven impeachable offenses. By January 1999, the impeachment trial began. By February 12, it was over, as transiting Uranus was trine Clinton's natal Mars/Neptune – continuing the pattern we have seen with Uranus transits to Mars/Neptune that allowed Clinton to wriggle free when pressed back into some tight corner.

From a spiritual perspective, one might assume that Clinton was allowed this modicum of grace, because the real work lie in moving beyond the out-of-control indulgences (Venus/Jupiter) and patterns of deception (Mars/Neptune) that had clouded his relationships with those he loved, and in learning to love with a clear heart. One additional heart *chakra* lesson in the midst of all this drama was conveyed to him during a visit to South Africa in spring of 1998. Of this encounter, Clinton says (782-783):

> By this time I had developed a real friendship with Mandela. He was remarkable not only because of his astonishing journey from hatred to reconciliation during twenty-seven years in prison, but also because he was both a tough-minded politician and a caring person who, despite his long confinement, never lost his interest in the personal side of life or his ability to show love, friendship, and kindness.
>
> We had one especially meaningful conversation. I said, "Madiba (Mandela's colloquial tribal name, which he asked me to use), I know you did a great thing in inviting your jailers to your inauguration, but didn't you really hate those who imprisoned you?" He replied, "Of course I did, for many years. They took the best years of my life. They abused me physically and mentally. I didn't get to see my children grow up. I hated them. Then one day when I was working in the quarry, hammering the rocks, I realized that they had already taken everything from me except my mind and heart. Those they could not take without my permission. I decided not to give them away." Then he looked at me, smiled, and said, "And neither should you."
>
> After I caught my breath, I asked him another question. "When you were walking out of prison for the last time, didn't you feel the hatred rise up in you

✕✕

again?" "Yes," he said, "for a moment I did. Then I thought to myself, 'They have had me for twenty-seven years. If I keep hating them, they will still have me.' I wanted to be free, and so I let it go." He smiled again. This time he didn't have to say, "And so should you."

Like his grandfather, Mandela was a role model for the heart *chakra* lessons Clinton was trying to learn. Whether or not Clinton will ultimately learn these lessons remains to be seen, or not seen. But it appears he at least took this wake-up call seriously. As he describes the aftermath of his impeachment (810-811):

I had asked three pastors to counsel me at least once a month for an indefinite period. . . Even though they were often tough on me, the pastors took me past the politics into soul-searching and the power of God's love. Hillary and I also began a serious counseling program, one day a week for about a year. For the first time in my life, I actually talked openly about feelings, experiences and opinions about life, love, and the nature of relationships. I didn't like everything I learned about myself or my past, and it pained me to face the fact that my childhood and the life I'd led since growing up had made some things difficult for me that seemed to come more naturally to other people.

I also came to understand that when I was exhausted, angry, or feeling isolated and alone, I was more vulnerable to making selfish and self-destructive personal mistakes about which I would later be ashamed. The current controversy was the latest casualty of my lifelong effort to lead parallel lives, to wall off my anger and grief and get on with my outer life, which I loved and lived well. . . . There was no excuse for what I did, but trying to come to grips with why I did it gave me at least a chance to finally unify my parallel lives.

Given Clinton's heartfelt effort to learn from his mistakes and grow as a human being, it would appear that his fourth *chakra kriya* had served its purpose.

As a postscript to this story, Clinton underwent successful open-heart surgery on September 6, 2004. Several months before the surgery, he had been complaining about shortness of breath and constriction in his chest. An angiogram showed extensive blockage, though "his heart muscle was strong with absolutely no damage (MacNeil/Lehrer Productions)," so surgery was arranged to improve his blood flow. While this event is not part of the Uranus cycle to his fourth *chakra* signature that we have been tracking, his surgery took place as his progressed Moon was semi-square natal Sun (a fourth *chakra* trigger) and his progressed Sun was conjunct natal Jupiter – a strong opening to *pranamaya*

◇◇

kosha, where unresolved heart *chakra* issues could potentially manifest as impeded blood flow to the heart.

Since 1988 (two years before the first public suspicions of Clinton's extramarital affairs began to surface), progressed Sun had been making its way through his troublesome 1st house stellium. Now with this open-heart surgery, it was finally making its exit. Clinton had kept his secrets for so long and so well, perhaps in resistance to the fourth *chakra* lessons he most needed to learn, that it had worked its way down to *pranamaya kosha* and manifest as physical blockage in his heart. Now that he had unburdened himself, and the lifeblood began to flow freely and openly again, the prognosis was good that he would recover to maximize the spiritual opportunities at the heart of his fourth *chakra* chart.

Chapter Nineteen
The Fifth Chakra Chart

As discussed in Chapter Five, the fifth *chakra* is the place of the teacher. It is where inner alignment with the truth of one's being produces outer alignment that is magnetic and illuminating for all who come into contact with it. One whose fifth *chakra* is open functions from a profound sense of place and time – of knowing his role within the larger whole of which he is part, and of playing it with the consummate skill of a surfer riding a wave. This heightened awareness produces the capacity to trigger recognition of truth in others. Such a being is capable of looking through the distortions caused by wounding and seeing the pure radiance of Spirit, dwelling as the animating force of the body hosting it. In the presence of such a being, self-doubt falls away and a more inviolable truth reveals itself.

Of course, at a lesser stage of enlightenment, the fifth *chakra* can also be an arena in which we work through our core issues. Such issues will invariably revolve around our capacity to assimilate the truth that is revealed to us as we live our lives, and our willingness to communicate that truth as openly and as honestly as possible. For many people, clear communication is a primary stumbling block on the path to harmonious relationships (fourth *chakra* fulfillment), worldly success (third *chakra*), getting what they need and want out of life (second *chakra*) and even, occasionally survival (first *chakra*) itself. For on the most fundamental level, each cell of our body must process information, and when that does not happen effectively – as for example, when a stroke interrupts communication between the brain and the muscles – existence itself is impaired.

In keeping with the pattern we have established so far, one would expect the fifth *chakra* to manifest as a *yang chakra*. But once the heart has been opened, this pattern begins to break down. The fifth *chakra* is a *yang* expression to the extent that in order to function through it, we must actively give our consent to the truth of our own being, as it seeks expression through us. If we seal our mouths with duct tape, and hide ourselves in a closet – metaphorically speaking of course – the fifth *chakra* atrophies. On the other hand, the inner alignment out of which the urge to speak our truth arises is one that only comes through surrender, through allowing the ego to entertain the possibility of a larger relationship with *bindu*. Until this *yin* process has established itself within the fourth and fifth *chakra*, the truth we speak will necessarily be partial, filtered through personal biases that may well be seriously distorted by wounding, and potentially the source of many difficulties in relationship to those with whom we are trying to communicate. It is the surrender to a deeper truth, and the willingness to give our consent to that truth – in thought, word and deed – that produces the balance between *yin* and *yang* necessary to a fully functional fifth *chakra*.

If we consider the fifth *chakra* circle within the context of the *yin-yang* symbol, it would be the small circular seed of *yin* at the heart of the *yang* half of the circle. We can also envision the fifth *chakra* in terms of the sinuous line between *yin* and *yang* as it is ridden down the curve from the *yang* to the *yin* portion of the circle. The more one surrenders to the inner voice of wisdom and knowing, the small still voice within, the more one's life becomes an act of grace, of doing by non-doing, and of being. Ultimately, the teacher does not teach. The teacher just is, and from the radiance of that being, students take what they need. As each of us learns to negotiate the fifth *chakra*, we eventually find the flow and then simply merge with it. At this level, the life force within us will move us when and where we need to be.

The Placement of Fifth Chakra Planets in Astrological Space

As mentioned in the preceding chapter on the fourth *chakra*, patterns related to the transcendence phase (of which the fifth *chakra* is the first) no longer exhibit preferences for one hemisphere or quadrant over another. They can be anywhere. At the fifth and sixth *chakras* especially, our task becomes perceiving the wholeness of psychic space, and living from a sense of integration within that space. Reflected astro-logically, this means that certain hemispheres are no longer taboo, nor fraught with danger, nor are others more comfortable or easier to navigate. All are part of the whole we are attempting to embrace, and the opportunity for that embrace is as easily found in the hustle and bustle of the southern hemisphere as it is in the secluded stillness of the northern, as available through relationships in the west as through solitary moments of self-discovery in the east.

Where a fifth *chakra* pattern does happen to land will say something about the *interchakra* dynamics that provide the arena for discovery and embrace of truth. If, for example, the pattern spans the north and the west, it may well be that the fifth *chakra* pattern in question plays itself out through some family melodrama with second *chakra* implications. If it is located primarily in the south and east, the same fifth *chakra* pattern may necessitate taking a more organic place in the world on the level at which the third *chakra* holds court. In this way, the fifth *chakra* can be freed from its hierarchical association with transcendence of "lower" *chakra* difficulties, and be understood within the more horizontal context of its relationships with the other *chakras.*

The Fifth Chakra and Cadent Planets

Having acknowledged the flexibility of fifth *chakra* patterns with regard to astrological space, I will also note an affinity between fifth *chakra* patterns and the cadent houses. In the trifold schema that divides the quadrants, we declare ourselves in the angular houses, and receive feedback to our declaration in the succedent houses. The cadent houses are where we assimilate this feedback, and incorporate it into our being as we move into the next angular house. This, at least, is a basic counterclockwise understanding embraced by most schools of contemporary astrology. It is also an astro-logical explanation for the *yin* component of our fifth house experience, for it is through listening to what life is telling us – to the feedback – and taking it in, that we absorb the information necessary to align with the truth of our being.

If we move through the quadrants in a clockwise direction – which in fact, is the way the planets actually move through the sky depicted by them – then we have a complementary perspective (Landwehr, "Clockwise Interpretation"). Assimilating our lessons in the cadent houses means little if it does not move us to live our truth. This is a realization that dawns in the cadent houses. The living itself takes place in the succedent houses, while the fruit of our alignment is a profound sense of place and timing manifest in the angular houses. Because this fifth *chakra* awakening begins in the cadent houses, it is to the cadent houses that we look for the core issues capable of triggering it.

In the 12th house, the miraculous fusion of Spirit and matter launches the experience of embodiment itself, which from this perspective, is an act of alignment. If this alignment had not taken place, there would be no life. On a deeper level, this is often the place of spiritual rebirth when confinement produces profound revelation and deep alchemical change. We alluded to such a possibility in the preceding chapter, when describing Nelson Mandela's unfathomable capacity for forgiveness after 27 years of imprisonment. Traditionally, the 12th house is not often associated with alignment, but that is only because the process is largely invisible – taking place in cloistered environments, prisons, ashrams or monasteries, long periods of hospital convalescence, or in the innermost chambers of a heart bound by an ordinary life. All we see when we look at 12th house experiences from the outside is the confinement itself. What we do not see is the inner transformation that takes place invisibly behind the walls of confinement, which are by design, consciously or unconsciously erected to keep out unwanted external influences. To the extent that these experiences of inner transformation can be understood to be a deeper alignment with the truth of one's being, then they can also be understood as fifth *chakra* experiences.

In the 9th house – normally associated with higher education, travel, and experiences beyond our everyday comfort zone – can also be found these outer triggers to alignment. I had such an experience in college, for example, when I was first exposed to the writings of Carl Jung. A spark of recognition was lit in me that has served as a guiding star ever since. Jung himself had many such experiences while traveling. In one experience, on a visit to the Pueblo Indians of New Mexico, his guide said to him (Memories 248):

◇◇

"The whites always want something; they are always uneasy and restless. We do not know what they want. We do not understand them. We think they are mad."

I asked him why he thought the whites were all mad.

"They say that they think with their heads," he replied.

"Why of course. What do you think with?" I asked him in surprise.

"We think here," he said, indicating his heart.

I fell into a long meditation. For the first time in my life, so it seemed to me, someone had drawn for me a picture of the real white man. It was as though until now I had seen nothing but sentimental, prettified color prints. The Indian had struck our vulnerable spot, unveiled a truth to which we are blind. I felt rising within me like a shapeless mist something unknown and yet deeply familiar.

However it manages to infiltrate our lives, it is this shapeless mist that produces the opening to fifth *chakra* wisdom that is found in both the 12th and the 9th houses. In the 12th house, this mist saturates our environment and we absorb it by osmosis, whether or not we intend to. In the 9th house – often traditionally associated with teachers – we make a more conscious choice, either to allow the truth that comes unbidden like mist into our lives, or to resist it. To the extent that we are willing to allow it, it changes us, and we learn what it is that we have to teach. We also learn from our resistance, although the process is more painful.

In the 6th house – normally associated with work and health issues – we find additional triggers to fifth *chakra* awakenings. The struggle to actualize a core sense of self through what the Buddhists call *right livelihood* is a central fifth *chakra* issue. To the extent that we settle for a mere job to pay the bills, eking out an existence through some form of drudgery utterly divorced from any sense of purpose or exercise of creativity that might be meaningful, we suffer from a fifth *chakra* malady that is all too common in a culture where people are largely valued for what they produce. To the extent that we seek to give voice to our vocation, or to follow what James Hillman and others have referred to as our "calling" is to empower ourselves on a deeper level of truth.

As discussed in *The Seven Gates of Soul*, it is often when something breaks down – we lose our jobs, or we get sick, to use two primary 6th house examples – that we experience our most profound openings to soul. As difficult as these experiences are, they force us to re-evaluate our sense of alignment with the truth of our being and make changes, sometimes radical changes, that realign us. This is perhaps never more true than when we are struggling with some chronic health issue, especially those that are a consequence of bad lifestyle choices, or of living in an environment that has in some way become toxic to our being.

Many otherwise healthy people, for example, must cope with cancers caused by chemical and/or radioactive contamination of the environment. On one level, this is a profoundly serious tragedy about which we are collectively still largely in denial. On the individual level, however, it can be an opportunity for profound alignment on the level of the fifth *chakra*. A friend of mine struggled in recent years with breast cancer, caused by a number of interrelated factors, including previous exposure to toxic chemicals. Even while my heart went out to her in her suffering, I marveled at the energy, determination and single-minded focus with which she pursued every possible avenue to healing she could find. In a rather paradoxical way, as she descended into the depths of her illness with as much loving awareness as she could muster, she became more alive. After her cancer went into remission (where it has thankfully stayed), she began counseling other women with breast cancer, speaking her truth about it from a renewed place of alignment with her spirit. In retrospect, I can easily see this as a fifth *chakra* awakening.

Lastly, in the 3rd house, associated with siblings, "lower" education – grade school, junior high and high school – and with communication itself, we have another cadent arena of opening to fifth *chakra* issues and concerns. Certainly our relationships with our siblings and our classmates at school is, for most of us, the first place in which we really become aware of who we are, and how we are uniquely who we are. This is also where we learn to communicate that truth to others – the very essence of fifth *chakra* experience, as it is understood from a *yang* perspective. Blockages to the communication process, often first played out in school, or with siblings, regularly appear when 3rd house planets are squared or opposed from other cadent houses.

Mercury's Role in Fifth Chakra Dynamics

It can not be surprising to note that Mercury – the planet most often associated with communication by traditional astrologers – would be the personal planetary agent of choice in fifth *chakra* dynamics[1]. Mythologically, Mercury (or Hermes in the Greek pantheon) was considered both the messenger of the gods and the patron saint of liars, con artists and thieves. At one end of the spectrum, we have a symbolic depiction of what happens when we do in fact listen to that small, still voice within, recognize our truth and honor as sacred communication from the very core of our being. At the other end of the spectrum, we have at least the appearance of dysfunction. I use the word, "appearance" because there is more going on here than meets the eye.

Mercury is also often associated with the archetype of the trickster, and not coincidentally, many of the greatest spiritual teachers have also been tricksters. This was certainly true of Swami Muktananda, and to a lesser extent also of Yogi Bhajan. Muktananda came from a lineage of Siddha saints, whose ranks included pickpockets, homeless derelicts of questionable repute, and an odd cast of characters who defied every stereotype any sane person would associate with enlightenment. We have already met Zippruana, the garbage dump saint. There was also Hari Das Baba, an amiable thief, who sometimes wore seven or eight coats, one over the other, and demanded money from everyone he encountered. If someone asked why, he would reply, "It is obvious – for wine" (Muktananda, Satsang 282). A third Siddha, Nrisinha Swami would walk naked from hotel to hotel and stuff his prodigious belly with as much food as each proprietor was willing to give him.

Or so the stories go. One can never tell with Mercury what is true and what is fiction, or even if there is a difference. As we struggle with the opportunity that Mercury presents us, as we would perhaps struggle with a Zen *koan*, the mind is wrestled into a place of submission, where it can potentially open to a higher truth – one that is invariably paradoxical and self-contradictory. The truth to which Mercury is our guide within the fifth *chakra* rarely conforms to the mind's notions about what ought to be true, but rather introduces a wobbly cog into the otherwise predictable rational machinery valued as the underpinning of truth in polite society. It is this wobbly cog that opens a more clandestine door to a subjective truth, quirky, unruly, out of sync with conventional wisdom, but ultimately the only truth capable of producing the kind of alignment we are seeking in the fifth *chakra*.

The enigmatic Russian mystic, Georges Gurdjieff (with natal Mercury in his cadent 3rd house, ruling both his cadent 9th and 12th houses) tells a remarkable story about the way Mercury operates in the fifth *chakra* to produce alignment. On the evening of the day he opened his Institute for the Harmonious Development of Man, he was boldly asked by one of his after dinner quests how he had financed such an ambitious undertaking. Though normally accustomed to dismissing questions about finances with a "none-of-your-business" joke, on this occasion, he chose to answer candidly. Prefacing his remarks, Gurdjieff said, "As I am now sitting here among you people who are fattened on what is called dollar-fat, and feel myself stimulated by the automatic absorption of these beneficent emanations, I intend by means of my reply, so to say, to 'shear' some of you a little" (249). This is the kind of comment Mercury, the Trickster, might make as an aside, before revealing the truth beneath the pretense of whatever charade he happened to be exposing at the time.

Gurdjieff then proceeds to tell a long, meandering tale, the details of which I will spare you, except for one small anecdote that will suffice to illustrate my point.

At one juncture in his quest for capital to finance his institute, Gurdjieff accepted a wager from the "fearless" Mme. Vitvitskaia, one of his nefarious traveling companions, challenging him to make a certain large sum of money in a relatively short time. In response, Gurdjieff set up what he called the Universal Traveling Workshop in the town of Ashkhabad in south central Russia, near the Iranian border. In a flyer advertising the services of the Universal Traveling Workshop, Gurdjieff promised to repair or mend everything from childrens' toys to grand pianos. "From the very first day, a whole procession of Ashkhabadians brought their things to be repaired. Lord! What on earth they did not bring" (256)!

If someone poor brought something in that required extensive, complicated repair, or if he was presented with a problem that interested him, Gurdjieff would work long and hard for very little money. If what he considered a pompous, rich person came in with a minor repair, Gurdjieff had no compunction about soaking them for all he could get. He tells with relish of how one "rich, fat Armenian, puffing and bathed in perspiration, accompanied by his daughter, dragged in a sewing machine to be repaired, which he had bought for her trousseau. . ." (259). The customer complained that for no apparent reason, the sewing machine had started working in reverse. In what must have been a superhuman effort to repress hysterical laughter, Gurdjieff informed the man that he would work overtime to make sure that he got the repaired machine back to him in three days, though it would cost him dearly. Then, before the man had even left the room, Gurdjieff flipped the switch that changed the sewing machine's direction, and put it on the shelf with the other finished articles, waiting for their owners to reclaim them.

Of course, it is natural to respond to such a story with mild outrage or astonishment, since such behavior is not what we would normally want to expect of someone who was supposed to be a spiritual teacher. But when the fifth *chakra* is activated through Mercury's participation, normal standards of moral or politically correct behavior cease to apply, however much we might like them to. No amount of righteous indignation, however well-deserved, will counterbalance the equally pressing realization that beyond our judgments, something extraordinary is going on.

During the time that Gurdjieff ran his workshop, he met with customers during the day and worked on the repairs they brought him at night. There was an intensification and acceleration of energy harnessed toward a specific end that could have only been sustained through a process of intense alignment between Spirit and the body – or what I imply in *The Seven Gates of Soul* is a profound awakening of the soul. Gurdjieff describes this awakening as "a change in the regulation of the tempo of the in-coming and out-going of energy which enabled me to sleep scarcely at all for several weeks, and even for months, yet at the same time to manifest an activity which, far from being reduced, was on the contrary even more intense than usual" (264).

<><><><><><><><><><><><><><><><><><><><><><><><><><><><><><><><><><><><><><><><><><><><>

Within the three and a half months that Gurdjieff's workshop was open, he made 50,000 roubles. This was over 80 times the annual salary of a well-paid, high-ranking officer in the Russian government, the gold standard to which all Ashkabhadians at the time aspired. Gurdjieff had earned this extraordinary sum, not as a privileged executive of some well-heeled capitalist venture, but through his own manual labor, and with the proceeds was able to finance his institute for spiritual development. The story illustrates what is possible in the place of alignment to the truth of one's being that is precipitated by a clear and open fifth *chakra*. This truth is not the sanctimonious truth of absolute truth seekers, but it is a galvanizing force capable of bending natural law to miraculous lengths, and where it does so, others will gather in awe to learn and grow – as they did with Gurdjieff, despite his "questionable" ethics.

Mercury's participation in fifth *chakra* patterns will not always result in such transcendence of ordinary limitations. More often than not, it will act on a more mundane level to create the impetus for smaller, more garden-variety improvements in our capacity to communicate, to live our truth, and to act from a more conscious sense of place and purpose. To the extent that we take advantage of these opportunities for modest learning and growth, however, doors will often be opened where it is possible to gain a glimpse of what true alignment looks and feels like. Mercury's invitation on the level of the fifth *chakra* will always be to walk through this door, whether we are ready to accept the invitation or not.

Uranus' Role in Fifth Chakra Dynamics

Seasoned astrologers often ascribe the primary role of Trickster to Uranus, with a somewhat lesser nod to Mercury, though Mercury retrograde has earned a reputation in its own right to rival the great master. Yet to the extent that we take our astro-logical cues from mythology, there is a distinct difference in flavor between these two planets that bears some elaboration – especially since both are likely to be involved in fifth *chakra* patterns, where the Trickster is hard at play.

In Homer's Hymn to Hermes, he describes Mercury as "devious, winning in his cleverness, a robber, a driver of cattle, a guide of dreams, a spy in the night, a watcher at the door. . . ." (qtd. in Morford 201).

> *Maia (his mother) bore him on the fourth day of the month. He was born at dawn, by midday he was playing the lyre, and in the evening he stole the cattle of far-shooting Apollo. After he leaped forth from the immortal limbs of his mother, he did not remain lying in his sacred cradle; but he sprang up and looked for the cattle of Apollo. When he crossed the threshold of the high-roofed cave, he found a tortoise and obtained boundless pleasure from it.*

◇◇

Over the course of his evolution as a god, Hermes/Mercury acquired (or perhaps revealed) additional dimensions – as messenger to the gods, psychopomp, patron saint of travelers, etc. It is clear, however, that from the very beginning, well before mortal children are even able to walk or talk, indeed fresh from the womb, Mercury was a full-fledged Trickster, no training or apprenticeship required.

Uranus, by contrast, is not very Trickster-like in these same familiar terms we readily associate with the archetype. He was born of an earlier generation of gods, primordial forces in grinding, tumultuous cataclysm at the dawn of creation. The sky god Uranus, along with his consort, the earth goddess Gaia, were descendants of Chaos, the "yawning void" out of which Creation itself originally sprang. Together, they gave birth to the Titans (precursors to the Olympic pantheon of which Hermes was a member), Brontes (Thunder), Steropes (Lightning), Arges (Bright), the Cyclops, and the Hecatonchires (Hundred-Handed monsters). According to the account given in Hesiod's *Theogony* (quoted in Morford 48):

> As each of his children was born, Uranus hid them all in the depths of Ge
> (Gaia) and did not allow them to emerge into the light. And he delighted in
> his wickedness. But huge Earth in her distress groaned within and devised
> a crafty and evil scheme. At once she created gray adamant and fashioned
> a great sickle and confided in her dear children. Sorrowing in her heart, she
> urged them as follows: "My children born of a presumptuous father, if you are
> willing to obey, we shall punish his evil insolence. For he was first to devise
> shameful actions.

So while Mercury is associated in early mythological writings with clever genius, playful creativity, and mischief, Uranus bears a much darker tone, more rightfully associated with perverse wickedness, arrogant domination, and malicious intent. If Uranus' story simply ended here, he would have undoubtedly rivaled Hades (the astrological Pluto) as the harbinger of everything dark and foreboding. But Uranus was instead castrated by a plot hatched between Gaia and Cronus, an event that altered the course of archetypal history[2]. That which was heavy and dark within him was passed on to Uranus' son and castrator, Cronus (known to astrologers as Saturn). His malicious capacity for inflicting suffering on others and then taking perverse delight in that suffering was given to the Erinyes, or Furies, avengers of blood guilt, and tormentor of sinners in the Underworld. His potent erotic creativity as father of the gods was passed on to his daughter, Aphrodite, who was born of the foam created when Uranus' genitals were thrown into the sea.

So what was left of Uranus himself? Hesoid and the chroniclers of myth who followed are strangely silent on that point. We can only project our own human responses to such catastrophic reversal of fate onto him, which is what we do to our gods and goddesses anyway. If something like that happened to me, I would take it as a wake up call. I would acquire a deepened sense of reverence in the face of awesome forces beyond my control, and I would be motivated to change my evil ways for a more constructive form of creativity. I would stop trying to dominate others, and control everything under the sun, and instead align myself to a more manageable individually meaningful truth that I could wield without such irreversible damage to myself and others.

This, in fact, is not far from the sort of transformation we have grown as astrologers to expect from Uranus. Uranus precipitates the unexpected break from business as usual, the abrupt fall from grace or reversal of fortune, the breakdown that is hell to experience but that ultimately leads to breakthrough. This is not so much the Trickster at work, but the force of Chaos, described most insightfully by Ralph Blum in his description of the Viking *rune*, Hagalaz (98):

> *The Rune of elemental disruption, of events totally beyond your control, Hagalaz has only an upright position, and yet it always operates through reversal. When you draw this Rune, expect disruption of your plans, for it is the great "Awakener," although the form the awakening takes may vary. Perhaps you will experience a gradual feeling of coming to your senses, as though you were emerging from a long sleep. Then again, the onset of power may be such as to rip away the fabric of what you previously knew as your reality, your security, your understanding of yourself, your work, your relationships or beliefs. . . . There is nothing trivial about this Rune: The more severe the disruption in your life, the more significant and timely the requirements for your growth.*

It is in this sense that Uranus participates in any pattern involving fifth *chakra* planets. In *The Seven Gates of Soul*, I speak of death in the metaphorical sense as the great awakener to the soul, the force that brings us to our knees and forces us to reevaluate who we are, what we are doing, and why we are doing it. Astrologers associate death with Pluto, but my sense is that this kind of death – the breakdown or breach of the familiar touchstones by which we measure our reality – more rightfully belongs to Uranus. When Uranus functions within the context of a fifth *chakra* pattern, its goal is always a deeper alignment with subjective truth, empowering us to fulfill our creative *dharma* with the consummate fertility of a sky god moving and shaking all that is at the dawn of creation.

Jupiter's Role in Fifth Chakra Dynamics

There is one more sky god we must account for in our discussion of the planetary dynamics of the fifth *chakra*. I refer to the god Jupiter, known to the Greeks as Zeus, grandson of Uranus, and chief deity of the more familiar pantheon of Mount Olympus. Given that Cronus had assumed the boorish ways of his father, swallowing his own children at birth to prevent them from one day usurping his position, Cronus' wife Rhea hid Zeus at birth in a cave on Mount Dicte, where he was fed by bees, nursed by nymphs, and guarded by fierce warriors who made constant noise with their weapons so that his cries would not be heard. Zeus grew to maturity, then fought a ten-year war against Cronus, which eventually resulted in Cronus' dethronement and Zeus' rise to power.

In Chapter Seventeen, we discussed Zeus briefly in association with infidelity, a correlation that derives from Jupiter's reputation as a philandering God, pulled this way and that by his prodigious lust. Here we must acknowledge his more fundamental stature as a hero-king, who vanquishes the forces of oppression, so that life might prevail. Zeus freed the children of Cronus and Hera, and is associated to this day, by astrologers and students of the deeper lessons of mythology everywhere, with the quest for freedom. Freedom, of course, has become one of those buzz words, at once describing a universal longing in every heart and yet at the same time giving the modern champions of oppressive Cronus the shield behind which they hide their quest for a return to the Golden Age of control and repression. In the sense in which Jupiter stands for freedom, however, it is the alignment of the individual with her own truth that leads to a fifth *chakra* awakening.

When Jupiter participates in a fifth *chakra* pattern, it will precipitate on some level a bid for greater freedom to be who one is, perhaps with all the excesses, exaggerations and imbalances to which Jupiter is also prone, but in genuine expression of unique individuality. The truth that leads to alignment is not one that is found by sticking to the middle of the road, or conforming to that which is acceptable to society. It requires breaking new ground, not because one is vainly trying to be different, but because one requires fresh ground in which to fertilize the growth of a soul too large to be bound by convention.

Neptune's Role in Fifth Chakra Dynamics

Just as Mars and Pluto tend to work together co-creatively in the first three *chakras*, so too do Jupiter and Neptune in the last three. We saw earlier, how Mars echoed Pluto's primary role in first *chakra* dynamics, then how Pluto echoed Mars' role as the dominant catalyst in the third *chakra*. In a similar way, Neptune will echo Jupiter's function in the fifth *chakra* – when it participates in a fifth *chakra* pattern – and increasingly come into its own as a primary player when we move to the sixth and seventh *chakras*.

We discussed Neptune previously in relation to the second *chakra*, where it served to dissolve the normal social barriers and boundaries to an unmitigated pursuit of pleasure,

285

often resulting in addiction, obsession, and escapist tendencies that quickly spiral out of control. Neptune actually serves a similar function in the fifth *chakra*, in that it likewise dissolves barriers to a less encumbered pursuit of the focus of the *chakra*. Here the focus is not pleasure, but subjective truth and what dissolves is not inhibition, but what Carlos Castenada referred to as consensus reality. Within the context of the fifth *chakra* process, Neptune is the planetary agency that allows us to peer through the veil imposed by consensus reality, and *see* what is true for us as individuals. The ability to see, in turn, changes everything. As Castenada (<u>Separate Reality</u> 186) describes the change:

> *A man can learn to see. Upon learning to see, he no longer needs to live like a warrior, nor be a sorcerer. Upon learning to see a man becomes everything by becoming nothing. He, so to speak, vanishes and yet he's there. I would say that this is the time when a man can be or can get anything he desires (second chakra). But he desires nothing, and instead of playing with his fellow men like they were toys, he meets them in the midst of their folly (fourth chakra expression of compassion). The only difference between them is that a man who sees controls his folly, while his fellow man can't. A man who sees has no longer an active interest in his fellow men. Seeing has already detached him from almost everything he knew before.*

Actually, what Castenada is describing here is the Neptunian pull into complete identification with Spirit that is more accurately understood as the province of the seventh *chakra*. The pull is first consciously felt in the fifth *chakra*, as a capacity to see, and evolves in the sixth *chakra* to become the capacity to move beyond the barrier of subject and object in the act of seeing – known to mystics of every stripe and persuasion the world over as a penetration of the veils of separation. Since the task in the fifth *chakra* is learning to function as a living embodiment of truth, however, one must take what one sees and use it in a functional way to create what the existentialists called a more authentic self. At this level, truth is experienced as a vision, which then must be incorporated into the daily life. Within the context of the fifth *chakra*, Neptune is what facilitates the experience of vision, while Jupiter and Mercury are what allow us to make sense of the vision, and find a personal pathway to liberation of soul within it.

Chiron's Role in Fifth Chakra Dynamics

Just as the handmaidens of Venus were seen to play a supplemental role in the fourth *chakra*, so can the asteroid Chiron[3] play a role in fifth *chakra* dynamics. Chiron – the mythical creature who was half horse, half man – is mostly understood by astrologers to be the wounded healer, after being accidentally shot by Hercules at a party at which his fellow centaurs were getting out of hand. But before he met his bizarre end, Chiron was the proverbial wise man, living somewhat reclusively in a cave on the top of a mountain (Mount Pelion). Occasionally, he would emerge from his hermitage to mentor exceptional humans – including the heroes Actaeon, Aeneas, Achilles and Jason, and the healer, Ascelpius. Chiron shared a broad range of knowledge with his protégés, drawn from herbal medicine, sacred mathematics, astronomy and astrology, prophecy and divination. Given this primal function – to which the wounding at the end of his life was a postscript – we would be hard-pressed to find a more fitting archetypal figure to represent the fifth *chakra* fully realized as the teacher.

To call Chiron a wounded healer is not irrelevant to his role in the fifth *chakra*, but it is not the arrow to his foot that should draw our primary attention. For what is most extraordinary about Chiron's function as mentor to heroes, healers, and leaders is the fact that he rose from the ranks of a species noted, not for its wisdom, but rather for its debasement. Chiron's fellow centaurs were creatures of raw instinct, given to wild and reckless bouts of drunken debauchery and violent sexual conquest. One can only assume that to become who he was known in mythology to be, Chiron had to first transcend his own genetically encoded tendencies toward excess and imbalance, wrench himself from the consensus reality of his tribe, and undergo a profound fifth *chakra* quest to find his own truth. This is not discussed – as far as I am aware – in the mythological literature, but like the missing years of Jesus, must compose a vital part of Chiron's story. To the extent that these speculations can be assumed valid, then Chiron becomes the archetype, not just for the fifth *chakra* fully realized, but also for the entire process of discovering, claiming, and living one's truth.

The Fifth Chakra Chart

When Mercury plus two or more of these other fifth *chakra* players – Uranus, Jupiter, Neptune or Chiron – participate together in a planetary pattern, especially across cadent houses, it is not unlikely to assume that some fifth *chakra* issue is a pivot point within the individual psyche, around which the spiritual life revolves. Other planets may be involved, adding color, nuance and *interchakra* references to the mix, but these primary players – sharing a love of quirky, individual subjective truth, as well as the passionate creativity necessary to find and live such truth – will more likely than not be the agents of conspiracy in any true fifth chakra awakening.

The fewer of these planets that are involved, and the farther away from the cadent houses the pattern lies, the weaker will be the pattern. If there is no pattern, a more pedestrian fifth chakra chart can still be constructed from any aspects formed by these planets to each other or to the rulers of the cadent houses.

Endnotes

1   Both Grasse (204) and Hodgson (138-139) consider Mercury to be the primary planetary agent ruling this *chakra*.

2   Oken assigns rulership of the fifth *chakra* to Saturn and the Earth (Gaia) (155).

3   Actually, astronomers are still debating whether or not Chiron is an asteroid, a planetoid, or a comet that became trapped by the Sun's gravitational pull. Though it resembles an asteroid, it orbits outside of the asteroid belt, and displays other anomalies that defy clearcut categorization.

Chapter Twenty
A Fifth Chakra Case Study

A given *chakra* signature doesn't always appear in the chart of an individual we would intuitively associate with that *chakra*, and sometimes it appears where we least expect it. In the case of our fifth *chakra* case study subject, however, there can be few surprises. Aside from his prodigious output in cataloguing and surveying the world's mythological heritage, Joseph Campbell is most often remembered for encouraging a generation of seekers to "follow your bliss." He considered a hero to be anyone who had the courage and depth of personal integrity to follow her personal calling into the unknown, and then return bearing gifts of singular beauty, but with meaning for the whole tribe. His own life was a vibrant example of this philosophy he espoused, and what is more important from our perspective here, it was a vivid demonstration of the fifth *chakra* process.

JOSEPH CAMPBELL

As with our fourth *chakra* case study, we will attempt to coax an understanding of Campbell's internal process through his own words, wherever possible, culled from interviews and his writings. Unlike Clinton, Campbell wrote no autobiography, but we will instead draw upon reflections offered in the sympathetic biography, *Fire in the Mind* by S. Larsen and R.A. Larsen, which quotes extensively from Campbell's actual words. As Larsen and Larsen note in their preface, though he "thought the corpus of his own writings should constitute the signature of the man, so to speak, not the incidental details of his life. . . . Campbell unselfconsciously left intact a wealth of personal autobiographical materials, correspondence, private diaries, dream journals. . . (xviii-xix)" and the like. It is from these that the authors draw in their attempt to document the life, along with extensive interviews with his wife, Jean Erdman, and others who knew him well, and it is these resources upon which we will also draw wherever possible in showing how Joseph Campbell embodied a fifth *chakra* process. Again our intent will be to dive below the surface of the known story to respectfully illuminate the more subterranean inner alchemy that fueled this great man's contribution to the world.

Campbell's fifth *chakra* pattern is formed by a loose out-of-sign square between Uranus in his cadent 3rd house and a tight Mercury/Jupiter conjunction in his cadent 6th house. The Mercury/Jupiter conjunction is part of a larger 6th house stellium, including the Sun and South Node, with the proximity of the nodal axis adding its usual emphasis and underscoring of importance. The Uranus-6th house stellium square, in turn, is part of a larger t-square pattern involving a cadent Neptune in the 9th house. As discussed earlier, and as we will see in the next chapter, the participation of Neptune in this pattern creates a bridge between the fifth, sixth and seventh *chakras*, adding to the potency of this signature.

Certainly the breadth of Campbell's vision, which encompassed not only world mythology, but also religion, psychology, anthropology, literature and film, demonstrates that he was an exemplar of the sixth *chakra* capacity for understanding reality from multiple interpenetrating perspectives. It is clear from his writings that he also knew the path beyond what we normally call reality into the complete identification with Spirit that takes place in the seventh *chakra*, but generally felt his calling to be within the realm of human culture. Campbell is best known for his admonition to "follow your bliss," which we might clearly understand as a Neptunian quest. Yet he also cautioned us that we "must return with the bliss and integrate it" (qtd. in Osbon 290) – a further task we might readily associate with the fifth *chakra*, and in his personal case, with the demands of everyday life concentrated in his 6th house stellium. In our analysis here, we will be primarily concerned with this more grounded aspect of Joseph Campbell's fifth *chakra* challenge.

In Chapter Ten, we refered to Campbell's chart as an example of activity on the level of *pranamaya kosha*. Here we would note that his fifth *chakra* pattern also manifests largely on that level, due primarily to the fiery potency of his 6th house stellium, containing two fire planets (Sun and Jupiter) in fire signs. These are fueled by air planet Mercury in fire sign Aries and air planet Uranus in the airy 3rd house in fire sign Sagittarius. The placement of Sun and Jupiter in the earthy 6th house creates an opening to *anandamaya kosha*, through the juxtaposition of earth and fire.

JOSEPH CAMPBELL'S FIFTH CHAKRA CHART

Campbell's Unwounded Soul Essence

To this point in our discussion of the *chakras*, we have observed that the unwounded soul essence that serves as the alpha and omega of our spiritual journey is generally most alive and often most visible around the age of 3 or 4. By this time in our development as human beings, there is sufficient sense of self to serve as a focal point around which significant experiences can register as ours, yet little capacity to resist or defend ourselves against their impact in the way we will later learn to do as adults. This combination of vulnerability, receptivity and impressionable identity makes us ripe for an awakening to soul that will set our spiritual journey in motion. Often this moment is both reflected astrologically and succinctly encapsulated by a potent image that describes - in a spiritual sense - who we are, and what we are here to do. It is this image, a psychic postcard of sorts that we send to ourselves at the outset of our journey that I have been calling the unwounded soul essence.

◇◇

Unfortunately, since biographies are always at least one step removed from the actual internal experience of their subject, they do not always capture the images that are most pertinent to their subject's spiritual evolution, and no such image of Campbell's soul essence at age 3 or 4 has been captured by the Larsens. Yet, since their biography begins with the tantalizing line, "Joseph Campbell was in his sixth or seventh year when the power of a mythic image first ensorcelled him" (3), we are encouraged to pay attention, and are rewarded instantaneously. For it turns out this mythic image, in retrospect, is also an apt image of Campbell's soul essence as it informed his lifelong journey toward a deeply personal truth worth living.

The mythic image in question arose in 1910, when Buffalo Bill's Wild West show came to his town, and his father took him to see it. This would have been around the time that transiting Jupiter was opposed natal Sun/Mercury/Jupiter, and square Uranus and Neptune (within one degree orb from April – July of that year). In any case, says Campbell of that event, "I early became fascinated, seized, obsessed . . . by the figure of a naked American Indian with his ear to the ground, a bow and arrow in his hand, and a look of special knowledge in his eyes" (qtd. in Larsen 3).

Looking at Campbell's chart astropoetically, it is not hard to see this Indian as Mars in Aries in the 7th house, conjunct the Descendant. If we consider the Descendant to be the horizon of the setting Sun, then we can imagine Mars in this position as an Indian (Aries = primal, naked energy, bows and arrows) with his ear to the ground. The special knowledge that Campbell intuited must be there would then be harbored by his 6th house stellium, just below the horizon, or threshold of consciousness. It was into this realm of knowledge that Campbell was compelled to go, and this Indian was his guiding image.

Campbell gained great respect for the Indian culture through his childhood studies, and clearly saw them as the true heroes in the battle for the American West. Mars is also an apt symbol for the hero's journey Campbell is so well-known for documenting, set in motion in his own life by this early identification with the image of an Indian warrior. To pursue this calling, Campbell had to essentially become this Indian, attuned to the natural world, a hero to his people, gathering secret knowledge from the underworld to bring back to his tribe. It should be noted here that both the Indian and Campbell's angular Mars in Aries are more accurately understood as indicators of a strong soul essence centered in the third *chakra*, but the real hero's journey for Campbell was down below the horizon of his chart into the cadent territory of his fifth *chakra* pattern.

Campbell's Primal Wounding

The flip side of this positive, compelling third *chakra* image of the Indian can be seen in an early image of the dark side of this quest for secret fifth *chakra* knowledge, which in truth, was not without its dangers. This darker image emerged in a nightmare that

Campbell had when he was about 2 years old, of "a whale about to swallow me" (12). This dream likely took place when transiting Uranus (natally 6 degrees out) formed an exact square to his natal Sun/Mercury/Jupiter stellium (within one degree of orb throughout all of 1906), although it is my sense that what Uranus was awakening him to, in this case, was the necessity for dealing with Neptune with which his natal Uranus is in opposition.

This dream obviously evokes the Biblical story of Jonah, who is swallowed by the whale – a story that astrologer Liz Greene associates with both Neptune and the devouring mother: "The fish (whale who swallowed Jonah) is simultaneously the phallus of the self-generating sea-mother, her voracious devouring mouth, and the god-child that she bears and will swallow up again" (11). Is it too far-fetched to suggest that Campbell was about to enter Neptune's realm, where the danger was being swallowed whole by archetypal forces way beyond his control? Or that already at age 2, he was on some level of his being, aware of this, or perhaps more accurately being warned about it by this dream? As Jung pointed out, one does not play with the archetypes for very long without being possessed by them, and becoming *their* plaything. Though Campbell was a hero Indian with ear to ground, the ground could at any time, crack open and becoming a yawning chasm with the power to consume him.

Late in life, Campbell discusses the story of Jonah and the whale with Bill Moyers, and relates it to the hero's journey (Power of Myth 180-181):

> CAMPBELL: *The story of Jonah in the whale is an example of a mythic theme that is practically universal, of the hero going into a fish's belly and ultimately coming out again, transformed.*
>
> MOYERS: *Why must the hero do that?*
>
> CAMPBELL: *It's a descent into the dark. Psychologically, the whale represents the power of life locked in the unconscious. Metaphorically, water is the unconscious, and the creature in the water is the life or energy of the unconscious, which has overwhelmed the conscious personality and must be disempowered, overcome and controlled. . . . In a story of the Jonah type, the hero is swallowed and taken into the abyss to be later resurrected – a variant of the death-and-resurrection theme. The conscious personality here has come in touch with a charge of unconsciousness energy which it is unable to handle and must now suffer all the trials and revelations of a terrifying night-sea journey, while learning how to come to terms with this power of the dark and emerge, at last, to a new way of life.*

Though we would perhaps not refer to such a "terrifying night-sea journey" as wounding in the way we have understood that term to this point, we must now consider the possibility that beyond the heart *chakra*, it is the gods themselves who wound us in order to initiate us into a realm of secret knowledge that cannot be entered by ordinary means. It is my sense here, that Campbell's early dream of being swallowed by a whale was his initiation – or at least, an image of what initiation would periodically feel like when the gods swallowed him alive.

The Astrological Timing of Campbell's Initiation Process

The whale god first swallowed Campbell when he was 13 years old. The day after Christmas, 1917, he suddenly became ill with a serious bronchial infection that persisted for months despite heroic treatment. In Chapter Six, I associate bronchial infections with a penetration of Spirit to the level of *annamaya kosha* in the fifth *chakra*. It should come as no surprise that the onset of this illness occurred during transiting Neptune's trine (and Uranus' semi-square) to natal Sun/Mercury/Jupiter, the acute manifestation of the disease erupting as transiting Sun-Pluto opposition squared this same fifth *chakra* trigger point. The opening to *annamaya kosha* comes through the concentration of planets in Campbell's earthy 6th house that is being triggered. Given Neptune's association with Jonah's whale, in Campbell's personal lexicon of symbols, we might suspect, however, that this was no ordinary (merely physical) illness. As it is described by his biographers (15):

> Through the opium-derived morphine, young Joseph entered a timeless time, the active world revolving around him at a dreamlike remove. His brother, sister, and friends were off to school; people were coming and going in the house all day; and in the center, like Vishnu dreaming the world, Joseph lay abed.

What happened in this semi-comatose state, no one – not even Campbell himself – can say. After this descent into the Underworld, Joseph spent many months recuperating, during which time he renewed his hero's journey in earnest. He resumed his study of the American Indian, reading through the entire multi-volume series of reports by the Bureau of American Ethnology, The Handbook of the American Indian and other weighty tomes to get at the heart and soul of the Indian psyche. He also began a serious studies of birds and stars, building his own telescope. When he was well-enough to go outside, he began hanging out with his first mentor – Elmer Gregor, an accomplished naturalist, whose expertise covered nearly everything Campbell was interested in. He also joined the Boy Scouts, whose leader was a friend of Gregor's. As the Larsens describe this dual mentorship (19):

> When he and Gregor would get together around a campfire, a kind of "powwow," or "feast of dreams," as the Iroquois called it, would begin, as

fact and folklore mingled with humor. Both men's rich life experiences, Indian stories, and legends of the American frontier must have taken on a preternatural life, in the flickering firelight, as young Joe sat with these two guides to the land of the imagination.

By the end of Neptune's transit to Sun/Mercury/Jupiter, Campbell was well enough to return to school. But by then, his education had already started in earnest and nothing he could possibly learn in school would rival the tutelage that came through his early immersion in the belly of the whale, his own self-study, and these two early mentors. Speaking later of his experiences at Columbia University, Campbell said (qtd. in Larsen 53):

Nature in the laboratory never quite convinced me as nature in the woods had convinced me; and the scholarship of the classroom never quite convinced me as the scholarship of my Indian books had convinced me. Laboratories and classrooms were indeed dealing with the things that moved me, but from a point somewhere off (my) center.

Before Campbell got to Columbia, however, his deeper education inside the belly of the whale was to encompass one more childhood lesson. At the onset of Neptune's last pass of natal Sun/Mercury/Jupiter, while transiting Jupiter and Pluto were also squaring Sun/Mercury/Jupiter from the 9th house, Campbell's grandmother, who was living with them at the time, died in a fire. His father became severely burned while trying to rescue her, and much of what Campbell had gathered to document and facilitate his early study was destroyed.

In one all-consuming event, Joseph Campbell lost the world of his childhood. The sudden death of his beloved grandmother was undoubtedly the deepest wound, but years later he would reminisce about what else had perished: his Indian books, and with the house, easy access to New Rochelle Public Library, his earlier journals and notebooks, all kinds of memorabilia and keepsakes . .

Whatever secret knowledge Campbell bore from this first round of initiation, he now carried inside of him. Neptune is not normally associated by astrologers with fire, but the loss which inevitably ensued, and relinquished his previous life to the mythic realm of memory and imagination was distinctly Neptunian. The event itself was reminiscent of Uranus, as we discussed him earlier – the harbinger of breakdown and abrupt reversal of fortune. At the time of the fire, transiting Uranus and Trickster Mercury were both sextile natal Uranus. Mars – the planet most readily associated with fire – was semi-sextile its natal position, with Campbell's Sun/Mercury/Jupiter at the midpoint between Mars' natal and transiting position.

◇◇

Campbell's Fifth Chakra Quest

What Campbell took with him from this early shattering of worlds was a restless, burning determination to seek the central truth of his own being, although it would be many years before he had a clue what he was doing. His college years – marked astrologically from October, 1923 – June, 1926 by transiting Neptune's sesquiquadrate to his natal 6th house stellium – were a grand youthful adventure, as was life in general to Joseph Campbell, but in the end an intellectual and spiritual disappointment. In many ways, his childhood adventures in the belly of the whale of his illness had spoiled him, and became the gold standard against all subsequent experiences were measured.

Campbell started college in Dartmouth at a time when he "was beginning to question the literality of the faith of his fathers. The profundity of the questions nagging at his soul somehow jarred with the blitheness of the Dartmouth College scene. He was "unhappy in a happy place" (31). He moved to Columbia, dedicated to "making the whole man" (32), but in the end, found it "a mildly interesting dustbin beside a track and a shower room" (53). In particular, he found it too compartmentalized to integrate his wide-ranging interests. Campbell was a cross-disciplinary scholar in a provincial era that understood such leanings only as dilettantism. Except for a few professors and his masters thesis advisor, who honestly told him that he would not find what he was looking for, were he to seek his doctorate at Columbia, he was reaching for something that no one in his world knew was there, much less could tell him how to attain.

The Yin Half of Campbell's Fifth Chakra Challenge

The one exception to this rudderless state of affairs was Krishnamurti, whom Campbell met on a steamship voyage with his family during the summer of 1924. Campbell had no idea who Krishnamurti was, and would not consciously embrace him for his wisdom and his spiritual teachings until years later in Paris. But the meeting – with Neptune sesquiquadrate Campbell's Sun/Mercury/Jupiter – was nonetheless a significant moment in Campbell's fifth *chakra* journey, and they instantly struck up what would become a lifelong friendship. Of this meeting, the Larsens wrote (43):

> *Nothing is mentioned in Joseph's reports of his knowledge of the powerful visions which, according to biographers, Krishnamurti was having at this time. Krishnamurti seems to have been passing through something like the classical kundalini experience of yoga and Tantric mysticism, with energies running up and down his spine; his followers reported strange experiences of their own, the consequences of a kind of "charged atmosphere" in his presence. No doubt, outside of the Theosophical Circle, Krishnamurti was*

reticent about his more mystical views and experiences. Krishnamurti was a designated spiritual leader, and Joseph Campbell, at the time, was only a student with a lovely manner and an inquiring mind. But there is no doubt that a strong attraction was pulling the two young men together. After these early experiences, Joe wrote about Krisnamurti, "I found him simply charming."

When clueless Campbell discovered later that Krishnamurti was pronounced by the Theosophists to be "the Living Vehicle of the Logos for this Age," he was a bit taken aback. Krishnamurti assured him that the title meant nothing to him. His task, as he saw it, "was to bring a new kind of spiritual awareness to the world, in which value was centered in the individual alone, not in systems of doctrines or dogmas" (64). This philosophy appealed greatly to Campbell, who was seriously questioning the provincialism of religions bound by rigid theologies.

Later, when Campbell was a graduate student in Paris, and he chanced upon his old friend, Krishnamurti modeling for the teacher of a friend, the two reconnected. Campbell began attending Krishnamurti's lectures and paying attention to what he had to say. After attending his first lecture, he stayed up talking with the spiritual master until 3 AM. Later, the friend who reunited them recalled, "he was so excited about it. It was a terrific turning point in his life" (qtd. in Larsen 89).

In Paris, Campbell's rudderless confusion began to subside, although the change had little to do with his academic studies (Larsen 84).

> *One day alone, in the little garden of Cluny, it came home to me that my official studies were having very little if anything to do with the central problems of my own life. They seemed to me to be running around the periphery of my field. It seemed to me that one should try to discover what was central and work out from there. With this, though my mediaeval studies continued, of their own momentum, until the end of the year (1927), my mind turned consciously to the problem of finding a center . . .*

Krishnamurti was one catalyst to Campbell's quest for center (Larsen 89), for as Campbell recognized:

> *What he said had to do with the problem of integrating all the faculties and bringing them to center. He used the image of the chariot drawn by the three horses of mind, body and soul. This was exactly in my line; and although I didn't feel that it could be classified as a New World Teaching, I was led to think of my problem now in terms of psychological centering.*

◇◇◇

The Yang Half of Campbell's Fifth Chakra Challenge

Yet, for Campbell, there was more to his problem than merely aligning with his center. To be sure, Krishnamurti had a valuable set of keys to the *yin* portion of the fifth *chakra* challenge Campbell had taken on, but he had little to say about the *yang* portion – taking one's truth out into the world and living it in a meaningful way. For Campbell, this was the function of art, and although he flirted for a time with the thought of becoming an artist, in the end, he decided that his true talents lie elsewhere, and that what really intrigued him most was the art of living. It was one thing to know the truth, but the real challenge was "bringing life back into the wasteland" (qtd. in Osbon 81) and sharing one's truth in such a way that it could also serve as a catalyst for awakening in the lives of others.

Art intrigued him, because not only did it often incorporate myth and symbolism and thus point toward deeper psychological and spiritual truths, but it was itself a manifestation of that truth within the world. During this fertile period – which coincided astrologically with the end of Neptune's sesquiquadrate to his 6th house stellium, and the beginning of transiting Uranus' conjunction to it – Campbell was introduced to the work of James Joyce. His initial reaction, upon opening *Ulysses* in 1927 was "Good God, what is this? I thought I had got my degree, but I don't know what he's talking about" (Larsen 83). Later, Joyce would prove to be instrumental in helping Campbell understand how art could embody archetypal truths and speak directly to the unconscious, where we were receptive to these truths, despite our conscious resistance.

Far more instrumental, however, in helping him tackle the second part of his problem – the art of living one's truth – was a wise and accomplished sculptor named Antoine Bordelle, who was the student and successor of Auguste Rodin. In a moment of supreme synchronicity, it was the mutual friend – Angela Gregory – who reunited him with Krishnamurti, who also introduced him to Bordelle. As it happened, Bordelle was both Angela's teacher and the artist for whom Krishnamurti had agreed to pose. At the time of this meeting (in December, 1927), transiting Uranus in Pisces, Neptune's sign, had formed a direct station exactly square Campbell's natal Uranus, while transiting Neptune was exactly trine natal Uranus. Transiting Jupiter was also in Pisces about 3-6 degrees from exact square to Uranus. All of the outer planets in Campbell's fifth *chakra* signature, in other words, were triggering his pattern.

Campbell began posing for his friend, Angela Gregory, who wished to sculpt a bust of Campbell's head. At the same time, he was taking copious notes while he listened to Bordelle talk about the relationship between life and art. Campbell took many pearls of wisdom from *Le Maître*, as Bordelle was called by his students. But among them were two oft-repeated phrases that would eventually become cornerstones of Campbell's philosophy and answers to the *yang* challenge of his fifth *chakra* dilemma (Larsen 94):

> *"It is the personality which tells the tale."* – By this, he essentially meant
> that one's life ought to spring from the center of one's being, and not be a
> mere adaptation to external circumstances. Who one was inside, what one
> passionately cared about, what one believed with all one's heart ought to be
> the source of one's existence in the world.

> *"Art vividly shows us the grand lines of nature."* – By this he meant that
> the job of the artist – which is to say anyone willing to live an authentic life
> – was not to manufacture something that didn't already exist, but to reveal
> the radiant splendor, the inner light, the truth and beauty of what was inside
> and everywhere around us.

Throughout the remainder of this seminal period (transiting Uranus' conjunction
to Sun/Mercury/Jupiter), Campbell traveled to Germany, where he read Goethe, Mann,
Nietzsche, Freud and Jung in German and discovered what he had been missing in the
"academic circus" (qtd, in Larsen 105). In Germany, Campbell also studied Sanskrit,
so that he could read the ancient scriptures in the language in which they were written.
While a voracious scholar like Campbell never really stopped learning, it can be seen in
retrospect that this Uranian period in the late 1920s in Europe was a fifth *chakra* initiation
into alignment with his center, and a concentrated exposure to ideas and attitudes that
would become cornerstones of the fifth *chakra* gift he would bring back to the "wasteland"
of the world.

Back Into the Belly of the Whale

Though by the ripe old age of 25, Campbell had it all figured out, one important
step had yet to be taken. Before he could make the contribution he was destined to make,
the young scholar had to get out of his head and into the world. Musing in his personal
journal (qtd. in Larsen 149), he wrote:

> *It seems, what I need is a cause! – something in which I might thoroughly
> lose myself. But all the causes I look at seem hardly worth the bother of doing
> much about them. – All is flux. All is illusion. Happiness is an illusion.
> Happiness is an absorption in a cause which in the end is but illusion.
> Perhaps the best cause, in the end, is Joseph Campbell. As Bourdelle used to
> say, "C'est la personalité qui conte" – seek out experience for myself – And it
> seems, the thing I need now for experience is contact with the world. I have
> been living aloof, in bookland. I must bump a bit, and rub elbows.*

◇◇

But how to do that without maintaining the starry-eyed idealism that had carried him this far? Upon his return from graduate school in Europe, Campbell saw firsthand how bumping and rubbing elbows could take a toll. Truth be told, he had been able to live the life of a freewheeling seeker of truth, co-mingling with the world's best minds in print and in person, gallivanting around the globe to follow his own intellectual bliss, because his father was back home, footing the bills. His lot was not so different than many college students, and Campbell was truly blessed to have parents that exalted in and gave full support to his unbridled pursuit of his passion, unconventional though it was. But upon returning to the family home in New York, shortly after the Stock Market crash, reality set in – as it did for many of that generation.

The first shock was his father, who had aged considerably in his absence, and was sick with a chronic cough. "I saw Dad at the foot of the gangplank looking old and pushed into his hat," he tells us, "and I knew that I was about to meet reality" (qtd. in Larsen 116). On one level, the reality Campbell met was the realization that life was fragile, precarious and short. On a deeper level, however, was the realization that he did not need another realization – that he was letting his own life go by, even as he passionately sought to articulate its ineffable essence.

His family moved to Woodstock, in part to downsize in the face of the Depression. Joseph hung out with them for awhile, and considered his future. Astrologically, this hiatus from his intense and unrelenting pursuit of knowledge came while transiting Neptune (in the 12th house) was quincunx his natal 6th house stellium. After Uranus' experience of enlightenment in Paris and Munich, he was back in the belly of the whale.

He thought briefly about going into business with his father, but then realized that would fly in the face everything he so passionately believed about how one ought to live one's life. He toyed with the idea of being a bohemian writer of fiction, but then decided that "all this intense living program seems to send people going up and down. Seizing the moment – and life so rich & all that. The point is, life is rather too rich to be taken injudiciously. Best carefully discriminate, and find what phases contribute to poise, sympathy, sensitivity & organic growth" (qtd. in Larsen 145).

Lastly, it occurred to him that with all the knowledge he had accumulated, it would be a natural extension of his path for him to teach. He returned to Columbia and spoke with his old teachers and mentors, all of whom were ready to hire him enthusiastically on the spot, with the one caveat that he had to be careful about interdepartmental politics, and crossing interdisciplinary lines. Campbell couldn't do it. After a seemingly inconsequential date with a sophisticated and intoxicating young woman, who told him, "Achievement is only dust," he decided instead to travel solo to the west coast. "I should live with a beautiful climate, and live perhaps with some Indians for awhile" (qtd. in Larsen 151) he told his bewildered family before hitting the road.

Campbell's Flirtation With the Anima

His journey began in the fall of 1931 (still well within orb of transiting Neptune's quincunx to his natal stellium). He stopped first in New Orleans to visit his old friend, Angela Gregory, who was rapidly becoming an accomplished artist in her own right. She introduced him to Franz Blom at Tulane University, who offered Campbell a job teaching archeology. As Larsen put it, "Campbell was to vacillate for months after leaving New Orleans before finally deciding that a lifetime of classifying antiquities seemed dry to the part of his soul that craved things live and juicy" (157).

After New Orleans, Campbell wound his way to Los Angeles, where another female friend (Campbell had lots of them), "a very socially mobile young lady" took him under her wing, and tried to introduce him to the Hollywood scene. Campbell instead expressed an interest in reading Tolstoy in Russian. Within a couple of months, Campbell was bored with both Los Angeles and Tolstoy and more restless than ever. "What I miss most," he wrote in his journal, "is the happy sense of getting somewhere. I'm stuck. I'm milling about" (qtd. in Larsen 160). Campbell did the only thing he could do. He kept going.

He went north, and wound up in Berkeley, visiting yet another female friend, Adelle Davis, whom he had met on a Carribean cruise with his family, several years earlier. "I was struck by the fact that I, who had been given everything," he wrote, "had learned to be melancholy over everything, whilst Adelle, who had been given nothing, was a twinkling, happy creature, tickled to death with the run of things. . ." (qtd. in Larsen 165). He also realized that part of what had been missing in his quest was the warmth and delight of sensual pleasures and the opening of the heart that could only come in the arms of a beloved. "We had a glorious week together; then Adelle went to her office; and I got up, like a pregnant Madonna, to wash the dishes and clean the house and pack my bags" (qtd. in Larsen 165).

After rebuffing Adelle Davis' desire for more than just a one-night stand, Campbell wrote, "I realized what an ape I had been through the whole thing. She had come, she said, because she had thought she might be able to give me something solid that I might build upon – an answer to one of my questions. And she found, instead of the chap she had known, another person off on another tangent, looking for answers in the skies" (qtd, in Larsen 168).

The problem – at least as far as his women were concerned – was that Campbell's was neither a second nor a fourth *chakra* quest. Though he was by all accounts a dashing young man, quite charming, witty, wise, from a wealthy family, he was not looking for a relationship, nor even sex. He could have had any number of women, and there were many opportunities for him that most men would sell their soul for. Not Campbell. At least at this point in his life, his infatuation with the *anima* was archetypal, ethereal, a symbolic quest. Though real flesh and blood women drew him, despite his resolve, like a bear to the honey pot, he largely felt this strange hormonal quiver to be a distraction.

It should be noted here, however, that his relationship to the *anima* was no less less a propelling force in his fifth *chakra* quest than his discovery of critical ideas. It is fitting that this walkabout to the west along the *anima* trail was undertaken during a Neptune transit, for Neptune is the planet through which the *anima* speaks most strongly to him. If his were a second *chakra* pattern, Campbell's dalliances on the way to paradise would ultimately prove to be the whole point of the journey. Since his was a fifth *chakra* Neptune, however, it instead led him from one teacher and/or soul companion on the quest for truth to the next. Angela Gregory had reunited him with Krishnamurti, and introduced him to Antoine Bordello. His Hollywood friend, Merle Sproull introduced him to a man named Ellery Walter, who had just been to Russia and who inspired Campbell, not just with his knowledge of Russia, but also with his adventuresome spirit – at a time when Campbell was wanting to study Russian and immerse himself in Tolstoy. At his next stop, the woman he went to see (yes, there is a pattern here) introduced him to John Steinbeck, with whom he felt an immediate philosophical kinship. And so it went, chasing the *anima* long enough to find the next nugget of truth down the street or around the corner from the real-life flesh and blood woman, who invariably failed to understand his priorities.

After meeting Steinbeck and through Steinbeck, Ed Ricketts, a philosophical naturalist whose earth-based spirituality Campbell greatly admired, Campbell decided to settle in Carmel, California. "At last," wrote Campbell, "a world of my contemporaries. I don't know why, but suddenly I felt that this was exactly what I had lacked" (qtd. in Larsen 173). After settling into a cheap cottage next door to Ricketts, Campbell resumed his perennial reading and his intellectual quest. But something was different about it now. Somehow the availability of creative companions, every bit as ruggedly independent in their thinking as he was, and the sheer beauty of his surroundings jogged something loose inside of him, and allowed the missing pieces to fall into place.

As he wrote to his friend, Angela Gregory on March 11, 1932 (as transiting Neptune was exactly quincunx Jupiter), trying to explain why he would not return to New Orleans and take the position he was offered to teach at Tulane (qtd. in Larsen 178):

> What I feel is this, that I am at present at last getting at my own self in the raw and that a contagious foreign enthusiasm might cloud my whole raw self over again and send me whirling off again in another wild direction. I'm sick of whirling off in wild directions, and this time, by jiggers, I'm going to hop after something that I'll be glad to catch if I catch it.

A couple months later in his journal (May 10, 1932 as transiting Neptune was forming a direct station exactly quincunx his natal Sun) (qtd. in Larsen 179), he wrote:

> In my enthusiasm for living as opposed to mere thinking, I have radically revised my attitude toward a great many matters. I have begun to react positively instead of negatively to the invitations of life, and as a result I find things wearing a warmer, more friendly light than they used to. . . I have found "the other side of my soul" and I know the difference at last between Life and Truth.

Part of Campbell's newfound enthusiasm for living stemmed from the fact that he had fallen in love with Steinbeck's wife, whereupon "All had shriveled to tertiary size in relation to love's primary size" (qtd. in Larsen 197). The three of them worked it out in friendly fashion, and Campbell left with Ed Ricketts for a trip to Alaska, before returning to New York. He showed up at his parents' doorstep, a bearded 28-year old "metaphysical vagabond" (Larsen 209) who had discovered not only the truth, but the Secret to Life.

By the end of this Neptunian period, he found himself with his first job as preparatory schoolmaster at the Canterbury School in New Milford, Connecticut, where he himself had been a student just a short time ago. Shortly after beginning, he wrote to his friend Angela Gregory, "I can already feel the compressions of the traditional molds around me. . . I am already having to barter off little pieces of my soul and the thrill of being alive is flickering out slowly, but surely" (qtd. in Larsen 214). He lasted one year, then returned to Woodstock and the relatively carefree life of a backwoods philosopher. But childhood was coming to an end for Campbell, and it was time for him to take his place somewhere in society. Astrologers will recognize this call to greater responsibility as a telltale sign of the Saturn return, and Campbell's came due in early 1934. From the perspective of the fifth *chakra*, it was also a matter of taking his quest to its destination in a sense of place, from which the alignment with personal truth that he had been seeking could take root, blossom and grow.

In March of 1934, as transiting Uranus was trine its natal position and sextile Neptune, Campbell was offered another job at Sarah Lawrence College, this time in a position that suited him and where he would remain for the next 38 years. It appeared that by the time of his first Saturn return, Campbell had typically put the folly of his youth behind him and settled into a more responsible adult life – on his own terms, of course. Given the dominance of his fifth *chakra* pattern, it was clear that under Saturn's tutelage, he was merely sinking the roots that would allow his ongoing quest to bear its most valuable fruit.

A Fifth Chakra Alchemy of Two Planetary Agents

It would be tempting to track Campbell's fascinating story all the way through, if space and time permitted. But by now, it should be clear that the formative years of his life were a trial-and-error fifth *chakra* process of gradually increasing alignment with the deepest truth of his being, and with that which made him feel most alive. Along the way, he also articulated the universal truth to be found spiraling around the axis of the *anima mundi* with a depth and breadth of vision that few have managed before or since.

From an astrological perspective, Campbell's fifth *chakra* process was an alchemy orchestrated by two planetary agents: Uranus and Neptune, each in their own way working the raw material of his 6th house Sun/Mercury/Jupiter. This vibrant stellium, core of his fifth *chakra* pattern, was the ongoing attempt that defined his life to distill a personal truth that allowed him to live from his center with as little compromise as possible.

"To be without principles, to be free-thinking; to be skeptical of all dogmas – to break whenever possible, the rule of the Golden Mean; to exercise restraint only for the fun of feeling formal – these are a few of the keys to a civilized permissiveness" (qtd. in Larsen 209). This was the credo that he carried with him through a prodigious career, in which he traversed the gamut of disciplines and ideas in parallel fashion to his travels across the physical globe and his wide-ranging love affair with life. Though he taught formally at Sarah Lawrence College for 38 years, more importantly, he became a spokesperson for a generation of truth-seekers, and was very much the embodiment of this archetypal fifth *chakra* function, as he both taught and lived what he had discovered to be the truth about life.

In this chapter, we have tracked the dual alchemy of Uranus and Neptune far enough to show how each contributed to the emergence of the man we remember today, and on a more personal level, to the awakening and activation of his fifth *chakra*. Uranus seems to have been primarily responsible for introducing him to those teachers and ideas that became seminal touchstones within his own emerging philosophy of life, while Neptune often plunged him back into the belly of the whale, where a restless longing for something just beyond his reach seemed to possess him and drive him forward unto the unknown. Jupiter also played its part – though we did not track it – undoubtedly most evident in Campbell's indomitable enthusiasm for the quest. Even when he was most unsure of his path, there was something driving him forward. Often his very frustration became the energy of breakthrough. I attribute this driving spirit to both his angular Mars in Aries – more peripheral to our discussion in this chapter, and to his Jupiter – situated at the very heart of his fifth *chakra* pattern.

In tracking his story, I have considered all major transits (conjunction, sextile, square, trine, and opposition) of both planets, as well as some considered minor (the semi-sextile, quincunx, semi-square and sesquiquadrate), all within a one-degree orb. The advantage of adding these minor transits to the mix is that it fills out the otherwise empty periods in Campbell's story, covering many more years of his life with the influence of either Uranus or Neptune, sometimes both. This is perhaps an exaggerated use of a technique I had used more sparingly in the other case studies in this book, but for a life as concentrated as Campbell's, it helps to bring the fifth *chakra* pattern into more detailed relief.

Normally, as the pattern unfolds throughout his life, either Uranus or Neptune would be in the ascendancy, while the other's influence was on the decline or relatively absent. The two exceptions to this alternating rhythm are:

August, 1917 – January, 1918:   Uranus semi-square stellium

Neptune trine stellium

October, 1959 – August, 1960:   Uranus sesquiquadrate stellium

Neptune quincunx stellium

During the first period, Campbell became sick with his childhood respiratory illness, and entered the belly of the whale, where I would argue the seeds of his deeper longings would first begin to germinate. Though always curious and excited by the possibility of learning something new, it was after this confluence of Uranus and Neptune that Campbell began his study of the American Indian and the natural world around him in earnest, and began a self-propelled quest for what – at this point – he could not say.

The second period saw the publication of the first volume of Campbell's *The Masks of God*, this one a summation of Primitive Mythology that was in essence a full-bodied extension of his earliest passionate interest in the American Indian, begun during the preceding period. The four-volume series as a whole can also arguably be understood as his magnus opus, the ultimate integration of all the various threads of interest he had pursued his entire life. Aside from the brilliance of the scholarship, Campbell put himself into the work, and the personal wisdom he had gathered in his own quest shines through from page one. After declaring the book to be the "confirmation of a thought I have long and faithfully entertained: of the unity of the race of man" (v), he tells us:

> I can see no reason why anyone would suppose that in the future the same motifs already heard will not be sounding still – in new relationships indeed, but ever the same motifs. They are all given here, in these volumes, with many clues, besides, suggesting ways in which they might be put to use by reasonable men to reasonable ends – or by poets to poetic ends – or by madmen to nonsense and disaster.

CHAPTER TWENTY

◇◇◇

In pursuing his fifth chakra journey, Campbell himself had madly pursued a passionate, at times shapeless obsession that could have ruined a lesser man. He had also tasted the sweet poetry of life, and with its juice still dripping down his chin, he had sat down to translate the whole experience into a prodigious body of work of magnificent numinosity. Anything less would have left his fifth chakra aching for more, and the rest of us lacking the guidance of the true fifth chakra hero he had become.

Chapter Twenty-One
The Sixth Chakra Chart

As discussed in Chapter Six, the spiritual task in the sixth *chakra* is to learn to see reality from multiple perspectives, and to adapt to the situation at hand from a place of maximum flexibility of spirit, creativity and resourcefulness. Unlike the fifth *chakra*, where we find our place and inhabit it from a place of optimal alignment to a relatively stable truth, the sixth *chakra* both invites and compels us to experiment with living from a mobile center, capable of embracing the relativity of truth as a blessing and source of liberation. We typically begin our work in the sixth *chakra* with a set of beliefs, normally conditioned by collective values and worldviews. To the extent that we opened and cleared our fifth *chakra*, these beliefs will be tempered by a discovery of individual truth, which may or may not corroborate what we were taught by the collective. But in the sixth, there is yet another step to be taken, which is to realize that all truth – even our most cherished personal beliefs, rooted in our most profound experiences – is relative to our perspective, and that perspective is capable of being shifted, shed, and/or traded for one more useful.

This is in fact what we do, throughout a lifetime of experience. As children, we are invariably wounded, and this wounding forms the core experience out of which arises our image of the world. As we move through life, we learn that the world does not always function the way we expect it to, based upon our wounded image. Sometimes we cringe when there is no bogeyman at our door. Sometimes we wait for surrogate parents to rescue us and no rescue comes. Inevitably we discover that we have strengths and resources that make us bigger than whatever laid us low, way back when. As we gain the competency and the confidence to face our issues head on, and to work creatively toward resolution, our image of the world shifts and we experience it in a different way. This is an experience of the sixth *chakra* opening and being cleansed.

Our first experience of such a possibility for shifting a wounded worldview typically takes a long time. If the astrological pattern reflecting the wound involves one of the transpersonal planets – Uranus, Neptune or Pluto – it can take a lifetime or longer. Yet, if we persist, and to the extent we are driven by the internal pressure of a sixth *chakra* pattern, eventually we will experience a breakthrough that alters the entire embodied existence of the soul. Change is no longer something we must struggle for years to achieve. It is available to us in the blink of an eye, as we step out of the story line of our own lives and approach the situation at hand in whatever way is most constructive in the moment. We need not be locked into a particular way of being just because it is our wounded habit. This is not to dismiss the pain or suffering that emanates from our wounds, both ancient and new. But beyond the pain and suffering is an understanding rooted in the core of our being that we are in essence larger than the biggest trials we must face. At the sixth *chakra*, we gain the capacity to return to the core at will, and then re-emerge along a different psychic spoke of the wheel to a state of being that is not quite so wounded.

In the sixth *chakra*, we also gain the capacity to see everything in perspective as part of the outworking of a larger ineffable plan in which we are all participants. Others appear to us as they are, but also as shining flawless diamonds, perfect in their imperfections, and we are able to relate to them with tremendous compassion. Despite the Buddha's admonition that life is suffering, we understand that some suffering we impose upon ourselves, and in the end, it is unnecessary to suffer as much as we do. Where suffering does exist, we embrace it in love, as an act of surrender to a larger Will, whose benevolence is unquestioned. Yet, when the sixth *chakra* is clear, we also see beyond our suffering to the evolutionary state that is gradually emerging through the pain. Our ability to see this way, in turn, serves as a source of healing to ourselves and others.

In the sixth *chakra* – the second in the transcendence phase of the evolutionary process – the distinction between *yin* and *yang* continues to break down. The expectation, in strict adherence to the pattern established in the first four *chakras*, is that the sixth *chakra* would be a continuation of the *yin* series. Certainly, the adoption of a belief system is largely a *yin* function, especially to the extent that early patterns of conditioning absorbed in childhood remain unexamined. The formation of an image and the projection of this image into the embodied world, however, is a *yang* function of consciousness, since it is an imposition of our worldview upon a screen which receives it, however unconsciously that imposition might be made. The penetration of the veils of illusion that allow us to see the relativity of our beliefs and shapeshift according to an alternate image is also a *yang* function of consciousness. As with the fifth *chakra*, both *yin* and *yang* are necessary to a balanced expression of the sixth *chakra*.

If we consider the sixth *chakra* circle within the context of the *yin-yang* symbol, then it is the small circular seed of *yang* at the heart of the *yin* half of the circle that allows us to make the shift that a cleansing of the sixth *chakra* requires. We can also envision the sixth *chakra* in terms of the sinuous line between *yin* and *yang* as it is ridden down the curve from the *yin* to the *yang* portion of the circle. The more deeply one understands that reality can be constructed along any number of spokes of creativity emanating from Source, the more intentional one becomes in aligning oneself with divine will. The clarity of the soul's intention then becomes an invitation to a deeper inhabitation of the body, the personality, and the embodied life by Spirit.

The Placement of Sixth Chakra Planets in Astrological Space

As with the fifth *chakra*, sixth *chakra* patterns can occupy any hemisphere or quadrant. Where they actually sit often determines which other *chakras* are central to the challenge of being able to break free from limited perspectives. According to the hierarchical yogic model from which the *chakra* system is derived, this *interchakra* exchange was generally considered to be a matter of some lower *chakra* blockage that prevented the *kundalini shakti* or life force from rising to the higher *chakra*. In the circular model of *chakras* I am presenting here, I prefer to think of the challenge as involving an additional layer of complexity, due to the fact that multiple interpenetrating and overlapping tasks are involved.

If, for example, a sixth *chakra* pattern spans the south and the west, it may well be that the pattern in question plays itself out in terms of relationship dynamics with fourth *chakra* implications. A common manifestation of this *interchakra* dynamic is a set of projected judgments that create disharmony in relationship. Often the judgments in question are rooted in some belief system that must change before harmony can be restored. We experienced this kind of fourth-sixth *interchakra* dynamic as a culture during the 50s, 60s and beyond in subtler forms to the present day, for example, as racism, born of the disparaging belief that blacks are inferior to whites. Similar beliefs have been carried to an extreme in Nazi Germany, and in far too many other acts of genocide, repression and ethnic atrocity. Judgmental beliefs also pervade many relationships on a more mundane level, as ordinary projections of endless variety.

On whatever level they manifest, working through such judgments presents a spiritual task which involves both fourth and sixth *chakras* – that is to say, the cultivation of a deeper level of compassion through changing one's beliefs, while simultaneously opening the heart wide enough to encompass a broader perspective. In my opinion, it is not, as the Hindu yogis intimated, that one must work through the issues blocking the lower *chakra* (in this case, the fourth) before one can experience an opening of the higher *chakra* (in this case, the sixth). It is instead a matter of working in both centers simultaneously. The necessity for doing this is reflected astrologically, when a sixth *chakra* pattern spans the southern and western hemispheres, or is rooted in the SW quadrant.

A sixth *chakra* pattern that spans the south and east, or that is rooted in the SE quadrant could potentially involve the third *chakra* – say for example, as the experience of a handicapped person with a bitter chip on her shoulder, badly in need of an attitude adjustment before being able to cultivate useful skills and seek gainful employment. Where the sixth *chakra* pattern spans the north and west, or sits in the 2nd quadrant, there can be an *interchakra* dynamic with the second *chakra*. Here, as one hypothetical possibility out of many, we may find a sexually impotent young man, who was raised by a strict Calvinist father to believe that sex was sinful and deserving of punishment. Where a sixth *chakra* pattern spans the north and east, or first *chakra*, we may well have an interaction with the first *chakra* that somehow adversely impacts survival itself.

I witnessed such a dynamic myself as a child, well before I knew anything about astrology or the *chakra* system, when a friend cut his wrist crashing through the backdoor window on his way to catch a football. His mother, a devote Christian Scientist, refused to take him to the doctor. We did manage to stop the bleeding with our Boy Scout training, and somehow found a doctor to stitch him up, but this was definitely a situation in which beliefs (centered in the sixth *chakra*) could have potentially jeopardized physical survival (anchored in the first).

Lastly, as we saw in Chapter Twenty, in the case of Joseph Campbell, fifth-sixth *interchakra* dynamics are also possible. In his case, they were precipitated through the dual impact of Uranus (predominantly a fifth *chakra* planet) and Neptune (predominantly a sixth *chakra* planet) interacting within the context of the same pattern. Though, for the most part, I have tried to choose examples, where the signature of a given *chakra* is clearly apparent, most of the time, it is these *interchakra* dynamics that will generate the most complex, challenging and ultimately rewarding core issues that we must face. We will cover these *interchakra* dynamics in more detail in Chapter Twenty Three, when we demonstrate how the system works as a whole. For now, suffice it to say that sixth *chakra* patterns can potentially be colored by *interchakra* dynamics, depending upon how they are placed in a birthchart. I say, "potentially," because as with all things astrological, just because a potential exists does not necessarily mean it will inevitably be manifest in the living experience of the person behind the chart.

The Sixth Chakra and Cadent Planets

Like fifth *chakra* patterns, sixth *chakra* patterns will also tend to involve the cadent houses. From the perspective of the fifth *chakra*, the cadent houses are where we discover our own truth through the assimilation of feedback. From the perspective of the sixth, this same truth – so pertinent to our fifth *chakra* challenge – is also the stuff of which our beliefs are fashioned.

This is not necessarily a bad thing. Beliefs are necessary to the creation of a stable existence with continuity and purpose. Without a philosophy of life, taken as the summation of our beliefs, we will be fairly rudderless, and blown about by the collective winds of change. Whatever image we form of the world through our sixth *chakra* activity in the cadent houses, it serves as the launching pad for our lives, in all of their multi-colored and at times unfathomable complexity.

Where the formation of beliefs, philosophies and images of the world becomes problematic is where it gels into something rigid – where the little subjective truth, fleeting and temporary to our navigation as souls, becomes Truth with a capital T. Or put another way, whenever we confuse our perceptions of reality with reality itself – a common occurrence for all of us – we have a potential sixth *chakra* issue. Normally, such a danger is reflected astrologically through a pattern involving hard aspects – such as a t-square, a grand cross, or a square with a third planet at the midpoint, semi-square to both ends. Tight stelliums can also be problematic in this regard, as can any pattern where Saturn plays a critical role. I have also observed some of this rigidity with grand trines, where the inherent inertia of the pattern seems to prohibit entertaining alternate points of view.

In any case, it is the cadent houses where beliefs either prove to be a useful foundation to a life of meaning and purpose, or become problematic blockages to the free-flow of sixth *chakra* adaptation to shifting life circumstances. In traditional astrology, it is generally the 9th house that is associated with beliefs, philosophies and worldviews, and the 9th house can certainly be a key location for sixth *chakra* issues, when planets functioning at that level are placed there, especially when they are part of a larger planetary pattern. Other cadent houses can also contribute to this picture.

The 6th house harbors beliefs about who we are in relation to the larger embodied world in which we participate, and what our place is within it. Such beliefs often become a determining factor in establishing our social station in life, our level of employment, our stature within the career we have chosen, and our overall level of satisfaction in both work and life in general.

In the 3rd house, we absorb the projections of our siblings, our peers at school, and later in life, our co-workers and anyone else with whom we must interact on a daily basis. These assimilated 3rd house projections in turn determine how we see ourselves through others eyes, how confident and comfortable we feel in social situations, and how capable we are of risking and investing ourselves emotionally. Sometimes we also absorb beliefs directly from the people we hang out with. If everyone in our social circle is a Republican, chances are we will be, too.

Lastly, in the 12th house, we encounter the most insidious beliefs of all, and often those that cause the most damage within the psyche. Here are all the unspoken family rules governing behavior – "big boys do not cry," "we don't speak about daddy's drinking problem – ever," "money is god" or whatever they happen to be for us. In the 12th house, we absorb the image of the world that is being lived by our family of origin, and unconsciously adopt it as our own. The 12th house will likely contain all the cultural norms, religious codes, political ideologies, and class dictums that have been embraced by the family, and passed on from generation to generation. As children, we absorb these rules by osmosis, and grow up thinking that this is the way it is, only learning later – often painfully – through our own experiences that this is not really what is true for us. To the extent that these beliefs and patterns of conditioning prevent a fluid adaptation to life's ever-changing panoply of demands, excessively rabid judgments of others, or self-defeating or negating behaviors, they may be linked to a sixth *chakra* pattern.

The Moon's Role in Sixth Chakra Dynamics

On their most basic level, beliefs can be understood as the collective memory of those who hold them. Those who fervently believe in Christ, for example, are embracing a history, and a body of mythological lore, passed down from generation to generation, preserved in The Bible and in countless sectarian permutations and adaptations of Christ's original teachings. The religion today known as Buddhism similarly arose in the 1st century CE, when the followers of Buddha, diminishing in number, wrote down his teachings to preserve them, while the collective memory of the *sangha* (community of seekers) was still relatively intact. In the Viking tradition, the god Odin drinks from Mimir's well (the well of remembrance) in order to attain the cumulative wisdom of the ancestors. Much of what is passed down from generation to generation as the social code, often deeply informed by religion, depends upon memory in both written and oral form for its transmission. The Moon is associated with the sixth *chakra*, mostly through its function as the planet of memory in general, and of emotional memory in particular[1].

Memories become an especially potent source for the image that we hold of the world when they are anchored by strong emotions. According to a number of scientific studies, pleasant memories tend to be more easily and more accurately remembered than unpleasant memories (Searleman 179-180). It is human to want to define ourselves in terms of our best moments, and to crystallize our beliefs, our worldview and our philosophy of life around hopeful ideas, which in turn are greatly reinforced by personal experiences of their truth and validity. Yet as Freud and several successive generations of psychologists have pointed out, it is the unpleasant memories of events, whose emotions are too difficult, paradoxical or complex to process that form the nucleus of our unconscious complexes.

These complexes can be understood from a spiritual perspective to constellate the core issues around which our soul's journey evolves. When the Moon participates in our sixth *chakra* patterns, then memories – both our more fondly remembered ones and those that have been repressed – become an important source for the images that we hold about ourselves and the world. To the extent that these memories are frozen, or unavailable to the conscious mind, then working through the issues they harbor will necessarily involve a process of remembering, feeling the difficult emotions around which these frozen memories have crystallized, and then releasing the charge we have invested in them. When this happens, a floodgate of psychic energy is opened within the sixth *chakra*, and significant change in a positive direction becomes possible.

Some astrologers believe that the Moon is the repository of memories not just from this lifetime, but also from past lives (Naiman 192). As discussed in *The Seven Gates of Soul*, I believe that information about past lives can be useful, when understood metaphorically

– that is to say, as an image of a process or dynamic playing itself out acutely in this present life. While I don't discount the possibility of past lives, I do believe that the emotional residues of past life experience reflected by the Moon must still be processed in the here and now, and released in present time, within the context of whatever experiences in this life are triggering past life memories. Assuming that some piece of core identity is maintained after death to become the nucleus of a new life, then it is not unreasonable to assume that which survives death will be tinged with unprocessed emotion.

Buddhists refer to the *bhavanga-sota* or subconscious life-stream, which provides the seed for a new incarnation, although there is no real guarantee of continuity for the soul claiming *bhavanga-sota* as her core identity. It is merely there for the taking, so to speak, in which case, it is not a matter of memory, but of vibrational resonance with the unresolved emotional residue. Whatever memories were attached to the unresolved emotional residue, while it was accumulating, no longer exist. What remains is the residue itself, which represents a piece of the larger puzzle we must all solve together. Some incarnating soul will be drawn to that residue, because its resolution can potentially produce growth – for the soul, and for the collective in which the soul participates. Astrologically, it is the Moon that binds us to the collective effort, and affords us the opportunity to participate in the release of toxic emotions that color a mindset that conditions us all. It is in this way that the Moon participates in a sixth *chakra* pattern, which in the end is largely about undoing the damage caused by collective investment in certain counterproductive ideas and beliefs.

Lastly, at this level, the Moon can also be associated with the faculty of intuition, which is a sixth *chakra* state of awareness. Intuition in this sense means an awareness of the whole pattern of which the individual is part. Awareness of the whole is a prerequisite toward relinquishing a tight identification with the part one plays within the whole, and an opening to the possibility of shape-shifting – that is to say, adopting another part, or another, or another. This is also a prerequisite to the seventh *chakra* realization that we are all One, which on any other level sounds trite, but is ultimately the *hieros gamos*, in which all polarities collapse into unity and the small separate soul merges back into the unity of Spirit. At the sixth *chakra*, the awareness of the possibility takes a more functional shape as sensitivity to the interconnection between seemingly separate parts within the whole. The parts are still separate, but they are related in rather profound and surprising ways that only become apparent when we feel our way into these relationships. This process of sensing the interrelationships between parts within a whole – otherwise understood as intuition – is the province of the Moon. Here, we have the aspect of the Moon that is associated with the High Priestess of the Tarot. When we cling tightly to a belief in separation that counterbalances our experience of interconnection, the resulting internal conflict can instead lead to a state of lunacy, associated with the Tarot card The Moon[2].

◇◇

Venus' Role in Sixth Chakra Dynamics

The second personal planet associated with the sixth *chakra* is Venus[3]. We have already met Venus in the second *chakra*, where it governed the pursuit of pleasure, and in the fourth, where it governed an opening of the heart in relationship through a process of resonance by affinity. In the sixth, this experience of resonance by affinity is taken one step further to encompass a network of affinity within which all resonant relationships are felt as an interconnected whole. This is similar to the awareness precipitated by the Moon, but the contribution that Venus makes to this awareness is more sensual and more viscerally attuned to the fertility of the earth, the cycle of the seasons, and the exchange of vital energies through the heart and the sexual organs. When both second and fourth *chakras* are open, there evolves an organic way of being that identifies less with a particular state of living embodiment and more with the primordial cycle of life and death – a cycle that by its nature transcends both life and death.

Such a state is depicted in the Tarot deck as The Star. The Rider deck, one of the original popular versions of the Tarot, developed by scholar of occultism Dr. Arthur Edward Waite, depicts the Star as a naked woman with one foot in a pool, the other on land, pouring water from two jugs, large vibrant stars overhead. As I see it, this card is quite sensual, and at the same time, quite cosmic. It depicts a fully embodied experience, yet it also shows how that experience is part of a larger cycle akin to the flow of water from source to destination and back again. At the sixth *chakra*, it is as though we begin to see beyond the veil of appearances into the inner workings of that which we call our life, and of life in general. There is less attachment, even as our capacity for enjoyment increases. Regardless of the *chakra* through which it functions, Venus is first and last associated with the capacity for enjoyment. In the sixth house, however, enjoyment is heightened by the very fact that this precious moment, this exquisitely unique configuration of identity, circumstance and opportunity will never come again. At this level, we know death not to be an illusion, as some mystical traditions maintain, but to be the flow of life back into Life that makes each life an experience to be treasured as deeply as one can.

At this level, Venus can be understood more accurately as Persephone, the goddess abducted into the underworld as the innocent maiden, Kore, who after living for a time in union with Hades or Pluto, transcends death. As neopagan activist Starhawk tells us (83), Kore-who-becomes-Persephone is:

> *she who descends into the underworld, into death, and rises again, eternally
> renewed. Kore is kin to Isis, Inanna, Astarte. The story of the rape of Kore is
> a late addition, an historical reference perhaps to the destruction of the early
> Goddess culture, or a patriarchal attempt to subvert the power of the myth.*

◇◇

> *The myth itself is a story strung together around the original experience, which was a ritual, the celebration of the Thesmophoria, in ancient Greece. The ritual was one of descent and rising . . . The ancient Kore shows us the power of life and death united; teaches us the secret that renewal cannot be separated from decay, that it is death that makes life fertile.*

Pluto's Role in Sixth Chakra Dynamics

It is mythologically impossible to talk about Persephone without also talking about Pluto or Hades, since they are consorts who represent the shadow of the *hieros gamos* to be experienced in the seventh *chakra*. Here I mean shadow, not in the Jungian sense of dark, repressed aspects of the psyche that need to be reclaimed – although that may be true at the level of the sixth *chakra* if polarized beliefs prevent one from seeing the ultimately unity of life and death within the context of a larger reality. What I mean by shadow here is a precursor, a foreshadowing and a lesser imitation of the real thing. Pluto and Persephone mirror the experience of union without actually achieving it. Persephone leaves Pluto and the underworld for several months out of the year to rejoin her mother Demeter above ground, and then returns. This coming and going establishes a cycle, which in turn is related to the fertility and dormancy of the Earth, and of everything taking shape or form within the embodied world. When true union is achieved, there is no longer any coming and going, the cycle dissolves, and the experience of embodiment is no longer necessary or possible.

Pluto is traditionally associated with death, and on one level it is Persephone's relationship with death that allows her to transcend it. Yet, Pluto the abductor is very different than Pluto the mate, and within the context of their relationship – which one must assume becomes intimate on some level – Pluto reveals a deeper dimension as the lord of inner wealth. For it is in transcending death, realizing it to be but the fertile soil out of which a more organic relationship to life arises, that one realizes everything in this life is much much more than it seems. It is a gateway into the experience of the Whole, and an awareness of the interrelatedness of everything contained within the Whole – not as an abstraction, but as a living experience available in each moment. This is the true wealth that Pluto governs, and it is only available through the sixth *chakra*, where one begins to see beyond the veil of mere material appearances.

Pluto's function at this level can be understood as reflected by The Hanged Man of the Tarot. About the Hanged Man, shamanic ceremonialist Dick Prosapio says this (28):

> *The Hanged Man is the one who must deal with being in a state of "liminality," of being in-between. (The limen is the sill of the door, that place between places.) This is a place of not-knowing, yet being content with*

◇◇◇

this lack of knowledge. Note the face of the Hanged Man. There is in his countenance a look of acceptance and peace with this state; the paradox being that not knowing, and accepting that experience is the ultimate contentment.... His legs form the figure four, completeness. His supports are sturdy trees, free of bough or ornament, perhaps indicating that this suspension of knowing is a more "pure" state of being than is knowing.

In this culture, we do not normally associate a state of liminality or not-knowing with wealth. Wealth in the usual sense is often understood as just the opposite – being in the know, having at one's disposal an accessible reservoir of knowledge for practical application. But at the sixth *chakra*, wealth comes instead from allowing the mind to empty out, becoming free of beliefs, and open to whatever wants to present itself in the moment, without preconceived ideas or assumptions. In this sense, Pluto is the agent that clears the mind[4].

This function of Pluto can be observed most succinctly in a mythological cousin of the Hanged Man, the Teutonic god Odin. By hanging upside down on Yggdrasil, the world tree, Odin realized in a single instant of inspiration, the entire runic alphabet. Since the word, "rune," means "secret," the implication here is that by hanging upside down, and allowing his conscious mind to empty of content, Odin was granted access to hidden wisdom. Through emptying the mind of beliefs, old patterns of conditioning, and assumptions about the nature of reality, the sixth *chakra* opens to reveal the underlying interconnective order that pervades the universe of apparently separate objects and entities.

I once had a glimpse of this possibility myself. During transiting Pluto's square to natal Pluto, I did a ritual ceremony with a Guatemalan shaman in Santa Fe, New Mexico. Although at the time, I thought I was taking advantage of this Pluto transit in order to access my power more consciously and intentionally, in retrospect, it seems more accurate to see my experience as an awakening of the sixth *chakra*. About the ceremony itself, I wrote in my journal that it "was a hypnotic, nurturing experience, but somewhat incomprehensible. Felt enfolded in cotton all day, peaceful, but tired and slightly headachy." And the next day: "Feeling quiet . . ., different in a subtle way – for one thing, my usual mind chatter seems to be off, or at least on vacation, which is nice for a change. Feels clear and clean and new again." For nearly a week after this experience, it took effort to think a thought. I was in the moment, the way I have never been before or since.

When Pluto participates in a sixth *chakra* pattern, its role is to facilitate the emptying of the mind. On a deeper level, it also demands that we relinquish our most cherished beliefs – usually through some experience or sequence of events that severely challenges them. In Chapter Six I spoke of the double bind as a critical moment in the sixth *chakra* process. Here I would add that it is often Pluto that places us in this critical bind and forces the reckoning with our beliefs that leads to change. Whatever image we previously held of the embodied world, we will be challenged to see the world differently under Pluto's often severe alchemical pressure. The old beliefs no longer explain what is happening to us, and we enter a state of liminality, like The Hanged Man, where we have the opportunity to simply be, without trying to explain. This state of pure being is the doorway to an open sixth *chakra*.

Neptune's Role in Sixth Chakra Dynamics

At this level, Neptune serves a similar function. Whereas Pluto operates most often through shocking the system, Neptune tends to operate through a more gradual, but no less intense pressure toward letting go. When Neptune aspects the Moon within the context of a sixth *chakra* pattern, the pressure is often toward the letting go of wounded memories, and releasing the emotional charge with which they are still invested. If we are angry, we must find a way to forgive. If we are sad, we must grieve. If we have regrets, we must make peace with what can no longer be and move on. Whatever feelings are attached to these memories, they will often come flooding through our system when Neptune triggers the natal sixth *chakra* pattern that contains Neptune. We will often be powerless at such times to resist these feelings, and can be easily overwhelmed by them. Usually there is nothing to be done, but to allow them to surge through us and have their way with our psyche. If we can surrender to that which overpowers us on the emotional level, it can be traumatic, but we will survive, often with a profound sense of having been cleansed, as after a refreshing rain.

If instead, we attempt to resist, like the little Dutch boy, putting his finger in the hole in the dike, our folly will soon overtake us. The anger we cannot release will turn toxic and make us sick. The sadness for which we cannot grieve will deepen into depression. The regrets we cannot make peace with will sap our energy and sink us into lethargy. In each of these states, there will come a forgetting and a letting go, despite our most heroic efforts to keep the old wounded memories alive. We can always choose to hang on to the bitter end, but if we do, all that will remain after Neptune has washed everything else away, will be a bitter aftertaste of the lost opportunity to live a less burdened life. If nothing else, old age and the forgetfulness that often comes with it - including in the most extreme cases, the state we call Alzheimer's - is Neptune's last parting gift, before we sink into the oblivion of final sleep. Better to accept Neptune's gift of liberation, while we are alive, as painful as it can be in the moment of release, than to cling to that which is destined to wash out from underneath us, and go out the portal to this life, leaving an unresolved pocket of *bhavanga-sota* behind us.

Neptune's second function within the sixth *chakra* is to dissolve the boundaries that keep us separate from each other and from the other living embodiments of Spirit within this world. We spoke of this process earlier in relation to Venus, and I would add here, that it is exaggerated and underscored when both Neptune and Venus participate in a sixth *chakra* pattern.

Jupiter's Role in Sixth Chakra Dynamics, Aided by Uranus and Prometheus

The last planet of major significance within the sixth *chakra* is Jupiter. Normally associated with perspective by astrologers, Jupiter provides the breadth of vision to be able to see the broader picture of the whole, as well as one's place within the whole that is the quintessential experience of the sixth *chakra*. As my friend and fellow backwoods philosopher Jann Burner recently described our predicament as human beings:

> It would seem that on one hand we have a person holding a glass orb in his hand and on the other hand we have this very same entity inhabiting the glass orb and trying to describe, understand or invent where it is and what it is doing – finally arriving at the fact it is, indeed, within the confines of a glass bowl, only when every other possibility has been eliminated – when, during this entire time, "it" was standing there holding the very same orb in its hand, experiencing it.

Jann's image is reminiscent of the famous MC Escher lithograph, Hand with Reflecting Sphere, which shows a hand holding a sphere in which is reflected an erudite bearded gentleman in his study (MC Escher himself?). It is also reminiscent of the famous Chinese proverb about the man who dreams he was a butterfly, and then wonders: was he a man dreaming he was a butterfly, or is he now a butterfly dreaming he is a man? The truth – discovered only in the sixth *chakra* – is that we are both. We are Spirit, and we are Spirit inhabiting a particular body, expressing ourselves within a particular perceptual framework as a distinct individual with personality, memories uniquely our own, and an intimately personal sense of identity. To the extent that we are identified with who we are within the context of the world inside the orb, we will not generally be able to see ourselves holding the same orb. To the extent that we are identified with Spirit, before incarnation, or perhaps between incarnations, we drink from the river of forgetfulness (Lethe), as the Greeks put it, and whoever it was we were inside the orb fades from memory.

The task, at the sixth *chakra*, is to be able to hold both images in consciousness simultaneously. This is not the same as intellectually understanding that both are true. It is an actual experience of being Spirit within a particular embodied state, not unlike lucid dreaming – of waking up within the dream to see that we are both the dreamer and the one being dreamt, of being fully present within the glass orb, while at the same time seeing through its self-reflective interior surface to the larger image of ourselves holding the orb.

Astrologically, it is Jupiter that allows us to be in these two perceptual places at once. Zeus' bird is the eagle, often associated with the perspective that comes from great height – that is to say, with identification with Spirit, or with the one holding the glass orb. But as chief deity of the Olympic pantheon, Zeus is also extremely active in the affairs of this world, chasing endlessly after earthly delights, constantly intervening in the affairs of humans and the other deities over which he has dominion. In some versions of the Greek myth, Zeus is the creator of human beings (Morford 57), although the dominant version, this accomplishment fell to Prometheus, who is potentially to Zeus what Zeus was to Cronus and what Cronus was to Uranus - his undoing and the chief deity of the next generation of gods and goddesses. Prometheus, whom we might understand as a more evolved version of Zeus, is celebrated in Aeschylus' play *Prometheus Bound* (Morford 66-67) as having given mortals many gifts enabling them to enjoy and learn from the embodied experience – mathematics, astronomy, carpentry, animal husbandry, mining, ship-building, medicine, and prophecy, to name a few. What are these, if not the demonstration of a full commitment to the embodied life?

Granted, this is Prometheus and not Jupiter, but it is my contention that as Jupiter works through the sixth *chakra*, it becomes more promethean in its function. Astrologer Richard Tarnas associates Prometheus with Uranus, and it may well be that Jupiter and Uranus work together within the context of the sixth *chakra* to generate the capacity to adapt most creatively to the embodied state. They do this by procuring just enough distance and perspective from that state to allow us to mold it as the holder of the sphere. Perhaps Jupiter provides the perspective, while Uranus provides the prerequisite detachment necessary to produce perspective, then allows a certain resourceful genius at tinkering with that which is now seen in perspective. Together, Jupiter and Uranus act like Prometheus in the sixth *chakra*[5].

Jupiter plays a second role in sixth *chakra* dynamics as the agent of shape-shifting. Although all the gods and goddesses in the Greek pantheon possess the power to change shape or form at will, it is Zeus who most often exercised it - usually in pursuit of some mortal with whom he was sexually infatuated. In addition to the eagle, Zeus has appeared at various times as a bull (in his seduction of Europa), a swan (in his seduction of Leda), a whirlwind (in his abduction of Ganymede), and the goddess Artemis (in his seduction of Callisto), to name just a few of his many permutations. Shape-shifting is a metaphor for the capacity to identify simultaneously with the Source, out of which spring the many myriad possibilities for manifest expression, and with these possibilities. Within the context of this current discussion, shape-shifting is having a collection of glass

◇◇

orbs at one's disposal, into which one can enter, or out of which one can exit, at will. It is Jupiter's function, at the level of the sixth *chakra*, to make possible this liberation from the limitations of the orb, while at the same time taking maximum advantage of the opportunity for self-realization within the life circumscribed by the orb.

The Sixth Chakra Chart

When three or more of these sixth *chakra* planets – the Moon, Venus, Pluto, Neptune or Jupiter (with or without Uranus' supplementary aid) – form a planetary pattern, especially across cadent houses, it is likely that we have a sixth *chakra* core issue at work.

A less potent signature is created by planetary patterns formed between these planets and/or the rulers of the cadent houses in angular or succedent houses. Planets in the cadent houses can also serve as triggers for sixth *chakra* processes, which will tend to manifest when aspected by progressed Moon or Venus, transiting Jupiter, Neptune, or Pluto.

Endnotes

[1] In the order of *chakras* presented by Grasse, he precedes the *ajna* (or sixth chakra) with the *chandra*. "Rarely mentioned in published writings," he tells us, "this center at the back of the head was described by Yogananda as the feminine counterpart of the solar, or third-eye chakra at the front of the head" (207). Grasse assigns the Moon to this chakra, noting its association with memory and psychic sensitivity. The *ajna* itself – which he associates with "such factors as will, higher rationality, creativity and one's sense of purpose or vision" – he assigns the Sun.

[2] Following the teachings of B. K. S. Iyengar, Hodgson divides the sixth chakra into three parts – the *ajna*, the *soma*, and the *lalata*. To the *soma*, she assigns the Moon (and Mercury), stating, "It is easy to see how the peaceful calm of the full Moon, shining on the waters of the soul, can balance the fiery heat of the Sun and Mars, which can become too strong if the *ajna* center is stimulated too soon" (150).

[3] Oken assigns sole rulership of the sixth chakra to Venus (155).

[4] Hodgson assigns Pluto to the *lalata*, along with Mercury. Once the *soma* has been activated, the soul is initiated into a deeper, esoteric knowledge that Hodgson equates with "cosmic consciousness."

> *The still water of the soul (soma – the Moon) becomes part of the ocean of divine life, every drop of which is illumined. In this state of absolute stillness and illumination, the lalata chakra, situated at the top of the forehead is activated and the soul can, at will, bring into the conscious mind any facet of*

knowledge which is required. This is cosmic consciousness, which we associate with Mercury, the messenger of the gods, manifesting his full power" (151).

My sense about this is that Mercury only realizes its full power – in the sense that Hodgson is talking about it – with ample help from Pluto, as the agent through which the mind is emptied and a deeper strata of knowledge, normally unavailable to the conscious mind, is accessed.

5   Hodgson assigns co-rulership of the *ajna* to Uranus. She does not elaborate, except to quote Alan Leo in stating that "where the head chakras are fully awakened, Neptune takes the place of the Moon and Uranus of the Sun in the horoscope" (151).

Chapter Twenty-Two
A Sixth Chakra Case Study

In exploring my collection of charts, three distinct possibilities for a sixth *chakra* case study stood out. The first was Kurt Cobain, the angst-ridden leader of the multi-platinum grunge-band, Nirvana, whose 1991 song, "Smells Like Teen Spirit" brought a generational mindset into focus. Cobain's chart contains a splendid water kite, involving four of five primary sixth *chakra* planets plus Uranus. The Moon sits in Cancer in a very wide conjunction to Jupiter, perhaps too far out of orb to be directly involved in the pattern. Of the planets that do participate, only Neptune lies in a cadent house, but Pluto, Uranus, and Venus rule cadent houses.

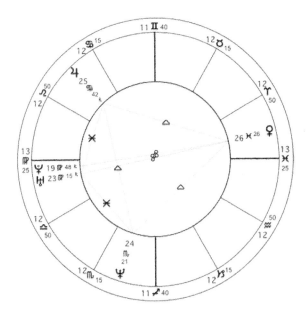

KURT COBAIN'S SIXTH CHAKRA CHART

The second possibility was Katherine Hepburn, considered by many to be the quintessential actress of the 20th century, holding the record for most Oscars awarded, second only to Meryl Streep in nominations. Hepburn's sixth *chakra* pattern is not apparent in the Porphry house system that I favor. If we use the Placidus system instead, the pattern comes into sharp relief as a cardinal t-square involving a Neptune-Uranus opposition at the base with Venus at the apex, all three planets in cadent houses. Jupiter, on the cusp of the cadent 9th house and conjunct cadent Neptune, also participates in this signature.

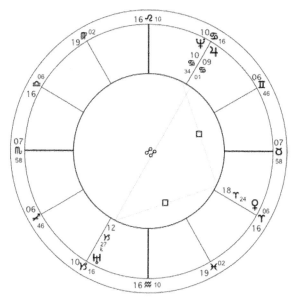

KATHERINE HEPBURN'S SIXTH CHAKRA CHART (PLACIDUS HOUSES)

Some astrologers might quibble with my decision to switch house systems in order to draw Hepburn's sixth *chakra* pattern into focus. Given the complexity of most lives, and the necessity for understanding them from multiple perspectives, however, I delight in the opportunity to turn a birthchart this way and that, as one might turn a kaleidoscope, in order to catch various dimensions of meaning that reveal themselves in slightly different light. Certainly Hepburn's stellar acting career can be understood as a spellbinding demonstration of the sixth *chakra* art of shape-shifting. Behind this public display was the tragic suicide of Hepburn's brother, endured within the context of a family belief system that insisted upon moving forward with life, regardless of its tragedies. Looking at her chart as a sixth *chakra* pattern, I believe it is possible to understand Hepburn's acting career, in part, as an attempt to come to grips with feelings that were not easily allowed by the belief system she inherited from her family.

If, however, we shift Hepburn's chart back to the Porphry house system, Neptune moves to join Jupiter in the succedent 8th house, suggesting a possible move in perspective from the sixth *chakra* to the second or fourth. If we then play around a bit with our intermediary house cusps, we find that using the Meridian system, popular with Uranian astrologers, a clear second *chakra* pattern emerges as Venus moves into the succedent 5th house to form a cardinal *t*-square with succedent 2nd house Mars and succedent 8th house Jupiter/Neptune. Certainly this approach to Hepburn's chart makes more sense within the system I am proposing, if our goal is to understand – for example – her life-long affair with Spencer Tracy.

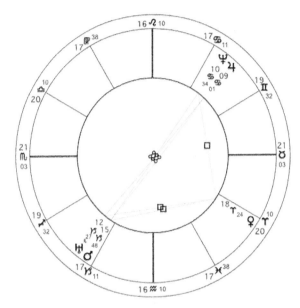

KATHERINE HEPBURN'S SECOND CHAKRA CHART (MERIDIAN HOUSES)

The fact that we had to shift to an obscure house system in order to "see" Hepburn's second *chakra* pattern may seem like a liberal use of the fudge factor by some, but it is in fact, itself a demonstration of the sixth *chakra* at work. The ability to view the same chart from multiple perspectives in arriving at our understanding of a complex, multi-dimensional life, is working through the sixth *chakra* – using what I like to call kaleidoscopic vision – in order to stretch the flexibility of a symbolic language that is often awkwardly cramped by an artificial scientific insistence on consistency. This insistence perhaps makes sense if our goal in the use of astrology is prediction, but unnecessarily limits us when the goal instead is exploration of the intricacies of real life.

In any case, as enticing as these two sixth *chakra* possibilities were, I opted for my third choice, an old friend whom I will call Susan – a massage therapist somewhat familiar with the *chakra* system and its application to matters of personal growth and healing.

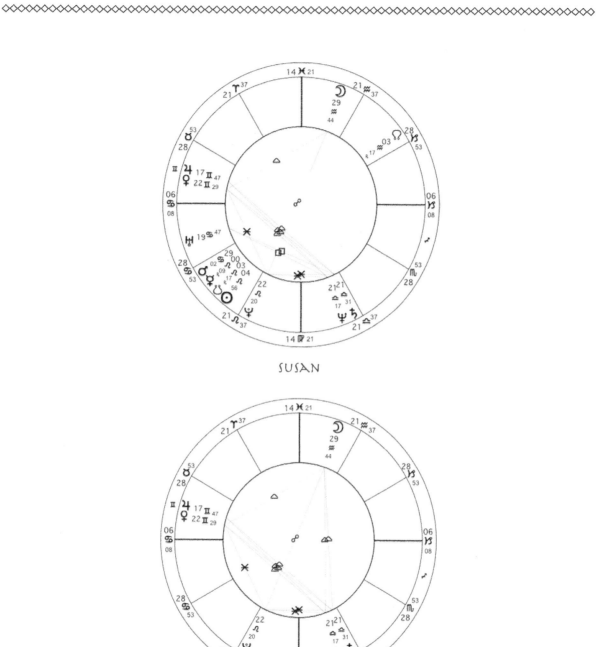

SUSAN

SUSAN'S SIXTH CHAKRA CHART

325

Susan's sixth *chakra* pattern is a half-kite, formed by Moon, Jupiter/Venus and Pluto all in cadent houses. The half-kite becomes a full air kite with the addition of angular Neptune/Saturn trine to Moon and Jupiter/Venus, and sextile Pluto.

Neptune/Saturn in the 4th house will arouse suspicion in the astute reader that a third *chakra* pattern of deficiency might also be a part of Susan's dynamic, particularly if Mars is implicated. As it happens, Susan's Mars is in the 2nd house loosely square to Neptune/Saturn, confirming this suspicion, and further suggesting that for Susan, clarity in the sixth *chakra* will be tied to her third *chakra* issues.

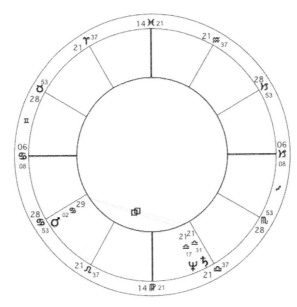

SUSAN'S THIRD CHAKRA DEFICIENCY PATTERN

This is corroborated by an additional observation that her primary sixth *chakra* pattern (the half-kite) lies predominantly in the east (3 of 4 planets) and the south (3 of 4 planets) – sections of astrological space associated with the third *chakra*.

With Jupiter in Gemini (a fire planet) in a water house, Venus in Gemini (an air planet) in a water house, and the Moon (the quintessential water planet) in an air sign and a fire house, there is strong juxtaposition of air and water, and fire and water in this pattern, providing significant openings to penetration by Spirit at the level of both *vijnanamaya* and *anandamaya koshas*. As the reader has no doubt already determined through the examples chosen thus far, whenever these two *koshas* of maximum penetration are implicated in a pattern, the potential is high for spiritual growth through approaching the pattern more consciously.

My Process in Choosing Susan
For My Sixth Chakra Case Study

Ultimately, I chose Susan as my sixth *chakra* case study for three reasons. First, while it is typical in astrological case studies to choose famous people, whose lives are on public display, I prefer to demonstrate that these patterns are also at work in the everyday lives of ordinary people whose personal issues will never register on the Richter scale of our collective attention. Secondly, we also tend to assume that the so-called higher *chakras* must be rigorously activated only in those who are noted for their spiritual achievements. A major premise of this book is the idea that the embodied life is by definition a spiritual adventure, often one that defies our definitions of spirituality, and that by looking at ordinary, everyday life through this lens, we can begin to appreciate just how precious an opportunity the mere fact of our existence in a body actually is. It was my feeling that Susan's life would demonstrate this far more poignantly than that of some public figure or spiritual teacher.

I also chose Susan as my sixth *chakra* case study with the idea that if this system had any validity at all, it ought to apply – not just to obvious examples, where the life in question cried out to be interpreted in a way that fit the profile, but also to cases where the application was less obvious, but the pattern was clear. Though I had done a couple readings for Susan over the years of our friendship, I frankly did not remember them when I found myself contemplating her chart anew in the context of this current project. Nor did I really know enough about her life story to intuit whether or not it would be a fit. But I decided to take the plunge and see what would arise if we explored her pattern together.

My choice was confirmed when I called Susan to propose the idea of interviewing her for my sixth *chakra* case study, and she said, "I'd been thinking about calling you for a reading. I have been feeling a volcano rumbling inside of me lately between my second and third *chakras* and I wanted to take a closer look at what might be going on in my chart." The rumbling volcano was an apt image of an acute eruption of whatever third *chakra* issues might potentially be impacting her sixth *chakra*, although I could see no immediately obvious astrological correlate to her Mars-Neptune/Saturn square. Nor could I be sure that it was her sixth *chakra* that was being impacted by this rumbling.

Despite these uncertainties, I could not help but note the synchronicity between choosing Susan as a suitable sixth *chakra* case study, and her apparently simultaneous interest in working with me. Astrologers are no stranger to the concept of synchronicity, since it is the "meaningful coincidence" (to use Jung's definition) between the movement of the heavens and life on earth that directly informs our art. It is also often the case that clients come to us at auspicious moments, when there is some meaningful coincidence between what happens to be going on in their lives, and our own process. I couldn't help but feel that such was the case with Susan.

The Astro-logic of Susan's Complex Sixth Chakra Process

On the day I called, transiting Neptune had returned for a second pass within one-degree of a trine to Susan's natal Jupiter, hardly the stuff of which erupting volcanoes are astrologically fashioned, but this was a transit that would be triggering her sixth *chakra* pattern in the days ahead. As mentioned earlier in this chapter, Neptune's function within the sixth *chakra* is to precipitate a letting go and a surrender to whatever it is we are resisting, while dissolving the boundaries that keep us separate from each other. It is through allowing Neptune to move us in these fundamental ways that we gradually open to a broader, more liberating perspective that transcends our beliefs and our limiting image of the world.

Here is where Susan's particular pattern connecting the sixth and third *chakras* becomes interesting, since the very same surrender to Neptune required of her in the sixth *chakra* would also potentially aggravate her third *chakra* issues, characterized by a relationship of deficiency between Mars and Neptune. For it is by clearly taking a strong individual stand - not allowing the dissolution of boundaries between self and other - that one is able to exercise the third *chakra* as vehicle for self-actualization. It is by sucking it up and keeping on keeping on - not by surrendering to something with the apparent power to derail us - that a deficient third *chakra* is strengthened.

It would appear then that Susan could either resolve her third *chakra* issues, or open her sixth *chakra*, but not both - entertaining a classic double bind potentially capable of radically shifting her perspective. Since she was on the cusp of a new opportunity to open and clear her sixth *chakra*, this was perhaps the source of the volcanic rumblings (of fearful anticipation) in her third *chakra*. Of course, this is only how it appears from within Susan's spiritual dilemma, while since this was a sixth *chakra* process, the answer would inevitably involve being able to see her predicament differently.

When I told her that I wanted her for my sixth *chakra* case study, she said, "How interesting! I have felt a darkness at my brow for years, and have been unable to move beyond it." I suggested to her then, not having yet noted the current Neptune transits, nor the astrological connection between natal Neptune and Mars, that perhaps there was a connection between the darkness at her brow and the volcano in her gut that we could explore within the context of this sixth *chakra* interview. Perhaps by moving more deeply into her core beliefs, the feelings that were implicated there, and the core issues requiring surrender, allowing the walls she had built up against this darkness to dissolve, there could come a shift in perspective that would allow her third *chakra* deficiency issues a bit more breathing room. At least that was the possibility I decided I wanted to take with me into the heart of our sixth *chakra* interview.

The Interview

Exploring a life in progress in real time within the context of the dynamic associated with a particular *chakra* is necessarily different than patching together quotes from an autobiography or even a journal in order to construct a case study. It is also very different than a traditional astrological reading, in which the goal is to impart information to the client. Though, as mentioned in the introduction to this book, my personal focus remains teaching individuals (including other astrologers) to use the language of astrology to gain perspective on their own lives, I also recognize and honor the noble efforts of the many competent professionals out there on the front line, whose primary intention is to use astrology as a therapeutic tool with their clients. Aside from illuminating the sixth *chakra* within the context of a living case study, it is my intention in the remainder of this chapter, to give a taste of what an astropoetic approach to astrology is like in exploring the pattern related to a given *chakra* dynamic in an actual session.

While a complete transcript of my two-hour phone consultation with Susan would bloat an already very full text, I will quote extensively from our conversation, interspersing comments about our process and about how her words illuminate a sixth *chakra* dynamic at work. In reading this edited session, I invite you to imagine yourself behind a plate glass window, watching me talk to Susan, while I am also simultaneously standing next to you, commenting on what Susan and I are discussing. I start the interview by setting the agenda for the session:

J: *Basically what I want to do with you is explore a pattern in your chart that fits the sixth chakra profile that I've worked out for my book. As you read in the chapters I sent you, the sixth chakra is mostly about belief systems. So what we're going to be looking for here is a belief system that possibly limits you in some way and that maybe seems ripe for transformation. But I really don't know what we're going to find. We'll just look and see what we come up with.*

Unlike a traditional astrology reading, in which the expectation is that I, the astrologer, will be telling you, the client, what your chart means, the astropoetic session is framed as an open-ended dialogue. You will notice as we proceed with this dialogue that I am not speaking astrology to Susan. Susan is not an astrologer, and the vocabulary of astrology is not particularly meaningful to her, so I will confine myself to speaking English.

Before the session, I have used my knowledge of astrology to structure the session around an exploration of the Neptune-Jupiter cycle, which is currently active through transiting Neptune's trine to natal Jupiter. Since Jupiter has the lowest degree number of all the planets in Susan's sixth *chakra* pattern, Neptune's transit to it marks the beginning phases of a potential sixth *chakra* awakening. In the session, I will explore the current transit and three previous periods, during which transiting Neptune brought a similar opportunity through prior Ptolemaic aspects to natal Jupiter. Though I will not speak astrology to Susan, I will use my knowledge of astrology to occasionally steer the dialogue in what I intuitively feel would be a productive direction, ask pertinent questions to draw out more of the story, or help her to see more clearly the pattern that the astrology reveals in conjunction with her story.

Unlike the case studies explored in previous chapters, my interview with Susan will begin in present time and then move backward toward her childhood. In real time, this approach is useful for two reasons: 1) Whatever is going on now is very close to the surface and often ready to be shared; and 2) The farther back in time we go, the fuzzier our memories tend to be. Establishing a context in discussing the more recent periods often acts as a subtle trigger to earlier memories attached to the various themes that are unfolding through the dialogue. As evidence for the validity of this approach, we might note how eager Susan is to take the lead. Though Susan and I have a certain rapport, built through years of intermittent friendship – and this would not always be the case, especially with someone not well known to the astrologer – the astropoetic approach is to let the client talk, while listening with astrological ears.

S: *I just want to say before we start that I think my John of God experience will play a big part in this, as we go back in time or forward in time, however you're going to do this.*

Susan recently completed a trip to Brazil to work with John of God, an indigenous healer, trained in western medicine, but also a channel with a profound and often inexplicable capacity to facilitate miraculous healings that western medicine is powerless to explain.

J: *Actually that was one possibility that had crossed my mind, because...*

S: *...because there's something there, and maybe if you ask me questions, we can unfold something. I'm not very analytical; you know, if it feels right, I go with it. I don't sit and try to figure it out, even though my mind tries to figure lots of things out (laughs).*

J: *And it's not necessarily about trying to figure it out, but on some level of your being, I'm sure being exposed to John of God has opened you up to a whole new realm of possibility.*

S: *Yeah, I do feel like I am, and I feel ready to work on it. You know, I'm more open to possibilities. I find it fascinating that I thought I should look into Reiki at this time, because I pooh-poohed it for so long. I thought maybe people weren't taking it seriously enough. But the reason why I decided to take the Reiki was something I think you had said many many years ago about discovering your own power or energy, you know, going on in your own body. That was the biggest reason why I decided to check into it.... Well now I'm working with this person whom I love... It's wonderful. I mean, I love what this woman's doing. I just love it....*

J: That's great, and this all fits well with what I want to talk about today. Sounds like you are opening up to new possibilities and something within you is beginning to shift. I think as we get into your story, exactly what it is that is shifting will become clearer. So, what I want to look at are four periods of your life that are all connected to each other. You don't have to know the astrology behind it, but these would all be periods of time in which your sixth chakra pattern was being triggered – in the same way that it's being triggered now.

S: Yeah, we did this before a couple of times. I don't remember what the patterns were, but we looked at several periods of turmoil.

J: Yes, I remember. Unfortunately I don't have my notes from those sessions any more. But I think this may be somewhat different, because this is not so much about turmoil as it is about opening up to new possibilities.

S: Oh, ok.

J: Although there is turmoil to the extent that we resist the process of opening, so there may be some of that there. But in terms of the sixth chakra, it's mostly about letting go of limiting beliefs about what's possible, both on a personal level, and probably in terms of your healing practice.

S: Right, ok.

What I'm essentially doing here is describing the impact of Neptune in Aquarius trine Jupiter in Gemini in the 12th house of Susan's chart, without speaking astrology to Susan. I'm not, however, interpreting transiting Neptune trine Jupiter in the sense that I would be if I were reading Susan's chart. I'm simply describing the transit as I hear it being expressed within Susan's opening remarks. "Awakening to new possibilities for healing that involve a deeper awareness of energy" certainly fits the astrological symbolism of the Neptune-Jupiter pattern we are exploring, and that is what I hear Susan talking about as she describes her experiences with John of God and Reiki, so that is how I am choosing to frame the conversation. I am also leaving open the possibility for talking about Susan's resistance to this awakening, or the various belief systems she may or may not have had to work through to get to this place of receptivity, at some other point within her story. But we are launched on a given track in relation to this current Neptune-Jupiter transit, and I am simply acknowledging where we are, based on her input. If instead of her John of God/Reiki experience, Susan began by speaking of her recent shocking discovery (Neptune in Aquarius) that (in the 8th house) she had developed a life-threatening case of cirrhosis of the liver (trine Jupiter), because of a longstanding habit of excessive drinking (in the 12th house) – also a fit to the symbolism – I would frame our conversation very differently.

J: So the first period is happening now. You're in the middle of it.

S: Oh yeah. Yeah.

331

◇◇

J: *It would have started somewhere around March of last year.*

S: *And I went to see John of God in April.*

J: *Ok, so there you go.*

S: *That was perfect, perfect timing, really.*

J: *Good. So why don't you talk a little bit about that. I know we've talked about it before, but I want to get some of this on tape.*

S: *Well, I was planning a trip to Costa Rica with a friend and really looking forward to that, but she ended up canceling. A couple of weeks later, R called me and said that he and W were going to go see John of God in Brazil, and did I want to go. At first I thought I don't really know if that's something for me.*

J: *Why did you think that?*

Here is the first possible hint of resistance, and I feel drawn to explore it.

S: *Well my first reaction was that I wasn't as in touch with the energy as those two were. You know, I don't work in that realm. Well, I actually do, but I was thinking that I don't, ok? My head stuff. I mean I don't sit in mediation. For me, meditation is more going out in nature and hiking . . . So anyway, R suggested that maybe I could suggest another female who would like to go, and I thought well that's kind of fun. So I called J, and she said, "I've been wanting to see him for years!" I said, "You have?" because we had never talked about it. She had heard about him from someone else, and they had brought a crystal back and said how powerful it was. So the more I talked about it, the more I shared that I had been asked to go, I got more excited, more excited, more excited. Then I knew it was the right thing to do. And J was able to go, too, even though she has two kids . . . J again is someone I would say is more out there with her intuition, feeling the energy, and that kind of thing, whereas I'm more touchy-feely, physical. And yet I have connection to energy.*

J: *Ok, so let me just point something out to you before we go on. You have a certain concept about yourself, about who you are and what you're capable of.*

S: *Right.*

J: *So this could be considered a sixth chakra belief.*

S: *Yeah. I agree. So, we go down there, and I say to myself I'm just going to be. I'm not going to judge. I'm going to follow whatever it is that they have as a group that they want. I'm just going to get as much of the experience as I can by allowing the experience to happen. And it was phenomenal for me, because I think out of the four of us, I got the most – I don't know, maybe movement is the right word.*

J: *Movement?*

S: Yeah. The first day there, I got put into surgery. She had physical stuff to deal with like her eyes . . . W was physically disabled, so he just needed a ton of work to get him to even be comfortable in his body. And R went for candida, the bloatedness in his stomach. So those three wanted something physical to happen. I, on the other hand, just said, "If I have any blocks, physical or energetic, can you help me with them?" And I really feel like I was helped. What happened when I came back was there was a feeling of much more self-confidence. I feel like I can express myself better. I'm more comfortable in situations that would have felt uncomfortable before. If I do feel anxiety, I'm able to try not to make it such a big deal, to relax into it. Again that mind thing comes in, but at least I'm asking different questions. And then, the answers that I get – and sometimes they're not even word answers – help me to calm down.

J: So that's quite a shift . . . It sounds to me like being with John of God just put everything into perspective.

S: Yes it did! It really did.

J: And so all the little stuff just doesn't matter. There's so much more going on than that.

S: Yes. Yes there is. So here I am with John of God, and being in mediation, you know, doing the best I can, and I'm just enjoying the heck out of it. I'm loving every minute of it . . . What I came back with was faith. Faith! I have faith now. I don't have to say anything, or even picture it. But I have faith. I can allow, if you want to call it, the universal energy, to flow through me. You know, come from me, as well as come from outside into me. We all have that spark of energy that makes us be able to have the gifts that we have. So that's what I got from that trip.

J: That's major, you know.

S: Yes, yeah.

J: Instead of just doing massage, you're allowing something to happen.

S: Right. And I've always felt like I'm being somewhat responsible, because I'm always learning, and I'm always wanting something to happen for the person, but also learning how to get out of the way, that it's not me at all, and create that space.

Here, with my astrological ears on, I can hear Susan describing what I would call a core issue related to her natal Jupiter-Neptune trine, now being echoed by this current Neptune-Jupiter transit. Neptune is tightly conjunct Saturn in her chart, and both planets trine Jupiter from the 4th house. Saturn trine Jupiter is reflected in her tendency to want to take responsibility for the well-being of other people, in this case, her massage clients. Neptune trine Jupiter is reflected in her desire to "get out of the way" and "create that space" in which healing can take place. "Getting out the way" in order to become an unimpeded channel for Spirit is rightfully understood as the province of the sixth *chakra*, and only occurs when this center is functioning in a place of optimum clarity and maximum penetration. Her concern with taking responsibility for the well-being of others – related astrologically to Saturn in the 4th house – is a third *chakra* concern, and within this apparent dichotomy between taking responsibility and getting out of the way, we can see the particular third *chakra*-sixth *chakra* dynamic we postulated would be in play at the beginning of the chapter.

I don't need to necessarily share this information with Susan at this point in our conversation, but I am curious to see how it will unfold throughout the other periods we will talk about, and how it translates – if it does – into a limiting belief system ripe for transformation. Here, I merely note – in plain English – how this Neptune transit is shifting her toward the Neptunian side of the line across which her Neptune/Saturn-Jupiter dilemma plays itself out.

J: *Well your faith will allow you to get out of the way much more easily.*

S: *Yeah. I've been working toward that for a long time. So we'll see.*

Here she confirms that this is a core issue, and that it is still a work in progress.

J: *Yeah, great!*

S: *You know, your work changes all the time. Even though you're doing the same thing, it's different, because you're different. I'm really enjoying it.*

J: *Well it sounds like a lot is opening up for you right now.*

S: *Yes, and Reiki's perfect.*

J: *Yeah, ok. Well that's basically it! (We both laugh). Yeah, this is exactly what I expected to find, although I didn't know the details.*

S: *Ok, good.*

J: *So is there anything else you want to say about this period. Do you notice any spillover to other areas of your life?*

S: *Well, look what I'm doing. I would have never done this.*

J: *House sitting?*

S: *I would have never house sat.*

J: *How is that a stretch for you?*

S: *Well, it's being responsible for someone else's stuff. And yet I'm a perfect person for it, because what I'm finding is that I do care, and I am making sure that everything is clean, and ok. You know, the place will be pretty close to how it was when they left. And that, I'm sure, for them is like a godsend.*

Here she further elaborates her ambivalence about responsibility, and I begin to suspect that we have uncovered one of the core beliefs that is ripe for shifting – the notion that responsibility is a burden that comes with moving beyond her comfort zone and with growth. I'm extrapolating a bit here, but what we are exploring is part of the sixth *chakra* pattern (reflected astrologically by this ambivalent natal Neptune/Saturn-Jupiter trine, and its time to make a connection between her emerging faith and the possibility for shifting this limiting belief.

J: *Yeah, well you are a conscientious person, so that's not in question. But what is in question is whether or not you'll be able to take on that responsibility. The old you would really rather have not.*

S: *God, yeah.*

J: *But here you are. It's almost like now that you've found your faith, you can relinquish that responsibility. You're not going to be irresponsible. but whatever happens is part of a larger package, and you're just the messenger. You're not the one doing it.*

S: *That's correct.*

It seemed to me that Susan was eager to grow into a more free-flowing expression of her being, which would take her to a higher level of possibility in her healing practice, and have far-reaching implications in other areas of her life. Her recent experiences with John of God and Reiki were facilitating a profound shift in her understanding of what was possible, and through the awakening of faith, she was able to let go of some of her fear of responsibility. Yet there was still something holding her back, some resistance – that rumbling in her third *chakra* noted earlier perhaps – that needed further exploration. I also suspected that the belief system we had partially exposed had roots and tentacles yet to be revealed. It was time to go back in time to the next period of her Neptune-Jupiter cyclical history.

J: *Good. Well I think we have a pretty good idea what's happening now. Let's go back a bit and see what the other stepping stones might have been.*

S: *Ok.*

J: *The next period back would have been January, 1992 – November, 1993, so pretty much all of 92 and 93.*

S: *Oh that's perfect, because that's when I graduated from massage school. I came out here in 91, and I graduated in February of 92.*

J: *Right on schedule.*

S: *That was a whole new life for me. Here I was going to have my – quote-unquote – own business,* because I'd always worked for someone else. Now what I did do – and I do think this was a safer way for me – was I ended up getting a part time job, and that helped me to meet my rent and you know, money stuff. And then I could expand from there with my massage.

J: Well ok, so you were trying to figure out how to do the practice, and make it work on a practical level.

S;   Yes.

J: But what about your actual experience of doing massage, of working on people. What was that like for you?

S: Oh wow. That was just wonderful. Yeah, I loved working on people. My whole life, even when I was in the restaurant business – which seems like another lifetime ago, which will probably come up a little bit – I enjoyed seeing people leave smiling, or feeling good, or that they had the best over-easy eggs that they could get, that whole thing. But that business was just too harsh for someone like myself, sensitive about caring that much. So finding massage was just like – oh man! . . . It did bring up some fear, because here I am thinking I could hurt someone.

J: The responsibility thing again.

Here, we have finally openly identified the pattern. Since it has come up now within two separate periods of the cyclical history we are exploring, it feels safe to give it a name, and to be on the lookout for its presence in subsequent experiences.

S: So I was a little tentative, I believe, as far as feeling and pressure and all that. But I'm much more comfortable with the interaction of one on one, and this was perfect. And to get complimented all the time was also a little hard, at first, because I probably didn't think I was very good. In my mind I was saying I'm still learning, which I mean, even today I'm still learning, so that's great. But I have the confidence of still learning (laughs). The school itself, and that was prior to this time, was such an important thing for me to have gone through . . . And boy, was that something to experience. But yeah – I knew I was going to be doing this for the rest of my life. Even if it grows into energy work or something, it's still going to be that work.

J: Yeah, well this was your foundation.

S: It was perfect. What I said when I was in massage school was I could be a student of this for the rest of my life. . . When that strong of a statement comes up, it's usually true.

J: So you're developing this foundation. And there's still this message about being responsible – "I am responsible for what happens to other people" . . .

S: Yeah . . .

J: . . . which will take a while to work through, though I think you're on the brink of that now. But you can see the core message being worked on here, during this earlier period, in a way.

S; Yes.

J: *And the other thing is you're moving into a whole new venue, and you're developing the confidence to be able to share your gifts with the world. Initially, there's a lot of fear and judgment and holding back, because you don't want to hurt somebody – all that stuff.*

S: *Yes. Yes, yes, yes.*

J: *But you are also stretching out beyond your comfort zone, and pushing the envelope, so from this period in 92 until now, you've moved the boundaries of that comfort zone way way back. So now you can give somebody a good experience, and not have to worry so much about . . .*

S: *. . . I don't worry about it. And now, when I don't feel a connection . . . I can say with great confidence, "We have a lot of different therapists here. You'd be more than welcome to try some other people . . ." And I can do that without worrying about whether I was good or bad, or any of that kind of stuff. So that's really what I've grown into.*

It is becoming clear, in listening to Susan talk about massage school, that one key to being able to relinquish this fear of responsibility is the development of skill and confidence. This is a natural course of development, astrologically associated with Saturn, and understood as a third *chakra* process. But given the connection between Susan's third and sixth *chakra*, we might begin to suspect that some progress in clearing the third *chakra* will be necessary before her sixth can open fully, and that in some way, the development of both *chakras* will unfold in tandem. Susan won't truly be able to "get out of the way" in order to allow Spirit to function more freely through her (a sixth *chakra* attainment) until she is secure in her identity and confident in her abilities (third *chakra* attainments).

It is also clear, however, that as Susan works to cultivate skill and confidence within her third *chakra* during this period in becoming a massage therapist, her sixth is already beginning to awaken. This becomes apparent, as she talks about her experience in massage school.

S: *It was a great time in that sense of working through a lot of my insecurities and lack of self-confidence in the work. But it was by leaps and bounds, because every massage that you did at that point was great . . . The other thing was getting out of my seriousness (giggles), you know going slow, making sure I'm not going to hurt anyone, all that, and just being able to play. That was a big deal then, too. When I gave the massage to my teacher to go into the clinic, she said, "You have a great touch, but I want you just to be able to play." And that was what I came out with. That was what I came out to do.*

J: *Yeah, it's about loosening up and being able to relax into the experience. It's partly about being more confident, which allows you to be able to play....*

S: *Yes.*

◇◇◇

J: . . . and also letting go of that sense of responsibility. As long as you feel like, "I might blow it here," then you get stiff, and you really can't relax, or play, or enjoy it.

S: Right.

The ability to play can be understood as a sixth *chakra* ability, because it necessarily involves forgetting the self that is self-conscious in the third *chakra*, and allowing a more flexible, less rigidly defined, more spontaneous being to take a variety of unpredictable shapes in response to the moment. As long as Susan believes she is responsible, but at the same time, not quite ready to assume that responsibility, her focus will be on shaping and honing her third *chakra* core. Once she develops the confidence to know that core will function reliably, she can relax enough to allow her sixth *chakra* to open. When it does, she becomes more playful, more fluid, more intuitive in her movements – as a therapist and as a human being.

J: There's one more thing I want to look at here, before we move backward. During this period, you were also getting together with R. So were there certain ways in which that relationship was opening you up to new . . . ?

S: Oh God, yes! Everything was opening me up here, Joe. I was really not . . . I don't want to say "aware," but maybe that is the word . . .

J: You'd been living a sheltered life.

S: Yeah. The first lunch we had, he had one of these beautiful macaw feathers . . . that an Indian shaman had given him, and he starts talking about that, and I'm like, "Oh! I know nothing about any of that." Before we got serious serious, we did do a couple of journeys, but it was hard for him to work with me, even from the beginning, because I wasn't visual. And he really likes to work with visual people. So it was a little tough for both of us. But what was nice was when he worked with J, and I sat and watched and listened, and that just opened up a whole new world to me . . .

J: So you got to see how that could work, even though it didn't necessarily work for you.

S: Yeah. And I think even then, I might have been a little hard on myself about that, judgmental about myself. I wasn't too much about judging other people, but I sure could judge myself, because being the perfectionist that I was, I would have thought that. But J and R were very supportive.

J: You were judgmental because you couldn't visualize?

S: Yes.

J: Ok. You thought maybe something was wrong with you, or something.

S: Right.

Susan's judgment about her inability to visualize is particularly interesting in light of the interplay between the third and sixth *chakras* in her chart. The third *chakra* is where we question our abilities, our capacity for living the lives we are living, and facing the challenges we face. The ability to visualize is a capacity specific to the sixth *chakra*, which Susan is being encouraged by life (including her relationship with R) to develop during this period. So here we have a poignant example of how her insecurities in the third were blocking her sixth *chakra*. I am also beginning to suspect that Susan's ambivalence about responsibility is more than just a matter of confidence.

J: Well that's also part of the belief package that you're working through. It's like you're responsible for everything that happens around you, or for the consequences of everything that you do. And then there's this other voice that says, "Well, you may not be good enough to do it."

S; Yes. And there's fear around whether I could do it or not. Yes, definitely.

J: So this is all about working through all of that and getting to different levels of awareness about it.

S; Yes it is.

J: And where you are now, you're becoming almost a transparent vessel, in a way.

S: Well, I hope so. I've been working on that. I want to be. Yeah.

J: It sounds like you're moving in that direction.

S: I do want to be that. and yet . . . boy, I guess the best way to put it is I really can share myself in my work. You know, I may not be able to share myself in an intimate relationship . . . I haven't been quite as successful in that, but . . .

J: Yeah, it's not like you just turn on a switch and you disappear . . . because you are definitely a part of the equation – what you bring to it – your personality, your energy field, your sensitivities, all of that comes into it. It's what makes you the channel that you are. What gets in the way is not any of that, but all the doubts and fears and the lack of confidence and the self-questioning. And that's what it sounds to me like you're slowly beginning to shed here.

S: I am. That's really the most important thing.

This fear that Susan will lose some piece of herself by becoming a transparent vessel (living with an open sixth *chakra*) is a third *chakra* fear. Our strongest sense of identity is rooted in the third *chakra*, and the potential loss of this sense of identity is quite threatening to the fear-based ego. As ego begins evolving toward identification with Spirit, as discussed in Chapter Fourteen, we begin to realize that the opening of the sixth *chakra* that appears to threaten ego is not a loss of identity at all, but actually

◇◇◇

an expansion. Susan is not quite there yet, so I offer her some reassurance. At the same time, I feel confident enough to suggest to Susan that she can have her cake and eat it, too.

J: *Well all this does tie into your core belief. There's almost two things going on at the same time. On the one hand, there's this message that you're not good enough, so you kind of back off from what's possible.*

S: *Yeah, right.*

J: *And on the other hand, you get into this space where you are able to let go, and back off from being responsible. So you're almost doing both things at the same time.*

S;   *What did you say? Being there, but not being responsible?*

The work that Susan and I are doing here involves becoming more conscious of a pattern, which is largely unconscious. This necessarily entails a lot of repetition. For Susan, the process will be a little bit like lucid dreaming, in that she will have moments of clarity, followed by a tendency to fall back into the dream. For me, it is a trial and error process of finding language that resonates with her own inner knowing, which requires saying the same thing over and over again, but using slightly different wording. The more we talk about it, the more intuitive I become about which words to use.

J: *Yeah. Being there means standing firmly in your truth and feeling confident enough to be who you are, in a more active way – on the one hand. And on the other hand, you're stepping back and allowing more.*

S: *Yes.*

J: *So those two things almost sound contradictory, but you're really working on the same thing from both ends of the spectrum.*

S: *Yes, I agree.*

J: *And R was a part of that.*

S: *Yeah, but I just wasn't able to do it. What ended up happening was we triggered each other on those deeper levels, and we weren't able to work it out together. We didn't change. I'm going to say we, because it's always a two-way street. It's never a one-way street. We couldn't change together.*

J: *Well, relationships can be like pressure cookers, and while we're in them often all we can do is try to hold it together. And it seems like nothing's happening, nothing's happening, nothing's happening. But look what happened when you got out of that relationship.*

S: *Oh, it was unbelievable.*

J: You were cooked. So you were ready to move and shake and get some things together.

S: Exactly. And I'll always love him for that. I'll always love that, because it happened. You know?

Here Susan is apparently judging herself for failure in her relationship to R. Even though she calls it a "two-way street," it is clear she is taking responsibility for something she didn't feel she could do. This is her pattern, and I am essentially inviting her to step out of her third *chakra* and experience what happened from the perspective of the sixth. In the third, we struggle to push back the boundaries of our living capacities, and inevitably butt up against our limitations. In the sixth, we are compelled to stop struggling, and experience the grace that is available to us – not because we have proven ourselves worthy, but simply because we are open enough to receive it. Letting go of all our third *chakra* judgments about success or failure is often the first step to such a sixth *chakra* opening.

J: Ok, so if we go back to the next period, that would have been January of 78 to November of 79. Again, it's about a two-year period here. You would have been 24, 25, 26 . . . mid twenties.

S: Oh my goodness. Ooh, that's fascinating. I was out in Los Angeles. That was a really crazy time, because I had been working at a place. They had money, so they were franchising. I was teaching franchisees how to run their stores.

J: Restaurants?

S: Yes. It was a salad bar, make your own soup, make your own quiche, sandwiches place. I thought, "Who am I to be doing this?" Yes, I know this store like the back of my hand, because I became the manager. I had a crew . . . Talk about playing it seriously, I was making sure everybody was doing their job. (laughs). But then what happened was they decided they were going to franchise. In my head, it was like, "Well, I don't think this store makes that kind of money," and also "Who am I to be showing these people how to run their stores?" And there they are, putting their homes up for mortgage. And I didn't feel right about that, because I didn't think they really should have done that.

J: Well, there's a lot of responsibility there, huh?

S: Yes. But I didn't say anything of course, because I was working for these people. What happened was I went and worked for a franchisee.

J: One of the people that were starting up?

S: Yes.

J: I remember you saying before that what you really enjoyed about the restaurant business was being able to leave a smile on the customer's face, when they felt like they had been well served.

341

S: *Yes.*

J: *So in a way, I think you're learning something here about yourself, because helping people to set up restaurants is not your thing, but leaving people with a smile on their face – that is your thing – and serving them well, and experiencing the satisfaction that comes with that. So I think maybe you got that during this period, maybe.*

S: *Well, being of service is really what I'm about.*

J: *Absolutely.*

When Susan says, "being of service is really what I'm about," my astrological ears perk up, because what I hear her describing is her Jupiter in the 12th house, ruling Sagittarius intercepted in her 6th house of service. Beyond her ambivalence about taking responsibility, and beyond her need to cultivate skill and self-confidence before she can take responsibility, is this deeper desire to be of service. Skill, confidence and the capacity to be responsible are the natural evolutionary stepping stones in the development of the third *chakra*, but the desire to be of service is a higher calling than just being able to do a good job. The awakening of this desire depends upon the clarity of the sixth *chakra*, where we begin to understand that however skilled we are at what we do, we are merely playing our part in a larger cosmic drama that transcends our individual contribution. In the sixth, it is no longer just about the individual and her development. It is about what she can contribute to the greater whole. The fact that Susan identifies so strongly with this desire suggests that beyond whatever third *chakra* struggles she must endure, her destination is the awakening of the sixth *chakra*, where she gains not just the competence to do a responsible job, but the inner strength to follow a calling where she can use her skills to be of service.

When Susan talks about wanting to be able to leave a smile on the face of those she serves, I hear her talking about her 12th house Venus conjunct Jupiter. I also hear Susan saying that during this period of her life, her sense of responsibility was being stretched to its limit, probably rebounding later as an awareness that she was being too responsible, and that there was a difference between being responsible and being of service. This awareness would in turn eventually create the opening to the sixth *chakra* that would allow her to get out of the way in order to better serve others as a massage therapist.

S: *You do serve people in the restaurant business. But this was a point in time when I was managing people. I mean it was just crazy, when I think about it. (Laughs).*

J: *Another lifetime, huh?*

S: *I don't even think I could do that now.*

J: *Well, that's like stretching your sense of responsibility way way out there.*

S: Oh God, yes. That was a hard time for me.

J: But on the other hand, here you were doing something that was way out of your league, but you were doing it, and I have no doubt you were doing a good job.

S: I was doing it.

J: So it's also got to be a tremendous confidence builder.

S: Yes it was. I mean people wanted me, and were willing to pay for me.

J: So you could carry that confidence with you later into your massage practice. It would help to serve as . . .

S: Well, it definitely helped me make the trip. It helped me get there certainly, because I came out here not knowing anybody, and just did it. That was one of the few decisions I made in my life, where I knew it was right and nothing was going to stop me. If anybody asked me why I was doing it, I would just look at them and say, "It's because it's what I need to do."

Obviously, learning the restaurant business was a powerful catalyst to development of Susan's third *chakra*, and as she developed her skill and confidence, she was able to assume increasing levels of responsibility. This essentially repeats the pattern we saw at massage school. During this prior period, however, a deeper sixth *chakra* longing began to stir in her, and as she found herself managing and teaching, she became acutely aware of having too much responsibility and too little of the sense of being of service that she craved. By this time, however, she had attained enough clarity in her third *chakra* that she was able to re-invent herself at a higher level of possibility – a change that only becomes possible as the sixth *chakra* is awakened. Ultimately, this awakening precipitated the quest to massage school. She needed a larger venue through which she could further develop her capacity to serve – not just through doing a job with confidence and skill, but also through "getting out of the way" and opening to a sense of play and of Spirit flowing through her.

At this point in our dialogue, we have identified the core belief – that she is responsible for doing a good job, while not really being sure that she can do it. This belief drives her third *chakra* agenda, and tends to dominate and block the opening of her sixth *chakra*. But what is missing from her story so far are the earliest formative experiences that would set such a belief in motion, along with the quest for balance between her third *chakra* and her sixth – the wounding of her soul essence, and the unwounded essence itself that would ultimately become the holy grail of her quest. To reach these experiences, we would have to turn our attention to the earliest station of her Neptune-Jupiter cycle, the waxing quincunx, when she was 10-12 years old.

J: Great. Well, let's just back up and do the last period, and then we'll kind of wrap this up. That would have been . . . when you were . . . 10–12.

S: *That's a time I don't have a really clear picture of. But it's actually become relevant to the Reiki stuff. I'm needing to go back a little bit, around my sister and I.*

J: *What do you mean, "go back around your sister . . . ?"*

S: *Well, I don't know at what age this was, but the first session I had with C—, she said, "My god, you have an awful lot of trauma around the right side of your head and neck and all that." And I had been run over by a car, I'm going to say when I was 7, or something like that. My Mom always had to buy extra milk or bread during the week, when she ran out, because my Dad did the shopping. So we went down to the corner store to get it. I just remember my Mom saying to watch me, to my older sister, who was two years older than me. So when we came to cross the street on the way home, my sister went to grab my hand, and I said, "I can do it myself," and I ran out and got hit by a car.*

J: *Oh, wow!*

On one level, it's pretty amazing that Susan would go immediately to the experience most relevant to the wounding of her sixth *chakra* soul essence. On the other hand, this entire dialogue has been preparation for returning to the earliest memories related to what we're talking about, and I've learned to trust that this is essentially how the process works. The astrological cycles somehow serve as tracks along which related memories are stored, and as we follow these tracks, our minds tend to gravitate toward experiences that illuminate the life lessons encompassed by the symbolism.

Of course, technically speaking, this event was not part of the Neptune-Jupiter cycle we are tracking. But it was clearly a key moment in the development of the sixth *chakra* belief that she is responsible for that which she is not sure she can do. After determining that the accident probably occurred during the spring or summer of the year Susan was 7, I was able to see that transiting Uranus was conjunct her natal Pluto at the time. This was also a potent trigger to her sixth *chakra* pattern, which involves natal Pluto as well as Moon, Venus and Jupiter.

I suspected that before this moment, Susan believed she could do anything, as many children tend to do, and the accident threw this belief into a state of cathartic suspension. She would then spend the next 22 years or so, working her way back to sense that she could in fact do quite a bit. Astrologically, transiting Uranus squared her natal Pluto at the same time that transiting Neptune was opposing her natal Jupiter (encompassing the period during which she was reaching the end of her involvement in the restaurant business, as discussed earlier). I didn't know all this until after the session, but I did want to at least explore the connection between Susan's accident and her limiting sixth chakra belief system.

J: *The fact that this happened at 7 doesn't seem to fit the cycle immediately, but it seems related to what we're talking about, because here you are at age 7, and you say, "I can do it myself," and wham, you get hit by a car. The message is, "Oh no you can't." Obviously, this must have completely changed your worldview.*

S; *Oh boy. It's hard to know, because some of the shamanic work I've had done says I was pretty good up to 3 or 4. Then something happened, which I don't remember. But you know, prior to that, I think I was in pretty good shape, not being so withdrawn.*

J: *Prior to 3 or 4, or prior to 7?*

S: *Well, I'm going to say prior to the accident, because I don't really remember anything else before that time.*

With this admission, Susan appears to fit the pattern we have observed with each of the case studies in this book so far – that something significant seems to happen at about age 3 or 4, which constitutes a major wounding of soul essence.

J: *I'll just mention that from my work with astrology, and especially in relation to this association with the chakra system that I'm developing, that is actually pretty common. I'm starting to realize that around 3 or 4 is usually – not always, but usually – when we get wounded. That's when the primal wound takes place.*

S: *I'll be darned.*

J: *Yeah. It's mostly unconscious and almost preverbal. I mean we're talking at that age, but I don't think we have words or concepts for what's happening. So it doesn't register on a conscious level. It's more of a subliminal thing. Whatever happened between 3 or 4 is probably lodged in your body on a cellular level, and I don't know if you've ever tried to get to it that way, but . . .*

S: *No, I haven't.*

J: *Well, it might be something worth exploring.*

S: *I can imagine, just as you're talking about this, that here you are as a kid, just wanting to experiment and play, and I probably got shot down, you know. It doesn't have to be with my parents. It could be my brother, sister, anything like that. And it probably just forced me to go inward, because . . .*

J: *Well it's probably an earlier version of the message you got with the accident that you can't do it by yourself . . .*

It is also possible to imagine that whatever happened at 3 or 4 shut down Susan's sixth *chakra*, and shunted the energy into her third. As mentioned earlier, the ability to "experiment and play" is a by-product of a sixth *chakra* that is functioning at its optimum level, while "going inward" implies a retreat from this experimental, playful way of being, to a safer, more circumscribed comfort zone marked by regularity, predictability, and routine.

S: On the outside I was this happy, nice kid, running around, but on the inside I was so unhappy, and always crying in my bedroom and that kind of thing.

J: What were you unhappy about?

S: I think it was because I couldn't connect with anybody. I didn't feel like I was being loved by my parents. I didn't have any connection with my brothers and sister. I did feel that I was alone, and I knew there was more. Because I was unhappy and nobody asked me why I was unhappy, I struggled with my parents not really knowing who I was, because they couldn't come out of their own comfort zone. I'm saying that in hindsight, but as a kid, what the hell do I know? But I always thought that they didn't know who I was.

J: Yeah, they didn't know who you were, and you didn't know who you were. (We both laugh). You wanted somebody to recognize you, but you weren't even able to recognize yourself yet.

S: That's true.

Both Susan's parents modeled life safely inside the circumscribed comfort zone. With Uranus in her 1st house, Susan is clearly someone who is ready to experiment and play, and embrace the kind of inherent flexibility of being that is available to her when her sixth *chakra* is opening and functioning at its optimal level. But she got no encouragement for this as a child (Saturn/Neptune square Uranus), and learned to shut down this part of her as a matter of survival.

S: And here's my father, who doesn't want anybody to touch anything, doesn't want anybody to try anything new. If you say something he doesn't . . . understand, he just bellows. Any time you opened your mouth to say anything different, you got slammed. So here you are as a young kid . . . and I see that with my nephew, who just . . . this kid is phenomenal, and he actually can take my Dad on. He doesn't take my Dad seriously. And I just love it. You know, I don't see him cowering, like we probably did. You know, my Dad may not be as strong, because he was younger then, so he has mellowed. But you can see through him a lot easier than when we were young and dealing with it.

J: So, basically any time you tried to spread your wings a little bit, you got the belt or some version of that.

S: Right. Yeah, or verbal abuse. But at least you knew what you were getting from him, which was actually, you never knew what he was going to be like (laughs) – whether he was going to be nice or he was going to be angry. With my mother, you wanted to kick her, just to see if she would do anything . . . There was a period of time – and again, I don't remember exactly when it was, though it was probably around that time of 10-12 – when I hated my mother, because I didn't think she was an individual. I didn't think she had any thoughts or did anything that she wanted to do. And that is something that I grew up with, because I didn't do anything that

I wanted to do for a long time. But I can remember specifically thinking that she was a robot, and that I just didn't like her, that I hated her actually.

Here, we're back on track – back within the cycle being covered, unexpectedly introducing Susan's mother into the dialogue. I note that Susan's unpredictable alcoholic father was probably the clearest embodiment of her 4th house Neptune/Saturn conjunction square Uranus. But I also note that her 9th house Aquarian Moon is more directly related to the sixth *chakra* pattern we are exploring and through its placement in the 9th house (where belief systems are often lodged), speculate that it probably lies at the root of her earliest messages about what she could and could not do – the limiting sixth *chakra* belief system she is struggling to transmute. Since Moon typically (though not always) = mother, this seems like a potentially fruitful path to take.

J: *So that message that you got during the accident, which was basically, "I can't do it myself" haunted you probably until your 20s, when you got into the restaurant business and realized yeah, you could do it. But I'm guessing that was also the message you got from your mother because that was the way she was relating to her own life. Is that true?*

S: *Yes. She told me when I moved out of the house when I was 17, she couldn't believe I was living on my own, and she could never do it, because she needed the security . . . Yeah, that was the message that I got, which is interesting, because I didn't see it like that.*

J: *Yeah, you were rebelling against your mother's projection onto you, but at the same time, unconsciously you probably bought into it, and then had to work your way through it.*

S: *Hook, line and sinker, yeah. It's amazing how we think want to be so different than our parents, and we end up having all that stuff, you know.*

J: *Well, we're taking it in by osmosis. Consciously, we're pushing them away, but we're so permeable at that age, that we really don't have a choice. We just take it on.*

By now, we have a pretty good idea of the belief system in need of transmutation before Susan's sixth *chakra* could function at its optimum efficiency. We also have both a specific incident and the general background atmosphere that contributed to this belief system. There was one additional piece of information yet to be revealed, however, that would bring her pattern into even sharper relief.

Throughout my interview with Susan, she kept returning to the subject of relationship. Already mentioned was her relationship with R, who was instrumental in her awakening, but also a pivotal point around which residual feelings of failure perhaps continued to revolve. There was also a relationship to a man in Los Angeles, during her restaurant days, who continually borrowed money from Susan, and essentially used her to enable his various addictions.

347

With my astrological ears on, I could hear her talking about the difficulties posed by her natal Saturn/Neptune square Uranus, with Saturn ruling her 7th house of intimate relationships. That a Neptune-Jupiter cycle should evoke these memories was not surprising, since these same Neptune transits to Jupiter we were tracking would also trigger her Saturn/Neptune-Uranus square. Neptune/Saturn did impact her sixth *chakra* half-kite pattern through its completion of a full air kite, but I still didn't quite understand how her relationships tied into this limiting belief system about what she could and could not do, and what she was or was not responsible for. In terms of her relationship, we spoke of boundary issues, but how the boundary issues she experienced in relationship impacted her beliefs about responsibility and capability was not at all clear. Quite graciously, Susan voluntarily filled in this missing piece of the puzzle with no prompting from me.

S: *The other thing that I can say about this time is that my mother was having an affair with this slimeball of a guy. My sister, younger brother and I would go over this guy's house, watch tv, smoke cigarettes. He'd give us money. If we kissed him, he'd give us a quarter or something like that. My sister was abused by him. For some reason, I can see my younger brother being abused also. It doesn't mean I was or wasn't.*

J: *So you think you were possibly abused by this guy, but don't remember?*

S: *I may not have been abused sexually like she was, but I was certainly emotionally abused, you know, with the kissy stuff and all that. But then I don't think I was too young for him either, because he ended up getting arrested for being a pedophile, which is why I say "slimeball." My sister says, "You never went there by yourself. You always went with me or G." And I said, "really," because see, I don't remember. She goes, "Yeah for some reason, you just didn't . . ." But of course, she went all the time when he was, you know . . . I don't know if they actually had sex, but he was certainly fondling her, and doing all kinds of stuff to her. When she approached my Mom about it, my Mom didn't believe her, and I was there at the time. My poor sister – that was just enough to put her over the edge.*

J: *So you think this might have been happening when you were 10 or 11?*

S: *Yeah, I think it would have been 10 or 11. But I don't have the exact time. It might be important for me to figure that out.*

J: *Well no. Just the fact that it's coming up suggests that it's probably related . . .*

S: *It's one of the few things I remember with my sister. And it's one of the sad things I remember. Here we all were, so much into our shells . . . you know, G was probably there, and he was on the couch with her, and we weren't even thinking that anything was going on. And even if we did, it didn't seem wrong or something, you know? I mean it's just weird.*

J: *Well you were an innocent kid . . .*

S: *I know, I know, I know. Even then we were all so much into our own selves that it was really tough for us to feel for anybody else. We were all there to survive in that environment, you know? We didn't bond with one another, which I think is sad. So we were pretty much on our own then. (Laughs). I was pretty much on my own . . .*

J: *The good news is that you developed a sense of self-reliance out of that.*

S: *Yeah.*

J: *You can do it on your own. But probably in terms of relationship, it's a lot harder, because you'll always be wondering, "Can I trust this person?" Again, it goes back to that boundary thing, you know. Where is the line? When you're 10, you're totally oblivious that there's a line there until you've already crossed it.*

S: *Yeah.*

J: *But then as you grow older, of course, you become more aware of it, and make more of a choice about it. But still, you had to go through that other relationship in Los Angeles, and then get to R, where it probably wasn't that much of an issue.*

S: *Right. But it was there.*

J: *Yeah?*

S: *Yeah it was, for me.*

J: *In terms of letting him making all the decisions and set the agenda . . .*

S: *Also the intimacy thing, of letting him in. That was a big part of it.*

J: *Yeah, so whatever this slimeball did or didn't do to you back at age 10 . . .*

S: *Yeah, exactly (laughs).*

J: *. . . probably somehow plays a part in that, I would guess.*

S: *Yes it does. It really does. But maybe that situation was there for me to get that first hit of the sixth chakra, because again I do picture myself as being in a protective shell, just to be able to survive in that environment. So it makes me think that there was something, maybe not with slimeball, but the interaction thing . . .*

J: *One thing we've talked about from time to time is learning how to trust your intuition. Well intuition is very much sixth chakra, and this is the opening of your sixth chakra. So you're in a place here where you better start trusting it or you're going to be in trouble.*

S: *Yes.*

J: *And I don't know if it actually dawned on you then, but I'm guessing that it did, sometime during this period. Because if you weren't going there by yourself . . .*

S; *Right.*

◇◇

J: Plus here you are. It's only 3 or 4 years after this accident. So you're kind of adjusting to that. You're wanting to get back to the place where you can say, "Yeah, I can do it myself."

S: Right, right, right.

J: So when you're in that vulnerable place of saying, "Well I don't know if I can do it or not," you become vulnerable to other people saying, "Well, here. Let me do it for you."

S: Right.

J: "And this is what I want you to do for me."

S: Oh boy, yeah.

J: See how that works?

S: Yes I do.

J: And where slimeball comes into it is probably in forcing you to look at that and say, "Yeah, well how much am I willing to do to get his help?" whatever help he could or couldn't provide, you didn't know. But you had to back off and say, "Well maybe I can do it myself. Maybe I have to do it myself. Maybe my life, my survival, my sanity depend on it."

S: Yeah.

J: "Maybe I have more to lose here than . . ."

S: Maybe I did know that he was not good. Maybe I didn't go by myself. But I allowed it to happen to my brother and sister.

J: Ok, well there's that responsibility thing again. They're making their own choices.

S: I know.

J: Are you really responsible for that? Especially at age 10 or 11.

S: Right.

J: But see all these questions are coming up, one way or the other.

S: Yeah.

What becomes apparent at this point is that Susan is not clear, even now, where the boundaries are in relation to her responsibilities and her capacity to respond. "What am I responsible for?" and "What is within my power to do?" are questions that – for her – have no clear or definitive answers. When she stays within her comfort zone, where she feels skilled and confident in her skills, she can relax a bit, and allow a more intuitive, experimental, playful flow of energy to flow through her sixth *chakra*. But when she crosses the line, outside of her comfort zone, often without knowing she has crossed the line, these primal questions are reawakened on some level of her being. As long as she believes, "I am responsible" at the same time that the thought that maybe "I can't do it by myself" is triggered by an awareness of being outside of her comfort zone, she will tend to feel an ancient rumbling in her third *chakra* and a dark cloud at the sixth.

Beyond the dark could is the possibility of trusting and of getting out of her own way enough to feel a certain grace and buoyancy more powerful than anything she could conjure for herself. The opening to this place of grace and buoyancy seems to lie in the faith that has begun to awaken in Susan as a consequence of her work with John of God, but it must also involve becoming more aware whenever she attempts to take responsibility for something that she is not rightfully responsible for or that transcends the reach of her personal power. With faith comes the possibility of taking a deep breath and simply allowing, even when it appears she is in some situation way over her head.

This possibility would not exist, of course, had she not already experienced at a deep cellular level, every bit as powerfully as the wounding brought about by her accident at age 7, and whatever happened at age 3 or 4. This, of course, is by now the familiar unwounded soul essence we have sought as the holy grail of images within every *chakra* pattern story we have explored. Susan's was no different, as evidenced by the following exchange at the end of our interview:

J: *What I want to ask you now is if you can remember what it was like before you shut down, when you were this happy kid and you were still unwounded. Do you have an image of that?*

S: *(Long silence). You know, again, it just all points back to playing outside. I can't express to you how important it was that we had a field to play in and woods. We had a park that we could go to, and I used to climb the trees in the park.*

J: *Yeah, climbing the trees in the park. That's an image. Can you remember climbing a tree?*

S: *Oh God yes. Because the tree felt alive, you know.*

J: *And how did you feel?*

S: *Oh, I felt great. I climbed high high high high. I don't know that I could even do that now. I'd be a little nervous doing it now. But you know, I'd be up high in the tree, and the wind would be blowing it, and I'd be hanging on. I felt safe. I didn't feel any fear.*

J: *That's kind of the ultimate experience of "I can do it," isn't it?*

S: *Yeah, I know. One of my biggest memories is being up in this one tree – I think I even put my initials in it – just swaying with the wind and holding on.*

J: *Yeah, that's cool.*

S: *Yeah, it is cool. That's something I won't forget actually.*

J: *Well, that's you.*

S: But those memories are few and far between.

J: Yeah, but that's you. That's an image of your essence, there, you know.

S: Yes. Yes it is.

It never ceases to amaze me how the images that we choose consciously or unconsciously to reflect our soul essence seemingly match the *chakra* patterns through which we are challenged to work toward restoration and healing. Aside from being the ultimate image of Susan's can-do spirit, the act of climbing a tall tree was, in ancient times, one kind of shamanic initiation. The world tree in Nordic mythology, Yggdrasil, from which Odin hung – which we spoke of in Chapter Twenty One with regard to Pluto's role in sixth *chakra* patterns – is a classic example of this quest for awakening of the third eye.

With branches that pierce the highest sky, and roots that penetrate to the bowels of the underworld, the living tree is a connecting link between the embodied world in which we live and the numinous world of essence, where everything visible is merely the container for an Invisible Force or Spirit that fills the embodied world with Its Presence. In the ethereal, yet grounded realm of the tree, it is possible to commune with that Invisible Force, while still in the body. This is the experience that shamans like Odin sought, so that they could gain the freedom to return along any spoke of the wheel they chose – moving freely from the body to the Source and back again, not merely waiting for death to recycle them, but intentionally evoking the experience of self-re-creation.

Visionary Ozarks author, Ken Carey tells of one such experience, sitting in top of a sixty-foot oak in the middle of a thunderstorm (55):

> Lightning flashes, thunder cracks, and in an instant the world I saw so recently in majestic springtime bloom appears dark, hideous. In the cold rain that follows, my mind contracts, but the image remains. I see a forest identical to the one I know and love, interpreted grotesquely somehow, as if in caricature. The image is so compelling that my fear, whatever merit it may or may not possess, seems suddenly of less relevance than the question of how this profound interpretive difference occurs.

Carey's answer to this question, drawn from that deeper place inside of him where all secret runic languages are revealed, was the essence of sixth *chakra* wisdom:

> How you understand yourself determines what you see; it determines your reality.

Most of us believe ourselves to be who we are, and the world to be what it is, because of our experiences. Many of us go through life, never questioning these experiences, nor the beliefs to which we are bound by them. But where a sixth *chakra* pattern dominates our chart, we will be compelled, perhaps despite ourselves, to climb the world tree for a broader view that puts our core beliefs into perspective.

In her own way, Susan has spent her entire life climbing such a tree. In its branches – far beyond her questions about the boundary between responsibility and getting out of the way, or between being able to do and being able to open to the grace that transcends doing – lies a great mystery, the immersion in which makes possible an intuitive fusion, where the questions, indeed all possible questions, dissolve. This is the knowing – beyond all belief – that Susan and other children of the sixth *chakra* are seeking.

Chapter Twenty-Three
The Seventh Chakra Chart

At the highest possible level, the seventh *chakra* chart is something of an oxymoron. When the seventh *chakra* is open, clear and fully functional, everything that we have identified as ours - including our birthchart - is realized to be nothing more than the proverbial finger pointing at the Moon. Or to be more accurate, it is the finger pointing at That Which Does Not Have a Name. Who we become once we have passed through the portal of an open seventh *chakra* is hinted at by the popular Sanskrit *mantra* known as the Heart Sutra: *Gate, Gate, Paragate, Parasamgate, Bodhi Svaha!* – translated roughly as Gone, Gone, Gone Beyond, Gone Beyond Beyond, Hail the Goer! Once the Goer has gone, the birthchart is rendered as useless as the molted skin of a snake.

When some astrologers speak of "transcending the birthchart," they are - knowingly or unknowingly - referring to the movement through the seventh *chakra* beyond the embodied realm to which the birthchart refers. All of us move beyond this realm at death, but whether or not we transcend our birthchart in passing is dependent on more than the mere shedding of our bodies. Most of us - even the most conscientious among us – will have failed to fully actualize our potential, and humbled ourselves before challenges that remain unmet, issues that remain unresolved, and obstacles we could not overcome. Time will erase the memory of most of our proudest achievements, and our birthcharts will remain only as silent testimony to a dream that was once taken to be real. Perhaps, if we do live more than one life, the chart will serve as the template for the seed of some future existence, and we will experience the same patterns - or some mutated variation of them – again.

In any case, from the perspective of the Goer, gone beyond consciously or not, the birthchart - transcended or not - does not mean anything at all. Others may ponder it, particularly if its former inhabitant was famous, and astrologers routinely do paw through the charts of the famous dead for clues that will help them understand the language of astrology as it applies to the living. But where we are going when we pass through the portal of the seventh *chakra*, the birthchart can no longer serve as a guide. In this sense, the seventh *chakra* chart is merely a description of the portal, above which is chiseled, "The Goer has left the building."

There is, however, another sense in which the seventh *chakra* chart can be useful, for the portal is both exit and entrance. As discussed in Chapter Seven, it is the opening through which Spirit infuses this life with its presence, and through which we become conscious of its handiwork within every detail of our experience. On this side of the Great

Beyond, the seventh *chakra* chart describes our capacity for this awareness, the kinds of experiences that will trigger it, and the cyclical time frame for the opening of the portal between this ordinary life and the realm of Spirit.

Those with strong seventh *chakra* charts will have the opportunity to move through the portal on a regular basis, and be hailed – within their sphere of influence – as mystics, poets, madmen, and geniuses whose contribution seems born of some other-worldly message. The rest of us will experience these same openings, albeit on a less dramatic scale, when the planetary alignments are right – that is to say, when transiting or progressed planets complete or amplify our relatively weak seventh *chakra* charts in real time. In such moments, the opportunity will exist to witness first-hand, the orchestration of our embodied lives from a place of Higher Intelligence that exists within us, but also transcends our limited capacity. We will see how the parts fit together to form the seamless whole fabric of this embodied world we are dreaming, and the source code behind the dream will become transparent for those with the eyes to see. Far from being useless, on this level, the seventh *chakra* chart becomes the key to understanding the other six *chakra* charts from their most enlightened perspective.

The Placement of Seventh Chakra Planets in Astrological Space

The astute reader will have observed a progression through the *chakras* toward an increasingly looser assignment of *chakra* patterns to segments of astrological space. The first four *chakras* tend to exhibit definite preferences for specific hemispheres, angles, quadrants and/or type of house (angular, succedent or cadent). Fifth and sixth *chakra* patterns also tend to gravitate toward specific areas, but with less regularity or reliability. Seventh *chakra* patterns can be anywhere, but by definition, they will cross boundaries and tie together opposite segments of the birthchart: southern hemisphere with northern; east with west; at least three of four quadrants; and angular, succedent and mutable houses. To some extent, any astrological pattern will do this, but it is the function of the true seventh *chakra* pattern to integrate parts into a seamlessly functioning whole, and any seventh *chakra* pattern worth its name will exhibit strong cross-category flavor.

There are two primary axes along which the integrative function of seventh *chakra* patterns takes place – represented astrologically by the horizon and the meridian of the birthchart. Along the meridian, or vertical axis, the integration is between heaven and earth – that is to say, between the divine will of Spirit, and the soul, which at the level of the seventh *chakra*, is the agent for the implementation of divine will. When planets involved in a seventh *chakra* pattern span the meridian or are relatively close to it (in the 9th, 10th, 3rd, and 4th houses), the soul will be called to a life of transpersonal surrender,

◇◇◇

gradually becoming a transparent vessel through which Spirit can function unimpeded by the resistance of a separate ego. There is no guarantee that such a lofty goal will be achieved, but when a seventh *chakra* pattern spans the meridian, the internal psychic pressure will be there, and ultimately, "resistance will be futile."

The second integrative function of the seventh *chakra* takes place along the horizon of the birthchart. Here the goal is Jung's *hieros gamos*, in which all opposites fuse into a seamless, integrated unity of expression. As discussed in Chapter Two, the experience of *hieros gamos* first becomes available to the soul within the second *chakra*, when that *chakra* has been penetrated to the level of *anandamaya kosha*. When this happens, the individual is no longer attached to a preference for hot instead of cold, no longer bound to cling to the light while pushing darkness away, nor so tightly identified with physical gender that she cannot embrace attributes, skills and predispositions of the opposite gender with equal facility. In the fourth *chakra*, the quest toward *hieros gamos* gets played out on the field of intimate relationships, where the soul learns to embody everything projected onto the partner, resulting in another evolutionary step toward integration and wholeness. This process is completed and taken to its penultimate expression in the seventh *chakra*, where the boundary between life and death itself proves to be illusion, and true immortality is attained.

Since every seventh *chakra* process is both horizontal and vertical by definition, immortality is made possible because the boundary between the individual soul and Spirit out of which all souls are endlessly recycled also ceases to exist. Through whatever seventh *chakra* process is initiated through the astrological pattern that describes it, the individual soul grows to identify less with the small identity of ego and increasingly with the generative power of the Source, which is unborn and undying.

Jung referred to this dimension of the *hieros gamos* as rejuvenation magic (Symbols 243-244), associating it with the cult legend of Samian Hera, in which Zeus had a "long-drawn-out clandestine love-affair" with Hera, his own wife. Zeus would kidnap Hera, and take her to a cave on Mount Cithearon, where they would fuse in the white heat of their cosmic passion, beyond the scrutiny of deity or mortal. In some variations of the myth, Hera would then bathe in the fountain of Kanathos, and become a virgin once again, at which point, the cycle would start over. In a sense, each of us is similarly kidnapped by Spirit and hidden in the cave of a mortal body, where we are ravished through the process of embodied life. In death, we return to the Fountain, where all is made new once again. Through the process of *hieros gamos* in the seventh *chakra*, we become Ravisher as well as ravished, Fountain as well as bather in the Fountain, and the dichotomies that make the myth so compelling to us on this side of that experience, collapse into Unity.

When the integrative function of the *hieros gamos* has done its work within the seventh *chakra*, the soul becomes thoroughly infused with Spirit, and a source of regenerative magic for anyone or anything drawn within its aura. That which needs to die, falls away, while that which is ready to be reborn, emerges from its gestation vibrantly renewed and ready for life. The soul also becomes the source of its own rejuvenation.

I saw this clearly in my work with Yogi Bhajan, who among his many other talents, served as a *Mahatantric* Master. Several times a year, he would sit before a gathering of hundreds of couples, guiding them through various meditations and exercises designed to channel the potent sexual polarity between male and female as an integrative agent, cleansing and fusing psychic disparities in the participants, and accelerating their spiritual growth. There is no way to adequately describe what happened during these sessions, other than to note a burning intensity that we were trained to associate with an activated *kundalini*, and that our lives were changed – sometimes radically – in retrospect. Through the entire process, Yogi Bhajan served as a psychic filter, channeling the astral flotsam and jetsam of his students through his own body, and sending it back out as purified energy. Doing this took a tremendous toll on Yogi Bhajan, who visibly aged ten years through the weekend-long ordeal, and often had to be helped from the podium when it was over. He would then typically disappear for a time, and return to continue serving us in some other capacity, completely restored and apparently at full vitality. In retrospect, I can easily see this power of self-rejuvenation as a by-product of an open and integrated seventh *chakra*.

The Soli-Lunar Dance and Seventh Chakra Dynamics

While a seventh *chakra* chart can occupy any section of astrological space, it must have a Sun-Moon aspect as its base, since the relationship between these two planets – more than any other astrological factor – symbolizes the seventh *chakra* process of integration, in both its vertical and horizontal dimensions. The Sun has long been associated with Spirit, at least in the West – since Egyptians identified it with the immortal Sun god, Osiris in the Pyramid Texts (c 2375 – 2200 BCE). In the 16th century, when Copernicus startled the world by proving that the Sun and not the Earth was at the center of the solar system, he took great spiritual delight at restoring God to His rightful place in the grand scheme of things. A century later, fired up by a vision of the Sun as the central image of God, Kepler worked out the "harmony of the spheres" on a mathematical basis.

Far more ancient still than these associations of Sun with Spirit are associations of Moon with embodied life on Earth. In 1965, archeologist Alexander Marshack analyzed the notches on a small carved figurine of a woman holding a crescent horn with 13 strokes (13 is the number of lunar cycles per year), dated from the Aurignacian period (c. 25,000 BCE), and determined them to be an early notational system for tracking the Moon in her cyclical motion (Cashford 16-17). A second artifact dated about 5,000 years later also refers to the Moon and seems to tie the lunar cycle with the feminine power of fertility and with the fertility of the Earth (20). Through thousands of years subsequent to these artifacts, the Moon was worshipped by matriarchal cultures around the world as the divine embodiment of the rhythms and life cycles of the embodied experience, governing birth and death and all organic evolution in between.

Within the astrological relationship between Sun and Moon, these two principles: the eternal, celestial, transcendent solar principle, and the cyclical, terrestrial, immanent lunar principle come together in a way that mirrors the inhabitation of physical form by Spirit that produces conscious life. On the deepest possible level of interpretation, the soli-lunar relationship symbolizes the basic experience of embodiment, discussed at length in *The Seven Gates of Soul* as the soul itself. On the level of the seventh *chakra*, these two planets together make possible the alchemical magic of vertical integration, particularly when they participate together in a larger seventh *chakra* pattern.

Given that the Sun and Moon are primary symbols for male and female, and the Sun is considered hot and dry, while the Moon is cool and moist, they also encompass the entire realm of polar opposites seeking horizontal integration within the *hieros gamos*. This is evidenced in a primordial lineage of paired deities: Osiris and Isis, Innana and Dumuzi, Ishtar and Tammuz, Uranus and Gaia, Cronus and Rhea, Shiva and Shakti, perpetually involved in a divine enactment of the quest toward integration of solar and lunar principles that underlies every human endeavor.

In the West, the Sun is generally considered to be masculine and the Moon feminine, but it should be noted here that this has not always been the case. The Moon was traditionally considered to be masculine in all Indo-European, Teutonic, and Semitic languages and among various peoples speaking these languages – including the Basques, Germans, Scandinavians, Hindus, Japanese, New Guineans, Australian aborigines, Eskimos, North American Indians of British Columbia, and many African tribes, to name just a few. Usually, though not always, whenever the Moon was masculine, the Sun was feminine. The Moon was feminine, and the Sun masculine among the Greeks, whose culture subsequently formed the bedrock of Western civilization (Cashford 151-152). Regardless of gender assignments, however, it is clear that at the level of the seventh *chakra*, we are moving toward a transcendence of gender that involves their synthesis. What Joseph Campbell says about pagan culture in the following quote (Occidental 163-164), can be understood to apply to the fusion of Sun and Moon, female and male, in the *hieros gamos* of the seventh *chakra*:

> A fundamental idea of all the pagan religious disciplines, both of the Orient and of the Occident. . . was that the inward turning of the mind (symbolized by the sunset) should culminate in a realization of an identity in esse of the individual (microcosm) and the universe (macrocosm), which, when achieved, would bring together in one order of act and realization the principles of

eternity and time, sun and moon, male and female, Hermes and Aphrodite (Hermaphroditus), and the two serpents of the caduceus. The image of the "Meeting of Sun and Moon" is everywhere symbolic of this instant.

Campbell goes on to remind us that in the Eastern *yogic* traditions, out of which our *chakric* model arises, it was the fusion of Sun and Moon through a specific exercise of *pranayama* (breath control) that effected the *hieros gamos* and the fusion of microcosm and macrocosm on a physiological level. By alternately breathing through the left and right nostrils, respectively governing a lunar channel called *ida* and a solar channel called *pingala*, a central channel called *sushumna* is opened through which *kundalini* can flow. This experience that marked the holy grail of *yogic* practice, for it lead to both vertical and horizontal integration within the seventh *chakra*. Yogi Bhajan taught this exercise as one of the most basic upon which all of *kundalini yoga* depended.

The Full Moon and Seventh Chakra Awakening

Because of these ancient associations, the seventh *chakra* chart is built upon an aspect between Sun and Moon[1]. While any aspect between Sun and Moon can serve as the platform for a seventh *chakra* pattern – when forming a larger planetary pattern with other seventh *chakra* planets – by far, the most integrative aspect and most potent opening to the seventh chakra is found in the opposition between Sun and Moon, more commonly known as the Full Moon. Technically speaking, the Full Moon is not a lunar phenomena; it is a depiction of the relationship between Sun and Moon at its most polarized arrangement (each on opposite sides of the Earth). Paradoxically, this extreme polarization creates the most potent impetus toward integration, because like a rubber band stretched to its optimum resiliency, the opposition produces accelerated momentum back toward the center.

Among many indigenous and traditional cultures, the Full Moon was a time of celebration, particularly well suited to marriages of both deities and humans (Cashford 60-61) – an historical fact that mirrors the symbolic depiction of *hieros gamos* by the Full Moon. Of course, marriage is more rightly understood as the province of the fourth *chakra*, where the possibility of *hieros gamos* is first encountered. Here the process takes place primarily on the level of *manomaya kosha*, where a truly satisfying intimate relationship requires each partner to work toward a certain level of healing and psychological integration with themselves. In particular, each partner must take back whatever they have projected onto the partner through the dance of anima and animus, as described by Jung.

At the level of the seventh *chakra*, the same dynamic is intensified through the addition of the vertical dimension, through which the partner essentially becomes Spirit, and the task of healing and integration becomes a matter of reclaiming all those projections one has aimed at God. Here the marriage is between the soul and Spirit, described in mystical literature everywhere. Christian mystic, Richard of St. Victor, for example, speaks of four stages by which the contemplative moves toward union with the Absolute: 1) betrothal, 2) marriage, 3) wedlock, and 4) "the fruitfulness of the soul". The first three stages are obvious references to the vertical *hieros gamos*. In the last stage, the soul (which is nearly always considered female in relation to the male polarity of Spirit) "is 'deified,' 'passes utterly *into* God, and is glorified in Him': is transfigured . . . by immediate contact with the Divine Substance, into an utterly different quality of being" (Underhill 139).

In Chapter Fourteen, we spoke of the journey between ego and *bindu* as a solar process of increasing identification with Spirit. This process is completed within the seventh *chakra*, through the incorporation into one's identity, everything that the Sun is not – symbolized astrologically by the Moon. At the New Moon, otherwise known as the dark of the Moon, the solar agenda predominates. But when the Moon is Full, the ego must expand to fill a larger space through the close encounter with something that cannot be encompassed within the ego's normal, everyday frame of reference. This, of course, is a symbolic understanding of the Full Moon, and not necessarily an actual description of what happens to each of us every Full Moon. To the extent that the seventh *chakra* chart is strong and activated by consciousness sufficient to embrace the opportunity that it presents, the Full Moon is the door through which the Goer goes beyond the beyond.

I was born on the Full Moon, and throughout my life I have noticed that major turning points often occur at or near the Full Moon. I bought the land where I now live during the Full Moon. I had my first book accepted for publication when the Moon was full. I met the woman introduced in Chapter Two as my "dancing star" at the Full Moon.

More importantly, however, the Full Moon in my chart is part of a seventh *chakra* pattern, which when activated, will produce a potential opening to the transcendent state of *hieros gamos*. I received *shaktipat* (spiritual initiation) from Swami Muktananda, for example, a few days before a Full Moon loosely square my natal Sun-Moon opposition. Over the days that followed this initiation, peaking at the time of the actual Full Moon, I settled into a much deeper state of meditation, and felt an intensification of the burning sensation in my spine I had come to associate with the awakening of *kundalini*. In retrospect, it is hard to know what if anything about me was permanently altered, and I cannot claim to have achieved any degree of lasting enlightenment or transcendence of this dualistic material world, but there was no question that during the experience itself, the opening to a more integrated state of consciousness was there.

There is also no question that beings far more powerful than I have walked through that opening and entered a realm of transcendent Unity beyond the beyond, from which the Goer did not return. The Buddha, for example, was supposedly born, achieved enlighenment and entered *Parinirvana* (the technical term for a buddha's death) on the Full Moon (Shaneman 4, 13, 14). Muktananda was also born at a Full Moon, received *shaktipat* from his guru, Swami Nityananda, on a New Moon square his natal Full Moon, and died (entered *Mahasamadhi*, the Hindu equivalent of *Parinirvana*) at the Full Moon (Bogart 175).

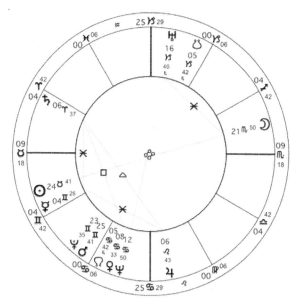

SWAMI MUKTANANDA

We will explore Muktananda's seventh *chakra* process in more detail as we progress through this chapter. Because the story line is far less important in the seventh *chakra* than an internal process that swirls beyond the reach of time – astrological or linear – we will not map the events of Muktananda's life in relation to astrological cycles the way we did for previous case studies. Instead, we will use his autobiography, *The Play of Consciousness* as a source for a firsthand account of the ways in which these various planetary agencies play their part in a seventh *chakra* process. His is not a story told by dates, although it is a very rich account of an inner adventure that few mere mortals are conscious enough to take, as well as a striking portrait of the inner landscape encompassed by the seventh *chakra*. As Paul Zweig claims in the introduction, "*Play of Consciousness*, in all of its complexity and apparent strangeness, but also in its strong emotions, its honesty, is neither more nor less than a portrait of the God within" (vi).

Each seventh *chakra* process will reveal a slightly different portrait of this God within in keeping with the individuality of the soul – at this level of consciousness, increasingly transparent – and we will explore the face of God as it was revealed to Muktananda momentarily. Here I only wish to make the point that the relationship between the Sun and the Moon, particularly the archetypal moment symbolized by the Full Moon, is a potent gateway through the seventh *chakra* awakening can proceed.

Other aspects between Sun and Moon may also be part of a seventh *chakra* pattern, provided they are in turn connected by aspect to a larger planetary pattern involving the transpersonal planets – Uranus, Neptune, and Pluto. Such is the case, for example, with Meher Baba (Sun trine Moon/Uranus quincunx Neptune/Pluto sextile Sun) and Ram Dass (Sun/Uranus trine Moon semi-square Neptune semi-square Pluto square Sun)[2]. Though the chart for Jesus Christ is an ongoing source of debate among some astrologers, at least one version of it (Jacobs) shows a New Moon (Sun/Moon) conjunct Uranus, opposed Pluto and trine Neptune, nicely fitting the profile presented here.

The primary agents of seventh *chakra* awakening are the transpersonal planets, Uranus, Neptune, and Pluto. Each works toward *hieros gamos* in a different way, and often more than one is involved in a potent seventh *chakra* pattern. If the natal pattern involves at least one of them in aspect to Sun and Moon, the others can and often do act as triggers to the activation of *hieros gamos* by transit.

Uranus' Role in Seventh Chakra Dynamics

Uranus is traditionally identified by most astrologers with Jung's individuation process – that is to say, the process by which any individual finds, celebrates and explores her unique individuality, apart from whatever conditioning by society and culture has compromised it. This sense of individuality evolves from a center that exists beyond the protective ego, but at the same time, is not yet completely identified – or ready to be – with Spirit. As noted elsewhere in this book, individuation is a critical phase of the spiritual evolution of any individual – particularly as it proceeds in the third, fourth and fifth *chakras*. It should be noted here, however, that individuation is – or can be – an impediment to the full awakening of the seventh *chakra*, which requires a surrender of individual identity to a larger Whole, to which that individual identity is only a stepping stone. To the extent that the individual is attached to identity, individuation is the ring-pass-not of the seventh *chakra*, the final obstacle to *hieros gamos*, particularly in the vertical dimension. To the extent that Uranus is the planetary agent of individuation, it can be a troublesome addition to any seventh *chakra* pattern in which it participates, since it will tend to facilitate the very sense of separation from the Source that the seventh *chakra* process is designed to transcend.

On the other hand, Uranus will serve to facilitate horizontal *hieros gamos*. Of great relevance here is the myth of Uranus' castration, for through the crude symbolism of this brutal act, we witness a god moving beyond gender, or the primary horizontal dichotomy between male and female. As discussed in Chapter Twenty One, Uranus was born of the primal goddess, Gaia, who then takes him as husband, and with him gives birth to the Titans (forerunners of the Olympians), the Cyclopes and the Hecatonchires (hundred-handed monsters). Because Uranus becomes overbearing and oppressive, and refuses to let his children see the light of day, Gaia crafts a plot with her son Cronus, who castrates his father and tosses his severed genitals into the sea. Out of the sea-foam churned in the wake of this brutal act is born Aphrodite, goddess of erotic love, as well as the Erinyes (Furies), a small army of giants, and the wood nymphs (called Meliae).

Approaching this myth as astrological metaphor, within the context of the *chakra* system, we might interpret it to mean this: Within the domain of the seventh *chakra*, Uranus is the uneasy agent of the Moon, introducing the Sun to that which is foreign to its nature and challenging it to integrate that which appears monstrous and incomprehensible. Uranus works through a process of extreme creativity, rips the veil between the norms of consensus reality and the unknown, and allows passage to and from unseen dimensions parallel to this one. Such a process can be seen at work in the lives of those who have Uranus in aspect to both Sun and Moon, within the context of a larger seventh *chakra* pattern – especially when Saturn and/or Venus (the two other major players in this myth) are also involved. Saturn provides the resistance to Uranus' impetus toward extreme horizontal integration, and out of this resistance comes the alchemical tension necessary to breakthrough. Venus facilitates the necessary psychic intercourse between the self, defined through a solar sense of identity, and the Uranian domain that encompasses everything that is foreign and incomprehensible to it.

Uranus in Muktananda's Chart

Such a pattern exists in Muktananda's chart, and is worth exploring here. Uranus is loosely sextile Muktananda's Moon and trine his Sun; Venus is semi-square the Sun and square Saturn; and Saturn and Venus are both sesquiquadrate the Moon.

The day after Muktananda received initiation from his guru Nityananda, he entered what he refers to as his "confused state of mind" (72-73).

> *I was in a very strange state. I was seized by restlessness. My whole body ached and every pore felt as if it were pierced by needles. I don't know why this suddenly happened. Where had my rapture, my ecstasy, gone? My pride and my elation had been taken away, and I was suddenly the same poor, miserable wretch that I had been before meeting Nityananda . . . Swami*

◇◇◇

Muktananda felt like a ruler gazing out as if in a dream at the ruins of his once-beautiful and beloved city, now destroyed by fate . . . This anxiety was burning me up. During the night I had a series of nightmares, and from the moment I got up I had felt this restlessness . . . I was tormented by anxious questions. . . . This anxiety grew in me and caused great anguish. Just as I had felt a surge of bliss before, now I was full of worry and was arguing with myself . . . I couldn't bring myself to do anything. Everything I saw around me terrified me . . . I was obsessed with impure, hateful, and sinful thoughts.

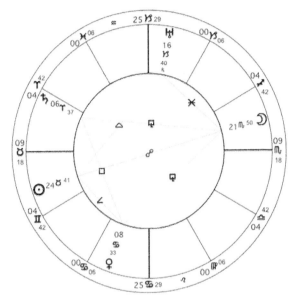

URANUS' CONTRIBUTION TO MUKTANANDA'S SEVENTH CHAKRA CHART

On whatever level it tends to function, Uranus is outwardly often associated with restlessness, anxiety and mental agitation. Here, it serves to precipitate a seventh *chakra* process in which the proud ego, enamored of its own special relationship to God or Spirit, must wrestle with the very antithesis of that – becoming "a ruler gazing out as if in a dream at the ruins of (a) once-beautiful and beloved city." This ruination is the mystical equivalent of Uranus' mythological castration – that is to say, from a spiritual perspective, it is the extreme experience of being cut off from God or Spirit. This process is described in the Biblical story of Job, and in countless variations throughout the mystical literature as the dark night of the soul. In *Holy Wisdom* (qtd in Underhill 387), Benedictine contemplative Augustine Baker describes her dark night of the soul in terms similar to those used by Muktananda, like him speaking of herself (appropriately at this level of consciousness) in the third person:

> Her former calmness of passion is quite lost, neither can she introvert herself; sinful motions and suggestions do violently assault her, and she finds as great difficulty (if not greater) to surmount them as at the beginning of a spiritual course. . . . If she would elevate her spirit, she sees nothing but clouds and darkness. She seeks God, and cannot find the least marks or footsteps of His Presence; something there is that hinders her from executing the sinful suggestions within her, but what that is she knows not, for to her thinking she has no spirit at all, and, indeed, she is now in a region of all other most distant from spirit and spiritual operations.

Within this region, Uranus – the extreme creator of monsters and incomprehensible other worldly creatures holds court, and as uneasy agent of the Moon, the catalyst to lunacy. As Cashford points out (282), "the term 'lunatic' comes from the Latin *lunaticus*, deriving directly from *luna*, which meant both 'Goddess of the Moon' and 'Moon', together with *tic*, which meant 'struck'." I would suggest here that it is Uranus – in its role as agent of the Moon – that provides the *tic* and that strikes the lunatic with an ego-shattering experience. On the level of the third *chakra*, or the fourth, this can be devastating to the psyche. On the level of the seventh *chakra*, though no less frightening, this experience serves the more deeply spiritual purpose of accelerating a horizontal *hieros gamos*. The vertical dimension of *hieros gamos* – the relationship between the individual soul and Spirit – has virtually collapsed. What is left is everything judged by the ego to be outside the normal bounds of creation, and a perceived internal pressure to integrate or die. It is a supreme test of the inherent malleability of the soul, with no guarantee of safe passage, integration, or psychic survival. It helps to have a well-developed sixth *chakra*, for this is where we become capable of entertaining alternate visions of reality, but on the level of the seventh, this capacity – under the tutelage of Uranus – is pushed to the extreme.

I would note here, in passing, that Muktananda's 9th house Uranus does contribute to a strong sixth *chakra*, particularly through its opposition to his 3rd house North Node/ Venus/Neptune.

He would need it, as Uranus began to churn its most bizarre outpouring of monstrous chimeras (76-77).

> My madness was growing all the time. My intellect was completely unstable.
> . . . My fear increased every second. I heard hordes of people screaming frightfully, as if it were the end of the world. I looked out of the small window

of my hut and saw strange creatures from six to fifty feet tall, neither demons nor demigods, but human in form, dancing naked, their mouths gaping open. Their screaming was horrible and apocalyptic. I was completely conscious, but was watching my madness, which appeared to be real. Then I remembered death.

I sat down on my asana (yogic position) and immediately went into the lotus posture. All around me I saw flames spreading. The whole universe was on fire. A burning ocean had burst open and swallowed up the whole earth. An army of ghosts and demons surrounded me. . . . I was quite aware that everything I was seeing was unreal, but I was still surrounded by terror. If I tried to close my eyes, they would immediately open again.

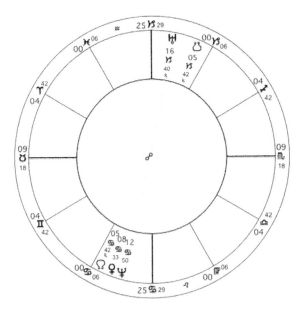

SWAMI MUKTANANDA'S SIXTH CHAKRA SIGNATURE

Neptune's Role in Seventh Chakra Dynamics

The impossible challenge posed by Uranus – integrating that which cannot be integrated – can only be met by taking refuge in Spirit. Here, we are not speaking of a whitewashed, sanitized version of the God of institutionalized religion, who always has our best interests at heart, but rather of a God that is large enough to encompass everything religion would decree to be not-God. To fundamentalist Christians, God is a refuge from Satan, but to the soul undergoing a seventh *chakra* rite of passage, God must include Satan to be truly useful. For the integration demanded at this level of spiritual intensity cannot exclude anything. During the Uranian phase of the initiation process, God appears to be entirely missing, and the vertical dimension in which *hieros gamos* is sought appears to collapse. This occurs only because everything on the horizontal plane of duality that our mind judges to be not-God must be integrated before vertical *hieros gamos* becomes possible.

Once Uranus has sufficiently terrorized the ego, shattered its illusion of God as refuge from not-God, Neptune becomes the agent of this renewed possibility for vertical *hieros gamos*. In the sixth *chakra*, we let go of the wounded memories of the story line with which we identify, but in the seventh *chakra*, it is the wounding imposed by embodied life itself that we must let go of. Our attitude toward the embodied experience – outlined in great detail in my previous book *The Seven Gates of Soul* – has consistently been to regard it as an unparalleled opportunity for spiritual growth. This does not negate the psychic fact, however, that incarnation is experienced as a separation from Spirit. Nowhere is this experience more acutely felt than by the soul undergoing its dark night in the seventh *chakra*. Conversely, the challenge at this level is to realize that separation is not possible, because at the most fundamental level of Being, each seemingly separate container for Spirit is Spirit. I am, you are, this book is, that Uranian monster in the darkest corner of your psyche also is.

Uranus – the astrological agent of separation – cannot help us to realize this; in fact, in some ways, it works 24/7 to undermine the possibility for such a realization. In the throes of a dark night initiation in the seventh *chakra*, a realization of unity is a virtual oxymoron – which is precisely why it is so profound when it actually does occur. From an astrological perspective, only an equally incomprehensible outpouring of Neptunian grace is sufficient to counterbalance Uranus' extreme creativity. In its own way, very different than Uranus', Neptunian grace can be a mixed blessing of utter possession by Spirit that results in megalomania, delusion, infantilism, escapist behavior, addiction to bliss or its many surrogates, dissociation into multiple personalities, and/or many other intractable varieties of psychopathology. To the extent that Neptune is part of a seventh *chakra* pattern within the chart of an individual psychically strong enough to entertain it, Neptune can provide healing reassurance in the midst of Uranus' dark night of the soul through an inner knowing that the tormented soul is not separate from That Which Cannot Be Tormented. As astrologer and Jungian psychologist Liz Greene suggests, "there has always been a curiously flexible interface between what is called madness and what is called union with the divine. To the ancient Greek, madness was the condition of being possessed by a deity. To the medieval Christian, madness was the condition of being possessed by a devil, which is simply another way of putting it" (xvii).

Union with a divine Source of Being large enough to encompass both deity and devil is Neptune's ultimate gift of grace. It is a gift, however, that cannot be prematurely accepted, for at every turn in the road, Neptune's dual capacity for enlightenment and delusion threatens to turn gold back into the humble etheric dust out of which dreams take shape. At the level of the third *chakra*, the desire for union with the divine can be a thinly veiled desire for a return to the womb, or the garden paradise of the second *chakra*, or some Golden Age in which all of the ills – personal and collective – which the soul is subject to miraculously disappear. At the level of the fourth *chakra*, the partner who promises rescue or redemption or simply a pleasurable distraction from the difficulties of life often becomes the false grail of the quest for union, which ends there and results in no true enlightnment. At the fifth, the messiah, *guru*, or cult leader seduces us into a limiting sense of allegiance, even as we learn from them, and at the sixth, the passage into other realms and other dimensions becomes an endless maze, out of which the soul cannot easily emerge.

It is only in the seventh *chakra*, where the task is identification with Spirit, that Neptune's guidance can be taken at face value – and even then, only if the soul has done the hard work of integration and healing demanded at each of the other *chakras*. There is no faking enlightenment, and traps along the path to it are too numerous to count. Genuine effort toward enlightenment seems necessary, but insufficient to take us there. What Neptune provides when the soul is ready, is a response to our longing for the divine that completes the circuit and dissolves the last shred of separation between soul and Spirit. Neptune resides in the tiny gap between God's finger and man in Michaelangelo's famous painting, waiting for us to discover in the seventh *chakra* that neither the gap, the fingers, nor the beings apparently attached to them actually exist, except as constructs of the mind.

Neptune in Muktananda's Chart

As previously mentioned, Muktananda's Neptune serves as a predominantly sixth *chakra* counterbalance to Uranus' penchant for extreme creation through the cadent opposition between them. Neptune also participates in Muktananda's seventh *chakra* pattern, albeit a bit more vicariously. Venus (the ruler of his chart) forms a fairly tight semi-square to Sun and sesquiquadrate to the Moon. Although Neptune is out of reasonable orb of these same aspects, it does conjunct Venus and through this conjunction, I believe, gets drawn into his seventh *chakra* pattern. The North Node is also conjunct Venus/Neptune, underscoring the importance of Neptune's role in Muktananda's seventh *chakra* pattern.

After Muktananda witnessed the ruination of his "once beautiful and beloved city" in the Uranian phase of his post-initiation ordeal, his experience shifted to reflect a distinctly Neptunian flavor (77):

Now, I saw the whole earth covered with the waters of universal dissolution. The world had been destroyed and I alone was left. Only my hut had been saved. Then, from over the water, a moonlike sphere about four feet in diameter came floating in. It stopped in front of me. This radiant, white ball struck against my eyes and then passed inside me. I am writing this just as I saw it. It is not a dream or an allegory, but a scene which actually happened – that sphere came down from the sky and entered me. A second later the bright light penetrated into my nadis (etheric nerve channels through which spiritual energy is channeled). My tongue curled up against my palate, and my eyes closed. I saw a dazzling light in my forehead and I was terrified. I was still locked in the lotus posture, and then my head was forced down and glued to the ground.

After a while, my eyes opened. I saw a very soft, red light shimmering all around. It was flickering slightly, and from it, sparks spread throughout the universe. As I watched, my legs unlocked, and I returned to body-consciousness. I got up, went outside, looked to the right, and looked to the left. The atmosphere was calm. I was astounded and dazed, recollecting everything I had seen. I went inside again and closed my eyes. The red light was there as before, I opened my eyes and went outside again, but there was nothing there.

NEPTUNE'S CONTRIBUTION TO MUKTANANDA'S SEVENTH CHAKRA CHART

CHAPTER TWENTY-THREE

◇◇

It would appear at first blush as though Muktananda was being given a reprieve. After the flood (a particularly potent Neptunian image, recurrent throughout mythology as a defining moment in human history), it would appear as though everything were made new through the descent and embodiment of divine grace. In this case, grace took the form of a moon-like sphere that entered Muktananda and then infused everything with a soft sparkling red glow. Alas, this reprieve was but a momentary respite.

We will return to the red glow when we speak of Pluto's role in Muktananda's seventh *chakra* awakening. First, I would note here that the visionary nature of Muktananda's experience was, in part, Neptune's contribution. Neptune governs the imagination and the image-making process, discussed at length in *The Seven Gates of Soul* as the soul's attempt to make subjective sense of the embodied world. This function is underscored by the fact that Muktananda's Neptune (a quintessential water planet in a water sign) sits in an air house amidst a minor stellium in water sign Cancer, all of which serves as a point of entry to *vijnanamaya kosha*, where the symbolic dimension of experience predominates. When Neptune is also part of an active sixth *chakra* pattern (as it is in Muktananda's chart), the image of the world ensconced in this symbolic dimension becomes quite malleable; in the seventh, the world as we know it essentially becomes undone. Thus, the catastrophic, apocalyptic nature of Muktananda's vision.

It was not the end of the world, however, that would pose Muktannanda's greatest challenge during the Neptunian phase of his seventh *chakra* initiation, but rather Muktananda's inability to see the world for what it truly was – the glorious embodiment of Spirit. Given that Venus governs Muktananda's chart and sits in conjunction to Neptune, it should come as no surprise that the imagery evoked by Neptune in raising this challenge would take on an erotic flavor (92-93).

> *Alas, alas. This was far worse than the experience of the end of the world that I had had on the first day. Now, everything was directed outward toward sex, sex, sex. I could think of nothing but sex! My whole body boiled with lust . . . When I shut my eyes, I saw, right in front of me, a beautiful naked girl inside the red light. Even though I didn't want to see her, she appeared. Full of fear and remorse, I opened my eyes. I saw the divine red light. Within it, Jagadmaba, the naked girl, still stood. If I shut my eyes, she was there, and if I opened them, she was there. What could I do? . . . At times she laughed; at times she smiled; at times she stood; at times she sat. I could not bear to see her anymore. . . . She would dance in front of me for awhile, moving her body suggestively, and jump and turn around. . . . She did not ask anything from me. She simply ruined my meditation, disturbed my sex organ, and did everything she could to make me break my vow (of celibacy). What had*

happened to me? It was one of the most painful times in my life; never before had I met with such trouble.

Though such a vision would perhaps be welcome were his focus within the second *chakra*, at the level of the seventh, it became the supreme distraction to his *sadhana* (spiritual practice), because it appeared to be drawing him back into the realm of duality that he was seeking to transcend. Muktananda struggled with this for what must have seemed an eternity, but held fast to his highest intentions. Then one day, the vision shifted. The woman began to appear adorned with jewels and became "extraordinarily attractive" (95). At first, this only seemed to intensify Muktananda's lust and amplify his agony. But then, through a series of fortuitous acts of grace, a new level of awareness about the true nature of his experiences began to dawn upon him.

First, in the midst of his agony, while he was roaring uncontrollably like a lion, he was visited by Harigiri Baba, a saint he loved and respected. Baba told him, "O Emporer, you are in a good condition. Things will be very good for you. You will become a god. You've got a beneficial fever. Through coming into contact with it, many people will be cured of their sickness and suffering. You will meet many people. . . . Go, go. You've got to go to come again. Don't be afraid" (96-97). No doubt, in these somewhat cryptic words, Harigiri Baba was speaking of the seventh *chakra* portal, and hailing Muktananda as the Goer.

After this visit, Muktananda felt ashamed, and decided to leave the village where he had "lived respectably . . . for a long time" to "go deep into the jungle where no one knows me" (97). His second moment of grace came when he encountered a meditation hut in his travels, and heard a voice telling him to "open that cupboard and read the book you find there" (98). The book described Muktananda's experience, but within a much more enlightened context. In great relief, Muktananda had a potent realization that altered the nature of the vision, so that the naked woman, now adorned with jewels, could reveal her true identity.

> *The naked woman I had seen in meditation caused so many difficulties only because of my ignorance and confusion of mind. She was, in fact, Mahadevi, the great Goddess Kundalini. I begged forgiveness of the Mother and recited a hymn in praise of Her. From then on, my meditations became very good.*
>
> *The next day Mother Kundalini stood in the red aura again, but this time I could see her supremely divine beauty. She was the lovely power of divine grace. As I gazed at Her, I realized my good fortune and bowed to Her, whereupon she merged into the red light. Now this Shakti became my Guru. It was only because my heart was naked, lacking true knowledge that She had*

371

appeared naked to me. The feeling of lust had arisen in me because I had not realized that She was the great Shakti Kundalini. I had taken Her for a mortal, an ordinary woman of the world, and my agony was a result of that ignorance. But now that was all over.

In the days that followed, Muktananda's meditation deepened, his awakening accelerated and moved relatively free of further impedance toward the ultimate realization – and Neptune's specific contribution to his seventh *chakra* experience of vertical *hieros gamos* (109):

Scriptural texts have distinguished the worldly from the spiritual, but when one has complete understanding, these two become one. This external world is the play of Chiti (consciousness), filled with Chiti; it is not different from Chiti, and it is the manifestation of Chiti. Chiti is constantly assuming ever-new forms through the unending stretch of beginingless time. The universe is the very body of Chiti.

From Neptune's perspective, the play of consciousness described by Muktananda is a distinctly feminine experience, in which everything is interrelated and interpenetrated on the horizontal level, and a manifestation of Spirit at its most immanent and intimate involvement in the vertical dimension of reality. Within the seventh *chakra*, Neptune represents Kundalini Shakti, the Divine Fertile Feminine, out of which everything is born and to which everything returns at the final dissolution of the body that carries the soul.

At this level, the concept of Feminine must not be confused with the female gender at other, more garden-variety levels of consciousness, nor even with what we might consider a feminine psychology of feeling, relationship, family, community and social consciousness. Instead, she is both the alluring ensnarement that seduces us into identification with the embodied life, and the guide to the Goer seeking to go beyond the beyond. At the distant shore of that seventh *chakra* journey is the understanding that there is ultimately nowhere to go, that the embodied life itself is Her sacred dance. As the *Tantric* texts (qtd in Neumann 333) remind us, speaking in Neptunian language:

The enchantress, the Great Maya, who delights in imprisoning all creatures in the terrors of samsara (deeply entrenched patterns of karma, core issues), cannot be pronounced guilty in her role of temptress who lures souls into multiform all-embracing existence, into the ocean of life (from the horrors of which she unceasingly saves individuals in her aspect as "boat woman"), for the whole sea of life is the glittering, surging play of her shakti. From this flood of life caught in its own toils, individuals ripe for redemption rise up at all times, in Buddha's metaphor like lotus blossoms that rise from the water's surface and open their petals to the unbroken light of heaven.

Pluto's Role in Seventh Chakra Dynamics

Shakti's consort in the sacred dance of life is Shiva. If Shakti can be associated with the experience of life – whether mired in the snares of a nasty core issue or reaching toward the unbroken light of heaven, then Shiva can be understood to represent the self-knowledge that allows the experiencer to put his experience into perspective. Muktananda struggled mightily with his experience of Shakti until he had a frame of reference. This frame of reference is what Shiva (and his astrological correlate, Pluto) bring to the seventh *chakra* experience of awakening.

We spoke of Pluto in relation to the sixth *chakra* as the bringer of hidden knowledge. Here our understanding of Pluto must deepen to encompass an awakening that transcends even the need to know. The frame of reference that Pluto provides in the seventh *chakra* bypasses the mind altogether, reverberating on the cellular level in a language that does not need to be interpreted in order to be understood.

In *yogic* parlance, Shakti is associated with *kundalini* energy, the potency of the Life Force itself, said to reside like a sleeping serpent at the base of the spine in the root *chakra*. Through spiritual practice – *yogic asanas* (postures), meditation, proper diet, ethical behavior and so on – the *kundalini* will become aroused and, according to *yogic* philosophy, rise up the spine, gradually awakening and cleansing each *chakra* in turn, until finally reaching the crown *chakra*, where it burns away the final veil, bursts into the light of a thousand suns, and precipitates a seventh *chakra* identification with the Source of All That Is. If Shakti is this energy rising, then Shiva is the force that awakens it, and induces it – against the gravity of this earthplane existence – to rise.

What is this force, capable of moving the Great Goddess Shakti Herself? It is the power of spiritual will, harnessed by the individual soul to the ultimate journey: utter annihilation of the soul in Spirit – a journey that American mystic Ram Dass refers to as the crisp trip, "because there's going to be no adventurer left to have had the adventure" (Be Here Now 9). Astrologers euphemistically talk about death and rebirth in relation to Pluto, but in its ultimate manifestation, Pluto serves as guide to a spiritual suicide mission from which there is no return. Once the Goer has gone, there is no coming back. Gone. Gone beyond. Gone beyond beyond. Hail the Goer.

It is the knowledge of this terrible truth – experienced not intellectually, but on the cellular level, in every fiber of the mortal body, and emotionally, in every aspect of one's life where identity holds court – that produces the frame of reference that Pluto brings to the seventh *chakra* process. Opening to Neptune's ultimate grace can perhaps cushion the psychological blow of self-annihilation, but it can't forestall the blow itself. Each of us experiences a dim echo of this blow upon death of the physical body, perhaps reassuring ourselves with thoughts of heaven, reincarnation, or whatever continuity we imagine for ourselves in an afterlife. But death is nothing compared to the understanding that the soul – this unique amalgamation of consciousness and substance that we call "I" – will no longer exist once it reaches the end of its spiritual journey. Of course, you and I both know – intellectually – that we will continue on as Spirit, but it is this lesser "I," this individual soul that will be annihilated, that must make the journey, and mere intellectual knowledge will not be sufficient to reassure this soul that there is anything at all at the other end.

Given the likelihood that this journey, culminating in a fully awakened seventh *chakra*, will end in obliteration of everything with which we identify before we depart, it takes a certain mad determination to take the first step, and an even more stupefying irrationality to continue, once the annihilation of the soul begins. It is this insistent, incomprehensible death wish that I am calling the power of spiritual will. You know how the crisp trip is going to end, and you sign up any way. That takes transcendent courage, an inexplicable conviction that moving with commitment against the flow of all human flesh is what you are here to do, and an utter disregard for the perks and pleasures of ordinary life. It is not simply a death wish. It is more than that.

Whatever it is, Christ had it, knowing he would hang on the cross and die for the sins of his torturers. The Buddha had it, walking out on a life of opulence and his earthly destiny as a king-in-waiting to plumb the depths of human suffering. Muktananda had it when he persisted with his meditation even when it conjured visions that tormented him, and his *sadhana*, even after he began to question his own sanity and his worthiness to call himself a *sadhu* (spiritual seeker). Everyone who has ever undergone the seventh *chakra* journey, whether history remembers them or not, had to leave behind more than most people will ever hope to have in order to embrace an uncertain future of no value that can be measured in earthly or human terms.

This insane, nonsensical heroism is Pluto's gift, if gift is what it can be called. Wherever Pluto sits in mutual aspect to both Sun and Moon, as part of a seventh *chakra* pattern, the possibility exists that one will bolt upright out of a sound sleep and head naked for the door, clutching this gift as a sole possession, obsessed and ruthless in mad pursuit of a treasure no one else can see[3].

Pluto in Muktananda's Chart

In Muktananda's chart, Pluto sits conjunct Mars in the 2nd house, semi-sextile to the Sun and quincunx to the Moon. Pluto's potency is amplified in this context by its conjunction to Mars, Pluto's little brother and the embodiment of ordinary human will, intention and courage – the earthly echo of Pluto's obsession with annihilation in the divine.

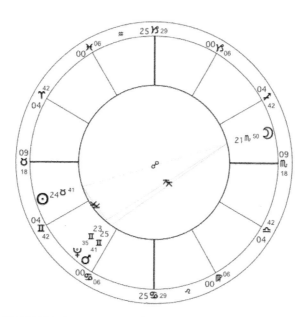

PLUTO'S CONTRIBUTION TO MUKTANANDA'S SEVENTH CHAKRA CHART

In his dedication to his mother at the beginning of *Play of Consciousness*, Muktananda says, "I was slightly over fifteen when one day I left the love of my mother and father far behind. I should not have done such a thing. But what could I do? I was destined to behave so callously. It was supposed to happen, so it did."

What happened, who can say? Muktananda touched thousands of people with the burning grace of his peacock feather, and thousands of lives are profoundly different because of this touch. But he himself had embarked on a journey that would leave a molted snakeskin where a man had been, and joyfully so. From birth, the mark of Pluto was upon him. Shortly before his departure on the crisp trip, transiting Pluto conjoined his natal Venus/Neptune conjunction, setting in motion his longing to merge with God, despite the cost. One day, a mysterious holy man came out of nowhere, patted Muktananda on the head, and disappeared into the jungle. Six months later, the Goer was off to find the beyond.

In August, 1947 – as transiting Pluto semi-sextiled natal Neptune, transiting Neptune squared natal Venus, and transiting Uranus conjoined natal Pluto/Mars – he found his guru, Baba Nityananda, and experienced the seventh *chakra* initiation we have been exploring in this chapter. Pluto's contribution to this process was to meet the madman's will that had brought Muktananda to this point with a movement of *kundalini* that would

375

burn him from the core the way a flute-maker reams a piece of wood to form a hollow tonal chamber. In the Plutonic red light aura in which he was constantly bathed, Muktananda experienced many strange and inexplicable *kriyas*, as they are called – spontaneous movements of energy with no predictable form. These are partly the work of Uranus, triggering extreme behavior in a human being turned inside out, and partly the work of Pluto, burning through residual pockets of psychic impurity to make unencumbered room for Spirit to completely inhabit the vessel that remained.

At various times, Muktananda would jump like a frog or roar like a lion, shake violently, or writhe like a snake. In keeping with Pluto's cellular awakening of body knowledge, Muktananda tells us (88, 113) that:

> *Meditation at the red stage, the stage of the red aura, is meditation in the gross body. As the red stage progressed, my body gradually became thinner and lighter. . . . Sometimes I could feel a force moving through the nerves of my hands. Sometimes prana would flow very quickly along the nerves of the lower part of my back. I couldn't understand what was working so dynamically inside of me. Sometimes my neck moved so violently that it made loud cracking sounds, and I became frightened. . . . Sometimes my neck would roll my head around so vigorously that it would bend right below my shoulders so that I could see my back. . . . Next, I started to feel a kind of warmth growing in my body. It grew so hot that it started to burn me everywhere. No matter what method I tried to cool my body, it went on burning as if on fire.*

Through these experiences and many more like it, Muktananda grew stronger and more purified, day-by-day. His meditations deepened, his visions broadened and became more tangible, at times a reflection of growing omniscience, and at other times increasingly bizzare. He visited many strange worlds, parallel dimensions to this one, other planets, the world of the ancestors. He was bitten by a black cobra (whether in this dimension or some other is unclear), and visited Yamaraja, the lord of death. Many strange adventures compose his madman's journey, far too many to share in this account of his seventh *chakra* awakening, and in the end, tangential to the real purpose of the journey. The red phase eventually passed, and Muktananda encountered a white light, a yellow light, a black light and eventually a blue light, at the center of which was the Blue Pearl, which proved to be the destination beyond the beyond that the spiritual madman was seeking (169).

> *The wonderful radiant Blue Pearl, with its countless different rays shining from within, came closer to me and began to grow. It assumed the shape of an egg and continued to grow into human shape. I could see it growing with*

◇◇

my own eyes and was lost in utmost amazement. . . . Suddenly divine radiance burst forth from it. For a moment, I lost consciousness. What had happened to Tandraloka (an inner world of bliss)? Where had Sarvajnaloka (a state of omniscience) gone? And what had become of the intuitive intelligence by which I had understood everything so far? Muktananda forgot himself for a few moments. Because he did not exist, everything else disappeared. . . . For a moment I was not conscious of anything. However, my state of meditation was still just as it had been. I was sitting firmly in the lotus posture, facing north. Then, I again saw a shining human form in the place of the oval. As it shone, Muktananda came back to himself.

In his meditation, the Blue Pearl assumed the form of a Blue Person, composed not of earthly elements, but of pure consciousness. It was through his encounter with the Blue Person that Muktananda realized who Muktananda really was (171, 184-186).

I was convinced that this was the divine Being who had been described in the Gita (13:13-14):

He has hands and feet everywhere. He has eyes, heads, and faces on all sides. He has ears everywhere. He knows all and exists pervading all.

He has all the qualities of the senses and yet is without any of the qualities of the senses, unattached and yet supporting all, free from the three attributes of manifestation and yet enjoying them.

He dwells in the sahasrara (seventh chakra) and appears in subtle form in the powers of all the sense organs. He can be experienced by the senses and yet is far beyond them and without them. While in the body, He says, "I am Muktananda, I am, I am," yet He is unattached to it. He is the nourisher of all. He is the sustainer of every cell within the 72,000 nadis (etheric nerve channels), the One who nourishes by giving vitality to the vital fluids and richness to the blood. . . . If someone gives him food, He eats it; if someone gives flowers, He accepts them; if someone gives clothes, He wears them; if someone bows, He accepts that too. The person giving all these things thinks, "I am giving them to Baba," but it is He who accepts them. . .

I still meditate now, but I have a deep certainty that there is nothing more for me to see. When I meditate, the certainty that I have attained full realization fills me completely. I say this because of the three visions I saw

> within the Blue Pearl, and because in the outer world I still see that same
> Light of Consciousness, whose subtle, tranquil blue rays I had seen spreading
> everywhere after the three visions. It has never gone away. . . . Now I really
> know that my Self pervades everywhere as the universe. I am completely
> convinced that there is no such entity as the phenomenal world, that indeed
> there never was such an entity. What we call the universe is nothing other
> than the conscious play of Chiti Shakti. I have naturally understood the
> significance of the sah, "He," and aham, "I," which combine to form So'ham.
> That knowledge is described in Vedanta as "Thou art That," whose fruit is
> the bliss of the Absolute, is my very own Self gently vibrating within me.

It is at this point that the language begins to falter in its ability to communicate the reality of the experience itself. But the fact that there are spiritual madmen like Muktananda who are brave and perhaps foolhardy enough to take the arduous, incomprehensible journey that a true seventh *chakra* awakening demands, and then attempt to share their experiences, ought to be encouraging to the rest of us. For even in the midst of this ordinary, fragile, temporary adventure most of us know as the embodied life, is living evidence of something more abiding, more alive than life itself, more central to who we are than any fleeting identity we could conjure. Those with strong seventh *chakra* charts – Sun and Moon in mutual aspect with one or more of the transpersonal planets – may add, in their own way, to this rarified literature, whether they ever write a word or not.

Each soul is a stone dropped into the pond we all share. Whatever stone is dropped from within a seventh *chakra* process will remind the rest of us that the pond itself, teeming with life, is Who we are, and every stone, Our gift to ourselves – a catalyst to our eventual awakening.

Endnotes

1   Though Grasse does not assign a planetary rulership to the *sahasrara* chakra (which in his system is the eighth), he implies that it is activated through "the culmination and perfection of the solar and lunar principles immediately below it" (208) in the *ajna* and *chandra* chakras respectively.

2   Both charts are noted and explored in some detail by Bogart in *Astrology and Spiritual Awakening*.

3   Quoting Alice Bailey, Oken assigns rulership of the seventh chakra to Pluto and Vulcan (a hidden planet within 8° 20' of the Sun) (155).

Part Three
The System Applied
and Transcended

Chapter Twenty Four
The System Applied

Thus far, I have outlined a system for approaching the birthchart as a multi-dimensional template for tracking consciousness through life experience. I have demonstrated how various astrological patterns lend themselves to activation at various levels of consciousness associated with the seven *chakras* of classical *yogic* tradition. I have shown how each of the *chakras* can be penetrated by Spirit to various levels of spiritual possibility associated with the five *koshas* (a less well-known component of that same *yogic* system), and how this distinction can also be mapped astrologically. Though I have presented this material in what I hope is an easily digestible piecemeal fashion, considering each *chakra* independently of the others, the book as a whole can be taken to be a delineation of an entire system.

Assessing the level of consciousness at which a birthchart is actually manifesting represents a departure from a more typical approach to birthchart interpretation. We are not interpreting the birthchart here, so much as we are establishing a context in which its meaning might be explored. In practice, one would look at the whole chart from the perspective of each *chakra*, and the interactions between *chakras*, as they are indicated astrologically by the most active of 35 potential derivative charts. Because of these differences from standard procedures, I feel it is worth showing in more detail how the system would be applied in actual practice to the exploration of a given birthchart.

It bears repeating here that the intent of the system is to better facilitate a process of self-discovery, which implies that the end-user of the system will also be the astrologer. I do not wish to discount the valuable services of the many competent professional astrologers out there in the trenches, who are applying their knowledge of astrology in assisting others to make better sense of their lives. My own focus for the past twelve years or so, has been to teach the language, primarily to those whose desire is for self-knowledge, rather than the acquisition of new professional tools. Thus it is to the student of self-application that this book is directed, although the principles of analysis – as outlined in this book and summarized in this chapter – can be applied to any natal chart, whether one's own or someone else's. I would only hope that the professional astrologer using this material would use it in the spirit in which it is given – as the conceptual framework for a process of exploration, rather than as a set of interpretive rules.

Perhaps the best way to summarize the system as a whole, and to show its practical application is to take a sample chart, and work through it. For this purpose, I have chosen the chart of spirited wise-woman and poet, Maya Angelou, whose six memoirs provide ample material for research for anyone wishing to explore her chart in relation to her life as a learning exercise. Having demonstrated how I correlate astrological data with real life experience in each of the other case studies I have presented in this book, I will not do that in detail here. Instead, our goal will be to analyze the chart in terms of the system, and lay the groundwork for the exploration that would follow.

MAYA ANGELOU

Analysis of Kosha Distribution Among the Planets

The first step in analyzing any chart in relation to the *chakra* system is to assess each planet separately for the depth at which Spirit is likely functioning, according to the *kosha* system outlined in Chapter Ten. The reader might be advised to review that chapter before proceeding with the following discussion.

Angelou's Sun is in a fire sign and a water house, creating an immediate opening to *anandamaya kosha*. Since the Sun is also ruler of her chart (or perhaps co-ruler with Neptune), this is significant in establishing her as one through which Spirit can operate with great capacity for expression. Her fiery Sun (a fire planet in a fire sign) also creates a secondary opening to *pranamaya kosha*.

The Moon (a quintessential water planet) in Angelou's chart is in an air sign in an earth house. The placement of a water planet in an earth house amplifies the water, creating an opening to *manomaya kosha*, while the juxtaposition of water and air creates an opening to *vijnanamaya kosha*.

Mercury is in a water sign and an air house, thus it functions primarily as an earth planet, although its placement in an air house creates the ability to also function at times as an air planet. An earth planet in an air house creates an opening to *anandamaya kosha*, while an air planet in a water sign creates an opening to *vijnanamaya kosha*.

Venus is also in a water sign and an air house, so the same astro-logic applies.

Mars is in an air sign and an air house, so functions as a fire planet. Given that it is conjunct the Descendant (the air angle), this creates a strong opening to *pranamaya kosha*.

Jupiter is in a fire sign in a water house, so it functions primarily as a fire planet, but also secondarily as a water planet. The juxtaposition of fire and water creates an opening to *anandamaya kosha*.

Saturn is in a fire sign and a water house, so functions primarily as an air planet (through its placement in a fire sign), but also at times as an earth planet (through its placement in a water house). An air planet in a water house creates an opening to *vijnanamaya kosha*, while an earth planet in a fire sign creates an opening to *anandamaya kosha*. These openings are given additional weight through Saturn's proximity to the South Node.

Uranus is in a fire sign in a water house, and functions as a strong air planet. The juxtaposition of air and water creates an opening to *vijnanamaya kosha*.

Neptune is in a fire sign and a fire house. Given that Neptune is a quintessential water planet, regardless of placement, and is angular, this creates a strong opening to *anandamaya kosha* through the juxtaposition of water and fire.

Pluto is in a water sign and an air house, functioning as a water planet. The juxtaposition of water and air creates an opening to *vijnanamaya kosha*.

Putting this information together, we see that Maya Angelou has the following distribution of planets among the *koshas*:

annamaya kosha:	0 planets
pranamaya kosha:	2 planets (Sun and Mars)
manomaya kosha:	1 planet (Moon)
vijnanamaya kosha:	6 planets (Moon, Mercury, Venus, Saturn, Uranus, and Pluto)
anandamaya kosha:	6 planets (Sun, Mercury, Venus, Jupiter, Saturn and Neptune)

We might surmise from this initial survey that Angelou is a woman endowed with a strong opening to Spirit (6 planets that provide openings to *anandamaya kosha*), and abundant capacity for expression of her relationship to Spirit (6 planets that provide openings to *vijnanamaya kosha*). We might initially speculate that her personal life will serve as the foundation for, but at times be subsumed by, the transpersonal function she has incarnated to assume (3 planetary openings to the energetic and psychological levels of penetration, compared with 12 to the more transpersonal levels). Angelous' personal life was often permeated by physical pain, emotional trauma, and psychological wounding, yet out of this tough existence, she was able to spin a legacy of pure gold, infused with the hard-won wisdom of a gentle soul who had been to the underworld and back again, yet lived to tell the tale. In this case, the real life evidence matches our speculation, and supports our overview of the five *koshas* as they manifest within her chart.

Analysis of Aspect Patterns Emphasizing Koshic Openings

The next step in this process is to observe the aspects in her chart and note where they tend to reinforce the *koshic* openings identified in step 1. Two or more planets working together to provide an opening are far more potent than one operating in isolation. Planets work together in many ways – some of which have been identified by astrologers and some that I believe have not. But for purposes of the following analysis, we will consider two. When planets providing an opening to Spirit at the same *kosha* share a dispositor relationship (one rules the sign in which the other sits), or form an aspect to each other, the opening they provide will be strengthened. Although I do think that the so-called minor aspects (particularly the semi-sextile, quincunx, semi-sextile and sesquiquadrate) can play a part in *chakra* dynamics, we will restrict ourselves in this analysis to the Ptolemaic aspects considered major by most astrologers (conjunction, sextile, square, trine and opposition).

It will perhaps be most revealing if we approach each *kosha* as a unit, and then explore the planetary interrelationships within that unit. In this way, we can essentially divide the natal chart into five separate *kosha* charts.

Immediately, we are faced with a conundrum, not all that uncommon: there are apparently no planets in Angelou's chart that provide an opening to *annamaya kosha*. This obviously does not mean that she will experience nothing on the physical plane – the mere fact of her embodiment attests to the foolishness of such a notion, not to mention her real life experience, including a rape at age 7, a teenage pregnancy at age 16, and struggles with arthritis in her later years.

In the absence of planets providing direct openings to *annamaya kosha*, we look instead to her earth houses – the 2nd, 6th and 10th – their rulers, and any planets in these houses. In Angelou's case, this would include Mercury (ruler of her 2nd house), Saturn (ruler of her 6th), Venus (ruler of her 10th) and the Moon (in her 2nd house). Of special note here would be the compound square between Saturn, Mercury and Venus. To complete the chart, we need only add the house cusps that bear the signs that these four planets rule – Taurus, Gemini, Cancer, Virgo, Libra, Capricorn and Aquarius – as this will show the arenas in which Spirit is likely to function most often and most intensively at this *kosha*. The fact that two of four angles, Descendant and Midheaven, are ruled by planets in this chart strengthens it, as does Saturn's proximity to the nodal axis. The letter "a" at the center of the chart wheel designates that this is an *annamaya kosha* chart, in keeping with the nomenclature presented in Chapter Nine.

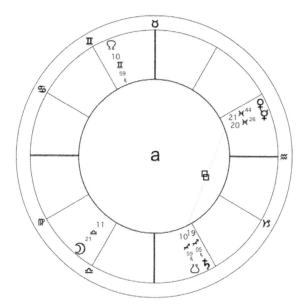

MAYA ANGELOU'S ANNAMAYA KOSHA CHART

Angelou's *pranamaya kosha* chart is formed by both Sun and Mars. Since the Sun in Aries is disposited by an angular Mars, this chart is actually stronger than the mere number of planetary participants would indicate. This chart is also strengthened by the participation of the Sun, which is the ruler of Angelou's chart, and the fact that Mars rules the nadir, encompassing half the angles in the chart.

The *manomaya kosha* chart is composed solely of the Moon and the house that it rules.

Not surprisingly, Angelou's *vijnanamaya kosha* chart is considerably more interesting, as it involves six planets with a number of important interconnections: a Mercury/Venus conjunction, a Mercury/Venus-Saturn square, a Pluto-Mercury trine, a Uranus-Moon

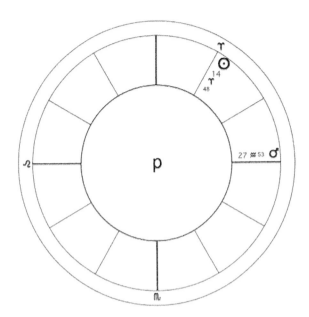

MAYA ANGELOU'S PRANAMAYA KOSHA CHART

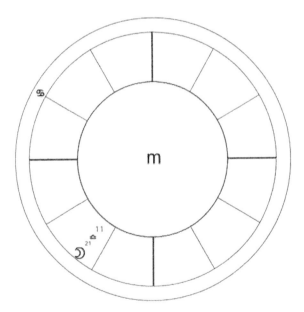

MAYA ANGELOU'S MANOMAYA KOSHA CHART

opposition, and a Moon-Pluto square that is made more potent by the fact that Pluto (in the sign Cancer) is disposited by the Moon. Uranus' rulership of the Descendant, and Venus' of the Midheaven, also add considerably to this chart, suggesting that her most important relationship and her career would both be vehicles through which Spirit could penetrate and function on the symbolic level. Certainly her career as a writer is testimony to that, while her numerous intense and colorful relationships were often a major source from which her images were drawn. Two-thirds of her house cusps are also represented, suggesting that this level of *kosha* penetration will tend to permeate nearly every aspect of her life. As with her *annamaya kosha* chart, Saturn's proximity to the nodal axis also adds to the weight of Angelou's *vijnanamaya kosha* chart.

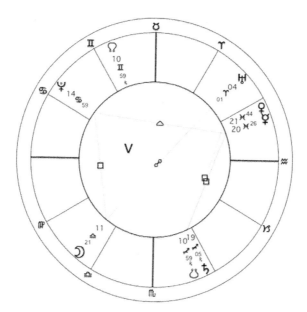

MAYA ANGELOU'S VIJNANAMAYA KOSHA CHART

Lastly, we have Angelou's *anandamaya kosha* chart, which is even stronger. This chart is intensified by two complex levels of interrelationship. First, we have four planets bound to Saturn loosely conjunct the South Node in the angular 4th house: Sun/Jupiter trines Saturn, while Mercury/Venus squares Saturn. Secondly, all six planets in this chart are bound together by rulership. Jupiter and Neptune are co-dispositors of Mercury/Venus (in Pisces) and Saturn (in Sagittarius), while the Sun is the dispositor of angular Neptune. Three of four angles are represented here, and nine of twelve house cusps, again suggesting at least the potential for a life deeply penetrated by Spirit.

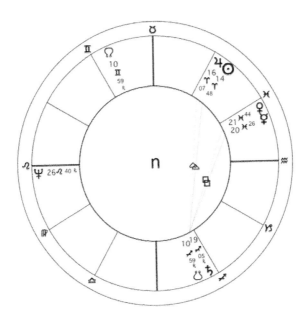

MAYA ANGELOU'S ANANDAMAYA KOSHA CHART

Analysis of Chakra Charts

Now that we have a fairly good idea of where Spirit is entering the life of the embodied soul, we turn our attention to how. The question of how has two interrelated dimensions: 1) to what extent (how much of) the life energy is focused in each *chakra*; and 2) what are the core issues around which consciousness is likely to revolve (how is Spirit being directed into the life). The first question is answered through an analysis of the seven *chakra* charts that can at least potentially be derived from the natal chart. The second question is answered through an assessment of the major planetary patterns in the chart, which then tie various *chakra* charts and kosha charts together. For our purposes here, a planetary pattern will be defined as three or more planets sharing mutual aspects. Though we will also note dispositor relationships, these will be insufficient in and of themselves to indicate a pattern capable of reflecting a complex of core issues.

Angelou's First Chakra Chart

To assess the strength of the first *chakra* chart, we look to planets near the angles (12th house side of the Ascendant, 6th house side of the Descendant and either side of the Nadir), particularly Moon, Saturn and Pluto. Angelou has nothing in any of these positions – not uncommon in real life, well-chosen case studies excepted, although she does have a square between two of the three classic first *chakra* planets – Moon and Pluto – strengthened by the Moon's dispositorship of Pluto. As we did in fleshing out her *annamaya kosha* chart, we would revert to plan B by looking to the rulers of those segments of astrological space associated with the first *chakra* – essentially the Ascendant, Nadir, and Descendant, and note any aspects or aspect patterns between them. In this case, we find a Sun/Uranus-Pluto square, which completes a larger cardinal t-square with her Moon, and a Sun-Saturn trine with nodal axis in tow – incidentally restoring all three classic first *chakra* planets to the pattern.

All this is just theory, of course, until we explore the life of Maya Angelou in relation to subsequent transits and progressions that activate this pattern, but for now, giving our analysis the benefit of the doubt, I would draw her first *chakra* chart as follows:

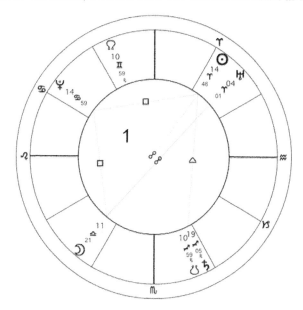

MAYA ANGELOU'S FIRST CHAKRA CHART

Certainly one label that Angelou has earned through her difficult, courageous life is "survivor," and we see that reflected here in her first *chakra* chart. Though it does not fit the classic profile, and we had to dig for it, it will serve as the basis for the exploration of any first *chakra* issues that might arise. We might want to pay special attention to this chart whenever it was activated by hard aspect (from 3-15 degrees of the cardinal signs) from transiting Saturn, Uranus and Pluto or the progressed Sun or Moon.

In exploring these cyclical histories, we would further note that her first *chakra* chart provides openings to all five *koshas* – through the participation of one or more of the planets of this pattern in all five *kosha* charts. Depending on the first *chakra* issues we are exploring, we would designate this chart as 1a, 1p, 1m, 1v, or 1n.

To understand the relationship between Angelou's periodic bouts with depression (here likely rooted in her Pluto-Moon square) and her will to live (embodied by the Sun), for example, we would approach this chart as 1a. To understand how the intensity of her relationships (Sun/Uranus) both threatened her literal survival (experienced by her Moon) and served as a potent opening to spiritual awakening, we would approach this chart as 1n. To be clear, this is the same chart we are talking about in each case, but a different level of consciousness likely being channeled through it. It is precisely this assessment of consciousness – missing from more traditional approaches to astrology – that this system is designed to address.

Angelou's Second Chakra Chart

The second *chakra* chart is formed primarily by planets in the succedent houses, particularly Venus, Mars, Neptune and Pluto, and sometimes Jupiter – usually as an adjunct to Neptune. In Angelou's succedent houses, we see a potent cardinal t-square involving half the planets in her chart. Of these, however, the only planet that can be considered a classic second *chakra* planet is Pluto. If we then look to the rulers of the succedent houses (2nd, 5th and 8th) for additional help, we potentially add Mercury (ruler of 2nd), Jupiter (ruler of the 5th), and Neptune (ruler of the 8th). Looking for aspects among these potential second *chakra* players, we see that Pluto forms a square to Jupiter and a trine to Mercury, which is conjunct quintessential second *chakra* planet Venus. Putting this all together allows us to construct Angelou's second *chakra* chart.

Because the planets in this chart also participate in Angelou's *annamaya*, *vijnanamaya* and *anandamaya kosha* charts, we would anticipate that her second *chakra* issues correlate primarily to these levels of penetration by Spirit. Her second *chakra* chart would consequently be designated as 2a, 2v, or 2n, depending on the context of the life questions we were considering. We would expect that one or more of these *chakra* charts would be activated when transiting Jupiter or Pluto, or progressed Mercury or Venus aspect one or more points in this pattern. Hard aspects of transiting Jupiter and Pluto to each other would be of special interest, as would soft aspects from transiting Pluto to Mercury/Venus.

Progressed Mercury triggered Angelou's Jupiter by conjunction in her 16th year, while progressed Venus reached this same point of her second *chakra* chart about five years later. At age 16, Angelou became pregnant after initiating sex with a boy to whom she was attracted, while at 21 she met and married the man whose last name she bears. With more input from Angelou, we might take these events to constitute part of her second *chakra* story.

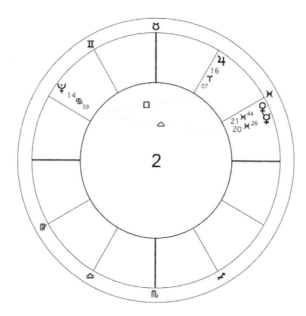

MAYA ANGELOU'S SECOND CHAKRA CHART

Angelou's Third Chakra Chart

Third *chakra* patterns are formed predominantly by Mars and the Sun, particularly when angular (on the 1st house side of the Ascendant, 7th house side of the Descendant, or either side of the Midheaven). When either of these planets aspects Jupiter, Uranus and/or Pluto, we have a potential third *chakra* pattern marked by excess, while aspects to Saturn or Neptune will tend to produce a third *chakra* pattern marked by deficiency. In considering Angelou's third *chakra* possibilities, we are drawn immediately to her potent angular Mars opposed her equally strong angular Neptune, suggesting a third *chakra* pattern of deficiency. We might also consider the rulers of her Ascendant, Descendant and Midheaven (Sun, Saturn/Uranus and Venus respectively), but since these planets contribute nothing further to the aspect pattern formed by Mars and Neptune, we would simply let it go at that and depict Angelou's third *chakra* by this simple aspect.

Looking at Angelou's prodigous output as a writer, as well as her involvement in the Civil Rights movement and her earlier career as a nightclub performer, we would not guess that deficiency would play any part at all in her third *chakra* dynamic. But that is precisely why this exercise is so valuable – especially were it to be used in Angelou's own attempt to come to terms with whatever psychic undercurrents tended to belie this exuberant, extroverted public persona, contributing for example to her periodic bouts with depression and low energy.

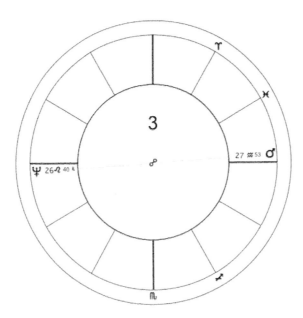

MAYA ANGELOU'S THIRD CHAKRA CHART

In any case, at this point in our analysis, we can simply designate her third *chakra* chart as revolving around this Mars-Neptune opposition, and let it be a template for further investigation. We would make special note of all Neptune transits to Mars (and Neptune), and look to Mars transits to Neptune (and Mars) for more details.

Since Angelou's Mars participates only in her *pranamaya kosha* chart, while Neptune participates only in her *anandamaya kosha* chart, it is these two *koshas* that will predominate in her third *chakra* – represented by the 3p and 3n charts respectively.

Angelou's Fourth Chakra Chart

Fourth *chakra* patterns are formed primarily by the Sun, Moon and Venus, particularly within the succedent houses. Other planets and asteroids can and often do play supportive roles[1]. Here our attention is immediately drawn to Angelou's Moon-Sun opposition in succedent houses, which forms a potential backbone to a fourth *chakra* pattern. Venus, on the cusp of her (Porphyry) 8th house is not connected to Sun or Moon by major aspect. If we consider the succedent house rulers (Mercury, Jupiter, and Neptune), we would add Jupiter (conjunct the Sun and opposed the Moon) to her fourth *chakra* pattern. In this case, I might also be tempted to include Uranus, since it sits in close proximity to this pattern and rules the SW quadrant often associated with fourth *chakra* issues. This is an intuitive departure from a strict application of the rules, but one that also makes good sense in terms of Angelou's story.

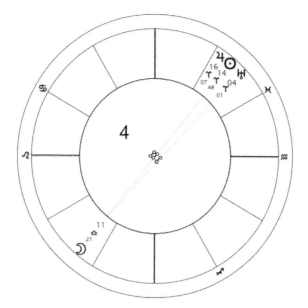

MAYA ANGELOU'S FOURTH CHAKRA CHART

In Chapter Seventeen, I suggested that in tandem with Jupiter, Uranus can produce relationship patterns in which commitment is elusive and multiple partners complicate the potential for *hieros gamos*. Angelou was married three times to three very different men, and although it would be presumptuous of us to jump to hasty conclusions about her fourth *chakra* process on the basis of this superficial fact, the astute astrologer using this system could reasonably postulate that Jupiter and Uranus are somehow players in this pattern.

As with her first *chakra* chart, Angelou's fourth *chakra* chart encompasses all five *koshas*, because of the participation of Sun and Moon, which cover all possible bases between them. We would note here – on a strictly analytical level – that Angelou's fourth *chakra* provides a very broad opening to Spirit, with details to be fleshed out through the appropriate cyclical histories. Of particular interest would be the cycles of transiting Jupiter and Uranus, and progressed Sun and Moon to all points in the natal pattern. The annual cycle of the Sun and the monthly cycle of the Moon could also provide narrower and more frequent windows of observation for the outworking of this pattern in Angelou's life.

◇◇

Angelou's Fifth Chakra Chart

Fifth *chakra* patterns are formed primarily by planets in cadent houses, particularly Mercury, Jupiter, Uranus and/or Neptune, and possibly Chiron. Angelou has no planets in cadent houses; nor are there any major aspects between these planets. Are we to conclude then, that Maya Angelou, noted wise-woman, award-winning poet, teacher and elder spokeswoman has no fifth *chakra*, does not function through the center of consciousness governing alignment with the truth of one's being, nor has any capacity for speaking, teaching and living her truth? Of course not. It just means that we must dig a little deeper for a dimension of her being that is perhaps so implicit in who she is, it does not need to be stated explicitly. Sometimes the absence of something in a birthchart can indicate utter lack of development; but at other times, it can also refer to an area of mastery, where no further development is necessary. I would not presume to make such a judgment in Angelou's case, but anyone who is capable of mesmerizing an audience with her voice, her grace of expression, and her message the way she can, must have a fifth *chakra* signature somewhere.

As with previous patterns related to her other more "invisible" *chakra* charts, we would look to the planets ruling her cadent house cusps (fifth *chakra* domain) for additional resources. Here we find Venus ruling the 3rd, Saturn the 6th; Mars and/or Pluto the 9th; and the Moon her 12th. We have already noted Angelou's Moon-Pluto square in relation to her first *chakra*, and would here speculate that it also serves as a point of entry to her fifth *chakra*. To this stalwart contributor, we would also add a loose trine between Venus and Pluto, and a square between Venus and Saturn. Since Venus is tightly conjunct Mercury, the pre-eminent fifth *chakra* personal planet, I would also include it in this pattern. Putting these aspects together, we arrive at the following fifth *chakra* chart.

Traditional astrologers will recognize an astrological signature for Angelou's power to mesmerize a crowd, in part through her melodious, entrancing voice, in Mercury/Venus in Pisces trine Pluto. As further intuitive confirmation of the validity of this pattern, we would note that this chart closely echoes Angelou's *vijnanamaya kosha* chart, which encompasses all five planets in this pattern (5v). The coincidence of the fifth *chakra* chart and the *vijnanamaya kosha* chart is befitting of a master poet, working on the symbolic level through the *chakra* associated with communication and speaking one's truth. The Moon provides an additional opening to *manomaya kosha* (5m), while Moon, Mercury Venus and Saturn provide an opening to *anandamaya kosha* (5n).

In tracking this pattern, we would be especially interested in hard aspects of transiting Saturn to Mercury/Venus; hard aspects of transiting Pluto to the Moon and soft aspects to Mercury/Venus; hard aspects of progressed Moon to Pluto; hard aspects of progressed Mercury and progressed Venus to Saturn; and soft aspects of progressed Mercury and progressed Venus to Pluto.

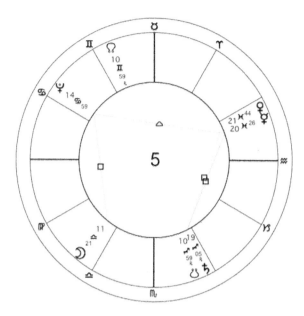

MAYA ANGELOU'S FIFTH CHAKRA CHART

Angelou's Sixth Chakra Chart

Sixth *chakra* patterns are formed primarily by Moon, Venus, Jupiter, Uranus and Neptune, particularly when placed in the cadent houses. Again, we must begin analysis of Angelou's sixth *chakra* chart by noting an absence of planets in cadent houses. Unlike the fifth *chakra*, where there were no aspects between the classic planets involved at that center of consciousness, the classic sixth *chakra* planets do form aspects in her chart – in particular oppositions between Moon and Jupiter, and Moon and Uranus. The rulers of the cadent houses add no additional aspects to the pattern. Since the Sun is sandwiched between Jupiter and Uranus and also in opposition to the Moon, we might suspect that it also plays a part in Angelou's sixth *chakra* chart, but this is a judgment call, the validity of which depends upon substantiating evidence from her life story.

Certainly the multifaceted nature of her career – ranging from poet to singer, to dancer to actress, to political activist to college professor – attests to her ability to periodically recycle her identity (symbolized most essentially by the Sun), as one might expect were the Sun to participate in her sixth *chakra* pattern. Adding her versatile career to her three marriages and her fluency in six languages – all suggesting maximum adaptability and relatively frequent self-reinvention – we see further evidence that a strong sixth *chakra* might pervade nearly every aspect of her life considered as a whole. Given that her Sun rules her chart as a whole, and fits into her sixth *chakra* chart like a hand into a glove, it seems an appropriate addition.

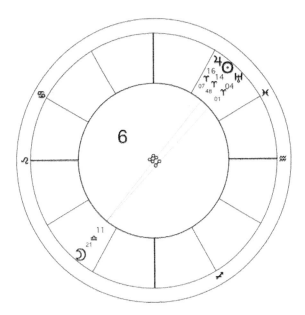

MAYA ANGELOU'S SIXTH CHAKRA CHART

Notice that Angelou's sixth *chakra* chart is identical to her fourth *chakra* chart. Even without the participation of the Sun, it is easy to see the connection between them. Obviously, any trigger by transit or progression to this pattern would affect both *chakras*, and one would expect to hear two parallel, overlapping stories in relation to any cyclical history we were tracking. This is not unusual. In fact, many of the strongest planetary patterns in any chart will participate in more than one *chakra* chart. The multidimensional nature of these patterns is, in part, what makes them so potent within the life of the individual. What the astro-chakra system allows us to do is to identify the various dimensions that contain the story behind the pattern, so that we can understand it – not just through interpretation – but through mapping the pattern to specific levels of consciousness with which it resonates. We also have an additional framework for understanding the pattern, as we consider which *chakra* charts are implicated in a given signature.

Knowing, for example, that this Moon-Uranus/Sun/Jupiter opposition in Angelou's chart spans the fourth and sixth *chakras*, we have reason to consider it as a signature for Angelou's role as sage wise woman. As discussed in Chapter Eight, when the heart is open, the capacity to see from multiple perspectives developed in the sixth allows one to see others more clearly, and share with compassion just the right piece of wisdom for the occasion or predicament at hand. One can see this in Angelou's dignified serenity, and the measured grace between her words that seems to softly illuminate any space she happens to occupy – whether a chair next to Oprah or a podium at a presidential inauguration. As astrologers we would look to her progressed Sun and Moon, and her transiting Jupiter and Uranus cycles to this pattern to tell the tale not only of the gradual opening of her heart (fourth *chakra*), but also the cultivation of her multidimensional wisdom (sixth) and her increasing capacity to share that wisdom from a place of personal power (fourth and sixth together).

Like her fourth *chakra* chart, Angelou's sixth *chakra* chart also provides an opening to all five *koshas*, suggesting it too is a potent signature for the full embodiment of Spirit within her soul's journey.

Angelou's Seventh Chakra Chart

The seventh *chakra* chart is typically composed of some aspect between Sun and Moon, primarily the opposition, bolstered by mutual aspects to one or more of the transpersonals – Uranus, Neptune or Pluto. Angelou does have a Sun-Moon opposition, serving as the base of a t-square with Pluto, as well as a Moon-Uranus opposition and a loose conjunction between Uranus and the Sun.

Does this mean that she is destined to attain enlightenment in the way of Buddha or Swami Muktananda? Not necessarily, especially since the mere existence of a strong signature for the seventh *chakra* (or any *chakra* for that matter) is no guarantee of anything. It is the consciousness that Angelou brings to her seventh *chakra* signature and not the signature itself that will tell the tale. Having the signature in her chart does mean that there will be internal pressure toward *hieros gamos* (particularly horizontal *hieros gamos* through Uranus' participation in the pattern), and toward identification with a transcendent Self that exists beyond the "slings and arrows of outrageous fortune" to which we are subject in this life.

Indeed, the very title of her famous autobiography, *I Know Why the Caged Bird Sings* can be taken as statement of awareness about the true nature of the soul as it is understood from the level of the seventh *chakra*. Of course, the journey Angelou documents in this book is to hell and back again, and the actual story of her life may or may not reflect the ripening of this awareness, but the seventh *chakra* pattern in her chart provides the template for a seventh *chakra* process nonetheless.

One distinction we might note between Angelou's chart and Muktananda's or the Buddha's is the fact that the latter two provide a much more potent opening to anandmaya *kosha*, which is ultimately where the seventh *chakra hieros gamos* and spiritual enlightenment must take place. 5 of the 7 planets in Muktananda's chart provide this opening, while 4 of 5 in Buddha's chart do. In each instance, there is pressure toward both horizontal and vertical *hieros gamos*. By contrast, in Angelou's chart, only the Sun provides an opening to *anandamaya kosha*, and there is only pressure toward horizontal *hieros gamos* (through Uranus' participation in the pattern).

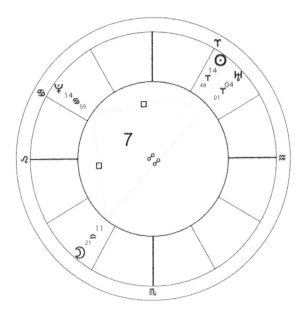

MAYA ANGELOU'S SEVENTH CHAKRA CHART

We should not underestimate the power of the Sun (ruler of her chart) to initiate a spiritual journey that could go all the way, though we would need to investigate the cyclical history of this cycle to truly grasp its meaning. Even if this pattern is not fully realized as an experience of enlightenment – we can see that it has already triggered a deep abiding faith, or awareness of divine grace, that touches countless thousands of the rest of us with its numinosity. In the end, as with all of these patterns in every chart, what becomes of this potential is entirely up to her.

The Use of Chakra Analysis To Understand the Natal Chart

The purpose of this investigation has not been to provide another set of techniques for interpretation of a birthchart, but rather to lay the conceptual groundwork for its more nuanced exploration. The possibilities for exploration are virtually endless, and fully capable of encompassing a lifetime study – as is true of every chart – for the serious student of astropoetics. Here I wish to outline just a few of the more important avenues that such investigation might take.

Now that we have a full set of *kosha* and *chakra* charts to work with, we would begin our investigation by simply taking stock of what we have. Of 35 possible *chakra* charts (7 *chakras* x 5 *koshas*), 29 are actively represented in Angelou's natal chart: 1a, 1p, 1m, 1v, 1n, 2a, 2v, 2n, 3p, 3n, 4a, 4p, 4m, 4v, 4n, 5a, 5m, 5v, 5n, 6a, 6p, 6m, 6v, 6n, 7a, 7p, 7m, 7v, and 7n. The others can be considered implied, or dormant, to be awakened occasionally by transit or progression.

An active 2p chart, for example, might come into play when progressed or transiting Sun or Mars (her *pranamaya kosha* planets) activates her natal Pluto- Mercury/Venus trine or her Pluto-Jupiter square (her second *chakra* chart). An active 3v chart would potentially come into play whenever transiting Moon, Mercury, Venus, Saturn, Uranus or Pluto, or progressed Moon, Mercury or Venus (her *vijnanamaya kosha* planets) formed an aspect to her natal Mars-Neptune opposition (her third *chakra* chart). Obviously in this later case, we might suppose that her dormant 3v chart would be frequently, if not constantly triggered, and technically this is true.

Realistically speaking, it is usually only a transit by the outer planets (from Saturn through Pluto) or a progression by Sun or Moon that have the power to draw a dormant *chakra* chart into sufficient awareness for an actual shift in consciousness to occur. Because the tracks for this level of awareness have not been laid in her natal chart, it would take a certain quantum leap in her growth to be able to effect an actual activation. The outer planet transits and soli-lunar progressions will graciously provide the requisite pressure for this quantum leap, but it is up to each soul what is made of the opportunity.

As any astrologer will attest, opportunities for growth during transits and progressions will depend largely – though not entirely – upon potentials encoded in the natal chart. Within this system, potentials are further differentiated in each of the 35 possible *chakra* charts, many of which will be active natally. Since all ten major planets (including Sun and Moon) cycle perpetually in relation to each other, within the context of these charts, there will be in any life an endless succession of opportunities for growth, triggered by the activation of one or more *chakra* charts.

The capacity to identify which *chakra* charts are being triggered in any given moment is one benefit to this system to which we will return in a moment. First, it is worth taking the time to consider the natal chart and the relative strength of its various derivative *chakra* charts as a broader overview of the way in which consciousness is being invited into Maya Angelou's life[2]. In Angelou's case, for example, aside from a broad opening to *vijnanamaya* and *anandamaya koshas* (involving 6 of 10 planets each), we would note a strong first, fourth, sixth and seventh *chakras* (involving penetration by all 5 *koshas*).

Where this level of analysis adds dimension to a more traditional approach to understanding a chart is in noting how the major planetary patterns in a given chart involve various *chakras*, and pairs of *chakras* that are associated with each other in various ways. The strongest pattern in Angelou's chart by far is her cardinal t-square, which encompasses half her chart. Not coincidentally, this same planetary pattern is implicated in every *chakra* chart but the third. The Moon-Pluto side of this pattern provides a trigger to her first, fifth and seventh *chakras*; the Pluto-Uranus/Sun/Jupiter side to her first, second and seventh; and the Moon-Uranus/Sun/Jupiter base to her first, fourth, sixth and seventh.

In a similar way, we might note that her Pluto-Mercury/Venus trine is implicated in her second and fifth *chakra* charts, perhaps generating the signature for her broad, multi-talented artistic abilities as discussed in the section on creativity in Chapter Eight. Her Mars-Neptune opposition will function primarily within the context of a third *chakra* deficiency pattern. Her Saturn-Mercury/Venus square will function as a catalyst to her first and fifth *chakra* processes, while her Saturn-Sun trine will predominantly manifest as a first *chakra* aspect.

In this way, we can observe that the ordinary aspects and aspect patterns that compose any birthchart are actually multi-dimensional openings to the activation of a variety of *chakra* charts at varying levels of consciousness. Consciousness will be applied to the chart by the native of the chart in ways that cannot always be reliably anticipated with reference to the chart alone, but when the story behind the chart is explored with reference to the dynamics related to the various *chakra* charts involved, the story can be brought into much sharper relief as the adventure in awakening of consciousness that it truly is.

The Use of Chakra Analysis To Understand Transits and Progressions

Not only can this adventure be described in some detail, but through the cyclical nature of astrology, it can also be timed. A fundamental tenet of basic astrology is that transits and progressions after birth (and some would say before birth) are the mechanism by which natal potentials are subsequently developed. Or more accurately put from an astropoetic perspective, they provide a window through which the developmental process can be observed. Now that we have a system for showing how various states of consciousness are implicated in the natal chart, we also have a mechanism for understanding this developmental process as an evolution in consciousness. This is the learning process discussed in some length in *The Seven Gates of Soul*, now mapped to a more specific schematic model based on the *chakra* system.

How this works in practice is through the technique of the cyclical history introduced in *The Seven Gates of Soul* and illustrated in each case study discussed in this book. Theoretically, we can map this history for any transit or progression of any planet involved in any *chakra* chart to any other planet in that same chart. A Uranus-Moon or Pluto-Sun cycle, for example, might potentially shed some light on Angelou's first *chakra* process, while a Jupiter-Mercury or Pluto-Venus cycle would provide clues about what actually goes on when her second *chakra* charts are activated. Under various circumstances, it might well be that a more rapid cycle (e.g. Moon-Uranus or Sun-Pluto for the first; Mercury-Jupiter or Venus-Pluto for the second) would provide the observational window of choice. In general, however, the most important cycles to track with regard to any *chakra* chart will be the slower moving cycles, in the following order of importance:

1)   Progressions of Sun and Moon (if both involved) to each other (Sun-Sun, Sun-Moon, Moon-Sun, Moon-Moon)

2)   Progressions of the Sun and Moon (if Sun and/or Moon are part of a given *chakra* chart) to the other planets involved in that *chakra* chart

3)   Progressions of Mercury, Venus and Mars

4)   Transits of Pluto, Neptune and Uranus (if involved) to Sun, Moon and/or personal planets

5)   Transits of Saturn and Jupiter to Sun, Moon, and/or personal planets

6)   Transits of outer planets (Jupiter – Pluto) to the same natal planet (i.e., transiting Pluto to natal Pluto; transiting Jupiter to natal Jupiter).

In Angelou's case, this would include (in order of importance) the following (p = progression; t = transit; undesignated = natal):

1st *chakra*:   p Sun-Sun, p Sun-Moon, p Moon-Moon, p Moon-Moon, t Pluto-Sun, t Pluto-Moon, t Uranus-Sun, t Uranus-Moon, t Saturn-Sun, t Saturn-Moon, t Saturn-Saturn, t Pluto-Pluto, t Uranus-Uranus

2nd *chakra*:   p Mercury-Pluto, p Mercury-Jupiter, p Mercury-Venus, p Mercury-Mercury, p Venus-Pluto, p Venus-Jupiter, p Venus-Venus, p Venus-Mercury, t Pluto-Mercury, t Pluto-Venus, t Jupiter-Mercury, t Jupiter-Venus, t Pluto-Pluto, t Jupiter-Jupiter

3rd *chakra*:   p Mars-Neptune, t Neptune-Mars, t Neptune-Neptune

◇◇◇

4th *chakra*: p Sun-Sun, p Sun-Moon, p Moon-Sun, p Moon-Moon, p Sun-Jupiter, p Sun-Uranus, p Moon-Jupiter, p Moon-Uranus, t Uranus-Sun, t Uranus-Moon, t Jupiter-Sun, t-Jupiter-Moon, t Uranus-Uranus, t Jupiter-Jupiter

5th *chakra*: p Moon-Moon, p Moon-Mercury, p Moon-Venus, p Moon-Pluto, p Mercury-Moon, p Mercury-Mercury, p Mercury-Venus, p Mercury-Pluto, p Venus-Moon, p Venus-Mercury, p Venus-Venus, p Venus-Pluto, t Pluto-Moon, t Pluto-Mercury, t Pluto-Venus, t Saturn-Moon, t Saturn-Mercury, t Saturn-Venus, t Saturn-Saturn, t Pluto-Pluto

6th *chakra*: p Sun-Sun, p Sun-Moon, p Moon-Sun, p Moon-Moon, p Sun-Jupiter, p Sun-Uranus, p Moon-Jupiter, p Moon-Uranus, t Uranus-Sun, t Uranus-Moon, t Jupiter-Sun, t-Jupiter-Moon, t Uranus-Uranus, t Jupiter-Jupiter

7th *chakra*: p Sun-Sun, p Sun-Moon, p Moon-Moon, p Moon-Moon, t Pluto-Sun, t Pluto-Moon, t Uranus-Sun, t Uranus-Moon, t Pluto-Pluto, t Uranus-Uranus

Generally, I use a one-degree orb on either side of exactitude to provide a relatively narrow window of observation. Obviously, several of these cycles will have implications for more than one *chakra* dynamic, in which case, information from the cycle in question can be applied to the appropriate *chakra* according to your understanding of that *chakra*. If, for example, a life experience in the progressed Sun-Moon cycle seems to precipitate an awakening of the heart through human relationship, it can be assigned to the fourth *chakra*; if it results in a modified belief system, altered worldview, or shift in identity, then it is more appropriately assigned to the sixth *chakra*; if it reflects more of a spiritual awakening – to the presence of Spirit within everyday life, it will be best understood as a seventh *chakra* process. The same event/process can sometimes be understood simultaneously in all three ways, and it can be somewhat artificial to make these distinctions. On the other hand, it can also add a depth of understanding to look at the same experience from different perspectives, and this is where knowing how the various cycles are mapped to the *chakras* can be enlightening. The more cycles related to a given *chakra* that are mapped, and more common themes can be identified, the more clearly a given *chakra* dynamic can be brought into view. The most informative periods will be those in which more than one cycle related to the same *chakra* pattern overlap.

The Use of Chakra Analysis To Explore Life Experiences

The third primary use to which this information can be put is in making sense of important life events. Most astrologers do this as a matter of course. *Chakra* analysis merely adds depth of understanding by allows us to understand events as stepping stones to the evolution of consciousness, mapped specifically to one or more *chakras*. Perhaps a real life example can be helpful in showing how this can be useful.

When Maya Angelou was 7 (or 8 – sources disagree), she was raped by her mother's lover. At his subsequent trial, Angelou lied and said that he had molested her more than once; then in the wake of the trial, her uncles kicked him to death in a vacant lot. Feeling guilty and responsible for her rapist's death, Angelou stopped speaking for five years, during which time she was nurtured and mentored by a neighbor, who saw her potential and encouraged her to read. Despite the horrific nature of the outer events (documented in her autobiography *I Know Why the Caged Bird Sings*), we might surmise that this was a powerful early station in her evolutionary journey, and then look to see how her *chakra* charts were being triggered at this time. Though specific dates are hard to come by, the outer planet transits (which move slowly) tell an interesting tale.

Traditionally, astrologers associate rape (and the potential for other violent crimes) with hard Pluto-Mars transits. From September, 1935 – June, 1938, transiting Pluto was moving in and out of orb of a quincunx to Angelou's Mars, covering the period of her rape and its immediate aftermath. So she does fit the profile, but this does not really tell us very much other than yes, in fact, she was the victim of a violent crime, just as her chart suggested (in the convenience of hindsight) that she might be. It does not shed any light on the significance of these events for her soul's evolutionary process. Nor does it begin to explain why she became mute for five years, or what was really going on during that five-year period, during which she discovered poetry.

Perhaps we will never know, since this is an internal, subjective and perhaps largely unconscious process, although a careful reading of her five autobiographies – especially *I Know Why the Caged Bird Sings* – might yield some helpful insights. We are not going to do that here, since our intention is not to do a case study, but rather to show how the astro-chakra system could be useful to Maya Angelou (or anyone) wishing to explore in more depth the events and processes of their lives. Of course, there are any number of ways of going about this exploration, and the actual process is an intuitive adventure with no set itinerary. Still, in demonstrating how I might go about it, hopefully the reader will get some idea of what is possible in the use of the astro-chakra system to understand major life transitions.

First I would note that in Angelou's chart, Mars registers primarily as part of her third *chakra* signature, so Pluto's immediate impact would be within the domain of the third *chakra*, which is where we grow in our capacity to deal with the demands of everyday life, cultivate a central sense of identity, and learn to exercise our personal power more effectively. We might surmise from this observation, that all these developmental

◇◇◇

processes were derailed during this violation of her sanctity, and that this constellation of events, including the murder of her rapist by her uncles, and the guilt she assumed from this chain of events can be understood, first and foremost, as a third *chakra* wound. Since Pluto in watery Cancer in the watery 12th house semi-sextile to watery Neptune functions as a strong catalyst to the opening of *manomaya kosha*, as well as to *anandamaya kosha* (through watery Neptune's placement in a fire sign and a fire house), while a watery Pluto quincunx a fiery Mars provides an additional opening to *anandamaya kosha*, we would further surmise that this was an activation of her 3m and/or 3n charts.

But this tells us only part of the story, since we would suspect from what we know about the *chakras*, that the shutting down of speech is also a fifth *chakra* wound. In discussing Angelou's fifth *chakra*, we mentioned an association between her melodious, spellbinding voice and her Mercury/Venus conjunction in Pisces, with both planets participating in her fifth *chakra* chart, and Mercury noted as the quintessential fifth *chakra* planet. Given that Neptune is a classic fifth *chakra* player, implicated indirectly in Angelou's fifth *chakra* pattern through its dispositorship of Mercury/Venus, it is not unlikely to assume that Pluto's transit to Mars (triggering her third *chakra* wound) and Neptune (opposed Mars within her third *chakra* signature) also had secondary repercussions in the fifth *chakra*. It is also impossible not to notice the natal square between Saturn and Mercury/Venus, which is also part of Angelou's fifth *chakra* signature.

As it happens, transiting Saturn was moving in and out of a conjunction to Mercury/Venus (from May, 1936 – February, 1937) while Pluto was transiting Mars-Neptune (September, 1934 – June, 1938). One noted manifestation of Saturn's participation in a planetary pattern is the shutting down of whatever it touches, and it appears this is what happened to Angelou as it transited her Mercury/Venus' fifth *chakra* signature for her voice and her later fluency in the poetic arts. Since Saturn in Pisces (an earth planet) triggering Mercury/Venus in Pisces (both earth planets) is a powerful opening to *annamaya kosha*, this can be understood primarily as an activation of her 5a chart – indeed literally affecting her physical capacity to communicate. This potential is indicated by her natal chart, but does not actually manifest until the transiting conjunction (the completion of one Saturn-Mercury/Venus cycle and the beginning of the next).

In the aftermath of the rape, and in the midst of her silence, other planets moved onto this same stage. From October, 1937 – June, 1940, encompassing almost her entire mute period, transiting Neptune was opposed natal Mercury/Venus. This was the period of her tutelage by the kind neighbor who introduced her to reading. We might also surmise that it was the nascent incubation of her real poetic voice, which emerged later as she began to write about her experiences. Neptune does not participate directly in Angelou's fifth *chakra* pattern, but it does disposit Mercury and Venus. Given this vicarious participation in Angelou's fifth *chakra* pattern, we might surmise that this was also an activation her fifth *chakra* chart. Since transiting Neptune in Virgo is watery while Venus/Mercury continues to be earthy, this would have been primarily an activation of her 5a chart. With Neptune (a water planet) transiting a fire house (the 1st), we also see some alchemical pressure on her 5n chart (especially since natal Neptune provides an opening to this *kosha*), that is to say, toward a stirring of Spirit within her throat *chakra*.

Since Mercury/Venus is also part of her second *chakra* chart, both Saturn and Neptune would also be triggering her 2a chart – Saturn, no doubt in shutting it down for protection and repair in the aftermath of physical abuse, but Neptune opening it again to new possibilities through the discovery of reading, poetry, and undoubtedly in her early teens, through the awakening of her natural (unforced) sexuality. Neptune would also trigger her 2n chart for reasons mentioned above, awakening Angelou to what would become the bliss that she would follow as a lifelong passion.

An additional activation of her second and fifth *chakra* charts was intensified by a subsequent Uranus transit sextile to Mercury/Venus (implicated in both her second and fifth *chakra* charts) from June, 1939 – March, 1941. Since Uranus (an air planet) in Taurus and 10th house (earth) is an opening to *anandamaya kosha*, this would have been a more specific activation of her 2n and 5n charts.

Lastly, from November, 1940 – February, 1941 (around the time she began speaking again), her progressed Moon was conjunct her natal Mercury/Venus, again triggering her 2a and 5a charts (Moon in Pisces = water; Mercury/Venus in Pisces = earth; water on earth = *annamaya kosha*). In this case, the Moon no doubt brought additional healing on both levels, allowing her to speak and to begin to enjoy life again.

Putting all this together gives us the following timetable:

9/34 – 6/38	*Pluto-Mars/Neptune*	*3m, 3n*
5/36 – 2/37	*Saturn-Mercury/Venus*	*2a, 5a*
10/37 – 6/40	*Neptune-Mercury/Venus*	*2a, 2n, 5a, 5n*
6/39 – 3/41	*Uranus-Mercury/Venus*	*2n, 5n*
11/40 – 2/41	*Moon-Mercury/Venus*	*2a, 5a*

This provides a conceptual framework in which Maya Angelou could come to understand this early wounding in her life, not merely as a series of literal events, but also as a spiritual process involving at least 6 different *chakra* charts, each with their own set of implications. This information is not meant to replace that which can be derived from a strictly astrological study of the chart, but it does provide a larger context in which the story and the chart might be integrated and understood on appropriate levels of meaning. Understanding each of these 6 *chakra* charts is a matter of exploring the various cycles that

◇◇◇

reveal them, as discussed earlier in this chapter, and then meditating on common themes. The system introduced in this book, and demonstrated as a system in this chapter is not meant to replace this introspective process, but will provide a useful template for it.

Endnotes

1   Generally, I only include the asteroids in a pattern if they participate within a very tight orb of 1 degree or less. Other astrologers may wish to experiment with looser orbs.

2   I use this phrasing to emphasize the fact that the existence of these various charts, even when strong, merely creates a pattern conducive to certain possibilities. Angelou's potent 6v chart, for example, does not necessarily guarantee a 6v experience. It does suggest that Angelou's life will be marked by a succession of powerful 6v opportunities to which she may respond or not. As we – or more in line with the spirit in which this system is being developed, she – explored the cyclical histories related to her 6v chart, we would be in a better position to assess how the opportunities being presented by the 6v chart were actually being met. But this is the case with any kind of astrological analysis. The chart merely provides a template of abstract possibilities, while it is the native of the chart that actualizes (or fails to actualize) them.

Chapter Twenty Five
Beyond the System

Those thinkers in whom all stars move in cyclic orbits are not the most profound: whoever looks into himself as into vast space and carries galaxies in himself also knows how irregular all galaxies are; they lead into the chaos and labyrinth of existence. – Friedrich Nietzsche (195)

In this book I have presented a system for tracking the evolution of consciousness that takes place surreptitiously through the seemingly ordinary events of any life. I have shown how this system works in the lives of a number of people, some of whom I know personally and a few famous people, whose autobiographies have provided the necessary connecting links between symbol and reality. In relation to the third *chakra*, I showed how I myself have used the system to understand my own process. In relation to the sixth *chakra* I showed how the system could be used in dialogue to help another person become more aware of their patterns. If you have read this far, then hopefully you would at least agree that it is possible to explore a birthchart within the context of an astro-logical system that intentionally takes an assessment of consciousness into account.

Yet even the best system is still only a template that we impose upon our experience after the fact, and any system will be but a pale reflection of that which it is tracking. The experience of life itself will always transcend the system we impose upon it, and consciousness is ultimately not something inherent to the system. However enlightened our interpretation of the birthchart might be, using this system or some other, the birthchart is only a piece of paper filled with hieroglyphics, waiting for its owner to infuse it with the real life experience necessary to give it meaning. Until we actually live the lives that the birthchart suggests are there to be lived, there is nothing to track, and any system – this one included – is merely an idle rosetta stone looking for something useful to decode.

Even when there is a life to be decoded, we are still but astrological archeologists, sifting through the artifacts of a life in order to speculate intelligently about its interior. In any life, it is usually only in retrospect that the various clues we leave to ourselves begin to make sense. In the moment of our most important experiences, there is too much raw data to be easily assimilated by the mind, too much vital life force to be contained in explanations, too little conscious appreciation of the true nature of our experience for it to register as a cogent idea. At best, the system is only something we can apply in hindsight, essentially establishing a site perimeter where there was none before, and digging carefully amidst the ruins in the settled dust for memories, peripheral impressions and shards of meaning. Life has moved on, and we are using the system to try to catch up with it – a strategy almost guaranteed to extract our attention from the present moment, which is where the soul perpetually dwells.

Given the limited usefulness of any system, one might reasonably ask, "Why have a system at all?" Socrates once said that "life without examination . . . is not worth living" (Plato), and it is human nature to want to understand, make sense of, and find retrospective meaning in our experience. In this endeavor, having a conceptual framework can be helpful. Astrology provides such a framework, while the astro-chakra system presented in this book adds depth to the astrological framework. I believe the system I have presented in this book is worth adding to the astrologer's toolbox – especially to the toolbox of the astrologer focused on contemplating his or her own journey. But it is the contemplation that is important. The system is only the mind shaft to a motherlode of subjective wisdom that has its own shape and its own internal logic.

What we will discover as we engage the system will as often contradict the system as confirm it. As we saw in working briefly with Maya Angelou's chart in Chapter Twenty Four, the patterns related to a given *chakra* often look nothing like the classic signature theory would lead us to expect. If you learn, in using this system as a point of departure, that your fifth *chakra* is not as I have described it in this book, or that for you, Mars is more a sixth *chakra* planet than a third, I will not be offended if you reconstruct the mind shaft to permit a more effective entry into your own process,

The system is only meant to facilitate an introspective journey, building upon what you already know about astrology, and adding various layers of information based upon a correlation of that knowledge with the *chakra* system. In reality, there are many more layers than seven, hidden dimensions parallel to those directly revealed by the system, that are personal to you, and nuances that seasoned astrologers will recognize as the fruit of experience. As discussed earlier, the best astrology can only expect to be a system of exoteric logic, capable of helping to increase awareness of an esoteric logic of life that transcends astrology altogether.

Having said that, I believe the astro-chakra system – as presented here – is flexible enough to allow discovery of this esoteric logic – which invariably means that as you use the system, the system will evolve. That is good. I would hate to think that I am merely adding to the dogma that litters the pathway to genuine understanding. The journey is what is important, and to the extent that the astro-chakra system does its job, you will inevitably shed the system as a child outgrows its clothes, when you find what you are looking for.

Send me a postcard (or drop me an email) when you get there – I'll be rooting for you with every bit as much passion as I am putting into the system you are leaving behind. Meanwhile, in the spirit of helping you with your introspective journey, I wish to note in this last chapter, an important chink in the system that it might be worth your while to explore.

The Inherent Flexibility of Astro-Chakra Patterns

As mentioned in Chapter Eleven, most astrologers who attempt to correlate the *chakras* to the planets assign one (or two) to each, and let it go at that. The earliest conceptual schemes tried to order the assignments from Saturn at the first *chakra* to the Sun at the seventh *chakra*, matching seven classical planets with seven *chakras*, although at least one system, developed by German mystic Johann Goerg Gichtel, moves more or less in the other direction (Leadbeater 18-21). Others have modified the system to include the outer planets discovered in modern times. Systems based on the esoteric teachings of Alice Bailey assign one ruler to each *chakra* in its undeveloped state, and another ruler in its more enlightened state (Oken 155). Some attempt to go beyond the planets to encompass emphasis on the signs the planets rule (Grasse 210-216, Bruyere)

Regardless of the scheme employed, however, the rationale has been that each *chakra* is in some way like the planet (and/or associated signs) that govern it, and that the governing planet can be understood to function primarily at a level of consciousness commensurate with the *chakra* it governs. I do think there is some truth to these assumptions, but that the correspondences between planets and *chakras* are not limited to a singular or even a dual rulership relationship. In my system, I have correlated signs with *koshas* (for reasons spelled out in my Introduction), while suggesting that more than one planet can be associated with each *chakra*, implying the *chakras* are multi-dimensional in their function, and that each governing planet is capable of a range of expression at various levels of consciousness,

My confession to you now is that this is only partially true. I do believe that certain planets have a natural affinity for certain *chakras* – explained in my discussion of the system. But I also believe that any planet can function at the level of any *chakra*, and every *chakra* expresses itself through every planet. In fact, I would go so far as to suggest that the very definition of Wholeness – the end point of the spiritual journey, in which Spirit functions freely and fully through the embodied soul that temporarily houses it – implies the capacity for every planet in the birthchart to function simultaneously through each *chakra*. Extending this concept to include the *koshas* as well as the *chakras*, we would further surmise that every planet will function through every *chakra* at the level of each of the five *koshas* (that is to say from an astrological perspective, in any sign). In this way, all

35 *chakra* charts become fully functional, and Spirit becomes fully incarnate within the embodied soul.

In this quest for wholeness, the birthchart merely represents the habitual tracks on which the soul is accustomed to running, and the point of departure for a broadening of the soul's behavioral repertoire. If, for example, someone has Venus in Virgo in the 2nd house square Neptune in Sagittarius the 5th, then according to the astro-chakra system, this will constitute a second *chakra* pattern, mostly manifest at the level of *annamaya* and *anandamaya koshas* – i.e. as active 2a and 2n charts. But all this really means is that this is the level of consciousness on which this soul will habitually respond to a triggering of this natal aspect.

Let's say that over time, this soul happily discovers her bisexuality (*anandamaya kosha*), but also develops a vaginal infection (*annamaya kosha*) because of a self-indulgent lifestyle that includes behaviors that are not particularly healthy. The vaginal infection diminishes her sexual pleasure, and she is motivated to seek a pathway to healing.

A moment's reflection should be sufficient to realize that this soul will not be able to heal herself by continuing along the same behavioral track that has contributed to her problem. What this means in terms of the astro-chakra system, is that she must find a way to jump the track – from the second *chakra* to some other, and from the two extreme *koshas* defining this aspect to the ones in the middle. Left to its own devices, Venus in the second *chakra* will seek pleasure without any real sense of self-restraint or moderation, yet this soul now finds herself in a situation where some self-restraint and moderation is apparently necessary. So where will Venus find this resource, which is not available to it in the second *chakra*? By moving to the third *chakra*, where its natural expression is the quest for balance. There may be other mitigating factors in this soul's chart that make such a shift in consciousness possible (say a sextile to Saturn in Scorpio in the 4th house), and these mitigating factors may well provide the mechanism for the necessary change, but the change itself can be characterized as Venus learning how to function on a new level of consciousness (the third *chakra*) that is not intrinsic to its nature (as reflected by the system).

In a similar way, Venus must allow Spirit to penetrate more deeply to the level of *pranamaya kosha*, where it is more attentive to the actual patterns of resonance within a given situation. At the level of *annamaya kosha*, Venus often simply allows itself to be drawn instinctively into experiences that feel good, but at the level of *pranamaya kosha*, there is a more developed awareness of the line between pleasure and excess, born of experience, and a sense of sufficient discrimination to back away before the line is crossed. Here is where Venus in Virgo becomes more discriminatory in its pursuit of pleasure, and how our troubled soul must shift in order to begin healing her vaginal infection. Again, the capacity for the shift is reflected by the chart, but the shift itself can be understood as a movement from one *kosha* that is built into the fabric of the chart to another one that is not.

As we make these *interchakric* and *interkoshic* shifts, we grow, our charts grow with us, and our understanding of the astro-chakra system must expand to encompass a possibility that is not intrinsic to the system. I would be remiss in my duties as the author of this system if I did not alert you to this inevitable progression in your work with it. While this is largely a matter of discovery, which will vary somewhat for each of you, and I do not want to spoil your fun, I also want to leave you with a framework for watching what happens as these planetary shifts are made. In the discussion that follows I will limit myself to briefly talking about *interchakric* shifts, and let the reader extract an understanding of *interkoshic* shifts within each *chakra* from a careful rereading of Part One of this book.

Planetary Scales

In her book, *Astrology and Spiritual Development*, Donna Cunningham introduces the concept of planetary scales, reminding us that "the planets are neutral in essence, yet are expressed in ways which range from lower expressions to higher ones" (105). Cunningham then prescribes meditations and other practices for moving planets up the scale, suggesting that "these scales have the potential to be a system of meditative or spiritual practice, as profound as the other recognized systems" (106). She does not mention the *chakras* by name, but it seems to me her idea is quite amenable to them, and speaks directly to the essence of the breathing room within the astro-chakra system that I am exploring here.

In any case, in the remainder of this chapter, I want to construct an outline of these planetary scales, as they relate to the astro-chakra system. The only caveat I would introduce in doing so is that in my view, we are not necessarily moving up the scale, but rather broadening our repertoire as our relationship to each planet expands to encompass *chakras* other than the ones in which it habitually functions. In the list that follows, I will devote a few phrases to the characteristic function of each planet in each *chakra*, with references to chapters where certain functions are discussed in more detail, and an implied extended invitation to the reader to mediate on those that are not.

THE SUN

1. the will to live; the consent given by the soul to the experience of embodiment

◇◇◇

2. instinctual gravitation toward that which sustains life; inhabitation of the body

3. learning to function within the body; coordination of will and physical movement; inhabitation of the embodied world; development of ego (discussed in Chapter 15)

4. cultivation of a personal center; development of relationship of ego to *bindu* and to the resonant field it centers; exploration of self in relation to others; discovery of *dharma* (discussed in Chapter 17)

5. the capacity to be a living embodiment of truth; development of a teaching presence; attractive charisma

6. surrender of individual will to divine will; expanded sense of self; disillusion of subject-object barrier

7. union of soul and Spirit (experience of vertical *hieros gamos*), surrender of ego and individual identity (discussed in Chapter 23)

THE MOON

1. the vulnerability inherent in embodiment; relationship to the mother (or nurturing parent); the wounding experienced in relation to the mother (or nurturing parent) (discussed in Chapter 11)

2. the *ouroborous* state of comfort, safety, and containment; the capacity to be nurtured and nourished; the development of a need-based relationship to the embodied world

3. the formation of habit patterns; instinctual protection of wounds; sense of self-worth and worthiness

4. *bodhichitta* and the capacity for caring, nurturance, empathy and compassion; emotional memory; longing for union with Spirit (discussed in Chapter 17)

5. the capacity to learn from experience; emotional expression and release; the cultivation of subjective wisdom

6. the formation of beliefs that revolve around emotional memories; patterns of familial and cultural conditioning passed on from one generation to the next; the cultivation of intuition (discussed in Chapter 21)

7. mystical identification with the embodied world (experience of horizontal *hieros gamos*) (discussed in Chapter 23)

MERCURY

1. awareness of the presence of the life force within the body

2. awareness of pleasure and pain and of the duality inherent in the embodied world; cultivation of the capacity for choice; awareness of gender

3. instinctual intelligence; self-awareness; the capacity to engage the embodied world and to learn from it

4. awareness of others; the capacity for relationship and for learning from others

5. the cultivation of communication skills; discernment of truth; the capacity to contemplate paradox; trickster energy; the capacity to teach (discussed in Chapter 19)

6. the capacity for self-contradiction; imagination; creative ingenuity; magic

7. awareness of the source code at the heart of all creation; the power of *vach siddhi* (creation through speech)

VENUS

1. discovery of the garden at the heart of the embodied world

2. instinctual gravitation toward pleasure; the capacity for enjoyment; the desire for a relationship to the embodied world (discussed in Chapter 13)

3   a sense of balance; the cultivation of values and a personal aesthetic; awakening of the desire to live in harmony with natural law; artistic creativity; creative passion

4   the desire for (sexual, emotional, spiritual) union with another; love; intimacy; joy; the capacity to cooperate with others toward a common end; co-creativity; awakening of group identification (discussed in Chapter 17)

5   the capacity to speak; the power of voice; the cultivation of personal grace and generosity of spirit; empowerment of others through appreciation; awareness of synchronicity

6 the power of creative manifestation; the development of tolerance for different points of view; desire for community; the capacity to mediate, build bridges and make peace between warring factions

7 divine ecstasy; abundance; the capacity to serve as a creative agent of divine will

MARS

1 warrior energy; the power to prevail against adversity; strength and vitality of body and spirit

2 the capacity to seek satisfaction of desires; the capacity to give pleasure (discussed in Chapter 13)

3 self-determination; cultivation of competence and expertise; establishment and defense of territory; development of personal sphere of influence (discussed in Chapter 15)

4 heroism, bravery and defense of the defenseless; identification with a cause; self-sacrifice for the common good

5 the power of persuasion; the cultivation of personal power; leadership abilities

6 the willingness to die for a belief; the impulse to seek out new experiences; the capacity to break with the past and begin anew

7 the power of *wu-wei* (non-doing); mastery of the power of intention; the capacity to serve divine will as a *bodhisattva*

JUPITER

1 freedom from fear, want, and struggle

2 the discovery of preferences; embrace of the power of choice; capacity for well-being; tendency toward excess in pursuit of pleasure

3 self-confidence; the impulse to broaden one's skills through education and training; the desire to excel (discussed in Chapter 15)

4 altruism; nobility of spirit; desire to make a contribution to the larger world of which one is part; capacity to make a difference in the lives of others

5   insistence on freedom of individual choice; impulse toward self-discovery; the capacity to teach; the awakening of a pioneering spirit

6   the awakening of perspective and vision; the capacity to make a unique contribution to the larger world of which one is part; the capacity for shape-shifting and self-reinvention (discussed in Chapter 21)

7   the power to bestow the blessings of Spirit on others through one's mere presence; omniscience; freedom from suffering and death

SATURN

1   the capacity to create safety and protection for oneself; self-limitation (discussed in Chapter 11)

2   inhibition and moderation in pursuit of pleasure; discrimination and discretion; the capacity for satiation (discussed in Chapter 13)

3   stamina and the capacity to preserve; the capacity to commit oneself to the pursuit of a goal; the will toward mastery; growth through challenge (discussed in Chapter 15)

4   the capacity for commitment in relationship, and to a sense of vocation or a calling; reliability; trustworthiness

5   personal integrity; the capacity to walk one's talk; impeccability; the power to earn the respect of others; appreciation for solitude and the power of silence; the capacity to teach by example and mentor others

6   the wisdom of experience; the capacity to discern truth in whatever guise it might appear; the capacity to be the eye of the storm in situations involving chaos and confusion

7   transcendence of the limitations of time and space; the capacity to embody Spirit without distortion

This list is necessarily incomplete, and is meant to be but a catalyst to further meditation and observation. For the most part, the listings of planetary functions related to each *chakra* are posed in positive terms as an expression of their unencumbered essence. In real life, there will of course be countless varieties of imperfection, and expression at less than optimum function will tend to be the norm, rather than the exception. Still, if one has a sense of what each planet is attempting to accomplish within each *chakra*, the many possible issues capable of compromising that intention will largely become self-evident. If, for example, the pure expression of Mars in the third *chakra* is heroism and bravery, then the opposite of that – cowardice and timidity – can be understood as a third *chakra* issue likely to be reflected astrologically by some difficult aspect to Mars, possibly by Saturn or Neptune. If formation of belief systems that revolve around emotional memories is the pure expression of the Moon in the sixth *chakra*, then dysfunctional beliefs rooted in wounded memories would be reflected astrologically by sixth *chakra* planets in difficult aspect to the Moon – most notably Neptune or Pluto. Other issues may not be so obvious, but their assignment to one or more planetary scales should nonetheless prove a valuable exercise in fine-tuning one's understanding and ability to employ the system.

The Transpersonal Planets as Alchemical Agents

The transpersonal planets, Uranus, Neptune and Pluto have not been included in this list, because their function is somewhat different. While the seven classical planets can be understood to have developmental functions, the transpersonal planets simultaneously complicate and accelerate development. These three planets are what I call *alchemical agents*, the suggestion being that their general purpose is to transmute the lead of wounded being into the gold of Whole (or healed) Being. The alchemical process is quite complex and has variously been depicted as a 3, 4, 6, 12, 20, 22, 50, and a 75-stage process (Hamilton 4). The three basic stages of one of these processes – *mortifacio* – can be understood to correspond to the alchemical function of the three transpersonal planets.

The term *mortifacio* refers to a deathing process, which as I discuss in *The Seven Gates of Soul* is the primary opening to soul available to us in the embodied life. The transpersonal planets serve, in various ways, as agents of deathing, by rendering our largely unconscious, habitual responses to the patterns in our chart ineffectual. When this happens, we are pressured to bring more consciousness to our patterns, to see them more clearly, and to experiment with approaching them differently. In terms of the astro-chakra system, it is under the alchemical pressure of the transpersonals that we are most likely to jump track, and force the system to expand in order to encompass our transcendence of it.

Each of the transpersonals will contribute in a different way to the deathing process that leads to this transformation. This is not news to anyone with even a modest understanding of astrology, but the difference bears elaboration in terms of the alchemical process of which I am proposing that they are agents.

Nigredo, a "blackening of the soul" at the start of *mortifacio*, can be understood in relation to Uranus. As we discussed in Chapter Twenty Three, Uranus is often manifest as an "extreme creativity" that shatters the boundaries of the familiar, and plunges the soul into a dark night that seems to be the absence or negation of everything it had been striving for. We discussed this process earlier primarily in relation to the seventh *chakra*, but here we can extrapolate to the other *chakras* and suggest that whatever the soul strives for in a given *chakra*, Uranus will appear to obliterate the possibility. The evolutionary goal of this obliteration is generally to force us to reach more deeply for resources we didn't know we had until we needed them.

The second stage of *mortifacio* is *albedo*, sometimes known as the "whitening phase." Here the soul experiences an intensified influx of spiritual energy that dissolves the duality that previously appeared to pervade the embodied world – a process we identified in Chapter Twenty Three as associated with Neptune. As discussed earlier, Neptune triggers a collapse of the barriers of separation between soul and Spirit, so that a sacred union, or a *hieros gamos* can take place. While *hieros gamos* per se takes place primarily in the fourth and seventh *chakra*, this same process can be understood to operate in each of the *chakras* as a process of lifting the veils of separation between the seeker and that which is sought, whether or not one is ready to see beyond the apparent dualities that condition the embodied world and the embodied soul that lives within it. If one is not, then one inevitably clings more fiercely to one's illusions, and experiences the sense of disorientation for which Neptune is well-known.

The third stage of *mortifacio* relevant to the transpersonals is *rubedo*, or the reddening phase. In *rubedo*, an embodied vehicle suitable for serving the increased identification with Spirit experienced during *albedo*, is reconstructed out the rubble of *nigredo*. As discussed in Chapter Twenty Three, this process involves the "death" of the individual soul and its subsequent "rebirth" as Spirit in embodied form. Death and rebirth are placed in quotations, because at this level of awareness, there is no one to die, and what is reborn has always been. In the other *chakras*, this same force, symbolized by Pluto, serves to facilitate the emergence of a more transcendent sense of identity. Again, the greater the resistance, the more agonizing the deathing process will be.

Having given this brief introduction to the alchemical function of the transpersonal planets, we can continue our list of phrases, illustrating their characteristic manifestation in each of the *chakras*. Again, these are obviously not meant to be definitive or exhaustive lists, but merely a point of departure for meditation by the student of the astro-chakra system.

URANUS

1   chaos; profound insecurity; discovery of hidden pockets of secret strength

2   attraction through resonance by wounding and/or contrast; exploration of the edge between pleasure and pain

3   challenges that transcend one's current state of readiness or ability; tendency toward excess (reckless, accident-prone, unreliable, unpredictable, and anarchistic expressions of ego); discovery of creative resourcefulness (discussed in Chapter 15)

4   emotional restlessness; challenges to intimacy; the shattering of relationships one has outgrown; awakening of true individuality

5   breakdown; alienation from one's culture; profound sense of isolation; creative iconoclasm (discussed in Chapter 19)

6   shattering of beliefs; compulsion to cut ties, burn bridges, and throw the baby out with the bathwater; spontaneous and uncontrollable shape-shifting; awakening of promethean genius (discussed in Chapter 21)

7   the dark night of the soul (discussed in Chapter 23)

NEPTUNE

1   the *ouroborous* state of stillborn protection; avoidance of pain; dependency on perceived sources of safety; transcendence of the fear of death

2   addiction to pleasure; irrational attachments to the source of pleasure; awakening of the capacity for ecstasy (discussed in Chapter 13)

3   self-doubt; spiritual sabotage of ego-centered goals; transmutation of warrior energy in service to a higher agenda (discussed in Chapter 15)

4   co-dependency in intimate relationships; difficulties in relationship due to projection of unconscious contents; psychic pressure toward dissolution of interpersonal boundaries and/or *hieros gamos*; awakening of compassion

5   piercing the veils of illusion imposed by cultural conditioning (discussed in Chapter 19)

6   letting go of outmoded belief systems; forgiveness of self and others; release of traumatic emotions; awakening of imagination and intuition (discussed in Chapter 21)

7   vertical *hieros gamos*; mystical identification with Spirit (discussed in Chapter 23)

PLUTO

1   awakening of *kundalini*; triggering of *tapas* (psychic heat that purifies as it burns)

2   sexual obsession; attraction to the forbidden; breaking familial and cultural taboos (discussed in Chapter 13)

3   ruthless, aggressive behavior; tendency toward excess in pursuit of personal goals; the will to address core issues (discussed in Chapter 15)

4   power struggles in personal relationships; the capacity of two people in relationship to trigger old wounds; the psychological chemistry of relationship as a force for personal growth

5   fanaticism in service of truth; the willingness to die for what one believes; the power to teach that comes from having lived what one teaches

6   the cultivation of shamanic healing abilities; the power of the cultural iconclast to change the society in which she lives; activism

7   the annihilation of ego and personal identity in the fusion with Spirit (discussed in Chapter 23)

Assessment of Planetary Levels Through Introspective Dialogue

Given that any planet can function on any level, it logically follows that the birthchart – even when analyzed by the astro-chakra system – tells only part of the story. The birthchart will show the tracks on which consciousness is accustomed to running, but consciousness itself is what the soul brings to the chart. Once our expectations are established through analysis of the relative strength of the 35 *chakra* charts inherent in the birthchart, we must engage ourselves (or our clients) in an introspective dialogue, so that we can get the rest of the story.

As demonstrated throughout this book, the cyclical history is the basic technique for exploring the chart in relation to the life story in which the exercise of consciousness at various levels is revealed. Which cyclical history to explore will depend upon what you wish to know, which natal patterns intuitively reflect your concerns, and how current transits and progressions are impacting those natal patterns. Each cyclical history will likely be related to one or more *chakra* charts, which then provide a context of expectations in relation to the memories associated with that history. If your cyclical history of choice is related to a 5a chart, for example, you would expect a story that somehow revolves around physical manifestations within the ear-nose-throat complex. If instead you are looking at a 3m chart, you would expect a story about the psychological implications of your struggle to acquire skill, function effectively within the world, and grow to excel at what you feel drawn to do. Many cyclical histories will implicate more than one *chakra* chart, in which case your expectations will be compounded accordingly.

But if your process has been one of learning and growth, your cyclical history will reflect a series of seminal moments in which you jumped track, and defied the expectations that your analysis of *chakra* charts has established. So the obvious question – after you have both the analysis and the raw data of memories associated with the cyclical history – is how does the story meet and/or defy expectations?

All the system really does is to establish a baseline against which the growth of any life in progress can measure itself qualitatively. Any cyclical history that does not defy the system is probably cause for concern, because it suggests a life that is spiritually stagnant. Taking into account the stubborn nature of many core issues, there should nonetheless be evidence within any cyclical history of experimentation in jumping track, even if the experiment ultimately proves unsuccessful. The system shows the default pattern, but the gradual transmutation of the default is the real story – and the real story will invariably transcend the system.

The Astro-Chakra System as One in a Series of Overlays

Taken as a whole, the astro-chakra system is but one of many possible overlays through which it is possible to view a birthchart. As discussed in the Preface, the language of astropoetics is multi-dimensional. It encompasses at the very least a qualitative understanding of number, a symbolic interpretation of astronomical phenomena, and a cosmic re-enactment of ancient, archetypal, mythological dramas meant to describe the actual movement of gods and goddesses within the embodied world. The birthchart can be seen through each of these lenses, one at a time, or simultaneously. Understanding how the various *koshas* and *chakras* are represented astrologically is an important lens through which we can glimpse the perceptual template through which consciousness flows as a primary manifestation of Spirit within human form – and it can be argued that it is a useful precursor to other templates that might be imposed. It is also one that is typically missing from most current astrological analysis. As important as this addition is, however, it is also important to understand that it is not by any means the only template through which a birthchart might be approached – nor even the only template through which consciousness might be assessed in relation to a birthchart.

The adaptability of the astrological language to multiple templates is, in fact, one of its most sophisticated features. Those who are more thoroughly conditioned by the scientific mindset might insist that only one of these templates is valid. But at its best, astrology represents what I would call a kaleidoscopic way of knowing. Just as turning a kaleidoscope this way and that to catch the light from different perspectives can be an endlessly fascinating exercise, so too can turning the birthchart this way and that be an endless source of useful information – provided the rationale for turning the chart a particular way is astro-logical. If the turning of the kaleidoscope has some basis as a measure of consciousness, number, astronomical reality, or applicable mythology, for example, it would make sense to turn it, and see what can be seen from the new perspective.

Modern eclectic astrologers do this as a matter of course, although they perhaps do not think of what they are doing in these terms. Nonetheless, harmonic charts, secondary progressions, the use of multiple house systems (turning by number); the use of Vedic astrology side by side with Western, the exploration of midpoint structures and/ or hypothetical planets and the use of solar return charts (to name just a few turnings by astronomy) all reflect the kaleidoscopic nature of astrological information. Some astrologers have their pet turnings, while others dismiss those with which they don't resonate. But astrology as a whole is kaleidoscopic by its very nature, and this is no small component of its strength as a language capable of mirroring complex realities.

In this book, we have explored a new, less familiar turning of the astrological kaleidoscope. In subsequent books in this series, we will explore others. To the extent that each is a system of astrology unto itself, all together are meant to demonstrate how the language itself transcends any given system. Ultimately astrology is not a system at all, but a symbolic language capable of giving rise to any number of logically coherent systems. It is in this spirit of expanding (or in some cases exploding) our limited notions of what astrology is or is not, that I have attempted to introduce the notion that considerations of consciousness can also serve as a legitimate basis for turning the astro-logical kaleidoscope.

Now that you have the astro-chakra system in your hands, I invite you to immerse yourself in it, then turn it this way and that. The rules of philosophical coherence by which the system makes intuitive sense are only meant to be an expansive jungle gym for the imagination – not necessarily to be transcended by superior rules, but to be used as a structural ladder to the cosmos capable of providing multiple pathways to fresh perspective on the soul's evolutionary journey. I now invite you to see what new light it can shed on yours.

Continue the Journey

Tracking the Soul is meant to provide a complete explanation of the theory and technique of the astro-chakra system, as well as instruction in its application for the diligent student wishing to explore it further.

For those who are intrigued by the ideas presented in this book, but who prefer to undertake their further study with guidance, a correspondence course is available through The Astropoetic School of Soul-Discovery.

Tracking the Soul serves as the textbook for this course, while homework assignments are tailored to each individual student and discussed in a series of phone consultations. The course includes a complete analysis of the student's birthchart with respect to all seven chakras and their koshic implications. In addition, core issues will be identified, analyzed within the context of the astro-chakra system, and explored in depth through the appropriate cyclical histories. Special attention will be devoted to chakra charts and correspondent issues currently being triggered by progression or transit.

Each year of study with The Astropoetic School will culminate in an annual workshop, where students immerse themselves in a more intensive experience of sharing, learning and growth with other students. Participation in the workshop is limited to ensure that each student receives individual and group attention, and so the group as a whole can focus with more depth in an atmosphere of intimacy and mutual support.

For students desiring a group experience without the intensive study of the correspondence course, a weekend workshop is available and can be scheduled whenever and wherever sufficient interest warrants.

More detailed information about the correspondence course and the workshop can be found at:

www.astropoetics.com

THE SEVEN GATES OF SOUL

Reclaiming the Poetry of Everyday Life

JOE LANDWEHR

Like a butterfly, whose seemingly random movements through the garden scatter beauty and pollen upon the dancing wind, something essential is lost forever when truth or beauty get pinned to a dissection board for closer scrutiny. This is not to say that the mystery of soul is inscrutable. We can glimpse it now and then, if we lean into it with open minds and hearts. The mystery is best approached humbly, however, with hat in hand, not with fiercely defended expertise or authority

In this landmark book, veteran astrologer Joe Landwehr discusses astrology's role within the larger context of a 6000-year dialogue about the soul, and who we are as human beings. Using the ancient Mesopotamian myth of goddess Inanna as a metaphor, the author explores the conceptual barriers to a true understanding of soul erected by religion, philosophy, science, and psychology, and outlines a poetic approach to astrology that transcends these barriers.

An ingenious, carefully laid out path not only to a deep practice of astrology, but also to the wisdom of the ages. – Thomas Moore, author of Care of the Soul

A huge book . . . vast, encompassing and a complete philosophy in itself. Highly recommended. – Erin Sullivan, International Astrologer

Joe Landwehr is a creative and imaginative thinker and has given us a rich treatment of a complex subject. – Mary Plumb, The Mountain Astrologer

Consider it a textbook on the anatomy and epistemology of soul. – Donna Van Toen, NCGR Newsletter

I think the book is quite special. It may be the kind of book that . . . will become a classic, growing slowly in popularity over the next decades. Thank you for writing this profound book. – Brita Adkinson, New Age Retailer

**Available at
www.ancient-tower-press.com**

Appendices

Glossary
Terms from Various Spiritual Traditions

ajna – Sanskrit name for the sixth chakra.

albedo – an alchemical process, sometimes known as the "whitening phase," in which the soul experiences an intensified influx of spiritual energy dissolving the duality that previously appeared to pervade the embodied world. Astrologically, albedo is associated with the planet Neptune.

anahata – Sanskrit name for the fourth chakra.

anandamaya kosha – state of bliss in which a full embodiment of Spirit is being realized in each moment; the deepest possible penetration of Spirit into matter, according to Hindu philosophy.

anima – a Jungian term, often used as a synonym for psyche or soul, but more accurately understood as a psychic force capable of dissolving limitations of identity imposed by the fear-based ego. The anima (or animus) is often projected onto a member of the opposite sex, who serves as the catalyst for this dissolution of limitations through the process of relationship.

anima mundi – literally, the soul of the world; an experience of the world as a soulful place through the projection of one's imagination into it.

annamaya kosha – the physical dimension of experience; the shallowest level of penetration of Spirit into matter, according to Hindu philosophy.

asana – yogic posture.

assemblage point – a term used by Carlos Castenada to describe the psychic vantage point from which an individual's perception of reality is constructed. Within the shamanic tradition espoused by Castenada. the assemblage point can be shifted and reality reconstructed according to an entirely different set of rules.

ashram – a community of spiritual seekers, living and studying together in one place.

bhavanga-sota – in Buddhist thought, the subconscious life-stream, which provides the seed for a new incarnation. Unlike karma – a concept to which it is related – bhavanga-sota is not specific to an individual, but rather serves as a source of attraction to an incarnating soul who resonates with it.

bindu – the core sense of self that is derived from Spirit. Through its evolutionary journey, the soul gravitates toward a more complete identification with bindu as the ego relaxes its defenses and allows Spirit to penetrate it more completely.

blue pearl – in Siddha yoga (Muktananda's tradition), a much sought after experience of bindu to be found in deep meditation.

bodhichitta – a Buddhist term used to describe the inherent vulnerability of the human condition. According to Pema Chodron and other Buddhist teachers, this experience of vulnerability is a gateway to a deeper experience of soul.

bodhisattva – a Buddhist term for one who, from a very high level of spiritual attainment, has chosen to serve humanity, rather than simply enjoy his or her solitary attainment.

chakra – a psycho-spiritual center of consciousness, associated by yogic tradition with various physiological correlates, psychological issues, and spiritual challenges.

chandra – a minor chakra at the back of the head, described by Parmahansa Yogananda as the feminine counterpart of the ajna, or sixth chakra at the front of the head.

ch'i – a Taoist term for the life force, similar to prana, élan vital, or kundalini.

consensus reality – a term used by Carlos Castenada to describe objective reality.

dark night – a mystical experience in which one's relationship to Spirit appears to be utterly negated, associated in this book with the planet Uranus.

darshan – the blessing of an enlightened being, said to have the power to heal and/or accelerate spiritual growth.

dharma – an eastern term (used by both Hindus and Buddhists) to describe a sense of purpose that derives from one's most essential identity; a deep calling or vocation.

granthi – a Sanskrit word for "knot;" another word for chakra, meant to denote the necessity for working through various blockages in order to attain clarity within the psychological domain encompassed by a chakra.

guru – a spiritual teacher with the power to serve as a catalyst for the growth of his or her students.

hatha yoga – a form of yoga based in the practice of physical postures or asanas.

heyokah – in Native American tradition, a contrary figure, whose job it was to mirror the fear-based ego and point toward its liberation; similar to a trickster, but perhaps with a more aggressive agenda.

hieros gamos – a Jungian term used to describe the reconciliation of opposites; a state of functional balance and psychological integration.

ida – in yogic practice, a lunar nerve channel (connected to the parasympathetic nervous system) activated through conscious breathing through the left nostril.

koan – in Buddhist practice, a riddle with no logical solution, designed to lead the practitioner away from dependence upon the rational mind and toward a more holistic, instinctual, spontaneous way of being.

kosha – a Hindu term used to describe the level of interaction between Spirit and matter, ranging from utter ignorance of the presence of Spirit at one end of the scale, to complete identification with Spirit at the other.

kriya – a spontaneous movement of energy within the body, resulting from the practice of yoga. Kriyas can take many forms, including but not limited to physical sensations, intense feelings, vivid imagery, or various life dramas.

kundalini – the life force, conceptualized by yogic practitioners as a coiled sleeping serpent at the base of the spine, which becomes activated through spiritual practice.

kundalini shakti – an alternate concept of kundalini, which conceptualizes it as an awakening precipitated by a dispensation of divine grace.

kundalini yoga – a form of yoga, involving physical posture, meditation, chanting and other spiritual practices, specifically designed to awaken kundalini.

lalata – in the yogic tradition taught by B. K. S. Iyengar, a minor chakra situated at the top of the forehead which, when activated by complete stillness of the mind, allows the yogic practitioner to bring into the conscious mind any facet of knowledge which is required.

magnetum – an element unknown to science, but mentioned in Hermetic texts, associated by energy medicine pioneer Rosalyn Bruyere with the seventh chakra.

mahasamadhi – a Hindu term to describe the death of an enlightened being, associated with his or her return to the Source.

mahatantric – a master at the art of tantric yoga; one who serves as a filter for the psychic cleansing of others engaged in tantric yoga.

manas – the Sanskrit word for mind, more specifically used to describe the interaction between perception and action; the function of the mind that allows us to respond to reality as we perceive it to be.

manipura – Sanskrit name for the third chakra.

manomaya kosha – the emotional, psychological realm, understood as an interaction between Spirit (as consciousness) and material reality.

mantra – in yogic practice, a Sanskrit word or phrase with the power to affect spiritual awakening through its repetition.

maya – a Hindu term evoked to describe the illusory nature of the world of duality.

mortifacio – an alchemical process associated with psychological death of the fear-based ego, necessary before psychological healing or spiritual awakening is possible.

GLOSSARY

mudra – in yogic practice, a position of the hands and fingers designed to stimulate various subtle nerve currents.

muladhara – Sanskrit name for the first chakra.

nadis – subtle nerve currents activated through yogic practice.

nigredo – an alchemical process, sometimes known as the "blackening phase," associated with the dark night of the soul, and a breakdown of limiting patterns of existence, associated with the planet Uranus.

ouroborous – a Greek word meaning a snake that swallows its own tail, often used by Jungian psychologists to describe a womb-like state of being in which psychological protection is exchanged for freedom and autonomy.

parinirvana – the Buddhist equivalent of mahasamadhi, in which an enlightened being attains final Buddhahood upon death of the physical body.

path with heart – a term used by Carlos Castenada to describe a life that revolves around one's dharma or calling; in the shamanic tradition, a primary source of empowerment.

pingala - in yogic practice, a solar nerve channel (connected to the sympathetic nervous system) activated through conscious breathing through the right nostril.

power-from-within – a phrase used by neopagan activist Starhawk to describe the power that arises when one connects and begins to live from a core sense of self, connected to all other living things.

power-over – a self-centered use of power that arises from a sense of separation and being in conflict with other beings, used by Starhawk to describe the more common misuse of power, in contrast to power-from-within.

prakriti – a state of being, at one end of the scale of koshas, marked by the presence of pure matter, utterly devoid of consciousness.

prana – Sanskrit word for the life force.

pranamaya kosha – the dimension of experience encompassing the movement of energy within the body, where awareness is directed to various physiological changes in one's state of being and their symbolic correlates.

psychopomp – a guide in the transition from life to death, usually associated with the Greek god Hermes (the astrological Mercury).

purusha – a state of being at the other end of the scale of koshas from prakriti, marked by pure consciousness, in which matter becomes a transparent vessel for the manifestation of Spirit in form.

430

right relationship – one of the Eight Noble Truths of Buddhism, recognizing the interconnectedness of all things, and the desirability of achieving harmony in all of one's relations as a way to honor and invoke that sense of interconnectedness.

rubedo – an alchemical process, sometimes known as the "reddening phase," in which the body and the embodied soul are reconstructed to be a more effective vehicle through which Spirit can function, astrologically associated with the planet Pluto.

rune – a letter of an esoteric Viking alphabet, composing a language of esoteric wisdom, channeled by the Norse god Odin, as he hung upside down from the world tree, Yggdrasil.

sadhana – spiritual practice.

sadhu – spiritual seeker, in ancient Hindu tradition, often a wanderer in search of truth.

sahasrara – Sanskrit name for the seventh chakra.

sangha – spiritual community.

sankhocha – an alternate term for chakra, meaning "contraction," suggesting that the work to be done in each chakra must necessarily involve relaxing an attitude of fear that causes the chakras to contract.

seeing – a term used by Carlos Castenada to describe the process of directly perceiving the "source code" out of which consensus reality is apparently constructed; the sixth chakra goal of the shamanic seer.

sefirah – one of ten qualities of divine nature represented in the Kabbalah.

shabda – a sacred subtle sound at the heart of creation, the perception of which facilitates awareness of the Source of all things.

shabda yoga – a form of yoga whose intent is the perception of the shabda, usually through the practice of mantra.

shadow – a Jungian term used to encompass all the rejected, disowned and projected parts of the self, the reintegration of which is necessary to individuation and wholeness.

shakti – a divine energy that pervades the manifest universe, usually conceived of as feminine in nature.

shaktipat – spiritual initiation with the tradition of Siddha yoga; an awakening of kundalini through the grace of a guru.

shushumna – a central subtle nerve channel, activated through yogic practice designed to bring the ida and the pingala into balance.

Siddha saint – a lineage of saints in India, known for their quirky ways, and power to initiate spiritual awakening through unorthodox methods.

Siddha yoga – a form of yoga that strives to activate kundalini through relationship to a guru of the Siddha lineage.

soma – according to the teachings of B. K. S. Iyengar, a division of the sixth chakra associated with the Moon and the cooling influence of a still mind.

story line – a term used by Buddhist nun Pema Chodron to describe our attachment to the melodrama of our lives. A goal of Buddhist meditation is to be able to drop the story line, and experience pure bodhichitta, the sense of vulnerability and openness to the truth of one's being that underlies all experience.

svadisthana – Sanskrit name for the second chakra.

tantra – in the West, a practice of conscious love-making; more commonly understood in the East as a transmutation of sexual energy to awaken the so-called higher chakras.

tapas – a manifestation of kundalini, usually experienced as a burning sensation in the spine, activated when a chakra is being cleansed.

tattwa – Sanskrit name for element.

trickster – in mythological tradition, the embodiment of the unpredictable; a force that defies logic, upsets rational plans, and ultimately forces one to be in the moment; astrologically associated with the planet Mercury.

vach siddhi – the power to manifest through speech, awakened when the fifth chakra is clear.

vijnanamaya kosha – the symbolic realm, as understood in yogic philosophy as the attempt of Spirit to communicate with the mind.

visuddha – Sanskrit name for the fifth chakra.

wu-wei – a Taoist word used to describe the art of doing by not-doing; going with the flow; getting out of the way, so that Spirit can operate through one, unimpeded by the self-important ego.

yang – a Taoist name for the active, initiatory, assertive principle at work in any process.

yin – the opposite of yang; a Taoist name for the passive, receptive, yielding principle, also at work in any process.

yoga – a path to spiritual integration, often involving physical postures and other practices designed to cleanse, strengthen and purify the body; meditation; chanting; sexual abstinence; selfless service; and devotion to a teacher or teaching.

yogi/yogini – a practitioner of yoga.

◇◇

Astropoetic Terms

alchemical tension – the pressure toward growth brought to bear through disparate combinations of elements, i.e., earth and fire; earth and air; fire and water; air and water.

alpha and omega – the relationship between the first and seventh chakra, signifying the circular nature of the chakra system in astropoetic thought.

astro-chakra system – an integration of astrology with the chakra system, outlined in great detail in this book.

astro-logic – another word for astrology, recognizing it to be a metaphoric language of symbolic logic, rather than a predictive science.

astropoetic impulse – the human longing to understand existence within a larger context of meaning and purpose that assumes a vital place for the individual within the whole.

astropoetics – a theory and practice of astrology that assumes its primary function to be that of symbolic language, capable of reflecting the subjective truth of everyday life through a study of the imagery – drawn from astronomy, mythology, culture and life itself – related to various planetary cycles.

awakening phase – the combined function of the third and fourth chakras, where the focus is awakening to the presence of Spirit within everyday life.

chakra chart – a depiction of the astrological factors in a birthchart related to the function of a given chakra.

clockwise motion – a basis for an astro-logical understanding of the houses, derived from the fact that planets appear to move through the houses on a daily basis in a clockwise direction. This is somewhat contrary to the teaching of traditional astrology, which relates the houses to their correspondent signs, and numbers them accordingly in a counterclockwise direction.

core issues – psychological issues that serve as the pivot point for a lifetime of opportunity for spiritual growth, usually depicted by the major astrological configurations in a birthchart.

creativity chakras – the second and fifth chakras considered in relationship to one another as a functional unit.

cross-polar relationship – an interchakra relationship involving one yang and one yin chakra, and one self-centered and one place-centered chakra.

cyclical history – a technique involving remembering events and processes related to a specific planetary cycle, useful in determining the real life correlations to a given natal aspect and the chakra charts in which it is implicated.

disparate elements - a combination of elements disharmonious with each other (i.e. air and earth, air and water, fire and earth or fire and water) that produces alchemical tension as a catalyst to growth

esoteric astro-logic - an understanding of the birthchart that derives from the observation of real life in relation to various astrological cycles.

exoteric astro-logic - an understanding of the birthchart derived from a consideration of the birthchart alone; a speculation about possibilities based on the symbolic logic of the birthchart.

horizontal hieros gamos - a reconciliation and integration of opposites - heat and cold, light and dark, male and female, etc. - inherent within life experience.

hybrid issue - an issue involving more than one chakra.

image - a subjective understanding of reality, projected into the world and experienced as its apparent nature.

incarnation phase - the combined function of the first and second chakras, where the focus is anchoring and securing one's existence on the physical plane.

interchakra relationship - the interaction of two or more chakras, especially when considered in the context of the outworking of some core issue.

interchakric shift - a shift in perception that allows one to consider any core issue from the perspective of a chakra other than those with which it is astrologically associated.

interkoshic shift - a shift in perception that allows one to consider any core issue from the perspective of a kosha other than those with which it is astrologically associated.

jumping track - the process of making interchakra and/or interkoshic shifts as a prelude to growth in relation to a core issue.

kaleidoscopic vision - the ability to see the same reality from multiple perspectives; a manifestation of an awakened sixth chakra; prized within astropoetic practice as the ability to look at the same birthchart from different complementary and sometimes contradictory perspectives.

patterns of deficiency - a core issue marked by insufficient energy to rise to the challenge of growth presented by a given chakra chart (particularly the third); often indicated astrologically by the participation of Saturn or Neptune.

patterns of excess - a core issue marked by more energy than can be effectively channeled through a given chakra chart (particularly the third); often indicated astrologically by the participation of Jupiter, Uranus or Pluto.

place-centered chakras – a term used to describe the fourth, fifth and sixth chakras, taken as a group, in which the intent is to take one's place within a larger integrated whole.

planetary scale – a term coined by astrologer Donna Cunningham to describe the range of possibilities for manifestation inherent in planetary symbolism; useful in astropoetic practice as an explanation of the primary mechanism at work in the astro-chakra system.

power chakras – the third and sixth chakras considered in relationship to one another as a functional unit.

primal wounding – the seminal life experience, often experienced around transiting Saturn's first semi-square to its natal position (age 3 or 4), that triggers a core issue.

resonance – the capacity of each soul to attract to itself that which is most conducive to its growth; in astrology, the constellation of imagery, life experience, and circumstance correlated within any given symbol or group of symbols.

resonance by affinity – the power of the soul to attract that which exists in harmony with its nature, i.e. like attracting like.

resonance by contrast – the power of the soul to attract that which exists in contrast to its nature, i.e. opposites attracting.

resonance by wounding – the power of the soul to attract people, experiences and circumstances that force a reckoning with core issues.

self-centered chakras – a term used to describe the first, second and third chakras, taken as a group, in which the intent is to discover one's identity as an individual.

transcendence phase – the combined function of the fifth and sixth chakras, where the focus is awakening to a larger sense of identity with Spirit.

unwounded soul essence – an image of the soul prior to the primal wounding, usually derived from some happy memory, which can be understood symbolically as well as in its literal interpretation.

vertical hieros gamos – an integration of the soul and Spirit, which can also be understood as a movement through the kosha system from total identification with material reality at the level of annamaya kosha to total identification with Spirit at the level of anandamaya kosha.

yang chakras – the first and third chakras considered together, in which the goal is to take active measures to establish anchor and further one's own agenda. The fifth chakra also has a strong yang component, which must be balanced by a yin opening to the

◇◇

deeper truth of one's being.

yin chakras – the second and fourth chakras considered together, in which the goal is opening to a deeper connection to all of life. The sixth chakra also has a strong yin component, which must be balanced by a yang effort to extricate oneself from the limited conditioning behind one's beliefs.

Tables of Koshic Placements

PLANETS IN SIGNS

	☉	☽	☿	♀	♂	♃	♄	♅	♆	♇
♈	p	n	-	-	p	p	-	-	n	p
♉	n	m	a	a	m	m	a	n	m	m
♊	p	v	-	-	p	p	-	-	v	p
♋	n	m	a	a	m	m	a	v	m	m
♌	p	n	-	-	p	p	-	-	n	p
♍	n	m	a	a	m	m	a	n	m	m
♎	p	v	-	-	p	p	-	-	v	p
♏	n	m	a	a	m	m	a	v	m	m
♐	p	n	-	-	p	p	-	-	n	p
♑	n	m	a	a	m	m	a	n	m	m
♒	p	v	-	-	p	p	-	-	v	p
♓	n	m	a	a	m	m	a	v	m	m

PLANETS IN HOUSES

	☉	☽	☿	♀	♂	♃	♄	♅	♆	♇
1	p	n	-	-	p	p	-	-	n	p
2	n	m	a	a	m	m	a	n	m	m
3	p	v	-	-	p	p	-	-	v	p
4	n	m	a	a	m	m	a	v	m	m
5	p	n	-	-	p	p	-	-	n	p
6	n	m	a	a	m	m	a	n	m	m
7	p	v	-	-	p	p	-	-	v	p
8	n	m	a	a	m	m	a	v	m	m
9	p	n	-	-	p	p	-	-	n	p
10	n	m	a	a	m	m	a	n	m	m
11	p	v	-	-	p	p	-	-	v	p
12	n	m	a	a	m	m	a	v	m	m

PLANETS IN HARD ASPECT

	☉	☽	☿	♀	♂	♃	♄	♅	♆	♇
☉	-	n	n/p	n/p	n/p	n/p	n/-	-	n	n/p
☽	n	-	a/v	a/n	m/n	m/n	a/v	v	m	m/n
☿	n/p	a/v	-	n	v/n	v/n	n	-/n	v/m	v/n
♀	n/p	a/n	n	-	v/n	v/n	n	-/n	v/m	v/n
♂	n/p	m/n	v/n	v/n	-	n	n/v	-/v	n/m	n
♃	n/p	m/n	v/n	v/n	n	-	n/v	-/v	n/m	n
♄	n/-	a/v	n	n	n/v	n/v	-	-/n	v/m	v/n
♅	-	v	-/n	-/n	-/v	-/v	-/n	-	v	v/p
♆	n	m	v/m	v/m	n/m	n/m	v/m	v	-	m/n
♇	n/p	m/n	v/n	v/n	n	n	v/n	v/p	m/n	-

Within the astro-chakra system, hard aspects include the semi-sextile, semi-square, square, sesquiquadrate and quincunx.

439

PLANETS IN SOFT ASPECT

	☉	☽	☿	♀	♂	♃	♄	♅	♆	♇
☉	-	n	p/n	p/n	p/n	p/n	-/n	-	n	p/n
☽	n	-	v/a	v/a	n/m	n/m	v/a	v	m	n/m
☿	p/n	v/a	-	-/a	p/m	p/m	-/a	-/n	v/m	p/m
♀	p/n	v/a	-/a	-	p/m	p/m	-/a	-/n	v/m	p/m
♂	p/n	n/m	p/m	p/m	-	p/m	-/a	-/v	n/m	p/m
♃	p/n	n/m	p/m	p/m	p/m	-	-/a	-/v	n/m	p/m
♄	-/n	v/a	-/a	-/a	-/a	-/a	-	-/n	v/m	p/m
♅	-	v	-/n	-/n	-/v	-/v	-/n	-	v	p/v
♆	n	m	v/m	v/m	n/m	n/m	v/m	v	-	n/m
♇	p/n	n/m	p/m	p/m	p/m	p/m	p/m	p/v	n/m	-

Within the astro-chakra system, soft aspects include the conjunction, sextile, trine and opposition.

Diagrams of Chakra Patterns

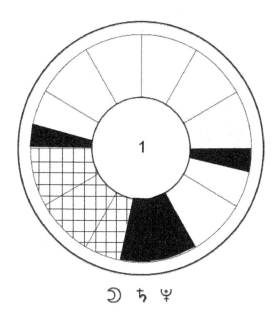

☽ ♄ ♇

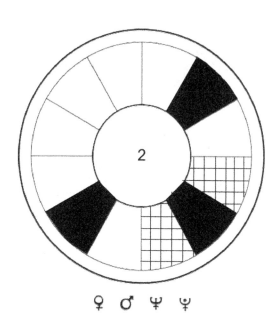

♀ ♂ ♆ ♇

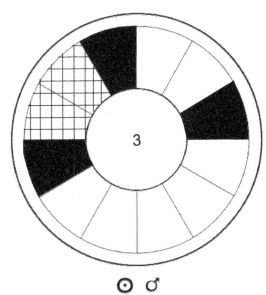

☉ ♂
+ DEFICIENCY: ♄ ♆
+/OR EXCESS: ♃ ♅ ♇

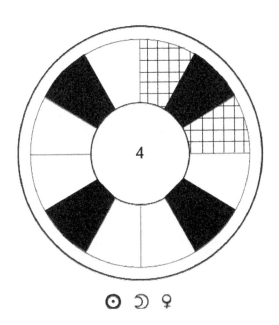

☉ ☽ ♀

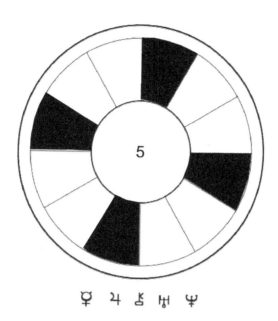

☿ ♃ ♁ ♅ ♆

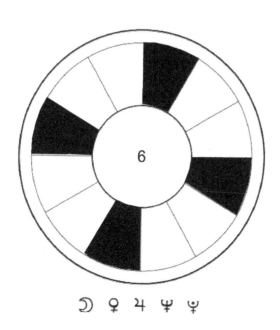

☽ ☿ ♃ ♆ ♇

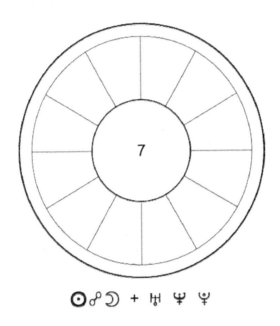

Works Cited

Avalon, Arthur. <u>The Serpent Power: The Secrets of Tantric and Shaktic Yoga</u>. New York: Dover, 1974.

Blum, Ralph. <u>The Book of Runes: A Handbook for the Use of an Ancient and Contemporary Oracle</u>. New York: Oracle Books, 1982

Bogart, Gregory C. <u>Astrology and Spiritual Awakening</u>. Berkeley, CA: Dawn Mountain Press, 1994.

Bolen, Jean Shinoda. <u>The Goddesses in Everywoman: Powerful Archetypes in Women's Lives</u>. New York: Harper Collins, 1984.

___. <u>The Gods in Everyman: A New Psychology of Men</u>. New York: Harper Collins, 1989.

Bruyere, Rosalyn L. <u>Wheels of Light: Chakras, Auras and the Healing Energy of the Body</u>. New York: Simon & Schuster, 1989.

Campbell, Joseph. <u>The Masks of God: Occidental Mythology</u>. New York: Viking Press, 1964.

___. <u>The Masks of God: Primitive Mythology</u>. New York: Penguin, 1959.

___. <u>The Power of Myth</u>. Ed. Betty Sue Flowers. New York: Anchor Books, 1988.

Carey, Ken. <u>Flat Rock Journal: A Day in the Ozarks Mountains</u>. San Francisco: Harper Collins, 1994.

Cashford, Jules. <u>The Moon: Myth and Image</u>. New York: Four Walls Eight Windows, 2002.

Castenada, Carlos. <u>A Separate Reality: Further Conversations With Don Juan</u>. New York: Simon & Schuster, 1973.

___. <u>The Fire From Within</u>. New York: Simon & Schuster, 1984.

Center for Disease Control. "Fast Stats A-Z." 11 October 2004. <http://www.cdc.gov/nchs/fastats/lcod.htm>

Chia, Montak. <u>Awaken Healing Energy Through the Tao</u>. .New York: Aurora Press, 1983.

Chodron, Pema. <u>When Things Fall Apart</u>. Boston: Shambala, 2000.

Clinton, Bill. <u>My Life</u>. New York: Knopf, 2004.

Cunningham, Donna. <u>Astrology and Spiritual Development</u>. San Rafael, CA: Cassandra Press, 1988.

Desai, Yogi Amrit. "Kundalini Yoga Through Shaktipat." Kundalini, Evolution and Englightenment. Ed. John White. Garden City, NY: Anchor Press/dDoubleday, 1979.

George, Demetra. Asteroid Goddesses: The Mythology, Psychology and Astrology of the Reemerging Feminine. San Diego, CA: ACS Publications, 1986.

Gibran, Kahil. "On Marriage." The Prophet. 17 October 2005. http://www.columbia. edu/~gm84/gibran3.html.

Grasse, Ray. The Waking Dream: Unlocking the Symbolic Language of Our Lives. Wheaton, IL: Quest Books, 1996.

Greene, Liz. The Astrological Neptune and the Quest for Redemption. Boston: Weiser, 1996.

Gurdjieff, G. "The Material Question." Meetings With Remarkable Men. New York: E.P. Dutton, 1974.

Hamilton, Nigel. "The Alchemical Process of Transformation." The Alchemy Web Site. 1 June 2006. <http://www.sufismus.ch/omega_dream/alchemy_e.pdf>

Harlow, H. F. and R. R. Zimmermann. "Affectional responses in the infant monkey." Science 130 (1959): 421-432.

Harrison, George. The Beatles: Past Masters, Vol 2. "The Inner Light." Apple Records, 1988.

Hillman, James. The Soul's Code: In Search of Character and Calling. New York: Warner Books, 1996.

Hodgson, Joan. The Stars and the Chakras: The Astrology of Spiritual Unfoldment. London: White Eagle Pub Trust, 1990.

Hopper, Dennis. "Quotes About James Dean." JamesDean.com. 28 August 2006. < http://www.jamesdean.com/about/quotesabout4.htm>

Jacobs, Jayj. SOS Consulting. "For Immediate Release: Happy Birthday Jesus." 11 May 2006. < http://users.netonecom.net/~sos/jesus.htm>

Judith, Anodea. Eastern Body Western Mind: Psychology and the Chakra System. Berkeley, CA; Celestial Arts, 1996.

Jung, Carl. The Archetypes and the Collective Unconscious. Trans. R. F. C. Hull. Bolligen Series XX, Vol 9, Pt 1. Princeton, NJ: Princeton University Press, 1959.

~. Psychology and Alchemy. Trans. R. F. C. Hull, Bolligen Series XX, Vol 12, New York: Pantheon Books, 1953.

~. <u>Symbols of Transformation</u>. Trans. R. F. C. Hull. Bolligen Series XX., Vol 5 Princeton, NJ: Princeton University Press, 1956.

~. <u>Memories, Dreams and Reflections</u>. Trans. Richard and Clara Winston. New York: Random House, 1965.

Landwehr, Joe. "The Clockwise Interpretation of Houses as a Gateway to Understanding the Soul's Evolutionary Process." <u>The Mountain Astrologer</u>. 93: Oct/Nov 2000.

~. "Cutting Away the Spider's Web." <u>Full Moon Meditations</u>. Mountain View, MO: Light of the Forest Primeval, 1993.

~. <u>The Seven Gates of Soul: Reclaiming the Poetry of Everyday Life</u>. Abilene, TX: Ancient Tower Press, 2004.

Lao Tzu. <u>Tao Te Ching</u>. Trans. Feng, Gia-Fun and Jane English. New York: Vintage Books, 1972.

Larsen, Stephen and Robin Larsen. <u>A Fire in the Mind: The Life of Joseph Campbell</u>. New York: Doubleday, 1991.

Leadbeater, C.W. <u>The Chakras</u>. Wheaton, IL: Theosophical Publishing House, 1927.

Myss, Caroline. <u>Anatomy of the Spirit: The Seven Stages of Power and Healing</u>. New York: Three Rivers Press, 1996.

MacNeil/Lehrer Productions. Online News Hour (September 6, 2004). "Clinton's Bypass." 26 October 2005. http://www.pbs.org/newshour/bb/white_house/july-dec04/clinton_9-6.html

Morford, Mark P.O. <u>Classical Mythology</u>. 5th ed. White Plains, NY: Longman, 1995.

Muktananda, Swami. <u>Play of Consciousness</u>. South Fallsburg, NY; SYDA Foundation, 1978.

~. <u>Satsang With Baba: Questions and Answers with Swami Muktananda, Vol 5</u>. Oakland, CA: SYDA Foundation, 1978.

~. <u>Understanding Siddha Yoga</u>. Ganespuri, India: Gurudev Siddha Peeth, 1978.

Naiman, Ingrid. <u>The Astrology of Healing - Vol 1: Stress: The Cause of Disease</u>. Santa Fe, NM; Seventh Ray Press, 1988.

Neumann, Erich. <u>The Great Mother: An Analysis of the Archetype</u>. Trans. Ralph Manheim. Bolligen Series XLVII. Princeton, NJ: Princeton University Press, 1963.

Nietzsche, Frederich. <u>On the Genealogy of Morals and Ecco Homo</u>. New York: Vintage Books, 1967.

Osbon, Diane K. Reflections on the Art of Living: A Joseph Campbell Companion. New York: Harper Collins, 1991.

Oken, Alan. Soul-Centered Astrology: A Key to Your Expanded Self. Freedom, CA: Crossing Press, 1990.

Plato. The Last Days of Socrates. Trans. Hugh Tredennick. London: Penguin, 1969.

Prosapio, Dick. Intuitive Tarot. New York: Morgan & Morgan, 1990.

Radha, Swami Sivananda. "Kundalini: An Overview." Kundalini, Evolution and Enlightenment. Ed. John White. Garden City, NY: Anchor Press/Doubleday, 1979.

Ram Dass. Be Here Now. San Cristobal, NM: Lama Foundation, 1971.

—. Miracle of Love: Stories About Neem Karoli Baba. New York: Dutton, 1979.

Reps, Paul, Compiler. Zen Flesh, Zen Bones: A Collection of Zen and Pre-Zen Writings. Garden City, NY: Doubleday, nd.

Rilke, Rainer Maria. "Buddha Inside the Light." Selected Poems of Rainer Maria Rilke. Trans. Robert Bly. New York: Harper & Row, 1981.

Rudhyar, Dane. The Astrology of Personality. Garden City, NY: Doubleday, 1970.

Searleman, Alan and Douglas Herrmann. Memory From a Broader Perspective. New York: McGraw Hill, 1994.

Shaneman, Jhampa & Jan V. Angel. Buddhist Astrology. St. Paul, MN: Llewellyn Publications, 2003.

Starhawk. Dreaming the Dark: Magic, Sex and Politics. Boston, MA: Beacon Press, 1988.

Taglilatelo, Pat. Astrodatabank. "Maya Angelou." 30 May 2006. <http://www. astrodatabank.com/NM/AngelouMaya.htm>

Tarnas, Richard. Prometheus the Awakener: An Essay on the Archetypal Meaning of the Planet Uranus. Woodstock, CT: Spring Publications, 1995.

Theodore, Pemo. "Unlocking the Mysteries of Love Through the Composite Chart." International Astrologer, Vol XXXIV, Number 2 (Winter/Spring 2006).

Underhill, Evelyn. Mysticism: The Nature and Development of Spiritual Consciousness. Oxford: Oneworld Publications, 1999.

Watts, Alan. Tao: The Watercourse Way. New York: Pantheon Books, 1975.

Web India 123. "Scientists unravel why smell triggers memory." 19 October 2004. <http://www.webindia123.com/news/showdetails.asp?id=49088&cat=Health>

Wilbur, Ken. "Are the Chakras Real?" <u>Kundalini, Evolution and Enlightenment</u>. Ed. John White. Garden City, NY: Anchor Books, 1979.

World Health Organization. "Cardiovascular Diseases." 11 October 2004. <http://www.who.int/cardiovascular_diseases/en/>

Chart Data

Maya Angelou, 2:10 PM CST, April 4, 1928, St. Louis, Missouri

Joseph Campbell – 7:25 PM EST, March 26, 1904, New York, New York

Bill Clinton, 8:51 AM CST, August 19, 1946, Hope, Arkansas

Kurt Cobain, 7:20 PM CST, February 20, 1967, Aberdeen, Texas

Ram Dass, 10:40 AM EST, April 6, 1931, Boston, Massachusetts

James Dean – 2:00 AM CST, February 8, 1931, Marion, Indiana

Isadora Duncan, 2:20 AM LMT, May 26, 1877, San Francisco, California

Bob Dylan, 9:05 PM CST, May 24, 1941, Duluth, Minnesota

Allen Ginsberg, 1:00 AM EST, June 3, 1926, Paterson, New Jersey

Hermann Goering, 4:00 AM CET, January 12, 1893, Rosenheim, Germany

Katherine Hepburn – 5:47 AM EST, May 12, 1907, Hartford, Connecticut

Timothy Leary, 10:45 AM EDT, October 22, 1920, Springfield, Massachusetts

Marilyn Monroe – 9:30 AM PST, June 1, 1926, Los Angeles, California

Swami Muktananda – 5:05 AM BDOT, May 16, 1908, Dharmasthala, India

Louis Pasteur – 2:00 AM LMT, December 27, 1822, Dole, France

Prince, 6:17 PM CDT, June 7, 1958, Minneapolis, Minnesota

Nancy Reagan, 1:18 AM EDT, July 6, 1921, New York, New York

Richard Speck, 1:00 AM CST, December 6, 1941, Monmouth, Illinois

Martha Stewart – 1:33 PM EDT, August 3, 1941, Jersey City, New Jersey

With the exception of Maya Angelou and Swami Muktananda, all chart data comes from the Famous Charts Collection that accompanies Graphic Astrology by Times Cycles Research. The source of the data is unknown.

Maya Angelou's data comes from Contemporary American Horoscopes, quoted from birth certificate/record, Rodden rating: AA.

Swami Muktananda's data was taken from *Astrology and Spiritual Awakening* by Greg Bogart, who quotes his source as Lois Rodden, Astrodata III, but gives no rating.

No data is given for my chart or for the charts of my ex-partner, students or clients to preserve confidentiality.

Index

A

I

yogic tradition.
  and Pluto 176
kundalini yoga 10-11, 99, 237

L

lalata 320 *See also* yogic tradition.
Laing, R. D. 90
Leadbeater, Charles 7, 16, 70, 95, 409 *See also* Theosophical Society.
learning 21, 26-27, 32-34, 36, 39, 43, 45-47, 49, 57-58, 62, 71, 75-77, 101, 107, 110, 115, 122, 166, 171-172, 196, 216-217, 223-224, 241, 248, 254, 257, 259, 267, 269, 272, 282, 286, 293, 299, 305, 311, 333, 336, 342-343, 349, 382, 400, 410, 412-413, 420
love 40-41, 44, 51-52, 57, 63-64, 66-67, 69-70, 72, 77, 79, 83-84, 99, 115-116, 173, 196, 198-199, 207, 211-214, 242-243, 246-247, 249-250, 252-257, 262-264, 266-268, 270-273, 287, 303-304, 308, 330, 341, 346, 352, 356, 363, 375, 413

M

magic 53-54, 71, 249, 168, 356-358, 413
mantra 354 *See also* yogic tradition.
Mars 124-125, 127-132, 134-136, 145, 148-152, 154, 156-157, 161-163, 174, 177, 179, 198-202, 203-206, 208-211, 213, 219, 221-222, 224-228, 230-236, 238-239, 248, 260-261, 264, 266-268, 270-273, 285, 292, 295, 304, 324, 326-328, 374-375, 383, 385, 399-401, 403-405, 408, 416
  and 1st chakra 179, 180, 183, 185-188, 414
  and 2nd chakra 199, 202, 203-206, 208-211, 213, 390, 414
  and 3rd chakra 221-222, 228, 391-392, 414
  and 4th chakra 414
  and 5th chakra 394, 414
  and 6th chakra 414
  and 7th chakra 414
  Mars-Venus xxv, 200
Matrix, The 99, 101
maya 44
medicine walk 54-55
meditation 27, 40, 223, 237, 278, 360, 370-374, 376-377
memory xxvi, 5, 8-9, 14, 20-21, 52, 63, 121, 191, 247, 251, 312-313, 317-318, 320, 330, 344, 348, 351-352, 354, 408, 412, 416, 420
  relation to esoteric astro-logic xxvi, 5
  relation to smell 80

◇◇